Kathee Golnick

MARKETING RESEARCH IN A MARKETING ENVIRONMENT

MARKETING RESEARCH IN A MARKETING ENVIRONMENT

WILLIAM R. DILLON

Bernard M. Baruch College
of The City University of New York

THOMAS J. MADDEN

University of South Carolina

NEIL H. FIRTLE

Market Facts, Inc.

with 130 illustrations

Times Mirror/Mosby College Publishing

St. Louis • Toronto • Santa Clara   1987

Acquisition Editor   Elizabeth J. Schilling
Developmental Editor   Catherine C. Bailey
Project Editor   Karen A. Edwards
Designer   Al Burkhardt
Editing and Production   Publication Alternatives
Cover Photograph   Eric Henlon

Copyright © 1987 by
Times Mirror/Mosby College Publishing
A division of The C. V. Mosby Company
11830 Westline Industrial Drive, St. Louis, Missouri 63146

Library of Congress Cataloging-in-Publication Data

Dillon, William R.
  Marketing research in a marketing environment.

  Includes index.
  1. Marketing research.   I. Madden, Thomas J.
II. Firtle, Neil H.   III. Title.
HF5415.2.D54   1987   658.8'3   86-23189
ISBN 0-8016-1303-5

C/VH/VH   9 8 7 6 5 4 3 2 1   03/C/366

To Jennifer
>
> the most enjoyable bundle of end benefits
> a father could experience

To my parents

> Thomas J. Madden and Winifred K. Madden

To Maureen

> a friend, colleague, and wife

Preface

In the past few years there has been a proliferation in the number of marketing research textbooks. This proliferation, in large part, is due to the fact that marketing research has become an integral part of undergraduate and graduate business curriculums. However, though teachers now have an increased number of texts from which to choose, the available books, in the opinion of these authors, are usually of the same genre. With few exceptions the primary emphasis is on the "scientific method" and general social science methodology with less emphasis on how marketing research is actually practiced.

In *Marketing Research in a Marketing Environment* we have attempted to bridge the gap between the theory and practice of marketing research. The danger in doing so is to give birth to a book that is too different and may not do justice to traditional content areas. Although we admit that this book is significantly different in its motivation, orientation, and presentation, it nevertheless preserves the integrity of all traditional marketing research content areas. We have tried to present the material in a way that is exciting and relevant as well as understandable. For the most part we do this by emphasizing the problem-oriented nature of marketing research and by discussing how marketing research is actually conducted in a realistic setting. Key features in *Marketing Research in a Marketing Environment* designed to achieve these goals include:

- *Introducing the reader to the world of commercial marketing research by discussing a job search scenario.* In the course of the interviewing process the student is exposed to some of the day-to-day activities that are routinely undertaken by marketing research departments.
- *Involving the reader in the marketing research community.* This community is discussed in terms of its principal parties and primary activities. The reader gains an appreciation for the primary players who conduct marketing research and their respective responsibilities.
- *Developing a framework that places marketing research within the*

well-known product life-cycle. Cross-classifying specific marketing research activities according to the marketing research stage and the focus of the research helps the student understand the problem-oriented nature of marketing research.

- *Introducing the reader to traditional content areas by discussing prototypical marketing research proposals.* Real-world marketing research proposals provide much of the motivation for the material presented in this book. The project proposals used throughout the book have been derived from actual marketing research projects. Though brand and research supplier names have been changed to ensure confidentiality, the illustrative proposals convey the essence of how marketing research is conducted in the real world.

- *Building on the secondary sources of information available.* In recent years the ability to locate and obtain secondary sources of market research information has been revolutionized by on-line computer-assisted data search technology. Scanner services are changing the face of commercial marketing research.

- *Introducing the reader to current sources of purchase and media data.* Syndicated sources of purchase and media data continue to be an important source of information that can be used to solve many marketing-related problems.

- *Involving the reader in a variety of marketing research studies.* The tools and techniques of marketing research take on greater meaning when discussed and illustrated in the context of real-world applications. The Case Studies at the end of each of the seven Parts in this text use real-world vignettes to demonstrate the important role that marketing research plays in providing relevant answers to marketing-related problems.

- *Reinforcing the major concepts introduced throughout the book.* Throughout each chapter marginal definitions are used to highlight key principles, and case studies and end-of-chapter questions ask the student to apply them. Further reinforcement is provided by learning objectives at the beginning of each chapter and by key concepts at the close.

We earnestly feel that these features represent a major step toward conveying the essence of marketing research.

Marketing Research in a Marketing Environment is divided into seven major parts. The book introduces the practice of marketing research through a scenario that describes the job search activities of a recent undergraduate marketing major and her discussions with the members of a marketing research department. This material sets the stage for the ensuing discussion in Part I and will interest the many students who are looking forward to a business-related career.

Part I, Marketing Research Environments, consists of two chapters. In Chapter 1, we describe what we mean by *realistic* marketing research environments and discuss the role and activities of marketing researchers. Chapter 2 discusses the necessary steps in designing a marketing research project.

Part II, Acquiring Data, considers tools and techniques that can be used to obtain the market information necessary to answer marketing-related questions. In Chapter 3, we describe secondary information from the perspectives of both traditional and newer on-line computer-assisted technologies. This material is up to date and is not covered in many current textbooks. Syndicated sources of information on purchase and media behavior are described in Chapter 4. The major suppliers of this sort of information are discussed and attention is focused on the new technology (i.e., scanner services) that is changing the face of marketing research. In Chapter 5, we provide a comprehensive treatment of survey interviewing methods, including the increasingly popular method of mall intercepts. Chapter 6 follows with a discussion of the issue of causality and, in particular, experimental research methods. All the experimental designs presented are discussed in the context of real-world marketing research studies to increase the relevance and understanding of this subject matter.

Part III, Sampling Theory and Practice, consists of two chapters. Chapter 7 presents the fundamentals of sampling. Further details on drawing probability samples are provided in Chapter 8. (For the reader not needing technical details on the procedures for drawing probability samples, Chapter 7 will suffice.)

Part IV, Measurement, Scaling, and Questionnaire Design, covers both theoretical and practical issues related to what to ask and how to ask it. In Chapter 9, the basic concepts of measurement are discussed, and the next two chapters expand on this material. Chapter 10 provides a discussion of the primary measurement scales used in marketing research. Because of the central role that attitudes play in answering many marketing-related questions, in Chapter 11 we have provided a treatment of attitude scales and measurement models. The final chapter in this part, Chapter 12, presents a comprehensive treatment of the issues that should be considered when designing a questionnaire and fielding a study. Because of the nature of this material all of the chapters are replete with examples.

Part V, Data Processing and Analysis, considers the tools and techniques of analysis. In Chapter 13, we discuss issues related to processing the data; in essence these procedures prepare the data for analysis. This is followed in Chapter 14 by a discussion of techniques that can be used to give the researcher an initial glimpse of the data. The next two chapters describe techniques that can be used to uncover and test hypotheses concerning a single variable or the relationships between two or more variables. Chapter 15 discusses hypothesis testing and is followed by two appendices that deal with Analysis of Variance. Chapter 16 discusses measures of association and regression analysis. A brief treatment of some popular multivariate data analysis procedures is presented in the appendices to this chapter. In all instances the discussion includes many examples and is directed to the unsophisticated reader.

Part VI, Applications, presents details on how several different types of marketing research studies are typically conducted. Specifically, Chapter 17 considers what are commonly referred to as *market studies*, Chapter 18 considers *concept and product studies*, Chapter 19 considers *package and name studies*, Chapter 20 considers *advertising testing studies*, and Chapter 21 considers *test market studies*, including *simulated test markets*. These applications are discussed in separate chapters for three reasons. First, these studies typify the practice of marketing research. Second, they provide a vehicle for illustrating how the concepts, tools, and techniques from the first five parts of the book can be used to solve real-world, marketing-related problems. Third, they provide exemplary material on which to build class projects. The final chapter in this part of the book, Chapter 22, discusses *marketing decision support systems*. With the recent advances in computer PC-based technology, marketing professionals are beginning to rely on marketing decision support systems with greater regularity and frequency. Although this trend is likely to increase in the future, marketing decision support systems receive only minimal coverage in many current textbooks. As part of our coverage of marketing decision support systems, an appendix to Chapter 22 discusses forecasting techniques.

Part VII, Report Preparation, consists of a single chapter, Chapter 23, in which we present suggestions for writing and orally presenting the results of a research project. The material in this chapter relies on the suggestions of practicing marketing researchers.

Supplements

We have prepared all of the supplements that accompany this textbook. In doing so, we have attempted to provide elements and features of value to the inexperienced as well as experienced instructor.

Instructor's Manual

- *Conversion notes.* A section labeled "What's Different and Why" begins each section of the manual. This material indicates where our coverage and terminology differ from other marketing research textbooks.
- *Learning objectives.* The learning objectives that appear at the beginning of each chapter are reproduced.
- *Key terms and concepts.* The key terms and concepts that appear throughout the textbook are reproduced.
- *Lecture notes.* A detailed outline of each chapter is provided.
- *Transparency masters.* Key exhibits, tables, and figures appearing in the textbook are reproduced as $8\frac{1}{2} \times 11$ transparency masters. Transparency masters are also provided for supplemental material not appearing in the textbook. The suggested spot for use of each of these is designed within the teaching suggestions.

- *Teaching suggestions.* These hints and ideas indicate how the authors would organize and present the material appearing in each chapter. Suggestions for where to integrate the transparency masters are also provided.
- *Author comments.* These describe the author's rationale for the major topics presented in each chapter.
- *Answers to end-of-chapter problems.* Detailed answers to every question are provided.
- *Case notes.* For instructors who decide to use any or all of the case studies appearing in the text, a detailed set of case notes is provided.

Test Bank

The test bank contains an extensive array of questions, categorized by chapter. In addition, correct answers are provided.

Test-Generation System

All questions appearing in the test bank are reproduced in a computerized test-generation system, for use with the IBM PC and compatible computers. The test-generation system provides the following features:

1. Individual test items can be added or deleted.
2. Individual test items can be edited.
3. A shuffle option is provided that allows different versions of the same examination.
4. Ample documentation.

Software

A unique set of contemporary interactive software programs are available to adopters. The software is pedagogical in nature and designed to enhance students' understanding of the concepts and techniques discussed throughout the textbook. Six individual modules are available:

1. The SAMPLE module demonstrates selected concepts related to drawing simple and stratified samples.
2. The SCALE module takes students through various types of monadic and comparative rating scales. Asking students to rate a set of brands on different types of scales enables them to gain an appreciation for the issues involved in selecting a rating instrument.
3. The QUESTION module is a computer-assisted interviewing program. Through this module students learn firsthand what it is like to use this form of collection. In addition, the question module generates a data file based upon students' responses that can be used to illustrate the tools and techniques of data analysis discussed in Part V of the text.

4. The ACA module illustrates how conjoint analysis works in an interactive PC environment. The module utilizes the Adaptive Conjoint Analysis (ACA) system developed by Richard Johnson of Sawtooth Software, Inc.

5. The ASCID module is a marketing decision support system for perceptual mapping. A unique feature of this system is the ability to position new objects in an existing perceptual space.

6. The FORCAST module is designed to demonstrate how the more popular forecasting techniques work.

Acknowledgments

In writing this textbook we have benefited greatly from the comments, suggestions, help, and last but not least, sympathy of many. The review process has been rigorous and constructive. The content of the textbook has been greatly influenced by the hundreds of comments and suggestions made by the reviewers. We gratefully acknowledge the help of the following reviewers:

David Andrus
Kansas State University

Richard Beltramini
Arizona State University

Norman Bruvold
University of Cincinnati

Lee Cooper
University of California at Los Angeles

Melvin Crask
University of Georgia

Dale Duhan
Michigan State University

Elizabeth Ensley
Oregon State University

Lawrence Feick
University of Pittsburgh

Roy Howell
Texas Tech University

Rajshekhar Javalgi
Marquette University

Michael Loizides
Hampton University

Nicholas Nugent
Boston College

Lawrence Patterson
Southwest Texas State University

Arno Rethans
Pennsylvania State University

Marsha Richins
Louisiana State University

Sandra Schmidt
University of Virginia

Richard Skinner
Kent State University

Gail Tom
California State University at Sacramento

Louis Volpp
California State University at Fresno

Gary Young
University of Massachusetts at Boston

Other individuals also deserve thanks. Nancy Podolak, the consummate administrative assistant, had the unenviable task of typing the manuscript. Her professionalism and skills allowed the manuscript to be finished on schedule in spite of an exceedingly long first draft. JoAnn Woo provided expert programming skills in connection with the software modules. Needless to say, without her help the software programs would still be in the developmental stages. Beth Schwartz provided administrative assistance and supervised the most difficult task of securing all of the permissions. Her perseverance and detective work is greatly appreciated. We were fortunate to be able to call on the expertise of Sal M. Meringolo, Head of the Reference Department, University of North Carolina at Charlotte, who prepared most of Chapter 3. Finally, Robert Johnson of Sawtooth Software, Inc., graciously provided the ACA software module.

The authors have greatly benefited from the help and suggestions of members of the business community. In particular, special thanks go to Lisa Myers of Shifrin-Blocher Research, Inc.; Jerry Leighton and Jeff Starr of CRC Information, Inc.; Steve Wilson, Bill Molts, and Ron Tatham of Burke Marketing Services, Inc.; Jody Burnstein of Adfactors, Inc.; Andy Boes of LINK Resources; and Mark Arkin of S. B. Thomas, Inc.

Several members of the academic community deserve acknowledgment. First, our colleagues at Baruch College and the University of South Carolina have been extremely supportive and helpful in class testing some of the material. Thanks are especially due Professors Gloria Thomas, Steve Schnaars, and Leon Schiffman of Baruch College and Professors Donald G. Frederick, Subhash Sharma, and Terry Shimp of the University of South Carolina. Second, while all the names are too numerous to mention, some other influential and helpful people have been David Brinberg at SUNY/Albany, Rajiv Grover at the University of Pittsburgh, Ajith Kumar at SUNY/Albany, and Narendra Mulani at Rutgers University/Newark.

Staff members and consultants at Times Mirror/Mosby deserve special thanks since they shared in the labors. We thank Mary Forkner and Joan Pendleton for their skills in bringing the manuscript through the production phase of the project. The conscientiousness and discriminating eye of Martha Simmons is greatly appreciated. Beth Lewis, Liz Schilling, and James Donohue made important contributions in the development and marketing of the textbook. Special thanks go to Cathy Bailey and Glenn Turner, who were the most actively involved in this project. Although the road was sometimes rocky, we owe them a great deal of thanks and gratitude.

This project began while two of the authors were at the University of Massachusetts. In addition, both of these authors started their careers at that institution and since most of our professional development took place at the University of Massachusetts, we would be remiss not to acknowledge our gratitude.

> William R. Dillon
> Thomas J. Madden
> Neil H. Firtle

Brief Contents

Contents

PART II

Acquiring Data: An Overview

Chapter 3

Secondary Information: Traditional Sources and New Technologies 75

PART III

Sampling Theory and Practices

Chapter 7

Chapter 8

PART IV

Measurement, Scaling, and Questionnaire Design

Chapter 9

Chapter 10

PART V

Data Processing and Analysis

PART VI

Applications

Chapter 17

Market Studies   576

Chapter 18

Concept and Product Testing 607

Chapter 19

Name and Package Testing 630

Chapter 20

Advertising Research Practices 642

PART VII

Report Preparation

Chapter 23

The Practice of Marketing Research

Introduction

The following items are all basic ingredients in conducting marketing research.

- Questionnaire design
- Sampling plans
- Data collection methods
- Data analysis procedures
- Report writing and presentation

Indeed, most of the subject matter covered in marketing research courses consists of these elements. However, in addition to understanding these technical "ingredients," we need to appreciate how they are used in practice. To successfully forge a path between theory and practice, we must understand that marketing research does not take place in a sterile, vapid environment. Rather, it is problem-oriented and directed toward satisfying consumer wants and needs. It often involves an interface between the company commissioning the research, a research supplier, a tab house, and an advertising agency. All of these organizations will become very familiar. ("Tab house" and other unfamiliar terms used in this introduction will be defined in later chapters.)

The various organizations mentioned form the basis of a "realistic marketing research environment." To help you better understand what this involves, we present an episodic tale that explores the marketing research business and the career opportunities it offers through the job-hunting activities of Judith Grath. Though most students will not pursue marketing research careers, knowledge of the technical aspects of marketing research coupled with a firm understanding and appreciation of realistic marketing research environments will enhance your overall managerial skills and employment potential.

Judith Grath, a recent graduate of State College, majored in marketing with a concentration in marketing research. She finished at the top of her class and is seeking a marketing research position, preferably at a

THE NEW YORK TIMES, SUNDAY, JUNE 15, 1986

Help Wanted	3200

MARKET RESEARCH FIELD ASST	**MARKET RESEARCH TRAINEE**
Major midtn supplier has entry-level position for bright hardworking college grad. Market research or marketing major. Familiarity with basic mktg research techniques a must. Send resume	Oppty for right person to join small research department in consumer package firm. Position reqs good communication skills and ability to work under pressure. Heavy telephone and field responsibilities. Contact . . .
MARKET RESEARCH CODERS	**MARKET RESEARCH FIELD DEPT TRAINEE**
Major research supplier seeks recent college grad. Must be familiar with basic mktg research techniques. Train to code openends, edit and tab. Send resume to	Small supplier seeks bright and personable college grad. Telephone contact with interviewing services. Write instructions. some travel. Send resume to . . .

Figure I-1

Listings for entry-level jobs in marketing research.

consumer products firm. All of the characters we introduce are fictitious, but the setting and discussion reflect what you may encounter, whether you pursue a career in marketing research or marketing management.

THE SEARCH

After graduation Judy threw her belongings into a rented trailer and returned to her parents' home in Queens, New York. Soon she began to canvass the "Help Wanted" section of the Sunday *New York Times*—dissecting the marketing research listings in hope of finding the "right" position.

Locating the right position would not be easy. Many of the market research listings were for coding, telephone interviewing, and field survey positions (Figure I-1). Judy thought that her strong academic training in marketing research and the experience gained in her honors project would allow her to land a position offering more managerial and direct research responsibilities.

Ideally, Judy wanted a marketing research analyst position. She wanted to participate in defining the objectives of specific research projects and programs as well as supervising the conduct of fieldwork, coding, and data analysis. Judy noted that most of the market research analyst listings required a minimum of two years' experience. This did not upset her because she felt that her specialized academic training would compensate for her lack of on-the-job experience.

THE NEW YORK TIMES, SUNDAY, JUNE 22, 1986

Help Wanted	3800

**MARKET RESEARCH
ANALYST**

Prestigious consumer package goods company seeks individual to join mktg research department. Position involves consumer market research projects, including testing of concepts, products, advertising and test marketing. The successful candidate will have responsibility for design, execution, analysis and oral and written reports.

Marketing degree plus minimum of 2 year's experience with a mktg research dept., advertising agency, or market research supplier are essential.

Position offers a very competitive compensation package and potential for career development. Please forward resume in confidence to . . .

Figure I-2

Listing for a marketing research analyst's job.

One Sunday Judy came across a very promising listing (Figure I-2). She decided to inquire about it.

FIRST INTERVIEW

On Monday morning Judy called the contact number; after she described her background and skills, she was given an appointment and asked to mail her resume right away. When she arrived at the company a few days later, she reported to the personnel department, filled out an application, and then met the personnel director, Mr. Robert Peel.

Mr. Peel was very low key and relaxed. He asked Judy several questions about her background and career aspirations: "What are your major strengths? . . . What are your major weaknesses? . . . Where do you want to be in five years?"

Then, "Tell me a little about your college experience," asked Mr. Peel.

"I graduated last May from State College," answered Judy, "completing the degree requirements for a bachelor's degree and majoring in marketing with a concentration in marketing research."

"Concentrating in a particular area within the general marketing curriculum is a bit unusual, isn't it?" injected Mr. Peel. "Tell me more about it."

"Among other things, the concentration meant that I took a two-course sequence in marketing research and an advanced seminar in re-

3

search methods. The first course in the sequence covered sampling design, questionnaire construction, data collection methods, and general field procedures; the second course involved data analysis and procedures," responded Judy.

"That sounds very impressive," said Mr. Peel. "Your academic training is perfect for an analyst position. But you know that ideally we are looking for someone with experience."

"Yes, that's clearly stated in the job listing," responded Judy. Before Mr. Peel could continue, Judy explained, "I realize the value of on-the-job experience, but I feel that my academic training coupled with my honors project compensates for my lack of practical experience."

"Tell me about your honors project," asked Mr. Peel.

"I consider my honors project as sort of practicum, or equivalent to an internship," began Judy. "Each student selected a new product concept. The assignment was to design and conduct a research project to investigate any aspect of the new product's marketing mix. The student was free to define the specific objectives of the project."

"Which new product concept did you choose?" probed Mr. Peel.

"I chose a product concept called Sergeant's Rug Patrol.[1] This product is positioned for those unfortunate people who have been forced out of their homes in the dead of night in fear of fleas and ticks. Sergeant's Rug Patrol claims to be the first product that actually kills fleas, ticks, and the insidious offspring that multiply in the carpet. Just sprinkle Sergeant's on and vacuum away the enemy."

The conversation then focused on the specifics of the honors project. Judy noted that the assignment was general, requiring each student to define the objectives of the research, design a questionnaire, collect and analyze the data, and finally prepare a written report and oral presentation.

"How did you collect the data?" interrupted Mr. Peel.

"Through a convenience sample," answered Judy. "In addition, I designed a *probabilistic sampling design* where each household residing in the State College area had a nonzero chance of being included in the study," she continued.

As the interview came to a close, Mr. Peel described the analyst position: "Marketing research analysts are accountable to the marketing research manager for conducting research on a specific brand or project. Responsibilities include consulting with brand managers and advertising agencies; defining objectives; designing studies; collecting data; and providing sound analysis in support of division profits, volume, new products, and competitive objectives."

Before Judy left, Mr. Peel asked her to send him a copy of her honors project and said that he would be in touch regarding a second interview. On the way home Judy reflected on her interview. She was happy with the meeting and was excited about the responsibilities of a marketing

---

[1]*New Product News* (New York: Dancer Fitzgerald Sample, Inc., March 1984).

research analyst. When she arrived home she typed a letter thanking Mr. Peel for his time and hospitality and included a copy of her honors project.

SECOND INTERVIEW

Two weeks later Judy received a letter from Mr. Peel indicating that although there was some concern about her lack of practical experience, her strong academic credentials and general enthusiasm were well suited for an analyst position. She was invited to spend a morning with John Richards, the director of marketing research. The letter also indicated that she would be meeting one of the marketing research analysts currently on board and thus would have a chance to better appreciate the role and responsibilities of an analyst. In closing, Mr. Peel thanked her for promptly sending the copy of her honors project.

On the appointed day, Judy reported to Mr. Peel's office. "It's good to see you again, Judy," he said, extending his hand. "We have a full day planned, so let's get started. Mr. Richards, the marketing research director, is expecting you."

Mr. Richards. As Judy entered Mr. Richards' office with Mr. Peel, Mr. Richards was examining a research report from one of the marketing research analysts. Mr. Peel introduced Judy and left the office.

Mr. Richards asked Judy to sit down and make herself comfortable. As he turned to file the report he was examining, he said, "This report is an excellent sample of how marketing research is problem-oriented and directed toward satisfying consumer needs. This report was submitted to us by the NutraSweet company. Are you familiar with this company?" asked Mr. Richards.

"Not really—but I do know about NutraSweet," replied Judy.

"Searle sells NutraSweet directly to food manufacturers and consumer products companies like ours," continued Mr. Richards. "Since we do a lot of business with Searle, they routinely furnish us with their research reports. This one is on their NutraSweet sampling projects."

"NutraSweet, a sugar substitute, has made good taste and low caloric intake compatible," injected Judy.

"Nicely put," said Mr. Richards.

Mr. Richards informed Judy that in 1983 Searle had wanted to get NutraSweet out of the box quickly by going directly to the consumer even though the product was sold directly to food and consumer products firms. "The objectives of the project were to increase awareness of NutraSweet sugar substitute and products containing it, to encourage trial, and to overcome traditional skepticism toward sugar substitutes," said Mr. Richards.

As Mr. Richards paused, Judy asked, "Was the sampling project targeted to any particular segments of the population?"

5

The best way to tell you what NutraSweet™ is, is to tell you what it isn't.

NutraSweet* is the brand name of a remarkable low-calorie sweetening ingredient made all the more remarkable because of what it isn't.

It isn't sugar.

And it isn't saccharin.

For that matter, it isn't like any other sweetening ingredient you've ever heard of.

NutraSweet™ is made of protein components like those found naturally in milk, eggs, fruit, vegetables and meats.

NutraSweet isn't sugar, but it tastes like it.

Sugar is a carbohydrate. NutraSweet isn't.

NutraSweet is made from two of the building blocks of protein.

Yet despite NutraSweet's lack of similarity to sugar in a molecular sense, sugar and NutraSweet are virtually the same in taste.

NutraSweet isn't bad for your teeth.

Because it's not a carbohydrate like sugar, NutraSweet doesn't encourage the growth of the bacteria that cause cavities.

So while you won't be able to tell the difference between sugar and NutraSweet in taste, consider the difference it could make at dental check-up time.

NutraSweet isn't saccharin.

Except for low calories, NutraSweet is unlike saccharin in every way.

It has no bitter aftertaste, for example.

And since NutraSweet is made from protein components, your body treats it as naturally as it treats all other protein you consume.

NutraSweet isn't fattening.

A cup of hot cocoa sweetened with NutraSweet instead of sugar has only 50 calories, not 110. A gelatin dessert only 8 calories, not 81.

NutraSweet is "low calorie" compared to sugar, because so much less of it is required to do the job.

In fact, NutraSweet is 200 times sweeter than sugar.

The average 12-year-old eats his own weight in sugar in a single year. Much of it in everyday foods like canned spaghetti.

That sweetness in mind, it's possible that NutraSweet will become an important way for your entire family to satisfy its "sweet tooth."

(The people who keep track of such things say that the average family of four eats 400 pounds of sugar a year, much of it "hidden" as an ingredient in foods like peanut butter, catsup, breakfast cereals and fruit-flavored drinks.)

NutraSweet isn't for sale.

If you're convinced you want NutraSweet in your family's menu and that you can't wait to buy it, *wait.*

You *can't* buy it, at least not by the bottle, bag or boxful. NutraSweet is an ingredient. You can only buy foods and beverages that *contain* NutraSweet.

To help you recognize these new products in your supermarket, food manufacturers are putting the NutraSweet brand name on packages and labels.

Look for it when you shop.

You'll love it for what it isn't.

*NutraSweet is a trademark of G.D. Searle & Co. for its brand of sweetening ingredient.

> Some of the innovative products using NutraSweet
> - ALBA* Hot Cocoa Mix
> - Alpine Sugar-Free Instant Spiced Cider Mix
> - Carnation* Sugar-Free Hot Cocoa Mix
> - D-ZERTA* Brand Dessert And Topping Mixes
> - Diet Hires Root Beer
> - Diet Orange Crush
> - Diet Squirt*
> - Featherweight* Gelatin & Pudding Desserts
> - Louis Sherry* Shimmer* & Dia-Mel* Dessert Mixes
> - Ovaltine's Sugar Free Hot Cocoa Mix
> - Shapely Shake™ Shake Mix
> - Swiss Miss* Sugar-Free Hot Cocoa Mix

A free taste of gum and discounts on other products sweetened with NutraSweet.™

Yes, I'm very interested in NutraSweet. Please send a sample of five gumballs along with discount coupons for other products sweetened with NutraSweet to:

Name_____

Street Address_____

City_____ State_____ Zip_____

Send to Searle Food Resources, Inc., P.O. Box 1174, Glenview, IL 60025. (Allow six weeks for delivery.)

NutraSweet™

Gumballs available while supplies last. Void where prohibited.

Figure I-3

Advertisement for NutraSweet designed to educate target segments of the population. (© 1983 The NutraSweet Company, Reprinted with Permission.)

"Good question," said Mr. Richards. "Yes it was. The sampling project was targeted to adults eighteen years or older, the food and beverage trade, and to health care professionals." Then, pulling out a copy of an advertisement, Mr. Richards said, "Take a look at this copy; it was developed by the advertising agency of Ogilvy & Mather." Mr. Richards handed the advertisement to Judy and continued, "Note that in order to educate key targets about the benefits of NutraSweet, the NutraSweet Company arranged for the development of a NutraSweet gumball and offered free samples through ads like the one you're looking at" (see Figure I-3).

Judy interrupted, "In what types of magazines were the ads placed?"

Glancing at the report, Mr. Richards replied, "Four-color, two-page ads with an order form were placed in consumer publications such as *Time* magazine, *Woman's Day, People, Reader's Digest*, and *TV Guide*; then there was a two-page ad that appeared in professional health care magazines. These ads offered professional samples and literature. The total circulation for the project was over 178 million." Mr. Richards asked, "What do you think the budget was?"

Judy thought a moment. Though her marketing research courses had discussed the relative costs of conducting personal, mail, and telephone surveys, she could not recall anything that would help her give an informed response. To avoid appearing foolish she meekly admitted, "I really don't have any idea."

"I didn't expect you to," Mr. Richards quickly injected. "The total budget, including gumballs, collateral materials, production, fulfillment, and print media, was over four million dollars."

Judy was shocked by the amount allocated to just one project. Before Mr. Richards could continue, she asked, "Was the campaign a success?"

Mr. Richards opened the report and read the summary: "Consumer response has been outstanding; more than 1.2 million readers have tried the gumballs. Unsolicited letters of thanks have been received by more than 25,000 consumers and health care professionals. The evidence clearly supports the contention that the promotion successfully reached their target markets. For example, post-evaluation research shows that more than 72 percent of the respondents now have tried products with NutraSweet."

Mr. Richards closed the report and added, "Searle's sampling plan has created a strong franchise that we are using in marketing our NutraSweet products. We expect this to become even stronger in the next few years."

Mr. Richards rose from his desk and filed the report. "I've been monopolizing the conversation: it's about time I let you do some talking." He asked Judy several questions about her research skills and general academic background. His questions were more specific than Mr. Peel's. He wanted to know the content of the marketing research, statistics, and computer courses that she had taken. He was particularly concerned with Judy's understanding of the practical aspects of marketing research. "Can you give me an example of how you have used your research skills?" he asked.

"My honors project involved all of the essential aspects of research—sampling design, questionnaire construction, data collection, coding, tabulation, analysis, and report writing."

Before Judy could continue Mr. Richards interrupted, "I certainly was impressed with the technical quality of the report, but I do have one or two questions."

"Fire away!" Judy responded, feeling very confident about her knowledge.

"Well to begin, didn't you collect data from a convenience sample of State College undergraduates?" asked Mr. Richards.

"Yes I did, but, in addition, a probabilistic telephone sampling plan in which each resident of State College Park had a known chance of being included in the sample was also designed," Judy added.

"I found your design to be technically correct," Mr. Richards responded, "but there appeared to be certain aspects of the overall design that were not taken into consideration."

"I'm not sure what you mean," Judy said. "The design followed acceptable sampling procedures."

Mr. Richards began by asking Judy about the type of household she wanted to include in the sample. "Does it represent the general population? Is it a household that has carpets? A household that has carpets and pets? Or is it a household that has carpets, owns a pet, and has purchased a powdered rug cleaner within the last six months? Obviously, the ease and difficulty in finding households with particular characteristics will affect the feasibility of the design."

Judy thought, "I didn't consider the *incidence rate* when designing my sampling plan. How many phone calls would an interviewer have to make to find a household having carpets and a pet, and that had purchased a powdered rug cleaner in the last six months?" she wondered. Before Mr. Richards could continue, Judy said firmly, "You're certainly right Mr. Richards, I should have more clearly defined the population of interest, especially since Sergeant's Rug Patrol may well be a low-incidence product."

"Precisely," responded Mr. Richards. He continued, "Your project explored a new product concept; as such, one could think of many interesting questions to investigate. For example, a basic question is the eventual market success or failure of this product. In this regard, are you familiar with some of the commercially available STM services such as Burke's BASES and Management Decision System's ASSESSOR models?" asked Mr. Richards.

Judy recognized the acronym as *simulated test markets* and recalled that her marketing research textbook provided a brief discussion. She even thought the ASSESSOR model was specifically discussed. However, the treatment was brief and she remembered very little about class discussion of such models. "I've heard of ASSESSOR, but my knowledge is very limited," she admitted.

"What about market/tracking studies?" probed Mr. Richards.

Once again Judy was frustrated at her inability to answer Mr. Richards. "I have an idea of what you mean by a tracking study, but I must admit that I'm not familiar with any specifics," she meekly responded.

Sensing Judy's frustration, Mr. Richards interrupted, "It's really not important, Judy. If you join us you'll become familiar with these services—remember there is such a thing as on-the-job training," Mr. Richards explained with a smile. "I asked about these services because it always surprises me that most marketing research textbooks pay such little attention to what are, for most consumer product companies, day-to-day marketing research activities."

Mr. Richards continued, "The plan is to have you meet with one of our analysts today to give you a close feel for what it's like to be in the marketing research department."

Mr. Richards then described the department. "Let me tell you how we are organized," continued Mr. Richards. "The department has seven marketing research managers, eight market research analysts, and six secretaries."

"Quite a large department," Judy thought. "Could you tell me a little about how various responsibilities are delegated within the department?" she interrupted.

"As director of marketing research, I am responsible for the validity, objectivity, reliability, and sensitivity of much of the information used by the division. This information is necessary for determining what products should be produced and how they should be named, packaged, advertised, and prototyped. Of course," he added, "I'm also responsible for the operation and maintenance of the marketing research department itself."

"Each of the seven marketing research managers reports directly to me. They are responsible for the management of the marketing research function for one or more brand groups. All the brands are classified into generic groups: for example, chewing gums. The managers have three primary functions: first, consulting, defining objectives, designing, and interpreting studies that further the attainment of division profit, volume, new product, and competitive objectives; second, administrative responsibilities assuring the proper interconnection of all projects; and third, administrative responsibilities for the management of marketing research department personnel at the analyst and secretarial level."

Judy anxiously awaited Mr. Richards' description of the analyst position. He continued, "The eight marketing research analysts are divided into junior- and senior-level positions. We currently have three junior analysts and five senior analysts. The position that you are interviewing for is at the senior level, and that's why experience is an issue," he explained. "I'm sure Mr. Peel gave you a general description of the position.

I'll only add that analysts have important administrative responsibilities. They directly oversee the work of research suppliers and tab houses and interface with the advertising agency people."

Pausing once again, Mr. Richards glanced at his watch and commented, "It's getting late, so let's go meet Cathy Samuels, one of the analysts."

Ms. Samuels. As they entered, Ms. Samuels' office Mr. Richards introduced Judy. "Judith Grath, this is Cathy Samuels, one of our bright, up-and-coming research analysts. I'll leave you two alone."

Ms. Samuels invited Judy to have a seat and make herself comfortable. She began to tell Judy about her background.

"I've been in the research department for five years now. I started as a junior research analyst. About three years ago I was promoted to a senior analyst. Let me tell you, I thoroughly enjoy being an analyst—I love the diversity."

Ms. Samuels then told Judy about the backgrounds of the other research analysts. "We have a diverse group of analysts here. Two of us have business degrees, with concentrations in marketing. One has a degree in psychology, and one a degree in economics. Your degree is in marketing, isn't it?" asked Ms. Samuels.

"Yes it is—marketing with specialization in marketing research," replied Judy.

Judy felt comfortable with Ms. Samuels. She was particularly interested in her background before she had become a junior analyst. She asked, "What type of marketing research experience did you have before joining the department?"

"Not a lot," responded Ms. Samuels. "While finishing my degree I had the opportunity to work part-time for a small research supplier. There I gained some experience in questionnaire construction, coding, field services, and tabulation. You see, although I received good technical training, I really didn't have a working knowledge of most studies that analysts are involved with on a day-to-day basis; for example, I knew very little about product testing, market surveys, and store audits."

As Ms. Samuels paused, Judy thought, "I really don't know much about these types of studies either."

"I don't mean to imply that research supplier experience, or its equivalent, is absolutely necessary," Ms. Samuels continued. "Here we give detailed marketing research guidelines to all the junior analysts. The guidelines explain all of our studies and projects. Actually, prior experience simply makes acclimation shorter and less pressured."

"I'm glad to hear that!" Judy exclaimed.

Smiling, Ms. Samuels asked, "Do you have any specific questions?"

Judy thought for a moment. "Yes," she replied, "Can you tell me about the project that you are currently involved with?"

"I have several interesting projects, all at different stages of develop-

Figure I-4

The PEAC microcomputer unit. (Reprinted with permission.)

ment," responded Ms. Samuels. "Let me tell you about one that's particularly interesting. I'm currently deciding whether we should commission a computerized *PEAC* analysis for one of our products."

Sensing Judy's puzzlement, Ms. Samuels explained that PEAC is a recently developed computerized methodology by Viewfact, Inc. for diagnostic pretesting of television and radio commercials.

Judy's interest was stimulated. "Tell me more," she requested.

"In principle, the PEAC procedure is very simple. It's a portable system that records second-by-second audience reaction to a commercial." Handing Judy a picture, Ms. Samuels explained, "At the heart of the PEAC system is the handheld microcomputer, which registers respondent reactions. The wireless unit in the picture records respondents' feelings" (see Figure I-4).

"While watching commercials, respondents press keys that correspond to their feeling state—for example, a typical unit will have five keys indicating 'very positive' to 'very negative' feelings; so, a respondent who particularly liked a segment of a commercial would press the 'very positive' key; a respondent who particularly disliked a segment would press

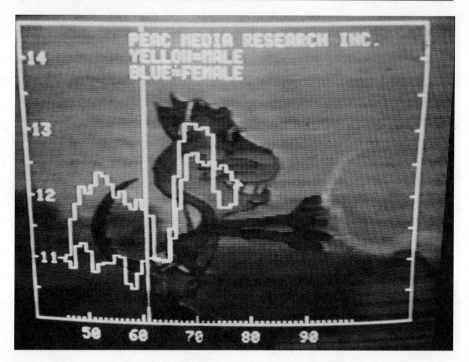

Figure I-5

A PEAC line for a soft-drink commercial. (Reprinted with permission.)

the 'very negative' key. The respondent continually depresses these keys throughout the entire commercial."

As Ms. Samuels paused, Judy asked, "How are these readings analyzed?"

"Well, after viewing the commercial, the individual microcomputers, which contain the registered feelings of each respondent, are plugged into a portable central processing unit. The individual responses are then aggregated and plotted. The plot traces the group's average response to the commercial. The commercial will be played back this time with the synchronized plot line superimposed over it. Thus, the end result is a second-by-second record of audience reaction to a particular commercial."

Ms. Samuels then handed Judy an illustration of the PEAC system (Figure I-5). As Judy examined the illustration, she continued, "Other diagnostics are also provided. As the plot is being computed, respondents, using paper and pencil, answer questions that examine such issues as the main point being communicated by the commercial. After the plot has been computed, respondents view the commercial again and participate in a group discussion that focuses on the points of greatest change in reactions. From the group discussions we can acquire information that helps reveal why these reactions occurred."

"What kinds of applications are you considering?" asked Judy.

"The most prominent PEAC applications to date have involved the *Ghostbusters* commercial, a Rick Springfield video, and the evaluation of President Reagan's performance in his second debate against Walter Mondale in the 1984 campaign. We plan on using PEAC on several recently developed advertisements that use different types of humorous appeals. We hope to find out which humorous delivery works best."

Before Ms. Samuels could continue, Mr. Peel walked into the office. "Excuse me Cathy, but it's almost one o'clock. I think Judy has heard enough about the marketing research business for one day," he chuckled.

After thanking Ms. Samuels, Judy and Mr. Peel walked to the elevator. Mr. Peel thanked Judy and noted that they planned to make a final decision in about two weeks.

THE LETTER

While waiting to hear from Mr. Peel, Judy reflected on her morning of interviews. As she thought about it, she came to realize that perhaps a senior marketing research analyst position was too high a position for a beginner.

The next day a letter from Mr. Peel indicated that although everyone had been impressed by her technical ability and communication skills, she lacked the practical experience necessary to handle the responsibilities of a senior marketing research analyst.

POSTMORTEM

Judy was still determined to land a research analyst position; however, she readjusted her sights and began to look at junior positions. The interview experience left her with a better understanding of the marketing research business and where she might fit in.

Some weeks later Judy landed a junior marketing research analyst position at a relatively large marketing research supplier. The position was just what she wanted—the responsibilities were demanding and promised to expose Judy to all of the varied aspects of the marketing research profession.

Summary

Whether you pursue a marketing research position, where you will *do* research, or a general marketing management position, where you will be responsible for commissioning and evaluating research projects,

13

Judy's experiences give you a realistic picture of what you can expect. Although Judy had to readjust her aspirations, she learned a valuable lesson—one that we continually emphasize in this textbook. Judy's experiences taught her to understand and appreciate the practical as well as the technical aspects of any position. Mastering the technique is simply never enough; it is a necessary but not a sufficient condition for success. The customs and practices of the marketing research profession need to be learned whether you end up in sales, management, or research.

Our objective in this book is to present the relevant technical material in a way that insures that you acquire a sound understanding and appreciation of how marketing research professionals practice the functions of marketing research. As we indicated in the Preface, our orientation is on the marketing research activities of consumer goods companies. The reason is simple: The marketing research practices of these companies are comprehensive and sophisticated and their expenditures on marketing research far exceed those of industrial or service companies. We will not ignore the marketing research practices of companies producing nonconsumer goods or services. By specifically focusing on consumer goods companies, however, we are able to expose you to a vast array of marketing research practices and projects, most of which can be used by other types of companies.

Key Concepts

"The mark of the true professional in any field is the rich vocabulary of patterns developed through years of formal education and especially through practical experience." (Peters and Waterman, *In Search of Excellence*)[2]

[2]Thomas J. Peters and Robert H. Waterman, *In Search of Excellence* (New York: Harper & Row, 1982).

MARKETING RESEARCH ENVIRONMENTS

Now that we've given you a brief introduction to marketing research, in Part I we focus on its environment and its role in the planning process. Our objective is to have you appreciate the environment in which marketing research takes place and the steps involved in planning and designing a marketing research study.

Chapter 1 defines marketing research and discusses its role in developing effective marketing strategy. A framework for understanding "realistic" marketing research environments is presented. Our discussion centers on the three principal components of such an environment: the intrastructure (in-house marketing research department), external parties that interface with in-house personnel, and the research cycle (in its relationship with the product life cycle).

After showing what happens when marketing research is not well-planned, Chapter 2 defines each step in a research project. Most importantly, we introduce the elements of a marketing research proposal. This book uses prototypical marketing research proposals throughout as a framework for introducing, discussing, and illustrating the various concepts, techniques, and principles that make up the essence of marketing research.

Realistic Marketing Research Environments

CHAPTER OBJECTIVES

- Define marketing research.
- Analyze the role of research in marketing strategy.
- Describe the characteristics of realistic marketing research environments.
- Explain the distinction between line and staff functions and its implications for the relationship between members of the marketing and research departments.
- Identify six principal parties outside the organization that play a crucial role in defining realistic marketing research environments.
- Describe the relationship between the research and product life cycles.
- State the ethical considerations involved in marketing research activities.

Introduction

This chapter continues our introduction to the theory and practice of *marketing research*. We want you to appreciate the role marketing research plays in developing effective marketing strategies and to understand the structure of the industry, including the available career opportunities. Our main point is that decisions on product positioning, price, promotion, and distribution for a brand or service should be based on intelligent, carefully conceived, and properly conducted marketing research. However, to understand and appreciate what is involved in making "good" marketing research decisions requires recognition of the *marketing research environment*. As a first step in understanding the important components that together constitute what we call "realistic marketing research environments," let us consider the following example.

"Luxury just isn't enough anymore." In years past, luxury, comfort, status, and style were the attributes emphasized in marketing cars like the Mark VII. Just a few years ago, the magazine ads for its predecessor, Mark VI, focused exclusively on luxurious good looks; in fact, the only

Figure 1-1

New-car advertisement emphasizes function and value as well as luxury. (Reprinted with permission.)

text accompanying the picture of the car was the phrase, "Fashion Shows."[1]

Not so today. In the new Mark VII ads Ford Motor Company's Lincoln-Mercury division spends 250 words on the car's "electronically controlled air suspension," its "vented four-wheel disk brakes," and its "fuel-injected 5.0 liter engine" (see Figure 1-1).

What has prompted this change in strategy? *Research!* In hopes of attracting auto advertising, Knapp Communications Corporation, publishers of the magazines, *Geo, Bon Appetit, Architectural Digest*, and *Home*, polled people with incomes of over $50,000 on their tastes in automobiles and gave the results to the automakers. With the help of J. D. Power & Associates, a market research firm, Knapp sent questionnaires to 1,450 households and obtained responses from 998.

---

[1]This discussion is based on "Affluent Buyers Want Value As Well As Luxury in New Cars," *Wall Street Journal*, 5 July 1984.

The responses suggested that affluent buyers indeed want something more than luxury from their cars. They want technology and performance, economy of operation, and "value for money." Surprising numbers want features such as four-wheel disk brakes and independent rear suspensions. Forty-six percent said they expect their next car to have a "higher performance engine," compared with only 18 percent who expect it to have a leather interior. "The affluent market is giving more credence to value and function," observes Mr. Brown, a vice president of Knapp. "That doesn't mean the affluent don't care about luxury and comfort, but they're more willing than we ever guessed to move to function."

As automakers design new models—and advertising campaigns to support them—they're trying to meet affluent buyers' demands for "function" and "value." The affluent buyer is important to all automakers, not just luxury-car makers. Although the average annual income of a Cadillac or Lincoln buyer is just above Knapp's $50,000 cutoff, most people with incomes over $50,000 don't buy Cadillacs or Lincolns. Among the Knapp respondents, the most widely owned car was Chevrolet (24 percent), followed by Oldsmobile, Ford, and Buick.

This example shows how marketing research aids strategy development. Information collected through marketing research can provide information on (1) changes in the firm's environment, (2) changes in competitive offerings, (3) changes in the firm's consumer base, and (4) reactions to new products or product modifications.

THE NATURE OF MARKETING RESEARCH

Marketing has not always held prominence in business organizations. However, in the past two decades, changes in the business environment and in philosophies of management have elevated marketing and the importance of marketing research.

Marketing Research Defined

Marketing research The systematic gathering, recording, processing, and analyzing of marketing data, which—when interpreted—will help the marketing executive to uncover opportunities and to reduce risks in decision making.

Put simply, marketing research helps the marketing executive to make better informed and less risky marketing and advertising decisions. Accordingly, the information obtained through marketing research must be *objective*, *impartial*, *current*, *translatable*, and *relevant*. Only then will this information help to uncover opportunities and reduce risks in decision making.

■ Marketing research is the systematic gathering, recording, processing, and analyzing of marketing data, which—when interpreted—will help the marketing executive to uncover opportunities and to reduce risks in decision making.

Several aspects of this definition warrant discussion. First, *systematic* refers to the requirement that marketing research be organized and objective. Marketing research projects must be well-thought-out, and the marketing researcher must be impartial and neutral, keeping an open mind about what a study might uncover; marketing researchers ought not to have a hidden agenda or an axe to grind. Second, *gathering* refers to the procurement of data used in marketing decisions. Note that the data may be primary or secondary. **Primary data** are collected specifically for the project at hand. **Secondary data,** which can come from internal sources (within the organization) or external sources (outside the organization) have been collected for another project and have generally already been published. Third, *recording, processing,* and *analyzing* refer to making the data useful. Recording involves the process of collecting the data; processing involves editing and coding, transforming the information into a form that can be tabulated by a computer; analyzing refers to the marketing researcher's attempts to make sense out of the data in light of the problem at hand. Fourth, *when interpreted* refers to the marketing researcher's inferences from the analysis—that is, determining what the analysis means in the context of the problem and the real-world marketing environment. And fifth, *will help the marketing executive to uncover opportunities and to reduce risks in decision making* refers to problem solving and identification of opportunities in marketing research—research should emphasize problem solving over an obsession with techniques.

History of Marketing Research

Though marketing research was conducted before 1900, the period 1910-1920 is generally recognized as its formal beginning.[2] Companies devoted exclusively to marketing research services surfaced during this period. For example, in 1916 R. O. Eastman started the Eastman Research Bureau, which provided data on magazine readership and circulation. Among his first clients were *Cosmopolitan* and the *Christian Herald;* a few years later the General Electric Company became a client and commissioned a consumer survey to determine the recognition of their trademark. During this period survey research methodology developed. Questionnaire construction and an awareness of the potential for bias induced from the interviewing process became the prominent methodological issue of the day.

During the 1920s and 1930s research departments became more common in all types of organizations, and several of the pioneering names in marketing research began to appear. For example, in 1922 Daniel Starch first used the *recognition method* for measuring the readership of advertisements and editorial content; in 1923 George Gallup,

[2]This material draws heavily from the work of Jack J. Honomichl, "Research Beat," *Advertising Age,* 19 April 1976.

Primary data Data collected specifically for the project at hand. *Secondary data* Data that have been collected for another project and have already been published. Sources can be in-house or external.

originator of the now-famous Gallup Poll, also became involved in measuring advertising readership; and in the same year Arthur C. Nielsen, the father of the largest marketing research operation in the world, entered the field with his concept of *share of market*.

By the end of the 1930s the number of companies providing marketing research information had vastly increased. In 1921 the first book totally devoted to the subject of marketing research was written by Percival White. The compelling methodological issues during this period involved sampling. Many of the early pollsters, including A. C. Nielsen, Elmo Roper, and Archibald Crossley, were labeled "charlatans" because it was *obviously* impossible to make accurate predictions about the population based on a small sample of it. As skeptical editors and commercial clients were won over to sampling, nonprobability sampling designs were dismissed and modern probability sampling approaches became the standard.

World War II did much to propel research. Social research was in heavy demand by all branches of the government, especially the Army, the Office of Price Administration, and the Office of War Information.[3] Social scientist's such as Paul Lazarsfeld, Elmo Wilson, and Rensis Likert headed government divisions responsible for conducting public opinion and attitude research. Following the war, Likert transported his research team to the University of Michigan and established the now-famous Survey Research Center; Wilson started his own company, International Research Associates.

The postwar period brought with it a boom in research companies and rapid advances in research methodology, especially in quantitative techniques and computer technology. Over two hundred marketing research companies had been formed by 1948;[4] indeed, of today's top ten research companies, only one, the A. C. Nielsen Company, was founded before World War II. Expenditures on marketing research also increased dramatically throughout the postwar period—by 1983 expenditures on marketing research exceeded $1 billion.[5]

The methodological explosion, sparked by the commercialization of the digital computer, gave rise to four new journals in the marketing research field: *Journal of Marketing Research* in 1964, *Journal of Advertising Research* in 1974, *Journal of Consumer Research* in 1974, and *Marketing Science* in 1982. Advances in marketing research methodology, computer technology, and quantitative techniques have altered the marketing research profession. Routine application of multivariate data analysis, advertising research by split cable TV, computer-assisted telephone interviewing, and the use of microcomputers and remote terminals in field operations are just a few examples of methodological and technological innovations.

[3]L. L. Lockley, "Notes on the History of Marketing Research," *Journal of Marketing*, April 1950, 733.
[4]"Market Detectives," *Wall Street Journal*, September 1947, 1.
[5]J. J. Honomichl, "Research Business Review—The Nation's Top 35 Market Research Companies," *Advertising Age*, 17 May 1984.

RESEARCH AND MARKETING STRATEGY

Objective and usable information obtained through well-conceived marketing research provides the foundation upon which marketing strategy is built. At each point in a product's evolution, strategic marketing decisions should be based on marketing research tailored to the particular needs of the product, dictated largely by the competitive and environmental factors facing the organization.

Strategy Considerations

To better appreciate the role of marketing research in strategy formulation, consider the case of a once top-selling product that has reached market maturity and is in danger of losing market share, awareness, and sales to newer competitors. One strategy would be to spruce up the aging product, reformulate the ingredients, add "new" to the packaging, and launch it as a "new and improved" product. An alternative strategy would be to define a new role for the aging product in the marketplace. This latter strategy, called **repositioning,** results less frequently from a marketing executive's inspirational brainstorm than from a company's research into its products and careful monitoring of category movement to detect subtle shifts before they become major trends.

Repositioning a product in a new category can be tricky but the potential rewards can be great. Let's look at one successful repositioning strategy.

Repositioning A strategy that defines a new role (new users or uses) for an aging product in the marketplace.

Snickers. In the late 1970s, marketers at Mars, Inc., noticed that consumer preferences were shifting to wholesome, nutritious food for snacks.[6] Thus, Snickers, the top-selling candy bar, was relaunched as a snack food. The repositioning ploy was a function of marketing opportunity, contends William Deeter, public affairs director for the company's M&M/Mars division. He notes: "The snack market is a bigger pond to go fishing in. Snickers has good food value and legitimate nutritional value." To add credibility to its claim of nutrition and good food value, Mars used the 1984 Olympic Games as a launching pad for the candy bar's new role—Snickers was the official snack food of the games.

Professional Brands. Another example of the role of marketing research in marketing strategy can be found in the health care arena. Over the past five years "professional" brands have appeared on the scene of the health care market.[7] The term *professional brands* refers to health care products once sold only on a prescription basis but now distributed over the counter (OTC).

[6]The repositioning of Snickers is discussed in D. Gallanis, "Positioning Old Products in New Niches," *Advertising Age,* 3 May 1984.

[7]This material was presented by Hanno Fuchs, Executive Vice President Director, Research, Sudler & Hennessey, Inc. at the AMA New Product Conference held in New York City in August 1984.

In 1981 Parke-Davis, a division of Warner-Lambert Company was ready to market several products that fit the professional brand category. However, very little was known about this emerging new segment in OTC health care. Parke-Davis marketing executives did have certain "gut" feelings about the structure underlying this market. Health care products were felt to fall along a *perceptual continuum* ranging from old-line proprietaries to prescription products. Proprietary OTCs were perceived to be consumer-focused, emotionally based, advertising intensive, folkloric and "good old. . . ." In contrast, prescription products were perceived to be professional-focused, rationally based, sales intensive, scientific, and state-of-the-art. The market executives at Parke-Davis thought that consumers would view the new product class, professional OTCs, as falling somewhere between proprietary and prescription products on the perceptual continuum. Faced with an emerging but unknown market segment Parke-Davis's marketing executives decided to undertake a research project to investigate their hypotheses about the product and consumer distribution concepts of professional OTCs. Sudler & Hennessey, a subsidiary of Young and Rubican, designed the study.

Step 1 of the research project involved a panel of twenty five physicians, pharmacists, and marketers who individually rated their patients'/customers' perceptions of 118 brands in seven product categories: analgesics, athlete's foot remedies, cold remedies, laxatives, nasal sprays, stomach remedies, and vitamins. Brands were rated along a high tech/low tech scale from 1 to 5 and a mean rating was computed for each brand. The results of this phase of the research project confirmed the perceptual continuum concept; based upon the mean rating scores, brands could be arranged along a perceptual continuum from lower-tech proprietary OTCs to higher-tech professional OTCs. The derived perceptual continuum for stomach remedies is shown in Table 1-1 (numbers in parentheses give mean rating scores).

Step 2 of the research project involved a survey of 8,600 respondents, each of whom assigned a tech (high-to-low) score for their "most used" brand in each of the seven product categories investigated in step one.

T A B L E 1-1
Derived Perceptual Continuum for Stomach Remedies

Low-Tech (1)				High Tech (5)
Bromo Seltzer (1.2)	Rolaids (1.8)	Gelusil (3.0)	Mylanta (3.4)	Gaviscon (4.2)
Alka Seltzer (1.1)	Bisodol (1.7)	Maalox (2.8)		
	Tums (1.6)	Di-Gel (2.8)		
	Phillips (1.5)	Alka-2 (2.6)		
	Chooz (1.5)			
	Pepto Bismol (1.4)			

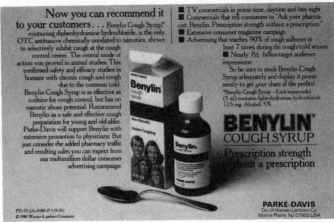

Figure 1-2

Advertisement for Benylin as an over-the-counter product, emphasizing its professional nature. Source: Parke-Davis, used with permission.

The results of this phase of the research indicated that users of professional OTCs are different from users of proprietary OTCs in a number of important ways. For example, compared to proprietary OTC users, professional OTC users tend to be younger and female, have higher incomes and social status, and be more educated. In addition the evidence indicated that users of professional OTCs perceived this product class as consumer and professional-focused, advertising-intensive, contemporary, sophisticated, more effective/more expensive than proprietary products, and less extreme/less expensive than prescription products. Along the perceptual continuum, professional OTCs were generally perceived to be more similar to prescription products than to proprietary products.

Based upon this research, marketing executives at Parke-Davis in concert with the account representative and researchers at Sudler & Hennessey set the communication goals for professional OTC products; these goals were to (1) communicate that the switch from prescription to OTC does not sacrifice full strength, (2) retain physician and pharmacist goodwill, and (3) project a professional-brand personality. The ad for Benylin shown in Figure 1-2 is consistent with these communication goals.

REALISTIC MARKETING RESEARCH ENVIRONMENTS

Look at Figure 1-3, a diagram of organizations that make up the marketing research community. The term *client* refers to the person or group that sponsors or commissions the research project. Through the marketing research department, the client usually contacts a marketing research

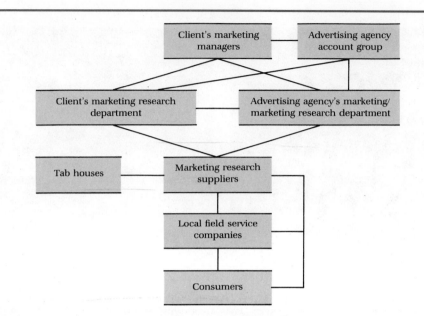

Figure 1-3

The marketing research community.

supplier, the research department of an advertising agency, or the local field service company directly. If the advertising agency is contacted, it can, in turn, either employ a marketing research supplier or deal directly with the local field service company. In any event, a tab house will be used to perform the tabulating work and other analyses, unless the marketing research supplier or advertising agency has tabulating capabilities.

By *realistic marketing research environments* we mean environments that accurately portray how marketing research is conducted and the context in which the research takes place. To be more specific, realistic marketing research environments have the following characteristics:

- Interface among involved parties in the marketing community is clearly recognized. These parties include the marketing executive, the marketing researcher, marketing research suppliers, tab houses, advertising agencies, local field services, and consultants.
- Research is problem-oriented, directed toward helping the marketing executive make better decisions with respect to satisfying consumer needs and wants as modified by societal considerations.

Although complex and characterized by many diverse problems and interested parties, realistic marketing environments comprise basic parts, easily described. Figure 1-4 presents an overview of the general structure of these environments. Notice that the framework shown in the figure

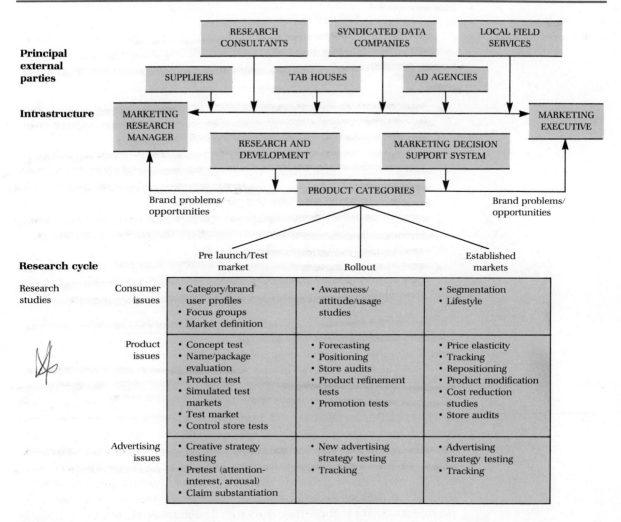

The figure shows a hierarchical diagram with the following elements:

Principal external parties (top row): RESEARCH CONSULTANTS, SYNDICATED DATA COMPANIES, LOCAL FIELD SERVICES; second row: SUPPLIERS, TAB HOUSES, AD AGENCIES

Intrastructure: MARKETING RESEARCH MANAGER, RESEARCH AND DEVELOPMENT, MARKETING DECISION SUPPORT SYSTEM, MARKETING EXECUTIVE, PRODUCT CATEGORIES, with "Brand problems/opportunities" on both sides

Research cycle and **Research studies**:

		Pre launch/Test market	Rollout	Established markets
Research studies	Consumer issues	• Category/brand user profiles • Focus groups • Market definition	• Awareness/ attitude/usage studies	• Segmentation • Lifestyle
	Product issues	• Concept test • Name/package evaluation • Product test • Simulated test markets • Test market • Control store tests	• Forecasting • Positioning • Store audits • Product refinement tests • Promotion tests	• Price elasticity • Tracking • Repositioning • Product modification • Cost reduction studies • Store audits
	Advertising issues	• Creative strategy testing • Pretest (attention-interest, arousal) • Claim substantiation	• New advertising strategy testing • Tracking	• Advertising strategy testing • Tracking

Figure 1-4

Overview of realistic marketing research environments.

has three major components: the intrastructure, external parties, and the research cycle. We'll now examine each in more detail.

The Intrastructure

First, marketing research is a staff function similar to legal, personnel, and accounting functions. Hence, the marketing research manager does not have the power to give orders to anybody in the line operation. The marketing researcher's role is advisory. Accordingly, compelling arguments presented persuasively are the marketing researcher's most important weapons; in other words, the marketing researcher must sell his or her ideas and positions.

The line/staff distinction is important and influences the relationship between respective members of the research department and of the marketing department. Four basic arrangements can describe this relationship:[8]

- *Noncompulsory consultation* reflects a system in which the marketing executive (line) can choose not to consult with the marketing researcher (staff) in development of research projects.
- *Mandatory consultation* reflects a system in which the marketing executive must consult with the marketing researcher in development of research projects; however, the marketing executive need not follow the advice of the marketing researcher.
- *Mandatory joint approval* reflects a system in which the marketing executive and the marketing researcher must jointly approve a research project before it is authorized.
- *Functional autonomous approval* reflects a system in which the marketing researcher has the power to authorize the development of a research project without the consent of the marketing executive.

Several reasons favor the mandatory-joint-approval arrangement, especially for the marketing researcher. In particular, by requiring the marketing executive to approve a particular research project, this arrangement increases the likelihood that (1) the objectives are actually "do-able" and have been translated into a workable project, (2) the research design is appropriate, and (3) the findings will be acted upon. A joint approval arrangement is implied by the double arrows shown in Figure 1-4 that connect the marketing executive and marketing research manager boxes. The double arrows signify that both parties play *proactive* as well as *reactive* roles in the marketing research projects of the organization. Moreover, in certain instances the marketing research manager may actually initiate the project, since it is common for larger marketing research departments to have their own research budgets. Such research budgets are usually allocated among the group managers and are frequently used for experimental and developmental projects.

The typical structure of a corporate marketing research department is headed by the director of marketing research, who reports directly to the vice president of marketing/marketing services. Reporting to the director of marketing research are a number of group managers, often titled associate directors. (This level may be absent in "leaner" organizations.) Group managers are responsible for marketing research for a specific group of products (such as beverages or health care products). Under each group manager is a marketing research manager who oversees the

[8]See N. Hollart, P. Golden, and M. Chudnoff, *Marketing Research for the Marketing and Advertising Executive* (New York Chapter: American Marketing Association, 1981), chap. V, 42–43.

senior and junior research analysts assigned to conduct research on a brand or on a small group of brands. The number of managers and analysts will vary.

Both the marketing executive and the marketing researcher interface with research and development (R&D) and the management information systems (MIS) groups. R&D provides technological support and advice and plays an instrumental role in product design decisions. MIS provides computer-based information that can be used strategically before, during, and after a marketing decision has been made. An important component is the **marketing decision support system,** (MDSS). This term refers to computer-based procedures and methods that regularly generate, store, analyze, and disseminate relevant marketing information. Three important components of an MDSS are a *data bank,* consisting of various kinds of external and internal data sources; a *statistical bank,* consisting of statistical procedures; and a *model bank,* consisting of mathematical optimization models designed to solve marketing problems. We will discuss MDSSs further in Chapter 22.

Principal External Parties

Six principal parties outside the organization play a crucial role in defining realistic marketing research environments. These parties interface with the marketing executive as well as with the marketing researcher and provide services that cannot be found within the organization. For example, in 1983 all manufacturers of consumer products spent an average of 58 percent of their total research budget on outside research.[9] Though there has been a decrease since 1978, a substantial percentage of total marketing research budgets still goes to such services, especially by manufacturers of consumer products.

Marketing Research Suppliers. The main business of marketing research suppliers is research—they are the primary data gatherers and analysts who execute studies and/or take ultimate responsibility for all of the technical aspects. The thousands of marketing research suppliers range from the extremely small one- or two-person shops to the extremely large multinational corporation. Two basic types of research suppliers are **full-service** firms, which can perform all aspects of a research project including research design, questionnaire preparation and production, interviewing, data processing, analysis, and interpretation, and **limited-service** firms, which specialize in only one or just a few aspects of a research project—for example, specific types of interviewing or particular types of studies. Table 1-2 gives the worldwide and United States research revenues for the top forty-four marketing research suppliers for 1985. Leading the field is the A. C. Nielsen Company, which had total

[9]Dick Warren Twidt, *1983 Survey of Marketing Research* (Chicago: American Marketing Association, 1983), 32.

Marketing decision support system (MDSS) Computer-based procedures and methods that regularly generate, store, analyze, and disseminate relevant marketing information.

Marketing research suppliers The primary data gatherers and analysts who execute studies and/or take ultimate responsibility for all technical aspects of a research project.
Full-service suppliers External parties that perform all aspects of a research project.
Limited-service suppliers External parties that specialize in only one or just a few aspects of a research project.

TABLE 1-2

Revenues for Forty-Four Leading U.S. Research Organizations, 1985

Rank	Organization	Total U.S. research revenues* (millions)	Research revenues from outside U.S. (millions)
1	A. C. Nielsen Co.	$517.0	$268.8 est.
2	IMS International	171.1	86.9
3	SAMI	138.5	—
4	Arbitron Ratings Co.	122.0	—
5	Information Resources	75.1	3.0 est.
6	Burke Marketing Services	73.1	3.7
7	M/A/R/C	46.3	—
8	Market Facts	37.8	—
9	NFO Research	34.3	—
10	NPD Group	33.1	—
11	Maritz Market Research	30.0	—
12	Westat	25.2	—
13	Elrick and Lavidge	24.6	—
14	Walker Research	20.7	—
15	YSW/Clancy Shulman	19.5	1.0
16	Chilton Research	19.1	—
17	Simmons Market Research Bureau	16.5	—
18	Louis Harris and Associates	15.8	5.5
19	ASI Market Research	15.7	—
20	Opinion Research Corp.	14.5	—
21	Winona Research	14.4	—
22	Decisions Center	13.8	—
23	Ehrhart-Babic Group	13.8	—
24	Harte-Hanks Marketing Services Group	11.7	—
25	Data Development Corp.	10.9	—
26	Custom Research	9.7	—
27	National Analysts	9.6	—
28	Mediamark Research	9.5	—
29	Admar Research	8.9	—

(United States and worldwide) research revenues of more than $780 million, a distant second is IMS International, which had total research revenues of about $258 million.

Full service marketing research suppliers are virtually structurally indistinguishable from each other. At the head of the organization is the president. Reporting directly to the president are the account group vice presidents and an executive vice president who supervises the staff functions relating to field operations, coding, secretarial services, data processing and tabulation, and production. The group vice presidents are responsible for servicing specific clients; typically there are "territorial sanctions" that do not permit one group vice president to service the clients of another group vice president, even if a particular client is not

T A B L E 1-2
(continued)

Rank	Organization	Total U.S. research revenues* (millions)	Research revenues from outside U.S. (millions)
30	Starch INRA Hooper	8.9	—
31	McCollum/Spielman Research	8.8	—
32	Gallup Organization	8.6	—
33	National Research Group	8.0	.9
34	Response Analysis	7.6	—
35	Decision Research Corp.	6.8	—
36	Decision/Making/ Information	6.7	—
37	Market Opinion Research	6.5	—
38	Guideline Research	6.5	—
39	Ad Factors Marketing Research	5.9	—
40	J. D. Power & Associates	5.8	—
41	Lieberman Research West	5.3	—
42	Marketing Research Services	5.1	—
43	Oxtoby-Smith	5.0	—
44	Kapuler Marketing Research	4.8	—
	Sub total, top 44	$1,652.5	369.8
	All other (56 CASRO companies not listed in top 44)	132.8†	
	Total (100 organizations)	$1,785.3	$369.8

*Total revenues that include nonresearch activities, for some companies, are significantly higher.

†Total revenues of 56 survey research companies—over and beyond those listed in top 44 list—that provide financial information on a confidential basis to CASRO (Council of American Survey Research Organizations).

Source: Advertising Age, 19 May 1986, S-5.

currently doing business with the company. Under the group vice president are a number of project directors, varying in experience and job responsibility. At the entry level is the trainee who reports to the assistant/junior project director. The number of project directors and trainees reporting to any one group vice president will depend on the size (dollar billings) of the accounts that vice president services.

The reasons for using outside research talent are simple: Marketing research suppliers provide economies of scale. In particular, (1) suppliers offer specialized talents that could be provided internally only at great cost; (2) by choosing different suppliers for different studies, the client gains considerable flexibility in scheduling and, most importantly, can better match the talents that a supplier offers with the requirements of a specific project; (3) the costs of going outside are often considerably lower than expenditures incurred if all aspects of the research are internalized; and (4) suppliers may be more objective and less subject to internal politics.

The services provided by marketing research suppliers can be classified into three categories:

Syndicated research services Companies that provide information from common pools of data to different clients.

- **Syndicated research services**—Companies that provide information from common pools of data to different clients are in the syndicated service business. Audits, purchase diary panels, audience share measurements, and advertising testing are the major types of syndicated services. Syndicated data companies tend to be among the largest in the research business. For example, all three of the top research suppliers listed in Table 1-2 deal largely in syndicated services. A. C. Nielsen Company offers a retail index audit that tracks volume and market share for food and drug products; IMS International offers a variety of syndicated reports on ethical pharmaceuticals, over-the-counter pharmaceuticals, medical diagnoses and treatments, and hospital laboratory supplies. SAMI provides category volume and market share data through computerized records of withdrawals from grocery chain warehouses. We will provide detailed information on most of the major syndicated data services in Chapter 4.

Standardized research services Studies conducted for different clients, but always in the same way.

- **Standardized research services**—A standardized research service is a research study conducted for different clients, but always in the same way. Advertising testing techniques are typically standardized so that the results of one study can be compared with norms of another study. Standardized services are often sold on a syndicated basis. Two popular standardized advertising testing techniques are Burke's day-after recall (DAR) procedure, which provides information on twenty-four hour day-after recall scores by telephone contact and McCollum/Spielman's advertising control for television (AC-T), which uses a controlled theater setting in twelve locations around the United States to measure attitude change in reaction to TV commercial exposures.

Custom research services Tailor-made, one-of-a-kind studies.

- **Custom research services**—Almost all marketing research suppliers offer clients tailor-made, one-of-a-kind studies. This type of service probably represents the largest number of studies conducted, but not the largest in dollar billings. Among the major marketing research suppliers offering custom research services are Burke Marketing Research, Market Facts, Inc., Elrick and Lavidge, and The NPD Group.

The following general factors should be considered in choosing a research supplier: *experience*—does the supplier have a reputation in the field? specific *people*—are there apt to be personality clashes between client personnel and supplier personnel? *approach*—are the services standardized or does the supplier understand the unique needs of the client? *flexibility*—does the supplier understand the position of the client? *quality*—does the supplier provide extensive field control and reliable validation procedures? *deadlines*—does the supplier complete projects on time? *cost*—does the supplier offer reasonably priced services and complete projects at estimated costs? and *marketing orientation*—does the supplier understand marketing and the role of research in developing strategies?

Tab Houses. Typically, neither the client nor the marketing research supplier has the necessary computing resources to generate tabulations of the data or other analyses. The tab house customarily gives the client or supplier a book of data containing tables that break down all of the response variables by key background and demographic factors. Tab houses generally give very quick turnaround; they are frequently open twenty four hours a day. They offer other specialized programming assistance and have libraries of canned statistical programs. Selection of a tab house is primarily based on cost and turnaround. The tab house is often chosen by the research supplier with ultimate responsibility for the project.

Tab houses Outside suppliers that perform tabulating work and other analyses when neither the client nor the marketing research supplier has the necessary computing resources.

Advertising Agencies. In 1981 the twenty five largest advertising agencies (in terms of gross income derived from United States operations alone) employed 1,550 research workers, of whom 1,162 were considered professionals.[10] However, not all advertising agencies place the same emphasis on research. Advertising research departments are generally more heterogeneous than research departments in other organizations. In some agencies a prominent individual with an impressive title runs the research operation; in others, an essentially autonomous research staff is scattered in branch offices and subsidiaries. Some agencies have their own internal data collection capabilities—for example, WATS phone centers, focus group facilities, and so on. Other agencies almost exclusively use marketing research suppliers or local field services. In some agencies research emphasizes the development of effective advertising copy, while in others it emphasizes the planning of marketing strategy.

The advertising agency research department is headed by a senior vice president who reports directly to the president. In some agencies the title for the second-in-command is research department head. Under the senior vice president are a number of research directors, all of whom may have vice president titles. Each research director has a different set of clients to service and conducts research on studies relating to commercial development and testing as well as advertising spending. Associate research directors supervise the activities of the research account executive. The entry position in agency research departments is the project director. All members of the agency research department interface, to varying degrees with account executives, client research departments, and brand/product management. For small clients, or clients with unso-

[10]J. J. Honomichl, "U.S. Agency Income Profiles," *Advertising Age*, 18 October 1982.

phisticated research functions, the agency research department will frequently conduct custom research studies.

The role of the agency researcher is undoubtedly diverse: The *advertising agency researcher* is essentially a consultant whose clients include agency management, account management, and outside clients; research projects originate from each of these sources. Extensive interfacing with agency management, account management, and outside clients can place the agency researcher in an uncomfortable situation, when the needs of the respective parties conflict. Frequently, the agency researcher becomes an arbitrator, who must balance the demands of different interest groups.

Local field services
Outside party used by market research suppliers to collect interviews.

Local Field Services. The marketing research supplier generally utilizes a local field service to collect interviews. A local field service is typically a single proprietorship, whose owner serves as the local field service supervisor. The supervisor secures the interviewers, typically part-time workers. The research supplier's field director sets the interviewer payment rates, the number of interviews to be completed, the time schedule, and other aspects of the project. The supervisor identifies the interviewers, assembles them, briefs them, and coordinates their efforts while in the field. Most interviewers free-lance and frequently work for many diferent suppliers. A research supplier may have its own exclusive group of interviewers who work for no one else. We will return to the interview process in Chapter 5.

Syndicated data companies Companies that collect certain types of data for sale by subscription to organizations.

Syndicated Data Companies. As discussed earlier, these companies supply information that is not client-specific; in other words, syndicated data companies collect certain types of data for sale by subscription to organizations. The most common types of syndicated data include retail sales and inventory, consumer panels, advertising media audiences, pricing, and advertising effectiveness. Major syndicated data companies include A. C. Nielsen, SAMI, and IMS International. See Chapter 4 for specific details.

Independent consultants
Individuals with unique and specialized marketing skills hired for research projects by the client or the research supplier.

Independent Consultants. Individuals with unique and specialized marketing research skills can be hired ad hoc for research projects by the client or research supplier. Many independent marketing research consultants have Ph.D. degrees and teach at universities and schools of business administration.

The Research Cycle

What the members of the marketing research community *do* is research, and the third part of a realistic marketing research environment is the research cycle. The concept of the product life cycle, which divides a product's evolution into four stages in terms of sales patterns over time (see Figure 1-5), is widely accepted; however, the idea of a research life

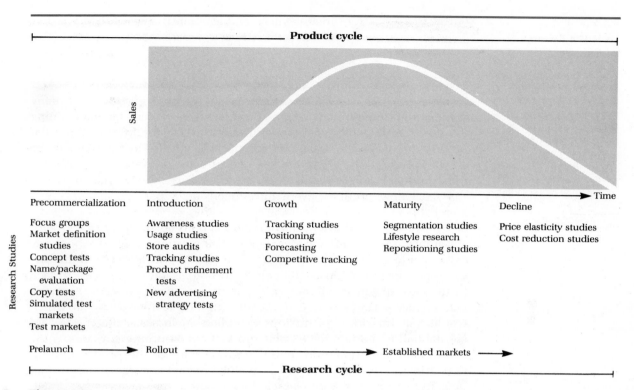

Figure 1-5

Interface between product and research life cycles.

cycle is not so widely recognized. Nevertheless, to develop effective marketing strategies we must understand the connection between the product and research life cycles. For example, the repositioning of Snickers, discussed earlier, underscores the importance of developing a *research strategy* that marries marketing research activities to the unique needs of the product at each point in its life cycle. To accomplish this, the marketing researcher must recognize the **research life cycle** as well as the *product life cycle.* The research cycle acknowledges the fact that as products move through their life cycle they have unique research needs. By dividing the research cycle into prelaunch, rollout, and established market stages, we can specifically match research activities to the unique needs of a product.

Figure 1-5 depicts this relationship. Notice that the product follows a sales pattern over time that can be divided into *introduction, growth, maturity,* and *decline.* Prior to introduction is an extremely important *precommercialization* period, though it is not specifically included as one of the four life-cycle stages. Over the course of this cycle, the marketing research needs of the product change correspondingly. The research cycle, which can be divided into *prelaunch, rollout,* and *estab-*

Research life cycle
Research activities in distinct stages matched to the unique needs of the product during each stage of its life cycle (prelaunch, rollout, and established markets).

33

**Precommercialization
stage** Developmental
stage of a product,
characterized by much
marketing research
activity designed to
ensure that the launched
product will be successful
in matching or exceeding
management's
performance objectives.

lished markets, recognizes such changes and specifically matches research activities to the unique needs of a product during each stage in its life cycle.

Precommercialization Stage. This developmental stage of the product is generally characterized by a great deal of marketing research. In many markets the development of new products is necessary for maintaining the health and vitality of the organization. It is painfully clear from the product life cycle that sales and profits will decline in the maturity or decline phases; this alone creates pressure to innovate and introduce new products. For example, *New Product News* reports that in March 1984, 163 new products were introduced, an 8 percent increase over March 1983.[11]

However, new-product introduction is both costly and risky. Proctor & Gamble, the perennial leader in advertising expenditures, spent nearly $100 million on each product when introducing Always, a feminine hygiene product, and Citrus Hill Select, an orange juice, in 1983.[12] In fact, in the case of Citrus Hill Select, expenditures exceeded sales. A classic failure story is Du Pont's CORFAM substitute for leather products, which resulted in hundreds of millions of dollars in losses. Failure rates are substantial. In a study of 366 new products in 54 prominent companies, Booz, Allen, and Hamilton found that one-third of the products introduced in the market were unsuccessful—10 percent were outright failures and 23 percent were classified as doubtful. For consumer products the outlook is even gloomier with estimates of product failures approaching 50 to 60 percent.[13]

All of the marketing research activities undertaken in the precommercialization stage are designed to ensure that if the product is rolled out nationally, it will be successful in matching or exceeding management's performance objectives. Several of the more commonly commissioned marketing research studies representing this stage include:

Concept testing. What is the appeal of the concept? To what market segment does it appeal most? What are the most attractive benefits?

Product testing. Does the product meet functional expectations? How does the product compare with competition?

Market studies. To what segment should the new brand be positioned? What is the competitive structure of the market?

Name/package testing. Do the name and package attract attention? Do they "fit" the product?

Copy testing. Does the copy execution communicate key product benefits?

[11]*New Product News*, (New York: Dancer Fitzgerald Sample, Inc., March 1984).

[12]"Leaders Rebuild Sales, Hike Advertising" *Advertising Age*, 14 September 1984, 1.

[13]Reported by G. Urban and J. Hauser, *Design and Marketing of New Products* (Englewood Cliffs, N.J.: Prentice Hall, 1980), 27.

Simulated test markets (STMs) and test marketing. What share of market can be expected? What volume will be realized?

Introduction Stage. The introduction stage is crucial to a product's future. At this stage, also called rollout, market research studies most commonly focus on the following activities:

- *Store audits.* Syndicated **store audits** monitor performance in the marketplace with respect to dollar and unit sales/share, distribution/out-of-stock, inventory, price, promotional activity, and feature ads.
- *Tracking.* A system for **tracking** the key sales components of customer awareness and trial and repeat purchases is set up very early in the introduction stage. Tracking is often accomplished through periodic waves of telephone interviewing and gives the client a basis for deciding whether sales are building as expected or whether changes need to be made. For example, if customer awareness is lower than expected and trial purchases are low as a result, then advertising may need to be reevaluated. On the other hand, if repeat purchases are low, product quality may be a problem.

Growth Stage. At this stage sales begin to take off. However, if growth is left unmonitored, problems can quickly arise. Among the more frequently commissioned marketing research studies are the following:

- *Positioning.* Is the advertising strategy communicating the appropriate product attributes and/or product image to the right target market? Are there other attractive target markets that we should be communicating to? **Positioning** attempts to set the mix of product, price, promotion, and distribution to maximize appeal to the target market.
- *Tracking.* A primary research activity deals with tracking issues. Monitoring of customer awareness and trial and repeat purchases as components of volume should be maintained. The objective of tracking is to look for two situations. An *unexpected success* occurs when what is planned as a modest new product turns out to be a runaway success; tracking research should be designed to spot this quickly, determine why it happened, and look for ways to expand, multiply, or accelerate the unexpected success. *Repairable failures* occur in the early stages of a product's growth cycle when most of the volume comes from first-time trial purchases. Growth proceeds when an increasing share comes from repeat purchases. First-time buyers can't be maintained forever. If the sales components of awareness and trial and repeat purchases aren't developing as planned, action needs to be taken.
- *Forecasting.* At this stage forecasting sales patterns, especially repeat purchases, is crucial. For example, sales frequently take a slight tem-

Store audits Studies that monitor performance in the marketplace among dollar and unit sales/share, distribution/out of stock, inventory, price, promotional activity, and feature ads.

Tracking System for measuring the key sales components of customer awareness and trial and repeat purchases.

Positioning A system for determining how to set the mix elements of product, price, promotion, and distribution so as to maximize appeal of a product to a particular target population.

porary dip during the growth stage as trial purchases trail off, but before repeat purchases pick up the slack. Unless the dip has been forecasted, management may come to the wrong decision regarding the viability of the product and abandon it just before a new sales spurt occurs.

■ *Competitive Tracking.* Tracking competitive products is the other function of a tracking system during the growth phase. The same measures of customer awareness and trial-and-repeat-purchase levels should be collected on competitive products as on the researcher's own product to see how much of a threat they pose. Samples of competitive products should be purchased and comparative testing undertaken. The objective is to know as much about competitive products' strengths and weaknesses as possible.

The Maturity Stage. At this stage, the product is established and sales tend to flatten out. The objective here is to successfully manage the product and find new ways to build interest, excitement, and sales. Marketing research activities should be directed at finding opportunities that will stimulate new interest in the product. Among the more commonly commissioned marketing research studies are the following:

■ *Repositioning.* Additional new volume can often be built by altering a product's position and appealing to a broader market or a different set of needs.

■ *Package testing.* A new or redesigned package is yet another way to try to stimulate sales by giving a product a "new look." **Package testing** should determine if the new package is better in impact, visibility, and connotations and not just different from the original package design.

■ *Segmentation.* To uncover additional uses or users for a product that can be promoted to stimulate new sales the researcher may undertake **segmentation studies.** The promotion of baking soda as refrigerator deodorizer is a classic example of this approach.

It is important to note that as possible product modifications emerge, the marketing researcher will undoubtedly consider undertaking precommercialization studies.

Decline Stage. At this stage sales and profits begin to decline. Improved products and/or technologies have surfaced in the marketplace, or perhaps the general public has simply grown tired of the product. Now marketing research should focus on attempts to salvage the product. However, when sales start to decline, the first reaction is likely to recommend cuts in research expenditures. It is unusual to find large, expensive studies designed to salvage a product in the decline stage. Price-elasticity and cost-reduction studies can help milk whatever profits still remain. In addition, another job of the marketing researcher is to determine the im-

Package testing A system for assessing the visibility of package alternatives, relative to one another and usually to a competitive brand, and the ability to package alternatives to convey product end-use benefits. **Segmentation studies** A system for identifying groups of consumers who exhibit differential sensitivity to one of the marketing mix elements.

pact of a deletion decision on the sales of other products, company image, and so on. This is especially important in industrial companies.

ETHICAL CONSIDERATIONS

Marketing research involves collecting information from people. This is, however, a two-edged sword. On the one hand, marketing researchers expect respondents to be willing participants who honestly and accurately respond to questions; on the other hand, respondents assume that marketing researchers will respect the following respondent rights:

- *Anonymity*—respondents will not be identified with their answers.
- *Privacy*—respondents may refuse to participate in the study.
- *Access to information*—respondents have a right to be informed about the purpose, procedure, and results of the study.

There are other ethical considerations. For example, marketing research suppliers must ensure that information about clients remain confidential. (Suppliers often have access to their client's confidential information about specific projects.) In addition, marketing research suppliers are ethically obligated to provide unbiased designs and honest and objective fieldwork, all of which may confirm or disconfirm their client's expectations about the outcome of a study. And finally, marketing researchers are ethically obligated not to pirate research designs and other relevant information—obtained, say, through soliciting project bids, which are seldom legally protected.

A number of industry groups in the marketing research field have developed codes of ethics to guide researchers. Among the industry groups publishing codes of ethics are The American Marketing Association (AMA), the American Association for Public Opinion Research (AAPOR), the Marketing Research Association (MRA), and Council of American Survey Research Organizations (CASRO).

Summary

If you recall our examples in this chapter, you'll realize that the role of marketing research in developing effective strategy is a major one. Marketing research made it possible to reposition Snickers and position Benylin and made it possible for American automakers to compete more effectively with foreign companies. Furthermore, research has a life cycle that parallels the product life cycle. Research is not possible, of course, without people and organizations. In the marketing research community the members of the intrastructure interact during every stage of the research process with people from the six external groups involved in marketing research.

Key Concepts

Marketing research

Realistic marketing research environments

Marketing research suppliers

Tab houses

Advertising agencies

Local field services

Syndicated data companies

Independent consultants

The product life cycle

The research life cycle

Review Questions

1. Define marketing research. Show how marketing research relates to the definition of marketing.
2. How could marketing research affect marketing strategy?
3. If companies have in-house marketing research departments, how can they justify going outside for research?
4. Describe the interface between the product life cycle and the research life cycle.

Planning a Research Project

C H A P T E R

CHAPTER OBJECTIVES

- Explain the importance of planning and well-thought-out marketing research.
- Describe the decision process and its relationship to information needs.
- List the various steps involved in the marketing planning process.
- Explain the importance of marketing research in the planning process.
- Describe the steps in the course of a research project.
- Delineate the key elements of a marketing research proposal.

Introduction

"Garbage in—garbage out" is a phrase we all have heard before. It succinctly captures a relationship between input and output that, unfortunately, characterizes far too many research projects. No one would deny that the final quality of a marketing research project is tied to the quality of the input. However, the quality of the input depends as much upon relevant background issues and the ability of the marketing executive and researcher to clarify the problem as it does upon the technical competence of the researcher.

Successful products don't just happen. Success comes about through careful planning and well-thought-out marketing research. Nevertheless, marketing executives sometimes fail to realize the value that can be derived from good marketing research. Take, for example, the case of the World Football League. Executives of the league were caught up in an air of enthusiasm and a sales pitch that was not realistic. Consequently, they failed to determine market potential for the new venture, to see if there was a reasonable chance to break even. Clearly, a well-thought-out market research program would have indicated that chances of success were less than likely and that a no-go decision was in order. The 1977 plight of Coors beer can also be traced to a lack of timely marketing research. In 1977–1978 Coors faced severe competitive pressure from Anheuser-Busch, resulting in market share losses and a significant decrease in per-share earnings. The reasons for this unfavorable trend? Simple—the Coors company was reluctant to conduct the marketing research that would have uncovered consumer preference for low-calorie beer and their dislike of Coors' hard-to-open press-tab can (a can that hardly satisfied most consumers' desire for convenience and ease of use).

How important is the marketing planning process? The value of well-conceived marketing research in the planning process cannot be overstated. Though many organizations recognize the value of a structured approach in the planning process, they often fail to follow through. In too many instances top management follows a "shoot from the hip" mentality, resulting in marketing research information that is neither objective nor actionable. Even in sophisticated organizations, enthusiasm and individual or career interests can render the best planning processes inept.

RESEARCH INFORMATION AND MARKETING PLANNING

As we indicated, the information obtained through marketing research projects must be objective and actionable and must help the marketing executive to reduce risks in decision making. However, the marketing executive must exercise good judgment in deciding what information to collect and whether the collected information is adequate—good enough to make the risk of error more tolerable than the delays and costs that would result from further data collection efforts.

Incorrect planning of marketing research studies can have several causes. For example, the marketing research supplier may not understand the marketing strategy and/or objectives of the sponsoring firm; the marketing manager directing the research may not understand the situation or may be operating under an erroneous set of assumptions; the marketing manager (or researcher) may have a hidden agenda for conducting the research; the marketing researcher may ask the wrong questions; the marketing manager may focus on an inappropriate response variable; and so on. In any of these events, poor research planning will undoubtedly lead to incorrect information and ultimately to bad management decisions. We'll look at two examples of poorly planned market research.

The Edsel

A classic portrait of marketing ineptitude is the much-publicized and commented-upon story of the Ford Motor Company's Edsel automobile.[1] Over a period of almost a decade Ford spent several million dollars on

[1]Much of this material is adapted from Robert F. Hartley, *Marketing Mistakes* (Columbus, Ohio: Grid Publishing, 1981) 115–128.

marketing research, focusing on such issues as owner likes and dislikes, market and sales analysis, and imagery studies that sought to determine the best personality for the car and the best name.

Eight hundred recent car buyers in Peoria, Illinois, and another eight hundred in San Bernardino, California, were interviewed about the various images they had of different automobile makes. Based on this research, Ford executives decided upon a personality for the new automobile that would be best suited for the younger executive or professional family on the way up. The Edsel was positioned as a smart, status-oriented automobile: It had a unique vertical grill and push-button transmission, hood, trunk lid, and parking brake lever as well as other luxury items reflecting engineering advancement and convenience. The Edsel was a big car; it had a 345-horsepower engine and many other high-speed performance features.

The Edsel was introduced on September 4, 1957. Though first-year sales were close to target projections, between 1957 and 1960 only 109,466 Edsels were sold. After recovering $150 million of its investment by using Edsel plants and tools in other Ford divisions, the Ford Motor Company still lost more than $100 million of its original investment plus an estimated $100 million in operating expenses.

The failure of the Edsel can be traced to many factors. The stock market collapsed in 1957, marking the beginning of the 1958 recession. Nevertheless, many factors contributing to the ultimate demise of the Edsel can be linked to poor research planning and marketing implementation. First, the personality/imagery research conducted was never effectively translated into tangible product features. Though the target segment of upwardly mobile young executives and professionals might have been the appropriate group of individuals to appeal to, one can question whether having horsepower and high-speed performance features were the appropriate characteristics to emphasize in an appeal to this segment. Second, the marketing research conducted on the Edsel was dated. For the most part, the research was completed several years before market introduction in 1957. Third, the heavy promotional build-up of the Edsel prior to its introduction led consumers to believe that a significant innovation was coming. Consumers were disappointed, for despite the new luxury style, the Edsel was also uselessly overpowered and gadget- and chrome-laden; in short, the Edsel wasn't worth the build-up.

What may become the Edsel of our times is the Coca-Cola Company's decision to market new Coke and the subsequent decision to return old Coke (Coke Classic) to the supermarket shelves.

New Coke/Old Coke

In April 1985 the Coca-Cola Company announced that it was replacing original Coke with a reformulated Coke. Never before in all the annals of marketing had a company voluntarily ceased production of a best-selling product and replaced it with an entirely new product—except for

automobile companies, whose products presumably benefit from new-
ness. What motivated this bold and shocking move? *Research!* According
to press releases, over a period of about 2½ years, 180,000 to 200,000 blind
taste-tests were done, pitting three or more "new" Coke formulas against
the original Coke formula, as well as rival Pepsi-Cola. The new formulas
were preferred to old Coke in blind taste-tests and, because they were
sweeter, competed more favorably against Pepsi.

As you are probably aware, consumers reacted violently against new
Coke and the plan to take original Coke off the market. Mail and phone
calls poured into the Atlanta headquarters and protests sprang up across
the country. In addition, Coke's ongoing research program indicated a
surge of interest in the old formula. By the first week in July, 70 percent
of the people interviewed said they preferred the old and only 30 percent
the new. In contrast, before May 30 the figures were 53 percent preferring
the new and 47 percent preferring the old.[2] In response, on July 10, 1985,
Coca-Cola announced that the old Coke formula would be brought back
under the name Coca-Cola Classic—a move as astounding as the introduction of new Coke.

How could Coca-Cola—with its sophisticated internal marketing research operation and a $4 million budget—so misread consumer reac-
tion? The research focused on taste preferences but did not measure the
abiding emotional attachment to Coke. Most of the taste-tests conducted
were "blind" comparisons that did not take into account the total product *gestalt*—name, history, packaging, image, and so on. Only 30,000 to
40,000 of the 180,000 to 200,000 taste-tests conducted involved the specific
formulation that eventually was introduced to the public.[3] Moreover, to
assure secrecy throughout the testing, people surveyed were not told
that the old Coke would be taken away and the new one substituted.
People participating in the taste-tests must have assumed that both the
new and the old formulas would be available side-by-side. Finally, inadequate research into preferences by segments also contributed to the
problem. While, in general, colas are consumed by a young segment,
Coke had an older segment. And though the younger segment liked the
sweeter taste, Coke's core market preferred the less sweet, more carbonated formulation.

The Edsel and Coke fiascoes might be perceived as examples of why
consumer research should be downplayed. But that isn't so at all. Instead, both examples reflect research that should have been done and
wasn't, or incorrect interpretation of what research was available. Marketing research does not guarantee a correct decision. The most one can
expect is that well-thought-out and implemented research will increase
the percentage of correct decisions. To this end, we devote this chapter
to discussing the roles marketing research play in the planning process.
Our recurring theme is that sounder and better-conceived research input
will undoubtedly produce more accurate and useful output. Most of the

[2]Nancy Giges, "Coke's Switch to Classic," *Advertising Age*, 15 July 1985, 82.
[3]Jack Honomichl, "Missing Ingredients in 'New' Coke's Research," *Advertising Age*,
(1985), vol. 56, 1.

discussion will outline the steps in the course of a research project. We will introduce some concepts that are the subjects of ensuing chapters and so will give only brief explanations here.

Weighing the Value of Information

Although information might be collected because of tradition, as a means to support a decision already made, for legal reasons, to serve as the basis for advertising claims, or simply to delay a decision, much information is collected explicitly to aid in making a particular decision. How, then, do we determine the value of the information that is collected?

If the information does not increase the likelihood of making a good decision, then it is of little value. If an executive, faced with two choices, each equally likely to be correct, is then given research information that increases the likelihood of making the correct decision from 50:50 to 75:25, the information is valuable though not perfect: There is still a one in four chance of making a wrong decision. In this case one is surely better off with information than without it. Information increases the likelihood of going ahead with a success or not proceeding with a failure. There are two conditions under which information generally proves to be most useful: (1) if there is a great deal of uncertainty concerning what is the best course of action to take, and (2) if the alternative courses of action would lead to either substantial losses or profits. The actual worth of information depends on three factors:

- the likelihood of making a correct decision on the basis of information collected
- the relative attractiveness (profitability) of the alternative decisions
- the cost of acquiring the information

As an example of how marketing executives weigh the value of information consider the decision to initiate a pretest market and/or test market for a new product. As we discuss in Chapter 21, test markets typically represent the final step in developing new, frequently-purchased consumer products. **Test markets** are intended to provide information about the market performance of a new product that otherwise would only be known after a national launch was in progress. But the direct costs of a test usually range from $1 million to $2 million, and the failure rate of new products in test markets can be substantial—recent reports estimate the incidence of such failures to be 64.5 percent.[4] Because test marketing is an expensive way to detect a new product failure, efforts have been directed at conducting more thorough evaluations of new products before initiating a test market. Over the past decade a number of pretest market models have appeared. In principle, at least, **pretest markets,** also called *simulated test markets* (STM), are not intended to

Test markets A system that allows the marketing manager to evaluate the proposed national marketing program in a smaller, less expensive situation with a view toward determining whether the potential profit opportunity from rolling out the new product or line extension outweighs the potential risks.

Pretest markets A system for providing management with information on the likely share or volume a new product will capture prior to conducting a test market.

[4]A. C. Nielsen Company, "New Product Success Ratios 1977," *The Nielsen Researcher*, (1979), no. 1, 2–9.

43

replace test markets but rather to screen out products with low probability of success in test markets. As we indicate in Chapter 21, pretest
markets cost only a fraction of what a test market costs.

The value of information provided by a pretest market and a test
market can be evaluated easily.[5] Suppose that the "ideal" program entails
the following procedure: (1) a go/no go decision based upon market share
or volume is applied to the pretest result; (2) if a go decision is reached,
another go/no go decision again based upon market share or volume is
applied to the test market result. Assume that the typical profit from a
new product that has been subjected to both a pretest and a test market
is $28.44 million. With neither a pretest nor a test market, the typical
expected profit is $16.74 million. Thus, the expected value of testing, fol-
lowing the "ideal" program, is $11.7 million:

$$\$28.44 - \$16.74 = \$11.70$$

If only a pretest is conducted, the typical expected profit is $28.02 mil-
lion. Thus, the expected value of a pretest is $11.28 million:

$$\$28.02 - \$16.74 = \$11.28$$

If only a test market is conducted, the typical profit is $28.16 million.
Thus, the expected value of a test market is $11.42 million:

$$\$28.16 - \$16.74 = \$11.42$$

Notice that either test can contribute the majority of value of the information provided by testing. However, the incremental expected value of
a test market, given that a pretest is conducted, is $420,000:

$$\$11,700,000 - \$11,280,000 = \$420,000$$

The incremental expected value of a pretest, given that a test market will
be conducted, is $280,000:

$$\$11,700,000 - \$11,420,000 = \$280,000$$

Thus, both pretesting and market testing provide worthwhile and valuable information.

This simple example illustrates the concept of value of information.
In Appendix 2-A we discuss a formal framework called *decision analysis*
for evaluating the worth of information.

Decision Processes and Information

The marketing decision-making process can be better understood by
examining its constituent activities:[6]

[5]The following material is adapted from G. L. Urban, G. M. Katz, T. E. Hatch, and A. J.
Silk, "The ASSESSOR Pre-Test Market Evaluation Systems," *Interfaces*, December 1983, 55–
56.

[6]The following discussion is adapted from John O'Shaughnessy, *Competitive Marketing: A Strategic Approach* (Boston: George Allen & Unwin, 1984), 125–128.

1. *Description.* A major function of marketing research is to collect basic descriptive data on the company, competitors, customers, served markets, and other aspects of the external environment. What specific information is collected and how depends on what is considered relevant by the marketing executive and on the value of the information.

2. *Explanation.* The purpose of explanation is to understand the event under study. This may involve describing the conditions under which the event varies or identifying its antecedents, causes, or effects. The purpose/objectives of the study will ultimately determine the type of explanation that is needed.

3. *Prediction.* By considering the effects of past, current, or proposed events, prediction attempts to make statements about future events. Depending on the problem setting, the marketing researcher may want to predict social and economic trends, market shares, competitor reactions, product acceptance, and so on. A class of statistical procedures called *forecasting* techniques are frequently employed for this purpose. (Forecasting techniques are discussed in Chapter 22.)

4. *Prescription.* Successful decisions are usually never guaranteed. Thus the activity of prescription involves selecting a course of action based upon the objectives of the study, while identifying relevant alternatives and assessing the likely consequences.

5. *Evaluation.* The activity of evaluation forms the basis for control; that is, by evaluating past performance or future potential the marketing executive can judge the success of what has been done or the likelihood of success in the future. Evaluation of past performance involves comparing actual performance against criteria—for example, planned performance—in order to assess the degree of accomplishment. Evaluation of future potential, in terms of a market share, for example, involves predicting and ranking probable future performances. In either case, evaluation requires clear standards called **action standards** to base the comparison on. Action standards define the performance criterion that will be used in evaluating the results of a marketing research study.

Table 2-1 summarizes the relationships among these elements and provides further details.

The Marketing Planning Process

Every marketing project goes through a planning process. Though the exact form of the process varies from organization to organization, the steps summarized in Figure 2-2 and discussed here are representative of what is generally involved.

Recognition. The first step, called recognition, is the identification of particular problems and opportunities. Frequently, marketing-related

---

Description Collecting basic descriptive data on the company, competitors, customers, served markets, and other aspects of the external environment.

Explanation An attempt to describe the conditions under which events vary or to identify its antecedents, causes, or effects so as to understand the event under study.

Prediction The attempt to make statements about future events on the basis of the effects of past, current, or proposed events.

Prescription Selecting a course of action based upon the objectives of the study and identifying relevant alternatives and their likely consequences.

Evaluation Judging the success of what has been done or the likelihood of future success.

Action standards A basis for defining the performance criterion that will be used in evaluating the results of a marketing research study.

T A B L E 2-1
Decision Processes and Information.

Description of: →	Explanation of: →	Prediction of: →	Prescription for: →	Evaluation of:
External environment	Social, technological and economic events	Social, technological and economic trends	Business-level planning: business in, investment objectives thrust	Business-level sales market share(s) earnings earnings per share return on investment/equity, etc.
Market	Market growth/decline, demand fluctuations, industry profitability	Market demand and sales	Market strategy product competitor segmentation promotion pricing distribution	Marketing-level *Sales* products territories customers channels sales people method of sale delivery size of order etc. *Costs* promotion selling transportation warehousing and order handling credit collection etc.
Customers	Customers' buying processes preferences perceptions attitudes	Buying behavior and product acceptance		
Competition	Competitors' behavior and performance	Competitor actions and reactions		
Company	Company success/low performance relative market share	Performance(s)		

Source: John O'Shaughnessy, *Competitive Marketing: A Strategic Approach* (George Allen & Unwin: Boston, 1984), 126.

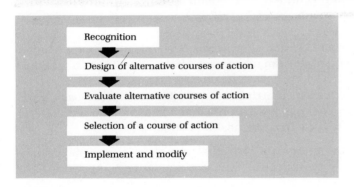

Figure 2-1

Stages of the marketing planning process.

problems and opportunities originate from the interaction of the organization's marketing program, the existing state of the market and consumer reactions to these factors. Evaluating the effectiveness of a marketing program can often help to isolate problem areas. Monitoring consumer responses to the marketing-mix elements can also help to identify potential opportunities. For instance, a market study may identify a brand whose share of the market has been increasing despite a shrinking advertising budget. This increase may signal that the size of the total market is in a state of flux, and so the marketing executive may decide to reevaluate the positioning, pricing, and promotional strategies of this brand. In new-product development, opportunity identification involves defining the best market to enter and the generation of ideas that can lead to entry.

Design of Alternative Courses of Action. To effectively develop alternative courses of action, the second step in planning, the marketing executive must clearly delineate the central issues and crucial factors that constitute the decision situation. Typically, alternative courses of action involve different specifications for the marketing-mix elements. For example, alternative courses of action might involve several different health-product ideas that are going to be concept tested to assess consumer interest and to establish priorities for further development.

Evaluation of Alternative Courses of Action. This third step involves evaluating the alternative courses of action on the basis of one or more response and/or performance variables. Here, again, adopting a formal framework for evaluating the various alternatives can be useful. Consider, for example, the following suggested procedure:

1. Delineate each possible alternative course of action, such as each new health-product idea.
2. List the possible result of each alternative course; for example, for

47

Top-box intention
scores The percentage of
individuals who indicate
that they "definitely"
would buy.

each new health-product idea obtain **top-box intention scores**
(that is, the percentage of individuals who say they "definitely"
would buy).

3. Estimate the payoff of each alternative course of action; for each new
   health-product idea, estimate market share or volume at national
   launch.
4. Assign probabilities to the different possible results for each given
   alternative; for example, assign probabilities to the market share or
   volume estimates of each new health-product idea.

More details on how to actually use this type of an approach are provided in the discussion on decision analysis appearing in Appendix 2-A.

Selection of a Course of Action. The fourth step involves making an
action decision. Deciding which course to follow or whether to maintain
the status quo is based on an evaluation of which course of action leads
to the most desirable results in relation to long-run (or short-run) objectives. The decision-maker selects the course of action that maximizes the
likelihood of attaining management objectives and goals. Because markets are generally becoming more competitive, some organizations, especially in the consumer goods industry, tend to resist making "do-noth-
ing," status quo decisions. Lacking good ideas, such organizations have
no alternative but to copy competitors' new products and follow them
into the market. Although this strategy has proved successful in some
markets for some organizations, parity products offering no real differential benefits produce marginal products with only a small chance of
success at best.[7]

Implementation. The final step in the marketing planning process is
implementation. After a concept test, for example, implementation might
involve the development of a product prototype and advertising copy,
and both can be tested in either a test market or a simulated test market.

The Role of Research in Planning

The role of research in the marketing planning process is quite simple: At each step in the process marketing research can help give direction to the marketing decisions that must be made. Table 2-2 outlines
research projects for each step of a problem involving new product introduction; comparable steps would be taken for any other component of
the marketing mix.

STEPS IN A RESEARCH PROJECT

Exhibit 2-1 presents an overview of the primary phases and steps
involved in a research project. Though a project's flow can be viewed in

---

[7]See, for example, J. H. Davidson, "Why Most New Consumer Brands Fail," *Harvard
Business Review*, March–April 1976, 117–121.

TABLE 2-2

**Planning Process and Marketing Research for
New Product Introduction**

Planning process	Marketing research
Identify opportunity	Focus groups
	Market definition study
	Idea generation
Design	Consumer measurement
	Product engineering and marketing mix
	Forecasting sales potential
Test	Name and package testing
	Advertising and product testing
	Pretest marketing forecasts
National launch (rollout)	Tracking studies
Evaluate	Market response analysis
	Store audits
	Product refinement tests

different ways, the figure shows the six primary phases and the fourteen
principal steps needed to take a project from beginning to end.

EXHIBIT 2-1

Primary Phases in the Course of a Research Project

 ← Standard

Planning the Research Design

1. Recognize and define problems — *most critical*
2. Research design and project proposal

Preparation

3. Sampling plan
4. Data-collection and questionnaire-design considerations

Fieldwork

5. Scheduling interviews
6. Conducting interviews
7. Check-in, editing, and validation — *Edit out problems; inconsistensies*

Processing

8. Coding and keypunching data
9. Constructing the computer tape

Tabulation, Analysis, and Interpretation

10. Generate tables
11. Analysis
12. Interpretation

Reporting

13. Written report/oral presentation
14. Follow-up

PLANNING THE RESEARCH DESIGN

Many more research projects fail because of inadequate preparation in developing the background of a study than because of insufficient technical knowledge. For example, in a 1983 Market Facts, Inc. survey of 183 of the largest consumer goods and services companies, better communication and more involvement in the problem were the most frequently mentioned ways of improving usefulness of research (see Table 2–3).[8] Planning the research design is perhaps the most important phase in the course of a research project; for many, if not all, of the qualitative and quantitative aspects of the study are conveyed by the chosen design. Put simply, the research design conveys the essence of a study.

The Problem

To clearly define the problem, the marketing executive and the researcher must understand its background. The key questions at the outset relate to objectives. Most marketing research studies begin with a problem provoked by some practical (or theoretical) difficulty associated with attaining objectives. In other words, problems occur when objectives are not met. Thus, without objectives, there would be no problems and no need for a decision. A decision presupposes a problem, and a problem presupposes an objective. Specifying what marketing seeks to achieve in a market, for example, provides the impetus behind and guidelines for the regular surveys and reports (for example, tracking studies or market share trends) that are routinely provided by marketing research. Ultimately all studies, including customized surveys and investigations, are related to overall objectives.

A good starting point in understanding the problem is to find out what happened before—to identify the history of the problem and avoid reinventing the wheel. The marketing executive and the marketing researcher must together define why the project is being undertaken, what the study is designed to measure, and how the information will be used.

[8]Market Facts, Inc., *Consumer Market Research Techniques, Usages, Patterns, and Attitudes in 1983*, p. 20.

TABLE 2-3

Market Research Needs

| | | Type of company | |
Answer*	Total sample (%)	Grocery & drug (%)	Durables & services (%)
Better communication	48	47	53
More involvement in the problem	46	38	55
Reporting to a higher level of management	23	22	26
Better research techniques	22	23	18
More research credibility	14	15	14
Less dissension on technique	9	10	6
Other factors	16	17	12
No opinion	5	7	4

*Based on Question 3b: "More and better use of marketing research in our company would be most enhanced by (check one or more)."
Source: Market Facts, Inc., *Consumer Market Research Technique Usage Patterns and Attitudes in 1983*, p. 20.

In other words, how will such data reduce risk and help the executive to make a more informed marketing decision? The following questions will help the executive and researcher examine the problem's history and plan for information gathering.

- What does the manager know about the situation?
- What assumptions are being used?
- Are the assumptions reasonable?
- If the assumptions turn out to be unrealistic how does this affect what is to be expected?
- Is anyone on the research project team biased?
- How precise does the information need to be?
- Will precision affect the choice of an alternative?

Exhibit 2-2 illustrates how these questions might have been answered by Coca-Cola marketing executives in planning a product-testing program for New Coke.

EXHIBIT 2-2

Problem Definition for New Coke Product-Testing Program

What does the manager know about the situation?

On a blind-test basis, cola drinkers prefer sweeter colas, hence Pepsi-Cola was preferred to Coke in blind taste-tests.

What assumptions are being used?

In order to counter the "Pepsi Challenge" campaign, Coke needs to be perceived as being sweeter.

Are the assumptions reasonable?

Before actual in-market distribution, blind taste-tests and in-home use tests appear to be the best approach to take to assess ultimate market acceptance.

If the assumptions turn out to be unrealistic, how does this affect what is to be expected?

The assumption is that a sweeter, better-tasting cola will lead to increased market share and will not alienate Coke's loyal franchise. If this assumption is unrealistic, market share could decrease.

Is anyone on the research team biased?

No! But blind acceptance of the taste testing program as the sole determinant of in-market acceptance could bias management in favor of introducing a sweeter formulation.

How precise does the information need to be?

Very precise—therefore a controlled testing program is needed.

Will precision affect the choice of an alternative?

Yes. The reformulated cola most preferred to old Coke and to Pepsi will be the winner.

Once the problem has been defined, marketing research is likely to be concerned with collecting informative data and other activities designed to solve the problem at hand.

Research Design and Project Proposal

When all of the background factors have been identified and the marketing executive and the researcher have agreed on why the project is being undertaken, what the study will measure, and how the information will be used, then the researcher can focus on the appropriate design of the study.

Project proposal A research written description of the key research design factors that define the proposed study.

Concept test A marketing study to determine what market segment a product idea appeals to and what is most attractive about the idea.

The design process culminates with a written **project proposal** that conveys the essence of the study. The project proposal describes the key research design factors that together define the proposed study. Project proposals are written by the organization's marketing research department or are solicited from outside research suppliers. Exhibit 2-3 presents a prototypical marketing research project proposal for a **concept test.** The proposal is relatively brief but precisely and informatively describes the key elements involved.

EXHIBIT 2-3

Marketing Research Project Proposal

Brand:	New products
Project:	Snack foods—Concept test
Background and Objectives:	The Brand Group has developed twelve new snack-food product ideas. The objectives of this research are to assess consumer interest in the concepts and establish priorities for further development.
Research Method:	Central location concept testing will be conducted in geographically dispersed markets. Each of the concepts plus one retest control concept will be evaluated by a total of 200 men and 200 women. The following age quotas will be used for both male and female groups within the sample:

18–34 = 50%
35–49 = 25%
50 & over = 25%

Each respondent will evaluate a maximum of six concepts. Order of presentation of concepts will be rotated throughout to avoid position bias.

Information to be Obtained:	This study will provide the following information to assist in concept evaluation:

Category usage	Believability
Purchase interest	Importance of main point
Uniqueness	Demographics

Action Standard:	In order to identify concepts warranting further development, top-box purchase-intent scores will be compared to the top-box purchase-intent scores achieved by the top 20 percent of the nonbranded concepts tested in earlier concept studies. (The top 20 percent of the concepts achieved top-box purchase-intent scores of 13 percent among all respondents and 16 percent among user groups.) Rank order of concepts purchase-intent scores and scores on the uniqueness, believability, and importance ratings will also be considered in the evaluation and prioritization of concepts for further development.
Material Requirements:	Fifty copies of each concept (color print format)
Cost:	The cost of this research will be $25,000 ± 10 percent.
Timing:	This research will adhere to the following schedule:

Fieldwork	1½ weeks	Computer tape	1 week
Topline	2 weeks	Final report	3 weeks

Selected Supplier:	ABC Research Service, Inc.

Background and Objectives. A project proposal should contain a clear explanation of the study's objectives and value. In the concept test proposal (Exhibit 2-3), for example, the stated objectives are to assess consumer interest in twelve new product concepts and to establish priorities for further development.

Research Method. The research method element involves important and interdependent decisions. Major decisions include the following:

- *Selection of the sample*—who and how many respondents to include.
- *Selection of the data collection method*—whether to use secondary data; a mail, telephone or personal interview; or perhaps a mall intercept.
- *Selection of the design element*—what are respondents going to be exposed to? Is a survey or experimental design most appropriate?

Information To Be Obtained. The project proposal presents crucial decisions relating to the following:

- *Measurement content*—what should be measured?
- *Measurement technique*—how should we measure it?
- *Analytical technique*—once we have collected the information, how are we going to analyze the data?

What should be measured and how the data are going to be analyzed are obviously greatly influenced by the purpose and objectives of the study. The measurement technique to be used largely depends on the analysis technique.

Action Standard. The action standard for the project proposal clearly defines the performance criterion that will be utilized. How the research results are judged is ultimately tied to the study's purpose and objectives and influences the choice of an analysis technique.

Cost and Timing. A project proposal will contain a statement of the projected cost and provide a schedule of when various aspects of the project will be completed. For example, **top-line** reports, which give the marketing executive highlights of the study's results (such as overall preference between two tested products) before all of the data have been tabulated, are generally due one week after the completion of field operations. Costs estimates typically are accompanied by a 10 percent contingency (on cost).

Top-line reports
Highlights of the study's results given to the marketing executive before all of the data have been tabulated.

Selection of a Supplier. The project proposal designates the participating research supplier.

PREPARATION

This phase of a study involves designing the sampling plan as well as data-collection and questionnaire design considerations.

Sampling

Most marketing research involves taking a **sample** of the target population. Rarely, if ever, will a census be taken, even if the entire population of interest could be interviewed. Chapters 7 and 8 are entirely devoted to sampling designs and related issues.

Sample Subset of respondents from the overall target population.

Information Gathering

The problem definition stage of the marketing research process will determine what information needs to be collected and how it should be collected. In some instances, secondary data will suffice, and in Chapter 3 we discuss various avenues for securing it. In other instances, the researcher will need to collect information directly from individuals by asking questions; Chapters 4–6 discuss a variety of ways of collecting informative data from respondents.

Questions can be asked in many different ways. In Chapters 9–11 we discuss measurement and scaling concepts and techniques, and Chapter 12 provides some general guidelines for constructing questionnaires.

FIELD OPERATIONS

Field operations are often farthest removed from the observation of the client and perhaps of the research supplier as well. Local field services usually have direct supervision and control over the fieldwork. Clearly, the conduct and supervision of field operations is critical to research quality. Various aspects of fielding a study are discussed in Chapter 12.

Interviews

The "field" is where we gather the respondents and administer the questionnaire. The local field service supervisor has responsibility for identifying the interviewers, training them, scheduling the interviews, and surpervising the interviewers while in the field. The supervisor is also responsible for *not* sending interviewers to homes in high-crime areas at night, scheduling interviews at dinnertime, or stopping weary, homebound shoppers in malls.

Check-in, Editing, and Validation

The local field service supervisor must insure that all questionnaires are completed properly and that the number of completed interviews meets the research design specifications for cost and schedule.

The supervisor must check to see whether interviewers are properly using the questionnaires. After the questionnaires are completed, they are checked in; at this time the field supervisor must spot-check for internal consistency. For example, respondents who indicated that they were not tuned-in to a particular television program should not provide information on ad recall for an ad airing only on that program. If not, impossible numbers can appear on the tab sheets. When errors are found they are edited out by either the field supervisor or the editing staff of the research supplier.

Ensuring the validity of the research findings requires checking whether the interviews were conducted according to the research design's specifications. The survey responses are validated by the research supplier. For example, standard practice in conducting telephone interviews is for the supervisor to recontact 15 percent of the respondents to make sure they actually completed the questionnaire.

PROCESSING

The next phase of the research project prepares the data for tabulation and analysis. Coding the questionnaire responses and preparing a computer tape are two of the crucial activities. Data processing activities are described in Chapter 13.

Coding

Questionnaires employ two basic types of question formats—closed-ended and open-ended. **Closed-ended questions,** which usually make up the majority of questionnaire items, are those for which the respondent has a limited number of answer choices; that is, the possible answers to the question have been limited by the researcher. Answers to **open-ended questions** are not limited by the researcher beforehand. For these types of questions, respondents can say whatever they want in their own words. Before responses to open-ended and closed-ended questions can be analyzed, numerical values or alphanumeric symbols have to be assigned. Various aspects of **coding** are discussed in Chapters 12 and 13.

Closed-ended questions Questions for which the respondent has a limited number of answer choices.

Open-ended questions Answers not limited by the researcher beforehand; respondents can say whatever they want in their own words.

Coding Process by which numerical values or alphanumeric symbols are assigned to represent a specific response to a question.

Constructing the Computer Tape

Once codes for all the open-ended questions have been decided upon, the questionnaires are delivered to the tab house. The tab house is responsible for cleaning up the data if necessary and constructing a master computer tape, which is typically returned to the research supplier.

TABULATION, ANALYSIS, AND INTERPRETATION

When all questionnaires have been edited, validated, and coded and the computer tape is ready, tabulation can begin. Issues related to tabulation and techniques of analysis are discussed and illustrated in detail in Part V.

Tabulation presents the data in tabular form, which allows the marketing researcher to effectively communicate with the marketing executive. Usually the tab house is given a list of required tables and instructions on how they should be constructed. Chapter 13 discusses tab specifications.

Analysis attempts to turn numbers into data, and then to turn data into actionable marketing information that can be effectively used by the marketing executive. Techniques of analysis are discussed in Chapters 14–16.

Interpretation involves a clear statement of implications derived from the study's findings. These implications define the alternative courses of action consistent with the objectives and nature of the study. "What does it all mean?" is a question the researcher must answer.

REPORTING

The reporting phase of a research study typically involves the written report, the oral presentation, and follow-up. Suggestions concerning how to present the results of a research study are presented in Chapter 23.

The *written report* reflects all of the marketing researcher's efforts and should justify the client's dollar outlay. An important feature is the *executive summary*, which capsulizes the essence of what has been done. If an oral presentation is also required, it should be tailored to the needs of the client and be adequately planned and prepared.

After the written report and/or oral presentation have been delivered, *follow-up* will involve comments and questions from the client about this material. The client may ask for clarification of certain points or for additional information—for example, a request for an additional cross-tabulation. Moreover, the marketing researcher follows up by determining from the client whether the study fulfilled its intended purpose.

Summary

This chapter has emphasized the importance of marketing research in the planning process. Inherent in the idea that well-planned research, conducted in a realistic environment, helps bring success is the idea that poorly planned research can lead to failure. We've seen what happened with the Edsel. To get you started thinking about doing marketing research correctly, we've outlined the steps in a research project and introduced the marketing research proposal. Marketing research proposals will serve as a framework for much of the material and examples introduced in ensuing chapters.

Key Concepts

Value of marketing research planning
Weighing the value of information
Decision analysis
Decision processes and information
Marketing planning process
Steps in a research project

Review Questions

1. Discuss what might contribute to incorrect planning of a research project.
2. Discuss the concept of the value of information.
3. Suppose you are the marketer of Sargeant's Rug Patrol (see Chapter I).
   (a) Discuss each element of the marketing planning process for this new product.
   (b) Discuss each step of a research project for this product.
4. Suppose you are involved in the commercialization of New Coke. From a decision-making perspective:
   (a) What concerns would you have?
   (b) How would you weigh the value of information obtained?

Decision Analysis

EXPECTED VALUE OF INFORMATION

Consider the situation where a brand manager is faced with deciding whether to roll out a new brand nationally. Past evidence indicates that a brand in this product category will (1) cost the company an estimated $3 million if it achieves less than a 2 percent share of market, (2) return about $1 million if it achieves a share of market between 2 and 2.25 percent, and (3) return about $2 million if it achieves a share of market greater than 2.25 percent. Suppose you were given the problem of choosing whether or not to introduce this brand. Perhaps you would first ask: What are the chances of realizing a share of market less than 2 percent, or a share of market between 2 and 2.25 percent, or a share of market greater than 2.25 percent? In other words, you would like to know the probabilities associated with each possible outcome.

If the probability of any one of the possible market share outcomes happens to be equal to one (the other two must therefore be equal to zero), then there is no uncertainty surrounding the decision. However, rarely will an outcome be known with certainty. The brand manager must make the decision to roll out the new product with uncertainty, because the probabilities for any of the three possible share outcomes will ordinarily not be zero or one.

How can the brand manager deal with uncertain outcomes? One strategy would be to somehow "guess" the likelihood of each possible outcome. We can frequently rely on past evidence in establishing the likelihood of some event or outcome. For example, the brand manager may know that historically 35 percent of new products launched in this category achieved a share of market less than 2 percent; 50 percent of new products achieved a market share between 2 and 2.25 percent; and the remaining 15 percent of new products achieved a market share greater than 2.25 percent. Using past evidence and the rewards and losses associated with the various market share outcomes we can calculate the *expected value of introducing the brand.* The expected value *(EV)*

TABLE 2A-1

**Expected Value of Introducing the
Brand (Prior Probabilities)**

Outcome	Payoff (millions)	Probability
<2% share	−3	.35
2–2.25% share	+1	.50
>2.25% share	+2	.15

$$EV \text{ (Introducing)} = (-3)(.35) + (1)(.50) +$$
$$= (2)(.15)$$
$$= -.25, \text{ or } -\$250,000$$

$$EV \text{ (Not introducing)} = 0$$

is found by summing the product of the payoff (or loss) of a particular outcome times the probability of that outcome.

$$EV = \sum_{\substack{\text{all} \\ \text{outcomes}}} (\text{payoff for outcome})(\text{probability of outcome})$$

The calculations for the expected value of introducing the brand are shown in Table 2A-1. Since, in this case, the expected value of introducing the brand is negative, the brand manager would probably decide not to go to national rollout.

As we indicated earlier, one purpose of marketing research is to reduce the uncertainty under which marketing executives must operate. The remainder of this appendix explicates a method for calculating the value of the additional information provided by a marketing research study. The method to be described uses an approach called *Bayesian analysis.* Probabilities associated with the particular outcomes without the additional information market research provides are called *prior probabilities*. The essence of Bayesian analysis is to use new information to revise the prior probabilities. The method relies on Bayes' Theorem and the basic laws of probability. Your basic statistics course probably covered probability theory. If you have forgotten this material we suggest that you review it before proceeding.

We now demonstrate how these revised probabilities are utilized to calculate the value of additional information.

VALUE OF ADDITIONAL INFORMATION

Before our calculations can begin, we need certain estimates from management. Specifically, we need (1) the payoff (or loss) associated with each particular outcome, (2) the prior probabilities associated with each outcome, and (3) the conditional probabilities of a particular research result, given that a specific outcome was realized. The conditional probabilities warrant further discussion.

Again let us consider the questions of launching a new product with three possible outcomes (outlined in Table 2A-1). Assume that the brand manager could commission a test market in order to help make the decision. Although the test market can help, the brand manager will still be operating under uncertainty, since there is no guarantee that the test market results will be perfectly reliable. In other words, sometimes the test market will indicate that the brand will achieve a relative "poor" share when in fact it achieves an "average" or "above average" share after national rollout. Letting R_j denote a particular test market result and O_i denote a specific outcome, then $P(R_j|O_i)$ is the probability that the test market will show a particular brand share, given that the product actually achieved that outcome after national rollout. The probabilities $P(R_j|O_i)$ are usually based on companies' past records, such as the association between test market results and actual results for category brands test-marketed in the past.

Table 2A-2 contains the estimates of these probabilities based on past records of test market projections (R_j) and actual results when the product was introduced (Oi). Notice that it is the columns that must sum to one, *not* the rows. Reading the table, we see that—in the past—85 percent of the time when the *actual*, after national rollout, brand share was less than 2 percent, the test market projected share was less than 2 percent, whereas in 10 percent of the cases the *actual* share was 2–2.25 percent when the test market projected share was less than 2 percent, and so on.

Our objective is to revise the probabilities of actual share for each of the possible test market projections. It is known from probability relationships that

$$P(O_i|R_j) = P(O_i) \cdot P(R_j|O_i)/P(R_j) \qquad (2A\text{-}1)$$

The $P(O_i)$ are the prior probabilities found in Table 2A-1. The conditional probabilities $P(R_j|O_i)$ are found in Table 2A-2. Consequently, we only need

T A B L E 2A-2
Estimated Probabilities (Conditional Probabilities)

Test market results (R_j)	Actual results (O_i)		
	<2%	2–2.25%	>2.25%
<2%	.85	.10	.05
2–2.25%	.10	.80	.20
>2.25%	.05	.10	.75

T A B L E 2A-3
Revised Probabilities

A. Full test market predicts poor brand share $[P(R_1)]$

Outcome (Share)	$P(O_i)$	$P(R_1|O_i)$	$[P(O_i) \cdot P(R_1|O_i)]$	$\Sigma[P(O_i) \cdot P(R_1|O_i)]$	$P(O_i|R_1)$
<2%	.35	.85	.2975	.355	.838
2–2.25%	.50	.10	.050	.355	.141
>2.25%	.15	.05	.0075	.355	.021

B. Full test market predicts average share $[P(R_2)]$

Outcome (Share)	$P(O_i)$	$P(R_2|O_i)$	$[P(O_i) \cdot P(R_2|O_i)]$	$\Sigma[P(O_i) \cdot P(R_2|O_i)]$	$P(O_i|R_2)$
<2%	.35	.10	.035	.465	.075
2–2.25%	.50	.80	.400	.465	.860
>2.25%	.15	.20	.030	.465	.065

C. Full test market predicts good share $[P(R_3)]$

Outcome (Share)	$P(O_i)$	$P(R_3|O_i)$	$[P(O_i) \cdot P(R_3|O_i)]$	$\Sigma[P(O_i) \cdot P(R_3|O_i)]$	$P(O_i|R_3)$
<2%	.35	.05	.018	.180	.100
2–2.25%	.50	.10	.05	.180	.278
>2.25%	.15	.75	.112	.180	.622

$P(R_j)$ to calculate the revised probabilities. The $P(R_j)$ can be calculated as follows:

$$P(R_j) = \sum_{i=1}^{I} [P(O_i) \cdot P(R_j|O_i)] \qquad (2A\text{-}2)$$

The calculations necessary to revise the prior probabilities for each possible test market result are provided in Table 2A-3, A, B, and C.

The next step in the procedure is to determine the expected value if the brand is introduced for each of the possible test market results. However, now instead of using the prior probabilities $[P(O_i)]$ to weight the outcome we use the revised probabilities $[P(O_i|R_j)]$. The expected value calculations are demonstrated in Table 2A-4. Remember that for each of the expected value calculations there is always the alternative of not introducing the brand which we will assume has an expected value of zero.

The expected value of additional information—that is, what you would be willing to pay for research—is found by subtracting the expected value without additional information from the expected value given additional information. From Table 2A-1 we already have the expected value without information, which is zero (not introduce). The expected value given additional information is calculated by taking the optimal alternative (introduce versus not introduce) for each test market

Revised Expected Value Calculations

	Decision
A. Test market projection < 2% share	
$EV = (-3)(.838) + (1)(.141) + (2)(.021) = -2,331,000$	Not introduce
B. Test market projection 2–2.25% share	
$EV = (-3)(.075) + (1)(.860) + (2)(.065) = 765,000$	Introduce
C. Test market projection > 2.25% share	
$EV = (-3)(.1) + (1)(.278) + (2)(.622) = 1,222,000$	Introduce

condition from Table 2A-4 and weighting it by the probability $[P(R_j)]$ of each test market projection. Hence the expected value (EV) given additional information (AI) is

$$EV|AI = (0)(.355) + (765,000)(.465) + (1,222,000)(.180)$$
$$= 575,685$$

Now the most that we would be willing to pay for the research is

$$\$575,685 - \$0 = \$575,685.$$

At first glance it may seem foolish to want to spend hundreds of thousands of dollars on a project that has an expected value of zero. However, notice that two of the alternatives (2–2.25 percent share and >2.25 percent share) have positive consequences. The research, then, aids management in rejecting an alternative with negative consequences or, on the other hand, selecting an alternative having positive consequences.

Decision Trees

A decision tree is frequently formed when Bayesian analysis is used. A decision tree is a network of decision nodes and branches. The branches represent alternatives. At each node nonoptimal branches are pruned (usually by using a double line). Figure 2A-1 is a decision tree representation of the brand introduction problem we have been working with.

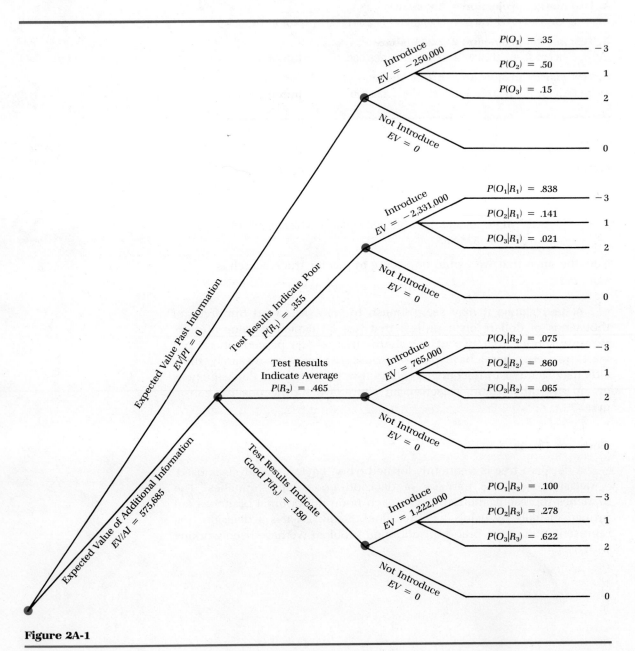

Figure 2A-1

Decision tree.

CASE STUDIES FOR PART I

Read

Case 1: Giving Smokers Added Value is Tobacco Firm's Latest Idea

By Margaret Loeb, Staff Reporter of *The Wall Street Journal*

The nation's 53 million smokers already have 214 styles of cigarettes to choose from, varying by flavor, tar, length, package, and the images conjured up in more than $1.5 billion of advertising yearly. Nevertheless, tobacco marketers have yet to run out of ideas to push on prospective customers.

The industry's latest brainstorm, following years of promoting brands with less tar, is to sell more value. Value, however, is defined quite differently by R. J. Reynolds and Philip Morris, each of which controls one-third of the $17 billion market.

Value, Reynolds says, is giving smokers more cigarettes in a pack. To attract what it calls the "smart shopper," Reynolds is bringing out Century, a brand that offers a carton of 225 cigarettes for the price of a normal carton of 200. Each Century has slightly less tobacco than a conventional cigarette, though.

Philip Morris says it too wants to give buyers more for their money but apparently doesn't believe that's as simple as giving them more smokes at no extra charge. "In economically hard times, we're adding something of value in the form of a very distinguished box," explains a spokesman at Philip Morris. Its latest introductions are Benson & Hedges 100's DeLuxe Ultra Lights, which come in a silver box with gold trim, and Players, in a black box with gold lettering.

Lorillard also defines value in terms of imagery, rather than substance. It recently introduced Satin cigarettes as "an affordable luxury" for women. Like the two new Philip Morris products, Satin has 20 cigarettes in a pack and sells for the same price as other brands.

"Players and Satin express value in a way," says James Johnston, a

Source: Wall Street Journal, 30 June 1983, 31. (Reprinted with permission.)

65

Reynolds executive vice president. "The issue is: Do consumers want fancier packages or more cigarettes?"

Although Reynolds says it thinks the latter, the company may be hedging its bets. Trade sources say Reynolds is preparing for the possible introduction of Sterling, a rival for Philip Morris's Players. And if the 25-cigarette Century proves successful, competitors doubtless will copy it. Reynolds also is testing a lower-price, 12-cigarette pack, sold primarily through vending machines.

Generally, though, U.S. tobacco marketers have been loath to tamper with industry practice of selling all their brands for the same price. Some tobacco executives predict that attitudes could change here soon. Overseas, so-called luxury cigarettes command higher prices, and brands that have little or no advertising sell for less than standard packs.

"We're the last country in the world not to have price and packaging segmentation," says John C. Maxwell Jr., a tobacco analyst at Lehman Brothers Kuhn Loeb. "Most countries have five, six, or seven price and package segments. Now that we're getting up to 80 cents or $1 a pack we can do some of this too."

Cigarette companies are paying so much attention to value, real or perceived, largely because the price of their product has jumped 35% in the past year. The chief reason: the doubling of federal excise taxes in January, the first increase in 30 years.

Tobacco makers also may have been surprised by the success of lower-price generic cigarettes, introduced three years ago by Liggett & Myers, an industry also-ran. Its no-name cigarettes now account for between 2.5% and 3% of the U.S. market.

A third reason for emphasizing value: Manufacturers may have gone as far as they can with "line extensions" of existing brand names. Marlboro now comes in six styles, Kool in 10, and Newport in eight. The proliferation reflects different tar levels, lengths, and flavors, as well as manufacturers' conclusions that it costs less to add a variation to an existing brand than to popularize a new name.

Introducing a major brand, says Reynolds, costs any cigarette company $80 million or more for advertising and promotion. In addition to such traditional marketing techniques as coupons, free samples handed out on street corners, and two packs for the price of one, tobacco merchants increasingly are offering samples to smokers who call toll-free telephone numbers.

For Satin, Lorillard ran ads in *People* magazine and women's magazines promising callers two free packs and a satin pouch. Lorillard won't disclose results, but AIS 800 Report, a telephone-marketing newsletter, says the company received 1.3 million calls within 11 days. Lorillard's original projection, the publication says, was 1.2 million calls in five weeks.

Money alone won't make new products into winners, though. Brown & Williamson's low-tar Barclay, introduced with considerable expense in 1981, declined in sales in its second year. Still, cigarette marketers justify the risk of product introductions by pointing out that just 1% of the market is worth $170 million in revenue and that a new brand needs only a 0.5% share to be considered a success.

One way to improve the odds is to rejuvenate a moribund brand. Reynolds has done that with Camel, and American Brands hopes to do the same with a filter version of Lucky Strike. The company says that, as of the end of March, Lucky Strike accounted for 0.62% of the market in cities where it was distributed.

Meanwhile, more new ideas are moving into test markets. Next month Liggett & Myers begins testing Superior and Dorado, which are aimed at areas with large Hispanic populations. K. V. Dey, president, says Liggett can't compete nationally with Reynolds and Philip Morris and instead plans to concentrate its resources in "the San Antonios, Miamis, and New Yorks of the world."

Questions

1. Define the marketing and marketing research problem(s) facing the tobacco industry in general and R. J. Reynolds in particular.
2. Identify which stage of the product life cycle Century is in and the implications for marketing research activities.
3. How might marketing research help R. J. Reynolds come to understand how consumers view Century?
4. Describe the importance of research in the marketing planning process.

Case 2: Why Bic Got Flicked *Read*

By Steven Flax

What's gone wrong with Baron Marcel Bich's marvelous marketing machine?

Bic Corp. of Milford, Conn., the U.S. arm of Bich's Sociéte Bic S.A. of France, was once the paradigm of a low-cost consumer products company. No more. Since the end of 1980 its earnings have declined by 33%. Operating margins, which once ran up to 29%, have fallen to 6.9% through the first half of 1982, and both total sales and net income are down from last year.

And last year was not a good year for Bic. On $218 million in sales, its profits were squeezed in lighters, it lost $2.3 million pretax on disposable shavers and, for the first time in its history, sales of ballpoint pens fell. Still the largest pen producer in North America, Bic has had up to 80% of the market in years past. The best estimate now has it at 60%. Obviously, the erosion must be stopped.

Source: Forbes, 27 September 1982, 38. (Reprinted with permission.)

67

That may not be easy. Despite the company's bullish public pronouncements, Bic's new roller ball pen, Bic Roller, has been disappointing so far. When the advertising behind Roller's introduction subsided, so did sales. Unit sales were down 50% in the first quarter of this year. Years ago, Bic had a chance to get into the erasable pen business early, but passed it up. "If people want to erase, they can use a pencil," one Bic marketing manager is purported to have said. Today, the erasable market is the fastest-growing part of the industry, and Bic is trying—so far without much luck—to play catch-up with Gillette and Scripto.

What happened? For one thing, Gillette woke up. Bic's traumatic 80% drop in operating profits in pens last year was largely due to savage price-cutting initiated by Gillette's Write Brothers line. This year, says Marc Binder of the Pen Shop in Culver City, Calif., a big West Coast distributor, his dollar sales of Gillette pens were up 249%, while Bic's fell about 30%. To judge from recent pretax earnings, Bic no longer has a cash cow. Says David Liebowitz, an analyst at American Securities Corp., "Gillette's strategy is hurting Bic dramatically." And $2.3 billion Gillette, 10 times larger than Bic, can afford to keep the price pressure on for a long time.

But Gillette is not the only cause of Bic's problems. The company has brought others on itself. These days, the Baron spends most of his time in France. The American company is largely in the hands of Chairman Robert Adler and Bich's son, Bruno, 35, who came to company headquarters in 1975 and has been president since last February. Neither Bich nor Adler wants to talk about it, but young Bich's training period appears to have been painful for the company, especially for its once-crackerjack sales force. In Europe seven years ago, insiders say the Baron spent part of a three-week Christmas holiday persuading Bruno to work up a five-year plan to get rid of highly paid salesmen and replace them with "order takers." Says one source: "If Bic could make disposable plastic clones that drove, spoke and wrote orders, they would much rather use them than human beings."

Since that time, insiders estimate that up to 80% of Bic's sales force, from national sales manager Ronald Shaw on down, have been fired or resigned. For those that remained, commission structures were changed so that salesmen earned less for the same amount of work.

Some of these dismissals have since come to haunt Bic. For example, Shaw became executive vice president of Pilot Pen Corp., the Japanese-owned company, which he quickly took from less than $2 million in sales to almost $30 million by getting into areas Bic ignored. Distributors complain that the overall quality of Bic's sales force has noticeably dropped. "Ten years ago the caliber of people at Bic was absolutely the highest in the country," says Ed Melugin, president of the Dallas Pen Co. "These guys that come in here now, you wonder how they found the door."

The strain is already beginning to tell. Bruno Bich has a hot temper, say some employees, and has been known to bellow at workers and slam telephones.

Will that old Bic magic ever work again? Bic still has a lot going for it. The name is still one of the most powerful consumer franchises in the world. Société Bic still stands behind the U.S. company with capital and resources. Despite industry skepticism, Bic is hopeful about its new line of pens called "Biro," its latest counterattack against Gillette. And the younger Bich, despite his inexperience and volatility, gets high marks from some of his employees as an intelligent, hard-working executive who is trying to learn.

But Bic has a long way to come back. Says the Pen Shop's Marc Binder, "Never before have they had to try to go get business back that they once had. And they've let a lot of it get away."

Questions

1. Define the marketing and marketing research problem(s) facing Bic.
2. In planning a recovery strategy, what marketing research issues should Bic consider?

Case 3: Toys for All

Toys for All, a manufacturer of children's toys, was interested in entering the educational toy market. To this end they established a new brand group whose responsibility was to develop and launch a new educational toy aimed at children under five years of age. Six months later, in direct response to this change, the brand group developed a new puzzle that they believed to be both enjoyable and educational.

A sample of 100 households with at least one child under the age of 5 was given the new puzzle and asked to evaluate it. The results were quite favorable and, in general, the product appeared to live up to its claims.

Based upon these results and past company records, the brand group determined that there was a 30 percent chance that the toy would capture less than 2 percent of the market, a 50 percent chance that the toy would capture 2–5 percent of the market, and only a 20 percent chance that the toy could exceed 5 percent of the market. The financial analysis indicated that if the new puzzle could get 2–5 percent of the market, the projected profit would be approximately $1.2 million; a share of market of less than 2 percent would translate into a loss of $1 million; and a share greater than 5 percent would likely return $1.9 million. The brand group was excited because they had a 70 percent chance of not losing any money on their first launch. However, they were also well aware that company records were solely for the general toy market, and the consumer testing was conducted on a small sample of households. Consequently, they decided to initiate a concept test with more representative sample.

Bradford, Inc., a research supplier specializing in concept testing of children's products was invited to submit a proposal to concept test the new puzzle. An account executive from Bradford, Inc., presented its basic methodology of concept testing toys. The brand group was presented with the choice between an in-home concept test at $95,000 and a mall-intercept concept test at $50,000. A member of the brand group asked how reliable the results were. The account executive indicated that it depends on the type of concept test selected (in-home or mall-intercept); in addition, he indicated that the company did keep records of share predictions and the actual shares realized by the products tested and that these records should help the brand group decide which type of concept test to choose.

In three days, the brand group received records from Bradford, Inc., showing the percentage of actual and predicted market shares for each of the two types of concept tests (Table 1):

TABLE 1
Records of Actual and Predicted Market Share

		Actual market share		
Predicted market share based on		< 2%	2–5%	> 5%
In-home concept test	< 2%	.70	.1	.05
	2–5%	.20	.8	.20
	> 5%	.10	.1	.75
Mall intercept concept test	< 2%	.65	.20	.10
	2–5%	.25	.60	.25
	> 5%	.10	.20	.65

Questions

1. Should the firm conduct a concept test?
2. If so, which type of concept test should they choose: in-home or mall-intercept?

Case 4: Hospital Marketers Lack Technical, Analytical Skills

By Keven T. Higgins, Senior Staff Writer

Analytical skills is an area of deficiency for today's hospital marketers, a point brought home repeatedly at the AMA's Sixth Annual Symposium on Health Services Marketing in Atlanta.

Marketing remains a middle-management function in many hospi-

Source: Marketing News 4/11/1986. (Reprinted with permission.)

tals, where many marketers formerly were PR directors, were hired because of their communications background, or have an academic background in marketing but lack line-management experience and the attendant skills in pricing, research, planning, and other marketing areas.

The bulk of the almost 1,000 attendees at the Symposium, sponsored by AMA's Academy for Health Services Marketing, were young professionals, and a recently completed national survey on the "State-of-the-Art of Hospital Marketing" suggests that audience was typical of the people in hospital marketing.

The study, performed by the Society for Hospital Planning and Marketing (SHPM) of the American Hospital Association, Chicago, found the average age of directors of marketing and vice presidents of planning and marketing to be 38. Directors of planning and marketing were even younger, averaging 34 years of age. Directors averaged about $40,000 in annual income, while VPs were in the $53,000 range.

Marketing and PR tend to be linked even at larger hospitals, said study coauthor Judith S. Neiman, SHPM director. "While people talk about the importance of marketing, it's not receiving the responsibility we think it deserves."

Guest relations are considered a major part of marketing at many hospitals, added coauthor Roberta Clarke, associate professor at Boston College. Consequently, the nursing director was identified as one of the top marketing officials at 21 percent of the hospitals surveyed.

"Political and communications skills are the strengths of (hospital) marketers today," Neiman said. "The weaknesses are in the technical and functional skills."

"PR was viewed to be the most effective of all marketing activities, marketing research was viewed to be the least effective," Clarke said. However, many of those respondents were spending a major portion of their time on research projects.

That assessment may be the result of hospital marketers' tight budgets and an inability to effectively manage research projects, another speaker suggested, Alan R. Andreasen, professor at UCLA's Graduate School of Management and a research consultant to nonprofit institutions, said "cheap but good research" is possible, but only if marketers collaborate closely with researchers to produce actionable findings.

"If you want your research money well spent, make it decision oriented, not ignorance oriented," Andreasen said. "Research is most valuable when you are most uncertain about what to do, not when you're ignorant."

Convenience samples instead of more expensive projectable samples, use of trained volunteers for field work, unearthing of data in hospital archives, and piggybacking hospital studies with other groups' projects are some ways to hold down costs, he said.

The deeper problem of ill-managed or poorly conceived projects can be overcome by taking a backwards approach to structuring research.

Traditionally, research projects begin with a definition of the problem, proceed to methodology selection, and conclude with collection and analysis of data. Andreasen advocated turning the process around by defining the decision you want to make, then letting that drive the research. Unless the hospital marketer knows what he intends to do with the findings, the research may fail to ask key questions or may talk around the problem, he warned.

The backwards approach also trains the marketer in methodology, and that permits more elaborate, effective approaches. "The manager ends up a part of the design process," he said.

"The worst thing is to get to the end of the study and decide that you should have done something different. That's what this is designed to avoid."

Questions

1. Comment on the suggested backwards approach to marketing research. Specifically, address the notion of not starting the process with problem definition.
2. How should, if at all, the approach to marketing research for hospitals differ from the more traditional consumer marketing research.

ACQUIRING DATA: AN OVERVIEW

In Part II we introduce, discuss, illustrate, and whenever possible critically compare approaches and procedures for acquiring informative marketing research data. Our objective is to thoroughly expose you to the principal sources of marketing research data and the variety of ways in which such data can be collected. The discussion is comprehensive, focusing on technologically based methods of accessing and collecting data as well as on traditional approaches.

Figure 1 outlines the general areas that will be considered. Note that a variety of data sources and collection methods

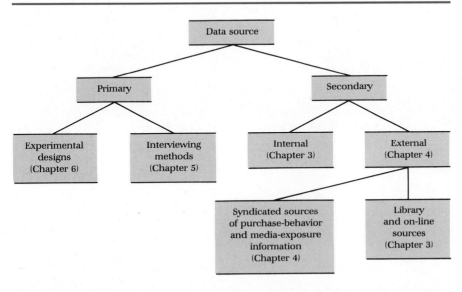

Figure 1

Acquiring market research information.

are available. The first distinction is between secondary sources (already existing) and primary sources (requiring data collection). Acquisition of secondary market information is easier than ever: Chapter 3 familiarizes you with on-line data bases, and Chapter 4 is a comprehensive treatment of syndicated sources of purchase behavior and media exposure information. The remaining two chapters focus attention on procedures for collecting primary research information. Chapter 5 considers the major interviewing methods, and Chapter 6 discusses experimental designs that can be used to assess cause and effect relationships.

Secondary Information: Traditional Sources and New Technologies*

CHAPTER OBJECTIVES

- Understand the distinction between primary and secondary sources of marketing information.
- Explain how to evaluate secondary information.
- Introduce new information technologies for the acquisition of secondary data.
- Describe on-line databases.
- Explain the role of database vendors who serve as information providers.
- Describe how on-line databases are accessed.
- Illustrate the unique features and capabilities of on-line databases.
- Describe off-line databases.

Introduction

Faced with a marketing-related problem or potential opportunity, the marketing manager wants to obtain information that increases the likelihood of choosing the best course of action. However, before spending time, money, and effort to collect data, the researcher needs to determine whether useful information exists and, if so, how to access it. Existing sources of useful marketing research information are more widespread than you might expect and should be considered first.

This chapter discusses sources of already-existing market research information. Specifically, we focus on library and other traditional sources of secondary data. We attempt to integrate the traditional print sources with on-line databases, powerful new tools for locating secondary market research. Without doubt, one of the most dramatic developments of the last decade is "the information revolution"—a term used to describe the rapid progress in computerizing information. The application of computerized information to marketing research is still in its in-

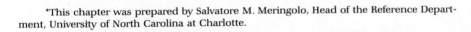

*This chapter was prepared by Salvatore M. Meringolo, Head of the Reference Department, University of North Carolina at Charlotte.

fancy; nevertheless, it has already had a substantial impact on the ways market information is disseminated to business. One analyst has predicted that mergers between "companies holding large databases and supplying secondary data reports . . . and the more traditional market research companies will be frequent enough to cause dramatic changes in the structure of the commercial marketing research industry estimated to be worth $3 billion in worldwide billings in 1983."[1] Indeed, the recent merger of SAMI, Arbitron, and Burke Marketing Research exemplifies the emergence of large research conglomerates. Although this chapter includes the traditional bibliographic essay on printed marketing research tools, it concentrates on the nature, size, and scope of interactive, on-line databases. We also introduce the mechanics of accessing on-line databases and some examples illustrating their use in marketing research.

PRIMARY VERSUS SECONDARY DATA

Primary data Data collected for a specific research need; they are customized and require specialized collection procedures.

Secondary data Already published data collected for purposes other than the specific research need at hand.

Internal secondary data Data available within the organization—for example, accounting records, management decision support systems, and sales records.

External secondary data Data available outside the organization from libraries and syndicated services.

At the broadest level, information sources available to the marketing researcher can be classified as primary or secondary. **Primary data** are collected for a specific research need; in this sense they are customized and require, in most cases, specialized data collection procedures. Interviewing methods and experimental designs used for collecting primary data are discussed in Chapters 5 and 6. **Secondary data** involve already-published data collected for purposes other than the specific research need at hand. **Internal secondary data** are available within the organization—for example, accounting records, management decision support systems, or sales records. **External secondary data** are available outside the organization from two main sources: library and other public sources and syndicated services that involve data collected under standardized procedures intended to service the needs of an array of clients. Syndicated services will be discussed in detail in Chapter 4.

For example, if Firm A conducts a survey to determine a demographic or psychographic profile of purchasers of solar heating equipment, it is collecting *primary data*. Firm B might query its sales force to get this same consumer information, rather than conduct a survey; in this case, the information is considered *internal secondary data*. It is secondary because it is a by-product of another activity (selling), and it is internal because the data are derived from existing information within Firm B. Alternatively, Firm C might conduct a search for external secondary data with regard to these same consumers. A consumer market study conducted by the U.S. Department of Energy and utilized by this firm would be considered *external secondary data* because the data were gathered for another purpose by an external agency—a government department needing to know and describe the extent to which government policy has influenced the use of an alternative energy source.

[1] E. Cole, *Advertising Age*, "Plotting Structural Changes in Industry," 1 November 1984, 34.

With these examples in mind, let's draw some conclusions about the characteristics of primary and secondary data:

1. Primary data are gathered for a specific purpose and conform to the objective of a particular research design.
2. Because gathering primary data requires specialized expertise (for example, survey design and administration), it can be both expensive and time-consuming.
3. Because secondary data have already been collected and may be published, their acquisition is relatively inexpensive; they can frequently be located quickly using appropriate printed reference tools or the newer information technologies.
4. The examination of available secondary data is a prerequisite to the collection of primary data; indeed, it can assist the researcher in defining the parameters of the primary research.
5. The examination of focused secondary data can be of critical importance in strategic marketing planning because it may alert management to future threats or opportunities in the marketplace.

EVALUATING SECONDARY INFORMATION

The quality of the information to be used in solving a marketing-related problem should be determined regardless of how the data were obtained. Researchers should especially examine external secondary information since the data were collected for a purpose other than the current one by someone outside the organization. Information obtained from secondary sources is not all equally reliable and/or valid. Secondary information can be misleading, and the data must be evaluated carefully in terms of recency and credibility.

When evaluating secondary information, consider the source of the data, measures used, the time period in which the data were collected, and the appropriateness of the analyses performed. The user of secondary information should routinely ask the following general questions.[2]

1. *What was the purpose of the study?* A fundamental question concerns why the information was collected in the first place. Rarely are data collected without some intent. The intent of the study ultimately determines the degree of precision, the types of scales used, and the method of data collection. Consider the Consumer Price Index (CPI), calculated monthly by the U.S. Bureau of Labor Statistics. The CPI measures price movements in the United States; it is based on 400 items of consumption. The index for each item is based on the average price paid for each item by a sample of wage earners and clerical workers in some key year. Specifically the index represents an

[2]The following material was adopted from David W. Stewart, *Secondary Research: Information Sources and Methods* (Beverly Hills: Sage Publications, 1984), 23-33.

average for a family of four, living in an urban area, with the following description: father, 38 years of age; mother, not employed outside the home; boy, 13 years of age; girl, 8 years of age. The index, therefore, is clearly not representative of the expenditures of most families. When using this index we must ask whether expenditure patterns for the group of respondents that we are interested in are different from those used to define the index. In addition, because the index is only a rough barometer of what is happening to purchasing power, we must question its usefulness in making specific decisions that may require a high degree of precision.

2. *Who collected the information?* Because secondary information is collected by someone outside the organization, a natural question concerns the expertise and credibility of the source. Organizations that provide secondary information vary with respect to their technical competence, resources, and overall quality. First, we can learn about the reputations of various sources of secondary information by contacting clients and others that have used the information provided by the source. Second, we can investigate how the data were obtained and the training and expertise present in the organization supplying the information.

3. *What information was collected?* One should always identify what information was actually collected by the organization supplying the data. In particular, it is important to identify (1) what was measured—for example, were fares or riders counted in a study on mass transit usage? (2) in what context were the data collected—were all the leading brands included in the taste study? (3) what was the relationship between what was measured and the event of interest— were self-report data used to infer actual behavior? (4) how were the data classified—were the data broken down by uses and markets or simply aggregated?

4. *When was the information collected?* The time period in which secondary information was collected plays an integral role in how the data should be interpreted. Factors present at the time the data were collected may influence the results obtained. For example, information on world affairs and, specifically, attitudes toward Russia should be examined when interpreting tracking data on the U.S. sales of and consumer attitudes toward Russian imports such as Stolichnya, vodka. Time may influence the definition measures, change the measurement instrument, or render the information obsolete altogether.

5. *How was the information obtained?* An essential ingredient in evaluating the quality of secondary information is the methodology employed to collect the data. For example, the size and nature of the target sample, the response rate obtained, the questionnaire used, the experimental procedures employed (if any), the interview procedure followed, and the analytical method utilized should be examined in some detail in order to adequately evaluate the quality of the data collection. When evaluating the procedure employed in collecting data, the critical issue is one of bias; that is, was there anything in the collection procedure that could potentially lead to a particular result, produce results that could not be generalized to the target population, or invalidate the results?

6. *Is the information consistent with other information?* In principle, two or more independent sources of secondary information should agree. When you are evaluating secondary information, a good strategy is to attempt to find multiple sources of the data and compare their conclusions. When differences exist, try to find the reasons for such differences and eventually determine which source is more reliable. However, this may be difficult or even impossible to do, depending on the amount of disclosure concerning the collection procedure employed.

A final caveat relates to numerical data obtained from secondary sources. The user of secondary information must understand what the numbers represent. Consider, first, the use of percentages from secondary sources. Percentages are relative and can be misleading. A 1-percentage-point change in share of market has very different implications depending on the size of the market. Percentages are not useful unless one understands what the percentage is based on.

Consider, next, index numbers, frequently used to summarize the differences among groups. Index numbers involve a transformation of percentages in which two percentages are compared. And therein lies the problem. For example, assume that 10 percent of the population own American Express Gold Cards. Among professionals 25 percent own Gold Cards, whereas only 1 percent of nonprofessionals own Gold Cards. An index number representing the likelihood of Gold Card ownership by occupation type can be constructed by dividing the percentage of ownership for each group by the incidence of ownership in the entire population.

Professionals $(.25/.10) \times 100 = 250$
Nonprofessionals $(.01/.10) \times 100 = 10$

Thus the index implies that professionals are more than twice as likely as a group to own Gold Cards compared with the entire population (250 compared to 100), while nonprofessionals are only one-tenth as likely as a group to own Gold Cards compared with the entire population (10 compared to 100). In general, especially small or large bases will result in very high or low indices because the index is a ratio of two percentages that are themselves relative measures. Therefore, any error contained in the index represents a combination of errors present in the two percentages used to form the index.

Finally, consider the use of other descriptive statistics, such as the mean. Without additional information relating to the variability present in the data and the number of observations upon which the mean was based, it is difficult to use such statistics in a meaningful way, especially when attempting to identify significant differences that might exist.

TRADITIONAL SOURCES OF SECONDARY MARKET DATA

Secondary market data are produced by many organizations, including federal, state, and local governments, quasi-governmental organizations, trade associations, nonprofit enterprises (such as research institutes and universities), commercial publishers, investment brokerage houses, and professional market research firms. These organizations, such as the U.S. Bureau of the Census, the National Sporting Goods Manufacturers Association, *Sales and Marketing Management*, Smith-Barney, and Frost & Sullivan, are all representative examples of secondary market data producers. Because the data-producing organizations turn out millions of data elements per year, it frequently becomes difficult to see the forest for the trees.

The first prerequisite for locating appropriate secondary data is intellectual curiosity. Never begin a half-hearted search with the assumption that what is being sought is so unique that no one else has ever bothered to collect it and publish it. On the contrary, assume there are corollary secondary data that should help provide at least definition and scope for the primary research effort. This game of "trivial pursuit" makes the search for published secondary market information both interesting and challenging.

Since the number of potentially useful print sources is considerable, we will concentrate on an important group of tertiary reference works that will lead the researcher to identify appropriate secondary source materials. These tertiary tools consist primarily of guides, handbooks, directories, indexes, and compilations that help the novice researcher move into a complex maze of secondary source documents. It is important to be familiar with these reference works, most of which can be located in large research libraries or specialized business libraries.

Guides to Business Information Sources

One of the best places to begin searching for secondary source information is with a guide to business information sources. A guide can help the researcher identify the important standard or recurring information sources on a specific subject. For example, in attempting to locate information on a specific industry, a guide may help identify the major statistical information sources, pertinent trade associations, trade journals, or directories. Some useful business information guides include:

■ *A Business Information Guidebook*
  Oscar Figueroa and Charles Winkle
  New York: ALACOM, 1980

- *Business Information Sources*
  Lorna M Daniell
  Berkeley, Calif.: University of California Press, 1976
- *Encyclopedia of Business Information Sources*, 5th edition
  Paul Wasserman et al.
  Detroit: Gale Research Company, 1983
- *Information Sourcebook For Marketers and Strategic Planners*
  Van Mayros and D. Michael Werner
  Radnor, Pa.: Chilton Book Company, 1983

If a guidebook fails to produce useful sources of information, this may indicate that the research strategy needs to uncover information of a one-time, nonstandard nature and that you need to turn to primary sources.

Directories

Because the pursuit of secondary market research frequently involves the identification of individuals or organizations that gather pertinent information, it may be necessary to use directories. One tool that is indispensable because it serves as a directory of published directories is

- *The Directory of Directories*, 3rd edition
  James M. Ethridge, editor
  Detroit: Gale Research Company, 1984

Two directories that receive heavy use and assist in the identification of trade associations are

- *Encyclopedia of Associations*, 19th edition
  Denise S. Akey, editor
  Detroit: Gale Research Company, 1985
- *National Trade and Professional Association of the United States*, 19th edition
  Craig Colgate, editor
  Washington, D.C.: Columbia Books, Inc., 1984

Data on the most specialized of products (such as tempered glass) are frequently collected by a trade association. Since these data may not be widely disseminated, a researcher may need to contact an association directly in an attempt to gain access.

Indexes to Business Literature

Indexes are useful because they help the researcher identify journal articles on a specific subject in any of hundreds of different periodical publications. Thus a researcher might use an index to locate survey data on supermarket shoppers contained in a pertinent trade journal article. The major business indexes, which differ in scope, retrospectiveness, frequency of update, and format, are

- *Business Index*
  Menlo Park, Calif.: Information Access Company, 1979 to present
- *Business Periodical Index*
  New York: H. W. Wilson Company, 1958 to present
- *F & S Index: Europe*
  Cleveland: Predicasts, Inc., 1980 to present
- *F & S Index: International*
  Cleveland: Predicasts, Inc., 1969 to present
- *F & S Index: United States*
  Cleveland: Predicasts, Inc., 1964 to present
- *Journal of Marketing*
  Chicago: American Marketing Association, quarterly (Every issue contains the section "Marketing Abstracts")
- *Topicator: Classified Article Guide to the Advertising/Communications/Marketing Periodical Press*
  Florissant, Colo.: Topicator, bimonthly

Indexes to Newspapers

Newspapers are also important sources of business/market information, but many local newspapers are not indexed in traditional indexes. Three major newspaper indexes provide subject indexing and are regularly updated:

- *National Newspaper Index*
  Menlo Park, Calif.: Information Access Company, 1979 to present (Indexes five newspapers: *New York Times, Wall Street Journal, Christian Science Monitor, Los Angeles Times,* and *Washington Post*)
- *New York Times Index*
  New York: The New York Times Company, 1851 to present
- *Wall Street Journal Index*
  New York: Dow Jones & Company, Inc., 1958 to present

Although these indexes are still useful, developments in the new information technologies address the historically poor access to information from our cities' important newspapers. For example, Vu/Text is a database vendor that provides on-line search and access to the contents of many major-market newspapers, such as the *Philadelphia Inquirer.*

Indexes to Statistical Information

Because the market researcher frequently attempts to identify particular statistical series, these indexes are extremely important tools. They provide detailed subject indexing of statistical contents of thousands of publications and are updated regularly:

- *American Statistics Index: A Comprehensive Guide to the Statistical Publications of the U.S. Government*
  Bethesda, Md.: Congressional Information Service, 1973 to present

- *International Statistics Index: A Guide to the Statistical Publications of International Intergovernmental Organizations*
  Bethesda, Md.: Congressional Information Service, 1983 to present
- *Statistical Reference Index: A Selective Guide to American Statistical Publications from Private Organizations and State Government Sources*
  Bethesda, Md.: Congressional Information Service, 1980 to present

Indexes to Specialized Business Information Services

Apart from the marketing information gathered from trade associations, business periodicals, government documents, and assorted other publishers of statistical information, commercial market research reports and investment brokerage house reports are two additional important bodies of literature now receiving subject indexing. Firms such as Frost & Sullivan, Business Communications Company, and Predicasts regularly publish market surveys on various products and industries. While these reports can be expensive ($1,000 is not uncommon), they may represent a low-cost alternative to primary research. One source that provides subject indexing of marketing research studies is

- *Findex, The Directory of Market Research Reports, Studies, and Surveys*
  New York: Find/Svp, annual and midyear updates

Other important sources of marketing information are the reports of investment brokerage houses such as E. F. Hutton & Company, Inc., and Kidder, Peabody & Company, Inc. The company and industry reports are prepared for these firms by expert professionals and can, for example, be a source of information on market share or industry trends and forecasts. One index to these reports is

- *CIRR/Corporate and Industry Research Reports Index*
  Eastchester, N.Y.: J. A. Micropublishing, Inc., annual

This index serves as a guide to a microfiche collection of these reports (in 1984, 13,000 research reports from forty investment firms), also available from J. A. Micropublishing.

Statistical Compilations

Unlike the statistical indexes that direct the researcher to specific statistical publications, the statistical compilation actually reprints the data contained in numerous secondary source documents. One can save considerable research time if needed data can be located in one of the following sourcebooks:

- Predicasts *Basebook*
  Cleveland: Predicasts, annual with quarterly updates (Time series statistics on the U.S. economy, industries, products, and services)

- Predicasts *Forecasts*
  Cleveland: Predicasts, annual with quarterly updates (Statistical forecasts on products, industries, services, and the U.S. economy)
- Standard & Poor's *Statistical Service*
  New York: Standard & Poor's Corporation, monthly (A current source for basic statistics on the U.S. economy, financial markets, and basic industries)
- *County and City Data Book*
  U.S. Bureau of the Census
  Washington, D.C.: Government Printing Office, irregular (Repackages census data relating to counties and cities)
- *State and Metropolitan Area Data Book*
  U.S. Bureau of the Census
  Washington, D.C.: Government Printing Office, irregular (Repackages census data relating to states and metropolitan statistical areas)
- *Statistical Abstract of the United States*
  U.S. Bureau of the Census
  Washington, D.C.: Government Printing Office, annual (An essential volume of social, political, and economic data form a variety of sources)

Because of their completeness and level of detail, the various censuses conducted by the U.S. Bureau of the Census form the statistical foundation for much of the extrapolation done on the U.S. population and economic activity. The various major components of the census series are

- U.S. Bureau of the Census
  Census of Housing (published every ten years)
  Census of Population (published every ten years)
  Census of Agriculture (published every five years)
  Census of Construction Industries (published every five years)
  Census of Manufacturers (published every five years)
  Census of Retail Trade (published every five years)
  Census of Service Industries (published every five years)
  Census of Transportation (published every five years)
  Census of Wholesale Trade (published every five years)
  County Business Patterns (published annually)

Survey of Buying Power

The statistical compilation considered by many marketing practitioners to be the most important single sourcebook for the marketing researcher is

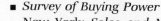

- *Survey of Buying Power*
  New York: *Sales and Marketing Management*, annual in two parts (Composite demographic and retail sales data for states, cities, and counties)

It is most valuable for its current population and income analysis of metropolitan statistical areas, counties, and states, as well as population and income projections for these same geographic areas.

Table 3-1 presents data taken from *Sales and Marketing Management's Survey of Buying Power* Data Service. The *Survey of Buying Power* Data Service consists of over 900 pages of maps and figures divided into three volumes. It includes, for each geographical area, population and detailed characteristics, effective buying income (EBI), total retail sales, **buying power index** (BPI), and three **graduated buying power indexes** (EPP, MPP, and PPP). The following describes how the EBI, BPI, and graduated EPP, MPP, and PPP are computed.[3]

- Effective buying income (EBI) is disposable personal income—that amount of gross income available after taxes to purchase goods and services. The EBI household distribution groups households into income classifications and geographic market detail.

- Buying power index (BPI) is a weighted index that converts three basic elements—population, effective buying income, and retail sales—into a measurement of a market's ability to buy and expresses it as a percentage of the U.S. potential. It is calculated by giving a weight of 5 to the market's percent of U.S. EBI, 3 to its percent of U.S. retail sales, and 2 to its percent of U.S. population. The total of those weighted percents is then divided by 10 to arrive at the BPI.

  The BPI is probably one of the *Survey of Buying Power's* most widely used single market measures. Because it is broadly based, it is most useful in estimating the potential for mass products sold at popular prices. The further a product is removed from the mass market, the greater is the need for a BPI modified by more discriminating factors—social class, income, age, sex, and so forth.

- Graduated buying power indexes are designed to correlate product potential and buying power of households with low income (under $15,000), moderate income ($15,000–$24,999), or high income ($25,000 and over). EPP, for economy-priced products, has the following weights applied to the respective percents of U.S. totals: 6 for households with incomes under $15,000, 3 for food store sales, and 1 for number of households. MPP, for moderate-priced products, has the following weights: 6 for households with incomes $15,000–$24,999, 3 for total retail sales, and 1 for three- or four-person households. PPP, for premium-priced products, has the following weights: 6 for households with incomes $25,000 and over, 3 for combined apparel and furniture-household-appliance store sales, and 1 for households with head 35–64 years old.

  Each index is calculated in the same manner as the more familiar BPI. That is, the market's share of the U.S. total of each indicator is multiplied by the given weight; the total of the weighted percents is then divided by 10.

Buying power index (BPI) A weighted index that converts three basic elements—population, effective buying income, and retail sales—into a measurement of a market's ability to buy, expressed as a percentage of U.S. potential.

Graduated buying power indexes Indexes that correlate product potential and buying power of households with low income, moderate income, or high income.

[3]The definitions were taken from *Survey of Buying Power Data Service (Sales and Marketing Management, 1985)*, 4, A-5, A-6.

T A B L E 3-1

Survey of Buying Power—Population, Effective Buying Income, Retail Sales, and Buying Power Index (BPI)

Metro area county	12/31/80 Population (thousands)	Percent of U.S.	Percent change 1970-80	Pop. per sq. mi. (density)	Percent white	12/31/80 Households (thousands)	Percent of U.S.	1980 EBI ($000)	Percent of U.S.	1980 retail sales ($000)	Percent of U.S.	Buying power index (BPI)	Graduated buying power indexes EPP (economy-priced products)	MPP (Moderate-priced products)	PPP (Premium-priced products)
New York	9,078.0	3.9727	−9.0	6,559	66.9	3,511.7	4.2877	82,157,498	4.5286	31,829,889	3.2959	4.0476	4.0949	3.9886	4.4931
Bronx	1,144.9	.5010	−22.2	27,924	46.7	422.9	.5164	7,112,721	.3920	2,362,342	.2446	.3696	.6088	.5004	.3465
Kings	2,201.8	.9636	−15.4	31,454	55.8	823.8	1.0059	14,574,961	.8034	4,560,002	.4722	.7362	1.0879	.9568	.7555
New York (Manhattan)	1,430.0	.6258	−7.1	62,174	58.7	712.6	.8700	18,312,841	1.0094	9,250,914	.9579	.9172	.8709	.8788	1.1869
Putnam	78.7	.0344	38.8	341	98.2	25.1	.0307	551,452	.0304	259,744	.0269	.0302	.0257	.0305	.0287
Queens	1,897.1	.8302	−4.5	17,566	70.3	718.9	.8777	16,400,005	.9040	4,700,340	.4867	.7639	.7051	.7674	.8142
Richmond	356.6	.1561	20.7	6,148	89.0	116.9	.1427	2,544,724	.1403	964,511	.0998	.1313	.1228	.1398	.1371
Rockland	262.1	.1147	14.0	1,489	89.3	79.4	.0970	2,416,930	.1332	1,015,830	.1052	.1212	.0795	.0773	.1327
Westchester	864.6	.3783	−3.3	1,952	83.9	309.7	.3781	10,619,178	.5854	4,100,831	.4247	.4956	.3106	.3148	.5220
Bergen, N.J.	842.2	.3686	−6.1	3,599	92.5	302.4	.3692	9,624,686	.5305	4,615,375	.4779	.4824	.2836	.3228	.5695
New York-Newark-Jersey City-Bridgeport Consolidated Area	16,558.4	7.2466	−5.4	3,146	74.8	6,028.6	7.3607	155,915,773	8.5943	64,611,379	6.6904	7.7535	6.5391	6.6893	8.6346

Source: *Sales and Marketing Management Survey of Buying Power Data Service* (1985), 5.

The data supplied in the *Survey of Buying Power* can be used in solving a variety of diverse marketing-related problems. The following examples illustrate the usefulness of this source of secondary market information.

EXAMPLE

Creating Customized BPI

Suppose that your firm has created a new line of gourmet, single-portion convenience-foods. To develop a customized BPI that reflects the market's ability to purchase this specific product, a consumer profile must first be specified. Typically, three factors are considered: demographic, economic, and distribution. For this line of foods, the target demographic subgroup consists of one-person households (HH) with incomes over $50,000. Initially at least, the gourmet items will be available exclusively in supermarket chains. Having selected an appropriate consumer profile, you can compute a customized BPI.

Step 1:   For each market compute the following percentages:

$$\text{Demographic percent} = \frac{\text{market's 1-person HH}}{\text{U.S. 1-person HH}}$$

$$\text{Economic percent} = \frac{\text{market's HH with income \$50,000+}}{\text{U.S. HH with income \$50,000+}}$$

$$\text{Distribution percent} = \frac{\text{market's supermarket sales}}{\text{U.S. supermarket sales}}$$

Step 2:   Determine the importance of each component of the consumer's profile.

Demographic = 50%

Economic   = 40%

Distribution = 10%

Step 3:   Calculate the BPI

BPI = .5 (Demographic%) + .4 (Economic%) + .1 (Distribution%)

Step 4:   Repeat for each market

Measuring Market Potential

Suppose that your firm manufactures women's dresses. Total U.S. retail volume is $3 billion. Your company does $2.10 million or a 7 percent share of market dollar volume. To measure market potential:

Step 1:   Select (identify) a geographic segment.

Step 2:   Identify the industry product sales for the given segment by multiplying a custom BPI by the U.S. total product sales of the industry.

Measuring Market Potential

	New Jersey	New York
Customized BPI	.0706	.1482
Industry sales	$2,118,000 ($3 billion × .0706)	$4,446,000 ($3 billion × .1482)
Company sales	$157,000	$230,000
Company share	7.41% [(157,000/2,118,000) × 100]	5.17% [(230,000/4,446,000) × 100]
Market potential index	105.9	73.9
Calculations	$2.10 million × .0706 =	$2.10 million × .1482 =
	$148,260	$311,220
	$157,000/$148,260 = 1.0590	$230,000/$311,220 = .739
	1.0589 × 100 = 105.90	.739 × 100 = 73.9

Step 3:   Identify company sales in the given segment.

Step 4:   Find your firm's share of market by dividing the results obtained in *Step 3* by *Step 2* results.

Step 5:   Identify the potential for a particular market by multiplying your total sales by the market BPI. Then divide your actual market sales by that potential number, and the result, after multiplying by 100, will be an index of your market performance. An index of 100 is par. Above 100 indicates that the market is performing above its basic potential. Under 100 means that the performance is under basic potential. In other words, an index of 80 would mean the market is 20 percent under potential.

Table 3-2 shows how this process works using a BPI already calculated for New Jersey and New York. Note that New Jersey has a performance index that is approximately 6 percent better than the estimated potential, whereas in New York the performance index is 73.9, which is 26.1% less than potential. The analysis would logically lead you to question why you are doing so poorly in the New York segment.

Other Sources

You should be aware of other sources of standardized market research information. The three sources described below provide standardized data covering either product usage and media habits, social trends, or consumer values and lifestyles.

- The Study of Media and Markets
  New York: Simmons Market Research Bureau, Inc. (SMRB)—Simmons Market Research Bureau is one of the most widely used sources of product usage and media audience data. SMRB produces a wealth of market information; data are available for some 750 product/ser-

vices categories, 3,500 brands, and numerous media audiences (print and broadcast). Sample SMRB breakouts for several brands of cold breakfast cereals are shown in Table 3-3. The table has been annotated for interpretation. SMRB data can prove useful in developing category and brand target segments and identifying media that reach them. Many libraries have SMRB volumes in their reference divisions; in addition, SMRB data can be accessed through vendors that provide time-sharing services.

- Yankelovich Monitor
  New York: Yankelovich, Skelly and White (1970 to present, annual)—The *Yankelovich Monitor* is a research service that tracks over forty social trends and provides information about shifts in size and direction and resulting market implications. Exhibit 3-1 presents a sample of social trends examined by the *Yankelovich Monitor* service. Social trend information as reported by the *Yankelovich Monitor* has proved to be useful in identifying likely shifts in demand for various product categories—for example, the shift to "white" liquors (such as vodka and gin) from "brown" whiskey (such as Scotch and rye blends).[4]

- SRI Values and Lifestyles (VALS^{TM})
  Menlo Park, California: SRI International—*VALS*^{TM} is a research service that tracks marketing-relevant shifts in the beliefs, values, and lifestyles of a sample of the American population. The *VALS*^{TM} system divides the population into segments consisting of three major groups of consumers, in turn divided into nine specific segments. Table 3-4 summarizes a variety of published findings about the segments. Tracking the shifts in the values and behavior of these segments can help in understanding the target segment one is appealing to.

EXHIBIT 3-1

A Sample of Social Trends Examined by the Yankelovich Monitor Service

Trend No. 1, Personalization

Monitor's measurement of the size of the group committed to Personalization comprises a series of scaled items including: (1) the emphasis placed on buying "products that reveal their style and personality"; (2) the need to add "one's own personal touch" to products; (3) the acceptance of nonconformity in appearance and lifestyle, even with some social and economic penalties; (4) the degree of desirability ascribed to being different from other people and showing it, rather than the value assigned to "fitting in."

[4]Olivia Schieffelin Nordberg, "Lifestyles Monitor," *American Demographics*, May 1981, 22; and B. G. Youovich, "Finding Answers," *Advertising Age*, 20 July 1981, 41–42 and 44.

T A B L E 3-3A
Sample Simmons (SMRB) Purchase Data

0096
P-20

BREAKFAST CEREALS (COLD): BRANDS (FEMALE HOMEMAKERS)

	TOTAL U.S. '000	QUAKER CAP'N CRUNCH				QUAKER LIFE				QUAKER PUFFED RICE				QUAKER PUFFED WHEAT			
		A '000	B % DOWN	C % ACROSS	D INDX	A '000	B % DOWN	C % ACROSS	D INDX	A '000	B % DOWN	C % ACROSS	D INDX	A '000	B % DOWN	C % ACROSS	D INDX
TOTAL FEMALE HOMEMAKERS	77506ᵃ	6014ᵇ	100.0ᵇ	7.8	100	4209	100.0	5.4	100	4417	100.0	5.7	100	3970	100.0	5.1	100
18-24	9335	1118	18.6ᶜ	12.0ᵈ	154ᵉ	652	15.5	7.0	129	•460	10.4	4.9	86	•289	7.3	3.1	60
25-34	18029	1820	30.3	10.1	130	1485	35.3	8.2	152	975	22.1	5.4	95	849	21.4	4.7	92
35-44	13417	1443	24.0	10.8	139	944	22.4	7.0	130	713	16.1	5.3	93	642	16.2	4.8	93
45-54	11632	998	16.6	8.6	111	•535	12.7	4.6	85	773	17.5	6.6	117	779	19.6	6.7	131
55-64	11283	•269ᶠ	4.5	2.4	31	•375	8.9	3.3	61	634	14.4	5.6	99	660	16.6	5.8	114
65 OR OLDER	13811	•366ᵍ	6.1	2.7	34	•217	5.2	1.6	29	862	19.5	6.2	110	751	18.9	5.4	106
18-34	27364	2938	48.9	10.7	138	2137	50.8	7.8	144	1434	32.5	5.2	92	1138	28.7	4.2	81
18-49	46197	4987	82.9	10.8	139	3346	79.5	7.2	133	2547	57.7	5.5	97	2150	54.2	4.7	91
25-54	43078	4261	70.9	9.9	127	2965	70.4	6.9	127	2461	55.7	5.7	100	2270	57.2	5.3	103
35-49	18833	2049	34.1	10.9	140	1209	28.7	6.4	118	1113	25.2	5.9	104	1012	25.5	5.4	105
50 OR OLDER	31310	1027	17.1	3.3	42	863	20.5	2.8	51	1870	42.3	6.0	105	1820	45.8	5.8	113
GRADUATED COLLEGE	9890	•422	7.0	4.3	55	715	17.0	7.2	133	503	11.4	5.1	89	441	11.1	4.5	87
ATTENDED COLLEGE	12236	948	15.8	7.7	100	861	20.5	7.0	130	720	16.3	5.9	103	742	18.7	6.1	118
GRADUATED HIGH SCHOOL	32853	3093	51.4	9.4	121	1843	43.8	5.6	103	1979	44.8	6.0	106	1665	41.9	5.1	99
DID NOT GRADUATE HIGH SCHOOL	22527	1552	25.8	6.9	89	789	18.7	3.5	64	1215	27.5	5.4	95	1122	28.3	5.0	97
EMPLOYED	37446	3008	50.0	8.0	104	2302	54.7	6.1	113	2029	45.9	5.4	95	1886	47.5	5.0	98
EMPLOYED FULL-TIME	29717	2270	37.7	7.6	98	1484	35.3	5.0	92	1495	33.8	5.0	88	1379	34.7	4.6	91
EMPLOYED PART-TIME	7729	738	12.3	9.5	123	818	19.4	10.6	195	•534	12.1	6.9	121	•507	12.8	6.6	128
NOT EMPLOYED	40060	3006	50.0	7.5	97	1907	45.3	4.8	88	2388	54.1	6.0	105	2084	52.5	5.2	102
PROFESSIONAL/MANAGER	10614	•640	10.6	6.0	78	562	13.4	5.3	98	501	11.3	4.7	83	462	11.6	4.4	85
CLERICAL/SALES	14780	1227	20.4	8.3	107	1038	24.7	7.0	129	922	20.9	6.2	109	850	21.4	5.8	112
CRAFTSMEN/FOREMEN	824	••108	1.8	13.1	169	••85	2.0	10.3	190	••61	1.4	7.4	130	••53	1.3	6.4	126
OTHER EMPLOYED	11229	1032	17.2	9.2	118	617	14.7	5.5	101	545	12.3	4.9	85	521	13.1	4.6	91
SINGLE	8267	626	10.4	7.6	98	522	12.4	6.3	116	423	9.6	5.1	90	•313	7.9	3.8	74
MARRIED	50768	4088	68.0	8.1	104	3138	74.6	6.2	114	2961	67.0	5.8	102	2649	66.7	5.2	102
DIVORCED/SEPARATED/WIDOWED	18471	1299	21.6	7.0	91	549	13.0	3.0	55	1033	23.4	5.6	98	1008	25.4	5.5	107
PARENTS	31500	4286	71.3	13.6	175	2630	62.5	8.3	154	1956	44.3	6.2	109	1588	40.0	5.0	98
WHITE	67876	5244	87.2	7.7	100	3925	93.3	5.8	106	4071	92.2	6.0	105	3684	92.8	5.4	106
BLACK	8235	700	11.6	8.5	110	•185	4.4	2.2	41	•296	6.7	3.6	63	••250	6.3	3.0	59
OTHER	1395	••70	1.2	5.0	65	••99	2.4	7.1	131	••50	1.1	3.6	63	••37	0.9	2.7	52

Market/demographic table for Quaker Cap'n Crunch (female homemakers). The four repeating column groups each consist of '000, % Down, % Across, and Index. The column-group headers at the top of the page are not legible; the first numeric column is the total number of female homemakers ('000).

	Total '000	(1) '000	% Dn	% Ac	Idx	(2) '000	% Dn	% Ac	Idx	(3) '000	% Dn	% Ac	Idx	(4) '000	% Dn	% Ac	Idx
NORTHEAST-CENSUS	16922	1342	22.3	7.9	102	1130	26.8	6.7	123	1493	33.8	8.8	155	950	23.9	5.6	110
NORTH CENTRAL	20200	2061	34.1	10.2	131	1227	29.2	6.1	112	1393	31.5	6.9	121	1533	38.6	7.6	148
SOUTH	26132	1805	30.0	6.9	89	1124	26.7	4.3	79	763	17.3	2.9	51	696	17.5	2.7	52
WEST	14252	816	13.6	5.7	74	729	17.3	5.1	••	768	17.4	5.4	95	792	19.9	5.6	108
NORTHEAST-MKTG.	17524	1440	23.9	8.2	106	1192	28.3	6.8	125	1454	32.9	8.3	146	879	22.1	5.0	98
EAST CENTRAL	11814	1204	20.0	10.2	131	710	16.9	6.0	110	913	20.7	7.7	136	972	24.5	8.2	161
WEST CENTRAL	13479	1236	20.6	9.2	118	932	22.1	6.9	127	912	20.6	6.8	119	1031	26.0	7.6	149
SOUTH	22875	1542	25.6	6.7	87	899	21.4	3.9	72	551	12.5	2.4	42	•567	14.3	2.5	48
PACIFIC	11814	593	9.9	5.0	65	•477	11.3	4.0	74	•586	13.3	5.0	87	•521	13.1	4.4	86
COUNTY SIZE A	31229	2468	41.0	7.9	102	1729	41.1	5.5	102	1917	43.4	6.1	108	1417	35.7	4.5	89
COUNTY SIZE B	23352	1792	29.8	7.7	99	1497	35.6	6.4	118	1213	27.5	5.2	91	1141	28.7	4.9	95
COUNTY SIZE C	12137	1026	17.1	8.5	109	•715	17.0	5.9	108	782	17.7	6.4	113	815	20.5	6.7	131
COUNTY SIZE D	10789	728	12.1	6.7	87	•268	6.4	2.5	46	505	11.4	4.7	82	597	15.0	5.5	108
METRO CENTRAL CITY	23359	1737	28.9	7.4	96	1220	29.0	5.2	96	1040	23.5	4.5	78	863	21.7	3.7	72
METRO SUBURBAN	34657	2799	46.5	8.1	104	2132	50.7	6.2	113	2296	52.0	6.6	116	2083	52.5	6.0	117
NON METRO	19491	1478	24.6	7.6	98	857	20.4	4.4	81	1080	24.5	5.5	97	1024	25.8	5.3	103
TOP 5 ADI'S	17725	1293	21.5	7.3	94	1055	25.1	6.0	110	1183	26.8	6.7	117	696	17.5	3.9	77
TOP 10 ADI'S	25079	2096	34.9	8.4	108	1556	37.0	6.2	114	1608	36.4	6.4	113	1114	28.1	4.4	87
TOP 20 ADI'S	35085	2839	47.2	8.1	104	1941	46.1	5.5	102	2143	48.5	6.1	107	1549	38.0	4.4	86
HSHLD.INC. $40,000 OR MORE	8818	•646	10.7	7.3	94	626	14.9	7.1	131	•505	11.4	5.7	100	•459	11.6	5.2	102
$30,000 OR MORE	18653	1521	25.3	8.2	105	1153	27.4	6.2	114	1122	25.4	6.0	106	1050	26.4	5.6	110
$25,000 OR MORE	25911	2178	36.2	8.4	108	1537	36.5	5.9	109	1514	34.3	5.8	103	1366	34.4	5.3	103
$20,000-$24,999	9349	787	13.1	8.4	108	848	20.1	9.1	167	•528	12.0	5.6	99	•508	12.8	5.4	106
$15,000-$19,999	8862	859	14.3	9.7	126	620	14.7	7.0	129	•397	9.0	4.5	79	•515	13.0	5.8	113
$10,000-$14,999	13844	1138	18.9	8.2	106	545	12.9	3.9	72	836	18.9	6.0	106	600	15.1	4.3	85
UNDER $10,000	19541	1041	17.3	5.3	69	659	15.7	3.4	62	1141	25.8	5.8	102	981	24.7	5.0	98
HOUSEHOLD OF 1 PERSON	11894	•178	3.0	1.5	19	375	8.9	3.2	58	604	13.7	5.1	89	510	12.8	4.3	84
2 PEOPLE	25454	949	15.8	3.7	48	791	18.8	3.1	57	1355	30.7	5.3	93	1211	30.5	4.8	93
3 OR 4 PEOPLE	28521	2756	45.8	9.7	125	1964	46.7	6.9	127	1521	34.4	5.3	94	1656	41.7	5.8	113
5 OR MORE PEOPLE	11637	2132	35.5	18.3	236	1080	25.7	9.3	171	937	21.2	8.1	141	•594	15.0	5.1	100
NO CHILD IN HSHLD	43986	1396	23.2	3.2	41	1425	33.9	•3.2	60	2353	53.3	5.3	94	2314	58.3	5.3	103
CHILD(REN) UNDER 2 YRS	5651	691	11.5	12.2	158	•583	13.9	10.3	190	•418	9.5	7.4	130	•295	7.4	5.2	102
2-5 YEARS	12521	1691	28.1	13.5	174	1133	26.9	9.0	167	893	20.2	7.1	125	725	18.3	5.8	113
6-11 YEARS	15766	2572	42.8	16.3	210	1436	34.0	9.1	168	962	21.8	6.1	107	757	19.1	4.8	94
12-17 YEARS	16144	2376	39.6	14.7	190	1252	29.7	7.8	143	910	20.8	5.6	99	798	20.1	4.9	97
RESIDENCE OWNED	55460	4079	67.8	7.4	95	3048	72.4	5.5	101	3282	74.3	5.9	104	3251	81.9	5.9	114
VALUE: $50,000 OR MORE	28563	2154	35.8	7.5	97	1768	42.0	6.2	114	1574	35.6	5.5	97	1511	38.1	5.3	103
VALUE: UNDER $50,000	26897	1924	32.0	7.2	92	1281	30.4	4.8	88	1708	38.7	6.4	111	1740	43.8	6.5	126

[a] There are 77,506,000 female homemakers in the United States.

[b] There are 6,014,000 female homemakers who are users/purchasers of Quaker Cap'n Crunch.

[c] 18.6% of the female homemakers who are users/purchasers of this brand are 18-24 years of age—1118/6014 = .1859.

[d] 12.0% of the female homemakers who are 18-24 years of age are users/purchasers of this brand—1118/9,335 = .1197.

[e] 154 is the index number found by 12.0/7.8 × 100 = 153.85, which means that the 18-24 age group purchases more of this brand than would be expected based on the portion of all female homemakers who are users/purchasers of this brand.

[f] A simple dot indicates that the projected population is relatively unstable because of small sample size.

[g] A double dot indicates that the number of cases is too small for reliability.

T A B L E 3-3B
Sample Simmons (SMRB) Media Data

BREAKFAST CEREALS (COLD): BRANDS (FEMALE HOMEMAKERS)

Program	Net	TOTAL U.S. -000	POST RAISIN BRAN A -000	B % DOWN	C ACROSS %	D INDX	POST SUPER SUGAR CRISP A -000	B % DOWN	C ACROSS %	D INDX	POST TOASTIES A -000	B % DOWN	C ACROSS %	D INDX	POST 40% BRAN FLAKES A -000	B % DOWN	C ACROSS %	D INDX
TOTAL FEMALE HOMEMAKERS		77506	17129	100.0	22.1	100	4740	100.0	6.1	100	4461	100.0	5.8	100	5217	100.0	6.7	100
WKDAY LOCAL EVENING TV NEWS																		
NETWORK AFFILIATES-EARLY		25416	5107	29.8	20.1	91	1247	26.3	4.9	80	1580	35.4	6.2	108	2007	38.5	7.9	117
NETWORK AFFILIATES-LATE		18757	4159	24.3	22.2	100	1205	25.4	6.4	106	1289	28.9	6.9	119	1257	26.0	7.2	107
INDEPENDENTS-LATE		2476	437	2.6	17.6	80	106	2.2	4.3	70	141	3.2	5.7	99	187	3.6	7.6	112
TV EVENING NTWK 6 PM-2 AM																		
SUN	A																	
ABC FRIDAY NIGHT MOVIE	A	4978	1250	7.3	25.1	114	307	6.5	6.2	101	329	7.4	6.6	115	287	5.5	5.8	86
ABC NEWS: NIGHTLINE	A	2266	579	3.4	25.6	116	136	3.0	6.2	101	140	3.1	6.2	107	163	3.1	7.2	107
ABC WORLD NEWS TONIGHT	A	5871	1355	7.9	23.1	104	236	5.0	4.0	66	391	8.8	6.7	116	481	9.1	8.2	122
ABC WORLD NEWS TONIGHT-SUN	A	2084	602	2.9	24.1	109	●●113[b]	2.4	5.4	89	●130[a]	2.9	6.2	110	●130	2.5	6.3	94
ARCHIE BUNKER'S PLACE	C	7966	1689	9.9	21.2	96	438	9.2	5.5	90	504	11.3	6.3	110	643	12.3	8.1	120
BARBARA MANDRELL	N	5626	1097	6.4	19.5	88	●279	8.9	5.0	81	426	9.5	7.8	132	548	10.5	8.7	145
BARNEY MILLER	A	8228	1757	10.3	21.4	97	401	8.5	4.9	80	551	12.4	6.7	118	532	12.1	7.7	114
BENSON	A	7000	1425	8.3	20.4	92	333	7.0	4.8	78	451	10.1	6.4	112	517	9.9	7.4	110
BOOK OF LISTS	C	5214	1337	7.8	25.6	116	●321	6.8	6.2	101	●242	5.4	4.6	81	●243	4.7	4.7	69
BRET MAVERICK	N	5453	1167	6.8	21.4	97	323	6.8	5.9	97	●266	6.0	4.9	85	353	6.8	6.5	96
CBS EVENING NEWS-DEAN	C	3645	797	4.7	21.9	99	●149	3.1	4.1	67	●182	4.1	5.0	87	●223	4.3	6.1	91
CBS EVENING NEWS-RATHER	C	7761	1625	9.5	20.9	95	451	9.5	5.8	95	509	11.4	6.6	114	599	11.5	7.7	115
CBS SAT NEWS-SCHIEFFER	C	3875	750	4.4	19.4	88	●176	3.7	4.5	74	256	5.7	6.6	118	308	5.9	7.8	118
CBS SAT NIGHT MOVIE	C	5273	1231	7.2	23.3	106	372	7.8	7.1	115	304	6.8	5.8	100	302	5.8	5.7	85
CBS SUNDAY NEWS-OSGOOD	C	2130	385	2.2	18.1	82	●●85	1.8	4.0	65	●●84	1.9	3.9	69	●132	2.5	6.2	92
CBS WEDNESDAY NIGHT MOVIE	C	6817	1398	8.2	20.5	93	465	9.8	6.8	112	506	11.3	7.4	129	477	9.1	7.0	104
CHICAGO STORY	N	3093	767	4.5	24.8	112	●●152	3.2	4.9	80	●216	4.8	7.0	121	●299	5.7	9.7	144
CHIPS	N	7786	1671	9.8	21.5	97	491	10.4	6.3	103	432	9.7	5.5	86	418	5.4	5.4	80
DALLAS	C	10915	2268	13.2	20.8	94	717	15.1	6.6	107	654	14.7	6.0	104	779	14.9	7.1	106
DIFFERENT STROKES	N	9535	2171	12.7	22.8	103	844	17.8	8.9	145	537	12.0	5.6	98	546	10.5	5.7	85
DUKES OF HAZZARD	C	7935	1723	10.1	21.7	98	616	13.0	7.8	127	485	10.9	6.1	106	521	10.0	6.6	98
FACTS OF LIFE	N	8082	1802	10.5	22.3	101	558	11.8	6.9	113	474	10.6	5.9	102	491	9.4	6.1	90
FALL GUY	A	8200	1847	10.8	22.5	102	569	12.0	6.9	113	413	9.3	5.0	88	475	9.1	5.8	86
FAME	N	6263	1205	7.0	19.2	87	556	11.7	8.9	145	331	7.4	5.3	92	304	5.8	4.9	72
FANTASY ISLAND	A	9027	1712	10.0	19.0	86	638	13.5	7.1	116	453	10.2	5.0	87	532	10.2	5.9	88
FATHER MURPHY	N	4724	956	5.6	20.2	92	●●259	5.5	5.5	90	331	7.4	7.0	122	323	6.2	6.8	102

TV VIEWING (ratings / audience data table)

Program	Code	N	V1	V2	V3	V4	V5	V6	V7	V8	V9	V10	V11	V12	V13	V14	V15
GIMME A BREAK	N	8983	11.5	21.9	99	839	17.7	9.3	153	477	10.7	5.3	82	466	8.9	5.2	77
GREATEST AMERICAN HERO	A	6628	8.8	22.3	103	510	10.8	7.7	126	436	9.8	6.6	114	368	9.0	5.6	82
HAPPY DAYS	A	8265	9.3	20.3	92	697	14.7	8.4	138	499	11.2	6.0	105	470	11.2	5.7	84
HARPER VALLEY	N	3816	4.1	18.6	84	●226	4.8	5.9	97	263	5.9	5.9	120	390	7.5	10.2	152
HART TO HART	A	11762	15.6	22.8	103	735	15.5	6.2	102	630	14.1	5.4	93	858	16.4	7.3	103
HILL STREET BLUES	N	9045	11.4	21.6	98	749	15.8	8.3	135	437	9.8	4.8	84	490	6.4	5.4	80
INCREDIBLE HULK	C	4712	5.4	19.8	89	297	6.3	6.3	103	289	6.5	6.1	107	325	6.2	6.9	102
LAVERNE & SHIRLEY	A	8279	10.5	21.8	99	699	14.7	8.4	138	445	10.0	5.4	93	436	8.4	5.3	78
LITTLE HOUSE-PRAIRIE	N	10207	10.6	17.6	80	606	12.8	6.0	97	603	13.5	5.7	103	604	11.6	5.9	88
LOU GRANT	N	8042	13.5	22.5	102	482	10.2	6.9	98	461	10.3	5.7	100	471	5.9	5.9	87
LOVE BOAT	C	11480	12.6	20.2	91	795	16.8	6.0	113	567	12.7	4.7	86	639	12.2	5.6	83
MAGNUM P.I.	A	10658	13.5	20.3	92	570	12.0	5.3	87	499	11.2	4.7	81	553	10.6	5.2	77
M*A*S*H	C	9369	13.5	24.0	109	733	15.5	5.3	128	687	11.4	7.3	127	694	13.3	7.4	110
MORK & MINDY	A	4737	7.2	25.9	117	289	6.1	6.1	100	307	6.9	6.5	113	352	6.7	7.4	110
NBC MAGAZINE	N	4118	5.1	21.2	96	●203	4.3	4.9	81	305	6.8	7.4	129	331	6.3	8.0	119
NBC MONDAY NIGHT MOVIES	N	7285	9.7	22.9	104	461	9.7	6.3	103	398	9.9	5.5	95	495	9.5	6.8	101
NBC NIGHTLY NEWS	N	5866	6.6	19.1	87	254	5.4	4.3	71	314	7.0	5.4	93	422	8.1	7.2	107
NBC NIGHTLY NEWS-SAT	N	2990	2.8	16.1	73	●100	2.1	3.3	55	●151	3.4	5.1	88	256	4.9	8.6	127
NBC NIGHTLY NEWS-SUN	N	3186	2.7	13.9	65	●87	1.8	2.7	45	●186	4.2	7.1	102	339	6.5	10.7	159
NBC SUNDAY NIGHT MOVIE	N	7514	10.5	23.9	108	384	8.1	6.1	84	530	11.7	7.1	102	463	8.9	6.2	92
ONE DAY AT A TIME	C	8157	10.2	21.4	97	498	10.5	6.4	100	521	11.7	6.4	111	600	11.5	7.4	109
ONE OF THE BOYS	N	3447	3.6	18.1	82	●219	4.6	6.4	104	268	6.0	5.7	135	331	6.3	9.6	143
QUINCY, M.E.	N	9880	11.8	20.7	94	557	11.8	5.4	92	525	11.2	5.3	82	724	13.9	7.3	109
REAL PEOPLE	N	9183	11.8	22.0	100	494	10.4	5.4	88	648	14.5	7.1	123	784	15.0	8.5	127
60 MINUTES	C	12666	16.5	22.3	101	582	12.3	4.6	75	874	19.6	6.9	120	1162	22.3	9.2	136
TAXI	A	8204	11.3	23.7	107	438	9.2	5.4	87	507	11.7	6.2	130	594	11.4	7.2	108
TEACHERS ONLY	N	6998	10.4	25.4	115	515	10.9	7.4	120	522	11.7	7.5	130	515	9.9	7.4	109
THAT'S INCREDIBLE	A	7495	9.7	22.2	100	447	9.4	6.0	98	418	9.4	5.6	97	498	9.5	6.6	99
THREE'S COMPANY	A	12031	17.1	24.3	110	894	18.9	7.4	122	671	15.0	5.6	97	758	14.5	6.3	94
TONIGHT SHOW	N	2727	3.7	23.1	104	115	2.4	4.2	69	209	4.7	7.7	133	214	4.1	7.8	117
TOO CLOSE FOR COMFORT	A	11418	15.9	23.8	108	864	18.2	7.6	124	716	16.1	6.3	109	756	14.5	7.8	98
TRAPPER JOHN, M.D.	C	11694	16.1	23.6	107	897	18.9	7.7	125	734	16.5	6.3	109	759	14.5	6.5	96
20/20	A	9204	11.9	22.1	100	444	9.4	4.8	79	571	12.8	6.2	108	664	12.7	7.2	107
WALT DISNEY	C	4583	5.9	22.1	100	277	5.8	6.0	99	●260	5.8	5.7	99	267	5.1	5.8	87

TV VIEWING SPORTS EVENTS

Program	Code	N	V1	V2	V3	V4	V5	V6	V7	V8	V9	V10	V11	V12	V13	V14	V15
BASEBALL		10670	15.2	24.5	111	528	11.1	4.9	81	899	20.2	8.4	145	1076	20.6	10.2	150
BASKETBALL-COLLEGE GAMES		4501	7.8	29.8	135	●448	9.5	10.0	163	●531	11.9	11.8	205	●371	8.2	8.2	122
BASKETBALL-PRO GAMES		4600	7.0	26.2	118	●332	7.0	7.2	118	●480	10.8	10.4	181	●456	8.7	9.9	147
BOWLING		4732	9.3	31.7	88	●375	7.9	7.9	130	●274	6.1	5.1	101	●399	7.6	8.4	125
BOXING		5042	—	31.6	143	—	14.7	13.8	226	●380	8.1	8.6	124	●409	7.8	8.1	121
FOOTBALL-COLLEGE GAMES		8758	16.1	31.6	143	725	15.3	8.3	135	771	17.3	8.6	153	851	16.3	9.7	144
FOOTBALL-PROFESSIONAL GAMES		14895	22.8	26.2	118	1312	27.7	8.8	144	1178	26.4	7.9	137	1148	22.0	7.7	115
GOLF		4057	6.7	28.2	127	●249	5.3	6.1	100	●356	8.0	8.8	152	●411	7.9	10.1	151
POST-SEASON COLL. FOOTBALL		6612	10.6	27.6	125	●468	9.9	7.1	116	●591	13.2	8.9	155	579	11.1	8.8	130
POST-SEASON PRO FOOTBALL		9284	15.0	27.7	125	747	15.8	8.0	132	754	16.9	8.1	141	758	14.5	8.2	121
TENNIS		3738	5.7	26.0	118	●216	4.6	5.8	94	●229	5.1	6.1	106	257	4.9	6.9	102

ᵃA single dot indicates that the projected population is relatively unstable because of small sample size.
ᵇA double dot indicates that the number of cases is too small for reliability.

Trend No. 10, New Romanticism

Monitor's measurement of the size of the group committed to New Romanticism is based on a series of scaled items including: (1) the recognition of a real need for "romance and mystery" in one's life; (2) the desire for "more excitement and sensation"; (3) the wish to "have lived in an age" when adventure and romantic concepts were in style.

Trend No. 14, Return to Nature

Monitor measures Return to Nature through a series of scaled items including: (1) the desire to live in a natural setting, i.e., in the country, as opposed to living in a city or its surrounding suburbs; (2) the perceived need to live in a way that is "closer to nature"; (3) the relative value to the individual of living in a "natural" way, as opposed to the benefits of widely available man-made modern conveniences.

Trend No. 33, Concern About Privacy

Monitor's measurement of Concern About Privacy is based on a series of scaled items including: (1) concern about maintaining one's right to privacy; (2) perceived violations of privacy by certain government agencies; (3) attitudes toward wiretapping under specified conditions; and (4) attitudes toward legislation designed to protect the consumer from perceived invasions of privacy by business.

Trend No. 44, Flirtation With Danger

Monitor's measurement of the size of the group committed to Flirtation With Danger consists of a series of scaled items covering: (1) the belief that the mastering of "dangerous" leisure activities can make one a better person; (2) interest in "dangerous" activities; (3) interest in taking potentially dangerous and/or illegal risks; (4) agreement that driving yourself to "the brink" is a path to better self-understanding.

Source: The Yankelovich Monitor, *Technical Description/Appendix* (New York: Yankelovich, Skelly and White, 1981), 50–58.

THE NEW AGE OF INFORMATION

With millions of pieces of potentially useful information floating about the information environment and with thousands of new documents becoming available every day, the data that could not be located a month ago may suddenly appear in the public domain. With the rapid development of on-line information databases, the researcher can frequently monitor developments without ever leaving the office. The task of gathering secondary data, once requiring a trip to a large research library in addition to numerous telephone calls to potential information sources, may now be largely accomplished in a fraction of that time.

To get some notion of the magnitude and development of on-line

T A B L E   3-4
A Profile of Selcted Characteristics for the SRI VALS™ Consumer Segments

	Millions of adults	Median age	Median household income	Ethnic minorities (%)	Are more experimental than conventional (%)	Believe a woman's place is in the home (%)
Survivors	6	66	Under $5,000	28	15	46
Sustainers	11	32	$11,000	30	12	32
Belongers	57	51	$17,500	5	6	34
Emulators	16	28	$19,000	20	10	9
Achievers	37	42	$30,000	3	7	16
I-Am-Me	8	21	$10,000	8	29	7
Experiential	11	28	$22,000	5	33	5
Societally conscious	14	37	$25,000	8	25	2

Source: Thomas C. Thomas, "Values and Lifestyles—The New Psychographics?" (Paper presented at the Advertising Research Foundation Conference, New York, February 24, 1981).

databases, consider the following: In 1968 there were fewer than 250,000 records in bibliographic databases (one category of on-line databases). By 1980 this number was estimated to have grown to 75 million records contained in over 600 databases.[5] Another source indicates that by the fall of 1983 these 600 databases had more than quadrupled to 2,453 databases, compiled by 1,189 different producers.[6] Thus, if the number of records or information elements captured by each of these databases also quadrupled, we could estimate that we now have access to on-line information containing approximately 300 million records!

A number of factors have contributed to this explosive growth in on-line information systems:

1. Publishers and other data compilers are now using computers as their primary production technology—witness the almost-extinct practice of manual typesetting in the newspaper industry. Thus, editing and publishing tomorrow's edition of the *New York Times* will automatically add hundreds of new stores to the *New York Times Info. Bank* database.

2. Companies referred to as on-line vendors serve as information supermarkets and provide easy access to hundreds of databases. These vendors greatly simplify the search process because they generally provide uniform search commands and protocol for each of the databases mounted on their computer.

[5]J. L. Hall and H. J. Brown, *Online Bibliographic Databases*, (Detroit, Mich: Gale Research Co., 1980), 17–19.
[6]Cuadra Associates, *Directory of Online Databases*, (Santa Monica, Calif., 1983), 6.

3. Telecommunications networks now provide low-cost access to remote databases with send or receive speeds of 1200 baud (120 characters per second).
4. Perhaps the most important development has been the rapid market penetration of personal computers. Until many potential users were able to interact with remote databases, the market for on-line services was quite limited—for example, to institutions such as research and corporate libraries. The personal computer outfitted for communications and in the possession of thousands of potential information-seekers has radically expanded the potential market for on-line information services. Thus, one current marketing strategy of the database producer and on-line vendor is to reach the end-user market—the information consumer—rather than relying solely on intermediaries such as librarians and information specialists.

DATABASES

As we pointed out earlier in the chapter, the databases available to the researcher are numerous and vary greatly with regard to the information they provide. Thus, knowledge of the different types of databases together with a directory of on-line vendors and database producers is indispensable for the beginning marketing researcher.

Bibliographic databases
Computerized files that
contain citations to
journal articles,
government documents,
technical reports, market
research studies,
newspaper articles,
dissertations, patents, and
so on.

Numeric databases
Computerized files that
contain original survey
data such as time series
data.

Directory databases
Computerized files
composed of information
about individuals,
organizations, and
services.

Full-text databases
Computerized files
containing the complete
text of the source
documents that make up
the database.

Database Varieties

The information represented in the hundreds of available databases varies from discipline to discipline. In addition to subject matter, databases may differ in scope, geographic and chronological coverage, and the frequency with which each database is updated. Databases also differ according to the type of information that they capture. These varieties may be categorized into the following groupings.

- **Bibliographic databases** contain citations to journal articles, government documents, technical reports, market research studies, newspaper articles, dissertations, patents, etc. Frequently, they provide summaries or abstracts of the cited material.
- **Numeric databases** contain original survey data such as time series data—for example, sales of sporting goods for the past twenty years.
- **Directory databases** are composed of information about individuals, organizations, and services. Through a directory database you could generate a listing of business establishments in a given geographic area that have incorporated within the last two years.
- **Full-text databases** are perhaps the variety of on-line databases that will experience the most rapid growth in the next decade. As their name implies, these databases contain the complete text of the

source documents making up the database. An example of a full-text database would be the *New York Times Info. Bank*, which contains the complete text of each issue of the *New York Times*.

Directories of Databases

Among the numerous database source listings are three directories that are quite useful because they are periodically updated:

- *Directory of On-Line Databases*
  Santa Monica, Calif.: Cuadra Associates, Inc., 1983
- *Information Industry Marketplace*
  New York: R. R. Bowker
- *Encyclopedia of Information Systems and Services*
  Detroit: Gale Research Company

Vendors

In addition to pursuing these directories, the researcher may wish to consult an information specialist who works with on-line services in a large library or a corporate information center. In many cases a specific database is accessed through a contract with an intermediary rather than directly from the database producer. These intermediaries, referred to as **on-line vendors**, generally mount numerous databases produced by many different organizations. The advantages of accessing a database through an on-line vendor are

On-line vendors
Intermediaries used to access databases rather than going directly to the database producer.

1. One contract with the vendor can usually provide access to many different databases.
2. Because there is only one contract, billing for the use of various databases is simplified with one periodic invoice.
3. Search protocol is generally standardized over all of the databases on the vendor's system, thereby simplifying the research process itself.
4. The availability of an on-line database index may assist the researcher in pinpointing the individual databases most appropriate for a specific search.

While there are hundreds of on-line vendors, a few of the larger ones include

- Bibliographic Retrieval Service (BRS)
- Compuserve, Inc.
- Dialog Information Service Inc.
- Dow Jones News/Retrieval
- Mead Data Central
- News Net
- System Development Corporation (SDC Search Service)
- Telmar Media Systems
- Vu/Text Information Services, Inc.

Exhibit 3-2 provides a description and additional information on the availability of each of these on-line vendor services.

EXHIBIT 3-2

On-line Vendor Services

Bibliographic   1200 Route 7
Retrieval Ser-   Latham, NY 12210
vice (BRS)

Provides access to over sixty databases in a variety of disciplines, including science, technology, and the social services, (including business and economics).

Compuserve,   5000 Arlington Ctr. Blvd.
Inc.   Columbus, OH 43220

Service access is provided to numerous business, financial, and economic databases.

Dialog Info.   3400 Hillview Ave.
Service, Inc.   Palo Alto, CA 94304

Provides access to approximately 200 on-line databases in all subject areas and claims to be the world's largest on-line database vendor.

Dow Jones   P.O. Box 300
News/Retrieval   Princeton, NJ 08540

Offers access to more than a dozen databases with emphasis on business and financial news and information useful in analyzing corporate financial performance.

Mead Data   P.O. Box 933
Central   Dayton, OH 45401

Through one of its two main database families known as NEXIS, Mead Data Central provides electronic access to the full text of hundreds of business databases, including selected newspapers, wire services, periodicals, newsletters, company annual reports, and investment firm reports.

News Net   945 Haverford Road
    Bryn Mawr, PA 19010

Specializes in the electronic publication of approximately 200 newsletters with a heavy emphasis on those that report on high-technology industries.

System   2500 Colorado Ave.
Development   Santa Monica, CA 90406
Corp.

One of the oldest, if not the oldest, vendor of databases in numerous subject disciplines.

Telmar Media   90 Park Ave.
Systems   New York, NY 10016

Provides access to over 40 numeric databases critical to market/media planning (such as Simmons Market Research Bureau, Nielsen, Arbitron, and MRI).

Vu/TEXT Info.   1211 Chestnut Street
Systems, Inc.   Philadelphia, PA 19107

Provides the electronic full-text delivery and search capabilities of a number of newspapers, including the *Washington Post, Boston Globe,* and *Miami Herald.*

Table 3-5 is a sample of the kind of information that can be obtained from an on-line vendor. In this hypothetical case, "Fogged-In-Airways" has used the Telmar Media Systems Service to help further identify its customer base (adults in the Pacific region who have taken three or more air trips in the past year). The company needs information about the target segment's age, income, education, marital status, occupation, and so forth. The table shows the demographic anaylsis performed using the Telmar system; the source of the data is the 1980 Simmons Market Research Bureau study consisting of answers from 15,002 respondents.

In selecting a vendor as a database supplier, you should examine the descriptions of the databases distributed. Be aware of the charges or fee structures, verify that the vendor's system will support communications with your terminal or personal computer, inquire about the availability of database documentation (a detailed description of a database's content and record structure), and determine the level of user support that the vendor is willing to provide (on-site system training, for example).

Once a vendor or vendors have been selected as information providers, the technology can be put to the test of problem solving and marketing research.

ACCESSING ON-LINE DATABASES

To fully understand how to use on-line databases, we need to be familiar with the system that is required as well as the fundamentals of on-line searching.

Required System

To use an on-line database, you first need a device that will support data communications. Thus, the initial prerequisite is access to a "dumb" terminal equipped for communication (with an acoustical coupler) or a personal computer with a modem and appropriate communications software.

The second requirement is a telephone through which the data

Demographic Analysis Using the Telmar System

Demographic analysis prepared for fogged-in-airways

		Total	Took 3+ Domestic Air Trips Past Yr.	
TOTAL*		26102	994	There are 634,000 men in the Pacific region who took 3+ domestic air trips in the past year. Men represent 63.8% of all adults in the Pacific region who took 3+ air trips in the past year, whereas 5.1% of all men in the Pacific region took 3+ domestic air trips in the past year. The index of 133.6 shows a higher concentration (33.6% higher) of men among adults who took 3+ domestic air trips, than among our *total* population.
	%COL	100.0	100.0	
	%ROW	100.0	3.8	
	INDEX	100.0	100.0	
SEX				
MALE		12462	634	
	%COL	47.7	63.8	
	%ROW	100.0	5.1	
	INDEX	100.0	133.6	
FEMALE		13640	360*	
	%COL	52.3	36.2	
	%ROW	100.0	2.6	
	INDEX	100.0	69.3	
AGE				
18-24		4928	170**	
	%COL	18.9	17.1	
	%ROW	100.0	3.4	
	INDEX	100.0	90.6	
25-49		12601	525	
	%COL	48.3	52.8	A single asterisk is SMRB's designation that the projected population is relatively unstable because of small sample base.
	%ROW	100.0	4.2	
	INDEX	100.0	109.4	
50+		8573	299*	
	%COL	32.8	30.1	
	%ROW	100.0	3.5	
	INDEX	100.0	91.6	
HOUSEHOLD INCOME				
LESS THAN		9973	198**	
$15,000		38.2	19.9	A double asterisk is SMRB's designation that the number of cases is too small for reliability.
	%COL	100.0	2.0	
	%ROW	100.0	52.1	
	INDEX			
$15-$24,999		7172	159**	
	%COL	27.5	16.0	
	%ROW	100.0	2.2	
	INDEX	100.0	58.2	
$25,000+		8957	638	
	%COL	34.3	64.2	
	%ROW	100.0	7.1	
	INDEX	100.0	187.0	

TOTAL = Adults in the Pacific Region

Source: SMRB Study, 1980, 15,002 respondents, 30 September 1980.

stream to and from the host computer to your local terminal will flow. The host computer may be hundreds or thousands of miles away. Thus, significant economies can be achieved by using a telecommunications network that provides local nodes in cities throughout the world (such as Telenet or Uninet). In this way a marketing researcher from New York is able to dial the local number of a telecommunications network and be able to log on to a computer in California in a relatively inexpensive manner.

Once the researcher has established the capability to transmit and receive information, the next task is to identify the host computer(s) containing the database(s) with the information needed for the marketing research problem at hand.

Fundamentals of On-Line Searching

While there are variations in search procedure from system to system or from vendor to vendor, one common theme in most of these systems is the use of the Boolean operators *and, or,* and *not*. These system commands help the researcher to link ideas together in different relationships.

The "And" search command requires that each term in the search statement exist in a document or record before it is retrieved. Thus, a simple search performed in one bibliographic database using the "And" operator may be illustrated by: *Find all documents relating to market data and personal computers*. This command would result in a set of references where both personal computers and market data are discussed.

The "Or" search command requires that any of the terms used in a search statement exist in the document before it is retrieved: For example, the command *Identify all documents dealing with personal computers or microcomputers* would result in a set of documents dealing with either personal computers or microcomputers and would eliminate duplicate records by counting items in the overlapped areas only once.

The "Not" operator makes it possible to eliminate an idea or concept represented by a word or phrase from the search result set. For example *Identify all documents dealing with personal computers, but not with minicomputers,* would eliminate from the set of documents those personal computer references that discuss minicomputers.

These three commands are best illustrated with the use of a Venn diagram and Boolean operators. For example, Figure 3-1 illustrates the command *Identify all documents containing market data relating to personal computers or home computers but not minicomputers*. The result is the shaded area that represents all of the documents dealing with market data for personal or home computers, but eliminates those that also deal with minicomputers.

Note that while these three Boolean operators are basic search commands in most on-line systems, they represent just a small percentage

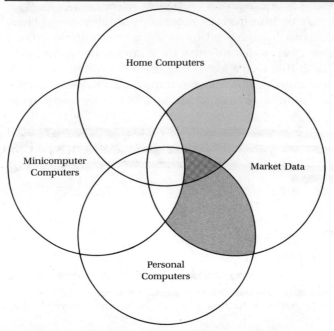

Home Computers

Minicomputer
Computers

Market Data

Personal
Computers

Figure 3-1

Venn diagram showing combination of "or" and "not" commands.

of the search options available to the researcher.[7] However, understanding and utilizing these basic search commands does allow us to examine more closely a few considerations of the application of on-line databases to the market research function.

EXAMPLE

Consumer Demographics

An automobile leasing company that specializes in exotic foreign cars is considering a local media advertising campaign in the tri-state region—New York, New Jersey, and Connecticut. Due to stringent IRS tax write-off requirements for automobile business use, this company plans to intensively market its leasing service to consumers rather than businesses. Company records indicate that past and current lessors are definitely young urban professionals; thus the company would like to identify communities with median household incomes above $35,000, where more than 20 percent of the labor force is engaged in managerial

[7]The database vendors (such as Dialog) generally provide manuals and training for the use of system commands. There are also a number of books on this subject, such as C. C. Chen and S. Schweizer, *Online Bibliographic Searching: A Learning Manual* (New York: Neal-Schumen Publishers, 1981) or C. L. Borgman et al., *Effective Online Searching* (New York: Marcel Dekker, 1984).

102

or professional occupations and where the median educational level goes beyond high school.

Database: Donnelley Demographics

Availability: Dialog Information Retrieval Service

Type: Numeric

Description: Produced by Donnelley Marketing Information Services, this database contains selected demographic information from the 1980 census, enhanced with current and five-year projections for some data series. Arranged by a variety of geographic subdivisions, the database contains information on demographic characteristics and is reloaded annually.

Exhibit 3-3 presents the search procedure that would be executed on the Dialog system.

This example illustrates the effective use of secondary market information available on the Dialog system. Note once again that in the interactive on-line environment, numerous vendors offer hundreds of databases that may be used in the search for relevant secondary market research information.

E X H I B I T   3.3

Consumer Demographic Analysis Using the Dialog System

Consumer demographic analysis prepared automobile leasing company

---

`Begin 575--`   [Database is selected from Dialog's menu of databases]

`File575:Donnelley Demographics 1/01/84--(Copr. 1984 DMIS)`

Set Items Description

`? s al=34999:al=99999--`   [The searcher(s) asks for communities with average household income (AL=) between $34,999 and $99,999.]

`   1 1933 AL=34999:AL=99999--`   [The system responds with set 1. There are 1933 communities in the U.S. that meet this requirement.]

`? s ga=10:ga=50--`   [The searcher(s) asks for communities which have between 10% and 50% of employed population in managerial positions (GA=).]

`   2 16473 GA=10:GA=50--`   [The system responds with set 2. There are 16,473 communities which meet this requirement.]

`? s gb=10:gb=50--`   [The searcher(s) asks for communities which have between 10% and 50% of employed population in professional positions (GB=).]

`   3 26738 GB=10:GB=50--`   [The system responds with set 3. There are 26,738 communities which meet this requirement.]

103

```
? s ha=12.0:ha=20.0--          [The searcher(s) asks for communities that have a me-
                                dian educational level between 12 and 20 years (HA= ).]

   4 46427 HA=12.0:HA-20.0--    [The system responds with set 4. There are 46,427 com-
                                munities which meet this requirement.]

? ss st=ny or st=nj or st=ct--  [The searcher(s) asks for all communities in New York
                                (NY), New Jersey (NJ), and Connecticut (ct) (ST= ).]

   5 2970 ST=NY                 [The system responds with set 8 which is the resultant
   6 1105 ST=NJ                 combination of sets 5, 6, and 7. There are 4,506 com-
   7  431 ST=CT                 munities in this tri-state region.]
   8 4506 5 OR 6 OR 7--

? c 1 and 2 and 3 and 4 and 8-- [The searcher(s) now asks that all of the above require-
                                ments be applied simultaneously.]

   9 519 1 AND 2 AND 3 AND 5 AND 8--  [The system responds with set 9. There are 519 com-
                                munities in the database that meet all of the above re-
                                quirements.]
```

OFF-LINE DATA FILES

So far we have emphasized computerized on-line information retrieval systems. Other important stores of computerized market information, although not directly accessible, may be accessed through a third-party service center—the computer data files of the U.S. Bureau of the Census, for instance.

While many large libraries are depositories for the print versions of the various census publications, the researcher should be aware that the published reports do not contain as much information as the magnetic data files. For example, at local levels there is greater demographic detail in the computer tape files than there is in the print version of the *Census of Population and Housing*. Use of data files also permits manipulation of data not possible in the printed documents. For example, use of a vendor like Telmar will allow one to manipulate (for example, cross-reference) SMRB data in a way not possible from the printed volumes. Two publications of the Census Bureau that will assist the researcher to identify appropriate census data are the *Users' Guide: 1980 Census of Population and Housing* and the *Bureau of the Census Catalog* (annual).

The researcher should be aware of a variety of access options to the census files. Commercial firms such as Donnelley Demographics database specialize in gathering and disseminating demographic information. This information most often consists of census data enhanced for marketing research (such as current-year estimate and five-year projections of population characteristics at a local level). The market researcher will, of course, pay a premium for the custom alterations generated by the commercial agency.[8]

[8]An excellent discussion and listing of these firms may be found in M. Farnsworth Rich, "Demographic Supermarkets of the Eighties," *American Demographics*, February 1981, 16–21.

Relatively low-cost access to portions of Bureau of the Census data archives can be achieved by working with state data centers, now accessible in most states. To facilitate dissemination of information from census data files, the Bureau of the Census has encouraged the establishment of a network of state data centers, frequently located at large universities in each state. You can identify the data center in your state by contacting the closest field office of the Bureau of the Census.

Summary

Appropriate secondary market research can be critically important to overall research. New information technologies are revolutionizing the researcher's acquisition of secondary-source market information. Since many college, university, and corporate libraries provide a computer search service and maintain contracts with some of the vendors mentioned in this study, you might inquire about a first-hand demonstration of an interactive, on-line database search. While the cost of these services may make a database search impractical for an undergraduate research assignment, access to these utilities is becoming a necessity in the real world of marketing research.

Although there has been an explosive growth in on-line databases, considerable information may still have to be gathered through a traditional manual search. Tertiary "print" tools remain indispensable to the gathering of secondary source materials.

Key Concepts

Primary data	*Directories*
Secondary data	*Indexes to business literature*
Evaluating secondary data	*Indexes to statistical information*
Effective buying income	*Statistical complications*
Buying power index	*On-Line Databases*
Customized buying power index	*Off-Line Databases*

Review Questions

1. Describe the roles of primary and secondary data in the research process.
2. When is primary data preferred to secondary?
3. Discuss the advantages and disadvantages of primary and secondary data.
4. What is "The New Age of Information?"
5. How would you assess the market potential for a new product?

Syndicated Sources of Purchase Behavior and Media Exposure Information

CHAPTER OBJECTIVES

- Explain the general characteristics, advantages, disadvantages, and uses of diary panels.
- Describe the leading diary panel services covering purchase and media panels.
- Explain the general characteristics, advantages, disadvantages, and uses of audit services.
- Describe syndicated audit services, warehouse withdrawal audit services, and custom audit services.
- Illustrate the increasing importance of electronic scanner services.
- Explain the general characteristics, advantages, disadvantages, and uses of electronic scanner services.
- Describe the major electronic scanner services.

Introduction

Having exhausted the available print tools for gathering secondary market information as well as the newer computerized on-line and off-line secondary sources, the marketing manager may want to consult a marketing research supplier. As we discussed in Chapter 1, many of these suppliers sell data and reports on specialized topics to client companies. The information collected by these suppliers is offered on a **syndicated service** basis—common pools of data and reports are sold to different client companies. The data are collected on a regular basis with standardized procedures and then "syndicated" to various users. Because the service is supplied to a number of client companies simultaneously, syndicated services are frequently less expensive than collecting the necessary data on one's own.

Unlike the secondary data discussed in Chapter 3, the information provided by syndicated sources has been collected to aid specific businesses with specific needs. The data and reports supplied to client companies are generally personalized to fit the specific needs of the client—

Syndicated services
Market research suppliers who collect data on a regular basis with standardized procedures. The data are sold to different client customers.

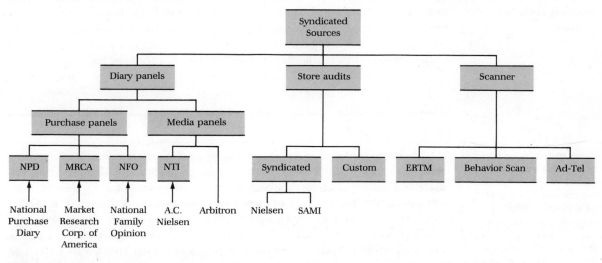

Figure 4-1

Typology of syndicated sources of purchase-behavior and media-exposure data.

for example, reports will be organized on the basis of the client's sales territories, the unit of reporting will be changed from ounces to pounds for a specific client. Most information from syndicated sources applies to consumer package goods. The competitive nature of this industry requires that firms have in-depth and timely information on purchase behavior and media exposure. Such information is invaluable in determining where a particular brand or product category is headed and the appropriate strategy to employ to solve a particular problem.

Chapter 4 is a comprehensive treatment of the syndicated sources of data on purchase behavior and media exposure. Figure 4-1 provides the framework for our discussion. We open with a discussion of **mail diary services,** which involve a sample of respondents who have agreed to provide information such as media exposure and purchase behavior on a regular basis over an extended period of time. Then we shift to the leading available retail, wholesale, and warehouse audit survey services, as well as the custom audit services that usually involve measurement of new-product movement in test markets and controlled store tests. Finally, we look at computerized electronic scanner systems that are revolutionizing marketing research and have proven to be formidable competition for traditional audit survey services.

Several comments on suppliers are in order. First, several factors influence the choice of a particular syndicated service. Aside from the characteristics and quality of the information supplied, the reputation, technical competence, experience, and personnel of the research supplier will be important (see Chapter 1). Second, the information presented in

Mail diary services
General term for services involving a sample of respondents who have agreed to provide information such as media exposure and purchase behavior on a regular basis over an extended period of time.

this chapter is not an endorsement or advertisement. Many marketing research suppliers provide information on purchase behavior and media exposure. We cannot discuss all of them. For the most part, the information we present is taken from promotional material supplied to client companies by the marketing research suppliers themselves.

DIARY PANELS

A **diary panel** is a special kind of mail diary service. Diary panels involve samples of households that have agreed to provide specific information regularly over an extended period of time. For this reason, they are frequently referred to as "continuous" panels. Although traditional diary panels are still very important for clothing, home durables, and other product categories in which the Universal Product Code (UPC) is not well entrenched, for consumer package goods the trend is to use electronic scanner services.

General Characteristics

Diary panels are maintained by commercial marketing research suppliers. Respondents are asked to *record* specific behaviors as they occur rather than merely respond to a series of questions. As a syndicated service, the same diary panel data are sold to a number of clients, although the analysis and presentation of the data are usually personalized to the client's needs.

Diary panels can be classified by the type of information recorded— either purchase behavior data or media exposure data. In most traditional diary panels, respondents are asked to use a self-administered questionnaire called a diary to record specific information periodically; in media panels electronic devices automatically record viewing patterns, supplementing a diary. Typically, the diary that contains the self-recorded data is returned to the sponsoring supplier every one to four weeks.

Comparative Evaluation

Because data in diary panels are recorded at the time of purchase as opposed to being retrospectively reported by the respondent as in other types of surveys, these panels are potentially more accurate. Though purchase data reported in surveys are fairly accurate in estimating relative magnitudes of the quantities of brands purchased, recall data on purchase behavior tend to either overestimate, for nationally advertised brands, or underestimate, for sensitive expenditure categories such as liquor or cigarettes and for local or chain brands, the "true" national

Diary panels Samples of households that have agreed to provide specific information regularly over an extended period of time. Respondents in a diary panel are asked to record specific behaviors as they occur, as opposed to merely responding to a series of questions.

aggregate purchase data.[1] In addition to typical response biasing factors—forgetting, ambiguous questions, reporting errors—the lack of accuracy in recall surveys of purchase behavior is due to the problems inherent in any effort to measure purchase behavior. These include mistaken identification of a brand perhaps due to similar packaging designs, lack of brand awareness, lack of knowledge of purchases made by other household members, and so on.[2]

Diary panels suffer from three primary practical weaknesses:

1. *Representativeness.* Despite extensive recruitment efforts, most diary panels underrepresent minority groups and low education levels. For example, the National Purchase Diary Panel (NPD) still reports that blacks are underrepresented in its panel.[3] Also, household turnover can seriously affect the representativeness of the panel.

2. *Maturation.* Over time the average age of the panel increases, and so the panel must be "rolled over" by periodically adding younger members.

3. *Response Biases.* Knowing that their purchases are being scrutinized, panel members may behave differently than they would otherwise. In addition, recording errors are always possible, since the panel member is responsible for entering the purchase or media data by hand.

4. People can develop promotional biases - may use coupons more than people not in the panel.

Uses

The two types of diary panels are diary purchase panels and diary media (TV and radio) panels. Diary media panels, such as the Nielsen ratings of TV shows, have been used primarily in establishing advertising rates (by radio and TV networks), selecting the appropriate media program or time to air a commercial, and establishing demographic profiles of viewer or listener subgroups. Diary purchase panels traditionally have been used in forecasting the sales level or market share of new products, identifying trends and establishing demographic profiles of specific user

[1] See, for example, L. Drayton, "Bias Arising in Wording Consumer Questionnaires," *Journal of Marketing,* October 1954, 140-45; J. Lansing, G. Ginsburger, and K. Braaten, *An Investigation of Response Error* (Urbana: University of Illinois, Bureau of Economics and Business Research, 1961); and J. Metz, *Accuracy of Responses Obtained in a Milk Consumption Study* (Ithaca, N.Y.: Cornell University, 1956).

[2] See, for example, J. H. Parfitt, "A Comparison of Purchase Recall with Diary Panel Records," *Journal of Advertising Research,* September 1967, 16-31; S. Sudman, "On the Accuracy of Recording of Consumer Panels I," *Journal of Marketing Research,* May 1964, 14-20; S. Sudman, "On the Accuracy of Recording of Consumer Panels: II," *Journal of Marketing Research,* August 1964, 69-83; S. Sudman and M. Bradburn, *Response Effects in Surveys* (Chicago: Aldine Publishing Co., 1974); and S. Sudman and R. Ferber, *Consumer Panels* (Chicago: American Marketing Association, 1978).

[3] *Sharing Marketing Decision with Diary Panels* (National Purchase Diary Panel, Inc., 1975), 20.

How Loyal Are My Brand's Buyers Vis-A-Vis My Main Competitor?

Of next 3 purchases same brand was bought	My brand	Competitor
0 of 3 times	25%	17%
1 of 3 times	33	24
2 of 3 times	21	24
All 3 times	21	35

The competitor has much higher loyalty among his buyers than my brand does.

Marketing Implication:
Efforts directed toward extending usage among existing buyers should increase loyalty. Options include in/on pack coupons, in-pack contests, premiums available for several proofs-of-purchase, etc.

How Does My Brand's Demographic Profile Compare To Other Brands? Am I Reaching My Target Audience?

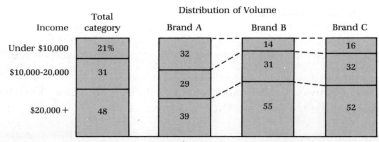

Income	Total category	Distribution of Volume		
		Brand A	Brand B	Brand C
Under $10,000	21%	32	14	16
$10,000-20,000	31	29	31	32
$20,000+	48	39	55	52

Relative to both the category and competition, Brand A is not doing well among upper income households.

Marketing Implication:
Advertising should be retargeted or revamped to reach the proper audience.

Should I Promote My Brand Using A Coupon Or Free Sample?

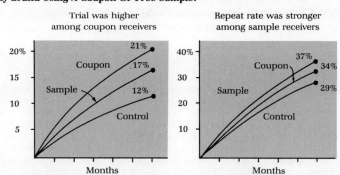

Both promotions encouraged more purchasing, with the stronger trial/weaker repeat for coupon receivers resulting in as much sales as the free sample.

Marketing Implication:
Since the sample cost three times as much, the coupon was chosen.

Figure 4-2

Using diary panel data to solve marketing-related problems. Source: National Purchase Dairy Panel, used with permission.

groups, evaluating test markets and controlled store tests, testing different advertising campaigns, and estimating brand switching and trier-repeat purchases. Figure 4-2 illustrates several ways diary panel data can be used to solve marketing problems.

Services

Three primary suppliers of diary purchase panels are National Family Opinion (NFO), National Purchase Diary Panel (NPD), and Market Research Corportaion of America (MRCA). The two principal suppliers of diary media panels are A. C. Nielsen and Arbitron. Before we briefly discuss each of these services we must emphasize that they are very fluid because of the competitive entry of electronic scanner services. In a changing market, services are constantly modified in light of new technology.

Diary Purchase Panels. Our description of diary purchase panel services is at best a snapshot of a feature length movie. These companies provide many services covering many product categories. We simply highlight the type of data available from these services.

In addition to its mail panel services, *National Family Opinion* offers special-purpose diary panels. The following list describes the product categories, size, and periodicity of the panels NFO maintains under its syndicated TRAC division. The Beverages panel uses a diary format, but the remaining panels are actually tracking studies because participating consumers are required to report in retrospect about purchases rather than record them immediately.

- Beverages: SIP—diary purchase panel consisting of 12,000 households that report quarterly on beverage consumption
- Carpet/rugs/home furnishings: CARS—tracking survey of carpet, rug, and home furnishings purchases mailed to 80,000 households quarterly
- Apparel: Men's and women's tailored apparel tracking survey mailed to 40,000 households three times a year
- Computers: Home computer and video games tracking survey mailed to 70,000 households twice a year
- Mail Order Purchasing: MOMS—tracking survey of mail order purchasing patterns mailed to 20,000 households quarterly

Special-purpose panel members are recruited from NFO's entire mail panel sample. Initial contact is by telephone and diaries are mailed out after securing cooperation. Unfortunately, response bias may be a serious problem, since NFO reports a dropout rate for panel members of between 30 and 40 percent. The information obtained is often used to analyze brand-switching patterns and track trial-and-repeat purchase levels. Figure 4-3 shows an NFO purchase record.

Monday, February 10 through Sunday, February 23

COUPONS RECEIVED

☐ NONE RECEIVED

DATE REC'D	FOR WHICH OF THE DIARY PRODUCTS? Please write in.	BRAND NAME:	HOW RECEIVED? ✓ OR WRITE IN:				
			By Mail	From Ad	From Pkg.	From Friend	Other
			☐	☐	☐	☐	
			☐	☐	☐	☐	
			☐	☐	☐	☐	
			☐	☐	☐	☐	

SAMPLES RECEIVED

☐ NONE RECEIVED

DATE REC'D	FOR WHICH OF THE DIARY PRODUCTS? Please write in.	BRAND NAME:	HOW RECEIVED? ✓ OR WRITE IN:				
			By Mail	From Ad	From Pkg.	From Friend	Left at Door	Other
			☐	☐	☐	☐	☐	
			☐	☐	☐	☐	☐	
			☐	☐	☐	☐	☐	

COFFEE

☐ NONE BOUGHT

DATE BOUGHT	Copy complete BRAND NAME from package	TYPE: (✓) ONE		Is it Decaf-feinated?		IF INSTANT, does label say "freeze-dried"?		IF GROUND COFFEE, check (✓) to indicate TYPE OF GRIND				SIZE: # lbs. or # of oz.	NUMBER BOUGHT	TOTAL PRICE PAID	WAS THIS A SPECIAL PRICE OR OFFER?		IF YES, DESCRIBE OFFER:					TOTAL AMOUNT SAVED (if any)–value of special offer, cents off, value of coupon, etc.
		Instant	Ground	YES	NO	YES	NO	Regu-lar	Drip	Fine	Elec-tric	Other			YES	NO	Coupon Used	Cents Off	Combina-tion deal	Store Special	Other - describe	

HOW MUCH DID YOU PAY? Don't include taxes.

JAM, JELLY, PRESERVES, FLAVORED REFRIGERATED SPREADS, MARMALADE, FRUIT BUTTER, etc..

☐ NONE BOUGHT

DATE BOUGHT	Copy complete BRAND NAME from package	KIND OF PRODUCT (jam, jelly, preserves, flavored refrigerated spread, marmalade, fruit butter, etc.)	FLAVOR (copy from the label - such as "raisin cinnamon", "grape", "strawberry", "fruit-nut", etc.)	TYPE OF PACKAGE			SIZE: # lbs. or # of oz.	NUMBER BOUGHT	TOTAL PRICE PAID	WAS THIS A SPECIAL PRICE OR OFFER?		IF YES, DESCRIBE OFFER:					TOTAL AMOUNT SAVED (if any)–value of special offer, cents off, value of coupon, etc.	WHERE BOUGHT?		
				Jar	Tub	Other				YES	NO	Coupon Used	Cents Off	Combina-tion deal	Store Special	Other - describe		Super-market	Indep-end-ent Grocery	Other - describe

HOW MUCH DID YOU PAY? Don't include taxes.

LAUNDRY DETERGENTS - liquid, powder, flakes, or tablets

☐ NONE BOUGHT

DATE BOUGHT	Copy complete BRAND NAME from package	FORM:				Is it mainly for use in COLD water?		Does it have active ENZYME ingredients?		SIZE - in lbs., ounces, quarts, pints, etc.	NUMBER BOUGHT	TOTAL PRICE PAID	WAS THIS A SPECIAL PRICE OR OFFER?		IF YES, DESCRIBE OFFER:					TOTAL AMOUNT SAVED (if any)–value of special offer, cents off, value of coupon, etc.	WHERE BOUGHT?		
		Liquid	Powder or Flakes	Tablets or Packets	Other; specify:	YES	NO	YES	NO				YES	NO	Coupon Used	Cents Off	Combina-tion deal	Store Special	Other - describe		Super-market	Indep-end-ent Grocery	Other - describe

HOW MUCH DID YOU PAY? Don't include taxes.

Figure 4-3

NFO purchase record.
Source: Natural Family Opinion, used with permission.

National Purchase Diary Panel operates a variety of consumer panels that address the various marketing research needs of its clients.[4]

- *National purchase panels.* Using a monthly diary, NPD collects continuous purchase data from a national panel of households. NPD guarantees monthly *returns* from 14,500 national panel members. Three different data collection vehicles are used: The N1 and N2 diaries are *each* completed by a minimum of 6,500 family households per month, and the NF diary is completed by a minimum of 1,500 nonfamily households per month. The use of multiple data collection vehicles gives NPD flexibility in tailoring sample sizes to meet the requirements of clients. For example, categories with low penetration (such as in-home blood pressure kits as opposed to shampoos) can be included in all three diaries, while categories with high penetration and short purchase cycles, dominated by national brands, may appear in only one or two of the three national diaries. Manufacturers use these data to track and analyze consumer purchasing of both established brands and new product introductions.
- *National CREST panel:* This panel of 12,800 national households completes the Eating Habit Study diary for two weeks during each quarter of the year. The syndicated CREST Report (Consumer Report on Eating Share Trends) is based upon these data and has become the primary source of consumer information for the food service industry.
- *National NET panel:* This household panel is a subset of the CREST panel and completes a daily meal diary for a two-week period each year. The syndicated NET (National Eating Trends) service uses this database to provide continuous tracking of in-home food and beverage preparation and consumption patterns.
- *Local market purchase panels:* Using a monthly diary, NPD collects continuous purchase data from 35,000 households in thirty-five test market areas across the country. These data are used for tracking new-product performance and evaluating consumer promotional plans.

Market Research Corporation of America maintains four major panels covering a variety of products. For example, the Soft Goods Information Service (SGIS) has been reporting since 1962 on purchase of women's wear, men's wear, intimate apparel, hosiery, children's wear, toddler and infant wear, footwear, accessories, jewelry, watches, home textiles, yard goods, sewing notions, patterns, craft yarn and kits, and luggage and leather goods. MRCA's newest panel, *Funds*, provides information on the day-to-day financial decisions of America's most active retail consumers of financial services. Funds is based on a nationwide household sample,

[4]The following panel descriptions were supplied by Rita E. Turgeon, Vice President, The NPD Group.

scientifically selected to represent households in the upper income range (above $25,000 annually), with a special concentration in the $75,000 and up segment.

Diary Media Panels. *Nielsen Television Index* (NTI) is perhaps the most famous of A. C. Nielsen's varied services. As a system for estimating national television audiences, NTI produces a "rating" and corresponding share estimate. A **rating** is the percent of all households that have at least one television set tuned to a program for at least six out of every fifteen minutes that the program is telecast. **Share** is the percent of households with a television set on who are tuned to a specific program at a specific time. Exhibit 4-1 describes these reporting devices.

Rating The percent of all households that have at least one television set viewing a program for at least six minutes out of every fifteen minutes that the program is telecast. *Share* The percent of households with television set on who are tuned to a specific program at a specific time.

E X H I B I T 4-1

NTI Measurement Techniques

1. Audimeter®

The Audimeter electronically stores minute-by-minute records of TV receiver tunings in NTI sample households. These tuning records are automatically transmitted by phone to the central computer. Audimeter records are inherently free of "response error," requiring no effort, recall, or reply from persons in the NTI sample concerning dial settings, station call letters, programs and the like. Portable sets are normally metered by supplying special connection points to the metering system in the rooms where the sets are used, so that the household may move a portable set from one room to another.

2. Audilog®

The Audilog is a closed-end diary requiring quarter-hour by quarter-hour entries for viewing and non-viewing by sample households. An Audilog is provided for each operable TV set in the household. Entries include station call letters and identification of viewers (two years old and over). The name, age, and sex of each person in the households, and home classification information, are obtained by periodic personal interviews conducted by the Field Rep. The names of each household member are pre-entered in appropriate columns on each Audilog by the office staff. The Audilog also provides space for entering new household members and viewing visitors.

3. Recordimeter®

The Recordimeter is a device installed on TV sets that registers hour and tenths of hours of set usage and that provides reminder signals every half-hour of set use as an aid to obtaining prompt entries in the associated Audilog. Set usage data obtained from the Recordimeter are used to check Audilog entries. Audilogs which significantly over- or understate actual set use are rejected and are not used in compiling the data.

Source: A. C. Nielsen, used with permission.

The NTI panel consists of approximately 1,200 households, matched according to United States national statistics, that have agreed to have an electronic device, called a **storage instantaneous audimeter,** attached to their television sets. The audimeter continuously monitors and records television viewing in terms of when the set was turned on, what channels were viewed, and how long the channels were tuned in. The data are stored in the audimeter and later transmitted via telephone lines to a central processing facility.

The viewing data collected by the electronic audimeter are augmented with diary panel records, called an **audilog,** on who was watching the program so that audience size and the characteristics of the audience (age, gender, and so forth) can also be determined. A **recordimeter** which registers hour and tenths of hours of set usage is used to check the audilog entries. Figure 4-2 shows the audilog and recordimeter devices. The viewing and audience characteristics data are combined to produce a report entitled **NTI-NAD (Nielsen Television Index, National Audience Demographics),** which is used to help companies decide which television programs are the best vehicles for their commercials; in other words, the NTI-NAD report can be used to identify a program (or programs) that will reach the appropriate and largest target audience. The NTI-NAD report gives ratings broken down by the following demographics:

- Households
- Women employed outside the home
- Women 18+, 12-24, 18-34, 18-49, 25-54, 35-64, and 55+ age groups
- Men 18+, 18-34, 18-49, 25-54, 35-65, and 55+ age groups
- Teenagers
- Children 2 and older and from 6 to 11

As we indicated, Nielsen NTI-NAD data are used by media planners to analyze alternative network programs. First, programs reaching the largest number of target audiences are identified using the NTI-NAD reports. Next, the cost efficiency of each program is calculated. Cost efficiency represents a television program's ability to deliver the largest target audience at the smallest cost. A **cost-per-thousand (CPM)** calculation is computed by taking

$$CPM = \frac{\text{Cost of a commercial}}{\text{Number of target audiences delivered}}$$

Exhibit 4-2 illustrates how the NTI-NAD data and CPM calculations can be used to select television programs.

Storage instantaneous audimeter Instrument that continuously monitors and records television viewing in terms of when the set was turned on, what channels were viewed, and for how long.

NTI-NAD (Nielsen Television Index, National Audience Demographics) A report combining viewing and audience characteristics used to identify a program (or programs) that will potentially reach the most appropriate and largest target audience.

CPM (cost-per-thousand) Cost-efficiency calculation that represents a television program's ability to deliver the largest target audience at the smallest cost.

E X H I B I T   4-2

Targeted CPM Calculations for NTI-NAD Data

The Nielsen ratings for three network shows on Thursdays, 10:00 P.M. to 11:00 P.M. indicate that 11.80 million households watched *20/20,* 17.32 million households watched *Knot's Landing*, and 15.03 million households watched *Hill Street Blues*. Assume we are interested in reaching men 25-54 years of age. The shares of the male 25-54 segment viewing these three shows are 9 percent for 20/20, 10.3 percent for *Knot's Landing*, and 14.9 percent for *Hill Street Blues*. Furthermore, let's assume the cost for a thirty-second commercial is $125,000 for 20/20, $160,000 for *Knots Landing*, and $100,000 for *Hill Street Blues*.

To determine CPM:

$$\text{CPM (individual show)} = \text{cost of commercial} \times 1,000/(\text{share for men 25-54} \times \text{base households})$$

The CPM for each target program is:

CPM *(20/20)*   = ($125,000 × 1,000)/(.09 × 84.92 million) = $16.36
CPM *(Knots Landing)*   = ($160,000 × 1,000)/(.103 × 84.92 million) = $18.29
CPM *(Hill Street Blues)* = ($100,000 × 1,000)/(.149 × 84.92 million) = $7.90

Hence, we can see that even though *Hill Street Blues* has fewer overall households than *Knots Landing*, the CPM is lower because of the lower cost of the commercial and higher percentage of viewers in this specific segment.

A subsidiary of Control Data, *Arbitron* maintains radio and TV diary panels locally and regionally. Prospective panel members are drawn primarily from lists maintained by Metro-Mail of households with listed telephone numbers. A preplacement letter is followed by a placement phone call. A diary is mailed to each member of the household twelve or older. Another phone call is initiated before the start of the survey and a second call is placed midway through the survey. This rather elaborate process produces a consent rate of over 80 percent, and over 65 percent of those consenting return usable diaries. Panel members receive anywhere from 25 cents to $2.00 per diary. The size of the panel varies with the size of the market. Both the radio and TV diaries cover one week.

The radio listening diary data are used to evaluate advertising alternatives (stations and programs) by estimating in each area the audience listening for fifteen-minute blocks of time. The key evaluative measures that can be computed for each fifteen-minute block are shown in Exhibit 4-3.

E X H I B I T 4-3

Arbitron Evaluative Methods for Radio

Average Quarter-Hour Persons

The average number of persons in a demographic group listening to radio for at least five minutes during an average quarter-hour in a given time period.

Cume Persons (Reach)

The estimated number of different persons in a demographic group listening to radio for five minutes or more within a specified time period.

Exclusive Cume

The number of different persons who, when they are listening, tune to only one station during the time period reported.

Rating

The percent of all people within a demographic group in a survey area who listen to a specific station.

$$\frac{\text{Listeners}}{\text{Population}} = \text{Rating (\%)}$$

Average Quarter-Hour Rating

The average quarter-hour persons audience for a demographic group expressed as a percentage of all persons estimated to be in that demographic group.

$$\frac{\text{Average quarter-hour persons}}{\text{Population}} = \begin{array}{l}\text{Average}\\ \text{quarter-hour}\\ \text{rating (\%)}\end{array}$$

Cume Rating

The Cume persons audience for a demographic group expressed as a percent of all persons estimated to be in that demographic group.

$$\frac{\text{Cume persons}}{\text{Population}} = \text{Rating (\%)}$$

Share

The percent of all listeners in a demographic group that are listening to a specific station.

$$\frac{\begin{array}{c}\text{Average quarter-hour}\\ \text{persons to a station}\end{array}}{\begin{array}{c}\text{Average quarter-hour}\\ \text{persons to all stations}\end{array}} = \text{Share (\%)}$$

Gross Impressions (GI)

The sum of the average quarter-hour persons audience for all spots in a given schedule.

Gross Rating Points (GRP'S)

The sum of all rating points achieved in a market area for a particular time span or spot schedule.

Cost per Thousand (CPM)

The cost of delivering 1,000 gross impressions.

$$\frac{\text{Cost of Schedule}}{\text{GI}} \times 1{,}000 = \text{CPM}$$

Cost per Rating Point

The cost of reaching an average quarter-hour persons audience of one percent (achieving an average quarter-hour persons rating of one) for a given demographic group.

$$\frac{\text{Cost of Schedule}}{\text{GRP}} = \text{Cost Per Rating Point}$$

Schedule Reach (Schedule Cume)

Estimated number of different persons who are listening at least once to a given spot schedule. (Unduplicated audience)

Frequency

The number of times a person is exposed to a radio spot schedule.

$$\frac{\text{GI}}{\text{Cume}} = \text{Frequency}$$

Time Spent Listening (TSL)

An estimate of the amount of time the average person spends listening during a specified time period.

$$\frac{\substack{\text{Quarter-hours} \\ \text{in time period}} \times \substack{\text{Average quarter-hours} \\ \text{persons audience}}}{\text{Cume audience}} = \text{TSL}$$

Away-from-Home Listening

Estimate of the amount of listening done away from home expressed as a percent of the total audience.

Cume Daypart Combinations

The unduplicated audience for combinations of dayparts. These data are only available in the Arbitron Report or through Arbitron on Information on Demand (AID).

Area of Dominant Influence (ADI)

The exclusive geographic area used by Arbitron Television to measure and report television viewing. Every county in the U.S. is assigned to one and only one ADI based on television viewing. Data are shown by ADI in the Arbitron Radio Report for the Top 50 markets whenever they are surveyed.

Source: Arbitron Rating Company, used with permission.

The age and gender makeup of each audience is also available so that their calculation can be based on audience profile. The TV diary panel is supplemented with a sample of households that have agreed to attach an electronic meter to their television sets. Meters automatically record viewing patterns in all of Arbitron's major markets. Telephone lines transmit the electronic data to Arbitron's central processing facility. Panel members are "rolled out" every five years.

Arbitron also produces custom reports for clients. Typically, these are based on an interactive computer-based system called **Arbitron Information on Demand (AID):**[5]

- **Radio and Television AID** can analyze any station's audience by selected demographics, specific geography, or nonstandard time periods. Subscribers use AID to select the audience estimates that best meet their needs.
- **Target AID** can categorize audiences by lifestyle, purchasing habits, and economic standing, allowing advertisers to choose the stations that deliver their target audience.
- **Product Target AID** is a microcomputer that categorizes television viewers by their purchasing patterns. *Arbitrends* delivers radio and television audience estimates directly to stations' and agencies' microcomputers. Radio Arbitrends updates radio listening information and selected markets each month and helps stations interpret and use these data.
- **The Arbitron County Coverage Report** measures audiences in every county in the continental United States and is conducted every year in television and every two years in radio.
- **Arbitron Marketing Research** produces special audience surveys conducted by telephone, personal interviews, and direct mailings to meet specific research needs expressed by clients.

AUDIT SERVICES

Many marketing decisions are ultimately based on how much product has sold. Audits indicate what is happening in the marketplace not only for a given marketer, but also for the competition.

General Characteristics

Audits are offered by commercial marketing research suppliers as part of their syndicated services portfolio. Although there are different kinds of audits, we will restrict the discussion to two basic types: retail (syndicated or custom) audits and warehouse withdrawal audits. As the name implies, an **audit** involves a formal examination and verification of either how much of a product has sold at the store level (retail audit) or how much of a product has been withdrawn from warehouses and delivered to retailers (warehouse withdrawal audits). Participating operators (such as retail chains, wholesalers, health and beauty-aid rack operators, frozen food warehouses) who have agreed to open up their doors or records so that audits can be performed receive basic reports and a cash

[5]The following material was taken directly from *Arbitron Ratings Today*, supplied by Shelly Cagner, Administrative Assistant in Communications.

Arbitron information on demand (AID) An interactive computer-based system that provides the basis for Arbitron custom reports for clients.
Radio and television AID Analysis of a station's audience by selected demographics, specific geography, or nonstandard time periods.
Target AID Categorization of audiences by lifestyle, purchasing habits, and economic standing.
Product target AID A microcomputer that categorizes television viewers by their purchasing patterns.
The Arbitron County Coverage Report Report that measures audiences in every county in the continental United States.
Arbitron Marketing Research A customized research service offered by Arbitron.

Audit A formal examination and verification of either how much of a product has sold at the store level (retail audit) or how much of a product has been withdrawn from warehouses and delivered to retailers (warehouse withdrawal audits).

payment. Again, like diary panels, audit services face stiff competition from electronic scanning syndicated services.

Comparative Evaluation

Audits provide relatively precise information on the movement of many different products. Because most consumer products are not sold directly to consumers, but to retailers, wholesalers, and distributors, the national consumer goods manufacturer does not have information on current sales at the retail level. Though factory shipments are known, warehouse inventories may be building due to limited retail sales, and the consumer goods manufacturer has no knowledge of the situation. Eventually, the consumer goods manufacturer finds out, but probably too late to develop corrective strategies to stimulate retail sales. Even when information about sales at the retail level is available, similar data for competitive products are rarely known. By reporting on these kinds of data, audit services provide a very important function.

One problem endemic to all auditing services involves limited or incomplete coverage. Not all areas or operators are included in the audit. For example, up until 1981 the Nielsen retail audit did not include one of the largest national grocery chains. Even though the operators included in the audit typically account for over 80 percent of the volume in the area, if a product tends to do better or worse in areas not included or with operators not included, then, as an absolute measure, the information reported in the audit can be misleading. In general, national data on market share is quite accurate, but the accuracy of regional breakdowns can be much lower. Another practical weakness involves the issue of information timeliness. There is typically a two-month gap between the audit cycle's completion and the publication of basic reports. Finally, there can be a problem in matching data on different types of competitive activity—for example, in matching advertising expenditures with the audit volume and share data, since the former information is usually purchased from other commercial sources and then integrated into basic reports.

Uses

Because varied sales data are provided by retail, wholesale, and custom audits, this service is particularly valuable in developing marketing strategies. Among the many uses of audit services are (1) measuring consumer sales relative to competition, (2) monitoring the full range of competitive activities, (3) identifying where new products are appearing and the volume of sales in each geographical location, (4) measuring the competitive impact of private brands, (5) analyzing and correcting distribution problems, if they exist, (6) developing advertising allocation schedules based on actual sales volume in a market, and (7) developing sales potentials for specific markets (category and brand development indices).

Services

A large number of commercial marketing research suppliers offer retail, warehouse withdrawal, and/or customized audit services.

Syndicated Audit Services. Retail audits involve in-store measurement of product-category movement. Periodically, auditors appear at participating stores and record such information as beginning inventory, ending inventory, receipts, price, deals, local advertising, and displays. Retail sales figures are computed by taking

Opening Inventory + Receipts − Ending Inventory = Retail Sales

The largest retail audit service for consumer packaged goods is the *Nielsen Retail Index*.[6] With this service, consumer responsiveness to products within the food, drug/health and beauty aid, and alcoholic beverage industries is measured at the actual point of sale on a bimonthly basis. In addition, Nielsen's national Scantrack service offers clients weekly sales data from a national sample of scanner-equipped stores. This program allows manufacturers to evaluate the effects of pricing changes and short-term promotions and to monitor unexpected events such as new product introductions, bad publicity (for example, the Tylenol poisonings), and so on.

Nielsen divides the country into strata based on geography, population, and store type and size characteristics. Outlets are then probabilistically drawn from each stratum. Over 76,000 separate audits are made annually in over 11,350 separate retail outlets. Nielsen employs over 600 full-time field representatives to gather the new data. These field representatives are college-educated and well-trained professionals with an average of approximately eight years in-field experience. The data provide information on a wide range of marketing variables and are typically provided on a bimonthly basis. Nielsen data are used to:

- Measure sales relative to competitors
- Measure sell-in to the retailer
- Evaluate brand's in-store position
- Analyze and correct distribution problems
- Evaluate pricing and promotion strategies
- Track advertising effects
- Monitor competitors' marketing efforts
- Analyze the effects of marketing variables by store type
- Analyze sales and marketing effects by territory

Figure 4-4 displays Nielsen Retail Index data for brands of muffin mixes, showing sales in thousands of dollars and percent change from the previous year for Betty Crocker, Duncan Hines, and all other brands for the bimonthly periods.

[6]The following discussion is based on material provided by the A. C. Nielsen Company.

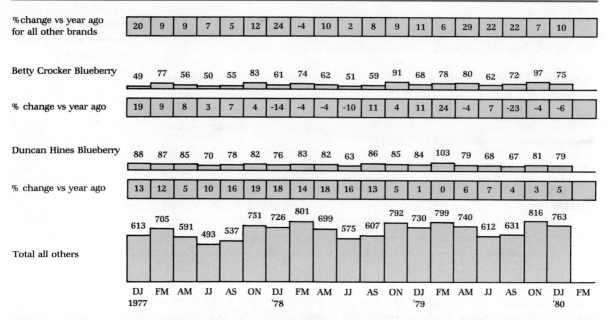

| %change vs year ago for all other brands | 20 | 9 | 9 | 7 | 5 | 12 | 24 | -4 | 10 | 2 | 8 | 9 | 11 | 6 | 29 | 22 | 22 | 7 | 10 | |

Betty Crocker Blueberry 49 77 56 50 55 83 61 74 62 51 59 91 68 78 80 62 72 97 75

| % change vs year ago | 19 | 9 | 8 | 3 | 7 | 4 | -14 | -4 | -4 | -10 | 11 | 4 | 11 | 24 | -4 | 7 | -23 | -4 | -6 | |

Duncan Hines Blueberry 88 87 85 70 78 82 76 83 82 63 86 85 84 103 79 68 67 81 79

| % change vs year ago | 13 | 12 | 5 | 10 | 16 | 19 | 18 | 14 | 18 | 16 | 13 | 5 | 1 | 0 | 6 | 7 | 4 | 3 | 5 | |

Total all others
613 705 591 493 537 751 726 801 699 575 607 792 730 799 740 612 631 816 763

DJ FM AM JJ AS ON DJ FM AM JJ AS ON DJ FM AM JJ AS ON DJ FM
1977 '78 '79 '80

Figure 4-4

Consumer sales of muffin mixes over a three-year period (equivalent 24-unit-case basis x 1,000). Source: A. C. Nielsen, used with permission.

Other prominent national auditing firms include *Audits and Surveys* and *IMS*. Audits and Surveys provides the National Total-Market Audit, which not only provides data on some of the packaged goods categories covered by Nielsen, but also allows for tracking of product movement in the automotive, sporting goods, photography, home improvement, and quite a few other industries. IMS provides audits of pharmaceutical products based on purchase invoices to both drugstores and hospitals.

Warehouse Withdrawal Audit Services. Warehouse withdrawal audits, as the name implies, are done at the wholesale rather than retail level. Periodically, perhaps every four weeks, warehouse withdrawals are monitored for those markets and warehouses that have agreed to participate in the audit service. Participating operators include supermarket chains, wholesalers, frozen food warehouses, and so forth. The operators included typically account for over 80 percent of the volume in an area and are enticed to participate by promises of information, and cash.

SAMI, a subsidiary of Time, Inc., is the leading warehouse withdrawal audit service available. It supplies warehouse withdrawal information on thousands of package goods items (in over 400 categories) sold through food stores. The data are gathered from fifty-four market areas that account for 88.4 percent of all commodity volume (ACV) and are reported separately for each region thirteen times a year. ACV is weighted percent of store figures that reflect the total of stores in which the brand is carried. In addition, SARDI (or SAMI retail distribution index) reports retail availability (distribution) for the same categories and market areas as SAMI.

Custom Audit Services. Research suppliers who provide these services offer two basic types of studies that depend solely on the level of control desired by the client. The highest level of control is known as a controlled store test. In **controlled store testing** (also known as mini-market testing), the supplier takes over warehousing and distribution of test product as well as total control of test variables (such as pricing, maintenance of out-of-stocks, display setup, couponing) within the market under examination—in addition to the basic task of measuring product sales. On the other hand, **store audits** represent the lowest level of control since suppliers do nothing to alter the test environment; they only measure product sales.

Costs for conducting these studies vary widely, depending on the test design. In designing custom audits, remember that costs vary based on degree of control, number of items in product category to be audited, number of stores to be audited, and length of time.

Some leading suppliers with this research expertise include:

- Marketest (a division of Market Facts, Inc.)
- Market Audits (a division of Burke Marketing Research)
- Audits and Surveys
- Burgoyne
- Ehrhart-Babic Associates

Three other important suppliers of these services who utilize state-of-the-art measurement systems, BehaviorScan, Ad-Tel, and ERIM, are discussed in the following section on electronic scanner services.

ELECTRONIC SCANNER SERVICES

Electronic scanner services began in the mid-1970s. With the advent of the universal product code (UPC) it became possible to record—through electronic optical checkout devices—information on *actual* purchase behavior as opposed to human reported behavior from a survey or diary.

General Characteristics

Since 1979 scanner data field services have been rapidly expanding, although development varies by geography and merchandising chain. By 1985 the estimated number of stores participating in scanner services was over 10,000, covering 40-50 percent of all commodity volume (ACV).

Controlled store testing Audit where the supplier takes over warehousing and distribution of test product as well as total control of test variables within the market under examination—in addition to the basic task of measuring product sales. *Store audits* Audit where the supplier does nothing to alter the test environment but only measures product sales.

Electronic scanner services Services that record information on *actual* purchase behavior, as opposed to human reported behavior, through electronic optical checkout devices.

The two major reasons for the increase in stores participating in scanner services are gains in labor productivity and tighter inventory control.

As with audit services, commercial marketing research suppliers offer electronic scanner services on a syndicated or custom basis. The two basic services offered by these companies are: national volume tracking and cable/scanner store facilities. *National volume tracking services* usually provide information on purchases by brand, size, price, and flavor or formulation based on sales data collected from the checkout scanner tapes. The information is collected from a sample of supermarkets that use electronic scanning systems. *Cable/scanner store facilities* involve scanner "panels," consisting of households that subscribe to one of the cable TV systems in the market. Scanner panel members are given plastic identification cards used whenever purchases are made in participating supermarkets. Specially equipped scanners read the identification cards and automatically record the purchases along with the identification number of the panel member. Because of the ability to target different advertisements into the homes of its scanner panel members, this service can be used to test alternative advertising copy executions or conduct market tests of new products. Also, because the specially designed scanner records identification numbers when purchases are made, an analysis of purchase behavior by demographic characteristics can be performed. Thus scanner panels provide an opportunity to conduct fairly controlled experiments in a relatively natural environment. Controlled experiments (experimental designs) are discussed in Chapter 6.

Comparative Evaluation

Electronic scanner services provide a number of attractive features. Compared to in-store audit services, electronic scanner national volume tracking services have three principal advantages with respect to:

1. *Accuracy*. National volume tracking via electronic scanner systems provides increased accuracy with respect to price information and eliminates the possibility that breakage or pilferage losses are counted as sales.
2. *Time*. National volume tracking via electronic scanner systems provides much shorter turnaround time, since the information is collected automatically. In addition, there is greater currency since scanner tapes are collected weekly as opposed to bimonthly (usually the case with in-store audits).
3. *Cost*. National volume tracking via electronic scanner systems is less expensive than *nationally projectable* volume tracking services.

Cable/scanner store facilities have three principal advantages with respect to:

1. *Accuracy*. Because purchases are recorded automatically, no biases are introduced by memory loss.
2. *Sample Control*. Because of the ability to target alternative advertis-

ing-copy executions into specific homes, an extremely controlled testing environment is possible.

3. *Quantity of Data.* Because demographic information about the panel is available, analyses of purchases by demographic characteristic of the consumer are possible. In addition, causal analysis is also possible in light of the highly controlled testing environment (see Chapter 6).

Compared to in-store audits, electronic scanner national volume tracking services have three principal disadvantages with respect to:

1. *Representativeness.* National volume tracking via electronic scanner systems may not produce projectable volume and share estimates because only the larger supermarkets have scanner capability.
2. *Quality of Data.* National volume tracking via electronic scanner systems is highly dependent upon the ability of the checkout clerk to use the equipment appropriately. Errors in recording can occur if clerks do not properly scan all of the purchases: For example, a clerk may use the register and ring up a heavy item to avoid lifting; or in scanning multipackage purchases (different flavors) of the same product, the clerk may simply scan only one package and then ring in the number of purchases, which incorrectly records the transaction as consisting of several packages of only one flavor.
3. *Quantity of Data.* National volume tracking via electronic scanner systems does not usually provide other causal data relating to coupon, point-of-purchase displays, advertising expenditures, and so forth, which are reported in store audits.

Two principal weaknesses in cable/scanner store facility services are

1. *Representativeness.* Three factors detract from the representativeness of data collected via cable/scanner store facility services. First, these services are in smaller markets. Second, they are small in number and hence have limited geographic dispersion. Thus, if geographic variations are important in a particular product category, the specific markets available may not be appropriate in terms of media or sample composition. Third, specific types of outlets are excluded. For example, certain types of drug stores are excluded, therefore, for certain product categories it is sometimes difficult to translate volume and share estimates. Mass merchandisers or department stores are also excluded, and thus trial or repeat purchase figures could well be distorted if some people buy exclusively in these outlets or if others make some purchases in groceries or drugstores and some in other stores.
2. *Quality of Data.* Five factors can potentially diminish the quality of data collected via cable/scanner store facility services. First, if the product category or the brand under study has a low incidence, the available sample sizes in the electronic scanner markets may be in-

sufficient, especially if more than one treatment is to be tested simultaneously. Second, while the technology enables one to monitor TV sets in use, it does so only for one set within the household—the primary one. For those products purchased by or for those in the household who tend to view a secondary TV set, there is a built-in limitation to projectability. Third, the system only provides information on TV sets in use (opportunities for exposure). Actual viewing by any particular members in the household still remains unknown. Fourth, until many markets become available, there is a potential danger of overuse—overuse that can influence and contaminate results. And finally, we should not forget that as important as behavioral and sales data are, to really understand what is happening and why, we may need other information as well—for example, interviews with triers, repeat buyers, nontriers, nonrepeats, and so forth.

Uses

Electronic scanner services provide a rich source of data that can be used in developing marketing strategy. Among the primary uses of national volume tracking via electronic scanner systems are price tracking, early warning signal analysis, and modeling. Because of the quantity of data available on purchase behavior and panel characteristics and the highly controlled nature of the environment, cable/scanner store facilities have been used in a variety of marketing research projects—for example, (1) new-product test markets, (2) product repositioning studies, (3) copy execution studies, (4) advertising expenditure level (high, low) analysis, (5) advertising/promotion mix analysis, and (6) resizing (up, down) investigations.

Services

ERIM (Electronic Research for Insights into Marketing). TESTSIGHT is a new service being provided by A. C. Nielsen under the ERIM division that provides a state-of-the-art measure of consumer purchasing behavior in a test market situation. Unlike the BehaviorScan and Ad-Tel systems, ERIM allows transmission of advertising into participating households without the use of a television cable system. Since the panels can be selected from *all* available TV households, not just those who have cable, the bias of cable-only testing is eliminated. The service is now being offered in two markets—Sioux Falls, South Dakota, and Springfield, Missouri—with consumer panels of equivalent size to BehaviorScan and Ad-Tel (2,500 respondents).

BehaviorScan. A service provided by Information Resources, Inc. (IRI), BehaviorScan is a network of eight mini-markets equipped for advertising transmission and controlled store testing. In each market, UPC scanners installed in supermarkets (accounting for better than 90 percent of all commodity volume) allow for the track of individual purchases of over

2,500 households as well as total movement through the stores. Using an IRI-developed technology, these markets are also equipped to target alternative advertising to custom-matched panels of households.

Ad-Tel. A division of Burke Marketing Research, Inc., Ad-Tel maintains diary purchase panels in seven markets in the United States: Three cities use electronic scanner data (Portland, Maine; Evansville, Indiana; and Orlando, Florida). Panel members complete purchase diaries in which purchase information for a wide variety of product categories is recorded. The types of data available from Ad-Tel reports include:

- Category Purchasing Dynamics (volume, share, penetration or percent of households buying, and purchase cycle)
- Brand Loyalty
- Test Brand Analysis (trial, repeat purchase, source of volume)

Summary

The marketing researcher who needs the standard or customized data available from syndicated services has a choice of many different kinds of information from three basic sources: diary panels, audit services, and electronic scanner services. The research project will determine which source provides the most appropriate data. Each type of syndicated service has advantages and disadvantages, related to representativeness of the sample, accuracy, quality and quantity of data, and so forth.

Key Concepts

Diary mail panels   *Syndicated audit services*
Diary purchase panels   *Custom audit services*
Diary media panels   *Electronic scanning services*

Review Questions

1. What are the advantages of syndicated services?
2. Distinguish between diaries and panels.
3. Should scanner services replace diary panels?
4. How would the marketing manager use a store audit?
5. The representativeness of sample data is always a prominent concern of the user of market research information. Evaluate the representation (or lack of representation) of:
   (a) diary panels
   (b) diary media panels
   (c) store audits
   (d) scanner services

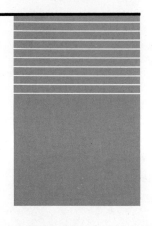

CHAPTER 5

Survey-Interviewing Methods

CHAPTER OBJECTIVES

- Describe the different types of survey interviewing methods.
- Understand the distinctive nature of mail, telephone, personal in-home, and mall-intercept interviews.
- Describe how new and more sophisticated computer technology is being used in survey research.

Introduction

If existing secondary and syndicated sources of market research information are not sufficient to solve the marketing problem at hand, then the researcher will probably have to collect primary data. We now shift our attention to procedures and methods that can be used to acquire such data. As *primary research*, these alternatives generally involve conducting a consumer or market survey of some kind. The term **survey** is generally used to describe a method of gathering information from a number of individuals (the respondents, who collectively form a **sample**) in order to learn something about a larger target population from which the sample has been drawn. The information collected will depend on the objectives of the research study. **Concept tests,** for instance, collect information on purchase intentions, likes/dislikes, and attribute ratings because this type of study aims to quantitatively measure the relative appeal of ideas or alternative positioning and provide direction for development of the product and product advertising. **Market penetration studies,** on the other hand, collect information on such measures as awareness, trial, and past-thirty-day use because their objective is usually to track brand awareness, purchase, and usage levels. Exhibit 5-1 provides a brief description of the types of information collected in marketing research surveys. Four broad categories of variables are listed: respondent background characteristics, personality traits, attitudes and lifestyle factors, and product-related variables.

Survey A method of gathering information from a number of individuals (the respondents, who collectively form a sample) in order to learn something about a larger target population from which the sample was drawn.

Concept tests Collection of information on purchase intentions, likes/dislikes, and attribute ratings in order to measure the relative appeal of ideas or alternative positioning and to provide direction for the development of the product and the product advertising.

Market penetration studies Collection of information on such measures as awareness, trial, and past-thirty-day

128

EXHIBIT 5-1

Types of Information Collected in Surveys

Respondent Background Characteristics

- Demographic variables
- Socioeconomic variables
- Ownership
- Media Habits

Personality Traits

- Innovativeness
- Dogmatism
- Risk taking
- Inner-other directedness

Attitude and Lifestyle Factors

- Attitude measures
- Activities, interests, and opinions

Product-Related Variables

- Usage data
- Determinants of brand choice
- Situational factors
- Intentions

Surveys can be classified in many different ways. We can classify them by the size and type of sample; for example, surveys can be conducted on a local, state, or national basis and may attempt to collect informative data from a few hundred or thousands of people. Surveys can also be classified on a temporal basis; for example, surveys can be distinguished according to whether a *cross-sectional* or *longitudinal* approach is adopted. **Cross-sectional surveys** collect informative data from a number of different respondents at a single point in time. The cross-sectional study typically examines the relationships among a set of relevant marketing-related variables across different cross-sections of respondents. Market segmentation studies that attempt to identify subgroups of respondents who will respond to a given marketing-mix offering in a similar manner are examples. **Longitudinal surveys,** on the other hand, question the same respondent at different points in time, examining the changes that occur with the passage of time. Market tracking studies that provide information on changes in the marketplace and consumer diary panels that provide weekly information on purchases, usage, and media viewing, for a group of respondents exemplify this type of survey. Alternatively, surveys can also be classified according to the interviewing method employed.

usage, where the objective is usually to track brand awareness, purchase, and usage levels.

Cross-sectional surveys Collection of informative data from a number of different respondents at a single point in time.

Longitudinal surveys Questioning of the same respondents at different points in time.

This chapter is devoted to a comprehensive discussion of survey-interviewing methodologies. The chapter is organized according to the alternative ways of surveying and interviewing individuals.

OBSERVATIONAL METHODS

At the broadest level, methods of data collection can be distinguished according to whether they involve asking the respondent to retrospectively report on some behavior or whether they directly or indirectly—by human or mechanical methods—observe the behavior under study. Observing behavior can be a particularly important research tool, especially in situations where the respondent is either unable or unwilling to report past behavior. In many situations it is the most accurate way to measure overt behavior. However, observation methods can not be used to measure variables that are directly unobservable, such as thoughts and other psychological variables, and can be extremely costly.

Direct versus Indirect Methods

Observational methods
Observation of behavior directly or indirectly by human or mechanical methods.

Most **observational methods** involve directly measuring behavior—a person or mechanical device records the behavior as it is taking place. Indirect observational methods have also been employed. For example, *garbology* studies, which involve checking the garbage cans of households and recording the goods consumed, as evidenced by the discarded cans, bottles, wrappers, and so on, is one approach to indirect observation. Another common approach to indirect observation is to audit the pantry of households to measure food-purchase behavior. Going through a kitchen and recording what is on the shelves provides an *estimate* of food shopping and consumption patterns—it's only an estimate since what is on the shelf may not necessarily be consumed. The Nielsen TV rating system discussed in Chapter 4 is yet another example of indirect observation. Program viewing is estimated by knowing what program the TV set is tuned to. Whether the individual is actually watching the program is another question. Finally, in the same vein, any audit (see Chapter 4) is a form of indirect observation.

Human versus Mechanical Measurement

The choice between human or mechanical measurement generally depends on which is easier to use in a given research situation. The advantage of mechanical observation is its accuracy. The advantage of human observation is its ability to provide additional insights into what is being observed—for example, following a consumer who moves from aisle to aisle through a supermarket provides insights into why certain goods were purchased.

We have already discussed one popular way to mechanically measure behavior in Chapter 4. Scanner services—and, in particular, optical scanning via Universal Product Codes (UPC)—allow extensive data on product category, brand, store type, price, quantity, and customer to be automatically recorded. *Physiological measures* represent another type of mechanical observational method. A pupilometer, which attaches to aperson's head and measures interest/attention by the amount of dilation in the pupil of the eye, and a galvanometer, which measures excitement levels by the electrical activity level in the person's skin, are two devices that have seen use in studies of shopping behavior and reactions to advertising. In contrast to these rather unnatural and obtrusive methods of mechanical observation are several less-obtrusive methods. Response latency and voice pitch analysis are two examples. The time it takes a person to respond to a question is a measure of response latency, based on the assumption that the longer it takes a person to respond to a question the more difficult is the decision. Voice pitch analysis attempts to measure a person's interest by monitoring his or her voice patterns.

QUALITATIVE INTERVIEWING METHODS

All surveys involve some sort of interview. In certain instances the interviewing is highly **structured;** the questions are completely predetermined. The interviewer cannot alter the interview by adding or omitting questions, change the sequence of questions, or change the wording of the questions. The use of predetermined questions may not be useful, particularly in early stages of research—in concept testing studies, for instance, where the respondent's feelings and beliefs are not well known and where the marketing researcher knows little about the specific criteria respondents will use to evaluate the concepts. In exploratory research studies that attempt to clarify or generate hypotheses about the issue being studied, the interviewer is generally allowed flexibility with respect to how the questions are asked and the degree of probing required to clarify the respondent's answers. The question format is typically **open-ended;** that is, no fixed response alternatives are presented and the respondent freely answers the questions presented by the interviewer. The focus group interview and the depth interview both use a relatively **unstructured format.** Both are viewed as **qualitative research methods,** as opposed to **quantitative research methods,** since they involve a small number of respondents who provide descriptive information on their thoughts and feelings not easily projected to the whole population.[1]

Focus Groups

The **focus group interview** is a frequently used data-collection method. Focus groups provide a unique opportunity to experience the

---

[1]Parts of the following discussion of depth and focus group interviews follows N. Hollart, R. Golden, and M. Chudnoff, *Marketing Research for the Marketing and Advertising Executive* (New York Chapter: American Marketing Association 1981), 93–97.

Structured interview
Method of interviewing where the questions are completely predetermined.

Open-ended question format Questions where no fixed-response alternatives are presented; instead, the respondent is permitted to respond freely to the question presented by the interviewer.

Unstructured interview
Method of interviewing where questions are not completely predetermined and the interviewer is free to probe for all details and underlying feelings.

Qualitative research methods Techniques involving small numbers of respondents who provide descriptive information on their thoughts and feelings not easily projected to the whole population.

Quantitative research methods Technique involving relatively large numbers of respondents and designed to generate information that can be projected to the whole population.

Focus group interview Interview where the interviewer listens to a group of individuals, belonging to the appropriate target market, talk about an important marketing issue.

"market" first-hand. The basic purpose of a focus group interview is to listen to a group of individuals, belonging to the appropriate target market, talk about an important marketing issue and to learn something from the group discussion. Focus group interviews generally involve anywhere from six to twelve people, prerecruited to meet defined characteristics—for example, age, gender, use of certain products, frequency of product use, and so on. The interview is led by an experienced moderator, who may be a clinical psychologist; it is usually held in a relaxed, informal setting to encourage conversation and interaction. The interviewing session can last between one and two hours and is usually recorded on audio and/or video tape. Sometimes the representatives of the sponsoring firm view the session through one-way mirrors or on closed-circuit television.

Focus groups have been conducted with all types of respondents—woman, men, children (six or older), and professionals. It is preferable to have homogeneous respondents attending a given session. If heterogeneous groups are assembled, the diverse backgrounds of respondents often lead to argumentative settings where important trends and patterns can be overlooked. In addition, the standard practice is to conduct several focus group interviews, usually three or four, and to spread them out geographically to achieve some indication of regional differences.

Focus group interviews are typically the first step in the research process for many types of marketing problems. Because they are used in the early, exploratory stages of the research process, their primary usefulness is not in providing precise quantitative information but rather in providing qualitative, descriptive information that bridges the gap between the firm and its products, and the consumer. Exhibit 5-2 briefly describes each of these uses. We cannot overemphasize the importance of the type of information that focus group interviews provide; in large measure, these interviews determine the quality of the research findings obtained in large-scale quantitative studies.

E X H I B I T 5-2

Specific Uses of Focus Groups

Generating New Creative Ideas

Listening to consumers talk about how they use a product or what they like or dislike about a product can provide input for creative teams in developing advertising copy. Advertising agencies often use focus group interviews for this reason.

Establishing Consumer Vocabulary

Understanding the words that consumers use in talking about a product or product category can be extremely useful in structuring questionnaires, particularly in phrasing the question and in determining permissible response categories.

Uncovering Basic Consumer Needs and Attitudes

In talking about a product or product category, consumers often express basic needs and attitudes that can be useful in generating hypotheses about what may or may not be accepted and about the factors responsible for the perceived similarity or dissimilarity among a set of brands.

Establishing New Product Concepts

Focus group interviews are particularly useful in providing information on the major strengths and weaknesses of a new-product idea. In addition, the focus group interview can be effective in judging whether strategy-supporting promises of end-benefits have been communicated clearly.

Generating New Ideas about Established Markets

Listening to consumers talk about how they discovered ways to put a product to alternative use can stimulate marketing executives to recognize new uses for old products.

Interpreting Previously-Obtained Quantitative Data

In some instances focus group interviews are used as the last step in the research process to probe for detailed reasons behind quantitative test results obtained in earlier marketing research studies.

A focus group project begins with a screening questionnaire used to locate potential participants who have specific characteristics. Once the group meets, the flow of the interview is usually from a general discussion of the product category to a discussion of a specific product or specific characteristics of a product. A **discussion guide** establishes the plan of the focus group interview, including the topics to be covered and sometimes the time allocated to each topic. The discussion guide is not a questionnaire; it simply provides an agenda for the group session that is flexible enough to be altered as the group discussion progresses.

Discussion guide Agenda that establishes the plan of the focus group interview, including the topics to be covered and sometimes the time allocated to each topic.

EXHIBIT 5-3

Focus Group Transcript

Group II 6:30 P.M.

Moderator: I'd like to go around the room first and hear a little bit about you. My name is Donna. I'd like to hear your names, what you do in the military, rank or specialty you have, and a little about your long distance telephone usage. If you don't mind, tell me the size of your bill, the number of calls you make, are they to family or friends or a side business you have, and where do you call. So we can get an idea whether you call Alaska once a month, or whether you make smaller calls. And do you place them during particular times of the days, or days you're off, and the brand of long distance you use. Who would like to start?

Respondent:	I'm a First Class Mate. I call my father once a week for maybe an hour. Sometimes I call my sister in Las Vegas, Nevada. My wife takes care of all the bills. My father was in an accident, is still recuperating.
Moderator:	So you call and kind of check on him once a week?
Respondent:	Yes.
Moderator:	If your wife takes care of the bills, do you know how much you spend on long distance?
Respondent:	I think the maximum has been about $49. It could be less than that. We call around 8:30–9:00 at night.
Moderator:	O.K. Curtis?
Respondent (Curtis):	I'm in the Navy. Some of the phone calls are made more or less, well a lot are long distance calls when I go overseas. I was in Canada and my father was in the hospital. My wife calls a lot to Virginia to her parents, maybe once a week. I call North Carolina, relatives there. I call Florida sometimes.
Moderator:	About how many long distance calls do you think your household makes every month in the United States?
Respondent (Curtis):	At least five.
Moderator:	Do you know what your average bill is?
Respondent (Curtis):	50-some dollars.
Moderator:	What brand of long distance do you use?
Respondent (Curtis):	AT&T. We just had Tel-something.
Moderator:	Telamco? It's what I saw today written on something downstairs.
Respondent (Curtis):	Yes, I think that's it.
Moderator:	Thank you, Curtis.

The moderator speaks informally and conversationally to the focus group participants and does not work from a formal prepared outline. Exhibit 5-3 presents a small portion from the transcript of a focus group interview done for an AT&T military residence research project in South Carolina.

Focus group interviews are useful because they can provide momentum and excitement as a base for discussing a wide range of information and ideas. The members of the group are often more at ease than they would be in a one-on-one interview and may speak more willingly or more freely—or may feel free to remain silent. The moderator can be more flexible in questioning; and several observers can stand by.[2]

On the other hand, participant interaction can also be disadvantageous. A dominant individual can take over; individual comments can be misread as representing the overall view of the whole group; and one focus group interview is not enough to get valid data. Several groups must be interviewed to counteract the possibility that the dynamics of one group will cause misinterpretation of the members' viewpoints. Focus groups are not a substitute for quantitative studies.[3]

Depth Interviews

The **depth interview,** often referred to as "one-on-ones," attempts to uncover underlying motivations, prejudice, attitudes toward sensitive issues, and so forth. Depth interviews are like long psychoanalytic sessions where free association and hidden sources of feelings are discussed, generally through a question guide or agenda administered by a highly skilled interviewer.

Depth interview ("one-on-one") Sessions in which free association and hidden sources of feelings are discussed, generally through a very loose, unstructured question-guide administered by a highly skilled interviewer. Attempts to uncover underlying motivations, prejudice, attitudes toward sensitive issues, etc.

Depth interviews can prove most useful where the marketing research issue under study deals with (1) a confidential, emotionally charged, or embarrassing matter; (2) a behavior for which socially acceptable norms exist and the need to conform in group discussions influences responses; (3) a complex behavioral or decision-making process that requires a detailed idiosyncratic step-by-step description; and (4) when the target population is difficult to schedule with group interviews—for example, doctors and other professionals. Depth interviews have been used in brand-name research to understand consumer's perceptions and responses to names.[4]

The depth interviewer must strictly follow certain rules. The interviewer should (1) avoid appearing superior or condescending and use familiar words; (2) ask questions indirectly and informatively; (3) remain detached and objective, letting the respondent first describe brand and product category thoughts—for example, feelings about the current brand most often used and the product category in general—before asking "why" questions; (4) not accept "yes" or "no" answers; (5) probe for all details and underlying feelings; and (6) encourage the respondent to talk freely, while keeping the conversation on-target for the study.

Depth interviews attempt to uncover content and intensity of respondents' feelings and motivations beyond the rationalized overt responses to structured questions. As such, they follow the method of psychoanalysis and psychotherapy and can be expensive. Because tape recordings are usually used, depth interviews take a long time to complete, transcribe and read, and must be analyzed by either an

---

[2]John M. Hess, "Group Interviewing," in *New Science of Planning*, ed. R. L. King (Chicago: American Marketing Association, 1968), 194.

[3]J. Pope, *Practical Marketing Research* (New York: AMACOM, 1981), 189.

[4]M. Z. Knox, "In-Depth Interviews Can Reveal 'What's In A Name,'" *Marketing News*, 3 January, 1986, 4.

experienced practitioner who knows the technique and the product category under study or a psychology specialist.

PROJECTIVE TECHNIQUES

In certain situations it may be beneficial to obtain information on respondents' feelings and beliefs indirectly. **Projective techniques,** taken from clinical psychology, exemplify this type of survey-interviewing method. Projective techniques presume that respondents cannot or will not communicate their feelings and beliefs directly. Instead, respondents are allowed to respond indirectly by projecting their own feelings and beliefs into the situation as they interpret the behavior of others. Among the more frequently used projective techniques are

1. **The Thematic Apperception Test (TAT).** This projective technique presents respondents with a series of pictures or cartoons in which consumers and products are the primary topic of attention. Cartoons are most frequently used in marketing research applications. The respondent is presented with pictures or cartoons that are neutral and is asked to indicate what is happening or what might happen next. This approach frees respondents to indirectly project their own feelings and beliefs onto the situation portrayed in the pictures or cartoons. The term *thematic apperception test* is used because themes (*thematic*) are elicited based on the perceptual-interpretive (*apperception*) use of the pictures and cartoons.

2. **Word Association.** We are all probably familiar with word association tests, which present respondents with a list of words, one at a time, and ask them to indicate what word comes immediately to mind. The respondent's response as well as the time it takes to respond are recorded and analyzed according to the frequency with which a response is given, the amount of time elapsed, and the number of respondents unable to respond within the time allowed. Elapsed time is important because a hesitation could indicate that the respondent was searching for a "socially acceptable" response.

3. **Sentence Completion.** Like word association, sentence completion tests are based upon free association. The respondent is asked to complete a number of incomplete sentences with the first word or phrase that comes to mind. Responses are then analyzed for content.

4. **Third Person/Role Playing.** The third-person technique and role playing presents respondents with a verbal or visual situation and asks them to relate the feelings and beliefs of a third person—for example, a friend, a neighbor, or a "typical" person, to the situation, rather than to directly express their own feelings and beliefs about

---

Projective techniques
A class of techniques which presume that respondents cannot or will not communicate their feelings and beliefs directly; provides a structured question format in which respondents can respond indirectly by projecting their own feelings and beliefs into the situation while they interpret the behavior of others.

Thematic apperception test (TAT) Projective technique presenting respondents with a series of pictures or cartoons in which consumers and products are the primary topic of attention.

Word association Projective technique where respondents are presented with a list of words, one at a time, and asked to indicate what word comes immediately to mind.

Sentence completion Projective technique where respondents are asked to complete a number of incomplete sentences with the first word or phrase that comes to mind.

Third person/role playing Projective technique that presents respondents with a verbal or visual situation and asks them to relate the feelings and beliefs of a third person to the situation, rather than to directly express their own feelings and beliefs about the situation.

136

the situation. It is hoped that the respondent will reveal personal feelings and beliefs while describing the reactions of some third party. A popular version of the third-person technique presents the respondent with a description of a shopping list and asks for a characterization of the purchaser.[5]

5. **Cartoon Completion Test.** A cartoon completion test presents respondents with a cartoon of a particular situation and asks them to suggest the dialogue that one cartoon character might make in response to the comment(s) of another cartoon character.

Like depth interviews, projective techniques require a highly skilled interviewer and must be analyzed and interpreted by experienced professionals. Not surprisingly, the cost per interview is high compared with other types of survey-interviewing methods. As a result, projective techniques are generally not used extensively in commercial marketing research except for word association, frequently used in brand-name studies.

Cartoon completion test Projective technique that presents respondents with a cartoon of a particular situation and asks them to suggest the dialogue that one cartoon character might make in response to the comment(s) of another cartoon character.

MAJOR DATA-COLLECTION METHODS

Most companies use a wide range of data-collection techniques. Market Facts, Inc., recently completed a survey on the major methods used by 183 of the largest American consumer goods and services companies for 1978 and 1983.[6] The major data collection methods are telephone (WATS) interviewing, followed by shopping-mall intercept, local telephone interviewing, in-home personal interviewing, and direct mail surveys. Most notable is the large decrease in the use of in-home personal surveys since 1978. The Market Facts survey also found that mall intercepts show the largest budget-share increase, whereas in-home personal interviews show the largest budget-share decrease since 1978.

"Cold" Mail Surveys

Mail surveys involve sending out a fairly structured questionnaire to a sample of respondents. Surveys are typically mailed directly to the respondent, and the completed questionnaire is returned by mail to the firm conducting the study. Alternatively, the survey can be dropped off to the respondent and arrangements can also be made for the completed questionnaire to be picked up.[7] Mail surveys can also be attached to

Mail surveys Data collection method that involves sending out a fairly structured questionnaire to a sample of respondents.

[5]Maison Haire, "Projective Techniques in Marketing Research," *Journal of Marketing,* April 1950, 649–656.

[6]Market Facts, Inc., *Consumer Market Research Technique Usage Patterns and Attitudes in 1983* (Chicago: April 1983).

[7]See C. H. Lovelock, R. Stiff, D. Cullwick, and I. M. Kaufman, "An Evaluation of the Effectiveness of Drop-Off Questionnaire Delivery," *Journal of Marketing Research,* November 1976, 358–64.

products, as is standard practice with warranty cards, or distributed as inserts in magazines and newspapers.[8]

A **"cold" mail survey** involves mailing questionnaires to a group of individuals who have not agreed in advance to participate in the study.

Flexibility and Versatility. Because mail surveys must be self-administered, they are not so flexible or versatile as personal or telephone interviews. Each question must be carefully structured, since no interviewer is present to clarify a question that the respondent doesn't understand; and there is no opportunity for following up on incomplete or unclear responses or for additional probing. The questionnaire must be simple and straightforward, and questions must be presented in fixed order. Finally, mail surveys are less versatile than personal interviews, since they do not employ certain visual cues. For example, full-scale product prototypes cannot be used, though it is possible to include drawings and photographs in a mailing.

Quantity of Data. A key factor determining the quantity of data that can be collected via direct mail is the length of the questionnaire. Personal interviews can be longer than either mail or telephone interviews, and mail interviews can be longer than telephone interviews. Short questionnaires have not been shown to generate higher response rates than longer questionnaires.[9]

Sample Control. Controlling who is in the sample with a "cold" mail survey can be difficult. Mail surveys require an explicit list of individuals or households eligible for inclusion in the sample. This list, called the **sampling frame,** must contain addresses, if not names and addresses, for the entire eligible population. In principle, then, mail surveys can reach geographically dispersed respondents and hard-to-reach areas (such as inner-city ghetto areas). In many instances, however, mailing lists are unavailable or, if available, are incomplete or dated. Telephone and street directories can prove to be ineffective sampling frames due to unlisted numbers, new residents, and households without phones. Moreover, even if a complete and accurate mailing list is available, researchers have little control over who fills out the questionnaire and whether it will be returned. Catalogs of mailing lists are available, containing thousands of lists that can be purchased.[10] (See Chapter 7 for further discussion of sampling practices.)

Quality of Data. On the positive side, the absence of an interviewer eliminates interviewer bias caused by altered questions, appearance or

---

[8]J. E. Klompmaker, J. D. Lindley, and R. L. Page, "Using Free Papers for Customer Surveys," *Journal of Marketing*, July 1977, 80–82.

[9]See L. Kanuk and C. Berenson, "Mail Surveys and Response Rates: A Literature Review," *Journal of Marketing Research*, November 1975, 440–453.

[10]For example, see *1973–1974 Catalog of Mailing Lists* (New York: Fritz S. Hotheimer, Inc., 1972).

speech, projection of cues to respondents, probing tactics, or cheating—that is, an interviewer's falsifying all or part of an interview. Also, because a mail survey does not involve any social interaction between an interviewer and a respondent, evidence suggests that for sensitive or embarrassing questions—for example, questions about drinking habits, sexual behavior, bank loans—mail surveys yield better-quality data than either personal or telephone interviews.[11]

On the negative side, however, the respondent cannot seek clarification without an interviewer, and the quality of data may be suspect due to inaccuracies caused by confusing questions. With mail surveys the respondent is free to read through the entire questionnaire before answering the questions, and—as a result of a response to a question appearing near the end of the questionnaire—change a response made to an earlier question. Finally, because of the lack of control over who is included in the sample, respondents who return the completed questionnaires are often not representative of the total sample. For example, in a mail survey about a new product, respondents who return the questionnaire may be more likely to have had either an extremely favorable reaction to the new product or a complaint about it.

Response Rates. Low response rates are among the most serious problems plaguing mail surveys. **Response rates** refer to the percentage of the total number of respondents sent questionnaires who complete and return the questionnaire:

$$\text{Response rate} = \frac{\text{Number of completed questionnaires}}{\text{Number of eligible respondents}}$$

where number of eligible respondents is equal to the number of questionnaires sent *minus* the number returned because of improper addresses, deaths, and so on. Because the response rate in mail surveys is related to the respondent's interest in the survey topic, nonresponse bias can be a serious problem. For a mail survey sent to a cold list of randomly selected respondents, without any pre- or post-mailing follow-up, typically no more than 10 percent of the questionnaires will be returned. With multiple pre- and post-mailing follow-ups it is possible to generate response rates of 80 percent, possibly more. Response rates will be considered again in Chapter 7.

Specific aspects of the questionnaire have been investigated for their potential to reduce refusals. The following list summarizes the available evidence.[12]

- *Questionnaire length.* Even though common sense suggests that short questionnaires should obtain higher response rates than longer questionnaires, research evidence does not support this view.
- *Survey sponsorship.* The sparse evidence that does exist concerning

---

[11]B. Dunning and D. Calahan, "Mail versus Field Self-Administered Questionnaires: An Armed Forces Survey," *Public Opinion Quarterly*, Spring 1972, 105–108.

[12]Kanuk and Berenson, 452.

Response rates The total number of respondents sent questionnaires who complete and return them expressed as a percentage.

the influence of survey sponsorship on response rates indicates that
official or "respected" sponsorship tends to increase response.

■ *Return envelopes.* The one study which tested the hypothesis that
return envelopes increase response rates suggests that the inclusion
of a stamped, return envelope does encourage response because it
facilitates questionnaire return.

■ *Postage.* Though a number of tests regarding postage are reported in
the literature, few studies have tested the same variables. Existing
evidence indicates that special delivery is very effective in increasing
response rates and that air mail is more effective than first class.

■ *Personalization.* Empirical evidence indicates that personalization of
the mailing has no clear-cut advantage in terms of improving response rates. For example, neither personal inside addresses nor individually signed cover letters proved to be effective in most cases
cited. The one study that tested the use of a titled signature versus
a signature without a title did show a significant advantage in favor
of the title.

■ *Size, reproduction, and color.* The few studies that examined the effects of questionnaire size, method of reproduction, and color found
no significant differences in response rates.

■ *Money incentive.* A number of studies indicate that a relatively small
incentive sent with the questionnaire is very effective in increasing
response rates. Large incentives will undoubtedly increase response
rates, but at a cost that might exceed the value of the added information.

■ *Deadline dates.* The few studies that tested the impact of deadline
dates found that they did not increase the response rate; however,
they did accelerate questionnaire return.

Speed. It usually takes several weeks for completed questionnaires to
come in. The elapsed time for completing a mail survey will be even
longer if follow-up mailings are required. Each follow-up mailing may
require two or more weeks to determine whether an acceptable response
rate has been achieved, so that a large mail survey may take several
months to complete. Unfortunately, the marketing researcher has very
little control over the time it takes for the completion and return of
questionnaires.

Cost. The relatively inexpensive cost of mail surveys is one of their most
attractive features. For mail surveys, the data-collection cost, excluding
analysis and report generation, can be as low as $2.50 per completed
interview.

Uses. Cold mail surveys are most often used in executive, industrial, or
medical studies; readership studies are often conducted with cold mailings. The selected respondents typically share a high interest in the survey topic, and the sample is small and geographically dispersed. On the

other hand, the cold mail survey is rarely used in attitude and usage studies of consumer products and services because of the potential of low response rates.

Mail Panels

A mail panel consists of large and nationally representative samples of households that have agreed to periodically participate in mail questionnaires, product tests, and telephone surveys.[13] Thus mail panels represent an important resource that offers marketing executives a pool of respondents ready to participate in research projects and to answer questions whenever they are asked to do so. Households that agree to participate in the mail panel are often compensated for their time and effort. Various forms of incentives are used.

Mail panels are maintained by commercial marketing research suppliers. There are four major players in the mail panel market: National Family Opinion (NFO), Market Fact's Consumer Mail Panel (CMP), Home Testing Institute (HTI), and Marketing and Research Counselors' National Neighborhood Panel (NNP).

Flexibility and Versatility. Like cold mail surveys, mail panels are not so flexible or versatile as personal or telephone interviews. Because the questionnaire is self-administered, the limitations associated with cold mail surveys apply to mail panels.

Quantity of Data. Compared with cold mail surveys, mail panels generally increase the quantity of data that can be collected. First, no time or effort is lost in qualifying or interviewing respondents and questionnaires are self-administered. Second, most panel members are available by phone for more in-depth information or more immediate response.

Sample Control. Mail panels afford much greater control over the characteristics of the sample. First, they can efficiently provide samples with greater geographic dispersion than can alternative data-collection methods. Second, mail panels also offer samples matched to U.S. Census Bureau statistics on key demographic criteria. Basic demographics usually include geographic region, population density, household income, age of panel members, and household size. Third, specific user groups within a panel can be identified and surveys targeted to households having specific characteristics. Fourth, specific members of any panel household can be questioned. Finally, hard-to-reach and low-incidence groups can be surveyed.

On the negative side, however, are the issues of representativeness

---

[13]This material follows the presentation found in Market Facts, Inc., *Why Consumer Mail Panels is the Superior Option* (Chicago 1986).

and response bias. The issue of representativeness involves the extent to which a panel can legitimately be considered representative of the overall population. Individuals who agree to serve on the panel are special merely because not everyone is willing to serve on a panel; in fact, only about 10 percent of those households approached agree to join. Moreover, cooperativeness may be unrelated to demographic variables which means that it cannot be compensated for by matching the entire panel, or some proportion of it, to census statistics.

Response bias involves the extent to which those panel members who respond to the mailing can be considered representative of the general population or, for that matter, of the entire panel of households. Again, interest in survey topic and extreme reactions can motivate a respondent to complete and mail back a questionnaire. There is little control over which household member actually fills out the questionnaire, although, compared with cold mailings, mail panels make it easier to question specific members of any panel household. Finally potential problems are caused by the natural tendency for panels to age *(maturation)* and by *conditioning/testing* effects that sensitize panel members over time to those products or services that have been the topic of the survey. Both maturation and conditioning effects can be reduced by "rolling out" panel members—by systematically adding younger, fresh panel members.

Quality of Data. Mail panels can enhance the quality of the data collected. First, because respondents have more time to answer than with telephone or in-home personal interviewing, they can be thorough and thoughtful in completing lengthy questionnaires. Second, aware of the confidentiality that mail panels provide, respondents can be more candid. Third, there is less risk of interviewer bias. Finally, consumer mail panels provide the prime tool for eliciting consumer answers in sensitive and/or personal areas where respondents would be reticent to answer interviewers.

Response Rates. Because of assured respondent cooperation, response rates in mail panels are typically in the 70–80 percent range.

Speed. As with cold mail surveys, it generally takes several weeks for complete questionnaires to come in. Because little follow-up is usually required, the data-collection process is completed much faster than with cold mail surveys.

Cost. Mail panels offer the lowest cost per respondent of any research medium. Access to a mail panel is often sold on a shared-cost basis. In a shared-cost mailing a limited number of firms have access to a proportion of the general panel sample for a specific dollar cost. As the name implies, each participating firm shares in the cost of the mailing. Restrictions are placed on the minimum number of mailings and the amount of information that can be obtained. For example, with the CMP service the minimum number of mailings is 1,000, with increments of 1,000, and the information is limited to a single two-sided card called a *Data Gage*. Figure 5-1 illustrates a Data Gage card. In a customized mailing, all aspects of the mailing have been tailored to the specific needs of a single firm. Essentially, for the right price, these mail panel services will allow almost any type of customized research project to be undertaken. In addition, mail panel firms also promote special subgroups of the total panel sample—for example, a baby panel or a student panel—and offer certain syndicated products such as beverage consumer mail panels. Because of economies of scale, monthly shared-cost computer card mailings can be as little as 30 cents per household. Mail panels are also cost-efficient because detailed demographic information on every household is already on file, and no additional data collection is necessary. No interviewing expenditures are necessary. The availability of demographic data permits identification of specific targets at reasonable cost.

Uses. Mail panels provide a vehicle for collecting meaningful data in virtually all areas of marketing research. Panels provide a very effective way to do in-home product testing, since specific user groups can be identified and targeted to receive the product and ultimately use it in a normal home environment. Another important application area is its ability to survey low-incidence groups in a cost-efficient manner by using the entire panel to identify users of a low-incidence product and then to follow up with a mail or telephone survey. This two-step procedure can greatly reduce the cost of surveying low-incidence groups.

Mail panels have also been used very successfully and innovatively to gather national and/or regional information. For example, panel members have been used as a national consumer field force to audit and report on a variety of products and services. Among other things, panel members have been asked to visit department stores and request catalogs, visit fast food restaurants and record prices, and buy products and report satisfaction.

Telephone Surveys

Telephone surveys involve phoning a sample of respondents drawn from an eligible population and asking them a series of questions. Although the use and percentage of dollar budget allocated to local telephone interviewing has decreased since 1978, WATS telephone interviewing continues to be a major data-collection method.

Flexibility and Versatility. Because an interviewer is involved with the questioning, telephone surveys can use complex questionnaires with features such as skip patterns, probes, refer-backs, and various termination points not possible in mail surveys. However, telephone surveys are not so flexible and versatile as personal interviews. An interviewer who observes the respondent can ensure that instructions are understood. Com-

Telephone surveys Survey that involves phoning a sample of respondents drawn from an eligible population and asking them a series of questions.

Please answer the following questions on this side <u>and</u> the other side of this card.

1. How frequently, if at all, do you purchase the following snack items? ("X" ONE FOR EACH ITEM)

	Once a Month or More	Every 2 - 3 Months	Less Often	Never
	1	2	3	4
Regular potato chips	[ ]	[ ]	[ ]	[ ] (9)
Flavored potato chips(Bar B-Q, Sour cream & onion, etc.)	[ ]	[ ]	[ ]	[ ]
Processed Potato Chips (Pringles, Munchos, etc.)	[ ]	[ ]	[ ]	[ ]
"Home style" Potato chips	[ ]	[ ]	[ ]	[ ]
	1	2	3	4
Cheese Puffs(Cheeto's etc.)	[ ]	[ ]	[ ]	[ ] (13)
Corn chips(Frito's etc.)	[ ]	[ ]	[ ]	[ ]
Tortilla chips (Doritos, etc.)	[ ]	[ ]	[ ]	[ ]
Pretzels	[ ]	[ ]	[ ]	[ ]
Peanuts/other nuts	[ ]	[ ]	[ ]	[ ]
Flavored Crackers(Not Saltines)	[ ]	[ ]	[ ]	[ ] (18)
	1	2	3	4
Dips(Canned or refrigerated)	[ ]	[ ]	[ ]	[ ] (19)
Dried fruit snacks (Fruit Roll-Ups, Fun Fruits, etc.)	[ ]	[ ]	[ ]	[ ]
Sweet baked goods (Hostess Snack Cakes, Twinkies, Dunkin' Sticks, etc.)	[ ]	[ ]	[ ]	[ ]
Frozen potato products (French fries, Tator Tots, etc.)	[ ]	[ ]	[ ]	[ ]
Frozen dessert snacks (Pudding Pops, Eskimo Pies, Dole Fruit Bars, etc.)	[ ]	[ ]	[ ]	[ ] (23)

2a. Within the past year, to which, if any, of the following charities have you contributed money? (RECORD UNDER 2a)

2b. To which of the following have you volunteered your time? (RECORD UNDER 2b)

	2a. Contributed Money	2b. Volunteered Your Time
American Cancer Society	[ ]1	[ ]1
American Heart Association	[ ]2	[ ]2
American Lung Association	[ ]3	[ ]3
Arthritis Foundation	[ ]4	[ ]4
Easter Seals	[ ]5	[ ]5
March of Dimes	[ ]6	[ ]6
Multiple Sclerosis (MS) Society.	[ ]7	[ ]7
Muscular Dystrophy Assn. (MDA) .	[ ]8	[ ]8
National Kidney Foundation	[ ]9	[ ]9
United Way	[ ]0	[ ]0
Other _____	[ ]-0	[ ]-0
None	[ ]-X	[ ]-X
	(24-25)	(26-27)

3. Do you own ...

	Yes	No
A programmable calculator?	[ ]1	[ ]2 (28)
A calculator with a tape print out? ..	[ ]1	[ ]2 (29)

4. Are you, or is someone in your household, a member of the American Automobile Association (AAA)?

    Yes .... [ ]1   No .... [ ]2   (30)

5. Does anyone in your household normally pack a lunch to school or work?

    School ... [ ]1   Work ... [ ]2   Neither ... [ ]3 (31)

6a. Which of the stores listed below have you <u>heard</u> of?

6b. Which, if any, have you visited <u>within the past year</u>?

Stores	Heard of?		Visited in past year?	
	Yes	No	Yes	No
Pier 1 Imports	[ ]1	[ ]2	[ ]1	[ ]2 (32-33)
Color Tile	[ ]1	[ ]2	[ ]1	[ ]2 (34-35)
Eckerd Drugs	[ ]1	[ ]2	[ ]1	[ ]2 (36-37)

(38-78 open)

79 [0][1] 80

Figure 5-1

Data Gage. Source: Market Facts, Inc., used with permission.

plex or lengthy scales or unstructured questions are difficult to administer via telephone. Consider a question that asks a respondent to allocate 100 points among several brands according to his or her likelihood of purchase. Also, the respondent may tire very quickly if repeatedly exposed to similar scales on the telephone instead of in person. Finally, it is impossible to show a respondent anything during a telephone interview. Thus, it is impractical to conduct advertising copy testing or package tests, for example, via telephone. In certain instances this can be overcome by mailing the respondent a visual cue before conducting the telephone interview. Nevertheless, inability to use visual cues remains an inherent problem with telephone surveys.

Quantity of Data. Telephone interviews typically last about fifteen to thirty minutes, although interviews of up to one hour have been successful.[14] Telephone interviews tend to be shorter than either mail surveys or personal interviews because (1) respondents can terminate the telephone conversation at their own discretion and (2) respondents may suspect telephone contacts. Of course, if respondents are extremely interested in the survey topic, then they will probably remain on the telephone.

Sample Control. Telephone surveys provide control over who is interviewed. Like mail surveys, telephone surveys can reach geographically dispersed respondents and hard-to-reach areas and are highly dependent upon a sampling frame. Households without telephones present an immediate problem, regardless of the sampling frame selected. Obviously, if telephone households and nontelephone households do not differ significantly, then the systematic exclusion of the latter group is no cause for alarm. However, the 1980 United States census shows that telephone ownership varies by geographical region (the South has the lowest penetration) and by race (blacks have a lower incidence of telephone ownership than do whites). Such differences between telephone and nontelephone households are not a major concern to commercial marketing research studies, however, since nontelephone households are typically considered to be low-consumption families. In addition, two issues must be considered when choosing a sampling frame. Ideally, the frame should be up-to-date, reflecting new phones in service and not excluding households without published telephone numbers. Estimates of the percentage of households with unpublished numbers varies considerably by geographical region. The national average is about 20 percent; for large metropolitan areas the median is about 27 percent; however, in certain parts of the country it can be as high as 48 percent.[15]

[14]S. Sudman, "Sample Surveys," *Annual Review of Sociology*, 1976, 107–120.

[15]For more details see C. L. Rich, "Is Random Digit Dialing Really Necessary," *Journal of Marketing Research*, August 1977, 300–301; A. B. Blankenship, "Listed versus Unlisted Numbers in Telephone Survey Samples," *Opinion Quarterly*, February 1977, 39–42; G. J. Glasser and G. D. Metzger, "National Estimates of Nonlisted Telephone Households and Their Characteristics," *Journal of Marketing Research*, August 1975, 359–61; and J. Honomichl, "Arbitron Updates Unlisted Phone Numbers," *Advertising Age*, 15 January, 1979, 40.

145

Directory and nondirectory sampling frames are used in telephone surveys. With traditional **directory-based sampling designs,** telephone numbers are selected from the directory in some prescribed way, and so the sample is restricted to households having published telephone numbers. If the directory is not current, then households that have moved into the geographical area covered by the directory cannot be included in the sample. Furthermore, if the geographic area to be sampled is not concomitant with the area covered by the telephone directory, then much of the ease of drawing the sample will be negated, since each selected telephone number must be identified as belonging to the eligible population by inspecting its address—a process that can prove cumbersome and can lead to inclusion errors.

To overcome exclusion bias, **random digit directory designs** have been used.[16] The first step in these random designs is to draw a sample of numbers from the directory, usually by a systematic procedure such as picking every tenth telephone number. Next, the selected telephone numbers are modified to allow all unlisted numbers a chance for inclusion. Three popular approaches for correcting exclusion bias with directory frames are (1) *addition of a constant to the last digit,* (2) *randomization on the r last digits,* and (3) *inverse sampling with probabilities proportional to size.* The first approach, addition of a constant to the last digit, calls for an integer (between 0 and 9) to be added (arithmetically) to the telephone number selected from the directory. The second approach, randomization on the *r* last digits, replaces the *r* last digits (*r* = 2, 3, or 4) of the selected telephone number with an appropriate number of random digits. The third approach involves a two-stage procedure. First the directory is used to select a sample of telephone numbers. The last three digits of each number are then removed. Next a block of three-digit random numbers, between 000 and 999, is selected and appended to the four digits remaining to form a complete seven-digit telephone number. Exhibit 5-4 briefly illustrates each of these approaches. If the geographic area to be sampled is concomitant with the area covered by the telephone directory, random digit directory sampling can prove effective. Out of the three methods, addition of a constant has been shown to produce high contact rates and representative samples.[17]

Nondirectory sampling designs do not make direct use of telephone directories. Instead, numbers are prescriptively added to working exchanges (also called prefixes). There are three kinds of nondirectory sampling designs: *simple two-stage, two-stage cluster,* and *stratified.*[18] A

Directory-based sampling designs Sample where telephone numbers are selected from the directory in some prescribed way.

Random digit directory sample designs Samples of numbers drawn from the directory, usually by a systematic procedure. Selected numbers are modified to allow all unlisted numbers a chance for inclusion.

Nondirectory sampling designs Telephone survey samples that do not make direct use of telephone directories. Instead, numbers are prescriptively added to working exchanges (also called prefixes).

[16] For example, see Mathew Hauck and Michael Cox, "Locating a Sample by Random Digit Dialing," *Public Opinion Quarterly,* Summer 1974, 253–60; and Seymour Sudmun, "The Uses of Telephone Directories for Survey Sampling," *Journal of Marketing Research,* May 1973, 204–207.

[17] E. L. Landon, Jr., and S. K. Banks, "Relative Efficiency and Bias of Plus-One Telephone Sampling," *Journal of Marketing Research,* August 1977, 294–99.

[18] For example, see Chilton Research Services, *A National Probability Sample of Telephone Households Using Computerized Sampling Techniques* (Radmor, Pa., 1976); Chilton

E X H I B I T 5-4

Description of Directory Sampling Designs

Addition of a Constant to the Last Digit

Selected telephone number: 456   6612

           exchange   block

Add one to the last digit to form the selected number 456-6613.

Randomization on the r Last Digits

Selected telephone number 456   8329

          exchange   block

Replace last two digits of block with randomly selected numbers 4 and 5 to form the number 456-8345.

Two Stage Procedure

Cluster one—selected exchange 265; selected telephone number

    265   9592

exchange   block

Replace last three digits 592 with randomly selected digits 045 to form selected number 265-9045. Repeat process until desired sample of households (telephone numbers) from this cluster is obtained.

---

simple two-stage sample randomly selects a working exchange and appends a block of four-digit random numbers. A two-stage cluster design first clusters telephone numbers by exchange. Next, a sample of exchanges is selected either randomly or systematically. Then, within these selected exchanges, four digits are generated to yield the sample of telephone surveys. The stratified sampling design also adds random digits to exchanges. However, in stratified designs, working exchanges and working banks are first determined. Each exchange consists of ten banks of 1,000 numbers each. For example, the 1,000 numbers between 8,000 and

---

Research Services, "Telecentral Communication: An Innovation in Survey Research," presented to the Advertising Research Foundation, 11th Annual Conference, New York City, October 5, 1965; Stanford L. Cooper, "Random Sampling by Telephone—An Improved Method," *Journal of Marketing Research,* November 1964, 45–48; J. O. Eastlack, Jr., and Henry Assael, "Better Telephone Surveys Through Centralized Interviewing," *Journal of Advertising Research,* March 1966, 2–7; Gerald J. Glasser and Dale D. Metzger, "Random Digit Dialing as a Method of Telephone Sampling," *Journal of Marketing Research,* February 1972, 59–64; Gerald J. Glasser and Dale D. Metzger, "National Estimates of Nonlisted Telephone Households and Their Characteristics," *Journal of Marketing Research,* August 1975, 359–61; William R. Klecka and Alfred J. Tuchfarber, Jr., "Random Digit Dialing as an Efficient Method for Political Polling," *Georgia Political Science Association Journal,* Spring 1974, 133–51; and E. Laird London, Jr., and Sharon K. Banks, *Boulder Shopping Survey: Shopping Habits and Attitudes of Boulder Residents* (Boulder, Colorado: Department of Community Development, March 1976).

8,999 are a bank. Information on working banks are kept by the telephone company; however, it may be difficult to obtain the information. Next, four-digit random numbers that fall within working banks are added to each working exchange to form the selected telephone number. The number of households taken from each exchange is based upon a pre-specified allocation rule. Stratified designs are typically used in local or regional telephone surveys, since it is not feasible to stratify by exchange at the national level—there are over 28,000 working exchanges.[19]

Quality of Data. Numerous studies have shown that telephone surveys produce data essentially comparable to that collected via mail surveys and personal interviews.[20] Telephone surveys do have several unique features, however. First, compared with mail surveys, telephone survey respondents show a greater tendency not to include information on income and personal finances.[21] Second, interaction between the respondent and the interviewer can create a tendency to give socially acceptable answers to sensitive or embarrassing questions.[22] In this regard, telephone surveys fall somewhere between mail surveys and personal interviews. Third, on the one hand, an interviewer reduces respondent confusion, permits probing, and allows respondents to clarify their responses; on the other hand, even though interviewers are not physically present during the interview they may still transmit cues that can bias respondent's answers. Interviewers can project a "warm" or "cold" image or, for that matter, convey their own attitudes through inflection and tone of voice, thereby either influencing the responses or suggesting the appropriate response.[23] Finally, on the positive side, telephone interviewing conducted at a central telephone facility allows the person supervising the survey to monitor a portion of each interviewer's work to ensure that the questionnaire is being administered properly and that no cheating is taking place.

Response Rates. The proportion of completed interviews in telephone surveys typically ranges from 60 to 80 percent.

$$\text{Response rate} = \frac{\text{No. of complete interviews}}{\text{No. of complete interviews} + \text{No. of refusals} + \text{No. of terminations}}$$

[19]Chilton Research Services, *National Probability Sample*, 2.

[20]See, for example, C. S. Aneshensed, R. R. Frerichs, V. A. Clark, and P. A. Yokopenic, "Measuring Depression in the Community: A Comparison of Telephone and Personal Interviews," *Public Opinion Quarterly* Spring 1982, 110–21; J. R. Hochstim, "A Critical Comparison of Three Strategies of Collecting Data From Households," *Journal of the American Statistical Association*, September 1967, 876–89.

[21]T. F. Rogers, "Interviews by Telephone and In Person Quality of Response and Field Performance," *Public Opinion Quarterly*, Spring 1976, 51–65.

[22]T. T. Tyebjee, "Telephone Survey Methods: The State of the Art," *Journal of Marketing*, Summer 1979, 68–78.

[23]E. Telser, "Data Exercises Bias in Phone vs. Personal Interview Debate, But If You Can't Do It Right, Don't Do It At All," *Marketing News*, 10 September 1976, 6.

Such high response rates are obtained by establishing contact with potential respondents. With telephone surveys, call-backs are easily implemented at little cost. Many telephone surveys use a three-call-back procedure.

Speed. When a central telephone facility is used, always the case in WATS telephone surveys, enough interviewers can be hired to ensure that several hundred telephone interviews can be scheduled and completed each day. Large national studies can then be collected in a week or two.

Cost. Because of economies of scale, the data-collection cost for WATS telephone surveys, excluding analysis and report generation, can be as low as $5 per completed interview.

Uses. Telephone surveys are used in studies that require national samples. In addition, when dealing with a small geographically-dispersed group of respondents, telephone interviewing may be the only practical way of reaching them. It has replaced door-to-door personal interviews for many attitude and usage studies, particularly in *market tracking studies* that periodically assess customer awareness, attitudes, and usage behavior in a product category. Telephone surveys are also used in *product tests* to obtain opinions after respondents have used the test product. Finally, telephone surveys are used increasingly as an efficient way to conduct call-back interviews with respondents previously contacted by a mail survey or personal interview.

Personal-In Home Surveys

The **personal-in home survey** involves asking questions of a sample of respondents face-to-face in their homes. With in-home personal surveys the responsibilities of the interviewer are to (1) locate the appropriate sample of respondents, (2) ask them a set of questions, and (3) record their responses. There has been a marked decrease in the use and percentage of dollar budget allocated to in-home personal interviewing.

Personal in-home survey Survey that involves asking questions of a sample of respondents face-to-face in their homes.

Flexibility and Versatility. Personal surveys are by far the most flexible and versatile of the data-collection methods. They afford the greatest freedom in questionnaire length and format. Complex questionnaires having involved skip patterns, lengthy scales, projective techniques, probes, refer-backs and various termination points can easily be used with an experienced interviewer. Since the interviewer and respondent interact, the interviewer can observe the respondent directly and thus can ensure that the instructions have been properly understood. In addition to asking and clarifying questions, an interviewer can also provide other valuable information. For example, in a *package test* study, the interviewer can record whether the respondent opens the package as it was designed or whether the package design is faulty. Finally, being able to present the respondent with visual cues is one of the most attractive features of in-home personal surveys.

Quantity of Data. Because the effort required by the respondent is substantially less than in a mail survey and often less than in a telephone survey, the quantity of data that can be collected with an in-home personal survey exceeds that of either of the other two data-collection methods. Open-ended questions are recorded by the interviewer and responses to lengthy scales can be made easier by presenting the respondent with a card listing the various categories.

Sample Control. In principle, by applying probabilistic sampling designs, a very representative sample of the total population can be drawn, using homes as a basis for the sampling; specifically, with in-home personal surveys the researcher can control which households are interviewed, who within the household is interviewed, the degree to which other members of the household participate in the survey, and other aspects of the data-collection process. Unfortunately, although the potential exists for a high level of sample control, serious execution problems can break down this potential. First, with nearly half of all women employed outside the home it is increasingly difficult to find respondents home during the day. The interviewer must contact the household either on weekends or at night and will likely have to make several call-backs to those respondents who are not at home or who are unavailable. Second, sample control with in-home personal surveys is seriously jeopardized by the increasing reluctance of interviewers to venture into inner-city neighborhoods. Furthermore, increasing crime rates have made many people cautious about letting a stranger into their home or even opening the door to a stranger.

Quality of Data. Because the interviewer can directly observe the respondent, ensuring that instructions are properly understood and can monitor exposure to the test stimuli, in-home personal interviews can yield more in-depth responses and more complete data than can telephone interviews.[24]

On the other hand, because of interaction between the interviewer and the respondent, the respondent may be reluctant to accurately answer potentially embarrassing questions and give socially acceptable answers to sensitive questions.[25] The interviewer is a dominant force in personal surveys, and so potential for interviewer effects is greatest with this method of data collection. Interviewers can alter questions, change the sequence of questions asked, change the appearance of questions, and give intentional or unintentional cues by their tone of voice, vocabulary, and verbosity as well as through probing; in effect each respondent could

---

[24]See, for example, E. Telser, *ibid.*, T. F. Rogers, *op. cit.*

[25]J. Colombotos, "Personal vs. Telephone Interviews Effect Responses," *Public Health Report*, September 1969, 773–820.

receive a different survey instrument.[26] Some evidence suggests that depending on the survey topic, the interviewer's age, gender, race, social class, authority, or opinions, can affect the respondent's answers to the questions asked.[27] Finally, the interviewer can cheat—intentionally falsify all or part of the interview. All of these potential effects can be minimized with proper control and design. The best advice is to hire only the best-trained and experienced interviewers. Since some degree of interviewer bias is always likely to be present, methods have been developed to account for such effects by subjective and statistical adjustments.[28] To safeguard against interviewer cheating, the standard practice today is to validate the interviewer's work by reinterviewing a sample of the respondents and asking several of the original questions again as well as determining whether the interview actually took place and if it was conducted properly.

Response Rates. Response rates with personal interviewers exceed 80 percent:

$$\frac{\text{Response}}{\text{rate}} = \frac{\text{No. of complete interviews}}{\text{No. of complete} + \text{No. of} + \text{No. of}}$$
interviews   refusals   terminations

Higher response rates can be obtained with increased numbers of call-backs. Most personal surveys vary the call-back schedule by time of day and day of week. The larger proportion of women employed outside the home (necessitating call-backs) and high-crime areas can seriously affect response rates.

Speed. If the total sample can be judiciously split among several markets, and if interviews can be conducted in each market simultaneously, it is possible to complete a large study relatively quickly. In general, personal surveys can be completed faster than mail surveys, but probably not so fast as telephone surveys.

Cost. Compared with mail and telephone surveys, personal surveys are relatively expensive. As the need for call-backs increases, the cost of a personal survey can skyrocket, since the interviewer may have to make repeated visits to a distant urban neighborhood just to complete a single interview. For in-home personal surveys, the cost of data collection, excluding analysis and report generation per completed interview, can be as low as $5 to $10; however, the cost per completed interview can be in

[26] See M. Collins, "Interviewer Variability," *Journal of the Market Research Society*, 2(1980), 77–95.

[27] See P. B. Case, "How to Catch Interviewer Errors," *Journal of Advertising Research*, April 1971, 39–41; J. Freeman and E. W. Butler, "Some Sources of Interviewer Variance in Surveys," *Public Opinion Quarterly*, Spring 1976, 84–85; and B. Bailar, L. Bailey, and J. Stevens, "Measures of Interviewer Bias and Variance," *Journal of Marketing Research*, August 1977, 337–43.

[28] For details see D. S. Tull and L. E. Richards, "What Can Be Done About Interviewer Bias," in *Research in Marketing*, 3rd Edition, ed. J. Sheth (JAI Press, 1980) 143–62.

the $100s or even $1,000s depending upon the length of the interview and incidence of the sample group under study.

Uses. Historically, in-home personal interviews were used frequently because of the low incidence of telephone ownership and the nonexistence of shopping malls; in addition, they were almost exclusively used when visual cues or exhibits needed to be shown and in complex attitude and opinion studies. Today, the trend is to use mall intercept interviewing.

Mall-Intercept Interviewing

Mall-intercept personal survey Survey method using a central location test facility at a shopping mall; respondents are intercepted on a convenience basis while they are out shopping.

A **mall-intercept personal survey** involves a central location test facility at a shopping mall where respondents are intercepted while they are out shopping. This type of data-collection method is extremely popular and showed the largest budget-share increase in the 1978 to 1983 period. Underlying this interviewing method is the rationale that it's more efficient to have the respondent come to the interviewer than to have the interviewer go to the respondent. This method has been around for more than twenty years, dating back to the first enclosed shopping mall. Today, there are more than 325 permanent mall research facilities.[29]

Flexibility and Versatility. Because an interviewer is present, the mall-intercept personal survey has even more flexibility and versatility than in-home personal surveys. Greater flexibility and versatility with visual cues and exhibits is possible—be they concepts, products, packages, or advertisements. In addition, marketing or technical people can easily observe or interact with respondents.

Quantity of Data. In contrast to in-home personal interviews, interview time with mall intercepts is generally limited because respondents are usually hurried. For example, General Foods, a heavy user of mall-intercept surveys, typically keeps the interview time to twenty-five minutes or less.[30]

Sample Control. Usually the interviewer chooses which respondents will be intercepted, and the choice is limited to mall shoppers, creating two primary problems. First, frequent mall shoppers have a greater chance of being included in the sample; and in fact, the problem is complicated further because interviewing is often limited to Thursday, Friday, and Saturday shoppers. Second, a potential respondent can intentionally avoid or initiate contact with the interviewer. Furthermore, the demographics of shoppers can vary drastically from mall to mall. On the pos-

[29]*Market Research Association Research Services Directory.* (Chicago: Marketing Research Association, 1986).

[30]Al Ossip, "Mall Intercept Interviews," *Second Annual Advertising Research Foundation Research Quality Workshop* (New York: Advertising Research Foundation, 1984), 24.

itive side, however, easy access to respondents is a clear benefit of mall intercepts: The limitations of night work involved with in-home personal surveys don't apply. Weather is not a problem. And finally, it is easy to determine which family member is the respondent.

Quality of Data. The overall quality of data from mall intercepts appears to be equivalent to that of telephone interviewing in terms of the ability to provide complete and in-depth responses.[31] In addition, because of the opportunity to closely supervise the interviewing process, interviewer bias can be reduced. Finally, limited evidence suggests that mall-intercept interviewing yields more accurate or less distorted responses in comparison to telephone interviews.[32]

On the negative side, however, the unnatural testing environment of the shopping mall can potentially produce biased responses from respondents—particularly in food testing and advertising test studies. Another factor detracting from the overall quality of data collected with mall intercepts is what can be called "mall burnout." The same people might be repeatedly interviewed. Finally, since sometimes only one-third of the people intercepted agree to participate, the potential for selection bias is quite serious.[33]

Response Rates. Response rates in intercept surveys are generally comparable to those obtained in in-home personal interviews. The percentage of people contacted who refuse to participate typically varies between 10 and 30 percent, which is slightly lower than in telephone surveys.[34]

Speed. By employing several central mall facilities, even moderately large studies (say, 500 respondents) can be completed in a few days. Next to telephone surveys, mall-intercept surveys are fastest.

Cost. Mall intercepts generally cost less than in-home personal surveys. Prerecruiting respondents to a central location is relatively cheap, and only limited quantities of the visual cues or exhibits are needed since such materials can be used repeatedly.

Uses. Mall-intercept personal surveys are regularly used in concept tests, name tests, package tests, product tests, copy tests, and in some simulated test market studies. In general, the type of visual cues and exhibits will dictate whether a mall-intercept personal survey should be used.

[31]A. J. Bush and J. F. Haire, Jr., "An Assessment of the Mall Intercept as a Data Collection Method," *Journal of Marketing Research*, May 1985, 158–67.
[32]Bush and Haire, 165.
[33]Ossip, 25.
[34]Bush and Haire, 165.

NEWER TECHNOLOGICAL APPROACHES

The marketing research business is constantly responding to the explosion in computer technology. Sophisticated computer technology is being introduced and integrated into existing services to create more flexible, easier-to-use, and more accurate data-collection methods. Computer-assisted interviewing is fast becoming a dominant force in collecting data from respondents.

CATI Interviewing

Computer-assisted telephone interviewing (CATI) Survey systems involving a computerized survey instrument. The survey questionnaire is either entered into the memory of a large mainframe computer, into a small microprocessor, or even into a personal computer. The interviewer reads the questions from the CRT screen and records the respondent's answers directly into the computer memory banks by using the terminal keyboard or special touch- or light-sensitive screens.

A **computer-assisted telephone interviewing (CATI)** system involves a computerized survey instrument. The survey questionnaire is either entered into the memory of a large mainframe computer, into a smaller microprocessor or minicomputer, or even into a personal computer. The interviewer conducts the interview in front of a CRT terminal, which has a television-like screen and typewriter-like terminal keyboard. The interviewer reads the questions from the screen and records the respondent's answers directly into the computer memory banks by using the terminal keyboard or special touch- or light-sensitive screens. In addition, the CATI system can provide labor-saving functions such as automatic dialing.

Flexibility and Versatility. CATI systems allow "individualized" questionnaires to be used for each respondent; that is, the set of questions that each respondent receives depends upon the respondent's answers to earlier questions. Complex skip patterns are done automatically; in addition, question wording, format, and sequence can be easily changed and the order of response alternatives can be rotated at virtually no additional cost.

Quality of Data. Because the questionnaire is computerized, such problems as respondents skipping over questions, misunderstanding instructions, ignoring skip patterns, or giving contradictory responses to two or more questions are solved.

Speed. Data analysis and report generation can be carried on as the data are being collected. Because the data are entered directly into computer memory, interim reports can be produced daily and preliminary data analysis (for example, top-line reports) can be generated in a more timely fashion.

Self-Administered CRT Interviews

Self-administered CRT interview An interviewing method where the respondent sits at a computer terminal and answers the questionnaire by using keyboard and screen.

Another recent innovation in data-collection methodology is the on-site **self-administered CRT interview.** In principle, a CRT self-administered interviewing station can be set up anywhere there is electrical and telephone service. Typically, self-administered CRT interviews have been used to collect data at trade shows, professional conferences, product clinics, central interviewing locations, and shopping malls.[35] The computer configuration of the on-site location can vary. The site can be computerized using personal computers, with each PC supporting three or four CRTs. CRTs can be hard-wired directly to a microcomputer or minicomputer, or the CRTs can be linked directly through telecommunications equipment to a centrally-located mainframe computer.

Flexibility and Versatility. Like CATI systems, on-site self-administered CRT interviews afford greater flexibility and versatility in handling individualized questionnaires, question wording, format, and sequence, response alternative ordering, and complex skip patterns. On the negative side, however, open-ended questions can be a problem. Open-ended questions require that the respondent type in answers—in this case phrases or sentences. While respondents generally have no difficulty in entering numbers, some may have poor typing skills. This problem can be handled by either minimizing the number of open-ended questions; having the respondent be assisted by a host or hostess; having the respondent handwrite the open-ended answers; or having the open-ended responses tape-recorded.[36]

Sample Control. Self-administered CRT interviews provide automatic control over who is sampled. Because CRTs are linked, and predetermined sample quotas are stored in the memory system, each respondent can be checked to determine which quota group he or she belongs to and whether the interview should be administered; in addition, respondent randomization can be accomplished automatically.

Quality of Data. Because the interview is self-administered, no interviewer is needed and interviewer bias is not a problem. These interviews may induce respondents to answer sensitive or socially embarrassing questions, since they may feel less threatened by a machine; in addition, as with CATI systems, self-administered CRT interviews solve such problems as respondents skipping over questions, misunderstanding instructions, ignoring skip patterns, or giving contradictory responses to two or more questions. The computer will simply not allow a respondent to make these kinds of errors.

Speed. As with CATI systems, data are entered into computer memory directly by the respondent. Data analysis can proceed quickly, and interim reports can be generated daily.

---

[35] For prototypical applications see B. Whalen, "On-Site Computer Interviewing Yields Search Data Instantly," *Marketing News*, 9 November 1984, 1–17.

[36] J. E. Rafael, "Self-Administered CRT Interview: Benefits Far Outweigh the Problems," *Marketing News*, 9 November 1984, 16.

Costs. A reasonable estimate of data-collection costs for 300–600 respondents, excluding data analysis and report generation, ranges from $6 to $10 per interview for a syndicated study or $18 to $23 per interview for a customized, exclusive study.[37]

Summary

In this chapter we have introduced issues involved in collecting primary research information; our emphasis has been on interviewing methodologies and the advantage and problems inherent in each. Selecting the appropriate method of data collection is not easy; no single interviewing method provides data more accurate than all the others. The choice among interviewing survey methods depends on two issues: (1) suitability of the data-collection method in light of the objectives of the research study and (2) the feasibility (that is, cost, speed, quality of data) of the method. Some of the newer computer-assisted data-collection techniques manage to solve serious problems of traditional methods, and use of these methods will probably increase.

Key Concepts

Survey
Observational methods
Focus group interviews
Depth interviews
Projective techniques
Cold mail surveys
Mail panels

Telephone surveys
In-home personal interviews
Directory-based telephone interviewing
Nondirectory-based telephone interviewing
Mall-intercept surveys
CATI systems
Self-administered CRT systems

Review Questions

1. How can the moderator affect the quality of data from a focus group interview?
2. What factors would you consider when choosing among mail, telephone, personal, and mall intercept interviews?
3. What specific research objectives would lead you to use the new computer approaches to interviewing?
4. Discuss and contrast directory and nondirectory telephone sampling methods.

[37]Whalen, 17.

Experimental Research Methods

CHAPTER OBJECTIVES

- Understand the distinction between laboratory and field environments.
- Introduce the concepts of experimentation and causality.
- Explain the necessary and sufficient conditions for inferring cause-and-effect relationships and what is meant by spurious correlation.
- Define the basic concepts of experimentation: *experimental design*, *treatments*, *experimental effects*, and *extraneous causal factors*.
- Discuss the various types of validity.
- Examine the factors that can jeopardize internal and external validity.
- Explain specific experimental designs in the context of prototypical marketing research projects.

Introduction

Primary research is frequently conducted in an attempt to shed light on the *causal* relationships between the marketing-mix elements and various consumer responses. For example, do consumers view price as an indicator of quality? Does an aggressive couponing program lead to more sales? Questions like these involve *cause and effect* and, consequently, the concept of *experimentation*.

Like scientists, marketing executives and researchers are practicing experimenters; however, their laboratory is often the marketplace and their subjects human beings—making cause and effect relationships more difficult to assess.

Chapter 6 considers the role of experimentation in marketing research. We begin with a brief discussion of research environments. Next we examine causality and the conditions necessary for testing cause-and-effect relationships. We turn to a discussion of validity and the factors that can jeopardize internal and external validity. Our major emphasis is on the more frequently used experimental designs, those that marketing researchers employ regularly. Throughout the discussion, we describe the factors that can jeopardize the validity of our experiments.

Realistic research environment Situation similar to the normal situation in which the behavior under study would naturally occur.

Laboratory experimental environment Research environment constructed solely for the experiment. The experimenter has *direct control* over most, if not all, of the crucial factors that might possibly affect the experimental outcome.

Field experimental environments Natural settings; experiments undertaken in the environment in which the behavior under study would likely occur.

Independent variable A factor in an experiment over which the experimenter has some control; if the experimenter manipulates its value, this is expected to have some effect upon the dependent variable.

Dependent variable The response measure under study in an experiment whose value is determined by the independent variable.

Causality Relationship where a change in one variable produces a change in another variable. One variable affects, influences, or determines some other variable.

RESEARCH ENVIRONMENTS

Research environments can be classified by the degree to which they provide a realistic or artificial setting. In a **realistic research environment**, the respondent is placed in a situation similar to that in which the behavior under study would naturally occur.

Laboratory Experimental Environments

The **laboratory experimental environment** allows the experimenter to have direct control over most, if not all, of the crucial factors that might affect the experimental outcome. Experiments take place in environments constructed solely for that purpose. The setting is rigorously specified and controlled. Laboratory experiments are used extensively in concept testing, taste testing, package testing, advertising effectiveness studies, and simulated test markets, though the degree of control exercised varies with the specific nature of the research project.

Field Experimental Environment

A **field experimental environment** is a natural setting—the environment in which the behavior under study would likely occur. Control is still a factor in field experiments. In fact, as the situation permits, the marketing experimenter should impose as much control as possible over those factors that could influence the experimental outcome.

EXPERIMENTATION

An experiment entails some sort of test. The test should allow us to discern the effects of an independent variable on a dependent variable, controlling for extraneous factors that might influence the outcome. An **independent variable** is a variable that the researcher has some control over. It can be manipulated in that its value can be changed independently of other variables. The independent variable is generally assumed to be related in some way to the dependent variable under study. This is why independent variables are sometimes referred to as *explanatory variables*. The **dependent variable** is the response measure or criterion that is under study. Its value is presumed to be determined at least in part by the independent variable that has been manipulated. To better understand experimentation we need to become familiar with the concept of causality and with several basic aspects of experiments.

Causality

By **causality** we mean that a change in one variable produces a change in another variable or, in other words, that one variable affects,

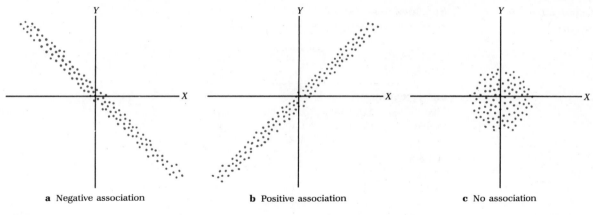

a Negative association   **b** Positive association   **c** No association

Figure 6-1

Patterns of association.

influences, or determines some other variable. We can rarely prove causality, since most effects have multiple causes. Hence, in attempting to establish causality, we must be particularly sensitive to competing explanations, to other extraneous variables that might have produced the observed cause-and-effect relationship. To infer causality requires three conditions: (1) concomitant variation, (2) time order of occurrence of variables, and (3) control over other possible causal factors.

Concomitant Variation. Without concomitant variation, causality cannot be proved or even inferred. Concomitant variation is the degree to which a variable X (for example, advertising expenditures) thought to be a cause covaries with a variable Y (for example, sales) thought to be an effect. Concomitant variation is another way of saying that two variables are associated. In Chapter 16 we present several different statistical measures used to compute the extent to which two variables are associated (that is, covary). For now, we will refer to association in a general way.

Consider, Figure 6-1, which shows three different patterns of covariation or association for two variables labeled X and Y, where X denotes the independent variable and Y denotes the dependent variable. In panel a the two variables X and Y are **negatively associated**—high values of X are associated with low values of Y. In panel b the two variables are **positively associated**—high values of X are associated with high values of Y. And in panel c the two variables exhibit no association—high values of X are associated with both high and low values of Y. The tendency is to say that the positive or negative association shown in panel a or panel b is evidence of causation between X and Y, whereas the lack of association shown in panel c is evidence of the lack of causation between X and Y.

Concomitant variation
The degree to which a variable (X) thought to be a cause covaries with a variable (y) thought to be an effect.

Negative association
Relationship where high (low) values of one variable are associated with low (high) values of another variable.

Positive association
Relationship where high (low) values of one variable are associated with high (low) values of another variable.

159

T A B L E 6-1

Spurious Association

Attitudes	Top-box intent score		Total
	No	Top-box	
a. Aggregate			
Like	116 (.18)	246 (.68)	362
Dislike	522 (.82)	116 (.32)	638
	638	362	1,000
b. User			
Like	60	240	300 (.80)
Dislike	15	60	75 (.20)
	75 (.20)	300 (.80)	375
c. Nonuser			
Like	56	6	62 (.10)
Dislike	507	56	563 (.90)
	563 (.90)	62 (.10)	625

Unfortunately, association by itself does not demonstrate causation. If two variables are causally related they must by necessity share association or covary, but the converse is not true. In fact, two variables can be associated because of a third variable that has not been accounted for. Consider the data shown in Table 6-1. The table gives hypothetical data on the relationship between top-box intent (percent definitely would buy) scores and respondent attitudes toward a new-product idea. One commonly accepted idea is that attitude change leads to behavior change and indeed in panel a we see a strong positive association between liking the product idea and top-box intent scores. Of the 362 respondents who indicated that they like the new product idea, 68 percent checked the top box on the purchase-intent scale; similarly, of the 638 respondents who indicated dislike, 82 percent also indicated that they would not likely purchase the product.

However, suppose that the marketing researcher suspects that the attitude-behavior relationship is actually influenced by another variable relating to whether the respondent has previously used items in this product category. The aggregate table is then split to form a prior-user panel b and a nonuser panel c. In the user group the chance of a respondent liking the new product idea is 80 percent (300/375); similarly, the likelihood of a respondent checking the top-box on the purchase intent scale is also 80 percent (300/375). On the other hand, in the nonuser group, the chances are 10 percent (62/625) in both cases. Thus, if we control for prior respondent use, we can "explain" the apparent cause-and-effect relationship between a respondent's attitude and purchase intentions. In trying to demonstrate cause-and-effect relationships, it is necessary to investigate whether some other variable is the source of the association.

In cases where a third variable is the actual cause of the observed association between other variables, we say that the original association was "spurious." **Spurious association** simply means an inappropriate causal interpretation of an observed association; it is not the association that is inappropriate, but rather the imputed cause-and-effect relationship.

Temporal Ordering of Variables. To say that a change in variable *A* produces a change in variable *B* requires that *A* occurs either before or simultaneously with *B* and not after it. This requirement is necessary to ensure the proper linkage between the cause and the effect events. A problem arises when two variables can legitimately be both a cause and an effect of each other. For example, increasing advertising budgets can lead to increases in sales volume, yet increases in sales volume can lead to increases in advertising expenditures, especially in cases where advertising budgets are a fixed percentage of sales. In any event, when demonstrating cause-and-effect relationships, be sure to justify the presumed causal time order among the respective variables.

Control over Other Possible Causal Factors. Even if we observe concomitant variation among two variables and can verify time order, causality is still questionable if the researcher has not searched for other factors that might have influenced the results. Cause-and-effect relationships must be inferred; therefore, to avoid misleading, and perhaps erroneous inferences, other competing explanations for the observed effect must be investigated.

Recall, for example, the role of marketing research in the decision to change the old Coke formula (Chapter 2). In discussing Coke, we briefly mentioned the Pepsi Challenge campaign. This campaign began in 1975 in the Dallas, Texas, market, where Pepsi-Cola had an 8 percent share of market compared with Coca-Cola's 27 percent share.[1] The Pepsi-Cola Company retained an independent research firm to conduct double-blind taste-tests, where cola drinkers tasted Coca-Cola and Pepsi-Cola without knowing which was which. The tests aimed to find out which taste cola consumers really preferred.

The results indicated that more than half the Coca-Cola drinkers tested actually preferred the taste of Pepsi. The research was translated into local television and print advertising and was called the Pepsi Challenge.

The Pepsi Challenge campaign was considered a success. In the Dallas area, for example, Pepsi's share of market increased 50 percent within a year after the Pepsi Challenge TV and local print campaign was launched. However, it is legitimate to ask whether there were other fac-

Spurious association
Inappropriate causal interpretation of an observed association.

---

[1]This material has been adapted from W. W. Talarzyk, *Cases For Analysis in Marketing* (Hinsdale, Ill.: The Dryden Press, 1977).

tors that might explain the apparent cause-and-effect relationship between Pepsi's increase in market share and the taste-test results as reported in the Pepsi Challenge campaign. Coca-Cola contended in a television commercial airing in the Dallas market that the blind taste-tests were misleading and inaccurate. Coke claimed that Pepsi was winning the taste tests only because respondents liked the letter "M" (the symbol for Pepsi) better than the letter "Q" (the symbol for Coke). Furthermore, price-cutting promotional activities conducted simultaneously by both Coke and Pepsi might have seriously confounded the taste-testing results. Our point is that although these alternative explanations for Pepsi's increased market share are conjecture, they nevertheless must be considered and controlled for in order to unequivocally substantiate the reasons for Pepsi's success occurring concurrently with the airing of the "challenge" campaign.

Each of the three conditions we have described is necessary but not sufficient for inferring causality. To appropriately infer causality requires that *all* three conditions be in place. Let's examine the difficulty of satisfying each of these conditions. Because many different types of variables covary, especially over time, concomitant variation is generally very easy to satisfy. Advertising expenditures and sales volume covary; top-box purchase-intent scores are associated with product-feature evaluations; favorable test-market results are related to the commercial success of a new product. The marketing researcher will find plenty of relationships; only the cause-and-effect inference is elusive.

In certain settings it is easy to say that *X* precedes *Y*, where in others it is almost impossible. Where the effect is measured after exposure to the cause agent, we can be sure of the time order of variables. Whenever the marketing researcher has control over exposing respondents to the cause agent (as in split-cable TV advertising effectiveness studies or a mall intercept), it is relatively easy to ensure that the cause variable precedes the presumed effect variable.

Because marketing-related effects can be produced by multiple factors, many difficult to control, the marketing researcher will typically find it difficult to present compelling evidence eliminating all other possible causal factors—unless the study is undertaken in rigorously specified, operationalized, and controlled settings.

Experimental Design and Treatment

Experimental design
Research concept where the researcher has direct control over at least one independent variable and manipulates at least one independent variable.

Nonexperimental designs/ex post facto Research that entails no manipulation. The effect outcome is observed and then an attempt is made to find the "causal factor" that indicates why the effect occurred.

In an **experimental design** the researcher has *direct* control over at least one independent variable and *manipulates* at least one independent variable. **Nonexperimental designs** entail no manipulation and are typically referred to as **ex post facto** ("after the fact") research, since the effect outcome is observed and then an attempt is made to find the "causal factor." An experimental design involves four elements: the treatment conditions that are to be manipulated, the respondents that are going to participate in the experiment, the dependent variable to be measured, and a procedure for handling extraneous causal factors.

A **treatment** refers to the independent variable that is manipulated. **Manipulation** means that the experimenter purposely sets the levels of an independent variable to test a specific cause-and-effect relationship. For example, to test the relationship between price and imputed quality the experimenter might expose respondents to four different price levels and record the quality ratings associated with each price level. In this case, price is the manipulated variable; a single treatment *factor*, price, has four treatment *conditions*, defined by the specific price levels used. Thus, the treatment conditions specify the manipulations under which the measurements on the dependent variable are taken.

Experimental Effects

The **experimental effect** denotes the impact of the treatment conditions on the dependent variable. We want to determine how each treatment condition influences the dependent variable; in other words, we want to determine the *effect* of each treatment condition.

To better understand the concept of an "effect" and how it might be computed, consider the following. Suppose that twenty respondents, who have agreed to participate in the experiment, are assigned to one of five treatment conditions, each reflecting a different advertising execution. In other words, there are four respondents per treatment condition and each treatment group is exposed to one of the five advertisements. The objective of the study is to measure the effects of the different advertising executions on aided 24-hour day-after recall scores. Aided 24-hour day-after recall scores could be collected by telephoning the respondents one day (24 hours) after exposure to the advertisement and asking whether they recall any features or aspects of what they saw—for example, brand name, price, or package design.

Let y_{ij} denote the 24-hour day-after recall score for the ith respondent who saw the jth treatment condition. Assume, for simplicity, that the 24-hour day-after recall has been coded so that the highest recall score is 10 and the lowest recall score is 0. Table 6-2 shows hypothetical data for each of the twenty respondents. The five different treatment conditions have been assigned the numbers 1 through 5. Notice that the table reveals a distinct ordering of the recall scores by treatment condition. Let $\bar{y}_{+j}$ denote the mean recall score in the jth treatment condition, where the "+" subscript indicates that we have summed over those respondents belonging to the jth treatment condition in computing the mean. From Table 6-2 we find that

$$\bar{y}_{+1} = (0 + 1 + 2 + 1)/4 = 4/4 = 1$$
$$\bar{y}_{+2} = (3 + 2 + 1 + 2)/4 = 8/4 = 2$$
$$\bar{y}_{+3} = (5 + 7 + 4 + 4)/4 = 20/4 = 5$$
$$\bar{y}_{+4} = (9 + 10 + 7 + 10)/4 = 36/4 = 9$$
$$\bar{y}_{+5} = (7 + 8 + 5 + 8)/4 = 28/4 = 7$$

TABLE 6-2

Hypothetical Data for an Advertising Experiment

				Treatments					
Ad1		Ad2		Ad3		Ad4		Ad5	
Person	Recall	Person	Recall	Person	Recall	Person	Recall	Person	Recall
1	0	1	3	1	5	1	9	1	7
2	1	2	2	2	7	2	10	2	8
3	2	3	1	3	4	3	7	3	5
4	1	4	2	4	4	4	10	4	8
Total (y_{++})	4		8		20		36		28
Average $(\bar{y}_{+j})$	1		2		5		9		7

Treatment conditions 4 and 5 produce much higher recall scores than treatment conditions 1 or 2. It seems that the variation in recall scores has something to do with which treatment condition a respondent saw. However, recall scores are not constant within a treatment condition; that is, not all respondents exposed to the same advertisement exhibit the same recall score. Each respondent would seem to have a unique reaction to the advertisement unshared by the other respondents who saw the same treatment condition. Based upon this line of reasoning, each respondent's recall score can be viewed in terms of three components: an overall mean, which does not depend on which advertisement the respondent saw; an estimated effect due to the particular advertisement that the respondent did see; and an error effect unique to each respondent. Some interesting insights follow. For example, the deviation of any respondent's recall score from the overall common mean is composed of two parts—namely, an estimated effect associated with the *j*th treatment condition and an estimated effect unique to the *i*th respondent.

The estimated effect of the *j*th treatment condition on a respondent's recall score can also be easily obtained by asking a simple question: Why should a respondent's score be higher or lower than the overall common mean? Well, one source of difference is due to the particular advertisement seen by the respondent. Thus, we can compare the treatment condition means with the overall common mean. We can say that the differences between the mean-treatment-condition recall scores and the overall-common-mean-recall score represents "explained" or "accounted for" variation, since we know that such differences exist because the treatment conditions have different effects on 24-hour day-after recall scores.

From the preceding discussion it also follows that the estimated error effect for the *i*th respondent in the *j*th treatment condition represents all of the effects on a respondent's recall score that are not due to or accounted for by the treatment condition seen by the respondent. In other words, we cannot explain why respondents who have seen the same advertising execution have different recall scores. In this sense, we can say that such differences are "unexplained" and due to the unique reactions of each respondent. For example, in Table 6-2 we see that respondent's recall scores in treatment condition 5 range from a low of 5 to a high of 8. This variation must be due to differences among the error components, since for respondents receiving the same advertising execution it must be that overall mean effect and the treatment effect are constants. What are the sources of error variation? Unique respondent effects, chance fluctuations in a respondent's behavior, extraneous factors—in short, all other effects not due to the treatment condition. These then constitute error effects whose size the researcher attempts to minimize using appropriate design and experimental controls.

Controlling Extraneous Causal Factors

Extraneous causal factors are those variables that can affect the dependent variable and therefore must be controlled. Such factors are typically referred to as **confounds** or **confounding variables** since, unless controlled for, they are confounded with the treatment conditions. They make it impossible to say that differences in the dependent variable are due to the different treatment conditions alone. For example, in the advertising execution/recall experiment of Table 6-2, it would have been incorrect to attribute higher recall scores to treatments 4 and 5 if we had found that respondents in these treatment conditions had greater brand familiarity than respondents who had been assigned to the other treatment groups.

There are four basic strategies for controlling extraneous factors: randomization, physical control, design control, and statistical control. All attempt to remove the differential effect of the extraneous causal variable across the various treatment conditions.

By randomizing respondents to treatment conditions one hopes that the extraneous causal factors will be equally represented in each treatment condition. Respondents can be randomly assigned to treatment conditions by using what are called *random numbers*. We can view the **randomization** process as being equivalent to pulling a respondent's name out of a hat and then assigning the respondent to one of the treatment conditions. We can "check" whether the randomization process worked by collecting measures on each possible causal factor and then examining the distribution of these extraneous variables across the treatment condition. The distribution of these extraneous variables should not be too different across the treatment conditions. In Chapter 15 we discuss different ways of statistically testing for group differences that can be used to perform a formal check on the randomization process.

Physical control involving possible causal factors means that we hold constant the value or level of the extraneous variable. For example,

Confounds or confounding variables Extraneous causal factors (variables) that can possibly affect the dependent variable and, therefore, must be controlled.

Randomization Process by which respondents are randomly assigned (e.g., pulling a respondent's name out of a hat) to treatment conditions for the purpose of controlling extraneous factors in an experimental setting.

Physical control An attempt to hold constant the value or level of the extraneous variable.

Matching Involves matching respondents on one or several background characteristics or other factors before assigning them to treatment conditions.

in our advertising execution/recall experiment the researcher could screen respondents for brand familiarity and sample only those with equivalent prior brand experience and usage behavior. Physical control often involves **matching** respondents. By matching we mean that respondents are matched on a set of background characteristics before being assigned to the treatment conditions. We discuss two different matching procedures later in this chapter.

Extraneous causal factors can also be controlled by using specific types of experimental designs. As we will see, several types of experimental designs are available; they differ according to the kinds of extraneous causal factors that they can control for. Later in the chapter we discuss several types of experimental designs.

Finally, extraneous causal factors can be statistically controlled for if the candidate causal variable can be identified and measured. Statistical control of a causal variable employs **analysis of covariance (ANCOVA).** ANCOVA removes the effects of the confounding variable on the dependent variable by a statistical adjustment of the dependent variable's mean value within each treatment condition. We will discuss ANCOVA in the appendix of Chapter 15.

Analysis of covariance (ANCOVA) A means of statistical control where the effects of the confounding variable on the dependent variable are removed by a statistical adjustment of the dependent variable's mean value within each treatment condition.

VALIDITY

There are two principal goals in conducting an experiment: (1) to draw valid conclusions about the effects of an independent variable and (2) to make valid generalizations to a larger population or setting of interest. We now discuss four types of validity.[2]

Statistical conclusion validity Involves drawing inferences about whether two variables covary.

- **Statistical conclusion validity** involves drawing valid inferences about whether two variables covary. Among other things, statistical conclusion validity considers the following issues: (1) Is the study sensitive enough to detect an effect of a desired magnitude? (2) Is there sufficient evidence to infer that the presumed cause and effect covary? (3) What is the strength of the covariation?

Internal validity Determination of whether the experimental manipulation actually produced the differences observed in the dependent variable.

- **Internal validity** examines whether the experimental manipulation (the treatment conditions) actually produces the differences observed in the dependent variable. In other words, internal validity focuses on evidence demonstrating that the variation in the dependent variable was the result of exposure to the treatment conditions rather than to other extraneous causal factors. Obviously, control is a key requisite in demonstrating internal validity and thus laboratory experimental settings offer greater internal validity than do field experimental settings.

[2]Our discussion of validity is based on the work of P. T. Campbell and S. T. Stanley, *Experimental and Quasi Experimental Design* for Research (Chicago: Rand McNally, 1963), and T. D. Cook and P. T. Campbell, Experimentation: Design Analysis Issues for Field Settings (Chicago: Rand McNally, 1979).

- **Construct validity** refers to whether the independent and dependent variables adequately represent the intended theoretical constructs.[3] Many of the measures that we collect supposedly tell us about concepts that cannot be measured directly. For example, we might use a simple five-point like-dislike rating scale to measure a respondent's attitude toward a brand. The respondent's attitude is not directly observable; it is a **latent theoretical construct.** However, we attempt to indirectly measure the attitude construct by using paper-and-pencil measures—five-point rating scales, for example. We generalize from our observable variables to the latent theoretical construct. And in essence, construct validity asks the question: To what extent do our variables represent the unmeasurable construct we are really interested in.

- **External validity** refers to whether the research findings of a study—cause-and-effect relationships—can be generalized to and across populations of persons, settings, and times.[4] In essence, external validity asks the question: To what extent do samples represent the population? Thus, because of their realism, field experimental settings offer greater external validity than do laboratory experimental settings.

This chapter will be primarily concerned with threats to internal and external validity. Chapter 15 will examine statistical conclusion validity; Chapters 9–11 will deal with measurement and related issues.

Construct validity
Determination of whether the independent and dependent variables in a study adequately represent the intended theoretical constructs. *Latent theoretical construct* Construct that is not directly observable.

External validity
Determination of whether the research findings of a study (cause-and-effect relationships) can be generalized to and across populations of persons, settings, and times.

FACTORS JEOPARDIZING VALIDITY

If not controlled for, extraneous factors pose threats that can jeopardize the internal and external validity of every experiment. To ensure that the experiment will not be confounded, the researcher must try to rule out all rival explanations that might produce differences in the dependent variable. Though this task is formidable, the following discussion of threats to valid inference making provides an excellent starting point.[5] Exhibit 6-1 offers a brief description of errors that can confound the results of an experiment.

EXHIBIT 6-1

Threats to Internal and External Validity

Internal

- History—events occuring simultaneously with the experiment
- Maturation—biological and/or psychological changes in respondents

---

[3]L. J. Cronbach and P. E. Meehl, "Construct Validity in Psychological Tests," *Psychological Bulletin*, no. 52, 1955, 281–302.
[4]Cook and Campbell, 38.
[5]Campbell and Stanley, 5–6; Cook and Campbell, Chapter 2.

- Testing—after-measurements taken on same subjects as before measures
- Instrumentation—changes in calibration of the measurement instruments
- Selection bias—improper assignment of respondents to treatment conditions
- Mortality—differential loss of respondents from treatment groups

External

- Reactive or interactive effects of testing—pre-exposure measurement sensitizes respondent to treatment
- Interactive effects of selection bias—improper (nonrandom) assignment of subjects to group results in different responses to treatment
- Surrogate situations—experimental setting (test units, treatment, or other elements) differs from real world

Threats to Internal Validity

As we discussed earlier, internal validity is concerned with whether the differences between treatment conditions are in fact due to the treatment conditions themselves, or whether rival hypotheses can explain the differences. We now turn to several common threats to internal validity.

History Threat to internal validity; refers to those specific events that occur simultaneously with the experiment, but that have not been controlled for.

History. History refers to those specific events that occur simultaneously with the experiment, but that have not been controlled for. Because these events occur at the same time as the experiment, they can affect the dependent variable and thus are confounded with the treatment conditions. For example, consider a "heavy-up" advertising program in which a greater-than-average amount of advertising money is allocated to a mature brand (say, for example, Bromo Seltzer), that is not currently being supported. The advertising program is launched in one or two test markets with sales monitored before and after the program launch. The difference between before-and-after sales levels is the assumed change due to the manipulated variable—the increased advertising expenditures. However, other factors related to competitor's attempts to "jam" the test (for example, trade promotions, couponing) that occur at the same time as the heavy-up advertising experiment could have produced (or nullified) the observed change in sales levels. In general, test markets are particularly vulnerable to historical factors because of the intentional jamming activities of competitors.[6] Or consider the effects of a feature news story about Bromo Seltzer aired nationally just after a pre- and post-advertising test is begun in several geographically dispersed markets. The news story could affect post-exposure rate levels. These effects are uncontrollable and are classified as history.

Maturation Threat to internal validity; refers to changes in biology or psychology of the respondent that occur over time and can affect the dependent variable irrespective of the treatment conditions.

Maturation. Maturation refers to changes in the biology (growing older, more experienced) or psychology (changes in beliefs, perceptions) of the

---

[6]N. Giges, "No Miracle in Small Miracle: Story Behind Failure," *Advertising Age*, August 16, 1982, 76.

respondent that occur over time and can affect the dependent variable irrespective of the treatment conditions. During the experiment respondents may become tired, bored, or hungry—influencing the response to the treatment condition. In general, tracking and market studies that span several months or years are particularly vulnerable to maturation factors, since there is no way to know how respondents might be changing over time. Also, maturation can be prevalent in experiments dealing with physiological responses, such as taste-testing studies.

Testing. Testing refers to the consequences of taking before- and after-exposure measurements on respondents. It occurs when the first measurement, before exposure to the treatment condition, affects the second measurement, taken after exposure to the treatment condition. Thus, the post-exposure measurement on the dependent variable is not due to the experimental treatment conditions alone but is a direct result of the respondent's pre-exposure measurement. For example, consider an advertising testing service in which respondents are prerecruited and asked to appear at a central testing location. These respondents are given a pre-treatment exposure questionnaire covering, among other things, attitudes and intentions to buy a certain brand, which the respondent is aware of but has never tried. After viewing an advertisement for the test brand they are again asked to fill out the questionnaire. Suppose that the experimenter finds no change when comparing pre- and post-exposure attitudes or intention-to-buy scores. The researcher might conclude that the advertising execution has had no effect. An alternative explanation is that respondents have sought to maintain consistency in their pre- and post-exposure measurement responses. Thus, what drove post-exposure measurement was not the experimental treatment condition but simply the respondent's pre-exposure responses. In general, testing effects occur because the respondent becomes expert at completing the measurement instrument, becomes annoyed at being asked to complete the same questionnaire twice, or becomes "frozen" in the sense of giving a consistent answer based on the initial questioning, and so on. If the respondent is not aware of being measured, then testing effects are unlikely to surface.

Instrumentation. Instrumentation refers to changes in the calibration of the measurement instrument or in the observers or scorers themselves. Instrumentation is most likely to occur when interviewers are used in a before-and-after exposure study. In such settings, interviewers may, with practice, acquire additional skills that make the second reading more precise. On the other hand, interviewers may become bored or tired, and by the time of the second measurement, their performance may have diminished and the recordings may have become less precise. Interviewer bias, discussed in Chapter 5, is an example of instrumentation.

Selection Bias. Selection bias refers to the improper assignment of respondents to treatment conditions. It occurs when selection assignment

Testing Threat to internal validity; refers to the consequences of taking before-and-after exposure measurements on respondents.

Instrumentation Threat to internal validity; refers to changes in the calibration of the measurement instrument or in the observers or scorers themselves.

Selection bias Threat to internal validity; refers to the improper assignments of respondents to treatment conditions.

169

results in treatment groups that differ on the dependent variable before their exposure to the treatment condition. In general, selection bias can occur if respondents are allowed to self-select their own treatment condition or if treatment conditions are assigned to groups. Consider a pricing study in which two price conditions are randomly assigned to various retail outlets. Because of size differences the experiment can become confounded. The problem is one of nonequivalence of groups. That is, store size affects sales levels irrespective of which price condition was assigned to a store.

Mortality Threat to
internal validity; refers to
the differential loss
(refusal to continue in the
experiment) of
respondents from the
treatment condition
groups.

Mortality. Mortality refers to the differential loss (that is, refusal to continue in the experiment) of respondents from the treatment condition groups. In general, experimental studies spanning a year or more, or even several months, are particularly vulnerable to mortality effects. This is a serious problem in purchase diary panel studies. In addition, mortality effects can surface in experiments where one (or more) of the treatment conditions is relatively undesirable. For example, the recent trend toward irregular-sized, shorter umbrellas has made it difficult to product-test normal-sized new-product versions because of their greater inconvenience. Over time, the treatment group with regular-sized umbrellas experiences some loss of respondents, and the respondents who do remain may be different from the other respondents participating in the experiment.

The threats to internal validity are not mutually exclusive. They can occur simultaneously and in certain instances can also interact with one another. For example, *selection-maturation-interaction* refers to the case where, perhaps because of self-selection, the treatment groups change with respect to the dependent variable at different rates over time.

Threats to External Validity

You will recall that external validity is concerned with generalizing research findings to and across populations of persons, settings, and times. Let's turn to several common threats to external validity.

Reactive or interactive
effects of testing Threat
to external validity that
occurs when a pre-
exposure measurement
increases or decreases the
respondent's sensitivity or
responsiveness to the
experimental treatment
conditions and thus leads
to unrepresentative
results.

Reactive or Interactive Effects of Testing. The reactive or interactive testing effect occurs when a pre-exposure measurement increases or decreases the respondent's sensitivity or responsiveness to the experimental treatment conditions and thus leads to unrepresentative results. In contrast to other testing effects with reactive or interactive testing effects, the pre-exposure measurement does not directly affect the post-exposure measurement; rather, the experimental treatment *condition* gains more notice and reactions than it would have if the pre-exposure measurement had not been taken. For example, in the advertising testing study the pretreatment exposure questionnaire could heighten respondents' interest, thus making them particularly sensitive to the advertising that they see. Reactive or interactive testing effects occur when the pre-

170

exposure measurement and the treatment conditions interact to produce a joint effect on the dependent variable.

Interactive Effects of Selection Bias. Interactive effects of selection bias is a situation that occurs when the improper selection of respondents interacts with experimental treatment conditions to produce misleading and unrepresentative results. Because of improper assignment of respondents to treatment conditions, some of the groups have a differential sensitivity or responsiveness to the experimental treatment conditions that cannot be generalized to the wider population.

Surrogate Situations. This threat to external validity occurs because of the use of experimental settings, test units, and/or treatment conditions that differ from those encountered in the actual setting the researcher is interested in. Surrogate situations produce ungeneralizable results. Consider the case where we are interested in measuring subjects' reactions to various advertisements—for example, the five ads used in the 24-hour day-after-recall experiment described earlier in this chapter. The subjects view the ads in a controlled environment and their attention to the ad is more or less forced as a result of the experimental procedure. We must ask ourselves if the ads will capture the same attention and subsequent information processing when viewed in a naturalistic setting. Recall scores could be lower or higher for all five treatment conditions simply due to the way people process the ad when it is aired outside the controlled laboratory setting.

Demand Artifacts

Demand artifacts are those aspects of the experiment that cause respondents to perceive, interpret, and act upon what is believed to be the expected or desired behavior.[7] Demand artifacts occur because human respondents do not respond passively to experimental situations. Suspicion about the purpose of the experiment, the respondent's prior experimental experience, and obtrusive pre- and post-measurements are just a few of the possible extraneous factors that can produce demand bias if these artifacts either increase the possibility that the respondent knows the true purpose of the experiment or if the artifacts influence the respondent's perceptions of appropriate behavior.[8]

Demand artifacts may have affected experimental studies investigating the quality connotations of price.[9] Early price-quality studies typically presented respondents with brands differentiated only by some letter

Interactive effects of selection bias Threat to external validity; situation where the improper selection of respondents interacts with experimental treatment conditions to produce misleading and unrepresentative results.

Surrogate situations Use of experimental settings, test units and/or treatment conditions that differ from those to be encountered in the actual setting that the researcher is interested in; threat to external validity.

Demand artifacts Those aspects of the experiment that cause respondents to perceive, interpret, and act upon what is believed to be the expected or desired behavior.

---

[7]A. G. Sawyer, "Demand Artifacts in Laboratory Experiments in Consumer Research," *Journal of Consumer Research*, March 1975, 20–30

[8]See, for example, R. Rosenthal and R. L. Rosnow, *Artifacts in Behavioral Research* (New York: Academic Press, 1969); and R. L. Rosnow and L. S. Aiken, "Mediation of Artifacts in Behavioral Research," *Journal of Experimental Social Psychology*, May 1973, 181–201.

[9]Sawyer, 21.

identification and the relative price (the brands were exactly the same) and found that respondents usually would choose the high-priced brand.[10] Respondents may have correctly guessed the purpose of the study and hypothesized that the experimenter expected them to choose higher-priced brands primarily for products which differ in quality.

Demand artifacts pose serious threats to both internal and external validity. They can confound the internal validity of an experiment when they interact with the experimental treatment conditions to produce misleading results. They also affect generalization of the findings since it is very unlikely that the same set of demand characteristics operating in a laboratory setting will characterize a real-life situation.

EXPERIMENTAL DESIGNS

Many different experimental designs are available—so many that it would be unrealistic to try to provide a complete and comprehensive treatment in one chapter. Our strategy is to introduce specific experimental designs frequently employed in marketing research studies and to provide examples of how they are used. These designs vary in the degree to which they control for extraneous factors that can jeopardize both internal and external validity. Before discussing specific experimental designs, let's look at the notation used to describe the various designs.

Notation

When discussing specific experimental designs, we use symbols that describe how each works.

- *RR* indicates that respondents have been randomly assigned to treatment conditions.
- *RM* indicates that respondents assigned to different treatment conditions have been matched on a set of characteristics.
- *EG* refers to the experiment group—that is, one of the treatment conditions.
- *CG* refers to the control group—the group that is not exposed to the experimental treatment.
- *X* represents the exposure of a group of respondents to one of the experiment treatment conditions.
- *O* refers to the observation or measurement of the dependent variable for each respondent.

In delineating each design we array symbols horizontally and vertically. A horizontal string of symbols indicates movement through time and refers to a specific treatment group. A vertical string of symbols indicates

---

[10]See, J. D. McConnell, "The Price-Quality Relationship in an Experimental Setting," *Journal of Marketing Research*, 5 August, 1968, 300–303.

events or activities that occur simultaneously. Subscripts delineate one treatment condition from another and denote order in the measurements.

To clarify how the symbolic scheme is used, let's use these symbols to describe five types of experimental designs.

1. *After-only design*—A single group is studied only once.
    EG: $X \quad O_1$
2. *One-group before-after design*—A single group is studied twice, once before exposure to the experimental treatment and once after exposure.
    EG: $O_1 \quad X \quad O_2$
3. *After-only with control design*—Two groups are studied; one group is exposed to the experimental treatment, one group is not.
    EG: $X \quad O_1$
    CG: $\quad\quad O_2$
4. *Before-after with control group design*—two groups are studied twice, with before-and-after exposure to the experimental treatment. In one case, they are studied under a random assignment rule, and in the other case under matched samples.
    Case 1 EG: $RR \quad O_1 \quad X_1 \quad O_2$
    　　　　 CG: $RR \quad O_3 \quad\quad\quad O_4$
    Case 2 EG: $RM \quad O_1 \quad X_2 \quad O_2$
    　　　　 CG: $RM \quad O_3 \quad\quad\quad O_4$
    Note that the subscripts on the X symbol simply indicate that one treatment, X_2, may differ from the other, X_1.
5. *Time series design*—A single group is studied over time, before and after exposure to the experimental treatment.
    EG: $O_1 \quad O_2 \quad O_3 \quad X \quad O_4 \quad O_5 \quad O_6$

Specific Experimental Designs

We now examine and illustrate some experimental designs frequently employed in marketing research. We emphasize the nonstatistical aspects of each design, how it is actually used in real-life marketing settings, and the extent to which it controls for extraneous factors. The testing of treatment effects for statistical significance will be treated in Chapter 15, which discusses *analysis-of-variance* (ANOVA) models.

After-Only Design. This design exposes respondents to a single treatment condition and follows it with a post-exposure measurement. Exhibit 6-2 presents an abridged marketing research proposal that describes an after-only design involving Burkes' Marketing Research Service 24-Hour Day-After Recall *(DAR)*. The design calls for telephoning 200 respondents who claim to have watched a particular TV show the night before in any of thirty-four cities. Respondents are asked both unaided and aided recall questions. First, respondents are asked if they remember

After-only design
Experiment that exposes respondents to a single treatment condition followed by a post-exposure measurement.

173

seeing a commercial for a product in the product category of interest (**unaided recall**). If they can recall, then they are asked what specific copy execution points of the advertisement they remember. If the commercial remembered is not for the test brand, then the respondent is asked whether he or she recalls the commercial for the brand being tested (**aided recall**). All results are compared to Burke category norm scores and are indexed for easier interpretation. The following example summarizes this design endeavor.

EXAMPLE

EG:	X	O
Respondents who claim to have watched a specific TV show the night before	Test market advertisement	Unaided, aided recall of specific copy points

---

EXHIBIT 6-2

Marketing Research Proposal: After-Only Design

Brand:	Brand Z hair conditioner
Project:	Day-after recall (DAR) study
Background & Objectives:	The brand group has developed a TV advertisement introducing Brand Z. The objective of this research is to evaluate this copy in a real-life setting.
Research Method:	A minimum of 200 respondents who claim to have watched a particular TV show the night before will be contacted by telephone in any of 34 cities.
Information to be Obtained:	This study will provide information on the incidence of unaided and aided recall along with specific information on which copy execution points were remembered.
Action Standard:	In order to be judged successful the percentage of unaided and aided recall scores must be significantly above category norms at the 80 percent confidence level.
Supplier:	Burke Marketing Research Service

Table 6-3 shows hypothetical results. Since this design lacks control over extraneous factors that could bias the results, product-category norms must be used in evaluation. In other words, this design so exten-

174

T A B L E 6-3

Unaided and Aided DAR Scores

	Recall	Index (relative to norm)
Unaided (% of time test ad is named)	27*	90
Norm	30	100
Aided (% of time test ad is named after prompting)	42*	111
Norm	38	100

*Not significantly different from the norm at the 80 percent confidence level.

sively lacks control that it is useless for inferring causality. However, the design does help assess whether or not the test advertisement produces recall scores that are significantly above (or below) category norms. To be statistically significant at the 80 percent confidence level we need percentage differences between actual and norm percentage scores of about 6–7 percentage points (see Chapter 15).

Before-After Design. In this design, a measurement is taken from respondents before they receive the experimental treatment condition. After the treatment a post-exposure measurement is taken. The treatment effect *(T.E.)* is computed by taking $O_2 - O_1$. However, to safely conclude that X and X alone produced the observed $O_2 - O_1$ effect, we must verify that no other possible extraneous factors could have produced the observed result.

Exhibit 6-3 is an abridged marketing research proposal that describes a before-after design involving McCollum-Spielman's Advertising Control for Television *(AC-T)* service. The following example summarizes this design.

Before-after design
Experiment where a measurement is taken from respondents before they receive the experimental treatment condition; the experimental treatment is then introduced, and post-treatment measure is taken.

E X H I B I T 6-3

Marketing Research Proposal: Before-After Design

Brand: Branded women's hair shampoo

Project: Advertising Control For Television (AC-T) study

Background & Objectives: The brand group has developed a new advertising campaign for branded women's hair shampoo. The objective of this research is to evaluate the effectiveness of a TV advertisement that portrays the brand's new image.

Research Method:	A minimum of 150 respondents will be recruited to central theater locations in four test cities. At the central testing location respondents are first given a personal interview. Then they view a TV show in which the test advertisement is embedded twice. After viewing they are again given a personal interview.
Information To Be Obtained:	This study will provide information on brand attitude, image, and purchase-intent change scores as well as overall reaction to the test commercial and recall scores.
Action Standard:	All results are compared to category norms at the 80 percent confidence level.
Supplier:	McCollum/Spielman

E X A M P L E

EG: O_1	X	O_2
Recruited respondents are given a questionnaire covering attitudes, images, and intention measures	Test advertisement	Respondents are again given a questionnaire covering attitudes, images, and intention measures as well as overall reaction to the test advertisement.

Table 6-4 presents hypothetical results. The test advertisement appears to have had substantial effects on before-after image and purchase-intent ratings. The principal extraneous factors that could have caused the observed before-after treatment effects appear to be testing, instrumentation, and interactive effects of testing. Moreover, the artificiality of the test environment (surrogate situation—TV program viewing in a theater) might also adversely affect the external validity of the study.

Before-after with control design Experiment that adds a control group to the basic before-after design; the control group is never exposed to the experimental treatment.

Before-After with Control Design. This design adds a control group to the basic before-after design just discussed. Respondents are assigned randomly to one of the treatment conditions or to the control group. Random assignment is an important characteristic of this design, which entails the standard before-after exposure measurement in the experimental treatment groups and an analogous before-and-after measurement in the control group, which is never exposed to the experimental treatment. The treatment effect is computed by taking

$$T.E. = (O_2 - O_1) - (O_4 - O_3)$$

176

TABLE 6-4
AC-T Test Results

	Norm		Test Advertisement	
	Percent change before-after	Index	Percent change before-after	Index relative to norm
Overall brand attitude				
Liked extremely	10	100	9	90
Brand image				
Strong agreement with:				
For today's woman	5	100	11	220
Gives hair body	7	100	12	171
Makes hair silky	7	100	13	186
Protection against dryness	8	100	5	63
For all kinds of hair	9	100	4	44
Purchase intention				
Extremely likely to buy	12	100	15	125

The difference ($O_2 - O_1$) reflects the effect obtained by using a before-after design. We are, in effect, adjusting the standard before-after treatment effect ($O_2 - O_1$) by the effect that would have been obtained without the experimental treatment ($O_4 - O_3$).

Exhibit 6-4 presents an abridged marketing research proposal that describes this type of design involving a dollar-off promotional program for a brand currently unsupported by promotional dollars. The following example summarizes this design.

E X H I B I T 6-4

Marketing Research Proposal: Before-After with Control

Brand:	Brand A mouthwash
Project:	Dollar-off promotional study
Background & Objectives:	The marketing management team has proposed a dollar-off promotional study for Brand A, a brand not currently supported. The object of this research is to assess the likely impact that such a program will have.
Research Method:	The Buffalo, N.Y., area was selected as the test market. A total of 30 retail outlets participated in the study. Stores were randomly assigned to an experimental treatment group (dollar-off promotion) and to the control group (no promotion).

Information To Be Obtained:	This study will provide information on before-and-after share of market.
Action Standard:	To be judged successful the promotional campaign should produce at least a 1.0 percent change in share of market.
Supplier:	Market Facts, Inc.

E X A M P L E

EG:	**RR**	O_1	X	O_2
	15 outlets randomly assigned	Share of market, week ending 11/17	Dollar-off promotion, week of 11/18	Share of market, week ending 11/24
CG:	**RR**	O_3		O_4
	15 outlets randomly assigned	Share of market, week ending 11/17		Share of market, week ending 11/24

Hypothetical results in terms of market share for the experimental and control groups are

- Before week ending 11/7—5.3 (experimental); 5.4 (control)
- After week ending 11/24—6.8 (experimental); 5.6 (control)

Note that with only a before-after design the estimated effect of the dollar-off promotional program would have been calculated to be 1.5 share points (6.8 − 5.3). However, it is necessary to adjust this effect by what would have been gained without the dollar-off promotional program. Hence, the true treatment effect is calculated to be

$$T.E. = (6.8 − 5.3) − (5.6 − 5.4)$$

or 1.3 share of market points, which exceeds the action standard requirement.

In general, before-after with control group designs control for all possible extraneous factors except mortality and the interactive effects of testing. History, maturation, and instrumentation should affect the treatment and control groups equally. Testing effects are also controlled for. Since both groups receive the pre-exposure measurement, any effect it has on the post-exposure measures should be the same regardless of treatment group. The effect of pre-exposure measurement can interact with the experimental treatment to affect the post-exposure measurement. In this application, however, interactive testing *effects* are unlikely, since the dependent variable is share of market, obviously measured unobtrusively via sales records.

After-Only with Control Design. In this design a control group is added to the standard after-only design to remove extraneous sources of bias. Respondents are randomly assigned to the treatment and control groups. Typically, in real-life applications respondents are also matched on one or a set of background characteristics. Without a pretest there is no way to assess whether the treatment and control groups are equivalent. The treatment effect is computed by taking the difference, $O_1 - O_2$.

Exhibit 6-5 is an abridged marketing research proposal that describes an after-only with control group design involving a two-cell monadic concept test. (In a monadic test the respondent rates the item in question on a scale without reference to other comparison items.) The following summarizes this design.

After-only with control design Experiment where a control group is added to the standard after-only design to control for extraneous sources of bias.

EXHIBIT 6-5

Marketing Research Proposal: After-Only with Control

Service:	Checking-account fee schedule
Project:	Two-cell monadic concept test
Background & Objectives:	The vice-president of a regional commercial bank must decide whether to initiate a new checking-account fee schedule. The new alternative considered is a variable .15 cents per-check-used fee schedule. The current program is a fixed $5.50-per-month fee schedule.
Research Method:	A two-cell monadic after-only concept test was selected. The design calls for 200 bank customers per cell with matched random assignment. Respondents will be matched on checking account balance and average number of checks used per month. Data collection will take place at four regional branches located in major shopping malls geographically dispersed within the state. Thus there are 50 respondents in each of the two cells in each of the four data collection cities. After being randomly assigned to one of the treatment groups, respondents are shown a concept board that describes one of the two checking-account fee schedules.
Information To Be Obtained:	The study will provide information on overall opinions, and purchase-intent scores, and account characteristics.
Action Standard:	To be judged superior, the following should hold: (1) the percentage of respondents checking top-box opinion ("excellent")

for one of the checking account fee schedules should exceed the other by at least 10 percentage points; (2) top-box purchase-intent scores in the experimental group should exceed 55 percent. If criteria 1 and 2 are both realized then the decision will rest on criterion 2.

Supplier: Market Facts, Inc.

EXAMPLE

EG: RRM	**X**	**O_1**
Respondents are matched and randomly assigned	15 cents per check condition	Overall opinion and purchase-intent scores
CG: RRM		**O_2**
Respondents are matched and randomly assigned	Fixed monthly fee of $5.50	Overall opinion

---

Note that we have introduced some new notation. The symbol RRM indicates that respondents have been matched and then randomly assigned to one of the two treatment groups. As we indicated, in this application there is no control group per se, but rather the current fee-schedule program acts as the control group.

Table 6-5 presents hypothetical results as the percentage of respondents who checked top-box opinion ("excellent"), and top-box purchase-

TABLE 6-5
Opinion and Purchase Intention Results

Location	Treatment composition	Excellent	Most definitely would use
A	$0.15/check	38	8
	$5.50/month	62	
B	$0.15/check	42	16
	$5.50/month	60	
C	$0.15/check	40	14
	$5.50/month	64	
D	$0.15/check	44	20
	$5.50/month	58	
Overall	$0.15/check	41	17
	$5.50/month	61	

intent (most definitely would use). It is clear from the table that the fixed $5.50 monthly fee schedule had greater appeal than the alternative 15 cents per-check-used fee schedule and exceeds the action standards.

In general, after-only with control designs do control for selection bias. Respondent matching coupled with random assignment can lead to certain efficiencies with respect to the estimation of treatment and error effects. Finally, since there is no pre-exposure measurement, this design also eliminates the possibility of interactive testing effects.

Nonequivalent Before-After with Control Quasi Design. This design is similar to the before-after with control design but does not use a random assignment rule; thus, we will use the term *quasi* when referring to experimental designs where the researcher is unable to achieve complete control over the scheduling of the treatments or cannot randomly assign respondents to experimental treatment conditions. *Quasi-experimental designs* are frequently used in marketing research studies simply because cost and field considerations often prohibit direct control over randomization of respondents or the scheduling of treatments. However, in the absence of such controls, the chance of obtaining confounded results is greatly increased and the marketing researcher must recognize what specific factors have not been controlled for and, wherever possible, incorporate their effects into the interpretation of the research finding.[11]

The quasi before-after with control design can be symbolically represented as

> EG: RM O_1 X O_2
> CG: RM O_3 O_4

Once again we have a standard before-after exposure measurement in the experimental treatment group and an analogous before-and-after measurement in the control group, which is never actually exposed to the experimental treatment. In this case, however, respondents are not randomly assigned to treatment and control groups. Instead, respondents are first matched on one or a set of relevant background factors to produce two groups of matched pairs and then a decision is made as to which respondent group will receive which condition, either experimental treatment or control. Thus, treatments are randomly assigned to groups as opposed to randomly assigning each member of a matched pair to a treatment. Figure 6-2 illustrates the difference.

Exhibit 6-6 presents an abridged marketing research proposal that describes a quasi before-after with control design involving a *heavy-up* advertising program for a branded antacid product not currently supported—that is, the brand's advertising budget has been held relatively

Nonequivalent before-after with control quasi design Experimental design similar to the before-after with control design except not utilizing a random assignment rule. Respondents are first matched on one or a set of relevant background factors to produce two groups of matched pairs and then one group receives experimental treatment.

Quasi-experimental designs Experimental designs in which the researcher is unable to achieve complete control over the scheduling of the treatments or cannot randomly assign respondents to experimental treatment conditions.

[11]For a comprehensive discussion of quasi-experimental designs see Cook and Campbell.

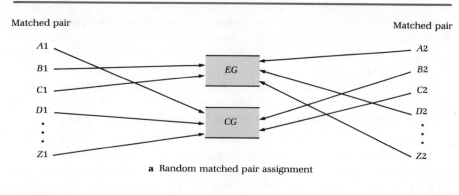

a Random matched pair assignment

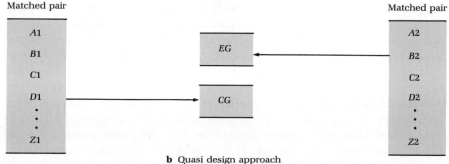

b Quasi design approach

Figure 6-2

Random material pair assignment versus quasi design approach.

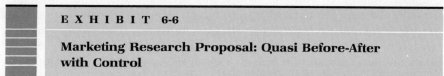

E X H I B I T 6-6

Marketing Research Proposal: Quasi Before-After with Control

Brand:	Branded antacid (mature product)
Project:	Heavy-up advertising tracking study
Background & *Objectives:*	The brand group has decided to investigate the potential impact of a heavy-up advertising program for a mature branded antacid product that has not been supported with promotional programs. The objective of the study was to measure changes in brand awareness, usage, and perceptions resulting from the advertising program.
Research *Method:*	The decision was to create a spending program in a definable test-market area. The Buffalo area was selected as the test market with a matched control market consisting of the Albany, Schenectady, and Troy areas. Matched samples of 400 antacid

182

users were contacted by telephone and measured with respect to brand awareness, usage, and perceptions before and three months after the advertising program began.

Information To Be Obtained: The study will provide information on before-and-after brand awareness, usage, and perceptions.

Action Standard: A necessary condition for management to recommend a national heavy-up advertising program for this brand is a test-market increase of at least 6.0 percent in the size of the group of people who have "ever" tried the test brand. Final decision rests on the perception and awareness results.

Supplier: Market Facts, Inc.

---

constant and has not been increased above maintenance-level expenditures. The following example summarized this design.

E X A M P L E

EG: RM	*O_1*	*X*	*O_2*
Matched sample of 400 users identified in the Buffalo, N.Y., test market	Measures of: brand awareness, brand usage (trial/most often used); perceptions of gentleness, efficacy	Translated heavy-up advertising program begins	3 months later—measures of: brand awareness, brand usage (trial/most often used); perceptions of gentleness, efficacy
CG: RM	*O_3*		*O_4*
Matched sample of 400 users identified in the Albany, Schenectady, and Troy, N.Y., control market	Measures of: brand awareness, brand usage (trial/most often used); perceptions of gentleness, efficacy		3 months later—measures of: brand awareness, brand usage (trial most often used); perceptions of gentleness, efficacy

---

Table 6-6 presents hypothetical results in terms of before-and-after brand awareness, trial, and perceived gentleness and efficacy for the test

183

TABLE 6-6

Results of the Tracking Study

	Test market Buffalo (%)	Control market Albany/Schenectady/Troy(%)
Before		
Aware of product	65	65
Ever tried	12.1	11.9
Respondents indicating product is		
gentle	35	36
efficacy	55	53
After		
Aware of products	66	65
Ever tried	18.7	12.0
Respondents indicating product is		
gentle	46	37
efficacy	56	54

and control markets. From the table we can calculate the treatment effects in the same way as with the standard before-after with control design. Hence, we calculate the effects to be

Awareness: $T.E. = (66 - 65) - (65 - 65) = 1.0$
Trial: $T.E. = (18.7 - 12.1) - (12.0 - 11.9) = 6.5$
Gentleness: $T.E. = (46 - 35) - (37 - 36) = 10.0$
Efficacy: $T.E. = (56 - 55) - (54 - 53) = 0.0$

It appears that though the heavy-up advertising program has not affected brand awareness, it has increased trial use by 6.5 percent, which exceeds the action standard requirement. Also, the advertising campaign appears to have increased the perception that this brand of antacid is gentle while preserving the perception of its effectiveness. Of course, the crucial questions about this interpretation is whether it is correct to attribute these results to the heavy-up advertising program alone. Though this application called for matched samples of respondents and matched test and control markets, a random assignment rule was not used; that is, members (respondents) of each matched pair were not randomly assigned to the experimental test and control groups, and thus we cannot be absolutely sure that the advertising program alone produced these results. The problem is that it is never possible to match respondents in test and control markets exactly.[12] There is always the chance that the experimental test and control groups are nonequivalent, that their pre-exposure measurement on the dependent variable(s) is significantly different. In general, the more similar the pre-exposure measurements, the more we can feel comfortable in asserting that the two groups are equiv-

[12]Electronic test markets (e.g., BehaviorScan) make an attempt to overcome this problem.

alent and the more effective is this design. In the present application, the two groups were matched and recruited similarly; thus, it is not surprising to note the similarity in the pre-exposure brand awareness, usage, and perception scores. Note, however, that this design does not generally control for interactive testing effects or interactive effects of selection bias, both of which can seriously confound the results.

Two-Factor After-Only with Control Design. This design differs from the previously discussed after-only with control group designs in having more than a single treatment—that is, the researcher manipulates more than one independent variable. Additional treatment factors are incorporated into a design so that the researcher can control for the interaction of the various treatment factors. With more than a single treatment, the number of cells in the study equals the number of possible combinations of treatment factors. For instance, with two treatment factors, each having three levels, there are nine (3 × 3) possible combinations or cells. Recall that by treatment factor we mean an independent variable that the researcher has manipulated (for example, price); by treatment level we mean the particular conditions or values of the independent variable that are of interest (for example, in the case of price, $1.00, $1.25, and $1.50 per unit). In such designs respondents are typically randomly assigned to the various experimental cells, though a matching procedure could also be used. Symbolically, a two-factor after-only (with control) design with six cells (2 × 3), two levels of treatment 1 and three levels of treatment 2 can be represented as

$$
\begin{array}{ccc}
 & X_{1a}X_{2a} & O_1 \\
 & X_{1a}X_{2b} & O_2 \\
 & X_{1a}X_{2c} & O_3 \\
EG: \quad RR & X_{1b}X_{2a} & O_4 \\
 & X_{1b}X_{2b} & O_5 \\
 & X_{1b}X_{2c} & O_6 \\
\end{array}
$$

Because each level of treatment 1 (X_{1a}, X_{1b}) is crossed with each level of treatment 2 (X_{2a}, X_{2b}, and X_{2c}), the (statistical) generic name for this class of designs is **completely randomized factorial designs.** In general, factorial designs allow us to estimate the respective effects of each treatment condition alone—commonly referred to as *main effects*—as well as joint effects of the two (or more) treatments—commonly referred to as *interaction* effects. Two treatments are said to interact if differences in the dependent variable under the level of one treatment are different at two or more levels of the other treatment. Note also that typically one level of each treatment represents the control condition, which provides a basis for comparing the individual effect estimates.

Exhibit 6-7 presents an abridged marketing research proposal that describes a two-factor, six-cell (3 × 2) after-only with control design involving a package and pricing test study for a mature woman's facial moisturizer. Figure 6-3 summarizes this design. Note that the control condition is the cream color package, priced at $6.29.

Two-factor after-only with control design Experiment differing from the after-only with control group designs by having more than one independent variable.

Completely randomized factorial designs Generic name for class of designs where each level of a particular treatment is crossed with each level of another treatment.

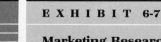

EXHIBIT 6-7

Marketing Research Proposal: Two-Factor After Only with Control

Brand: Womens' facial moisturizer

Project: Package/pricing test study

*Background &   The beauty-aid brand group is considering replacing the cur-
Objective:*   rent package design for a mature women's facial moisturizer. In
                        conjunction with a possible change in package, the brand
                        group is also considering pursuing a premium pricing strategy.
                        Two alternative packages (green and yellow) have been devel-
                        oped to possibly replace the current cream color package. The
                        alternative pricing structure being considered is to retail a 6-
                        ounce container for $6.79 as compared to the current price of
                        $6.29. The objective of the study is to assess consumer reactions
                        to the alternative package and price strategies in terms of visi-
                        bility, consumer perceptions of product end-benefits and pur-
                        chase intentions.

*Research   Three alternative packages (cream and green and yellow) and
Methods:*   two alternative prices ($6.29 and proposed $6.79) will be evalu-
                        ated monadically in central-location shopping centers in Des
                        Moines, Iowa, and Minneapolis, Minnesota. Each combination
                        of package and price alternatives will be viewed among 300 fe-
                        male facial-moisturizer users aged 18–64. Age quotas will be es-
                        tablished in each of six package–price cell combinations as fol-
                        lows:

Age	Percent
18–24	27
25–34	25
35–49	35
50–64	13

Fifty respondents will be randomly assigned to each of the six
cells according to these age quotas. In order to determine consumers' reactions to each alternative package-price combination, respondents in each cell will be exposed to a slide containing the package and price variation and competitive leading
brands. The test brand is shown in three positions within each
cell to control position order bias. Each slide is shown for one
second and then respondents are asked to recall the brands
they have seen. After this questioning the test brand is shown
again for a prolonged period, and respondents are questioned
about purchase likelihood and product imagery. After-exposure
reading is then taken.

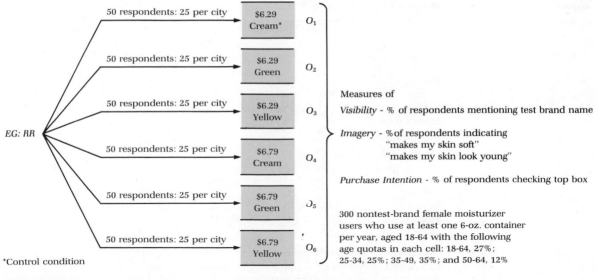

Figure 6-3

Design for two-factor after-only experiment, with control.

Information To Be Obtained:	Information on visibility (percent of respondents mentioning test-brand name after one-second exposure), package imagery (percent of respondents indicating that test brand makes their skin soft and young-looking), and purchase intentions.
Action Standard:	A recommendation to replace the current package with either of the two new designs (green or yellow) will be made if the following conditions are met: (1) one of the new designs must be found to be more visible (at the 80 percent confidence level or higher) than the current design; and (2) the new design that generates greater visibility must also produce higher ratings (80 percent confidence level or higher) on the "keeps skin soft" and "keeps skin younger-looking" attributes.
	A decision to change the price from $6.29 to $6.79 per 6-ounce container will be made if there are no significant differences (at the 80 percent confidence level or higher) between the respective top-box purchase-intent scores.
Supplier:	Burke Marketing Research.

Table 6-7 shows hypothetical results in terms of visibility, brand imagery, and top-box purchase-intent scores. The elements in the table give percentages for each cell in the design computed across the two cities. Also shown in the table are the "total" percentages computed for the package and price treatment factors separately—that is, the total per-

TABLE 6-7

Results of the Package/Price Study

a. Visibility

Package design	$6.29	$6.79	Color totals*
Cream	25	26	25.5
Green	38	39	38.5
Yellow	30	31	30.5
Price totals	31	32	

b. Imagery
"Makes My Skin Soft"

Package design	$6.29	$6.79	Color totals
Cream	39	41	40
Green	33	58	45.5
Yellow	35	31	33
Price totals	35.7	43.3	

"Makes My Skin Look Young"

Package design	$6.29	$6.79	Color totals
Cream	36	38	37
Green	35	63	49
Yellow	38	40	39
Price totals	36.3	47	

c. Purchase Intention

Package design	$6.29	$6.79	Color totals
Cream	55	40	47.5
Green	58	62	60
Yellow	56	43	49.5
Price totals	56.3	48.3	

*Totals give row and column margin averages.

centages for a factor are computed by averaging the appropriate percentages over the levels of the other treatment factor; in part **a** of the table
the total percentage of respondents who mentioned the test-brand name
when exposed to the cream color package was 25.5% ([25 + 26]/2), regardless of the retail price.

Though these total percentages can give us a rough feel for the effects of each treatment factor, they must be interpreted carefully because,
if interaction effects are present, sole reliance on the main effect estimates can lead to erroneous conclusions. We will demonstrate how main
effects and interaction effects are estimated in the appendix of Chapter
15. However, for now, let us examine Table 6-7 and Figure 6-4 and attempt to make some tentative conclusions. Figure 6-4 shows bivariate
plots based upon the data given in Table 6-7. In each figure, percentages
are on the vertical axis and package design occupies the horizontal axis.

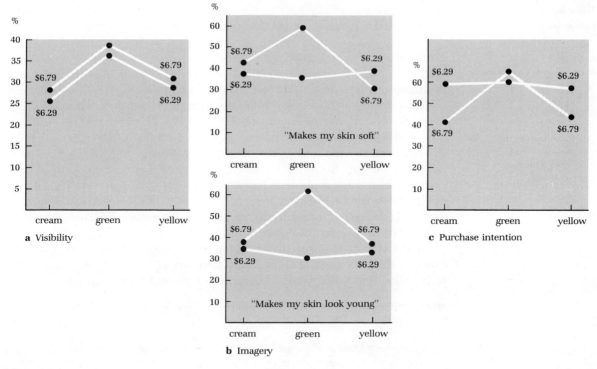

Figure 6-4

Plots of interaction for two-factor after only with control design.

The two solid lines in each figure trace the movement in percentages for each price level. For example, if the solid lines cross, there is evidence to suggest that the treatment factors interact. (Actually, any nonparallelism is a sign of interaction.) First, consider panel **a,** which reports on the percentage of respondents who mentioned the test-brand name after a one-second exposure. Notice that the solid lines are parallel and do not cross. In this case there appears to be a clear effect due to package color. Regardless of price, the green package produces greater visibility. In panels **b** and **c** the results are not so simple. For both imagery questions and purchase intentions there is some indication of an interaction between package and price. For the image questions there is not much difference between the various cell percentages with one important exception: green at $6.79 does appreciably better than the others. Thus, there appears to be some synergistic effect produced by pairing these two treatment conditions. A similar result is obtained for top-box purchase intentions. In general, and as expected, the low price condition generates a greater percentage of top-box purchase-intent scores than does the higher price condition with one important exception; green at $6.79 does slightly better than any of the other package and price variations. Barring

*Time series quasi
design* Experiment that
involves periodic
measurements on some
group or individual,
introduction of an
experimental
manipulation, and
subsequent periodic
measurement.

problems of selection bias, which can always confound after-only with control designs, the results of the study will likely lead management to recommend a green package design and a retail price of $6.79.

Time Series Quasi Design. This design involves periodic measurements on some group or individual, introduction of an experimental manipulation, and subsequent periodic measurements. We use the term *quasi* to describe this design because there is no randomization and because the timing of treatment presentation as well as which respondents are exposed to the treatment may not be directly under the control of the researcher. This design appears to be very similar to the before-after $(O_1 \ X \ O_2)$ design discussed at the beginning of this section. As we demonstrate in the example that follows, although this design bears a basic similarity to the before-after design, because we take many pre-exposure and post-exposure measurements, the time series designed provides more control over extraneous factors.

Exhibit 6-8 presents an abridged marketing research proposal requested by the Chewing Gum Brand Group for a national tracking study to be conducted next year.[13] Figure 6-5 summarizes this design.

E X H I B I T   6-8

Marketing Research Proposal: Time Series Design

Brand:	Chewing gum
Project:	National tracking study
*Background &
Objective:*	The chewing gum brand group has requested that a national tracking study be conducted next year. The objective of the study will be to track changes in awareness, consumer perceptions, and use resulting from any proprietary or competitive changes in the chewing gum market.
*Research
Method:*	The study will be conducted over the next year in monthly waves beginning in February. Interviewing will be conducted by long distance from a central location. Strict probability methods will be used to select telephone numbers from all working exchanges and numbers in the continental United States. Respondents will be randomly selected within a household. Two hundred (200) past-30-day chewing-gum users will be interviewed for eleven months, February through December, yielding a total sample of 2,220.
*Information
To Be
Obtained:*	The study will provide information on changes in brand awareness, consumer perceptions, and use patterns.
Supplier:	Market Facts, Inc.

---

[13]In commercial marketing research studies using this type of design, respondents would be marketed so that there would be 200 different respondents in each month.

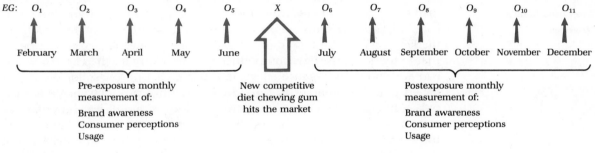

Figure 6-5

Time series quasi design.

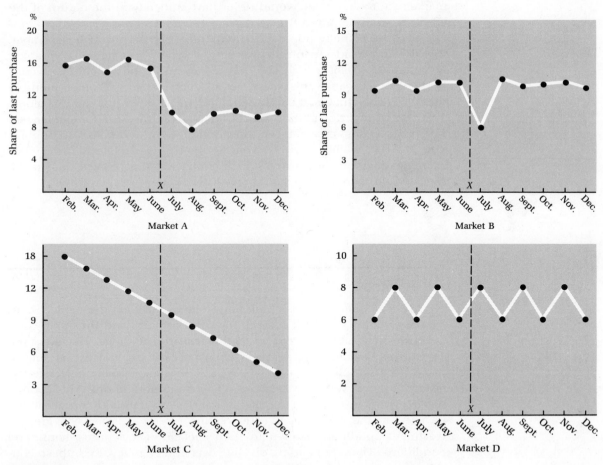

Figure 6-6

Share of last purchase for established brand.

To better understand the effects of the new competitive entry on the market, we have plotted the share of last purchase data for the established brand in Figure 6-6. In the figure, the X denotes the approximate market entry of the new diet chewing gum. From the figure it appears that in market A the new competitive product entry has had both a short-run and long-run negative effect on share of last purchase for the established brand. In market B, the new competitive product entry has had only a temporary short-run negative effect on share of last purchase, as our share of market has bounced back to pre-entry levels by the end of the year. In markets C and D, the new competitive product entry has not had a real effect, for the changes that have occurred since its introduction are consistent with the prior pre-entry share of last purchase history. It is important to note that if we had examined only the change between June and July, as would be done if a one-group after-only design was used, the conclusion would have been that the new competitive product entry had a detrimental effect on our share of last purchase in all four markets; in addition, we would never have understood the nature of the effects in markets A and B.

Because of the multiple measurements, February through December, this design provides controls over several types of extraneous variables. A maturation effect, which could have produced the June–July change, is ruled out because this effect would show up in the other monthly measurements; that is, it would not affect the June to July months alone. Testing and instrumentation effects can also be ruled out for similar reasons; and if some care is taken, selection bias and mortality can be minimized. The possible uncontrollable sources of bias relate to history (for example, competitive activity) and interactive testing effects due to the repeated measurements taken on each respondent.

Summary

We have seen that experimental designs providing the tightest controls over internal validity may be the most artificial and thus may compromise our ability to generalize the research findings. However, the pragmatics of marketing research often necessitates that we be able to project the sample results to the larger untested population. Hence the issue of internal versus external validity is an important one. This conflict has led many researchers to suggest that designs tight in internal validity be used in the early stages of marketing research projects to identify treatment conditions known to have specific effects under controlled conditions. Then, depending on the costs and risks involved, these conditions can be subjected to further testing in more natural settings through the use of quasi-experimental designs.[14] Quasi-experimental designs, if properly developed, can provide the marketing researcher with a vehicle for extending experimentation into real market settings.

Key Concepts

Laboratory experiment
Field experiment
Causality
Concomitant variation
Spurious association
Temporal ordering
Control
Experimental design
Treatment
Manipulation
Effect
Confounding variables
Validity
History
Maturation
Testing
Instrumentation

Selection bias
Mortality
Interactions
Reactive or interactive effects of testing
Interactive effects of selection bias
Surrogate situations
Demand artifacts
After-only design
Before-after design
Before-after with control design
After-only with control design
Nonequivalent before-after with control design
Two-factor design
Time series design

Review Questions

1. Discuss the advantages and disadvantages of laboratory versus field experiments.
2. What are the requirements for a causal relationship between two variables?
3. Discuss the various methods for controlling extraneous sources of variation.
4. Discuss the differences between internal and external validity.
5. Compare the before-after with the before-after with control experimental designs with respect to controlling for threats to internal validity.

[14]See A. G. Sawyer, P. M. Worthing, and P. E. Sendak, "The Role of Laboratory Experiments to Test Marketing Strategies," *Journal of Marketing*, Summer 1979, 60–67.

CASE STUDIES FOR PART II

Case 1: Peoria Isn't Average Enough for One Ad Agency Anymore

By Eugene Carlson, Staff Reporter of *The Wall Street Journal*

Peoria, Ill., in the eyes of at least one Madison Avenue advertising agency, is no longer Middle America. For years, Peoria has been considered an ideal test market for new products, a community so close to the national average in income and mix of ages that it's sort of a U.S. in miniature. If a new brand of soap or antifreeze plays well in Peoria, the theory goes, there's a good chance it will be a sales winner across the country.

Peoria isn't the only Middletown, U.S.A. Marketing executives have a short list of cities that seem to work well as test markets because they're so normal. One widely read list is compiled by the New York advertising agency Dancer Fitzgerald Sample Inc. The agency has just revised its list for the first time in three years and, alas, Peoria and 16 other cities have been dropped. At the same time, 18 cities were added, bringing Dancer Fitzgerald sample's total of recommended test-market communities to 46.

How does a city get cut from the ranks of the super average? Paducah-Cape Girardeau, Mo., lost out because its household income has slipped well below the national norm, says Ira Weinblatt, a Dancer Fitzgerald Sample senior vice president. Tampa-St. Petersburg, Fla., no longer qualified because its elderly population is far higher than in most communities.

Fresno, Calif.'s citizens are average enough, but the city was dropped as an ideal test market because Mr. Weinblatt thinks newspaper and television advertising rates there are too high. "Some markets exploit the fact that they are test markets and charge high media prices," he says. That can add a lot to the cost of promoting a new product.

Peoria's downfall was twofold. Unemployment has been unusually high, largely the result of big employee layoffs and a seven-month strike at Caterpillar Tractor Co. Also, television rating services report that more

Source: Wall Street Journal, 27 September 1983, 35.

and more Peoria homes are picking up programs beamed from TV stations in Chicago, Springfield, Ill., and the Quad Cities (Davenport, Iowa–Moline, Ill.). As this "spill in" of programs from outlying stations grows, market researchers have difficulty measuring the effectiveness of new-product advertising that's being shown strictly on local channels. "When you test, you want the market to be as clean as possible. You want at least 80% of the market listening to its own stations," Mr. Weinblatt says.

Peoria, for its part, likes the benefits that flow from being average. "We have a regular stream of test-market business coming into Peoria," says David Schlink, marketing manager of the Peoria Journal Star. While new-product advertising isn't a big chunk of the newspaper's total ads, loss of some of these accounts "would be important to us," he says.

A new-product city also runs the danger of becoming too popular. Market researchers believe that consumers who are barraged with new-product advertisements in newspapers and on television, and who see strange varieties of peanut-butter and mouthwash every time they go to the supermarket, react differently than normal shoppers. Buffalo, N.Y., Milwaukee, and Minneapolis-St. Paul are in this category, Mr. Weinblatt says. They haven't been dropped from his agency's recommended list. "But we sort of flag them. We say be careful; they've been used a lot. If you can, use some place else."

Here are the other cities that Dancer Fitzgerald Sample dropped from its latest recommended test-market roster: Albuquerque, N.M.; Amarillo, Texas; Columbia-Jefferson City, Mo.; Davenport, Iowa–Moline, Ill.; Jacksonville, Fla.; Memphis, Tenn.; Mobile, Ala.; New Orleans; Norfolk–Portsmouth, Va.; Richmond, Va.; San Antonio, Texas; Savannah, Ga.; and Tucson, Ariz.

Cities added to the list this year are: Boise, Idaho; Charlotte, N.C.; Cincinnati; Columbus, Ohio; Erie, Pa.; Fort Wayne, Ind.; Green Bay, Wis.; Greensboro, N.C.; Greenville, S.C.; Lexington, Ky.; Omaha, Neb.; Phoenix; Roanoke, Va.; Sacramento, Calif.; Salt Lake City.; Seattle; Spokane, Wash.; and Syracuse, N.Y.

Finally, Mr. Weinblatt names eight cities on the test-market list that are closest to the U.S. population and income norms. A sort of Middle America honor roll. "The most average of the average," he calls them. They are Cedar Rapids and Des Moines, Iowa; Cincinnati, Omaha; Portland, Ore.; South Bend, Ind.; Springfield, Ill.; and Syracuse.

Questions

1. Using secondary sources of information, determine the distribution of income and age in the United States.
2. Again using secondary sources of information, validate the extent to which the cities recommended by Mr. Weinblatt provide the closest match to population distributions.
3. In addition to income and age, what other characteristics available from secondary sources would you consider to be useful in assessing potential test-market cities? Identify these sources.

Case 2: Consumers' Attitudes and Perceptions Toward Seafood when Eating Out: Preliminary Phase

The lack of acceptance by the consumer of squid, mackerel, pollock, whiting, hake, and other underutilized species impedes the fishing industry from developing and using these existing fisheries in spite of the abundance of product available. The specific problems being encountered are in the marketplace. Although problems of quality and handling techniques also exist, solutions to these problems are to little or no avail unless consumers will accept the product.

All sectors of the fishing industry concerned with these species, from harvesting to processing to distribution, are affected by the problem of consumer non-acceptance. Even popular species are underused at certain times of the year. In this area of scarce resources, the result is to deny use of abundant resources to all sectors of the fishing industry. Such denial affects the costs of other processing and distribution resources and capabilities, contributes to greater cyclical fluctuations within the industry, denies greater employment opportunities, and inhibits commercial food-service establishments from providing lower-cost seafood menu items, which would benefit the consumer and increase consumption of all species.

A major market for fish is the food-service industry. As viable as this industry is, however, it selects only certain seafood products and sells them with a minimum of marketing effort and much ignorance about the consumer who eats seafood away from home.

Marketing research has explored the attitudes, perceptions, and behavior of the food-market seafood buyer and resultant home-consumption patterns. The away-from-home seafood buyer, however, consumes twice as much seafood as the at-home eater and provides a vital link not only in total consumption, but also in the exploration of new uses and species. Yet he or she orders seafood or fish only about 7 percent of the time in all restaurants.

This research is directed at understanding the marketing process that is most effective in expanding consumption of both traditional and nontraditional fish in commercial food-service establishments. This knowledge is essential to the stabilization, maintenance, and growth of the fishing industry and is advanced by empirical identification of consumers' beliefs, attitudes, intentions, and behaviors toward seafood products and their promotion. Specifically, the broad objective of the full research project is threefold:

1. To provide an analysis of consumer beliefs, attitudes, intentions, and

Source: Material for this case was supplied by Dr. Robert C. Lewis, Department of Hotel Administration, University of Massachusetts.

behavior toward product characteristics of fish eaten in commercial food-service establishments, especially underutilized species, both fresh and frozen.

2. To develop an effective foundation for generating marketing tactics and strategies for food-service operators in preparing, serving, merchandising, advertising, promoting, menu listing, naming, and pricing of fish products, especially underutilized species.

3. To provide an analysis of delineated market segments that will orient the food-service operator toward optimal marketing effectiveness for fish and fish products, especially underutilized species.

The research was confined to Massachusetts for funding and resource-limitation reasons. As such, it pays particular attention to fish species of the northeastern seaboard and to the attributes of Massachusetts consumers. Generalizations beyond Massachusetts should be made with caution, but it is believed that the findings have nationwide implications.

Part I of the Research

The purpose of this part of the research project was to provide a foundation and qualitative basis for the more extensive quantitative research that would follow. As the first phase of a comprehensive study, it examines.

- general attitudes and perception toward seafood
- factors affecting those attitudes and perceptions
- attitudes, feelings, and beliefs that influence consumers' behavior patterns toward eating fish when dining out

  Specific objectives were to explore

- tastes and preferences
- familiarity with the product
- knowledge of nutritional attributes
- previous consumption
- present consumption
- home versus away-from-home usage
- associations
- awareness, knowledge, familiarity, consumption, and attitudes toward nontraditional species

Focus group research was undertaken to collect data. Four focus group interviews of eight to ten persons each were held in geographically different areas, including both inland and coastal markets. This enabled us to examine any differences that might exist between those consumers who have immediate access to a wide variety of fresh fish and those who are farther removed from it.

197

Sample

Two focus groups, one male and one female, were held in the Boston and Springfield, Massachusetts areas. Participants for the interviews were prescreened on several factors so that they would represent a cross-section of the restaurant-eating public. These factors included age, income, education, marital status, frequency of eating in restaurants, type of restaurant visited, and frequency of selecting seafood when eating out.

Virtually all participants had attended high school and most had completed college. The groups were about evenly divided between married and single or divorced participants. Representative job descriptions included clerk, secretary, homemaker, bookkeeper, supervisor, draftsperson, teacher, and contractor. About 75 percent were Massachusetts natives.

All participants had eaten dinner at least twice in a table-service restaurant during the previous month. Approximately one-third claim they eat out at least eight times a month; some claim they eat out as often as five times a week.

All participants order finfish for their main course at least occasionally when dining out. Over half reported they eat fish frequently when at restaurants. Half of these say they always eat fish at restaurants.

METHOD

Each focus group session began with an introduction to what a focus group is and how one is conducted. The moderator emphasized that there were no right or wrong answers and strongly encouraged participants to express their own opinions. Discussion was free-flowing and generally exploratory, but also probing and directed to certain topic areas. (The full moderator's guide for conducting the sessions is shown in Exhibit 1).

EXHIBIT 1

Moderator's Guide

Introduction

A. Moderator
B. Focus group technique, taping, etc.
C. Participant introductions (name, where live, where born, how often eat out [non-fast food])

Background Information

A. Favorite restaurant/why?
B. What influences our choices of food?

1. Things in childhood—As a child did you try new foods?
2. Peer group
3. Religion
4. Geographical preferences (where)
5. Parental pressure

Seafood Consumption

(not shellfish such as crab, lobster, shrimp; talk about fish such as sole, halibut, cod)

A. How frequently eat seafood when eat out?
   1. What kinds?
   2. Why? (benefits)
      a. health
      b. taste
      c. price
      d. nutrition
   3. More or less than in the past?
   4. Eating habits change as get older
   5. Why not others?
B. Present consumption habits
   1. Home
   2. Away from home
      a. Why at restaurant and not at home?
      b. Is restaurant an experience or just a place?
C. Favorite seafood
   1. Why/what makes it a favorite?
      a. fish itself
      b. sauce
      c. texture
      d. manner in which it is prepared
   2. Elements that appeal the most
   3. How important familiarity?
D. Describe a typical dining out experience—in terms of menu selection
E. Influencers/preconceived ideas
   1. Waitress
   2. Menu
   3. People you are with
   4. Specials of the day
   5. Table tents on tables
   6. Any particular tastes or names that may influence
F. Do you try new dishes?
   1. Why?
   2. Why not?
G. What catches your attention?
   1. Description
   2. Name
   3. Price
   4. Others
H. Expectations
   1. What will it taste like?
   2. What kinds/names?

199

I. Types of restaurants
  1. More likely to trust a particular type of restaurant
  2. More likely to try something new in a restaurant you trust
  3. How does type of restaurant influence choice?

Menu Evaluation (Hand-Cut Menus)

A. What catches your eye first?
  1. Price
  2. Descriptions of fish
  3. Benefits seen in eating fish
B. Probe for specifics of factors making favorite/underutilized species
  1. Would you eat this kind? (Try few terms)
  2. Why?
  3. Why not?
  4. Would you try it?
  5. How familiar are you with these species? (some on menu, others like monkfish, dog fish)
C. Fresh fish vs. frozen
  1. Likes/dislikes
  2. Do you trust the menu?
  3. Trust the waitress?
D. Methods of preparation
  1. Broiled
  2. Baked
  3. Fried
  4. Steamed
  5. Sautéed
  6. In chowders

Marketing Influence/Strategy

A. Restaurant's role in educating the consumer
  1. Waitress
  2. Special promotions
  3. Descriptions
B. Other media used to influence
  1. TV
  2. Articles
  3. Commentaries
  4. News item
  5. Julia Child-type program

Question

1. Critique and evaluate the approach taken in the focus-group phase of this study.

Case 3: Survey Carried Day for Anheuser's LA

By Scott Hume

An Anheuser-Busch consumer survey proved a deciding factor in federal Judge Roy W. Harper's recent ruling that its LA name for its low-alcohol beer can be protected as a valid trademark (AA, May 28).

According to the 21-page decision, A-B entered as evidence results of a survey that the judge concluded showed "consumers do not generally recognize the term LA to immediately connote low alcohol when they see such on [Anheuser-Busch's] product."

Because that study convinced the judge the LA name "stands for an idea which requires some operation of the imagination to connect it with the product," he ruled the LA name to be "suggestive" rather than "descriptive" or "generic," and thus deserving of protection.

A-B initiated the suit, heard in federal district court in St. Louis, against Stroh Brewery, which markets Schaefer L.A. low-alcohol beer. (Court records show that Detroit-based Stroh also obtained approval from the Bureau of Alcohol, Tobacco & Firearms for an Old Milwaukee L.A. brand not currently marketed.)

The research study was conducted by Yorum Wind, Professor of marketing and management at the University of Pennsylvania's Wharton School of Business. At shopping malls in 15 cities (eight of which were among the dozen initial LA test markets), respondents were divided into two groups: Those familiar with the product and its advertising and those who were not.

Those unfamiliar with the product were shown the can (whose label says only "LA from Anheuser-Busch") and asked what type of beer it is. Less than 6% described it as "low alcohol," "light alcohol" or a variation.

However, nearly 25% of those respondents who had seen, heard of or tried LA described the product as a reduced-alcohol beer. The researcher concluded that the difference between the two sets of responses was attributable to the effect of advertising.

For Judge Harper, the Wind study provided compelling evidence "LA" is not a generally recognized generic term, as Stroh Brewery had maintained.

Because Stroh showed that A-B's agency, D'Arcy MacManus Masius, St. Louis, had prepared preliminary reports on the low-alcohol beer market in Australia, Judge Harper dismissed A-B's contention that its choice of LA as a brand name was "arbitrary and fanciful." Several brands with the LA designation are sold in Australia, including Tooth's LA, Resch's Premier LA and S.A. Brewing LA Draught.

But while granting that "it is conceivable that Australian beer consumers perceive LA as a designation for a category," the judge ruled

Source: Advertising Age, 4 June 1984.

Stroh had "failed to show any relevant connection to what prospective consumers' perceptions of LA are in the United States."

In his summation, Judge Harper ruled that A-B had "presented the industry with sufficient notice of its selection of LA as a brand name." He also noted that Stroh had "appropriated the designation LA in order to dilute its distinctiveness in the marketplace and therefore create confusion in the marketplace between plaintiff's product and defendant's product."

Stroh has said it will appeal the decision and market its Schaefer low-alcohol beer under an as-yet-undetermined name.

Question

1. Assume the role of an independent marketing researcher asked to provide technical advice and comments to Judge Harper on the interviewing methods used by Professor Wind. Specifically, you are asked to prepare a statement detailing the advantages and disadvantages of the method used by Professor Wind and to offer any suggestions as to how the interviewing should have been conducted.

Case 4: Bristol-Myers Claims Anti-Anxiety Drug is Safer Than Valium and Just as Effective

By Michael Waldholz, Staff Reporter of *The Wall Street Journal*

A new anti-anxiety drug is making some drug makers anxious.

The new drug, called Buspar and developed by Bristol-Myers Co.'s Mead Johnson Pharmaceutical division, isn't available yet. But if, as expected within a few months, the U.S. Food and Drug Administration approves prescription use of Buspar, it would become the first new type of medicine available for treating anxiety since Hoffmann-La Roche Inc.'s Valium was approved 21 years ago.

Researchers—many of whose work is partially funded by Bristol-Myers and other drug makers—consider Buspar the first drug that is based on a chemical structure different from Valium's but is as effective as Valium in relieving anxiety. "We've looked at perhaps several dozen experimental compounds over the years and none before Buspar have compared favorably" with Valium, says Dr. Samuel Gershon, head of the psychiatry department at Wayne State University in Detroit.

Source: Wall Street Journal, 20 December 1984.

Unlike Valium, Buspar doesn't hold the potential of becoming addictive, according to researchers. Tests also indicate it neither makes users sleepy nor interacts dangerously with alcohol, both potential problems with Valium. Says Dr. Harold Goldberg, a researcher at Boston State Hospital, "I think it's going to beat the hell out of the benzodiazepines," the chemical family of about seven minor tranquilizers that includes Valium.

MONTHS OF STUDY

Finding out whether Buspar lives up to Dr. Goldberg's expectation will require months of study once large numbers of Americans are using the drug. While some benzodiazepine advocates are skeptical about the new drug's claims, anticipation among doctors is rising as news spreads of its imminent release. "I'm anxious to get to use it, and so are others," says Dr. Robert Rakel, a family practice physician in Iowa City and professor at the University of Iowa. . . .

Bristol-Myers isn't talking either, but it has generated interest in Buspar by funding symposiums for doctors about anxiety treatment in which independent researchers discussed their Buspar findings. "A good doctor will prescribe tranquilizers with trepidation, especially with patients with chronic anxiety, who may get hooked," says Dr. Rakel. "If Buspar is what is being claimed, I can see a lot of doctors being more relaxed."

Valium itself has become a household word. When released, it quickly eclipsed an earlier generation's favorite, Miltown, which in the 1950s had itself become a synonym for tranquilizer and the butt of so many jokes that its marketer, Carter-Wallace Inc., eventually changed the drug's name, to Deprol.

Compared with previous drugs for treating anxiety, Valium generally causes few adverse reactions. Over two decades, only two deaths in the U.S. have been blamed on its use alone, a low statistic among even the safest drugs.

But use of Valium and the entire benzodiazepine class has declined recently. About 10 years ago, it began to be reported that some people taking the drug for long periods became physically or psychologically dependent on it. Withdrawal was painful and, for some, quite dangerous. By 1979, enough of these studies had surfaced to persuade the company and the FDA to change the information sent to doctors with the drug, warning them about the dependency problem.

Other problems have become associated with the benzodiazepines. The drugs can increase the intoxicating effects of alcohol and are dangerous in combination with large amounts of alcohol and narcotics. Because it is a sedative, Valium isn't recommended for people who work machinery or drive for a living.

Newer benzodiazepines—including Ativan, sold by American Home Products Corp.'s Wyeth Laboratories, and Xanax, sold by Upjohn Co.—

have been marketed as causing fewer problems. But "all benzodiazepines really work similarly, even though the companies claim the differences are significant," says Dr. Darrell Abernethy, an associate professor of medicine at Baylor University Medical Center.

As the basis for its claim that Buspar isn't addictive, Bristol-Myers uses a series of animal studies and one human study. Based on this and other data, an FDA committee recommended that Buspar, unlike the benzodiazepines, needn't be regulated as a "controlled substance." Such a rating requires greater physician and pharmacist surveillance and is given to drugs thought to be prone to abuse.

But some doctors who have prescribed and studied the benzodiazepines for years are skeptical, especially of claims that Buspar isn't addictive. "We've been disappointed before about nondependency claims," says Dr. David Greenblatt, a pharmacologist at Tufts University. He notes that researchers made similar claims about Valium when it was released.

Anticipating such concerns. Mead-Johnson has begun a large-scale study of patients taking Buspar and a benzodiazepine, to see which are most likely to develop dependency problems. Company officials won't discuss the study but have told several researchers that it's "going well," according to a researcher.

DEPENDENCY WORRIES OVERBLOWN

Still, Dr. Greenblatt and others argue that worries of Valium dependency are overblown. They say dependency occurs in only a very small population of patients, particularly those with other addictions. Dr. Greenblatt says the "adverse publicity" is what has caused the decline in use of benzodiazepines.

Indeed, some researchers suggest that patients familiar with Valium may dislike Buspar. Dr. Karl Rickels, a professor of psychiatry and pharmacology at the University of Pennsylvania, says patients who like Valium because it provides quick anxiety relief or those who take Valium to relieve insomnia may be disappointed in Buspar's slower response.

But in preparation for a market shake-up, all drug makers are scurrying to expand FDA-approved uses of their products. Upjohn is testing Xanax for use against depression. Several others are studying use of their tranquilizers against something called "panic disorder," a recently identified type of severe anxiety attack. Even Bristol-Myers is testing Buspar for other uses, including whether it can relieve pre-menstrual stress. . . .

Question

1. Design an experiment to test for the product claims, both pro and con, being made about Buspar.

Case 5: The Performance Test™

According to the Nielsen clearing house, four of every five households in the United States use coupons. Moreover, the coupon redeemer is upscale, economically and educationally. While the primary source of coupons is Sunday newspaper inserts, direct-mail coupons have, by far, the highest average redemption rate—8.1 percent.

Knowing about the ubiquity of the coupon redeemer and desiring to provide a behavioral base evaluation of print advertising, Final Analysis developed the Performance Test,™ described below.

A DEFINITION

The Performance Test™ is a marketing research technique that rapidly, economically, and reliably evaluates relative effectiveness of alternative package goods print ads through actual behavioral measures.

The Stimulus

- The stimulus is an 8½×11 test ad with redeemable coupon appended.
- The ad and coupon are direct-mailed to households in preselected areas.
- The mailing contains *only* the single test ad and coupon.

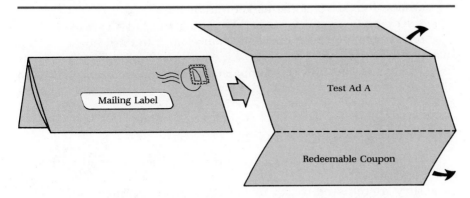

Figure 1

Test ad with detachable coupon.

Source: This material supplied by Final Analysis, New York.

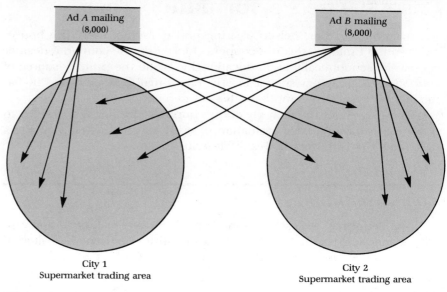

Figure 2

Alternate-household mailing system.

The Sample

- Each test ad is sent to 8,000 households, on an alternating-*household* basis within select supermarket trading areas.
- For example, in any supermarket trading area, ad A is mailed to first house on street, ad B to second house, ad A to third house, ad B to fourth house, etc.
- This system ensures the comparability of samples receiving each alternative ad.

The Criterion-Measure

- Redeemed coupons for each alternative ad are retained at the test supermarkets.
- They are retrieved weekly by Final Analysis personnel.
- Five weeks after the ad coupon mailing, a report is submitted reflecting the proportion of coupons redeemed for each test ad.

Since sample compositions for each test ad are the same and coupon values for each test ad are identical, the redemption level differences are attributable only to the ads themselves.

Other Utilities of the Performance Test

The technique lends itself to evaluating

- *Alternative strategies*, in addition to traditional print-ad executions of a strategy.
- *Alternative coupon values*, keeping the product advertising constant.

Questions

1. Critique and evaluate "The Performance Test" with particular attention to issues that surface in testing cause-and-effect relationships.
2. What improvements would you suggest?

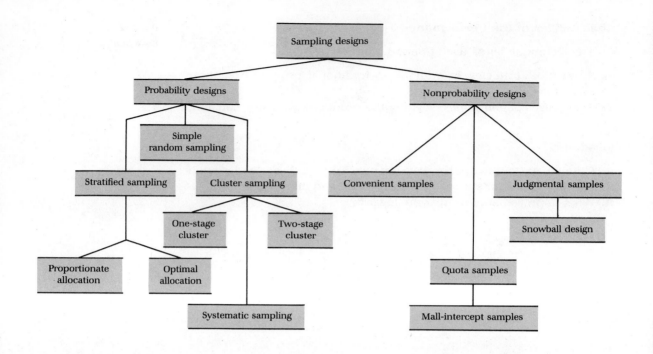

SAMPLING THEORY
AND PRACTICES

Having decided how the data are to be collected, the
next concern focuses on the question of how to obtain a sample of
respondents that is representative of the target population of interest. In
Part III, attention is directed to sampling theory and practices. There is
voluminous literature on the theory and practices of sampling; indeed,
entire textbooks are devoted to this subject. Nevertheless, the next two
chapters will expose you to the major sampling techniques and how
they are used in marketing research studies. The figure on the facing
page presents a taxonomy of the specific sampling techniques that will
be considered. Note that sampling techniques can be divided into
two broad categories: *probability designs* and *nonprobability designs*.
As we will come to understand, in a probability sampling design
each element of the population has a known nonzero chance of
being selected. In such cases sampling variation can be computed
and results can be projected to the entire population. In contrast,
because in nonprobability sampling designs (also called *purposive
samples*) the chance of selecting any particular population element
is not known, sampling variation cannot be computed and results
cannot, in a strict sense, be projected to the entire population. This
is not to imply that probability sampling designs are "good" and
nonprobability sampling designs "bad." As we will see, both
probability and nonprobability procedures have appropriate use in
marketing research.

The subject of sampling can be technically rigorous.
The level of technical rigor required ultimately depends on the specific
application context. In certain instances, only a few basics and some
common sense are needed, whereas in other instances sampling
decisions involve complex statistical concepts and the use of a host of
computational formulas. Because some of you will never be responsible
for designing a sampling plan, nor have to evaluate the technical
aspects of a sampling design, whereas others may want to know a little
about the technical aspects of sampling theory, we have presented two
chapters on the theory and practice of sampling. In Chapter 7 we

present a nonquantitative treatment of sampling fundamentals with particular emphasis on the decisions that must be made by a manager or research analyst. Chapter 8 is devoted to a more technical treatment of sampling and should be of interest to those of you who want to know how to actually draw various kinds of probability samples.

Sampling Fundamentals

- Discuss the key elements involved in devising a sampling plan.
- Explain the importance of properly defining the target population of interest.
- Illustrate the distinctive features of probability and nonprobability samples.
- Describe the major types and primary practical uses of both probability and nonprobability samples.
- Discuss the primary approaches for determining sample size.
- Define the concepts of *sampling* versus *nonsampling* errors.
- Explain what factors contribute to *nonresponse* and *response* errors.
- Describe how response rates can be improved.
- Discuss the proposed remedies for nonresponse error.

Introduction

Put simply, **sampling** involves identifying a group of individuals or households who can be reached by mail, by telephone, or in person, and who possess information relevant to solving the marketing problem at hand. A logical first question is: *Why sample at all?* The answer is simple and straightforward: Sampling is practical and economical. Recall that the objectives of survey research are to describe and explain selected characteristics of a prespecified group of individuals, households, institutions, or objects. However, complete enumeration of the group, called a **census,** is rarely undertaken because it is usually much too expensive in terms of time, money, and personnel. Even the most notable exception, the *U.S. Census of Population*, conducted each decade, generates an enormous amount of data about many subjects by surveying a small sample of the entire population. As we will see, there is simply no need to survey every individual to obtain an accurate representation of the group as a whole. With proper care and control, only a very small fraction of the entire population is needed to obtain an accurate representation of the group as a whole.

Sampling Identification of a group of individuals or households (or institutions or objects) who can be reached by mail, telephone, or in person, and who possess the information relevant to solving the marketing problem at hand.

Census A complete enumeration of the prespecified group.

211

Remember that sampling may not always be necessary. Instead of immediately running out and asking a group of individuals a series of questions, the marketing analyst should first exhaust all relevant sources of secondary data—reinventing the wheel is often costly, time-consuming, and potentially embarrassing.

With this caveat in mind, let us begin our treatment of the theory and practice of sampling. The discussion begins by describing the key elements that a marketing manager or researcher must consider when devising a sampling plan. These elements, which together form the overall sampling design, provide the organization for the remainder of this chapter. Although many of you may never actually draw a sample or compute sample-based statistics in a real-life marketing research setting, at some point you may be responsible for overseeing the sampling design and play an important role in evaluating the overall plan. Consequently, you need to understand the basic issues of sample design.

SAMPLING DESIGN CONSIDERATIONS

In devising a sampling plan, the marketing analyst must make several decisions ranging from who should be included in the sample to whether the sample should be statistically adjusted. In certain instances, the marketing analyst will rely on a trained sampling professional who has been called in to devise the sampling design; in other instances, the marketing analyst will rely on a few basic principles plus his or her own knowledge of the problem at hand. In either case, the analyst must clearly understand the implications of the decisions made, since these decisions determine the quality of the information collected.

A sampling design usually involves five decision issues:

1. *Target population and frame issues:* Who should be included in the sample? How can these individuals be identified? How many contacts will be required?
2. *Data-collection issues:* What data-collection method should be used? How does the choice of a data-collection method influence other aspects of the sampling design?
3. *Sample-size determination issues:* What method of determining how many to sample should be used? How many should be sampled?
4. *Sampling techniques issues:* How will the sampling points (individuals) be selected? What is the relationship among the various techniques that can be used to draw the sample?
5. *Nonresponse-bias issues:* What are the potential sources of nonresponse bias? How does nonresponse bias affect the survey results? How can nonresponse be handled?

We have already discussed some of these issues, and so our treatment of them here will be brief.

TARGET POPULATION AND FRAME ISSUES

The object of sampling is to acquire information about a population. The elements that make up the population are called **sampling units.** For instance, a sampling unit may contain individuals, households, institutions, or stores. Sampling units are used to select the elements that will go into the sample. For example, in directory telephone sampling (Chapter 5), the element possessing the information sought by the survey is typically a particular member of the household; in this case, a sampling unit contains households—specifically, each household's telephone number. The first decision in designing the plan is to define which sampling unit is appropriate: in other words, to decide who should be in the sample.

Sampling units The elements that make up the population.

Target Population

A sample does not have to be representative of the general population but rather it must be representative of the population of interest. The population of interest is called the **target population.** Precise definition of the target population is absolutely essential. If you define your target population improperly, then the research will likely be ineffectual in solving your problem.

Target population The population of interest; contains the sampling units (and elements) that possess the information sought by the survey.

The key in defining the target population is the ability to translate the objectives of the study into a definitive statement specifying who should or should not be included in the sample. What may at first appear to be simple, seldom is. Consider the market research proposal for a new facial-moisturizer concept test described in Exhibit 7-1. What is the appropriate target population? All females? Females who have used facial-moisturizer creams? Females who have used a facial-moisturizer cream within the last thirty days? Females 18 years or older? Answers to these questions are critical to the proper definition of the target population. Different answers produce different target populations. The specifications given in Exhibit 7-1 define a target population of females who are past-thirty-day users of facial moisturizer products, are 18 years of age or older, and live in the greater Cincinnati, Ohio, area.

E X H I B I T   7-1

Marketing Research Proposal: Concept/Product Test

Brand:	Facial Moisturizer
Project:	Concept/Product Test
Background & Objectives:	The brand group has requested that research be conducted to determine: (1) consumer reaction to each of two positionings for a new facial moisturizer product and (2) fit of the new facial-moisturizer product with each of the concepts.

Research
Methods:

(handwritten: used w/in the last 30 days)

Each of the two concepts will be tested among 200 females who are past-thirty-day facial-moisturizer users. The following quota will apply for each cell

45%	age 18–34
30%	age 35–54
25%	age 55+

The concepts will each be evaluated monadically in five central locations located in the Cincinnati, Ohio, area. Respondents will then be given one package of the product to use at home for a period of one week. Telephone call-backs will be made at the end of the use period to obtain reactions to the product.

Information
To Be
Obtained:

Concept:
Purchase interest
Likes and dislikes
Key benefit
Overall and attribute ratings
Other diagnostic questions

Product:
Purchase interest
Likes and dislikes
Overall and attribute ratings
Performance versus expectations
Other diagnostic questions

Action
Standard:

The concept that produces the highest percentage of respondents reacting positively to *both* concept and product (as determined by the purchase-intent scale), provided that said concept did not earn lower positive purchase interest in the *concept only* phase, will be selected for further development. In the latter event, changes in either the concept or product will be recommended.

Timing &
Cost:

The following schedule has been established:

Field	3 weeks
Top-line	1 week
Final Report	6 weeks

The cost will be $25,000 ± 10%

Supplier:

Burke Marketing Research

You need to remember three points about defining target populations. First, the target population must be consistent with the objectives of the study; it must contain individuals, households, or other units that possess the information sought by the survey. Second, any other "qualities" that respondents need to have in order to be included (or excluded) in the sample must also be clearly specified. For example, many commercial marketing research studies require that respondents not have participated in a marketing research study in the past three months to be considered for inclusion in the sample. Finally, *all* decision rules for inclusion or exclusion of respondents from the survey must be clearly explained.

Once you have defined the target population, you next must determine how to *identify* the target population of interest. We now turn to issues involved in specifying a *sampling frame.*

Sampling Frames

Selecting a sample means that one selects some number of sampling units from the target population. To select a sample of elements or units from a target population presumes that we are able to identify (locate) the target population of interest. A **sampling frame** is simply a list or set of directions (such as a geographic breakdown) that identifies the target population. A sampling frame can be a list of names and telephone numbers, as in a telephone survey; an area map of dwellings, as in an in-home personal survey; or a list of household addresses obtained from a local utility company, as in a mail survey. If no list or organized breakdown of the target population exists, then location sampling (as in mall-intercept surveys) or random-digit dialing (as in telephone surveys) is probably the only alternative. One of the biggest problems in probability sampling, and especially in simple random sampling, is obtaining appropriate lists.

Sampling frame A list or set of directions that identifies the target population.

Actually, lists or other geographical breakdowns are available from a variety of sources. Local community utility companies have a fairly complete list of households. Local area telephone branches frequently cooperate and give out a list of working exchanges. Magazine subscriptions, organization membership rosters, credit card companies, and professional associations are all well-known sources of lists. Many companies are in the business of selling lists. For example, the Donnelley Company maintains a list drawn from telephone directories and automobile registrations that contains around 88 percent of U.S. households. Some companies compile catalogs of lists. Though costs do vary, a list can generally be obtained for between $50 and $120 per thousand names.

Although lists or other geographic breakdowns exist, the list rarely matches the target population exactly. For example, a list of residents of a given community usually does not include new arrivals or households living in dwellings built since the list was created. Lists are rarely current; in addition, lists frequently contain duplication—households with multiple telephone numbers or individuals whose names and addresses appear on two or more lists (combined in hope of better representing the target population) have an increased chance of being selected. Thus a list can overrepresent or underrepresent a target population.

The list (sampling frame) used defines what can be called the **operational** or *working* **population.** If a sampling frame consists of all the sampling units in the target population *plus* additional units, then it suf-

Operational population The sampling frame that is used.

215

fers from **overregistration.** If, on the other hand, a sampling frame contains fewer sampling units than the target population, it suffers from **underregistration.** The difference between the operational population and the target population is commonly referred to as the sampling **gap.** It is probably safe to say that a gap exists in most surveys, including the majority of market research studies. In selecting a sampling frame you should try to minimize gap, since the larger the gap the greater the potential for misleading results.

Once the target population has been properly defined and an appropriate list or geographic breakdown selected, you must address the question of how many contacts (telephone calls, mailings, and the like) will be required.

Incidence Rates

One of the key components of estimating both the cost and timing of a research study is the incidence rate.[1] The incidence level determines how many contacts need to be screened for a given sample size or quota requirement.

In most commercial marketing research studies a criterion for inclusion in the survey is past use of the brand or product/category under study. Product/category use incidence is ordinarily known and supplied by the client (the firm commissioning the research). This defines the **gross incidence**—the percentage of the entire population who are product-category users. **Net incidence** is the factored-down gross incidence, which includes *all* target population qualifications. It is also called the *effective* or *overall* incidence. To illustrate, we consider a survey in which a qualified respondent must meet the following requirements:

- female head of household
- 18–55 (no specific age breakouts)
- used any OTC cold remedy in the past month
- no known health restrictions, drug allergies
- no one in household employed by advertising agency, marketing research company, or drug manufacturer
- has not participated in a marketing research study in the past three months

The product/category use incidence was quoted at 60 percent. This was confirmed to be the gross incidence level—that of "past one-month OTC cold-remedy usage." The next step is to calculate the net incidence level. This involves taking the gross incidence of 60 percent and reducing it for all other qualifications. Note that the screening/data-collection method affects the qualifcation percentages. Let us assume an in-person mall-intercept screening method. Calculating the net incidence is a mul-

---

[1] Much of this material has been adopted from G. Lee, "Incidence is a Key Element," *Marketing News* 13 September 1985, 50–52.

tiplication process. As shown below, the gross incidence is multiplied by the qualification percentages for all inclusion components.

Net incidence = Gross incidence × qualification percentages

Qualification percentages = 87% female heads of households
92% age 18–55
88% no health restrictions/drug allergies
97% no household employment
96% no past research participation

Qualification percentage = 87% × 92% × 88% × 97% × 96%
= 65.6%

Net incidence = 60% × 65.6% = 39.4%

The net incidence will determine the number of contacts required for a given sample size or quota. The relationship between incidence and the number of contacts needed is given by

Incidence = Total qualifed (needed) ÷ Total contacts asked qualifying questions

Thus for a quota of 100 qualified respondents and a net incidence level of 39%, the number of contacts required, assuming no refusals, will be

100 ÷ 39% = 256

Using the gross incidence level of 60 percent we would need only 167 contacts. You can see that serious problems surface if the gross incidence is mistakenly used as the net. Moreover, the magnitude of the error in miscalculating the net incidence escalates as the overall sample size or quota increases.

As we indicated earlier, the actual screening/data-collection method that will be used must be considered in estimating the various qualification components. Due to visual screening in-person recruiting results in high qualification percentages; for example, an interviewer can quickly ascertain a person's sex and even age. In contrast, with telephone screening, the interviewer knows less about the person picking up the phone, and so a lower net incidence is to be expected. Using our hypothetical quota of 100 qualified respondents, Table 7-1 compares the number of contacts required for in-person versus telephone screening.

DATA-COLLECTION ISSUES

An important decision in devising a sampling plan involves the choice of a method for collecting data. For survey research you have a choice between telephone, mail, in-person at-home, or mall-intercept interviews, among others. We discussed various survey-interviewing methods in Chapter 5. In review, the choice of a data-collection method affects

T A B L E 7-1

Comparison of Net Incidence—In-Person versus Telephone Screening

Qualifications	In-person	Random telephone
Female head of household	87%	72%
18–55	92	86
Used any OTC cold remedy in the past month	60	60
No health restrictions/drug allergeis	88	88
No prior research participation	96	96
No employment by advertising agency, marketing research company or drug manufacturer	97	97
Net incidence	39%	30%
Contacts required	256	333

(1) the quality of data, (2) the quantity of data that can be collected, (3) the types of questions that can be asked, (4) the speed with which the data can be collected, (5) the incidence of nonresponse, and (6) the cost of the study. In addition, with respect to sampling design, the choice of a data-collection method directly influences (1) the number of contacts required, (2) the type of sample to be drawn, (3) how sample size is determined, and (4) the approach to handling nonresponse.

SAMPLE SIZE DETERMINATION ISSUES

An important issue in survey research is how large a sample to draw. Large samples are generally more precise than small samples. In other words, all else the same, with large samples the researcher is generally more confident that the results are representative of what is being measured. However, large samples are also generally associated with higher costs. Marketing researchers use at least five different methods of determining sample size. Sample size can be determined based upon (1) blind guesses, (2) statistical precision, (3) Bayesian considerations, (4) cost limitations, and (5) industry standards.

Blind Guesses

Blind guessing Using informed intuition to determine how many units to sample.

Blind guessing, clearly the most unsatisfactory method of determining sample size, uses informed intuition as the basis for determining how many units to sample. This approach to determining sample size is completely arbitrary and does not consider the likely precision of the survey results or the cost of obtaining them.

Statistical Precision

The term **precision** refers to the level of uncertainty about the characteristic being measured. Recall from your basic statistics course the concept of a **confidence interval.**[2] A confidence interval gives a range into which the true population value of the characteristic being measured will fall, assuming a given level of certainty. The smaller this range the more precise are our conclusions about what the true population value of the characteristic is.

$$C.I. = \overline{X} \pm (z_{1-\alpha/2} \, s_X/\sqrt{n})$$

where

Precision Level of uncertainty about the characteristics of the construct being measured.

Confidence interval Range into which the true population value of the characteristic being measured will fall, assuming a given level of certainty.

$C.I.$ = range (confidence interval) in which the true value of the characteristic lies

$\overline{X}$ = estimated value of population characteristic (the mean) based on sample

$z_{1-\alpha/2}$ = reliability coefficient (confidence level), constant drawn from standard normal table based on desired level of certainty (α) ($1 - \alpha$)

s_X = standard deviation of estimated value

n = sample site.

A confidence interval is determined by the estimated value, say, the mean ($\overline{X}$), of the characteristic, the confidence level or reliability ($1 - \alpha/2$), the standard deviation of the estimated value of the characteristic (s_X), and the sample size (n). A confidence interval (range) will become smaller as the sample size is increased. However, since statistical precision (the range or confidence interval) is related to the square root of the sample size, in order to double the precision of an estimate the sample size must be quadrupled (50 to 200, 100 to 400, and so on).

With larger samples sizes one can generally expect greater reliability from the results. The level of reliability is determined largely by the objectives of the survey. For example, for a one-cell concept test the marketing brand group might feel that if fewer than 70 percent of the respondents interviewed check the top two boxes of the purchase-intent scale, then the concept should be dropped from further consideration. Thus, in this setting, the marketing brand group would be concerned with overestimates of the true population value but would probably not worry if the estimated value were 70 percent when the true population value was 65 percent. The marketing brand group might say that it would like to be "virtually certain" that the estimated proportion of respondents who checked the top two intention boxes differs from the true proportion by no more than $100 [(70 - 65)/70]$ or 7.14% of the true proportion.

---

[2]If you do not recall what a confidence interval is, do not worry. We will explain this concept later. In addition, you may want to skip ahead and quickly read the first few sections of Chapter 15.

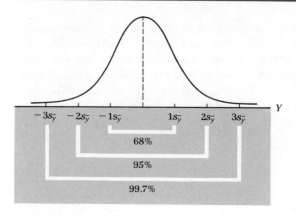

Figure 7-1

Areas under normal curve.

But what is meant by the term "virtual certainty"? Assuming that the sample estimate is normally distributed, it is possible to translate "virtual certainty" in terms of reliability. Figure 7-1 shows the areas under normal curve. Under the assumption that the sample estimates are normally distributed, we know that for approximately 997 of every 1,000 samples the true population value will fall within the following interval:

$$\text{Estimated value} \pm 3 \, s_X/\sqrt{n}$$

The problem then is to draw a sample of size n that is large enough to satisfy this condition.

The level of precision is determined once the sample has been drawn. Obviously, the trick is to determine the level of precision required and then calculate the sample size necessary to achieve the desired level. First, decide on an acceptable **tolerance level,** which represents the allowable difference permitted between the estimate and its known true population value. One approach is to take one-half of the desired confidence interval (range). Let h denote the tolerance level. Next determine $z_{1-\alpha/2}$, the *reliability coefficient* (that is, the virtual-certainty factor discussed above), which is based on the estimated sample value being normally distributed—for virtual certainty $z_{1-\alpha/2} = 3$; for 95 percent confidence $\alpha = .05$ and $z_{.975} = 1.96$. To determine the required sample size we need to obtain an estimate of the standard deviation of the characteristic to be measured in the target population ($\hat{\sigma}_X$). This can be based on prior studies or on small-scale pilot study, or subjectively—by guessing. Alternatively, assuming normality, a useful method for estimating the standard deviation is to take one-sixth of the estimated range of the distribution associated with the characteristic being measured. As shown below, the required sample size (n^*) can be determined by the reliability

Tolerance level The allowable difference permitted between the estimate and its known true population value.

220

coefficient $(z_{1-\alpha/2})$, the estimated standard deviation $(\hat{\sigma}_X)$, and the acceptable tolerance level *(h)*.

$$n^* = \frac{(z_{1-\alpha/2})^2(\hat{\sigma}_X)^2}{h^2}$$

where

n^* = required sample size

$z_{1-\alpha/2}$ = reliability coefficient

$\hat{\sigma}_X$ = estimate of the standard deviation of the population characteristic

h = tolerance level—allowable permitted difference between estimate and population value

Note that it is also possible to specify the level of *relative precision* desired—that is, a researcher may want to ensure that the estimated value is within a fixed percent (perhaps 5 percent) of the true population value. In such cases, the tolerance level acceptable would be set equal to 5 percent of the anticipated value.

The use of statistical precision to determine sample size strictly applies to **probability sampling designs** only—that is, samples drawn in such a way that each member of the population has a known, nonzero chance of being selected; in fact, the discussion of statistical precision given above is based on a simple random sample design where each member of the population has a known *and* equal chance of being selected. Depending on the type of probability design used, the exact method of calculating the required sample size for a given level of precision will change; however, the critical elements in deciding on sample size do not. In most marketing research surveys, the researcher will undoubtedly be interested in more than one characteristic; we suggest, therefore, that the discussion of statistical precision presented here be used as a general guideline rather than as a definitive way to determine how many units must be sampled.

Probability sampling designs Samples drawn in such a way that each member of the population has a known, nonzero chance of being selected.

Bayesian Considerations

Bayesian decision analysis can also be used to determine sample size. The Bayesian approach, although not used much in practice, bases the decision regarding how large a sample to draw on both the expected value of the information obtained by the sample and the cost of taking the sample (see Appendix 2A). This approach involves computing a difference known as *expected net gain* from sampling for various sample sizes and choosing the sample size with the largest positive expected net gain.[3]

Bayesian decision analysis Process that bases the decision on how large a sample to draw on both the expected value of the information obtained by the sample and the cost of taking the sample.

[3]Because the Bayesian approach is not frequently used in practice (primarily due to its complexity and perceived difficulty) we do not discuss it further. The interested reader can consult P. Schlaifer, *Analysis of Decisions Under Uncertainty* (New York: McGraw-Hill, 1969) for a comprehensive treatment.

Cost Limitations

The cost limitations method, or "all-you-can-afford," determines survey sample size on the basis of the budget allocated to the project. This approach involves (1) subtracting from the available budget all nonsampling-related costs (for example, fixed cost of designing the survey, questionnaire preparation, data analysis, and report generation), and (2) dividing this amount by the estimated cost per sampling unit to arrive at the desired sample size. This approach is unsatisfactory since it emphasizes *cost* to the exclusion of all other factors, especially precision.

Industry Standards

Industry standards
Those rules of thumb,
developed from
experience, that have
become standard industry
guidelines for determining
how large a sample to
draw.

Industry standards refer to those rules of thumb, developed from experience, that have become standard industry guidelines for determining how large a sample to draw. Conventional guidelines on sample size vary with the type of marketing research study as well as with the number of cells included in the study. The conventional approach to determining sample size is frequently used in nonprobability design, especially in *quota samples.* In quota samples, for example, the minimum number of respondents per cell is typically no less than 50. Table 7-2

T A B L E 7-2

Typical Sample Sizes Used in Different Types of Marketing Research Studies

Study	Mimimum size	Typical size (range)
Market studies	500	1,000–1,500
Strategic studies	200	400–500
Test-market penetration studies	200	300–500
Concept/product tests	200*	200–300/cell
Name tests	100*/name variant	200–300/cell
Package tests	100*/package variant	200–300/cell
TV commercial tests	150/commercial	200–300/commercial
Radio commercial tests	150/commercial	200–300/commercial
Print ad tests	150/advertisement	200–300/commercial
Test market audits		
Projectable-number of stores accounting for:		
Food	50% of ACV†	
Drugs	50% of ACV†	
Controlled		
Food	10 stores	10–12 stores
Drugs	10 stores	10–12 stores
Focus Group	6/region	8–12/region

*If quota samples are used, the minimum cell size for analysis is 50 respondents.
†ACV—average all commodity volume

presents a summary of minimum sample sizes and typical sample sizes for various commercial marketing research studies. For example, 1,000–1,500 is usually considered to be a reasonable sample for a national (probability) market study. And 200–300 per cell is the convention for a typical concept or product test.

Although we have discussed the various methods of determining sample size separately, rarely will the marketing researcher rely on any one approach. The practicing marketing researcher has to consider statistical precision along with financial constraints as well as company policy (industry standards) when deciding on how many to include in the sample.

SAMPLING TECHNIQUE ISSUES

An important issue that must be resolved in sampling design concerns the method of drawing the sample. There are two broad categories: *probability samples* and *nonprobability samples.*

Probability Samples

All probability sampling procedures share two fundamental characteristics.[4]

1. Before the sampling takes place, it is always possible to specify every potential sample of a given size (samples of size two, of size three, and so on) that could be drawn from the population and the probability of selecting each sample.
2. Every sampling unit must have some nonzero chance of being selected.

Thus, in probability sampling designs, the population must be clearly defined, enabling the researcher to tell which sampling units belong to the population of interest and which sampling units do not. This means that a sampling frame (a list or other organized breakdown of the target population) must be available. There is no requirement that every potential sample have the same probability of selection, but that the probability of selecting any particular sample of a given size can be specified.

The ability to determine this probability means that the precision of the estimated value of the characteristics under study can be computed. In other words, confidence intervals into which the true population value will fall with a given level of certainty can be computed. And, in essence this allows the researcher to make inferences (projections) to the target population from which the sample was drawn. The primary probability

[4]R. J. Jaeger, *Sampling in Education and the Social Sciences* (New York: Longman, Inc., 1984), 28–29.

*Simple random
sampling* Design
guaranteeing that every
sample of a given size as
well as every individual in
the target population has
an equal chance of being
selected.

sampling methods are simple random sampling, systematic sampling, stratified sampling, and cluster sampling.

Simple Random Sampling (SRS). The simplest method of drawing a probability sample is randomly. This method is equivalent to a lottery system in which names are placed in an urn and drawn out randomly. Simple random sampling guarantees that every sample of a given size, as well as every individual in the target population, has an equal chance of being selected. To draw a simple random sample requires a list or other organized breakdown that specifically enumerates each individual, household, or other element in the target population. Numbers from 1 to N (the size of the target population) are assigned to each element in the list and a random number table (see Table 1 in the Statistical Appendix) is used to select n (the desired sample size)—in other words, the elements with numbers corresponding to the random numbers are selected into the sample.

Simple random samples have many desirable features; for example, they are easily understood and used, and allow one to project sample results to the target population. Nevertheless, simple random samples are rarely used in practice. First, SRS may be infeasible—it requires that all elements in the target population be identified and labeled (numbered) prior to sampling. Prior identification is often impossible. Second, SRS can be expensive—it can result in especially large samples or in samples spread out over a large geographic area, making data collection time-consuming and costly. This occurs because SRS gives each element in the target population an equal chance of being included in the sample. Consider the use of SRS in a study designed to compare various brand-user groups of a target population. Under SRS the expected representation of a brand user group is its population proportion, or market share. If a brand has 3 percent market share we would need a simple random sample of 7,000 or so to adequately represent users of this brand. Finally, SRS does not guarantee that the sample drawn will be representative of the target population—it may not include specific subgroups of the population. Consequently, the sample ultimately drawn may contain too few or too many individuals from certain subgroups. A simple random sample of past-thirty-day facial-cream-moisturizer users, for example, could result in a sample where specific brands of the category are overrepresented or underrepresented in relation to their actual market shares. In such a case, resulting brand profiles could be quite distorted. In other words, though random samples will represent a population well *on average*, a given random sample (and particularly a small one) may not represent the target population well at all. For this reason, some sample procedures attempt to guarantee that the correct proportion of subpopulation elements find their way into the ultimate sample.

Systematic sampling
Design where the target
sample is generated by
picking an arbitrary
starting point (in a list)
and then picking every
nth element in succession
from a list.

Systematic Sampling. With **systematic sampling** the target sample is generated by picking an arbitrary starting point (in a list) and then picking every *n*th element in succession from a list. For example, if one wanted a target sample of 60 from a target population of 3,600 and assuming that the twenty-first element (or any number between 1 and 60) was selected as the arbitrary starting point, then elements 81, 141, 201, . . . , 3,561 would make up the remaining fifty-nine elements of the target sample. Systematic sampling is very easy to use. Note also that although a list of all individual elements in the population is required, there is no need to generate a set of random numbers and therefore the random numbers do not have to be matched with individual elements as in SRS. Since some lists contain millions of elements, considerable time can be saved by not having to scan the entire list and pull off, say, the names and addresses or phone numbers of the designated elements. Thus it is not too surprising to note that many consumer phone and mail surveys use a systematic sampling procedure.

Stratified Sampling. Stratified sampling involves partitioning the entire population of elements into the subpopulations and then selecting elements separately from each subpopulation. Consequently, stratified sampling necessarily involves two types of variables: a **classification variable,** which is used to place each population element into a particular subpopulation, and a **sampling variable,** which represents the characteristic of the population that we wish to estimate.

Stratified sampling can be described by four steps:

1. Based upon some classification variable, the entire population of sample units is divided into distinct subpopulations called *strata.*
2. Within each stratum a separate sample of elements is selected from all of the elements composing that stratum, usually by SRS.
3. For each separate sample an estimate of the characteristic of interest is calculated and properly weighted and then added to obtain a combined estimate for the entire population.
4. The variances of the estimates are also computed separately for each stratum, and these are also properly weighted and added to form a combined estimate for the entire population.

Stratified sampling
Design that involves partitioning the entire population of elements into subpopulations, called strata, and then selecting elements separately from each subpopulation.
Classification variable
Variable used to place each population element into a particular subpopulation.
Sampling variable
Variable that represents the characteristic of the population that we wish to estimate.

Stratified sampling is more complex than SRS and, because at least one classification variable must be observed for each sampling unit, potentially more costly. On the positive side, however, stratified sampling can be much more efficient than SRS. For a given sample size, the standard deviation of the estimated value can often be significantly reduced through the use of a stratified sampling design—a smaller confidence interval is often obtained. This is frequently accomplished by stratifying to preclude the selection of undesirable samples that might be selected under some other sampling design. For example, suppose we wish to estimate the total number of interviews completed per day by all of the field service companies that have performed field operations for our company last year. Further, suppose we know that the majority of the field services are small and primarily perform mall-intercept surveys,

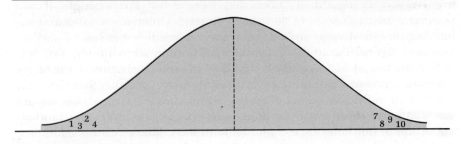

Figure 7-2

Stratified sampling. In this case the classification variable has divided the population into two halves. We choose a sample of one from each stratum. Thus the procedure rules out undesirable samples like 1, 2; 2, 3; 9, 10; 8, 9; and so on.

while the few large field service companies perform the vast majority of in-home personal interviews. Under these conditions, an SRS taken from the list of all field service companies may not necessarily represent the population since it might contain too few or too many of the very large field service companies.

A solution to this problem might be to stratify on the basis of the size of the field service company; that is, we could stratify each sampling unit (field service company), prior to sampling, into two groups (small, large) and then using SRS techniques, select certain numbers of field service companies from each of the two strata. A very simple illustration of this is shown in Figure 7-2.

The efficiency of stratified sampling is directly tied to the efficacy of the (classification) variable used to classify the sampling units into strata. We want the sampling units assigned to a particular stratum to be very similar to each other with respect to the characteristic being measured (within-strata homogeneity), but very different from the elements assigned to other strata (between-strata heterogeneity). In most applications the population is stratifed on the basis of a variable that can be conveniently measured—for example, geographic region, age, gender, and so on. Remember that a good classification variable for one study may be quite unsatisfactory for another.

An important decision in stratified sampling is the number of elementary units to be sampled from each stratum, under the constraint that a total of n elements is to be sampled over all strata. In practice, two procedures have been extensively used for allocating the total sample size among the strata. One procedure, **proportional allocation,** guarantees that stratified random sampling will be at least as efficient as SRS. In proportional allocation the number of elements selected from a stratum is directly proportional to the size of the stratum—that is, the population in that stratum. In other words, with proportional allocation the proportion of elements taken from each stratum is simply given by n/N.

***Proportional
allocation*** Sampling design guaranteeing that stratified random sampling will be at least as efficient as SRS. The number of elements selected from a stratum is directly proportional to the size of the stratum.

226

The second procedure, called **disproportional** or **optimal** allocation produces the most precise (reliable) estimates. Optimal allocation essentially involves a double weighting scheme since the number of sample elements taken from a given stratum is proportional to the relative size of the stratum and the standard deviation of the distribution of the characteristic under consideration among all elements in the stratum. The rationale for this dual weighting procedure is simple. First, size is important since the strata with the larger numbers of elements are the most important in determining the population mean. These strata should also be more important in deriving estimates. Second, optimal allocation of the sample across the strata will result in relatively more elements being drawn from strata having large standard deviations and relatively fewer elements being drawn from strata having small standard deviations. Note that optimal allocation reduces to proportional allocation if the distribution of the characteristic under study has the same standard deviation within each stratum.

Stratified random sampling is a popular sampling procedure because it combines the conceptual simplicity of SRS with potentially significant gains in precision. An increasing trend today is the use of stratified sampling designs in telephone interviewing (see Chapter 5). Exhibit 7-2 and Table 7-3 describe the telephone sampling procedure used by Survey Sampling Inc., a research supplier specializing in survey sampling methodology. This sampling procedure combines systematic and stratified sampling concepts to gain efficiency for nondirectory telephone interviewing.

Disproportional or optimal allocation
Double weighting scheme where the number of sample elements taken from a given stratum is proportional to the relative size of the stratum and the standard deviation of the distribution of the characteristic under consideration among all elements in the stratum.

E X H I B I T 7-2

Description of Sampling Procedure for Telephone Interviewing

Stratification to Counties

To equalize the probability of telephone household selection from anywhere in the area sampled, samples are first systematically stratified to all counties in proportion to each county's share of telephone households in the survey area. After a geographic area has been defined as a combination of counties, the sum of estimated telephone households is calculated and divided by the desired sample size to produce a sampling interval:

$$\text{Total estimated telephone households} \div \text{desired sample size} =$$
$$750{,}000 \div 6{,}000 = 125$$

A random number is drawn between 0 and the interval (125) to establish a starting point. Assuming the starting point is 86, then the 86th, 211th, 336th, 461st, . . . , records would be selected for the sample, each time stepping through the database by a factor of 125. This is a systematic random sample—as the sample is selected in a systematic "nth" fashion from a random starting point. Any

TABLE 7-3

Proportionate Distribution Through Systematic Sampling

	Total households	Percent with phone	Estimated phone households	Percent of sample
County A	223,404	94	210,000	28.0
County B	393,258	89	350,000	46.7
County C	204,301	93	190,000	25.3
Total	820,963		750,000	100.0

county whose population of estimated telephone households equals or exceeds the sampling interval is automatically included in the sample, while smaller counties are included with a probability proportionate to their size.

Using our example, where the sample size is 6,000, let us also assume that the geographic area selected covers three counties. The sampling interval allows the proportionate distribution of the sample over three counties as shown in Table 7-3.

Selection of Numbers Within Counties

For each county included in the sample, one or more unique telephone numbers is selected by systematic sampling from among all working blocks of numbers in all telephone exchanges assigned to the county. A working block is defined as 100 contiguous numbers containing three or more residential telephone listings:

> the phone number 266/7558
> exchange/block

In this example, for the exchange 266, the entire block comprises the number 7500-7599. Exchanges are assigned to a single county on the basis of where listed residents live. For those overlapping county lines, the exchanges are assigned to the county with the highest number of listed residents.

Selection Among Exchanges

Once the sample has been allocated, a second sampling interval is calculated for each county by dividing the number of listed telephone households for the county by the portion of the sample allocated to that county. In our earlier example, it was determined that 28 percent of the sample (1,680 numbers) would be drawn from County A. Each exchange and working block within an exchange are weighted by their share of listed telephone households. If the total number of listed telephone households in the data base for this county is 159,600, then that number divided by 1,680 gives us an interval of 95.

Next, from a random start between 1 and 95, those exchanges and working blocks falling within the interval are sampled on a systematic basis. Two more digits are then randomly chosen from the range 00–99 and added to each of the blocks selected. The result is a complete number made up of the exchange, the block, and the two random digits (for example, 266 + 75 + 59).

Source: Survey Sampling, Inc., used with permission.

Cluster Sampling. Cluster sampling procedures can be described broadly by the following features:

1. Based upon some classification variable or natural grouping, the entire population of sampling units is divided into mutually exclusive and exhaustive subsets, called **clusters.**
2. Clusters are then selected based upon a specified probability design such as SRS.
3. Elements are either probabilistically drawn from each selected cluster, or for each selected cluster all of the elements are included in the sample. Note that in contrast to SRS and stratified sampling, with cluster sampling, a sampling frame is needed only for those clusters selected into the sample.

There are many different types of cluster sampling designs. At the most general level, cluster sampling can involve either a single stage or multiple stages. By a stage we simply mean a step in the sampling process. For example, if stores participating in a test-market study are the clusters and calendar weeks are sampling units, then there might be two steps involved in selecting the sample of calendar weeks on which to base the estimate of volume sold for the test brand under study. The first step might involve selecting a sample of stores, and the second step might involve selecting a sample of calendar weeks for each of the stores selected at the first step. The clusters used at the first stage of sampling are generally referred to as **primary sampling units** (PSUs) and the sampling units selected at the second stage of sampling are generally referred to as **secondary sampling units** (SSUs).

A **single-stage cluster sample** entails one step in that once the sample of clusters is selected, every sampling unit within each of the selected clusters is included in the sample. If the clusters are chosen by SRS and within each cluster all sampling units are selected, then we refer to this design as **simple one-stage cluster sampling.**

Multiple stage cluster sampling designs entail two or more steps. For example, in a telephone survey we might first take a sample of states. Second, we might take a sample of counties within each sample cluster (states). Third, we might take a sample of working telephone exchanges within each of the counties selected at the second stage. And finally, we might take every telephone number within each working exchange selected at the third stage. Note that in multistage cluster sampling more than one sampling frame is likely to be used in drawing the sample. However, after each stage, the sampling frame for the next stage involves only those clusters chosen at the preceding stage. If the clusters at the first stage are selected by SRS, and if at the second stage the sampling units are selected probabilistically by SRS from each sample cluster so that the same fraction of sampling units is drawn from each sample cluster, then we refer to this design as **simple two-stage cluster sampling.** In cases where the clusters are of unequal size, then it is not always possible for the fraction of sampling units at the second stage to be ex-

Cluster sampling Design where a sample of clusters is first selected and then a decision on which sampling units to include in the sample is made.
Clusters Groups or collections of sampling units.

Primary sampling units (PSUs) Clusters used at the first stage of sampling.
Secondary sampling units (SSUs) Sampling units selected at the second stage of sampling.
Single-stage cluster sample One-step design where, once the sample of clusters is selected, every sampling unit within each of the selected clusters is included in the sample.
Simple one-stage cluster sampling One-step design where first stage clusters are selected by SRS and within each selected cluster all sampling units are chosen.

Simple two-stage cluster sampling Design where the clusters at the first stage are selected by SRS, and at the second stage the sampling units are selected probabilistically by SRS from each sample cluster—so that the same fraction of sampling units is drawn from each sample cluster.

actly the same within each sample cluster. A frequently used type of two-stage design that does not entail SRS of clusters at the first stage is called sampling with **probability proportional to size, PPS sampling.** Under PPS sampling, clusters are sampled at the first stage with probability proportional to the number of sampling units in the cluster.

The two primary advantages of cluster sampling are feasibility and economy. For these reasons, cluster sampling is frequently used in practice, especially in surveys covering large geographical areas. The practical feasibility of cluster sampling comes about because in many settings the only sampling frame readily available for the target population is one that lists clusters. Lists of geographical regions, blocks, telephone exchanges, and the like can usually be compiled relatively easily, and the researcher can thus avoid compiling a list of all individual elements for the target population, a process almost never feasible in terms of time and resources for populations of any reasonable size.

Cluster sampling is generally the most cost-effective means of sampling. Cost efficiencies come about because of the relative ease with which sampling frames can be assembled and the reduced costs associated with traveling. For example, with in-home personal surveys, if a geographical area such as a census tract defines the clusters, then once the sample of census tract clusters is selected and households are selected from within the sample census tracts, then the cost of traveling from household to household will usually be relatively low. Cost economies arise from selecting a relatively small number of census-tract clusters and sampling many households from the sample census tracts, as opposed to taking a SRS of households (of a given size) spread across many census tracts: The traveling costs for visiting households living in different census tracts are considerably higher than the traveling costs of visiting households in the same tract.

Though practical and economical, cluster sampling is not without its disadvantages, however. First, and perhaps most serious, for a given sample size the estimates obtained from cluster sampling designs are frequently not as precise as those obtained from samples drawn with the use of other sampling designs. The reliability of cluster samples will be poor depending upon the extent to which sampling units within a cluster are homogeneous. The procedure with cluster sampling is to select many sampling units from very few clusters to capitalize on traveling-cost savings. However, if the within-cluster sampling units are homogeneous, then selecting more than one of these sampling units provides very little additional information on the population characteristic under study. Thus, the ultimate sample selected from the small number of cluster PSUs can be unrepresentative of the entire target population and highly unreliable estimates can be obtained. In cluster sampling, we want the within-cluster sampling units to be somewhat heterogeneous with respect to the sampling variable to ensure representativeness. However, in practice, clusters tend to be homogeneous—for example, households on the same block are frequently similar with respect to socioeconomic

230

and demographic factors; patrons who regularly frequent the same store are often similar with respect to social class as well as other variables.

The aim in choosing a sampling design is to select the one that yields the most precise estimates at a specified cost, or conversely, the design having lowest cost that yields estimates with specific precision. If cost and feasibility were the sole concerns, then rarely would one choose any design other than cluster sampling. On the other hand, if reliability of estimates were the sole concern, then one would rarely choose cluster sampling. In choosing between cluster sampling and other designs we must incorporate reliability *and* cost *and* feasibility.

The second principal disadvantage associated with cluster sampling designs is their complexity. The most complex cluster sampling designs occur when each cluster in the population does not have the same number of sampling units. The complexity of cluster sampling manifests itself in several difficulties. The procedure for drawing the sample becomes more difficult and estimation formulas become much more involved; in fact, standard statistical software packages cannot usually be used to estimate population parameters under cluster sampling except in simple one-stage designs where formulas for estimates resemble the formulas used in SRS.

Use of Probability Samples. In commercial marketing research studies, probability samples are drawn when the need is for highly accurate estimates of share of market or volume that can be statistically projected to the entire market. Heterogeneous markets favor the use of nationwide studies and probability samples. In nationwide studies a high degree of accuracy is generally worth the extra cost because of the information needed and the decisions to be made. For example, national market tracking studies provide information on category and brand-use incidence rates and demographic and psychographic user profiles. Among other things this information is used to measure the relative effectiveness of the organization's marketing program, to define target audiences, to identify marketing opportunities, and to provide direction for developing marketing strategies. Such decisions are vitally important to the organization and require accurate estimates that can be statistically projected to the entire market. Finally, as we indicated in Chapter 5, the clear trend is away from in-home personal surveys. It is not surprising that most studies that use probability samples are conducted via the telephone. These designs generally call for a two-stage procedure in which systematic and stratified sampling are combined with some form of random digit dialing (see Exhibit 7-2).

Nonprobability Samples

All **nonprobability sampling procedures** share a common characteristic. There is no way of determining exactly what is the chance of selecting any particular element into the sample. Consequently, esti-

Nonprobability samples
Form of sampling where there is no way of determining exactly what the chance is of selecting any particular element or sampling unit into the sample.

mates are not statistically projectable to the entire population. We don't mean that nonprobability samples are necessarily inaccurate and always inferior to probability samples. Rather, nonprobability samples can be good (representative) or bad (unrepresentative) depending on the approach and controls used in selecting who is included in the sample. Certain nonprobability designs produce what are called purposive samples, since certain "important" segments of the target population are intentionally overrepresented in the sample. Some of the major nonprobability sampling approaches include convenience sampling, judgmental samples, and quota samples.

Convenience samples Studies in which respondent participation is voluntary or which leaves the selection of sampling units primarily up to the interviewer.

Convenience Samples. With convenience sampling, there is very little or no control over who is included in the sample. If respondent participation is voluntary or if the interviewer selects sampling units, then convenience samples are produced. For example, 100 women might be intercepted in a shopping mall and interviewed with no quotas or qualifications for participation in the study. There is no way to assess the representativeness of the sample. Mail surveys often produce convenience samples. Because of the self-selection and voluntary participation that accompany this data-collection method, the issue of nonresponse is extremely important. We will discuss nonresponse bias shortly.

Judgmental sampling Studies where respondents are selected because it is expected that they are representative of the population of interest and/or meet the specific needs of the research study.

Judgmental Samples. Judgment sampling involves selecting certain respondents for participation in the study. Respondents are selected because they are presumably representative of the population of interest and/or meet the specific needs of the research study. Judgment samples are frequently used in commercial marketing research studies. For example, the concept product test described in Exhibit 7-1 specifies that only past-thirty-day facial-moisturizer category users should be interviewed. Test markets exemplify judgmental samples—the specific community, neighborhood, or metropolitan area is presumed to be representative of the entire market. Scanner services also use what must be considered judgmental samples of cities. As we discuss in Chapter 21, a debate centers on whether the judgmentally selected sample of cities represents only those specific cities or actually the entire United States.

Snowball design Sample formed by having each respondent, after being interviewed, identify others who belong to the target population of interest.

A special kind of judgmental sampling is the **snowball design,** frequently used when it is necessary to reach a small, specialized target population. Under a snowball design, after being interviewed, each respondent is asked to identify others who belong to the target population.

Quota sampling Design that involves selecting specific numbers of respondents who possess certain characteristics known, or presumed to affect, the subject of the research study.

Quota Samples. Quota sampling involves selecting specific numbers of respondents who possess certain characteristics known or presumed to affect the subject of the research study. It is extremely common in commercial marketing research studies to set quotas on interviews based on age, gender, or income. Quota samples are designed to ensure that the proportion of the sample elements possessing a certain characteristic is approximately the same as the proportion with the characteristic in the

232

population of interest. In other words, the sample is representative of the entire population. The concept/product test described in Exhibit 7-1 uses a quota sampling design. The age quota specifications shown presumably reflect the actual age distribution of all category users in the entire facial-moisturizer market, or a subsegment of category users who constitute the target market. An interviewer at the testing location, who is responsible for conducting twenty interviews, might be instructed to intercept and interview nine female past-30-day category users, aged 18–34, six female past-30-day category users, aged 35–54; and five female past-30-day category users, 55 years or older. Table 7–4 presents some representative

TABLE 7-4
Representative Quota Sample Requirements

	Chewing gum		Breath sweeteners		Antacid		Cough drop	
	% of users	% of volume	% of users	% of volume	% of users	% of volume	% of users	% of volume
Male	45	45	45	45	45	NA	40	45
Female	55	55	55	55	55	NA	60	55
8–11	10	10	—	—	—	—	10	5
12–17	20	25	20	20	—	—	15	10
18–24	20	20	20	20	15	NA	25	25
25–34	20	20	20	20	25	NA	25	25
35–49	15	15	25	25	25	NA	15	20
50 +	15	10	15	15	35	NA	10	15

	Razor blades % of volume			Hand/body lotions % of volume			Cough syrup % of volume
	Males	Females		Males	Females		Females
18–34	45	60	18–34	60	30	18–34	60
35–49	25	20	35–54	30	60	35–49	40
50–65	30	20	55–65	10	10		

	Mouthwash % of users
Male	45
Female	55
16–24	20
25–34	25
35–49	25
50–64	25
65 +	5

quota sample requirements based on category users and/or category volume for several product categories.

Whether quota samples actually produce representative samples is often a difficult question to answer.[5] If an important characteristic that affects the subject of the research study is overlooked, then the quota sample will not be representative. Because quota samples are frequently used in mall-intercept surveys, there is potential for overrepresenting the kinds of people who frequent high-traffic shopping malls (see Chapter 5). To improve the quality of mall-intercept quota samples we suggest the following guidelines[6]:

- Use several different shopping malls in different neighborhoods so that differences between them can be observed.
- To minimize biases caused by traffic and parking flows, stratify by mall-entrance location and take a separate sample from each entrance.
- To minimize biases caused by shopping patterns, stratify by time segments—such as weekdays, weekday evenings, and weekends—and interview during each segment.

Use of Nonprobability Samples. Nonprobability samples are frequently used in commercial marketing research studies. In many instances the cost of conducting a national probability sample is prohibitively expensive, given the information needed and the decisions to be made. In practical settings the objectives of the study dictate what method of sampling will be used. For example, in concept tests, product tests, package tests, name tests, focus groups, and copy tests, all using nonprobability samples, projectable totals are usually not needed; rather we need to know only the proportion of the sample checking top-box purchase-intent scores or favorable brand attitudes. Moreover, since these studies typically focus on brands for which shopping mall customers represent a major share of the market, mall shoppers can provide an adequate population, and mall-intercept quota samples are frequently used.[7]

NONRESPONSE BIAS ISSUES

The quality of the data collected in a particular survey is a function of what can be called the **total survey error.**[8] Total survey error reflects the difference between the overall population's true mean value (on the

Total survey error The difference between the overall population's true mean value (on the variable of interest) and the mean observed value (of the variable of interest) obtained from the particular sample of respondents.

[5] See Leslie Kish, *Survey Sampling* (New York: John Wiley & Sons, 1965) 562–566, for a discussion of the problems in quota samples.

[6] The following guidelines were adapted from Seymour Sudman, "Improving the Quality of Shopping Center Sampling," *Journal of Marketing Research* November 1980, 423–31.

[7] *Ibid.*, p. 423.

[8] The discussion of total survey error and its components follows the presentation in H. Assael and J. Keon, "Nonsampling vs. Sampling Errors in Sampling Research," *Journal of Marketing*, Spring 1982, 114–123.

characteristic of interest) and the mean observed value (of the characteristic of interest) obtained from the particular sample of respondents. A matter of some importance is what causes the information obtained from a sample of respondents to differ from that of the entire population. Total survey error is composed of two components: **random sampling error** and **nonsampling error.**

Total survey error = random sampling error + nonsampling error

Random sampling error occurs because the particular sample selected is an imperfect representation of the overall population. Random sampling error represents how accurately the chosen sample's true mean value reflects the population's true mean value. It can be controlled by employing appropriate statistical design considerations and by increasing the sample size.

Nonsampling error represents the degree to which the mean observed value (on the characteristic of interest) for the respondents of a particular sample agrees with the mean true value for the particular sample of respondents (on the characteristic of interest). The size of nonsampling error depends on two factors: **nonresponse error** and **response error.** Nonresponse error occurs because not all of the respondents included in the sample respond; in other words, with nonresponse, the mean true value (on the characteristic of interest) of those sample respondents who do respond may be different from the entire sample's true mean value (on the characteristic of interest). The other component of nonsampling error, response error, occurs when respondents give inaccurate answers.

Nonsampling errors are more complex and harder to control than are sampling errors. And some evidence suggests that nonsampling errors are a much larger part of the total survey error than are sampling errors.

Response Errors

Response errors occur when respondents do not provide accurate answers. A respondent may give inaccurate responses intentionally or unintentionally, because of interviewer effects and biases as well as other external or societal factors:

1. *Intentional factors.* Respondents may purposely misreport their answers because they want to "help" the researcher and therefore either agree or disagree with all statements; called **acquiescence bias,** it is particularly prominent in new-product tests. When faced with a new-product concept, certain respondents will respond very positively to the concept regardless of their true feeling.

2. *Unintentional factors.* Even though a respondent intends to respond accurately, response errors arise because of a faulty recall, fatigue, question format, question content, or some other unintentional fac-

Random sampling error Error caused because the particular sample selected is an imperfect representation of the overall population and therefore the true mean value for the particular sample of respondents (on the variable of interest) differs from the true mean value for the overall population (on the variable of interest).

Nonsampling error Degree to which the mean observed value (on the variable of interest) for the respondents of a particular sample agrees with the mean true value for the particular sample of respondents (on the variable of interest).

Nonresponse error Error that occurs because not all of the respondents included in the sample respond; in other words, with nonresponse, the mean true value (on the variable of interest) of these sample respondents who do respond may be different from the entire sample's true mean value (on the variable of interest).

Response error Error that occurs because respondents (who do respond) may give inaccurate answers or a respondent's answers may be misrecorded.

Acquiescence bias Tendency to agree or disagree with all statements.

tor. (We discuss the proper way to construct and format questions in Chapter 12.)

Response errors also arise when respondents are unfamiliar or have little experience with the topic of the survey. For example, asking low-income respondents about what is most important in choosing a European vacation spot and their intentions about which vacation spots they will go to may result in intention scores that have little or no relationship to the respondent's actual behavior.

3. *Interviewer effects and biases.* Remember that interviewers can influence respondent's answers, misrecord respondents' answers, or even cheat by falsifying respondents' answers.

4. *Extended or societal factors.* Respondent errors can arise because the respondent is influenced either positively or negatively by the organization conducting the study. Also, the desire to give socially acceptable answers to sensitive or potentially embarrassing questions leads to response errors.

Nonresponse Errors

Very few studies achieve a 100 percent response rate. The problem of nonresponse error occurs because those who agree to participate in the study are different, in some way, from those who are unable or unwilling to participate. In general, the higher the response rate, the lower the probability of nonresponse effects. However, response rate can be a poor indicator of nonresponse error. First, response rates provide no information about whether the respondents are good representatives of the original target sample. Second, an increasing response does not necessarily reduce nonresponse error. For example, if those nonrespondents who are induced to respond, through call-backs or some other method, are no different from the respondents already in the sample, nonresponse bias may still be a problem.[9] Third, the notion of response rate is ambiguous since the number of eligible respondents used in the calculation of response rates frequently differs across studies; in some instances, for example, poor health or an inability to communicate in English are considered acceptable reasons for not counting a contact in the response rate calculation, whereas in other instances, they are not considered legitimate. Finally, another difficulty is that researchers often fail to report the way in which the response rate was calculated.[10]

Unfortunately, the extent of the differences between respondents and nonrespondents can seldom be directly determined. Indirect methods sometimes provide very limited checks for respondent and nonre-

[9]See L. Leslie, "Are High Response Rates Essential to Valid Surveys," *Social Science Research*, September 1971, 332–34.

[10]See J. Williams-Jones, "Lack of Agreement on the Standardization of Response Terminology in the Survey Research Industry," in K. B. Monroe, *Advances in Consumer Research VIII* (Association for Consumer Research, 1981), 281–286.

spondent differences. For example, if the sample is drawn from available records, (e.g., personnel files or warranty cards) whatever information is available from those sources can be used to check for respondent-nonrespondent differences.[11] If the sample is supposed to be representative of the general population, then comparisons can be made against the United States Census.[12] Note, however, that indirect comparisons may be of little use and may even be misleading if the characteristics employed for comparison purposes are not closely related to the variable under study. For example, if age and occupation information are available from warranty card records, but these variables have no relationship to receptivity to a new direct-mailing appeal, then to use them as a basis for comparing respondents and nonrespondents may be of little value.

With personal and telephone surveys the interviewer can make limited judgments about a person's background characteristics when a refusal occurs. For example, the interviewer may be able to make judgments about the nonrespondent's age, gender, marital status, family size, socioeconomic status, and so on. This is not the case with mail surveys; with no interviewer, nonrespondent characteristics cannot be determined. Mail surveys present the researcher with much more serious respondent-nonrespondent differences than do either personal or telephone surveys. The reason is the chance for response selectivity.[13] Recipients of mail questionnaires can examine the instrument thoroughly before deciding to respond. Interest in the particular survey topic is likely to be a primary factor in whether the questionnaire is completed and returned. As a result, respondents may not be representative of the original target sample.

Improving Response Rates

Because a low response rate increases the probability of nonresponse error, researchers have tried to develop procedures to improve response rates. Low response rates can be caused by not-at-homes and refusals.

Not-At-Homes. Low response rates caused by not-at-homes can be a serious problem with in-home personal and telephone surveys; however, employing a series of call-backs can drastically reduce the percentage of not-at-homes.

The minimum number of call-backs in consumer surveys is typically three to four. The percentage of not-at-homes will vary with such factors as (1) the nature of the respondent—individuals more likely to be at

[11] D. A. Dillman, *Mail and Telephone Surveys: The Total Design Method* (New York: John Wiley and Sons, 1978), 53.
[12] D. A. Dillman, J. A. Christenson, E. H. Carpenter, and R. M. Brooks, "Increasing Mail Questionnaire Response: A Four-State Comparison," *American Sociological Reviews*, 1974, 744–756.
[13] Dillman, 53.

home include married people with small children, as opposed to single or divorced people, (2) the day and time of call—contact is more likely on the weekend than on a weekday, in the evening as opposed to in the afternoon; and (3) the interview situation—all else the same, advance appointments made by telephone or by mail notice increase contact.

Available data clearly indicate that (1) people are generally not home as much as they used to be, and (2) the best time to contact an individual is in the evening. For example, societal and lifestyle changes, working wives, fewer children, higher divorce rates, and the diminishing role of the family can explain why it is becoming increasingly more difficult to contact respondents.

The successful use of call-backs is based on two assumptions: (1) the number of nonresponses due to not-at-homes and the probability of response must be large enough to justify the effort—if the number of hard-core zero responses is large, then call-backs will be fruitless; and (2) call-backs should be different from those respondents already in the sample.

There should be a prescribed plan for and control over call-backs. A control sheet is commonly used in telephone surveys to record the outcome of each attempted contact. Typically, the first call yields the most responses, but the second and third calls have higher responses per call.[14] The first call frequently provides information about the respondent that allows subsequent calls to be scheduled more efficiently. The ultimate decision concerning the number of call-backs involves weighing the benefits of reducing nonresponse bias by initiating further call-backs against their additional cost. As call-backs are initiated and completed, an evaluation of the difference between the call-back respondents and the respondents already in the sample should be conducted. If the differences are minor or if a trend develops on the survey variable of interest, fewer call-backs may be warranted or no further call-backs may be warranted at all.

Refusals. The second component contributing to low response rates is refusals. The unwillingness or inability of respondents to answer specific questions or participate in the survey at all is a potential problem for in-home personal, mail, telephone and mall-intercept personal surveys. Procedures for reducing refusals vary depending on the method of data collection.

The proportion of refusals depends upon a diverse set of factors. As we indicated in Chapter 5, refusal rates in *personal and telephone surveys* can be high. Procedures for reducing refusals in these surveys have emphasized prior notification, motivating the respondent, and proper writing and administration of the questions.

1. **Prior notification** involves sending potential respondents an advance letter to notify them of the impending telephone or personal contact. Advance letters appear to positively affect response rates for

Prior notification
Method of reducing nonresponse that involves sending potential respondents an advance letter to notify them of the impending telephone or personal contact.

---

[14]Leslie Kish, *Survey Sampling* (New York: John Wiley & Sons, 1965), p. 552.

samples of the general public.[15] The rationale behind this procedure is simple: Respondents often react with suspicion when reached by an unexpected telephone call or contacted by an interviewer either in their home or at a shopping mall. This element of surprise and uncertainty contributes to refusals and diminishes the overall quality of the data collected. The advance letter seeks to relieve potential anxiety regarding inclusion in a survey while at the same time creating a cooperative atmosphere. With mall-intercept personal surveys, respondents can be prerecruited; that is, respondents are screened ahead of time by telephone. If the respondent qualifies, then he or she is asked to come to the central mall-testing location at a specific time to be interviewed. A prerecruiting strategy works best in situations where the proportion of qualified respondents is low—for example, with low-incidence product categories and when the interview is lengthy. Prior notification cannot be used in all instances, however. For example, it is not possible with random digit dialing.

2. *Motivating the respondent* involves procedures that can potentially increase respondents' interest or involvement and thereby gain their cooperation. One type of procedure called the **foot-in-the-door technique** involves first getting respondents to complete a relatively short, simple questionnaire and then, at some later time, asking them to complete a longer questionnaire on the same general topic. The rationale behind this procedure is based on **self-perception theory,** which proposes that individuals come to know their attitudes through interpreting the causes of their behavior.[16] To the extent that one's behavior is attributed to internal causes and not to circumstantial pressures, a positive attitude toward the behavior develops; and these attitudes, or self-perceptions, exert a direct influence on subsequent behavior. Thus, the self-perception paradigm predicts that persons who actually comply with the small request will view themselves as persons who engage in such activities and so will be more likely to perform similar, more substantial activities. Though the evidence indicates that this procedure generally increases response rates, it may not be significant in view of the substantial added expense.[17]

3. *Proper writing and administration of the questions* relates to the skills and expertise of the person putting together the questionnaire and the interviewer who administers it. Interviewers who have learned how far to probe and encroach on respondents' privacy and patience without outraging their stamina will reduce the proportion of

Foot-in-the-door technique Method of reducing nonresponse involves first getting respondents to complete a relatively short, simple questionnaire and then, at some later time, asking them to complete a larger questionnaire on the same general topic.

Self-perception theory Theory proposing that individuals come to know their attitudes through interpreting the causes of their behavior. To the extent that one's behavior is attributed to internal causes and not to circumstantial pressures, a positive attitude toward the behavior develops, and these attitudes, or self-perceptions, exert a direct influence on subsequent behavior.

[15]D. A. Dillman, J. G. Gallegos, and J. H. Frey, "Reduce Refusal Rates for Telephone Interviews," *Public Opinion Quarterly*, 1976, 66–78.

[16]D. Bem, "Self-Perception Theory," in *Advances in Experimental Social Psychology*, edited by L. Berkowitz (New York: Academic Press, 1972), 1–62.

[17]R. M. Graves and L. J. Magilavy, "Increasing Response Rates to Telephone Surveys: A Door in the Face For Foot-In-The-Door," *Public Opinion Quarterly*, Fall 1981, 346–58.

refusals. Skilled interviewers can reduce the proportion of refusals by not accepting a no answer to a request for cooperation without making an additional plea. This procedure, called **refusal conversion** or **persuasion,** has been found to decrease refusal on the average by about 7 percent.[18]

Second, refusals to specific questions can be reduced by proper attention to question wording and format. Interviewing respondents by telephone or in person means that the questions asked are usually communicated orally. Oral communication means that many questions appropriate in mail surveys will not work if asked in the same form on the telephone or in person. Finally, question format and wording also affect respondents' willingness to answer socially threatening or embarrassing questions. We return to this issue as well as some general guidelines for properly writing and administering questionnaires in Chapter 12.

A relatively large number of procedures have been investigated as potential ways to improve refusals in *mail surveys.* Among these are prior notification, characteristics of the cover letter and questionnaire, and follow-up procedures.

1. *Prior notification* to inform or motivate respondents has successfully increased response rate.[19] In addition, it can also accelerate the rate of return. An advance letter or phone call generally informs respondents that they will be receiving a questionnaire shortly and requests their cooperation. The *foot-in-the-door* technique previously described can also be used, although the evidence seems to indicate that this approach does not generate higher response rates than does standard prenotification.[20]

2. *Characteristics of the cover letter and questionnaire* that could be useful in reducing refusals have been extensively investigated. The cover letter is integral to the mail survey and may be the most logical and efficient vehicle for persuading individuals to respond. The cover letter is the first part of the mail-out package that respondents will likely read. It introduces the survey and motivates the respondent to fill it out and return it as quickly as possible. Specific elements that should be included in the cover letter are discussed in Chapter 12.

3. *Follow-ups* involve contacting the respondent periodically after the initial mailing. **Follow-ups** or reminders are almost universally successful in reducing refusals and usually are less costly than prior

[18] *Ibid.,* 357.

[19] See, for example, B. J. Walker and R. B. Burdick, "Advance Correspondence and Error in Mail Surveys," *Journal of Marketing Research,* August 1977, 379–83.

[20] For experimental results on the foot-in-the-door technique, see C. T. Allen, C. D. Schewe, and G. Wijk, "More on Self-Perception Theory's Foot Technique in the Pre-Call Mail Survey Setting," *Journal of Marketing Research,* November 1980, 498–502; and R. A. Hansen and L. M. Robinson, "Testing the Effectiveness of Alternative Foot-In-The-Door Manipulations," *Journal of Marketing Research,* August 1980, 359–364.

E X H I B I T 7-3

Sequence of Follow-ups in Mail Survey

One week: A postcard reminder sent to everyone. It serves as both a thank you for those who have responded and as a friendly and courteous reminder for those who have not.

Three weeks: A letter and replacement questionnaire sent only to nonrespondents. Nearly the same in appearance as the original mailout, it has a shorter cover letter that informs nonrespondents that their questionnaire has not been received, and appeals for its return.

Seven weeks: This final mailing is similar to the one that preceded it except that it is sent by certified mail to emphasize its importance. Another replacement questionnaire is enclosed.

Source: Dillman (1978)

notification procedures. Follow-up procedures involve a sequence of mailings. Exhibit 7-3 describes a typical sequence identified by the number of weeks that elapsed after the original mailout.[21]

Remedies for Nonresponse[22]

Several different remedies for nonresponse error have been proposed. We discuss five approaches to dealing with it.

Estimation of Effects. Whenever possible, the researcher should attempt to estimate the effects of nonresponse. However, this process is complicated by the fact that direct validation rarely will be possible. One approach is to link nonresponse rates to nonresponse effects.

As a first step, nonresponse rates should always be reported. As we indicated, though high response rate is not in itself enough evidence to conclude that nonresponse bias is small, it does reduce the probability of nonresponse effects. In most instances, it seems reasonable to assume that a small nonresponse is unlikely to produce a large effect on the sample mean value of the variable of interest. To estimate the effects of nonresponse, nonresponse size must be linked to estimates of differences between respondents and nonrespondents. How? The key is to find out information about these differences. This information can be obtained from the sample itself—for example, from follow-ups on a subsample of the nonrespondents or from extrapolating any differences found through call-backs. Another frequent source of information on these differences is the knowledge base accumulated in past studies.

Estimation of Effects
Method of handling nonresponse error by linking nonresponse rates to nonresponse effects; to estimate the effects of nonresponse, nonresponse size is linked to estimates of differences between respondents and nonrespondents.

[21]Dillman, 183.
[22]Parts of this treatment follow the discussion in Kish, 557–60.

241

Simple Weighting
Procedures that attempt to remove nonresponse bias by assigning weights to the data that in some sense account for nonresponse.

Simple Weighting. Weighting procedures attempt to remove nonresponse bias by assigning weights to the data to help account for nonresponse. Suppose that in a national survey, response rates differed in each of four major geographical regions. Assume that the response rates were 80 percent in the East, 50 percent in the South, 75 percent in the North, and 60 percent in the West. For the East the weight would be 1.25 (100/80); for the South 2.00 (100/50); for the North 1.33 (100/75); and for the West 1.67 (100/60). Weighting subclasses inversely to their response rates can correct for differences between them; however, this weighting destroys the self-weighting nature of a sample design, and the complications of weighting can sometimes be expensive. We comment on this issue further in Chapter 13.

Substitutions Method of handling nonresponse; nonresponses are replaced with other substitute respondents expected to respond.

Substitutions. Substitutions for nonresponse simply involve replacement—nonresponses are simply replaced with other respondents—that is, substitutes that are expected to respond. This approach is based on dividing the overall sample into subclasses. The subclasses should be internally homogenous for respondent background characteristics but should vary greatly in terms of response rates. If the subclasses are so constructed, then a substitute can be identified who is similar to a particular nonrespondent and not to respondents already in the sample. The substitution approach is useless for reducing nonresponse bias when replacing a nonrespondent with a respondent who resembles other respondents in the same way.

Imputation Approach that imputes nonresponses to specific questions or an entire questionnaire on the basis of a set of characteristics available for both respondents and nonrespondents.

Imputation. This approach attributes nonresponses to specific questions or an entire questionnaire on the basis of a set of characteristics available for both respondents and nonrespondents. Imputation is based on the notion that if there is high correlation between a set of characteristics and the response variable under study, then a reasonably good prediction of the "missing" variable (nonresponse) may be obtained from capitalizing on this correlation. In many surveys imputation for nonrespondents is carried out by adjusting the weights of the respondents to account for nonresponse, similar to the simple weighting approach described above, or by a replacement procedure, as was done in the 1960 Census where a nonresponding household was replaced by the questionnaire responses of the previously listed responding household.[23]

Replacement Approach to reducing nonresponse; included in the survey are the addresses (or telephone numbers) of nonrespondents from an earlier survey that used similar sampling procedures. When a response is obtained in the current survey, the interviewer replaces the nonresponse address with an address for a nonresponse in a previous study.

Replacement. The replacement approach works as follows: Included in the survey are the addresses (or telephone numbers) of nonrespondents from an earlier survey that used similar sampling procedures. When a nonresponse is obtained in the current survey, the interviewer replaces the nonresponse address with an address of a nonrespondent in a pre-

[23]A comprehensive review of alternative and weighting imputation procedures can be found in D. W. Chapman, "Survey of Nonresponse Imputation Procedures," *Proceedings of the Social Statistics Section, American Statistical Association* Part I (Washington: American Statistical Association, 1976), 245–51.

vious survey. This approach was originally proposed for in-home (dwelling) personal surveys; through minor modification it can be applied in other survey settings. Obviously, the replacement approach works best in situations where a firm conducts surveys routinely involving similar survey sampling procedures.

For the replacement approach to be successful, three conditions must be in place: (1) the earlier survey nonresponse addresses must be numerous enough and have significantly high chance of response to justify the effort; (2) the relationship of the probability of response to the survey should be strong so that additional responses tend to yield correspondingly large reductions in nonresponse bias—in other words, nonresponse addresses in the earlier survey should be different from respondents already in the sample; and (3) nonresponses of the current survey must be similar in nature to nonresponse from the earlier survey from which the replacement addresses have been taken—ideally, the time between the two surveys should be brief and both surveys should use similar kinds of respondents.

Summary

In this chapter we have presented a treatment of the fundamental concepts of sampling. We organized our discussion in terms of the five key decision issues that a marketing manager or researcher must consider when devising a sampling plan. Sampling decisions are complex; there is no single "right" way to make sampling decisions. As we emphasize, cost, reliability of the estimates, industry practices, and convenience all influence the choice of a sample design. Because of the interrelationships among the decision issues (for example, the method of data collection is related to the method of drawing the sample), compromises will undoubtedly have to be made. Since most serious errors in sample design occur because of nonsampling errors we suggest that the researcher be particularly sensitive to nonresponse bias and errors in logic.

Key Concepts

Target population
Sampling frames
Incidence rates
Sample size determination
Probability samples
Simple random samples
Stratified samples
Cluster samples
Nonprobability samples

Convenience samples
Judgment samples
Quota samples
Nonresponse bias
Nonresponse errors
Response errors
Improving response rates
Remedies for nonresponse

Review Questions

1. What is a target population?
2. What are incidence rates?
3. Discuss how each of the components of a confidence interval can affect sample size determination.
4. Compare stratified sampling to cluster sampling.
5. When would a researcher most likely use (1) probability samples and (2) nonprobability samples?

Procedures for Drawing Probability Samples

CHAPTER OBJECTIVES

- Discuss the mechanics of probability sampling designs.
- Explain how to draw simple random samples, systematic samples, stratified samples, and cluster samples.
- Illustrate how population characteristics are estimated under simple random sampling, systematic sampling, stratified sampling, and cluster sampling.
- Demonstrate how required sample sizes are calculated under various probability sampling designs.

Introduction

This chapter presents the mechanics of drawing probability samples. The material will be of interest to those of you who want (or need) to understand more about how the various probability sampling designs work and specifically how probability samples are drawn. In our discussions of simple random sampling, systematic sampling, stratified sampling, and cluster sampling, we emphasize various issues likely to arise in practical application and, wherever possible, compare the benefits of each.

SIMPLE RANDOM SAMPLING PROCEDURES

As we indicated in Chapter 7, simple random sampling (SRS) is based upon the simplest probabilistic model: A *simple random sample* (**SRS**) of n elements from a target population of N elements is one in which each of the M samples in the target population has the same chance of being selected, equal to $1/M$. In addition, the probability of selecting any individual element is equal to n/N, the ratio of target sample size to target population size.

Selecting the Sample

If a sampling frame is available, a simple random sample is drawn according to the following steps:

1. Assign a number from 1 to N to each element.
2. Using the random number table (Table 1 in the Statistical Appendix) and as many digits consistent with N, begin at some arbitrary point and proceed either up, down, or diagonally until n different numbers greater than zero but less than or equal to n have been selected. If you reach the bottom line of a particular page, proceed to the top line of the very next column on that same page. If you run out of columns on the current page then proceed to the next page of random numbers.
3. The numbers selected identify the elements to include in the sample.

T A B L E 8-1

Completed Interviews per Day, Mall-Intercept in Cincinnati, Ohio, XYZ Field Service

Interviewer	Completed interviews/day (Y_i)
1*	4.5
2	3.5
3	6.5
4*	2.5
5	5.5
6*	3.5
7	3.5
8	2.5
9	4.5
10	5.5
11*	6.5
12*	6.5
13	5.5
14	4.5
15	2.5
	67.5

*Interviewers selected into the sample—see text discussion.

E X A M P L E

Suppose that, as part of your duties as a junior analyst, you are responsible for overseeing field service operations. Specifically, you are responsible for estimating the average number of interviews completed daily by all of the field services that have conducted mall-intercept surveys for your department in 1987. This information is to be used for 1988 budget planning purposes. You are beginning to plan the 1987 sampling design. To decide on how many field services to include in the sample, you take a simple random sample of field interviews from an "average" field service operation in order to obtain sample estimates of the mean and variance of the number of interviews completed per day. Table 8-1 lists the number of completed interviews per day for fifteen field interviewers employed by the XYZ Field Service—a presumably average field service operator.

The following procedure is used to draw a simple random sample of $n = 5$ field interviewers. Because $N = 15$, two-digit random numbers are used. Beginning at some arbitrary point in a random number table (Statistical Appendix, Table 1), at row 16, column 2 for example, you use the first two columns to select the needed interviewers. Moving down the column pick out five different numbers between 01 and 15. Numbers equal to 00 or greater than 15 are discarded as well as any duplication. From the random number digit table we find that the first two-digit number satisfying these conditions is 12, followed by 04, 01, 06, and 11. Note that the number 04 was encountered twice, but it was discarded the second time. Also note that when the bottom of the page is reached, you proceed to the top line of the very next column on the same page.

Estimating Population Characteristics

Estimates obtained under SRS are unbiased estimators of their corresponding population values. If, for simplicity, we assume infinite (or at least very large) target populations, we can estimate the mean and variance of the characteristic being measured in the entire target population under SRS as follows[1]

$$\bar{y} = \sum_{i=1}^{n} y_i/n \tag{8-1}$$

$$s_y^2 = \frac{\sum_{i=1}^{n} (y_i - \bar{y})^2}{n-1} \tag{8-2}$$

where

n = total sample size

y_i = value of the characteristic being measured for the ith element in the target sample

$\bar{y}$ = estimated mean value (unbiased estimator of population mean)

s_y^2 = estimated sample variance (unbiased estimator of population variance)

In Chapter 7 we introduced the concept of reliability in discussing sample size determination. The reliability of an estimated *population parameter* (for example, a mean value or a proportion) refers to its reproducibility—how reproducible the estimate of a population parameter is over different samples of a given size. Assuming no measurement error, the reliability of an estimate of a population parameter can be judged in terms of its **standard error.** For instance, the estimated standard error of the sample mean is given by

$$s_{\bar{y}} = \frac{s_y}{\sqrt{n}} \tag{8-3}$$

Standard error ($s_{\bar{y}}$)
Indication of the reliability of an estimate of a population parameter; it is computed by dividing the standard deviation of the sample estimate by the square root of the sample size.

[1]For computational purposes we recommend the following algebraically equivalent form for calculating the variance and standard deviation.

$$s_y^2 = \frac{\sum_{i=1}^{n} y_i^2 - \dfrac{\left(\sum_{i=1}^{n} y_i\right)^2}{n}}{n-1}$$

or

$$s_y = \sqrt{\frac{\sum_{i=1}^{n} y_i^2 - \dfrac{\left(\sum_{i=1}^{n} y_i\right)^2}{n}}{n-1}}$$

where $\sum_{i=1}^{n} y_i^2$ = summation of the squares of each observation

$\left(\sum_{i=1}^{n} y_i\right)^2$ = square of the total summation.

The smaller the estimated standard error associated with the sample mean, the greater the reliability of the sample estimate.

The standard error of an estimate can be used to form confidence limits on *population estimates.* To construct confidence intervals, we must make certain assumptions about the sampling distribution of the sample estimates. For reasonably large sample sizes (say $n > 30$), the sampling distributions of sample estimates (such as means or proportions) are close to the normal distribution, and normal theory can be used to construct confidence intervals for the unknown population parameters being estimated. For example, an appropriate 100 $(1 - \alpha/2)$ percent confidence interval for the true population mean is

$$\bar{y} \pm (t_{1-\alpha/2} s_y / \sqrt{n}) \tag{8-4}$$

All of the terms appearing in (8-4), except t, have been previously defined. The symbol t refers to students' t-distribution. We use the t-distribution instead of the standard normal z-distribution since in most cases the population variance will be unknown. Tabulated values for the standard normal z-distribution and the t-distribution are given in Tables 2 and 3, respectively, in the Statistical Appendix. The value of t is read from the table of students' t-distribution for n - 1 degrees of freedom.[2] If the sample size is greater than 30 then the value of t is the same as the value of z read from a standard normal table for the same level of significance.

The preceding formulas strictly apply to situations in which the target population is infinitely large. When the target sample is large in relation to the target population these formulas will overestimate the estimated variance (standard deviation) of a population parameter (mean or proportion). A correction factor is used whenever the target sample represents 10 to 20 percent or more of the target population. The **finite**

Finite population correction factor (fpc) Correction for overestimation of the estimated variance (standard deviation) of a population parameter (such as a mean, or proportion) when the target sample represents 10–20 percent or more of the target population.

population correction factor (fpc) is given by $\left(\dfrac{N - n}{N - 1}\right)$. The fpc "corrected" variance formula is thus

$$s_y^2 = \left(\frac{\sum\limits_{i=1}^{n} (y_i - \bar{y})^2}{n - 1}\right) \left(\frac{N - n}{N - 1}\right) \tag{8-5}$$

Essentially, the fpc depends upon the relation of n to N. If the population size N is very large and the sample size n is small, then the fpc will be close to 1; if, on the other hand, the sample size n is close to the population size N, then fpc will be less than 1 and will decrease the numerical value of the estimated population variance. In most consumer goods studies the assumption of infinite target populations is probably reasonable—target populations typically include millions of individuals or households.

---

[2] Recall from your basic statistics course that the term "degrees of freedom" refers to the total number of observations in the sample ($=n$) less the number of independent restrictions (parameters estimated).

E X A M P L E

Having drawn the sample (see Table 8-1), you, the junior analyst, turn to estimating the mean and variance of the number of interviews completed per day. Noting the finite nature of the population and that $n/N > 20$ percent you decide to use the fpc "corrected" variance formula. Applying expressions (8-1) and (8-5) yields the following results:

$$\bar{y} = \frac{4.5 + 2.5 + 3.5 + 6.5 + 6.5}{5} = 4.7 \text{ interviews/day}$$

$$s_y^2 = \frac{(4.5 - 4.7)^2 + (2.5 - 4.7)^2 + (3.5 - 4.7)^2 + (6.5 - 4.7)^2 + (6.5 - 4.7)^2}{5 - 1}\left(\frac{15 - 5}{14}\right)$$

$$= (3.2)\left(\frac{10}{14}\right) = 2.29$$

Thus the estimated standard error of the mean number of interviews completed per day is

$$s_{\bar{y}} = s_y/\sqrt{n}$$
$$= \sqrt{2.29}/\sqrt{5} = .68$$

Finally you compute a 95 percent confidence interval around this estimate. Setting $\alpha = .05$, we find from Table 3 in the Statistical Appendix, that $t_{1 - \alpha/2; n - 1} = 2.776$ and therefore

$$\bar{y} \pm t_{(1-\alpha/2); n-1}s_{\bar{y}}$$
$$4.7 \pm 2.776\,(.68) = 4.7 \pm 1.89$$
$$= \text{between 2.81 and 6.59 interviews/day}$$

In certain instances, the researcher may want to estimate population proportions. Appendix 8A, Exhibit 1 presents the necessary details.

Sample Size Determination

It is frequently necessary to determine the size of the sample required to estimate a population parameter with a certain level of precision. Following the discussion provided in Chapter 7, the procedure for determining such a sample size is

1. Specify the acceptable **tolerance level** *(h)*. This is the difference between the estimate and its unknown true population value. One approach to specifying the acceptable tolerance level is to take one-half of the desired confidence interval (range).
2. Determine the reliability coefficient $(z_{1-\alpha/2})$, which depends on the desired level of certainty $(1 - \alpha/2)$.
3. Obtain an estimate of the standard deviation $(\hat{\sigma}_y)$ of the characteristic to be measured in the target population. This can be based on prior

studies, on a small-scale pilot study, or subjectively by guessing or by taking one-sixth of the estimated range of the distribution of the characteristic (if normal).

4. Apply the following formula to obtain the required sample size n^*

$$n^* = \frac{(z_{1-\alpha/2})^2 \, (\hat{\sigma}_Y)^2}{(h)^2} \qquad (8\text{-}6)$$

To ensure an estimate within a fixed percent of the anticipated mean value, the following procedure should be followed:

Relative tolerance level (**r**) The difference between the estimate and its unknown true population value, expressed as a percentage.

Coefficient of variation (C_Y) A measure of relative dispersion given by dividing the population mean by its (true) standard deviation.

1. Specify the acceptable **relative tolerance level** (r), which is expressed as a fixed percent (for example, 5 percent or 10 percent).
2. Determine the reliability coefficient ($z_{1-\alpha/2}$).
3. Obtain an estimate of the **coefficient of variation** of the characteristic to be measured in the target population. The coefficient of variation (C_Y) is a measure of relative dispersion given by σ/μ, where σ is the (true) standard deviation of the population mean, and μ is the (true) population mean value. For the purpose of determining the required sample size, obtain an estimate of the anticipated mean value of the characteristic in the target population ($\overline{Y}$) and the estimated standard deviation ($\hat{\sigma}_Y$) of the characteristic in the target population and compute the estimated coefficient of variation

$$\hat{C}_Y = \hat{\sigma}_Y/\overline{Y}$$

4. Apply the following formula to obtain the required sample size n^*:

$$n^* = \frac{(z_{1-\alpha/2})^2 \, (\hat{C}_Y)^2}{(r)^2} \qquad (8\text{-}7)$$

Appendix 8A, Exhibit 1, gives the appropriate formulas for determining the required sample size in the case of proportions.

E X A M P L E

At this point, you the junior analyst, have all of the information needed to determine the sample size required to achieve a desired level of precision. Because results of the survey are to be used for budgetary purposes, your estimate of the mean number of interviews completed per day needs to be virtually certain ($z_{1-\alpha/2} = 3$) to be within 10 percent of the true population value. Using the "anticipated" mean ($\overline{Y} = 4.7$) and standard deviation ($\hat{\sigma}_Y = \sqrt{2.29} = 1.51$) obtained in the preliminary study, you first compute an estimate of the coefficient of variation:

$$\hat{C}_Y = 1.51/4.7$$
$$= .32$$

Next, formula (8-7) was applied:

$$n^* = (3)^2 (.32)^2/(.10)^2$$
$$= 92.16 \rightarrow 92$$

Since fractional interviewers cannot be sampled, the 92 will not give quite enough precision. In this case, you decide to include 93 interviewers in the target sample.

SYSTEMATIC SAMPLE PROCEDURES

In Chapter 7 we briefly mentioned an extremely easy-to-apply approach to drawing samples, namely, the method of systematic sampling. All systematic sampling designs have two characteristics in common: (1) the elements of a population are treated as an ordered sequence and (2) elements are selected according to some fixed interval from an ordered sampling frame. Put simply, systematic sampling consists of taking every kth sampling unit (or element) after a random start. Application of systematic sampling is quite easy, since it typically involves selecting every kth line from listing sheets or every kth block from numbered maps. In systematic sampling of one in k elements, there are k possible samples; and although each element has the same chance $(1/k)$ of being included in the sample, the particular sample selected depends on the random number used as the starting point. Thus, each of the k possible samples can be viewed as a "cluster" of n elements with each element being k units apart. In addition, because each sampling unit (or element) appears only once in each possible sample, each unit has a probability of selection also equal to $1/k$. For this reason, systematic sampling is actually a one-stage cluster sampling design (Chapter 7).

To draw a systematic sample, certain elements (or sampling units) in the target population will need to be identified; for example, one may want to select the elements labeled $j, j + k, j + 2k, j + 3k, \ldots$. Note, however, that in contrast to SRS the size of the target population (N) need not be known prior to sampling, nor does a list or other organized breakdown of the elements in the target population need to be available beforehand; in other words, the list can be compiled during the sampling process. An example of such a list would be the situation where you are sampling one of every five customers entering an entrance of a mall shopping center. The sampling can be done while the frame is being constructed.

We must emphasize two features of systematic sampling. First, the order of elements (or sampling units) in the list is not irrelevant. For example, consider the case of a researcher looking at supermarket sales over 365 consecutive days who decides to select every seventh day's sales into the sample. In this case, the sample of 52 days of sales (365 ÷ 7) would produce misleading results, since depending on where in the list of sales data the researcher started, the samples would reflect the sales for all Mondays, all Tuesdays, and so forth. The ordering of elements can affect the efficiency of the estimates obtained under this sampling design. Second, in contrast to SRS, in which *every one* of the *(N)* samples has the same chance of being selected, a systematic sample of one in *k* contains only *k* possible samples, and the particular sample selected depends upon which random number was originally selected.

Selecting the Sample

Assuming that some list or other organized breakdown of the elements in the target population is available, a systematic sample can be drawn by the following procedure.

Sampling interval
Computed by taking *n/N* together with *r*, the first chosen element to be included in the sample, determines which elements will be included in the sample.

1. For each element in the target population assign the numbers 1 to *N*. We will refer to the number assigned to an element as its *index*.
2. Suppose *n* elements are to be sampled. Compute $k = N/n$ where *k* is called the **sampling interval.** If *k* is a fraction, choose that integer closest to the ratio *N/n*.
3. Using a random number table, select a number, *r*, in the range 1 to *k*.
4. Select as the first element for inclusion in the sample the element with the index *r*.
5. Continue to select elements according to the following scheme

   $r + k$

   $r + 2k$

   .

   .

   .

   $r + (n - 1)k$

An example will help to clarify the procedure.

EXAMPLE

Let us return to the data on the number of completed interviews per day for the mall-intercept package test conducted in Cincinnati, Ohio, by the XYZ Field Service Company (see Table 8-1). However, suppose now that we wish to effect a systematic sample of size $n = 5$; in other words, we desire a sample in which 1 out of every 3 interviewers of the $N = 15$ interviewers will be selected. We have already assigned index numbers to all of the population elements so that we can go directly to step 2 and compute

$k = N/n = 15/5 = 3$

Since k is an integer we need neither round up nor down. Next, using Table 1 in the Statistical Appendix, we need to select a random number, r, between 1 and 3. Assume that $r = 2$. Thus, the systematic sample would consist of elements

$$r = 2$$
$$r + k = 5$$
$$r + 2k = 8$$
$$r + 3k = 11$$
$$r + (5 - 1)k = 14$$

We indicated earlier that a list need not be available prior to sampling. The following example illustrates how to draw systematic samples when no list is available.

EXAMPLE

Suppose that detailed records on all of the field service companies employed by the marketing research department over the last year are located in 6 file drawers, each having a depth of 32 inches. If a sample of 75 records is needed, a systematic sample could be drawn as follows:

1. Determine the total length of field records (that is, $32 \times 6 = 192$ inches).
2. Determine k, where in this case $k = 192/75 = 2.56$ inches, or the total length divided by the number of records.
3. Using a random number table select a number between 0 and k—that is, between 0.00 and 2.56. (Suppose that $r = 1.65$).
4. Using some kind of measuring device, take the record that is $r = 1.65$ inches from the front of the first file drawer. Select next the record that is $k = 2.56$ inches from the first record selected. Continue this process, moving onto other drawers when necessary until the end of the last drawer.

Estimating Population Characteristics

In general, estimation of population parameters and, in particular, the estimate of the variance of the characteristic under study in the target population can become quite complex. However, if the list from which the systematic sample is drawn represents a random ordering with respect to the variable being measured, then the estimates obtained under systematic sampling will be identical to those obtained under SRS; in other words, we can use the same formulas as in SRS.

Sample Size Determination

In general, the determination of sample size for systematic samples is quite difficult. However, if we assume that the list from which the systematic sample was drawn represents a random ordering with respect to the variable being measured, then the methods for determining sample size developed for SRS can be used. If the assumption of random ordering is not defensible, then little can be done. The problem is that the variance of estimates obtained under systematic sampling is dependent upon the sampling interval. For example, a one-in-four systematic sample from a list of 100 observations will yield a sample of size 25; a one-in-five systematic sample will yield a sample of size 20. Intuition coupled with what we now know about sampling theory would lead us to expect that the variance of estimates from the larger sample should be smaller than the variance estimates obtained in the smaller sample. However, depending on the ordering of elements in the list, the smaller sample may produce estimates that have smaller variances than those obtained in the larger sample. The point here is that, in practice, we will rarely know the nature of the list (that is, its ordering) and, therefore, it will be difficult for us to determine the appropriate sampling interval.

STRATIFIED SAMPLING PROCEDURES

In many studies, the target population of interest can be divided into different segments (strata), where each segment has a distinctive character. Under *stratified random sampling*, the information about the strata is used in designing the overall sampling plan. As discussed in Chapter 7, the following steps describe the essence of stratified sampling:

1. Based upon some classification variable, the entire population of sample units (or elements) is divided into distinct subpopulations called strata.
2. Within each stratum a separate random sample of elements is selected from all of the elements composing that stratum.
3. A separate mean (or proportion) is computed for each stratum from the sample selected from each stratum, and these separate estimates are properly weighted and added to obtain a combined estimate for the entire population.
4. The variances of the estimates are also computed separately for each stratum, and these are also properly weighted and added to form a combined estimate for the entire population.

The objective of stratification is to maximize the homogeneity of the sampling elements *within* strata. Thus a reasonable approach would be to use a classification variable highly associated with the sampling variable. Indeed, the stronger the relationship between the classification variable and the sampling variable, the greater will be the effect of stratification.

A decision about how many strata to form can be based on efficiency. In terms of efficiency, many strata should be used: Increasing the number of strata provides increased precision since the variance of the estimates is determined by the within-stratum variation;[3] in principle, more strata provide finer delineations of the population—which, all else the same, should yield more homogeneous stratum elements. However, in practical applications the number of strata that should be formed depends on such considerations as (1) the classification variables available for stratification, (2) their degree of association with the sampling variable, (3) the cost of defining the strata, and (4) the cost of allocating the population elements among the strata. The general consensus is that most practical applications do not demand the use of many strata. The gains from stratification are proportional to the relative size of the stratum. With many strata, many of them will likely be small (containing few population elements) and contribute little to the gains from stratification. Typically, only a few strata yield most of the gains from a given classification variable.[4]

Selecting the Sample

The procedure for selecting a stratified random sample is as follows:

1. Decide on a classification variable and the number of strata to employ.
2. Obtain a list or other organized breakdown of all elements in the target population; and on the basis of the classification variable, assign each element to one of the H strata.
3. Number each element in each stratum from 1 to N_h.
4. Decide on the number of sample elements (n_h) to be selected from each stratum, where $\sum_{h=1}^{H} n_h = n$.
5. Using a random number table (see Table 1 in the Statistical Appendix), draw a simple random sample of size n_h from each stratum.

EXAMPLE

Table 8-2 presents results in terms of units sold for a controlled store promotion test conducted in five geographical regions. Data on shelf space measured in 5-inch length increments [the brand under study is packaged in a 5-inch (length) × 2-inch (width) × 3-inch (height) box] and whether the promotion included an exclusive newspaper feature are also given in the table. Consider the stores participating in the promotion test as the elements, and volume (in units) sold as the characteristic being measured. Assume further that the junior analyst assigned to this study has decided to use geographical region as the classification variable. Note that in Table 8-2 the stores appear by region (the stratifying vari-

[3]W. Cochran, *Sampling Techniques*, 3rd edition (New York: John Wiley & Sons, 1977), 132.
[4]For additional details see L. Kish, *Survey Sampling* (New York: John Wiley & Sons, 1965), 102.

able) and within a region each store is identified by a number between 1 and N_h.

The junior analyst decided to take a sample of twelve stores from the fifty stores participating in the study with the following breakdown: three stores from stratum 1 (Buffalo), three stores from stratum 2 (Cincinnati), two stores from stratum 3 (Kansas City), two stores from stratum 4 (Minneapolis) and two stores from stratum 5 (Phoenix). Having determined how many stores to sample from each of the five strata, the Junior Analyst then employed a random number table (Table 1, Statistical Appendix) and randomly selected the appropriate number of elements from each stratum. The procedure for selecting the elements from the five strata parallels that used in SRS. For each stratum we will begin with an independent random start and select the elements whose within-stratum numerical label matches the random number that is between 1 and N_h. Table 8-3 presents the sample drawn following this procedure.

TABLE 8-2

Strata for 50 Stores—Controlled-Store Promotion Test

Store	Volume (units)	Shelf-space (inches)	Exclusive feature	Store	Volume (units)	Shelf-space (inches)	Exclusive feature
Buffalo Store (Stratum 1)				**Kansas City Store (Stratum 3)**			
1 $(Y_{1,1})$	55	15	0	1 $(Y_{1,3})$	109	30	1
2 $(Y_{2,1})$	35	10	0	2 $(Y_{2,3})$	57	15	0
3 $(Y_{3,1})$	68	20	0	3 $(Y_{3,3})$	71	15	1
4 $(Y_{4,1})$	38	10	0	4 $(Y_{4,3})$	49	10	0
5 $(Y_{5,1})$	90	20	0	5 $(Y_{5,3})$	75	15	0
6 $(Y_{6,1})$	98	25	0	6 $(Y_{6,3})$	39	10	0
7 $(Y_{7,1})$	62	15	1	7 $(Y_{7,3})$	81	20	1
8 $(Y_{8,1})$	42	10	1				
9 $(Y_{9,1})$	89	20	0				
10 $(Y_{10,1})$	36	10	1	**Minneapolis Store (Stratum 4)**			
11 $(Y_{11,1})$	51	15	0	1 $(Y_{1,4})$	43	10	1
12 $(Y_{12,1})$	65	15	0	2 $(Y_{2,4})$	83	20	0
Cincinnati Store (Stratum 2)				3 $(Y_{3,4})$	131	35	1
				4 $(Y_{4,4})$	98	25	0
1 $(Y_{1,2})$	30	10	0	5 $(Y_{5,4})$	73	20	0
2 $(Y_{2,2})$	85	20	0	6 $(Y_{6,4})$	35	10	0
3 $(Y_{3,2})$	66	15	1	7 $(Y_{7,4})$	69	15	1
4 $(Y_{4,2})$	40	10	0	8 $(Y_{8,4})$	21	5	0
5 $(Y_{5,2})$	100	25	0	9 $(Y_{9,4})$	87	20	0
6 $(Y_{6,2})$	67	15	1	10 $(Y_{10,4})$	100	25	1
7 $(Y_{7,2})$	72	20	1	11 $(Y_{11,4})$	29	5	0
8 $(Y_{8,2})$	84	25	0				
9 $(Y_{9,2})$	51	10	1				
10 $(Y_{10,2})$	19	5	0	**Phoenix Store (Stratum 5)**			
11 $(Y_{11,2})$	65	15	0	1 $(Y_{1,5})$	63	15	0
12 $(Y_{12,2})$	113	30	1	2 $(Y_{2,5})$	60	15	0
13 $(Y_{13,2})$	21	5	0	3 $(Y_{3,5})$	121	30	1
14 $(Y_{14,2})$	78	20	1	4 $(Y_{4,5})$	140	35	1
15 $(Y_{15,2})$	110	30	1	5 $(Y_{5,5})$	100	25	1

Sample Elements from Table 8-2

Population label	Sample label	Volume units	Shelf space (inches)	Exclusive feature
Buffalo Store (Stratum 1)				
5 $(Y_{5,1})$	1 $(y_{1,1})$	90	20	0
6 $(Y_{6,1})$	2 $(y_{2,1})$	98	25	0
10 $(Y_{10,1})$	3 $(y_{3,1})$	36	10	1
Cincinnati Store (Stratum 2)				
1 $(Y_{1,2})$	1 $(y_{1,2})$	30	10	0
6 $(Y_{6,2})$	2 $(y_{2,2})$	67	15	1
11 $(Y_{11,2})$	3 $(y_{3,2})$	65	15	0
Kansas City Store (Stratum 3)				
3 $(Y_{3,3})$	1 $(y_{1,3})$	71	15	1
7 $(Y_{7,3})$	2 $(y_{2,3})$	81	20	1
Minneapolis Store (Stratum 4)				
2 $(Y_{2,4})$	1 $(y_{1,4})$	83	20	0
10 $(Y_{10,4})$	2 $(y_{2,4})$	100	25	1
Phoenix Store (Stratum 5)				
2 $(Y_{2,5})$	1 $(y_{1,5})$	60	15	0
4 $(Y_{4,5})$	2 $(y_{2,5})$	140	35	1

Estimating Population Characteristics

In defining the estimation of population characteristics for stratified random sampling we use the same type of notation as for simple random sampling. All the formulas that follow assume infinite populations and appy only to the estimation of a population mean using stratified random sampling. Appendix 8A, Exhibit 2, contains the formulas that apply to the estimation of a population proportion.

Consider a population containing N elementary units grouped into H mutually exclusive and exhaustive strata. Let $N_1, N_2, \ldots, N_H$ denote the number of elements in each of the strata, that is, the size of the subpopulations. Since the total population (N) was divided into H strata, $N = \sum_{h=1}^{H} N_h$. The size of the sample chosen from each stratum is denoted as n_h, and $n = \sum_{i=1}^{H} n_h$ where n is the total sample size. In a later section we discuss how to determine the sample size in each stratum (n_h) given an overall sample size (n) under two types of allocation rules.

Under stratified random sampling, the mean and sampling error associated with a characteristic in the entire target population can be estimated as:

$$\bar{y}_{(ST)} = \sum_{h=1}^{H} w_h \bar{y}_h \qquad (8\text{-}8)$$

and

$$s_{\bar{y}(ST)} = \sqrt{\sum_{h=1}^{H} w_h^2 s_{yh}^2}$$

$$= \sqrt{\sum_{h=1}^{H} w_h^2 \frac{s_{yh}^2}{n_h}} \qquad (8\text{-}9\text{A})$$

or

$$s_{\bar{y}(ST)} = \sqrt{\sum_{h=1}^{H} w_h^2 \left(\frac{s_{yh}^2}{n_h}\right)\left(\frac{N_h - n_h}{N_h - 1}\right)} \qquad (8\text{-}9\text{B})$$

if the sample represents 10–20 percent or more of the large population. Note that in expressions (8-8) and (8-9)

w_h = weight attached to the hth stratum equal to N_h/N

$\bar{y}_h$ = mean in the hth stratum

s_{yh}^2 = variance in the hth stratum

The variance in the hth stratum is calculated from

$$s_{yh}^2 = \sum_{i=1}^{n_h} (y_{ih} - \bar{y}_h)^2/(n_h - 1) \qquad (8\text{-}10)$$

Most importantly, from formula (8-9) we see that the estimate of the standard error of the mean under stratified sampling depends *only* on the within-stratum variability.

E X A M P L E

Having drawn the sample (Table 8-3), the junior analyst focused on estimating the mean number of units sold and the sampling error of the estimate.

The estimated mean volume in units sold per store in the entire target population can be estimated from (8-8) as follows:

$$\bar{y}_{(ST)} = \left(\frac{12}{50}\right)\left(\frac{90 + 98 + 36}{3}\right) + \left(\frac{15}{50}\right)\left(\frac{30 + 67 + 65}{3}\right) + \left(\frac{7}{50}\right)\left(\frac{71 + 81}{2}\right)$$

$$+ \left(\frac{11}{50}\right)\left(\frac{83 + 100}{2}\right) + \left(\frac{5}{50}\right)\left(\frac{60 + 140}{2}\right)$$

$$= 74.89 \text{ units per store}$$

Similarly, the estimated within-stratum variances are, according to (8-10):

$$s_{y1}^2 = \frac{(90 - 74.67)^2 + (98 - 74.67)^2 + (36 - 74.67)^2}{2} = 1137.33$$

$$s_{y2}^2 = \frac{(30 - 54)^2 + (67 - 54)^2 + (65 - 54)^2}{2} = 433.00$$

$$s_{y3}^2 = \frac{(71 - 76)^2 + (81 - 76)^2}{1} = 50.00$$

$$s_{y4}^2 = \frac{(83 - 91.5)^2 + (100 - 91.5)^2}{1} = 144.50$$

$$s_{y5}^2 = \frac{(60 - 100)^2 + (140 - 100)^2}{1} = 3200.00$$

Now to obtain the estimated standard error of the mean units sold per store in the target population, the junior analyst applied the appropriate fpc "corrected" formula

$$s_{\bar{y}(ST)} = \sqrt{\left[\left(\frac{12}{50}\right)^2\left(\frac{1137.33}{3}\right)\left(\frac{9}{11}\right)\right] + \left[\left(\frac{15}{50}\right)^2\left(\frac{433}{3}\right)\left(\frac{12}{14}\right)\right] + \cdots + \left[\left(\frac{5}{50}\right)^2\left(\frac{3200}{2}\right)\left(\frac{3}{4}\right)\right]}$$

$$= \sqrt{44.56} = 6.68$$

Thus a 95 percent confidence interval for the true population mean number of units sold per store is

$$\bar{y}_{(ST)} \pm t_{(1-\alpha/2);\, n-1} s_{\bar{y}(ST)}$$

$$74.89 \pm (2.201)(6.68) = 74.89 \pm 14.70$$

$$= \text{between } 60.19 \text{ and } 89.59 \text{ units sold per store}$$

Sample Size Determination

We can estimate the sample size required to estimate a population mean within a specified error limit at a specified level of confidence. As in SRS, estimates of the anticipated variance of the characteristic to be measured in the target population must be known; however, for stratified random sampling, estimates of the within-stratum variances must also be known for all strata.

Following standard notation, under stratified random sampling, the formula for determining the (approximate) number of elements needed to be $100(1 - \alpha/2)$ percent certain of obtaining an estimated mean that differs from the true population mean by no more than a fixed percent is, for reasonably large N, given by

$$n^* \approx \frac{N(z_{1-\alpha/2})^2(\hat{\sigma}_{WY}^2/\bar{Y}^2)}{(z_{1-\alpha/2})^2(\hat{\sigma}_{WY}^2/\bar{Y}^2) + Nr^2} \tag{8-11}$$

where with the exception of $\hat{\sigma}^2_{WY}$ all terms have been previously defined.[5] In expression (8-11) $\hat{\sigma}^2_{WY}$ is the "anticipated" or estimated weighted average of the individual within-stratum variances:

$$\hat{\sigma}^2_{WY} = \sum_{h=1}^{H} N_h \, \hat{\sigma}^2_{yh}/N \tag{8-12}$$

E X A M P L E

Suppose that for the last five years records of all in-store promotion studies have been maintained. Among the information routinely recorded are (1) product category of test brand, (2) volume (in units), (3) shelf-space allocation, (4) promotional activity, and (5) testing location. Table 8-4 gives information on the distribution of units sold in 250 stores located in the Buffalo (stratum 1), Cincinnati (stratum 2), Kansas City (stratum 3), Minneapolis (stratum 4) and Phoenix (stratum 5) test markets. The junior analyst decides to use this information in planning a controlled store-promotion test that will be conducted in these areas. Believing in history, the anticipated mean number of units sold in the future promotion test will likely be

$$\frac{45(55) \,+\, 70(68) \,+\, 50(70) \,+\, 60(74) \,+\, 25(101)}{250} = 70.8$$

The weighting factors are, respectively

$$w_1 = (45/250) = .18$$
$$w_2 = (70/250) = .28$$
$$w_3 = (50/250) = .20$$
$$w_4 = (60/250) = .24$$
$$w_5 = (25/250) = .10$$

To calculate the estimated number of stores needed to be virtually certain of estimating the mean number of units sold to within 20 percent of the true mean under stratified random sampling, an anticipated value for $\hat{\sigma}_{WY}$ is needed. Using Table 8-4 and relation (8-12) the junior analyst computes the anticipated value of the weighted average of within-stratum variances to be

$$\hat{\sigma}^2_{WY} = \frac{45(82) \,+\, 70(121) \,+\, 50(110) \,+\, 60(132) \,+\, 25(75)}{250}$$

$$= \frac{27455}{250} = 109.82$$

Thus applying relation (8-11)

$$n^* \approx \frac{250(3)^2 \,(109.82/70.8)}{(3)^2(109.82/70.8) \,+\, 250(.20)^2} = \frac{3490.04}{23.96} = 145.66$$

so that the junior analyst plans to sample 146 stores.

---

[5] In a strict sense expression (8–11) is applicable only when the sample is to be allocated across the strata in relation to the relative size of each stratum. Allocation of the sample across the strata will be discussed shortly.

TABLE 8-4
Distribution of Units Sold

Strata	Size	Mean units sold	Variance of distribution of mean units sold
Buffalo	45	55	82
Cincinnati	70	68	121
Kansas City	50	70	110
Minneapolis	60	74	132
Phoenix	25	101	75

Allocating the Sample

An important decision in stratified sampling is the number of elementary units to be sampled from each stratum, under the constraint that a total of n elements is to be sampled over all strata. In practice, two procedures are used for allocating the total sample size n among the H strata. One procedure, *proportional allocation,* guarantees that stratified random sampling will be at least as efficient as SRS. The other procedure, *optimal allocation* or *disproportional allocation,* minimizes the standard errors of the estimated population parameters for a fixed sample size n and a predetermined number of strata, though it is more difficult to apply than proportional allocation.

In this section we illustrate these two allocation procedures. We are confining our discussion to stratified random sampling, and so, regardless of the allocation procedure, once the number of elements n_h is determined, an SRS procedure is used to select elements from each stratum.

Proportional Allocation. In proportional allocation the number of elementary units selected from stratum h is directly proportional to the size of the population in that stratum. In other words, with proportional allocation the sampling fraction $f_h = n_h/N_h$ is constant for all strata, which implies that the overall sampling fraction $f = n/N$ is the fraction taken from each stratum. Under this allocation procedure the size of the sample to be drawn from each stratum is easily calculated. The number of elements drawn from each stratum, n_h is given by

$$n_h = \left(\frac{N_h}{N}\right)n \tag{8-13}$$

Optimal Allocation. The goal in optimal allocation is to allocate a fixed sample size among the strata to minimize the variance of the characteristic to be measured in the target population. Assuming equal per-element sampling costs, it can be shown that the allocation of n sample

units into each stratum, which will yield a minimum variance estimate
of a population parameter, is given by

$$n_h = \left(N_h \hat{\sigma}_{Yh} \middle/ \sum_{h=1}^{H} N_h\, \hat{\sigma}_{Yh} \right) n \qquad \text{(8-14)}$$

Optimal allocation essentially involves a double weighting scheme;
the number of sample elements taken from a given stratum is proportional to (1) the relative size of the stratum and (2) the anticipated standard deviation ($\hat{\sigma}_{Yh}$) of the distribution of the characteristic under consideration among all elements in the stratum. As we mentioned in Chapter
7, the rationale for this dual weighting procedure is simple. First, size is
important since strata with larger numbers of elements are the most important in determining the population mean. Second, stratum variability
is important since, if the distribution of the characteristic under consideration has a large standard deviation in a particular stratum, then a
relatively large number of elements must be selected from that stratum
to obtain a reliable estimate of a stratum parameter. A smaller number of
elements must be selected from a stratum in which the distribution of
the characteristic under consideration has small standard deviation.

EXAMPLE

Having decided to sample 146 stores, the junior analyst next examined how
the sample would be allocated among the strata under proportional and optimal
allocation.

Under proportional allocation the sample would be allocated to the five
strata as follows:

$$n_1 = \frac{45}{250}(146) = 26.28 = 26$$

$$n_2 = \frac{70}{250}(146) = 40.88 = 41$$

$$n_3 = \frac{50}{250}(146) = 29.20 = 29$$

$$n_4 = \frac{60}{250}(146) = 35.04 = 35$$

$$n_5 = \frac{25}{250}(146) = 14.60 = 15$$

If an optimal allocation plan is used, some estimate of the anticipated standard deviation of the characteristic under study must be available. Using the information presented in Table 8-4 and expression (8-14), the sample would be
allocated among the strata as follows:

$$n_1 = \left(\frac{45\sqrt{82}}{45\sqrt{82} + 70\sqrt{121} + 50\sqrt{110} + 60\sqrt{132} + 25\sqrt{75}} \right) 146 = 22.9 = 23$$

$$n_2 = \left(\frac{70\sqrt{121}}{45\sqrt{82} + 70\sqrt{121} + 50\sqrt{110} + 60\sqrt{132} + 25\sqrt{75}} \right) 146 = 43.2 = 43$$

$$n_3 = \left(\frac{50\sqrt{110}}{45\sqrt{82} + 70\sqrt{121} + 50\sqrt{110} + 60\sqrt{132} + 25\sqrt{75}} \right) 146 = 29.4 = 29$$

$$n_4 = \left(\frac{60\sqrt{132}}{45\sqrt{82} + 70\sqrt{121} + 50\sqrt{110} + 60\sqrt{132} + 25\sqrt{75}} \right) 146 = 38.7 = 39$$

$$n_5 = \left(\frac{25\sqrt{75}}{45\sqrt{82} + 70\sqrt{121} + 50\sqrt{110} + 60\sqrt{132} + 25\sqrt{75}} \right) 146 = 12.1 = 12$$

To apply optimal allocation, we need to know the standard deviation of the distribution of the variable under consideration. In practice, this will rarely be known. There are, however, two ways in which to proceed.

1. Based upon prior research surveys that have investigated similar sampling variables and used similar classification variables, obtain—through averaging or some other method—estimates of $\hat{\sigma}_{yh}$, the standard deviation of the distribution of the sampling variable within each stratum. Next, use these estimates to calculate the optimal allocation of elements to draw from each stratum.

2. Draw a small "subordinate" sample from each stratum. Denote the subordinate sample elements by $n_1^*, n_2^*, \ldots, n_H^*$ with values of the sampling variable given by $y_{i1}^*, y_{i2}^*, \ldots, y_{iH}^*$. Next, on the basis of the subordinate sample calculate s_{yh}^* the estimated standard deviation of the sampling distribution of the sampling variable. Using s_{yh}^*, calculate the optimal allocation of elements to draw from each stratum. As a precautionary step, after drawing the sample on the basis of the *pseudo* optimal allocation procedure, check the estimated standard deviations against those obtained in the subordinate sample. If consistent, proceed. If not, then draw another subordinate sample and continue following the same procedure as before.

CLUSTER SAMPLING PROCEDURES

The sampling methods discussed so far all require sampling frames that list or provide an organized breakdown of all elements (or sampling units) in the target population. An alternative strategy is to construct sampling frames that contain groups or clusters of elements (or sampling units) without explicitly listing the individual elements. Sampling can be performed from such frames by taking a sample of clusters, obtaining a list or other breakdowns only for those clusters that have been selected in the sample, and then selecting a sample of the individual sampling units. These sample designs are known as *cluster samples* and are widely used in practice because of their feasibility and economy. In this section we discuss and illustrate two-stage cluster sampling designs and, in particular, PPS sampling.

Two-Stage Cluster Sampling Procedures: PPS Sampling

As we indicated in Chapter 7, to the extent that the elements within clusters exhibit homogeneity with respect to the variables being measured, cluster sampling and especially simple one-stage cluster sampling, will be relatively inefficient compared with other sampling designs. Because there is likely to be much redundancy among the elements within a cluster, it may be better to take a sample of the elements rather than to select all of them. In such cases, the sample would be drawn in two stages: In the first stage a sample of clusters from the population would be selected, and in the second stage a sample of the elements (or sampling units) within each sample cluster would be drawn.

There are several types of two-stage sampling designs. One type is called simple two-stage cluster sampling since it involves SRS at both the first and second stages in the sampling design. In other words, SRS sampling is used at the first stage to select a sample of clusters from the population, and at the second stage to draw a sample of elements from each sample cluster. Under this design the fraction of elements selected at the second stage is the same for each sample cluster. This design is strictly appropriate only when each cluster contains the same number of sampling units. If the cluster sizes are different it is impossible to take the same percentage of elements from each sample cluster.

Because it is extremely unlikely that clusters will contain exactly the same number of elements (or sampling units), we confine our discussion to a two-stage cluster sampling design that accommodates clusters of varying sizes. This design, called probability proportionate to size, or PPS sampling, results in the same number n of sampling units (or a multiple of n) being selected from each sample cluster.

In PPS sampling, clusters are sampled with probability proportional to the number of sampling units within the cluster. Thus, large clusters are more likely to be included in the sample than small clusters. PPS sampling is self-weighting in that the probability of selecting a sampling unit in a cluster, given that the cluster has been selected at the first stage of sampling, varies inversely with the size of the sample cluster. PPS sampling results in selecting approximately equal numbers of sampling units from each sample cluster.

Selecting the Sample

Let M denote the total number of clusters available and m the number of clusters to be sampled. The following outlines the steps involved in drawing a PPS sample.

1. Generate cumulative measure of size, denoted by *MOS*. The measure of size for a particular cluster will be denoted by MOS_j, where $MOS_j = N_j$. Note that the cumulative *MOS* simply equals N, the total population.
2. Compute the sampling interval, s, where $s = MOS/m$.
3. Consulting a random number table, or some other device, choose a random number between 1 and s; let r denote the first random number chosen.
4. Select clusters having the following numeric labels

   r

   $r + s$

   $r + 2s$

   $r + 3s$

   .

   .

   .

   $r + (m - 1)s$

   A cluster is selected if the selection number falls into its sequence of numbers; that is, the selection number is greater than the *MOS* of all previous clusters, but less than or equal to the *MOS* including the designated cluster.
5. Selection of sampling units within each sample cluster proceeds as follows: Select n_j sampling units from each sample cluster based on SRS or systematic sampling; the number of sampling units selected from a sample cluster is given by

$$n_j = f_2 \times N_j$$

where f_2, the second-stage sampling fraction, is equal to f/f_1. Noting that f, the overall sampling fraction, is equal to n/N, then f_1, the first-stage sampling fraction, is equal to N_j/s.

PPS results in an equal number of sampling units being selected from each sample cluster. In general, the number of sampling units selected from each sample cluster will be (approximately) equal to

$$n_j = \bar{n} = n/m.$$

It can happen that a cluster's *MOS* can exceed the sampling interval. In such cases, the cluster will automatically be included in the sample; that is, this cluster will be selected with certainty. Because of the existence of clusters that will be included in the sample with certainty, we must modify the PPS sampling selection procedure to identify and remove such clusters.

To be more specific, after computing s, the sampling interval, we check whether $MOS_j > s$ for each cluster j in the population. If

265

$MOS_j > s$, cluster j is removed from further consideration and new cumulative MOS's are computed. Denoting the new sampling interval s^*, we again check whether any $MOS_j > s^*$. If a cluster's MOS is greater than s^*, then that cluster is also removed and a new MOS is once again computed. This process continues until no remaining cluster has a MOS greater than s^*, the relevant sampling interval. For the remaining clusters, the PPS sampling procedure then continues in the manner described above. However, note that from the remaining clusters we will select only $m^* = m - c$, where c denotes the number of clusters selected with certainty. For clusters selected with certainty, we would sample

$$n_c = (f \times N_1) + (f \times N_2) + \ldots + (f \times N_c)$$

so that we end up selecting

$$n^* = n - n_c$$

sampling units from the sample of clusters selected under PPS sampling.

E X A M P L E

Let us consider the ten test-market cities given in Table 8-5 and suppose that the junior analyst responsible for this study wishes to take a PPS sampling of $n = 25$ stores from $m = 5$ cities. The first step in the procedure is to form the cumulative MOS, which is generated by cumulating the number of stores in each city. From the data presented, $MOS = 500$.

Next the junior analyst computes s where

$$s = \frac{500}{5} = 100$$

T A B L E 8-5
Procedure for PPS Sampling

City	Number of stores (MOS)	Cumulative MOS	Cumulative MOS—excluding Buffalo	Random number	Random number chosen
Erie, Pa.	20	20	20	001–020	
Fargo, N. Dak.	10	30	30	021–030	26
Green Bay, Wis.	40	70	70	031–070	
Pittsburgh, Pa.	90	160	160	071–160	125
Portland, Oreg.	20	180	180	161–180	
Cincinnati, Ohio	75	255	255	181–255	224
Buffalo, N.Y.	105	360	—		
Lexington, Ky.	20	380	275	256–275	
Minneapolis, Minn.	70	450	345	276–345	323
Nashville, Tenn.	50	500	395	346–395	
Total	500	500	395		

and notes that MOS_7 (Buffalo) exceeds 100. Consequently, following the procedure described earlier, Buffalo is selected with certainty. The new MOS is then calculated. The cumulative MOS for the remaining 9 cities (excluding Buffalo) is 395 (500 − 105 = 395) and therefore

$$s^* = MOS/(m-1)$$
$$= 395/4$$
$$= 98.75 \text{ or } 99$$

Noting that no city exceeds s^*, the junior analyst now uses Table 1 of the Statistical Appendix to generate a random number between 1 and 99. Assume the number 26 is selected. Thus

r	26
$r + s^*$	26 + 99 = 125
$r + 2s^*$	26 + 198 = 224
$r + 3s^*$	26 + 297 = 323

The sample cities, from Table 8-5, are

Fargo, N. Dak.
Pittsburgh, Pa.
Cincinnati, Ohio
Minneapolis, Minn.

with Buffalo being included (from step 1) to obtain the required 5 clusters.

We will not discuss or illustrate how to estimate population characteristics under PPS sampling, nor will we consider sample size determination. The fact that cluster samples have unequal numbers of sampling units create some problems when it comes to estimation and sample size determination that are beyond the scope of our discussion.[6]

In closing our discussion of PPS sampling we should note that two-stage cluster sampling designs are generally more cost-effective than SRS and, in many instances, can provide cost efficiencies over simple one-stage cluster sampling designs. In addition, as we mention in Chapter 7, PPS sampling procedures can be used to improve mall-intercept surveys.

Summary

Sampling is often referred to as being more of an art than a science. This sentiment reflects the fact that a great deal of creative ingenuity is generally required in reaching the individual households that possess information relevant to solving the marketing problem at hand. As we

---

[6]See, for example, Cochran, *op. cit.*; P. S. Levy and S. Lemeshow, *Sampling for Health Professionals* (Belmont, Calif.: Lifetime Learning Publications, 1980), 75–78, for a discussion illustrating this procedure.

indicated in Chapter 7, sampling decisions are often complex and there is no single "right" way to make them. Deciding on the specific sampling design to use may often not be straightforward; sampling professionals may be needed. This chapter has explained the mechanics of probability sampling designs for those of you who want (or need) to understand how such designs work.

Key Concepts

Selecting the sample

Estimating population characteristics

Sample size determination

Simple random sampling

Systematic sampling procedures

Stratified sampling procedures

Allocating sample units to strata

Cluster sampling procedures

PPS sampling

Review Questions

1. What is a standard error?
2. What information is necessary to determine a sample size to achieve a desired level of precision?
3. Discuss the differences between proportional and optimal allocation in stratified sampling.
4. What are the relative benefits of stratified sampling compared to simple random sampling?
5. What are the relative benefits of probability proportional to size cluster sampling compared to other two-stage cluster sampling designs?

Appendix 8A
Population Proportions

E X H I B I T 1	
Population Proportions: SRS	

Proportion

$$p = \sum_{i=1}^{n} y_i/n$$

where y_i equals 1 or 0.

Standard Error

$$s_p = \sqrt{\frac{p\,(1-p)}{n-1}}$$

Standard Error, With fpc

$$s_p = \sqrt{\frac{p\,(1-p)}{n-1}}\sqrt{\frac{N-n}{N-1}}$$

Sample Size Determination

$$n^* = \frac{(z_{1-\alpha/2})^2\,(1-P)}{Ph^2}$$

Sample Size Determination, With fpc

$$n^* = \frac{(z_{1-\alpha/2})^2\,(1-P)}{Ph^2}\left(\frac{N-n}{N-1}\right)$$

where
  P = anticipated (or estimated) value of the proportions in the entire target
  population

E X H I B I T 2

Population Proportions: Stratified Random Sampling

Proportion

$$p_{(ST)} = \sum_{h=1}^{H} w_h p_h$$

Standard Error

$$s_{p(ST)} = \sqrt{\sum_{h=1}^{H} w_h^2 \frac{p_h(1 - p_h)}{n_h}}$$

Standard Error, With fpc

$$s_{p(ST)} = \sqrt{\sum_{h=1}^{H} w_h^2 \frac{p_h(1 - p_h)}{n_h} \left(\frac{N_h - n_h}{N_h - 1}\right)}$$

Sample Size Determination

$$n^* \approx \frac{N(z_{1-\alpha/2})^2 \, (\hat{\sigma}_{WP}^2/P^2)}{(z_{1-\alpha/2})^2 \, (\hat{\sigma}_{WP}^2/P^2) + Nr^2}$$

where

P = anticipated (or estimated) value of the proportions in the entire target population

$\hat{\sigma}_{WP}^2$ = anticipated (or estimated) weighted average of the individual within-stratum variances.

CASE STUDIES FOR PART III

Case 1: The Yellow Page Operator

By Alan M. Field

It's nearly midnight and you've locked yourself out of your car. You need a 24-hour locksmith who accepts Visa cards, but there's no Yellow Pages next to the nearest telephone. In most localities that spells frustration, if not panic. But if you're in Houston, help is as near as 622-1411, where a call is answered by a polite operator who will give you the names, addresses, and phone numbers of up to four locksmiths in your area, all of whom accept Visa cards.

Introducing the electronic Yellow Pages, a new service that, despite its name, is brought to you not by deregulated Southwestern Bell but by an upstart outfit named The 1411 Co. "We have created a whole new way to advertise," says Edward J. Guinan, the New York-born, 37-year-old president of 1411, who founded the company last November.

Guinan's idea was to offer a service combining features of the traditional Bell Yellow Pages and directory assistance, at slightly lower rates. The cheapest 1411 ad, in two product categories—auto sales and service, for example—and in only one of Houston's 65 geographical zones, costs $230 a month.

That's only a little cheaper than the smallest display ad in the Bell Yellow Pages—one-sixteenth of a page—which costs $244.75 per month. The Bell ad is distributed in all of Houston, but very few 1411 advertisers, mostly small businesses, have markets outside their local neighborhoods.

Moreover, Guinan's 1411 uses four mainframe computers to provide custom service for both caller and advertiser that no written directory can offer. When a caller tells a 1411 operator the first three digits of his phone number and asks for a Maserati repair shop, the operator quickly searches through the database to identify from one to four shops in the caller's neighborhood. She then reads detailed information, such as "Joe's Maserati Service, 5000 Main, is open from 9 A.M. to 5 P.M., takes Visa

Source: *Forbes*, 15 July 1985, 106.

cards, friendly service." If the first shop sounds fine, the operator will stop there, but the caller can request information on up to four shops.

1411 guarantees advertisers that their pitches will be heard by 25% of callers in any given geographical zone. Because most businesses target their products to only one such zone, that is the equivalent of a quarter-page Bell ad worth $912 per month. Also, 1411 ad copy, which is stored in computer memory, can be changed on 24 hours' notice; Yellow Pages ads, by contrast, are frozen in print for a year.

The service has had an immediate appeal to busy Houstonians. They made 700,000 calls to 1411 in May, up from 50,000 in January, the first month of operation. That, in turn, has fed sales: In May 1411's sales staff sold as much as $84,000 a day in advertising, up from an average of $5,000 in January.

But none of this comes cheap. The 1411 Co., capitalized at $14 million by venture capitalists and private investors, spent over $2 million just on telephones and computer hardward and software. Since the new year the staff has grown from 70 to nearly 270, including 150 phone operators and 55 ad salesmen. Says Guinan, an investment banker and venture capitalist who lists operations in New York and London, "It's like starting in cable TV. The front-end expense is very substantial and is paid out before any revenues come in." Nevertheless, Guinan thinks that he can turn a profit by the spring of next year.

He will have to watch his costs to do it. Most of 1411's advertisers so far are small businessmen, such as Tom Carby, who owns Sunrise Movers, or Julio Villarreal Jr., owner of AARK Pest Control, who like 1411's more focused approach to their local markets. But they may be forced to drop out at contract renewal time because Guinan's ad rates have risen 30% since January, as he has pushed for profitability.

Question

1. Mr. Guinan has decided to roll out the electronic *Yellow Pages* service in the state of California. The problem is to decide which counties (geographical zones) to concentrate on. Design a sampling plan to answer this question.

Case 2: A Head & Shoulders Study

A market researcher calls with the following specs:

> 300 interviews with females 18 or older who shampoo their hair at home. One hundred will be with Head & Shoulders users, the rest with users of any other shampoos. The effective telephone incidence for Head & Shoulders users is 20 percent; all-other-brand users is 75 percent. The interview length is 15 minutes.

In response to these specifications, the junior research analyst estimates that 767 contacts will be needed, 500 for the Head & Shoulders quota and 267 for all-other-users quota (100 ÷ .20 = 500; 200 ÷ .75 = 267). With 767 contacts required and assuming a 30 percent productive dialing ratio (finding a respondent home), the number of dialings needed was estimated at 2,557 (767 ÷ .30 = 2,557). The total hours required for interviewing was estimated as

$$2{,}557 \text{ dialings} \times 1.5 \text{ minutes} = 3{,}835.5$$
$$767 \text{ contacts} \times 3 \text{ minutes} = 2{,}301$$
$$300 \text{ completes} \times 15 \text{ minutes} = \underline{4{,}500}$$
$$10636.5 \text{ minutes}$$
$$\text{or } 177.28 \text{ hours}$$

The junior research analyst also included time spent on qualified refusals and break-offs, estimated at 10 percent. Thus, the estimate of total hours of interviewing was 195 hours. At $20 an hour, the bid submitted was $3,900.

Questions

1. Comment on the incidence rate projections.
2. Develop a probabilistic sampling design for this study. What potential problems do you anticipate?

Case 3: Changing Complexion of Restaurant Industry

In response to the dramatic changes that have taken place in the restaurant industry, the Restaurant Association of America recently commissioned a survey of restaurant owners. The study called for a national probabilistic sample; its objectives were to estimate the incidence of the following types of eating establishments:

1. fast-food
2. casual
3. dinner
4. fine dining

Another objective was to collect various data on menu offerings and price structures. Subgroup analysis is to be undertaken by restaurant type and geographical region. Assume that you have been retained to evaluate the procedures used. The necessary details follow.

Sampling Plan

Selection of Firms to Conduct the Sampling. Various firms specializing in drawing probabilistic telephone samples were solicited and asked

273

to supply a national probability sample of restaurant establishments; in addition, several county samples were also requested. These samples were judged for accuracy and completeness in relation to census and county data. A single firm was selected.

Selection of Sampling Frame. The sample eventually used was based on a frame of all restaurant establishments located in the contiguous United States.

Sample Selection Procedures. The design ultimately used was that of a probability-replicated sample, comprising twenty randomly selected, stratified, matched samples of fifty restaurants, each from a frame of all eligible United States restaurants and each having a known chance of selection.

The total database was filtered to create a population consisting only of telephone numbers falling into the *Yellow Pages* categories of restaurants. The filtering process resulted in a population of 302,247 restaurants. The file was then geographically sorted by area codes and exchange, and a systematic selection was made to produce the final sample. A sample of 10,000 restaurants were first sampled from this list, verified, and then 5,000 restaurants were selected into the final target sample.

Sample Size Considerations. The objective was to estimate the incidence (proportion) of each of the five categories of eating establishments within ±5 percent. After some discussion it was felt that a sample of 1,000 establishments would be sufficient.

Response Rates. Great care was given to achieving high response rates by completing five call-backs. The total number of calls made exceeded 3,000, representing about a 30 percent response rate.

Survey Instrument (Questionnaire Construction and Administration). The following procedures were undertaken:

1. Questionnaire was subjected to rigorous pretests, and the instrument was constructed according to acceptable standards.
2. Questionnaire was administered by executive interviewers, especially those trained in the food-service industry, to insure objective and accurate responses.
3. Computer-driven CRT interviewing center was employed.
4. 25 percent of the interviews were verified.

Question

1. Prepare in memo format an evaluation of the sampling design and procedures used.

Case 4: Born to Sun

Jane Goldman

The best ride on the shore, I'd heard, was the Sea Serpent, in Wildwood. The line snaked around the metal guideposts four times—a good twenty minutes' wait, said a boy who'd been on it three times that night. In front of me, a couple in their thirties with enormous bellies—hers zipped into her blue jeans, his hanging over the top—held hands and stared straight ahead. Behind me, a boy of around sixteen in a PARTY NAKED T-shirt and sleeveless denim jacket leaned his whole weight against a dark-haired girl in a tank top and short shorts, curving her backward over the metal fence.

Around us on the boardwalk, people elbowed through mobs to get to the bumper boats, the 146-foot Ferris wheel, the fun house, the games. Bells, bangs, pops, shouts, and canned music made it hard to hear a conversation, so everybody in line just watched silently as the roller-coaster cars strained up the first incline and then let go, screamed down-hill, looped upside down twice, and then creaked back uphill for another go-round, this time backward. Just watching was nauseating, but after twenty minutes I figured at least I knew what I was in for.

I had no idea. I have never been on such an abusive, battering, loud, scary ride—it's the mechanical equivalent of getting rolled by a righteous wave. But when I got out and wobbled down the exit steps, I wasn't sure I didn't want to go back and do it again.

That's pretty much how I feel about the Jersey shore. It's a pain in the neck to get there, and when you do, you're assaulted by noise, crowds, smells. But I always want to go back. You don't need a lot of money or the right connections or a friend with a house. Bring a few bucks and come as you are and you've got water slides, great rock and roll, an old-fashioned revival meeting, and a six-story cement elephant, just for starters.

From Sandy Hook to Cape May there are 127 miles of coastline, mostly back-to-back towns that are as different as kids in a fourth-grade chorus line. In one six-mile strip you'll find the urban wasteland of Asbury Park right next to party-hearty Belmar, which is smack up against the anachronistic religious retreat of Ocean Grove, which is next to wealthy, conservative Spring Lake.

The places do run in types—the boardwalk towns, like Seaside Heights and Point Pleasant; the party towns, like Belmar and Wildwood; their brothers, the rock-and-roll towns, Asbury Park and Long Branch; the tasteful resorts, like Spring Lake, Bay Head, and Cape May; the family-vacation spots, like Ocean Grove, Ocean City, and Long Beach Island. Atlantic City stands alone.

Since the 1984 State Supreme Court ruling on beach access, all of the New Jersey coastline is open to visitors, but it'll cost you. Only Wildwood,

Source: *New York Magazine*, 30 June–7 July 1986, 43.

Cape May Point State Park, and a few out-of-the-way beaches are free. Beach badges are for sale right on the water at public beaches; in other areas, you'll have to buy one from the town, usually at the police station. Prices vary: $2 for a weekday at Seaside Heights, $4 to $5 a weekend day at Point Pleasant Beach, $5 a season at Beach Haven, $110 a season, with bathhouse, in Deal. The public beaches have bathhouses, with changing rooms and toilets, right on the beach or boardwalk.

To get to all points on the shore, take the New Jersey Turnpike south to Exit 11 and get onto the Garden State Parkway South. The weekend traffic is legendary, and there's no back way. The delays are especially maddening at the bottle-necked approaches to tollbooths, where you drop a quarter in a basket every 25 miles (or less).

Question

1. The New Jersey State Tourist Commission wants to determine tourists' evaluations of the Jersey shore. A primary objective is to determine the origination and destination of travelers vacationing on the Jersey shore and their opinions and evaluations of the Jersey shore as a vacation spot. Assume the role of a marketing researcher who must devise a sampling plan for a study of the opinions and evaluations of summer vacationers visiting the New Jersey shore.

MEASUREMENT, SCALING, AND QUESTIONNAIRE DESIGN

We now turn our attention to the topics of measurement, scaling, and questionnaire design. Specifically, in Part IV we present four chapters that together provide a comprehensive treatment of the process of measurement, both theory and application.

Chapter 9 introduces basic concepts of measurement and discusses the concepts of reliability and validity—which give meaning to the measurements we take. Chapter 10 presents details on different types of measurement scales. Chapter 11 is totally devoted to attitude scaling and measurement models; here we apply several of the scaling techniques discussed in Chapter 10 to the problem of measuring attitudes and, in addition, discuss and illustrate compositional and decompositional attitude-measurement models. In Chapter 12 we turn to issues involved in questionnaire design and field execution; now that we know what measurement is and how its techniques work, we use them to form our questions.

9

Basic Concepts of Measurement

CHAPTER OBJECTIVES

- Introduce and define basic concepts of measurement and scaling.
- Explain the classical true score model of measurement.
- Discuss the theory and measurement of reliability.
- Discuss the theory and measurement of validity.
- Describe a procedure for developing sound constructs.

Introduction

We have discussed methods of obtaining primary information and methods of choosing a sample; now we turn to more specific details on the theory and application of measurement techniques. Because the information collected will be analyzed, numbers must be assigned to the responses to the questions that are asked. As we will see, the numbers assigned have important implications in terms of how the answers to questions can be interpreted and analyzed. Thus we need to understand the properties of the various scaling techniques and the proper way to use them.

MEASUREMENT DEFINED

Measurement Process of assigning numbers to objects to represent quantities of attributes.

Measurement involves "rules for assigning numbers to objects to represent quantities of attributes."[1] Stated somewhat differently, **measurement** relates to the procedure (the rules) used to assign numbers that reflect the amount of an attribute possessed by an object, person, institution, state, or event. Think of the everyday occurrence of rating a movie on a scale of 1 to 10. That is very simple measurement. Note that measurement does not pertain to objects themselves—we never measure an object or a person, per se—but rather the amount of an attribute or

[1]J. C. Nunnally, *Psychometric Theory* (New York: McGraw-Hill Book Company, 1967), 2.

278

characteristic possessed by the object. To be more specific, we never measure consumers—only their age, income, social status, perceptions of brand benefits, purchase intentions, or some other relevant characteristic.

The most important and critical aspect of measurement is specifying the rules for assigning numbers to the characteristics to be measured. Once a measurement rule has been selected, the characteristics of objects or persons take on meaning only in the context of the numbers assigned; therefore, if we don't know the rule being applied, we cannot completely or accurately understand the characteristic in question. Consider the characteristic of consumer *brand loyalty* and the following pattern of purchases for two hypothetical consumers during a given period:

consumer 1:   A B C A B B

consumer 2:   A C B C C C

If, for example, brand loyalty is measured by computing the proportion of total purchases devoted to the most frequently purchased brand, then the brand loyalty score for consumer 1 is 3/6 = .50 and for consumer 2 it is 4/6 = .67. On the other hand, if brand loyalty is measured by counting the number of different brands purchased, then both consumers would be given the same brand loyalty score. Conclusions about the brand loyalty of these two consumers depend upon which measurement rule the researcher adopts.

A question that follows naturally from this illustration is: Which of the two measurement rules is more correct? This question is difficult to answer. Many characteristics that we investigate in marketing research studies can be measured in a variety of ways. Particular attention must be given to the objectives of the study, the precise definition of the characteristic to be measured, and the correspondence between the measurement rule and the characteristic.

Concepts, Constructs, and Definitions

The term **concept(s)** refers to the name(s) given to characteristics that we wish to measure. The terms **construct** and *concept* are frequently used interchangeably. Concepts and constructs are abstractions that are formed for a specific research purpose. For example, in Chapter 11 we discuss the **attitude** construct in some detail. Attitude is a concept that most of us would say relates to a person's feelings about or predispositions toward an object. However, when used in a research setting, attitude becomes a construct that must be specifically defined and measured by the researcher.

Constitutive Definitions. A constitutive definition delineates the major characteristics of a given construct. Constitutive definitions allow us to distinguish the concept in question from other similar but different concepts.

Concept/construct Names given to characteristics that we wish to measure.

Attitude Concept that relates to a person's feelings about an object or thing.

Constitutive definition Specifications for the domain of the construct of interest so as to distinguish it from other similar but different constructs.

For certain concepts the definition found in a dictionary will serve as an appropriate constitutive definition, while for others the constitutive definition will need to be more precise and tailored to the specific research question under study. We cannot overemphasize that the constitutive definition must be consistent with the objectives of the study. If, for example, we are interested in consumer attitudes toward purchasing new Coke, then the attitude concept in question is not the object (new Coke) but instead a consumer's attitude toward *purchasing* new Coke on the next purchase occasion.

Measurement definitions
Specifications as to how unobservable constructs are related to their observable counterparts; that is, the procedure that provides a correspondence between the concept and the real world.

Measurement Definitions. The proper specification of a concept also involves linking the constitutive definition to observable events. A measurement definition translates the constitutive definition into actionable steps that must be followed in order to assign numbers to the characteristics being measured. The numbers must be assigned in such a way as to reflect the properties of the construct under study; in other words, the measurement definition provides a correspondence between the concept and the real world. As such, a measurement definition clearly defines which observable events (traits, characteristics, variables, and so on) are to be measured and the procedure for assigning a value to the concept. It determines which question will be asked.

E X A M P L E

Attitude

*Constitutive
Definition:*   A predisposition to react to a brand in a favorable or unfavorable way.

*Measurement
Definition:*   On your next purchase occasion, do you intend to purchase Brand X?

0_____X_____100%
Definitely   Definitely
will not buy   will buy

0_____X
|←——1"——→|

1" = 25 percent chance of buying

Many of the constructs measured in typical marketing research studies are directly observable, while many are not. For example, the concepts of sales and market share have easily observable physical referents; that is, each of those concepts can be directly tied to observable events. In contrast, the concepts of attitude, product perceptions, or consumer satisfaction involve an individual's mental states and consequently must be measured indirectly. Whether a concept is directly or indirectly observable is not the critical issue. In either case, the researcher must define precisely what is meant by the construct under study.

To summarize, constitutive definitions specify the characteristics of a construct—what the construct is—while measurement definitions link the construct, as reflected by its constitutive definition, to the real world.

LEVEL OF MEASUREMENT

To the extent that we have identified the proper characteristics to measure (constitutive definition) and have applied the correct rules for assigning numbers to reflect the quantity of the characteristic possessed by an individual, household, or object (measurement definition), we will have captured the construct that we wish to study. The end result of measurement is to assign to each individual, household, or object a number that reflects the amount of a characteristic possessed; in this way, individuals, households, or objects can be distinguished according to how much of the underlying construct they possess. However, depending on the characteristics being measured, the numbers assigned have different properties that determine the kinds of statements we can make about the amount of a characteristic possessed by one individual relative to another.

Measurement can be undertaken at different levels. The levels reflect the correspondence of the numbers assigned to the characteristic in question and the meaningfulness of performing mathematical operations on the numbers assigned. The numbers assigned to reflect the amount of a characteristic possessed by an individual, household, or object can be described in terms of the following properties:

- Order—the numbers assigned produce an ordering with respect to a characteristic.
- Distance—the differences between the numbers assigned produce an ordering with respect to a characteristic.
- Origin—the number zero indicates the true absence of a characteristic (that is, a unique origin).

There are four basic types of **measurement scales** that can be distinguished by the underlying assumptions regarding the correspondence of numbers assigned and the meaningfulness of performing mathematical operations on the numbers—that is, on the basis of order, distance, and origin. Table 9-1 describes some of the most important features of each.

Nominal Measurement Scales

Nominal-scaled data are described in terms of classes; that is, the numbers assigned allow us to place an object in one and only one of a

Measurement scales Measurement devices that can be distinguished according to the underlying assumptions regarding the correspondence of numbers assigned to the properties of objects and the meaningfulness of performing mathematical operations on the numbers.

T A B L E   9-1

Types of Measurement Scales

Scale	Basic empirical operations	Some permissible statistics
Nominal	Determination of equality	Number of cases Mode
Ordinal	Determination of greater or less	Median Percentiles
Interval	Determination of equality of intervals or differences	Arithmetic mean Standard deviation Product-moment correlation
Ratio	Determination of equality of ratios	Coefficient of variation

Source: Adapted from S. S. Stevens, "On the Theory of Scales of Measurement," *Science*, 7 June 1946.

Nominal scales
Measurement device where the numbers assigned allow us to place an object in one and only one of a set of mutually exclusive and collectively exhaustive classes with no implied ordering.

set of mutually exclusive and collectively exhaustive classes with no implied ordering. **Nominal scales** provide a system that "maps" an object to a number; in other words, a number is assigned that identifies a specific object. For example, a person's telephone number, or social security number are examples of nominally scaled data. The numbers assigned have no specific properties other than to identify the person assigned the number.

Nominal-scaled variables are frequently referred to as *qualitative* or *nonmetric.* For example, such variables as gender, religious denomination, political affiliation are generally viewed as qualitative, since the numbers assigned actually do not reflect the amount of the attribute possessed by an individual.[2] In fact, any reassignment of the numbers (such as reversing the numbers assigned) would have no effect on the numbering system, since nothing is implied by the numerals in the first place. Therefore, only a limited number of statistics are permissible. To be more specific, with nominal-scaled data it is not meaningful to compute the mean, since average gender or average political affiliation, for example, has little meaning. Nominal-scaled data can be counted—it is legitimate to say that 55 percent of the sample is female. The correct measure of central tendency is the *mode*—the value that appears most frequently.

Ordinal Measurement Scales

Ordinal scales
Measurement device where the response alternatives define an ordered sequence so that the choice listed first is less (greater) than the second, the second less (greater) than the third, and so forth. The numbers assigned do not reflect the magnitude of an attribute possessed by an object.

Ordinal-scaled data are ranked data; consequently, all that we can say is that one object has more or less or the same amount of an attribute as some other object. Thus, with an **ordinal scale** the response alternatives define an ordered sequence so that the choice listed first is less

[2]For this reason some have argued that nominally scaled variables do not actually represent measurement.

(greater) than the second, the second less (greater) than the third, and so forth. The numbers assigned do not reflect the magnitude of a characteristic possessed by an object. If, for example, a person's rank ordering of four brands according to overall preference is A(2), B(1), C(4), D(3), where the number in parentheses is the respective brand's rank order, we can say nothing about the difference in overall preference among the brands. In addition, even though the difference between the rank order numbers 1 and 2 equals the difference between the rank order numbers 2 and 3, we cannot say that the difference in overall preference between the first- and second-ranked brands equals the difference in overall preference between the second- and third-ranked brands.

With ordinal scales any transformation is permissible as long as the basic ordering of the objects is maintained. Thus, we could have assigned the numbers 40 to brand C, 35 to brand D, 30 to brand A, and 10 to brand B. Note that this assignment preserves the relative preference rank ordering of the four brands. Because only order is implied, with ordinal-scaled data the appropriate measures of central tendency are the *mode* and the *median*—the value below which 50 percent of the observations lie.

Ordinal measurement scales are frequently used in commercial marketing research studies. Preference data and purchase intentions are typically collected with ordinal measures. In the following example, we illustrate two questions that produce ordinal data.

EXAMPLE

Read the list of packaged ice cream brands on the card I just gave you.

Breyers
Sealtest
Haagen Dazs
Frusen Gladje
Hood
Borden

Tell me which packaged ice cream brand you prefer most. Now excluding that brand, mention the brand of packaged ice cream that you next most prefer. (Continue until all brands have been considered.)

(1) _____   (3) _____   (5) _____
(2) _____   (4) _____   (6) _____

Interval Measurement Scales

Interval-scaled data allow us to say how much more one object has of an attribute than another; thus, with **interval scales** we can tell how far apart two or more objects are with respect to the attribute, and so the

Interval scale
Measurement device that allows us to tell how far apart two or more objects are with respect to the attribute and consequently to compare the difference between the numbers assigned. Because the interval scale lacks a natural or absolute origin, the absolute magnitude of the numbers cannot be compared.

difference between numbers assigned can be compared. In other words, with an interval scale the difference in the amount between scale points 2 and 3 on a scale is equal to the difference in the amount of the attribute between scale points 3 and 4; further, the difference between scale points 1 and 2 is one-half the difference between scale points 2 and 4. With interval scaled data, the arithmetic *mean, median,* or *mode* can be used as a legitimate measure of central tendency; and virtually the entire range of statistical analysis can be applied to interval measurement scales (see Chapters 15 and 16). Because of the arbitrary nature of the zero point, any positive linear transformation (that is, $y = a + bx$, where x is the original scale value, y is the transformed scale value, a is any constant, and $b > 0$, will preserve the interval scale properties of the scale.

This is not to say, however, that the absolute magnitude of the numbers across objects can be compared. Stated differently, we cannot say that the object assigned the number 4 has twice the characteristics being measured as the object assigned the number 2 on an interval scale. The reason is that while an interval scale possesses the characteristics of order and distance, it lacks a natural or absolute origin (zero point). Thus, with interval data neither ratios nor differences are unique; however ratios of differences are. To see this, consider the following example.

E X A M P L E

Person	Original scale value (x)	Transformed scale value ($y = 5 + 3x$)
A	5	20
B	10	35
C	15	50

The data consist of the interval scaled values for three hypothetical individuals. The original scale values have been transformed according to the transformation $y = 5 + 3x$. We can see that it is incorrect to conclude that Person B has twice the characteristic being measured as Person A—for the transformed values, 35 is not twice 20. We can, however, conclude that the difference in the characteristic possessed by Person A and Person B is the same as the difference in the characteristic possessed by Person B and Person C; that is

Person B		Person A			Person C	−	Person B
10	−	5	= 5 =		15	−	10

And we see a corresponding equality of differences in the transformed values.

Person B	−	Person A			Person C	−	Person B
35	−	20	= 15 =		50	−	35

The ratio and differences between the scale values of the individuals are not unique, but the ratios of the differences are:

$$(10 - 5)/(15 - 10) = 1 = (35 - 20)/(50 - 35)$$

To summarize, the difference in the characteristic possessed by Person A and Person B is the same as the difference between Person B and Person C, using either scale. Thus, within-scale comparisons across people are permissible. However, Person A does not have 5 more units of the characteristic than Person B, since while Person B_O − Person A_O = 5, Person B_T − Person A_T = 15, where the subscripts O and T refer to the original and transformed scale values, respectively.

Interval measurement scales are also frequently used in commercial marketing research studies, especially in collecting attitudinal and overall brand rating information. For example, consider the following two prototypical question formats.

EXAMPLE

Please indicate your degree of agreement or disagreement with each of the following statements by selecting the appropriate response.

Breyers Ice Cream is:	Strongly agree	Agree	Neither agree nor disagree	Disagree	Strongly disagree
Wholesome	———	———	———	———	———
Healthy	———	———	———	———	———
Premium-priced	———	———	———	———	———
Unique	———	———	———	———	———
Good value	———	———	———	———	———

I would like you to rate the six brands of packaged ice cream on an overall basis. *(Hand respondent the card)* Using the phrases on this card, please tell me how you would rate *(Brand checked following "x")* overall? *(Record in appropriate place below.)* And how would you rate *(Insert next brand)?* *(Record in appropriate place below. Continue for each checked brand.)*

	Excellent	Very Good	Good	Fair	Poor
( )Haagen Dazs	5	4	3	2	1
(x)Breyers	5	4	3	2	1
( )Hood	5	4	3	2	1
( )Frusen Gladje	5	4	3	2	1
( )Sealtest	5	4	3	2	1
( )Borden	5	4	3	2	1

It is unlikely that the interval between each of the scale categories in both of the questions shown above is exactly equal. In fact, the data resulting from either of these two scales are, strictly speaking, ordinal, but typically analyzed as if they are interval. If the interval between successive scale categories is grossly unequal, then applying statistical analysis that requires interval measurement can produce badly misleading results.

Ratio Measurement Scales

Ratio scales
Measurement device with
the same properties as
interval scales. In
addition, ratio scales have
a natural or absolute
origin.

Ratio scaled data have the same properties as interval scaled data—with one important difference. **Ratio scales** possess a natural or absolute origin. Thus, we can legitimately say that the object assigned the number 4 has twice the characteristic being measured as the object assigned the number 2 on a ratio scale. Ratio scales are frequently associated with directly observable physical events or entities. Directly observable relevant marketing constructs that can be measured on a ratio scale include market share, sales, income, number of salespersons per territory, and so forth.

Because of the legitimate zero point, ratio scales only allow for proportionate transformation of scale values. For example, the proportionate transformation of the form $y = bx$, where x is the original scale values, y is the transformed scale value and $b > 0$, will preserve all of the relationships among the objects. Ratio scales are the most powerful of the scale types; they have the properties of the other scale types and more, since they possess the characteristics of order, distance, and unique origin.

We need to make three points before proceeding. First, the measurement level categories (nominal, ordinal, interval, and ratio) we've discussed are not necessarily exhaustive. It is possible to have a nominal scale that conveys partial information on order or an ordinal scale that conveys partial information on distance.[3] Second, keep in mind that the measurement level adopted for the given characteristic being measured ultimately defines the construct's metric. For example, if the characteristics that purportedly reflect the construct in question are measured at the ordinal level, then the construct's metric will also be ordinal. Finally, the progression from nominal to ratio scaling implies an increasingly restrictive set of measurement rules. The arithmetic operations that are permissible for a higher scale of measurement should never be applied to a lower scale of measurement, as Exhibit 9-1 illustrates.

[3]Between nominal and ordinal scales lies the *partially ordered* scale; between the ordinal and interval scales is the *ordered metric* scale. It is beyond the scope of this text to discuss these scales in any detail. Further discussion can be found in C. H. Coombs, "Theory and Methods of Social Measurement," in *Research Methods in the Behavioral Sciences*, ed. L. Festinger and D. Katz (New York: Holt, Rinehart and Winston, 1953).

EXHIBIT 9-1

Be Careful What You Do With Numbers

Consider the following scenario:

In a recent taste test 100 respondents were asked to indicate their purchase intentions for two brands of soft drinks. The soft drinks were tasted blind. After tasting the first soft drink, respondents indicated their purchase intent on the following scale:

A. Definitely would buy _____
B. Probably would buy _____
C. Might or might not buy _____
D. Probably would not buy _____
E. Definitely would not buy _____

After recording their intentions, respondents were instructed to drink some water (to clear their taste buds) and then to taste the second soft drink. After tasting the second soft drink they were again asked to indicate their purchase intent (on the identical scale). The order of tasting the two brands was randomly assigned across the respondents.

The following summarizes the results:

	Brand X	Brand Z
A. Definitely would buy	15	20
B. Probably would buy	50	15
C. Might or might not buy	20	50
D. Probably would not buy	10	10
E. Definitely would not buy	5	5
Total	100	100

These results were forwarded to the brand group responsible for this category. At a general meeting of the group some time later the three brand managers who had worked on this study presented their conclusions. Brand Manager 1 concluded that, "Based on the data our brand (Brand X) is 50% more preferred than the competition (Brand Z)." Brand Manager 2 concluded that, "Based on the data our brand (Brand X) is 7.5% more preferred than the competition (Brand Z)." Brand Manager 3 concluded that, "Based on the data our brand (Brand X) is 9.4% more preferred than the competition (Brand Z)."

The apparent inconsistency among the brand managers is a bit puzzling, especially since the same data and computational procedure were used by each manager. Each calculated an average score for each brand, took the difference, and then divided the difference (ignoring sign) by the competitive brand's score to obtain a percentage.

You might be wondering, What possibly could account for the different conclusions? Well, it seems that each brand manager used a different coding system in computing the mean scores. Brand Manager 1 decided to code category A as $+2$, category B as $+1$, category C as 0, category D as -1, and category E as -2. This resulted in mean scores of .6 (Brand X) and .3 (Brand Z) and since the .6 score is 50 percent more than the .3 level obtained by the competition, this brand manager concluded that Brand X is 50% more preferred. In contrast to Brand

Manager 1, the second brand manager assigned category A at $+1$ and continued up to $+5$ for the category E. This yielded mean scores of 3.6 (Brand X) and 3.35 (Brand Z). Finally, Brand Manager 3 essentially used the same coding system as the second brand manager but assigned a $+5$ to category E and a $+1$ to category A. This resulted in means scores of 2.4 (Brand X) and 2.65 (Brand Z).

Which brand manager is right? Well, as you might suspect, none of them. The reason is that, for this type of data, calculation of ratios is not appropriate.

RELIABILITY AND CONSTRUCT VALIDITY

After the construct has been constitutively defined, its measurement definition determines the specific questions to be asked and how numbers are to be assigned. Because the conclusions drawn about the construct under study are ultimately determined by the responses to the questions that we ask, we need to consider the properties of the measurement instrument itself. Concerns about the measures used in marketing research have been voiced by many. For example, in a 1978 issue of *Marketing News*, Burleigh Gardner, President of Social Research, Inc., made the following comment:[4]

> Today the social scientists are enamored of numbers and counting. . . . Rarely do they stop and ask, "What lies behind the numbers?"

> When we talk about attitudes we are talking about constructs of the mind as they are expressed in response to our questions.

> But usually all we really know are the questions we ask and the answers we get.

In this section we discuss two standard measurement criteria—reliability and validity. *Reliability* indicates the precision of measurement scores, or how accurately such scores will be reproduced with repeated measurement. *Construct validity* refers to the extent to which differences in observed measurement scores reflect true differences in the characteristic being measured. Before we give further details on these two criteria, we introduce what is called the *true score model* of measurement, which will provide a perspective on the issue of reliability and construct validity.

True Score Model

The **true score model** provides one framework for understanding what requirements our measures must satisfy.[5] Consider, for example,

True-score model A person's specific attitude toward buying and using the brand, denoted by X_T. The true score is composed of X_O, the observed score component, and X_E, the error score component. $X_O = X_T + X_E$.

---

[4]Burleigh Gardner, *Marketing News*, 5 May 1978, 1.
[5]Note that the true score model is not the only theory of measurement. For further details see F. M. Lord and M. R. Novick, *Statistical Theories of Mental Test Scores* (Reading, Mass.: Addison-Wesley, 1968).

the attitude construct. We assume that a person holds a specific attitude toward buying and using a brand. This specific attitude is called his or her "true" attitude, and we denote this level by X_T. To capture the person's attitude, we use a particular measurement scale that produces an observed score, denoted by X_O. The measurement scale is usually composed of a number of scale items (questions), all presumed to be measuring the construct under study. These items represent a sample of items from the population of items that define the domain of the construct.

Ideally, we would like the measurement scale to produce an observed score equal to the person's true attitude level, that is $X_O = X_T$. It rarely happens, however, that the observed scale score will equal the true score. The discrepancy between the two is usually referred to as the error score, given by the difference between the observed score and the true score:

$$X_E = X_O - X_T \tag{9-1}$$

where X_E denotes the error score. By simple manipulation, we have the classic true score model of measurement

$$X_O = X_T + X_E \tag{9-2}$$

which states that the observed scale score is composed of a true score component and an **error component.** The true score component represents the person's actual score on the construct of interest, whereas the error component is due to all those factors that cause the person's observed scale score to differ from the person's true score.

Error component Those factors that cause the person's observed scale score to differ from the person's true score.

The variation in a set of measurements obtained from a given measurement instrument arises from a variety of specific sources or factors. Exhibit 9-2 summarizes the possible sources of variation in measurement scores. Note that the true score is only one of nine possible sources of variation. All of the remaining sources constitute the error component in the classical true score model.

EXHIBIT 9-2

Possible Sources of Variation in Measurement Scores

1. *True differences* in the characteristic being measured.
2. Characteristics of individuals that affect scores: for example, intelligence, extent of education, information processed.
3. Short-term personal factors: health, fatigue, motivation, emotional strain, among others.
4. Situational factors: for example, rapport established, distractions that arise.
5. Variations in administration of measuring instrument: interviewers, for example.

6. Sampling of items included in instrument.
7. Lack of clarity of measuring instrument: ambiguity, complexity, interpretation, for instance.
8. Instrument factors: lack of space to record response, appearance of instrument, and so on.
9. Analysis factors: For instance, scoring, tabulation, statistical compilation.

RELIABILITY

Reliability The extent to which measures are free from random error and yield consistent result.

Reliability in a measurement context is not really different from the layperson's definition.[6] Essentially, reliability denotes stability or consistency; that is, reliable measures are consistent—stable from one administration to the next. Consider Table 9-2, which shows three sets of scale scores for five individuals. The first column in the table displays each person's true score. The second and third columns show observed scale scores obtained under an unreliable test and a reliable test, respectively. Notice that the rank orders of the first and third columns covary exactly; in other words, even though the observed scale scores obtained with this test are not identical to the true scores, they are in the exact rank order. And in this sense, this test is reliable. In contrast, the observed scale scores appearing in the second column do not covary with the true scores. And in this sense, this test is unreliable.

T A B L E 9-2
True, Reliable and Unreliable Test Scores*

(1) True scores	Rank	(2) Scores from unreliable test	Rank	(3) Scores from reliable test	Rank
42	1	27	4	45	1
35	2	44	1	37	2
31	3	30	3	33	3
28	4	20	5	27	4
22	5	36	2	21	5

*Adapted from F. N. Kerlinger, *Foundations of Behavioral Research*, 3rd ed. (New York: Holt, Rinehart and Winston, 1973).

[6]Parts of this section are based on the work of J. P. Guilford, *Psychometric Methods* (New York: McGraw-Hill Book Company, 1954); K. N. Kerlinger, *Foundations of Behavioral Research*, 3rd ed. (New York: Holt, Rinehart and Winston, 1973); F. M. Lord and M. R. Novick, *Statistical Theories of Mental Test Scores* (Reading, Mass.: Addison-Wesley, 1968); J. C. Nunnally, *Psychometric Theory*, 2nd ed. (New York: McGraw-Hill Book Company, 1978); J. P. Peter, "Reliability: A Review of Psychometric Basics and Recent Marketing Practices," *Journal of Marketing Research* 16, February 1979, 6–17.

Reliability Theory

The error score is an increase or decrease from the true score caused by measurement error. Measurement error is the primary source of unreliability. Unreliability comes about primarily because the items making up the measurement scale do not measure the same construct. The error component in the classic true score measurement model (see relationship (9-2)) is itself composed of two components. That is,

$$X_E = X_S + X_R \qquad (9-3)$$

where X_S denotes **systematic sources of error** representing stable characteristics such as *instrument factors*, which affect the observed scale score in the same way each time the test is administered, and X_R represents **random sources of error** such as *short-term personal factors*, which affect the observed scale score in different ways each time the test is administered (see Exhibit 9-2).

From Table 9-2 we saw that a test is reliable if it consistently rank-orders individuals. Since systematic errors do not contribute to inconsistency, they affect the observed scale scores in the same way each time the test is administered and consequently do not adversely affect reliability. However, random error does and therefore lowers reliability. Based on this discussion, reliability can be simply defined as the extent to which measures are free from random error and yield consistent results. Stated somewhat more formally, a measure is reliable if independent but comparable measures of the same construct agree. Since reliability depends on how much random error is present in our measures, we can say that if $X_R = 0$, the measure is perfectly reliable.

Reliability Measurement

The general approach for assessing reliability is to determine the proportion of systematic variation in a measurement scale. To accomplish this, the various methods determine the association between scores obtained from two scales, where one of the scales is a similar replicated version of the other. If the association between the scores derived from the two scales is high, the scales are consistent in yielding the same results and are therefore reliable.

Several methods for calculating the reliability of a measurement scale involve the use of a correlation coefficient. Since measures of association and specifically correlation coefficients will be discussed in some detail in Chapter 16 we will not present the computational formula here. We should note, however, that the correlation coefficient used to assess reliability must be consistent with the measurement level of the scale. Chapter 16 provides the necessary details.

Systematic sources of error Denoted by X_S, component made up of stable characteristics that affect the observed scale score in the same way each time the test is administered.

Random sources of error Denoted by X_R, component made up of transient personal factors that affect the observed scale score in different ways each time the test is administered.

Test-Retest Reliability. In the test-retest method of reliability assessment, respondents are administered identical sets of scale items at two different times under similar conditions. The suggested retest period is two weeks after the initial test. The **reliability coefficient** is computed by correlating the scores obtained from the two administrations.

There are several problems with the test-retest method. First, it is sensitive to the time interval between test occasions. All else the same, the longer the time interval between test occasions, the lower the reliability.[7] Second, a low reliability coefficient will be obtained if a change in the phenomenon under study has occurred between the first and second administrations; however, it may be difficult to distinguish this change from unreliability. Finally, the reliability coefficient as computed in the test-retest method can be inflated due to the correlation of each scale item with itself. In computing the reliability coefficient, the correlation of each scale item with itself across the two administrations is considered. It is reasonable to expect that these correlations are likely to be much higher than correlations between different scale items across administrations; thus, the reliability coefficient can be high simply because of the high correlations that are present between the same scale item measured at different times, even though the correlation between different scale items is quite low.[8]

Internal Consistency Reliability. There are a number of different approaches to computing internal consistency reliability. With these approaches the item scores obtained from administering the scale are in some way split in half and the resulting half scores are correlated. Large correlations between **split-halves** indicate high internal consistency. The simplest approach is to split the scale items in terms of odd- and even-numbered items or randomly. There is, however, one fundamental problem with using split-halves to assess internal consistency: Depending on how the scale items are split in half, different results will be obtained. This raises the important question of which one is the "real" reliability coefficient.

A popular approach to overcoming this limitation is to form all possible split-half partitions of a measurement scale and to compute the mean reliability coefficient. **Cronbach's alpha**[9] (α) is the most commonly accepted formula for assessing the internal consistency of a multi-item measurement scale. Computationally, alpha is given by

$$\alpha = \left(\frac{k}{k-1}\right)\left(1 - \frac{\sum_{i=1}^{k}\sigma_i^2}{\sigma_T^2}\right) \tag{9-4}$$

[7]G. W. Bohrnstedt, "Reliability and Validity Assessment in Attitude Measurement," in G. F. Summers, ed., *Attitude Measurement,* edited by G. F. Summers (Chicago: Rand McNally, 1970), 85.

[8]For further discussion of this point see J. C. Nunnally, *Psychometric Methods.*

[9]L. J. Cronbach, "Coefficient Alpha and the Internal Structure of Tests," *Psychometrika* 16, September 1951, 297–334.

where

k = the number of items in the measurement scale

σ_i^2 = variance of the ith item

σ_T^2 = variance of the entire measurement scale

Noting that the total variance equals the sum of the individual scale item variances plus two times the sum of the scale item covariances, relationship (9-4) can be expressed in computational form as

$$\alpha = \left(\frac{k}{k-1} \right) \left(1 - \frac{\displaystyle\sum_{i=1}^{k} \sigma_i^2}{\displaystyle\sum_{i=1}^{k} \sigma_i^2 + 2\sum_{i>j}^{k} \sum_{j}^{k} \sigma_{ij}} \right) \tag{9-5}$$

where σ_{ij}, $i > j$, denote the $k(k-1)/2$ covariances. The expression shown in (9-5) is more convenient computationally. Also, in this form we can see an interesting property of coefficient α related to what might happen to the internal consistency of a measurement scale, as indicated by coefficient α, as the number of scale items increases.

Consider the results of increasing a given scale measurement by m items. With m additional scale items, $(k+m)/[(k+m)-1] < (k/k-1)$, and this component of the formula decreases; however, there are m additional variances and $m(m-1)$ additional covariance terms; thus, the number of additional variance terms increases arithmetically, while the number of additional covariance terms increases geometrically. Since the former component appears in the numerator and the latter component appears in the denominator, the quotient in expression (9-5) increases. In general, although $(k/k-1)$ in the formula decreases with an increase in the number of scale items and the additional variance terms would have a negative effect on coefficient α, the geometric increase in the number of covariance terms that appears in the denominator of expression (9-5) more than offsets these effects. Thus, an important property of coefficient α is that unless the covariance of each of the additional scale items with each original item is almost zero and the variance of each of the added items is not, an increase in the number of scale items will increase the reliability of the scale, as measured by coefficient α. It also naturally follows that coefficient α can be maximized by asking what are essentially the same questions several times. Note, however, that this is *not* good measurement practice.

Alternative Form Reliability. In the alternative form approach to reliability assessment, the same subjects are measured at two different times, usually two weeks apart, with two scales designed to be similar in content but not so similar that the scores on the scale administered first affect the scores on the scale administered after two weeks have elapsed. The reliability coefficient is obtained by correlating the scores from the two administrations of the alternative scale forms.

Alternative form reliability Method of calculating reliability; the same subjects are measured at two different times, usually two weeks apart, with two scales designed to be similar in content but not so similar that the scores on the scale administered first affect the scores on the scale administered after two weeks have elapsed.

Alternative forms implicitly assess the equivalence of content of sets of scale items. And herein lies the problem. Using this approach presumes that substantially equivalent alternative forms can be developed. Strictly speaking, alternative forms require that the alternative sets of scale items used have equivalent means, variances, and intercorrelations.[10] Even if these conditions are satisfied, it may be difficult to assess the equivalence of the alternative sets with respect to content. Low correlation between the alternative form scores could be due to low reliability or nonequivalence of content. This approach appears best suited to situations in which the construct under study is expected to vary over short time periods. In such cases, alternative form measures can allow one to investigate these changes.

CONSTRUCT VALIDITY

Even if a measurement scale is reliable, it may or may not be construct valid. In other words, a measurement scale can consistently yield the same (or similar) scores, but the scores obtained need not reflect the construct that the researcher wishes to study. Reliability does not guarantee that a measurement scale will be construct-valid, since construct validity is most directly related to the question of what the measurement scale is in fact measuring. Stated more formally, a measurement scale is said to possess **construct validity** to the extent that differences in the observed scale scores reflect true differences in the characteristic or construct being measured.

Construct validity The extent to which differences in the observed scale scores reflect true differences in the characteristic or construct being measured.

Construct Validity Theory

At the heart of construct validity is nonrandom error. Matters of construct invalidity arise when other factors (confounds—see Chapter 6) affect the characteristics being measured in addition to the one underlying construct and random error. The presence of nonrandom errors can result in scale items representing something other than the intended construct, perhaps an extremely different construct altogether. For instance, if a researcher uses a particular set of scale items to represent brand loyalty but later discovers that the scale actually taps only repeat purchase behavior irrespective of attitude, then the scale is an invalid indicator of loyalty.

Validity depends on the extent of nonrandom error present in the measurement process. And just as reliability is a matter of degree, so is validity. One can probably never attain a perfectly valid measurement scale—one that represents the intended construct and no other. For example, high scorers on a brand-loyalty scale may be not only persons who exhibit loyalty (both favorable attitude and purchase behavior) but also people who buy the same brand(s) because of limited availability. This is another way of saying that validity critically depends on the ex-

[10]H. Gulliksen, *Theory of Mental Tests* (New York: John Wiley & Sons, 1950).

294

tent of nonrandom error—that is, confounds—and, like reliability, is a matter of degree.

Types of Construct Validity and Measurement

The term construct validity is often used amorphously, meaning different things to different researchers. Construct validity has come to be used generically and provides a broad umbrella under which the other types of validity are subsumed. We now describe several types of construct validities that you should be aware of and briefly comment on how each is measured.[11] In the course of the discussion, we refer to the attitude construct in order to provide specific illustrations of what is meant by the various types of validity.

Content Validity. This type of validity is concerned with the representativeness of the content of a measurement scale. Content validity focuses on whether the scale items adequately cover the entire domain of the construct under study. Consider, for example, the attitude construct, which is presumably composed of three subdimensions relating to a person's likes/dislikes, beliefs, and behavioral intentions. An attitude score, to be content-valid, should contain scale items that tap all three subdimensions. The content validity of a measurement scale would be assessed by evaluating the closeness of the scale items to the characteristic or construct under study.

Content validity
Indication of the representativeness of the content of a measurement scale; focuses on whether the scale items adequately cover the entire domain of the construct under study.

Convergent Validity. This type of validity indicates that measurement scales designed to measure the same construct should be related. In attitude measurement, the scale items purportedly measuring the affective (like/dislike) subdimension of attitude should be related to the scale items purportedly measuring the cognitive (belief) subdimension—since both measurement scales presumably reflect a person's attitude. Convergent validity is generally assessed by the extent to which two (or more) measurement scales designed to measure the same construct correlate.

Convergent validity
Indication of the extent to which measurement scales designed to measure the same construct are related.

Discriminant Validity. This type of validity examines the extent to which the measurement scale is novel and not simply a reflection of some other variable. Measurement scales can correlate too highly. To quote a seminal article on convergent and discriminant validity: "Tests can be invalidated by too high correlations with other tests from which they were intended to differ."[12] If two presumably distinct measurement scales correlate very highly, then they may be measuring the same characteristic or construct rather than different characteristics or constructs.

Discriminant validity
Indication of extent to which the measurement scale is novel and not simply a reflection of some other variable.

---

[11]Our treatment of how to measure validity will be elementary. Details on validity measurement require a level of sophistication beyond the scope of this textbook. Readers wanting further details can consult N. Schmitt, B. W. Coyle, and B. B. Saari, "A Review and Critique of Analyses of Multitrait-Multimethod Matrices," *Multivariate Behavioral Research* 12 (1977), 447–478; N. Schmitt and D. M. Stults, "Methodology Review: Analysis of Multitrait-Multimethod Matrices," *Applied Psychological Measurement* 10(1986), 1–22.

[12]Campbell and Fiske, 8.

Suppose that in measuring attitude the correlation between the affective (like/dislike) measurement scale items and cognitive (belief) measurement scale items approaches unity; in this case the two measurement scales would be indistinguishable, and we would conclude that the two scales are not reflecting *separate* and *distinct* components of attitude but rather just a single component. Discriminant validity is assessed by examining the correlation between the measure of interest and other measures that purportedly measure a different, but related, characteristic or construct.

*Criterion validity
(predictive validity)*
Indication of whether the
measurement scale
behaves as expected in
relation to other
constructs.

Criterion Validity. This type of validity investigates whether the measurement scale behaves as expected in relation to other constructs. For example, in the context of the attitude construct, we might investigate whether persons with positive attitudes, as indicated by the measurement scale being used, also have a tendency to perform favorable behaviors with respect to the attitude object. Criterion validity is generally assessed by determining the extent to which the observed measurement scale scores can predict some criterion measure. For this reason, this type of validity is sometimes referred to as *predictive validity*.

DEVELOPING SOUND CONSTRUCTS

Based upon the discussion presented so far, we can outline a recommended procedure for developing sound constructs in terms of five essential steps.

1. *Specify constitutive definition*. This involves a clear and precise definition of the domain of the construct in question.
2. *Specify measurement definition*. This involves specifying the items (questions) to be asked and the rule for assigning numbers to the characteristics of interest—that is, specifying the scale of measurement.
3. *Perform item analysis*. After the items have been placed in an appropriate format, data should be collected from members of the relevant target market of interest and an *item analysis* performed. The items making up a scale should correlate highly with the total score for the overall measurement instrument; in this sense the scale can be said to be *internally consistent*. Items showing low correlation with the total score for the overall measurement instrument should be deleted. The exact procedure for conducting an item analysis will depend on the specific type of scale used. We will demonstrate how an item analysis is performed for different types of attitude scales in Chapter 11.
4. *Perform reliability checks*. Once an item analysis has been performed, new data should be collected with the purified measurement instrument and a reliability check performed. We have discussed various tests for reliability.

5. *Perform validity checks.* After the reliability of the measurement instrument has been established, a validity analysis must be performed. Where appropriate, each type of validity should be examined.

Unfortunately, the procedure for developing sound constructs described above is rarely completely followed in commercial marketing research studies. The reason for this is simple; time and cost constraints often make it impossible to completely follow such an elaborate procedure. Nonetheless, we suggest that the steps described above serve as a framework for construct development that can be implemented in whole or in part, depending on the resources available.

Summary

The objectives of the research study ultimately determine the constitutive and measurement definitions adopted and the set of scale items used. The researcher must define the construct clearly—in constitutive and measurement terms—and then choose an appropriate measurement scale that establishes the proper correspondence between the numbers assigned and the quantity of characteristics possessed, as well as the set of mathematical operations that can be performed. The measurements taken are subject to tests of reliability and validity. The researcher who follows the procedures for developing sound constructs is apt to be measuring more than just the questions asked and answers received.

Key Concepts

Measurement
Concept/construct
Constitutive
  definition
Measurement
  definition
Scales of
  measurement

Nominal scales
Ordinal scales
Interval scales
Ratio scales
True-score model
Reliability
Test-retest reliability

Reliability coefficient
Internal consistency
Validity
Convergent validity
Content validity
Discriminant validity
Criterion validity

Review Questions

1. Discuss what is meant by measurement and distinguish between constitutive and measurement definitions.
2. Distinguish among the four basic types of measurement scales (*nominal, ordinal, interval,* and *ratio*) in terms of order distance and origin properties.
3. Discuss the concept of the true score model and its implications for reliability and validity.
4. Explain the concepts of reliability and validity.
5. How should constructs be developed?

297

Measurement Scales

CHAPTER OBJECTIVES

- Distinguish among the various types of measurement scales.
- Describe and illustrate *comparative* types of measurement scales.
- Describe and illustrate *noncomparative* types of measurement scales.
- Discuss and illustrate purchase-intent scales.

Introduction

This chapter is totally devoted to describing and illustrating a variety of frequently used measurement scales. We start by distinguishing between two general types of measurement scales: *comparative* and *noncomparative*. Then we describe many of the commonly used comparative and noncomparative scales with particular emphasis on how these scales are used. The final section of the chapter considers the *purchase-intent* scale, one of the most frequently used scales in commercial marketing research studies.

SCALE TYPES

The various types of measurement scales fall into two broad categories: *comparative and noncomparative scales.*

In **comparative scaling** the subject is asked to compare one set of stimulus objects directly against another. For example, a respondent might be asked to directly compare, on the basis of a set of salient attributes, his or her current brand against the other brands that are considered when making a purchase from this product category. Because the scaling is comparative, results must be interpreted in relative terms and have ordinal or rank order properties; that is, the scores obtained indicate that one brand is preferred to another, but not by how much. An attractive feature of comparative scales is that relatively small differences among the objects being compared can be detected. Note, however, that since the respondent is instructed to directly compare objects, differ-

Comparative scaling
(nonmetric scaling)
Scaling process in which the subject is asked to compare a set of stimulus objects directly against one another.

ences are effectively "forced" to surface. Finally, comparative scales are generally easily understood by the respondent.

In **noncomparative scaling** the respondent is asked to evaluate each object on the scale provided independently of the other objects being investigated. Because each object is rated independently, noncomparative scaling is frequently referred to as **monadic scaling.** Monadic scales are the most widely used scaling technique in commercial marketing research studies.

C H A P T E R   10
Measurement Scales
Noncomparative scaling (monadic scaling)
Scaling method whereby the respondent is asked to evaluate each object on the scale provided independently of the other objects being investigated.

COMPARATIVE SCALES

Comparative scales ensure that all respondents approach the rating task from the same known reference point.

Paired Comparisons

The **paired comparison scale** presents the respondent with two objects at a time and asks the respondent to select one of the two according to some criterion. Paired comparisons yield ordinal scaled data; for example, brand A is preferred to brand B: brand A tastes better than brand B, and so on. This type of scale is frequently used, especially when the objects are physical products. As the following example illustrates, paired comparison scales are extremely easy to administer; and the resulting data are generally easy to analyze and interpret.

Paired comparison Scale that presents the respondent with two objects at a time and asks the respondent to select one of the two according to some criterion.

E X A M P L E

To scale consumers' response to four alternative package designs for a new product, a mall-intercept study of 100 consumers was used. After qualifying the respondents, the interviewer presented each one with an 8-inch by 8-inch poster. The poster contained a color picture of two alternative package designs, and the respondent was asked to indicate which he or she preferred most. Because there were a total of four package designs, the respondent was presented with six posters, one at a time in random order.

To tabulate the paired comparison data, a matrix was formed that indicated the percentage of people choosing each package design when paired with the other three designs. Table 10-1 presents this matrix with the four package designs labeled, A, B, C, and D. The numbers in the matrix represent the proportion of people choosing the column entry over the row entry. For example, A was chosen 80 percent of the time when paired with B (consequently, B was chosen 20 percent of the time when paired with A); A was chosen 25 percent of the time when paired with C, and so forth.

Notice that package design C was preferred to all other package designs, and package design B was not preferred to any of the other designs. A rank ordering of the designs with respect to preference would be C > A > D > B. To obtain this ranking, we form another matrix. In this matrix, shown in Table 10-2,

TABLE 10-1

Proportion of Times Column Package Design Chosen over Row Package Design

	Package design			
	A	B	C	D
Package design A	—	.20	.75	.40
B	.80	—	.90	.70
C	.25	.10	—	.35
D	.60	.30	.65	—

TABLE 10-2

Calculation of Rank-Order Values from Table 10-1

	A	B	C	D
A	—	0	1	0
B	1	—	1	1
C	0	0	—	0
D	1	0	1	—
Sum	2	0	3	1

if the column design was preferred (that is, a proportion $> .5$) to the row design, we place a 1 in that cell, whereas if the column design was not preferred (that is, a proportion $< .5$), we place a zero.[1] The rank-order value is calculated by simply summing the columns. (Proportions equal to .5 are randomly assigned a value of one or zero).

This example entails four brands and six comparisons. In general, with n brands there are $n(n - 1)/2$ comparisons along one criterion; and therefore with k criteria, there are $k \times [n(n - 1)/2]$ comparisons in total. Obviously, with many brands and/or criteria, the number of comparisons can become unwieldly. In addition, because objects are compared two at a time, respondents' judgments may not obey the rule of transitivity; that is, if brand A is preferred to brand B, brand B preferred to brand C, then, by the rule of transitivity, brand A should be preferred to brand C; however, if brand C is preferred to brand A, then an intransitivity exists. If a large number of intransitivities exist, then the paired comparison data will be uninterpretable.

Another important property of paired comparison scales is that the ordinal data obtained can be easily converted to interval scaled data, as the following example illustrates.

EXAMPLE

To convert the ordinal data resulting from the paired comparison procedure reported in Table 10-1, we use an approach that, in essence, converts the proportions to z-values (standard normal deviates—see Chapter 15).[2] For example,

[1]An alternative approach to handling paired-comparison data used in commercial marketing research is to look at the proportion of times a given package design is chosen out of the total number of comparisons involving that package design.

[2]L. L. Thurstone, "A Law of Comparative Judgment," *Psychological Review* 34 (1927), 273–286.

Z-Values Resulting from Table 10-1

Brand	A	B	C	D
A	0.00	− .84	.67	− .25
B	.84	0.00	1.28	.52
C	− .67	− 1.28	0.00	− .39
D	.25	− .52	.39	0.00
Total	.42	− 2.64	2.34	− .12
Mean	.105	− .66	.585	− .03
I^*	.765	.00	1.245	.63

from Table 10-1 the proportion of people choosing A over B is .80. From the cumulative normal distribution shown in the Statistical Appendix, Table 2, we see that the z-value for .80 is approximately equal to .84. If the proportion is less than .5, we subtract the proportion from 1 and the resulting z-value carries a negative sign. For example, only 10 percent of the people chose B over C; consequently, this cell would contain a z-value of − 1.28. Table 10-3 contains the z-values corresponding to the proportions reported in Table 10-1.

Let us determine the interval scale value for package design A (column one). From Table 10-3 the value would be [0.0 + .84 + (− .67) + .25]/4 = .105. As previously noted, the zero point of an interval scale is arbitrary. For ease of interpretation we can rescale the interval scale values just obtained. This involves adding the absolute value of the smallest mean scale value to original mean scale values. For instance, in this example, alternative B has the smallest mean scale value (− .66); thus we add .66 to all four mean scale values. The resulting scale values (I^*) are shown in Table 10-3. Based upon these scale values we would conclude that C is preferred to A, A is preferred to D, and D is preferred to B.

Dollar Metric Comparisons

An extension of the paired comparison method is the **dollar metric (scale or graded paired** procedure.[3] The dollar metric scale extends the paired comparison method by asking respondents to indicate which brand is preferred and how much they are willing to pay to acquire their preferred brand. As the following example demonstrates, this scaling technique allows one to obtain an interval scaled measure of preferences.

Dollar metric scale (graded paired comparison) Scale that extends the paired comparison method by asking respondents to indicate which brand is preferred and how much they are willing to pay to acquire their preferred brand.

E X A M P L E

As we indicated above, the dollar metric scale is an extension of the paired comparison method. The respondents are presented with pairs of brands and, in

[3] E. A. Pessemier, *Experimental Methods of Analyzing Demand for Branded Consumer Goods with Application to Problems in Marketing Strategy.* Bulletin 39 (Pullman: Washington State University, Bureau of Economic and Business Research, June 1963).

T A B L E 10-4
Dollar Metric Method

With respect to fruit juice, which container do you prefer?				How much more in cents would you be willing to pay for the preferred container?
glass	✓	can	___	$.07
box	___	plastic	✓	.06
glass	✓	box	___	.07
plastic	___	glass	✓	.02
can	✓	box	___	.03
plastic	___	can	✓	.05

the same manner as with paired comparisons, are asked to select the one they prefer most. However, with the dollar metric scale respondents are also asked how much more, in dollars, they would be willing to pay for the brand selected. For example, suppose a manufacturer of fruit juices wanted to scale preference for different types of containers (glass, plastic, can, or paper box). Table 10-4 presents the responses of one hypothetical person.

A preference scale can be created by summing the dollar (cents) amounts reported for the various comparisons. For each comparison when the alternative is preferred the additional amount willing to be paid carries a positive sign, whereas if it is not preferred the sign is negative. From the data presented in Table 10-4 we can compute the following preferences:

Glass:	$.07 +$	$.07 +$	$.02 =$	$.16$
Plastic:	$.06 +$	$(-.02) +$	$(-.05) =$	$-.01$
Can:	$-.07 +$	$.03 +$	$.05 =$	$.01$
Box:	$-.06 +$	$(-.07) +$	$(-.03) =$	$-.16$

Thus glass is most preferred, followed by can, plastic, and finally box.

Rank-Order Scales

Next to paired comparison scales, the most widely used comparative scaling technique is simple rank-order scaling. With a rank-order scale, respondents are presented with several objects simultaneously and requested to "order" or "rank" them. The following example illustrates how this scale type works.

E X A M P L E

To illustrate the use of simple rank order, consider that we have ten people ranking four brands with respect to preference. We show each subject a list of the four brands and ask them to place a 1 beside the brand they most prefer, a 2 beside their second choice, and so forth. Table 10-5 presents the ordering of the

T A B L E 10-5
Rank-Order Data

Person	A	B	C	D
1	2	1	3	4
2	1	2	4	3
3	2	1	3	4
4	4	2	1	3
5	3	1	2	4
6	2	1	3	4
7	1	3	2	4
8	4	2	1	3
9	2	1	4	3
10	3	1	4	2

T A B L E 10-6
Tabulated Rank-Ordered Data

Brand	Ranking			
	1st	2nd	3rd	4th
A	2	4	2	2
B	6	3	1	0
C	2	2	3	3
D	0	1	4	5

ten subjects; for example, the first subject ranks B first, A second, C third, and D fourth, while the second subject ranks A first, B second, D third, and C fourth, and so on. Notice that B was ranked first by 60 percent (6/10) of the subjects, whereas D was never ranked first. Table 10-6 tabulates the raw data presented in Table 10-5. Here the numbers in the table represent the number of times each brand was ranked either first, second, third, or fourth; for example, brand A was ranked first twice, while brand B was ranked first six times, and so forth.

One way to scale the brands with respect to preference is to multiply the frequency times the rank. The resulting scale values represent an ordinal scaling with low numbers representing higher preferences. If we want higher numbers representing increased preference, we can simply recode the rankings; that is let 1st = 4, 2nd = 3, 3rd = 2, and 4th = 1. The ordinal scale values for the four brands follow:

A $(2 \times 4) + (4 \times 3) + (2 \times 2) + (2 \times 1) = 26$
B $(6 \times 4) + (3 \times 3) + (1 \times 2) + (0 \times 1) = 35$
C $(2 \times 4) + (2 \times 3) + (3 \times 2) + (3 \times 1) = 23$
D $(0 \times 4) + (1 \times 3) + (4 \times 2) + (5 \times 1) = 16$

The ranking is therefore B > A > C > D where ">" indicates preference.

Constant Sum Scales

The **constant sum scale** is a popular technique that overcomes the problem of having respondents evaluate objects two at a time. Rather, respondents are instructed to allocate a number of points or chips—say, for example, 100—among alternatives according to some criterion (for example, preference or importance). Respondents are instructed to allocate the points or chips in such a way that if they like brand A twice as much as brand B, then they should assign it twice as many points or chips.

The use of the constant sum scale can differ depending on the type

Constant sum scale
Procedure where respondents are instructed to allocate a number of points or chips among alternatives according to some criterion—for example, preference, importance, and so on.

of interview. For example, with a mall-intercept or personal interview, we may actually give a respondent 100 *chips* and have them allocate the chips among a set of alternatives with respect to some criterion, (for example, importance). This method has the advantage of allowing visual inspection of the actual height or number of chips allocated, and the respondent is free to move the chips around to represent his or her feelings. In a mail interview we probably would ask the respondent to allocate 100 *points* among the alternatives. The respondent is still free to change his or her allocation; however, since chips are not actually being distributed, inspection is more difficult. Exhibit 10-1 contains a typical application of the constant sum method.

E X H I B I T 10-1

Constant Sum Scale

Below are five characteristics of an automobile. Please allocate 100 points among the characteristics such that the allocation represents the importance of each characteristic to you. The more points a characteristic receives, the more important the characteristic is. If the characteristic is not at all important, it is possible to assign zero points. If a characteristic is twice as important as some other characteristic it should receive twice as many points.

Characteristics	Number of Points
1. Styling	50
2. Ride	10
3. Gas mileage	35
4. Warranty	5
5. Closeness to dealer	0
	100

To scale the characteristics, we simply count the points assigned to each characteristic by each person. Note that the scale, using 100 points, ranges from 0 to $n \times 100$ for each object, where n equals the number of respondents (the sample size).

There are two primary problems with using a constant sum scale. First, the respondent may allocate more or less of the points or chips available. Thus, if the respondent is instructed to allocate 100 points but instead allocates 112 points, the researcher must adjust the data in some way or throw out this respondent. Second, if too few points or chips are used, then there are likely to be rounding errors. On the other hand, using a large number of points or chips will cause respondent fatigue, confusion, and possibly refusal problems.

Magnitude Estimation

The scaling device called **magnitude estimation** was developed in the area of psychophysics and adapted for use in product and attitude research.[4] Respondents assign numbers to objects, brands, attitude statements, and so on such that ratios between the assigned numbers reflect ratios among the objects on the criterion being scaled. In attitude research, respondents are simply asked to indicate agreement or disagreement with the attitude statement. Once the respondent has indicated the direction of feeling, he or she is then instructed to freely assign numbers that indicate the intensity of the feeling.

Exhibit 10-2 contains the typical instructions provided to respondents for magnitude estimation. Following the instructions is an example of a magnitude estimation scale used to measure opinions of a particular toothpaste.

Magnitude estimation
Scale in which respondents assign numbers to objects, brands, attitude statements, and the like so that ratios between the assigned numbers reflect ratios among the objects on the criterion being scaled.

E X H I B I T 10-2

Magnitude Estimation

HAVE RESPONDENT READ THE INSTRUCTIONS ALONG WITH YOU.

At the bottom of this page, there is a series of characteristics that may or may not describe the brand of toothpaste that you purchased last time.

Please indicate how much you agree or disagree that each characteristic printed below describes this brand. Enter an "X" in the appropriate box and a number to show how strongly you agree or disagree. If you neither agree nor disagree that the characteristic describes your brand, leave both boxes blank and enter a zero (0) on the line under the column labeled "HOW MUCH"

Large numbers mean that you *agree strongly* or *disagree strongly* that a particular characteristic describes this brand. For example:

	Agree	Disagree	How much
Is easy to store	X	___	(large number)
Is easy to store	___	X	(large number)

Small numbers mean that you *agree moderately* or *disagree moderately* that a particular characteristic describes this brand. For example:

	Agree	Disagree	How much
Is easy to store	X	___	(small number)
Is easy to store	___	X	(small number)

[4]See, for example, H. R. Moskowitz, B. Jacobs, and N. Firtle, "Discrimination Testing and Product Decisions, *"Journal of Marketing Research,"* February 1980, 84–90.

A *zero (0)* will mean that you *neither agree nor disagree* that the characteristic being considered describes this brand. For example:

	Agree	Disagree	How much
Is easy to store	____	____	0

PLEASE REMEMBER THAT THE SCALE YOU USE IS ENTIRELY YOUR OWN. THERE ARE NO LIMITS ON THE SIZE OF THE SCALE THAT YOU USE.

	Agree	Disagree	How much
( ) Cleans teeth	_____	_____	_____
( ) Leaves your mouth feeling fresh	_____	_____	_____
( ) Prevents cavities	_____	_____	_____
( ) Prevents bad breath	_____	_____	_____
( ) Whitens teeth	_____	_____	_____
( ) Prevents tooth decay	_____	_____	_____
( ) Has a good taste	_____	_____	_____
( ) Rinses easily	_____	_____	_____
( ) Protects teeth	_____	_____	_____
( ) Has an attractive color	_____	_____	_____
( ) Contains fluoride	_____	_____	_____
( ) Has a gel-like consistency	_____	_____	_____
( ) Is a good value for the money	_____	_____	_____
( ) Is approved by the dental association	_____	_____	_____
( ) Eliminates a bad taste in your mouth	_____	_____	_____

Q Sort Scales

Q-sort scales Rank-order procedure in which objects are sorted into piles based on similarity with respect to some criterion.

A **Q sort scale** uses a rank order procedure in which objects are sorted into piles based on similarity with respect to some criterion. Respondents are given a set of objects—for example, brands, concepts, words, or phrases—and are instructed to sort them into piles according to some criterion. For example, a respondent might be given a set of brands and asked to sort them according to which are most similar to that person's ideal brand. The following example illustrates how a Q sort scale works.

E X A M P L E

One of the major airlines was interested in determining the magazines that frequent flyers would most prefer to have available for reading while in flight. Management had a list of 75 magazines and wanted to scale the preferences of frequent flyers with respect to these.

To employ the Q sort method, each magazine cover was photographed and reduced to a "3 × 5" picture. A cluster sample, clustering on major airports, of 100 frequent flyers was used to scale preferences.

Exhibit 10-3 presents the instructions and rating form used to scale the preferences.

E X H I B I T   10-3

Q-Sort Procedure

The deck in front of you contains pictures of 75 magazines. Please choose the 9 magazines you most prefer of the 75. Once you have selected the 9 you most prefer, please list the magazine name on the form provided under the column "prefer most." Now we would like you to select the 9 magazines you *least* prefer from the remaining 6 magazines. Now please list these nine under the column "prefer least." Of the remaining 57 magazines, please select the 15 you most prefer and list these 15 under the column labelled "like." Of the remaining 42 magazines, please choose the 15 you like the least and place these names under the column "dislike." There should be 27 magazines remaining; please list the titles of these magazines under the column "neutral."

Tabulation Sheet

Prefer most	*Like*	*Neutral*	*Dislike*	*Prefer least*
(9)				(9)
	(15)		(15)	
		(27)		

The number of items included in a Q sort scale should not be less than 60 nor more than 140; 60 to 90 items appears to be a good range.[5] The instructions on how the items should be sorted determine the Q distribution, though in general Q distributions are an arbitrary matter. In the preceding example, respondents are specifically instructed to sort the magazines to produce a distribution that will probably be reasonably close to a normal distribution.

NONCOMPARATIVE SCALES

With noncomparative rating scales, the respondent is not instructed to compare the object being rated against either another object or some specified standard. Thus, in rating a specific brand, the respondent assigns the rating based upon whatever standard is appropriate for that individual; no comparison baseline such as "your ideal brand" is provided. Of course, in assigning the rating, each respondent must use some standard; however, the researcher has not provided it.

Continuous Rating Scales

Continuous rating scale
(graphic rating scale)
Procedure that instructs
the respondent to assign
a rating by placing a
marker at the appropriate
position on a line that
best describes the object
under study.

A **continuous rating scale,** is sometimes called a graphic rating scale, instructs the respondent to assign a rating by placing a mark at the appropriate position on a line, usually 5 inches long, that best describes the object under study. The following exhibit demonstrates two versions of a continuous rating scale.

E X H I B I T   10-4

Continuous Rating Scales

Type A

```
 _____
 0   10   20   30   40   50   60   70   80   90   100
Unfavorable              Neutral              Favorable
```

Type B

```
 _____
Unfavorable                                   Favorable
```

In one case (type A), the respondent is assisted in localizing the rating by the use of numbers and descriptions along the continuum. However,

[5]K. M. Kerlinger, *Foundations of Behavioral Research*, 3rd ed. (New York: Holt, Rinehart and Winston, 1973) 583–592.

in the other case (type B), the respondent is free to check anywhere on the line. After the respondent has assigned a rating with scale type B, a score is determined usually by dividing the line into as many categories as desired and assigning the respondent a score based on the category into which his or her mark falls, or by measuring the distance, in millimeters or inches, from the left- or right-hand end of the scale and coding the distance from 0 to 127 (millimeters) or 0 to 100 ($\frac{1}{20}$ inch). In either case, the resulting scores are typically analyzed as interval data.

Itemized Rating Scales

With an **itemized rating scale** the respondent is provided with a scale having numbers and/or brief descriptions associated with each category and asked to select one of the limited number of categories, ordered in terms of scale position, that best describes the object under study. Several different types of itemized rating scales are demonstrated in the following exhibit.

Itemized rating scale
The respondent is provided with a scale having numbers and/or brief descriptions associated with each category and asked to select one of the limited number of categories, ordered in terms of scale position, that best describes the object under study.

E X H I B I T   10-5

Itemized Rating Scale

Type A

Favorable   Unfavorable

_____ : _____ : _____ : _____ : _____ : _____ : _____

extremely   quite   slightly   neither   slightly   quite   extremely

Type B

Favorable   Unfavorable

_____ : _____ : _____ : _____ : _____ : _____ : _____

Type C

Favorable   Unfavorable

_____ : _____ : _____ : _____ : _____ : _____ : _____

    7   6   5   4   3   2   1

Type D

Favorable   Unfavorable

    7   6   5   4   3   2   1

As demonstrated in the exhibit above, itemized rating scales can take on many different formats depending upon the number of categories, the nature and degree of verbal description, the number of favorable and unfavorable categories, the presence of a neutral position, and the forced or nonforced nature of the scale.

Figure 10-1

Picture itemized rating scale.

1. *The number of categories.* Conceivably, any number of response categories can be created. The issue involved with selecting the number of categories concerns the respondent's ability to discriminate. To be more specific, researchers who favor using a large number of scale categories argue that respondents are capable of making fine discriminations, whereas those who favor using only a limited, and usually small, number of scale categories argue that respondents are not capable of making fine discriminations and to force them to do so would produce ambiguous data at best. Is there an optimal number of categories to employ in all situations? Probably not. In most marketing research applications rating scales typically have between five and nine response categories; however, as we indicated, little can be said about an optimal number of response categories that can be generalized to all circumstances.[6]

2. *Nature and degree of verbal description in itemized rating scale.* Various types of verbal descriptions and numeric formats can be used. Verbal category descriptors help to ensure that each respondent is operating from the same base; however, note that the presence and nature of verbal category descriptors will affect the responses.[7] In addition to verbal category descriptors, pictures have also been used, especially if the respondents are children. A picture itemized rating scale is shown in Figure 10-1.

3. *The number of favorable and unfavorable categories.* If an equal number of favorable and unfavorable scale categories are used, the scale is called **balanced;** otherwise, the scale is said to be **unbalanced.** An unbalanced itemized rating scale is shown below.

Balanced scale Scale using an equal number of favorable and unfavorable categories.

Unbalanced scale Scale using an unequal number of favorable and unfavorable scale categories.

[6]For additional evidence, see E. P. Cox II, "The Optimal Number of Response Alternatives for a Scale: A Review," *Journal of Marketing Research*, November 1980, 407–422; A. M. Givon and Z. Shapira, "Response to Rating Scales: A Theoretical Model and Its Application to the Number of Categories Problem," *Journal of Marketing Research*, November 1984, 410–419.

[7]A. R. Wildt and M. B. Mazis, "Determinations of Scale Response: Label Versus Position," *Journal of Marketing Research*, May 1978, 261–267; R. I. Haley and P. B. Case, "Testing Thirteen Attitude Scales for Agreement and Brand Discrimination," *Journal of Marketing*, Fall 1979, 31; and H. H. Friedman and J. R. Leefer, "Label Versus Position in Rating Scales," *Journal of the Academy of Marketing Science*, Spring 1981, 88–92.

E X H I B I T 10-6

Unbalanced Rating Scale

Excellent   _____
Very good   _____
Good   _____
Fair   _____
Poor   _____

When should unbalanced rating scales be used? It seems reasonable that when the distribution of responses is likely to be skewed, either positive or negative, an unbalanced scale with more categories in the direction of the skewness should be used. For example, unbalanced scales are frequently used when asking socially threatening questions (see Chapter 12).

4. *The presence of a neutral position.* If a balanced rating scale is used, the researcher must decide whether to employ an *even* or *odd* number of scale items. With an odd number of scale items, the middle scale position is generally designated as a neutral point. The argument against neutral positions is that respondents really are not neutral and should be forced to indicate their feelings. On the other hand, proponents of scales with neutral positions argue that it is possible for the respondent to be neutral. If respondents can indeed be neutral with regard to the object under study, then they should be able to express their neutrality. A balanced, odd-number itemized rating scale is presented below.

E X H I B I T 10-7

Balanced Rating Scale with an Odd Number of Items

Strongly agree	Agree	Neither agree nor disagree	Disagree	Strongly disagree
_____	_____	_____	_____	_____

5. *The forced or unforced nature of a scale.* In a **forced itemized rating scale** the respondent indicates a response, even though he or she may have "no opinion" or "no knowledge" about the question. In

Forced itemized rating scale Procedure in which a respondent indicates a response on a scale, even though he or she may have "no opinion" or "no knowledge" about the question.

such cases, the respondent may mark the midpoint of the scale; however, if enough respondents have no opinion or knowledge, marking the midpoint will distort measures of central tendency and variance. Thus, it is reasonable to suggest the use of a scale with a "no opinion" or "no knowledge" category.

Semantic Scales

Semantic scale
Procedure where respondents describe their feelings on a rating scale with end points or categories associated with labels having semantic meaning.

Semantic differential scale Semantic scales utilizing bi-polar adjectives as end points.

With a **semantic scale,** the category descriptors refer to semantic labels. Respondents describe their feelings on a rating scale with end points or categories associated with labels having semantic meaning. When bipolar adjectives are used as end points, the scale is called a **semantic differential scale.**[8] Depending on the specific type of semantic scale used, the resulting data have ordinal or interval properties. We will discuss the semantic differential scale in more detail in Chapter 11, which considers attitude measurement. The following exhibit demonstrates how a semantic scale works.

E X H I B I T 10-8

Instructions for a Semantic Scale

Instructions[9]

Many of the questions in the survey use rating scales with seven places. Make a check mark in the place that best describes your opinion. For example, if you were asked to rate the weather in Amherst on such a scale, the seven places should be interpreted as follows:

good _____ : _____ : _____ : _____ : _____ : _____ : _____ bad
    extremely quite slightly neither slightly quite extremely

If you think the weather in Amherst is *extremely good,* then you would place your mark as follows:

The weather in Amherst is:

good __X__ : _____ : _____ : _____ : _____ : _____ : _____ bad
    extremely quite slightly neither slightly quite extremely

If you think the weather in Amherst is *quite bad,* then you would place your mark as follows:

The weather in Amherst is:

good _____ : _____ : _____ : _____ : _____ : __X__ : _____ bad
    extremely quite slightly neither slightly quite extremely

---

[8]C. Osgood, G. Suci, and P. Tannebaum, *The Measurement of Meaning* (Urbana: University of Illinois Press, 1957).

[9]These instructions were adopted from I. Ajzen and M. Fishbein, *Understanding Attitudes and Predicting Social Behavior,* (New Jersey: Prentice Hall, 1980), Appendix B.

312

If you think the weather in Amherst is *slightly good,* then you would place the mark as follows:

The weather in Amherst is:

good _____ : _____ : __X__ : _____ : _____ : _____ : _____ bad
    extremely quite slightly neither slightly quite extremely

If you think the weather in Amherst is *neither good nor bad,* then you would place your mark as follows:

The weather in Amherst is:

good _____ : _____ : _____ : __X__ : _____ : _____ : _____ bad
    extremely quite slightly neither slightly quite extremely

In making your ratings, please remember the following points: (1) Place your mark in the middle of spaces, not on the boundaries:

good _____ : __X__ : _____ : _____ : _____ : _____ : _X___ bad
     (this)   (not this)

(2) Be sure to answer all items—please do not omit any.
(3) Never put more than one check mark on a single scale.

The following example presents a semantic differential scale used in a study on vacationing in Florida during Spring Break.

EXAMPLE

Semantic Differential Scale

Going to Florida on spring break is:

important ____ : ____ : ____ : ____ : ____ : ____ : ____ unimportant

worthless ____ : ____ : ____ : ____ : ____ : ____ : ____ valuable

good ____ : ____ : ____ : ____ : ____ : ____ : ____ bad

rewarding ____ : ____ : ____ : ____ : ____ : ____ : ____ punishing

useful ____ : ____ : ____ : ____ : ____ : ____ : ____ useless

pessimistic ____ : ____ : ____ : ____ : ____ : ____ : ____ optimistic

hard ____ : ____ : ____ : ____ : ____ : ____ : ____ soft

boring ____ : ____ : ____ : ____ : ____ : ____ : ____ interesting

active ____ : ____ : ____ : ____ : ____ : ____ : ____ passive

compulsory ____ : ____ : ____ : ____ : ____ : ____ : ____ voluntary

serious ____ : ____ : ____ : ____ : ____ : ____ : ____ humorous

pleasant ____ : ____ : ____ : ____ : ____ : ____ : ____ unpleasant

Stapel scale Procedure using a single criterion or key word and instructing the respondent to rate the object on a scale.

Stapel Scales

A modification of the semantic scale, the **stapel scale** uses a single criterion or key word and instructs the respondent to rate the object on a scale from—for example—"does not describe" to "describes completely." This type of scale may be useful in situations where the respondent can like the object, but dislike certain aspects of it. The following exhibit demonstrates how a stapel scale works.

E X H I B I T 10-9

Stapel Scale

Below are a list of words that may or may not describe your attitude toward compact cars. Please choose a number from the scale immediately preceding the adjectives that best describe your attitude toward compact cars and place the number on the space provided.

Perfectly   7   6   5   4   3   2   1   Not at all

Describes   Describes

safe	_____	boring	_____
pleasant	_____	status	_____
risky	_____	enjoyable	_____
necessary	_____	old	_____
useless	_____	valuable	_____
attractive	_____	cold	_____

Likert scale Procedure where series of terms are used and a summated score computed.

Likert Scales

A **Likert scale** is a summated instrument scale. The items making up a Likert scale are summed to produce a total score. In essence, a Likert scale is a composite of itemized rating items. Typically, each scale item will have five categories, with scale values ranging from −2 to +2 where 0 is a neutral response. Likert scales are *presumed* to have interval-scale measurement properties. The Likert scale is frequently used in attitude research, and we will discuss this scale in more detail in Chapter 11. The following exhibit demonstrates how a Likert scale works.

E X H I B I T 10-10

Likert Scale

The statements below describe different opinions of big business in the United States. Please indicate how strongly you agree or disagree with each of the statements by circling the category that best reflects your opinion.

	Strongly agree	Agree	Neither agree nor disagree	Disagree	Strongly disagree
If companies were left to themselves and not regulated the consumer would get a much poorer deal.	5	4	3	2	1
On the whole, government regulation has done more to help business than to help consumers.	5	4	3	2	1
On the whole, government regulation has done a good job of protecting the interests of consumers.	5	4	3	2	1
Most companies are so concerned about making a profit that they don't care about quality.	5	4	3	2	1
Most companies do a good job of providing reasonable products at a fair price.	5	4	3	2	1
Most companies don't really care about giving consumers a fair deal.	5	4	3	2	1

Purchase-intent scales Procedure attempting to measure a respondent's interest in a brand or product.

PURCHASE-INTENT SCALES

One of the most widely used scales in commercial marketing research studies is the **purchase-intent** scale. In the most general sense, purchase-intent scales attempt to measure a respondent's interest in a brand or product. More specifically, they provide information to get at the key issue: How likely is a respondent to purchase a given brand, product, or concept? Two popular types of purchase-intent scales are frequently used: a five-point itemized rating scale and an eleven-point purchase probability scale. The following exhibit presents each type of scale.

E X H I B I T 10-11

Purchase-Intent Scales

Five-Point Scale

—Definitely would buy (top box)
—Probably would buy
—Might or might not buy
—Probably would not buy
—Definitely would not buy

Eleven-Point Scale

10—Certain, (99 in 100) (top box)
9—Almost sure (9 in 10)
8—Very probably (8 in 10)
7—Probable (7 in 10)
6—Good possibility (6 in 10)
5—Fairly good possibility (5 in 10)
4—Fair possibility (4 in 10)
3—Some possibility (3 in 10)
2—Very slight possibility (2 in 10)
1—Almost no chance (1 in 10)
0—No chance (0 in 100)

The five-point itemized rating scale at the top is the more commonly used purchase-intent scale, at least in commercial marketing research. Typically, interest focuses on top-box purchase-intent scores. **Top box** indicates the percentage of respondents rating the brand, product, or concept in the most favorable category on the rating scale—or in other words, the number of respondents in the "definitely would buy" category on a five-point scale. Top-box percentages are routinely used as a criterion of performance in marketing research; that is, the brand, product, or concept achieving the highest top-box score is deemed the strongest or most acceptable.

Summary

In this chapter we have discussed and illustrated a variety of comparative and noncomparative scaling techniques and have attempted to show the advantages and disadvantages of the major types. Now we'll put what we've learned to use in the measurement of a particular construct, namely, *attitude*.

Key Concepts

Comparative scaling
  (nonmetric scaling)
Noncomparative scaling
  (monadic scaling)
Paired comparison
Dollar metric (graded
  paired comparison)
Rank-order scale
Constant sum scale
Magnitude estimation
Q-sort scales
Continuous rating scale
  (graphic rating scale)

Itemized rating scale
Balanced scale
Unbalanced scale
Forced itemized rating scale
Semantic scale
Semantic differential scale
Stapel scale
Likert scale
Purchase-intent scales
Top-box scores

Review Questions

1. Discuss the distinction between comparative and noncomparative rating scales.
2. Describe several of the more popular comparative scales.
3. Describe several of the more popular noncomparative scales.
4. Discuss the two primary purchase-intent scales.

CHAPTER

11

Attitude Scaling and Measurement Models

CHAPTER OBJECTIVES

- Explain what is meant by an attitude.
- Describe and illustrate various scaling techniques for measuring attitude.
- Introduce compositional and decompositional attitude measurement models.
- Clarify the differences between and the advantages and disadvantages of compositional and decompositional attitude measurement models.
- Describe and illustrate compositional attitude models.
- Describe and illustrate two decompositional attitude measurement models.

Introduction

In Chapters 9 and 10, we introduced basic measurement concepts and discussed and illustrated various measurement methods (scale types). Now we continue our treatment of measurement and scaling, with particular emphasis on issues and problems that surface in measuring directly unobservable constructs—specifically the concept called *attitude.* You may wonder: Why the concern with attitudes? To put it simply, attitudes are presumed to be a precursor of behavior; that is, attitudes are thought to reflect a person's beliefs and in some sense determine that person's ultimate behavior. Indeed, the vast majority of commercial marketing research studies contain questions to measure the respondent's attitude. The term *attitude* is, however, inexact and amorphous, meaning different things to different researchers.

Though our attention is primarily on the measurement and scaling of attitude, we must also understand what is meant by an attitude and its relationship to other constructs. Thus the first step in understanding how attitudes can be measured is to provide a brief description of (1) what we mean by an attitude, (2) its constituent components, and (3) the conceptual framework linking attitudes to behavior. We next discuss specific scale types that have been used to measure attitude components. These range from simple single-item scales to many-item composite scales, some already presented in Chapter 10. Then we turn to two types of popular attitude measurement models—*compositional* and *decompositional* models.

ATTITUDES

What is an **attitude?** Each of you probably has a different definition. However, it is reasonable to suspect that in describing an attitude such terms as *feelings, emotions,* and *likes/dislikes,* would be used. This is not too surprising, since attitudes represent a person's *evaluation* of an object, based upon the person's beliefs about that object; and, to some degree, attitudes determine how the person will *respond* to the object in the future.

Attitude A learned predisposition to respond in a consistently favorable or unfavorable manner with respect to a given object. The three components of attitude are cognition, affect, and conation.

Definition

Though there have been many definitions of attitudes, most researchers would probably agree with the following description:

Attitude is a learned predisposition to respond in a consistently favorable or unfavorable manner with respect to a given object.[1]

This description involves three fundamental characteristics: the notion that attitudes are learned, the notion that attitudes are a precursor to behavior, and the notion that behavior is consistently favorable or unfavorable toward the object.

Components of Attitudes

The concept of attitude is generally viewed as being structured into three interrelated components: *cognitions* (beliefs), *affect* (feelings), and *conation* (behavioral intentions).[2]

- **Cognitions** refer to a person's knowledge, opinions, beliefs, and thoughts about the object. Put simply, cognitions represent the information that a person has about an object.
- **Affect** refers to a person's feelings toward an object. Feelings denote the person's overall evaluation (that is, like/dislike, goodness/badness) of an object.
- **Behavioral intentions** refer to a person's intentions to perform a specific behavior with regard to an object.

Cognitions A person's knowledge, opinions, beliefs, and thoughts about the object.
Affect A person's feelings toward an object. Feelings denote the person's overall evaluation (like/dislike, goodness/badness) of an object.
Behavioral intentions A person's intentions to perform a specific behavior with regard to an object.

[1]M. Fishbein and I. Ajzen, *Belief, Attitude, Intention and Behavior* (Reading, Mass.: Addison-Wesley, 1975), 6.
[2]M. J. Rosenberg and C. I. Hovland, *Attitude Organization and Change* (New York: Yale University Press, 1960), 1–14.

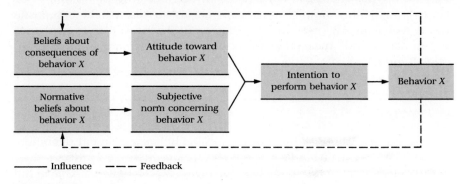

Figure 11-1

Conceptual framework relating beliefs, attitudes, intentions, and behaviors with respect to a given object. *Source:* M. Fishbein and I. Ajzen, *Belief, Attitude, Intention and Behavior* (Reading, Mass: Addison-Wesley, 1975), 6.

Conceptual Framework

To fully understand the concept of attitude we need to provide a conceptual framework that clearly delineates the relationships among cognitions, affect, behavioral intentions, and—finally—behavior. Figure 11-1 presents one well-accepted conceptual framework relating beliefs, attitudes, intentions, and behaviors with respect to a given object.[3]

As you can see from the figure, beliefs are the fundamental building blocks in this conceptual structure. Through a variety of information sources (such as direct observation and inferences), a person forms beliefs about an object by associating it with specific attributes or lack thereof. All one's beliefs taken together provide the base that determines what a person's attitudes, intentions, and behaviors are. Notice that this model does not distinguish between affect and attitudes; that is, it treats attitude as primarily affective or evaluative, representing a general predisposition. Thus, a person's attitude toward a particular brand is assumed to be based on his or her beliefs about that brand. If those beliefs about the brand involve mostly favorable attributes, the person's attitude will be positive. If, on the other hand, those beliefs about the brand involve mostly unfavorable attributes, the person's attitude will be negative. Thus, a person's attitude toward a brand is determined by the set of beliefs associated with the brand rather than by any single belief. Similarly, attitudes (that is, total affect), determine the person's intentions to behave with respect to the object, but again the relation is between attitudes and the set of intentions as a whole. Because attitude is viewed as a general predisposition, it is not necessarily related to any specific behavior. Each

[3]Fishbein and Ajzen, 15.

intention *is* related to a specific behavior. And given that behavior is volitional, a person should perform intended behaviors, barring any unexpected events.

ATTITUDE MEASUREMENT TECHNIQUES

Several types of scaling techniques have been employed to measure a person's overall evaluation of an object. We discuss and illustrate three popular scaling techniques: single-response formats, semantic differentials, and Likert scales. As we demonstrate, these standard methods are based on responses to statements of beliefs or intentions and yield a single score that represents the person's location on an evaluative scale.

Single-Response Formats

Single-response measures involve asking the respondent to make a judgment about the object in question. Typically, single-response measurement scales use a verbal, self-report, nonforced choice, monadic format, although formats do vary with respect to the labels used. Graphic scales (Chapter 10) are frequently employed. With such scales, the respondent places a check mark on the scale, which may be a continuous line or a line divided into categories.

Single-response formats Scaling technique that involves asking the respondent to make a judgment about the object in question.

EXAMPLE

Single-Response Format

My attitude toward the commercial just seen is

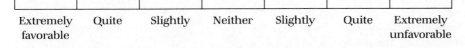

| Extremely favorable | Quite | Slightly | Neither | Slightly | Quite | Extremely unfavorable |

Likert Scales

We illustrated a **Likert-type scale** in Chapter 10. Assuming that a constitutive definition of attitude has been agreed upon, the measurement process continues by specifying a measurement definition; this involves generating a large number of items that are statements of beliefs or intentions. Each item is judged according to whether it reflects a favorable or unfavorable attitude toward the object in question. Ambiguous and neutral items are immediately eliminated. Respondents are then asked to rate the attitude object on each scale item in terms of a five-point labeled scale shown in the following example.

Likert scales Scaling technique where a large number of items that are statements of beliefs or intentions are generated. Each item is judged according to whether it reflects a favorable or unfavorable attitude toward the object in question. Respondents are then asked to rate the attitude object on each scale item in terms of a five-point category-labeled scale.

E X A M P L E

Likert Labeled Scale

5	4	3	2	1
Strongly agree	Agree	Neither agree nor disagree	Disagree	Strongly disagree

Exhibit 11-1 presents several examples of Likert scale items developed in an attitude-measurement study of a particular commercial.

E X H I B I T 11-1

Likert Scale Items

	Strongly agree	Agree	Neither agree nor disagree	Disagree	Strongly disagree
1. The commercial was soothing	5	4	3	2	1
2. The commercial was not entertaining	5	4	3	2	1
3. The commercial was insulting	5	4	3	2	1
4. The commercial was silly	5	4	3	2	1
5. The commercial was too "hard-sell"	5	4	3	2	1
6. The characters in the commercial were realistic	5	4	3	2	1
7. The commercial was not creative	5	4	3	2	1
8. The commercial clearly demonstrated the product's advantages	5	4	3	2	1
9. I will remember this commercial	5	4	3	2	1
10. The commercial had meaning to me personally	5	4	3	2	1

A person's attitude score is determined in several phases. In the preliminary phase, responses are scored from 1 to 5. To be more specific, strong agreement with favorable items is scored 5, whereas strong disagreement with favorable items is scored 1. The reverse is true for unfavorable items so that strong disagreement with an unfavorable item yields a high score. A preliminary attitude score for each person is obtained by summing across all of the item scales, with higher scores indicating more favorable attitudes. (If there are 25 items, for example, attitude scores could range from a low of 25 to a high of 125.)

The second phase involves an **item analysis.** In this specific context, items are checked to ensure that Likert's **criterion of internal consistency** is satisfied. According to the criterion of internal consistency, the relationship between attitude score and the probability of endorsing a given item should be linear. To be more specific, the more favorable a person's attitude, the more likely he or she should be to endorse favorable items and, conversely, the less likely he or she should be to endorse unfavorable items. From the assumed linear relationship between attitude score and probability of item endorsement, it follows that an individual item satisfies the criterion of internal consistency if the item score significantly correlates with the attitude score. Thus, in the second phase, the preliminary attitude score is correlated with each constituent item. We will discuss how to compute a correlation coefficient in Chapter 16. The fifteen or twenty items that correlate the highest with the attitude score constitute the final Likert scale.

Item analysis Procedure for checking scale items to ensure that Likert's criterion of internal consistency is satisfied.
Criterion of internal consistency An individual item satisfies the criterion of internal consistency if the item score significantly correlates with the attitude score.

EXAMPLE

Generally we start with a large set of items and choose the 15 or 20 items that correlate most with the overall score. Here we use a small-scale example. Assume we have ten individuals rate the ten Likert scales shown in Exhibit 11-1.

Table 11-1 presents the responses and the level of association between each

T A B L E   11-1
Responses to 10 Likert Items Shown in Exhibit 11-1 and Item-to-Total Correlations

Individual	1	2	3	4	5	6	7	8	9	10	Sum of ten items
1	5	5	1	3	1	2	5	2	5	2	31
2	3	4	2	2	2	1	5	3	4	3	29
3	4	2	4	2	5	4	2	4	5	5	37
4	1	4	2	3	2	1	4	1	4	3	25
5	3	1	5	3	4	4	2	4	5	5	36
6	3	5	2	4	2	2	5	1	4	3	31
7	4	3	3	3	2	3	3	3	4	4	32
8	3	4	2	3	1	1	4	2	4	3	27
9	4	2	5	3	5	5	2	4	5	5	40
10	3	5	1	3	1	2	5	2	4	2	28
Item-to-total correlations	.58	−.75	.84	−.14	.87	.96	−.77	.82	.79	.81	

item and the overall scale. On the basis of the magnitude of the individual item-to-total correlations, item 4, would be deleted because of its relatively low correlation with the overall scale. To calculate attitudes we would first reverse the scoring on the two items (2 and 7) having negative correlation and then sum the items.

Semantic Differential

Semantic differential
Scaling technique where a measure of the person's attitude is obtained by rating the object or behavior in question on a set of bipolar adjective scales.

We illustrated the **semantic differential** scale in Chapter 10. The semantic differential is used in attitude measurement because a person's attitude toward an object is defined in terms of evaluations (likes/dislikes), and so a person's attitude can be measured by rating an object or behavior on a set of bipolar adjective scales known to be associated with evaluation of the construct being measured. Exhibit 11-2 presents a set of bipolar adjectives that have been used in attitude studies.

E X H I B I T 11-2

Bipolar Adjective Scales That Have Been Shown to be Associated with an Evaluative Dimension

good-bad
likable-unlikable
kind-cruel
pleasant-unpleasant
grateful-ungrateful
harmonious-dissonant
beautiful-ugly
successful-unsuccessful
true-false
positive-negative
reputable-disreputable
wise-foolish

The semantic differential is one of the most frequently used procedures for measuring attitudes. The typical procedure involves identifying five to ten bipolar adjective scales that are associated with an evaluative dimension. Respondents are then asked to rate the attitude object on each scale. Responses to each evaluative bipolar adjective scale are scored from $+3$ to -3, with positive values reflecting favorable evaluations. The scores for a respondent are summed across all of the bipolar adjective scales and the resulting sum or average is taken as the index of attitude. Item analysis should be performed on individual bipolar adjective items; for example, a correlational analysis similar to that used with the Likert scale can be performed. Scales with high correlations are retained and this set constitutes the semantic differential scale for the measurement of attitude toward the object in question.

EXAMPLE

To measure reactions to a new type of shaving cream, management had men use the shaving cream in their home for one week. At the end of the week, the men were given a ten-item semantic differential scale and were asked to evaluate the "shaving experience" using the new type of shaving cream (referred to as code 4-11). Exhibit 11-3 contains the semantic differential scale used. Six of the scales were thought to reflect evaluative meaning: "likable-unlikable," "good-bad," "pleasant-unpleasant," "useful-useless," "beneficial-harmful," and "attractive-unattractive."

Table 11-2 presents the item-to-total correlations for the six scales thought to reflect qualities used in making an evaluation. These correlations are calculated as the product moment correlation between each item and the total score, that is, the sum of the remaining five items. Note again that we will discuss how to compute the product moment correlation in Chapter 16. For now, note that all the correlations are quite strong, the lowest being .77. Hence attitudes toward shaving with the new type of shaving cream would be calculated by summing individuals' responses to the six items shown in Table 11-2.

To summarize, the attitude scaling techniques we have discussed arrive at single attitude scores based upon responses to statements of beliefs or intentions. The attitude score represents where the person would stand on an imaginary scale, with favorable at one end, unfavorable at the other. This "scale" measures attitude toward a product, object, or behavior.

T A B L E 11-2
Item-to-Total Correlations

Item	Correlation With Total
Likable-unlikable	.88
Good-bad	.91
Pleasant-unpleasant	.82
Useful-useless	.77
Beneficial-harmful	.93
Attractive-unattractive	.78

EXHIBIT 11-3

Semantic Differential Scale

In my opinion, the shaving experience using shaving cream code 4-11 was

Likable	____ : ____ : ____ : ____ : ____ : ____ : ____	Unlikable
Good	____ : ____ : ____ : ____ : ____ : ____ : ____	Bad
Cold	____ : ____ : ____ : ____ : ____ : ____ : ____	Hot
Unpleasant	____ : ____ : ____ : ____ : ____ : ____ : ____	Pleasant
Sharp	____ : ____ : ____ : ____ : ____ : ____ : ____	Dull
Useful	____ : ____ : ____ : ____ : ____ : ____ : ____	Useless
Boring	____ : ____ : ____ : ____ : ____ : ____ : ____	Interesting
Beneficial	____ : ____ : ____ : ____ : ____ : ____ : ____	Harmful
Attractive	____ : ____ : ____ : ____ : ____ : ____ : ____	Unattractive
Active	____ : ____ : ____ : ____ : ____ : ____ : ____	Passive

ATTITUDE MEASUREMENT MODELS

Attitude measurement models provide a framework for understanding how consumers make decisions. By a *model* we mean a representation of the consumers' mental events and feelings—a representation that can be used to explain their ultimate behaviors.

We now discuss and illustrate three basic approaches to modeling consumer preferences. The first approach, *affect referral*, is the simplest and assumes that a person's overall impression—that is, likes and dislikes—drives the choice process. The second approach begins with a set of explicit perceptions or beliefs about brand characteristics or attributes and uses them as a basis for predicting brand evaluations. Such methods are commonly referred to as *compositional models.* The third approach begins with measures of overall evaluations of general attributes and uses them to infer the weights or values attached to individual, underlying characteristics. Such methods are commonly referred to as *decompositional models.*

Affect Referral

Under the simplest of all of the attitude measurement models, **affect referral,** consumers are thought to form wholistic images of the various alternatives and to choose the best alternative from the set of products/brands available. Thus, the consumer choice process is driven by an overall impression—that is, likes and dislikes—and little or no cognitive processing of attribute-based beliefs is required.

In what situations are a person's overall impressions likely to drive the choice process? In general, if no clear brand/product differences ex-

Affect referral Model based on consumers forming wholistic images of the various alternatives and the consumer chooses the best alternative from the set of products/brands available. The consumer choice is driven by one's overall impression and little or no cognitive processing of attribute-based beliefs is required.

ist, then it is unlikely that any information processing will occur, and consumers will rely on their overall likes and dislikes in decision making. Another situation is in mature markets where consumers have had extensive experience with the brands/products making up the market. If consumers have had extensive experience with a product category, it is likely that prior processing of attribute-based beliefs and other information has led to strong product/brand preferences. Therefore, when a particular need arises, no further cognitive processing of attribute information is needed, since the consumer will select that alternative already preferred.

The affect referral has limited marketing relevance since it provides no insights into the structure of attitude. The affect referral model can reveal which brands are liked or disliked, but it does not indicate the reasons for this evaluation. Given that the marketing manager can, to some extent, control the physical characteristics and associated images of brands, knowledge of the attribute-based beliefs that determine overall impression and evaluation are important in formulating effective marketing strategies. Because the affect referral model provides no such data, direct measures of affect (like/dislike) are complemented by measures that provide a diagnosis of brand strengths and weaknesses on relevant product attributes.

Compositional Models

Compositional models focus on the relationship between evaluative judgments and subjective attribute perceptions. Linear compensatory models exemplify this approach to attitude measurement.

Basic Compensatory Model. Compensatory strategies view a consumer as weighting—through either an adding or averaging rule—attribute-based information about alternative product/brands in such a way that the presence of one or more attributes can compensate for the absence of other attributes. The particular product/brand with the highest "score" derived from applying the relevant combinatorial rule is presumed to be the chosen alternative. In general terms, we can express the way in which consumers make judgments as

$$J(X) = \sum_{i=1}^{n} w_i X_i \qquad (11\text{-}1)$$

where

$J(X)$ represents the consumer's overall judgment of product/brand X;

X_i is the amount of attribute i possessed by product/brand X;

w_i is the weight associated with the ith attribute;

and

n is the number of attributes.

Compositional models
Models that focus on the relationship between evaluative judgments and subjective attribute perceptions.

Compensatory models
Models based on weighting, either through an adding or averaging combinatorial rule, attribute-based information concerning the alternative product/ brands under consideration such that the presence of one or more attributes can compensate for the absence of other attributes.

327

Marketing Adaptations. The usual form of the attitude measurement model as adapted to marketing research problems is

$$J(X) = \sum_{i=1}^{n} w_i b_i \qquad (11\text{-}2)$$

where

$J(X)$ is the consumer's overall judgment of product/brand X;

b_i is the extent to which a consumer believes the product/brand X possesses the ith attribute;

w_i is the importance weight attached to the ith attribute;

and

n is the number of attributes.

Models such as these are referred to as *multiattribute attitude models*.

E X A M P L E

Assume that a brand manager of a leading brand of toothpaste, say, Brand X, wanted to measure consumers' attitudes towards the brand. Furthermore, the brand manager is fairly certain that consumers consider only three salient attributes when choosing toothpaste: *decay prevention, whitening ability*, and *breath freshener*. Exhibit 11-4 contains the belief (b_i) and importance (w_i) scales. Note that the importance statements (w_i) refer to toothpaste in general, whereas the belief statements (b_i) refer specifically to the attitude object, in this case Brand X toothpaste. Note also that ratings are collected on the respondent's ideal brand.

Table 11-3 contains data on the responses to the belief and importance scales for two hypothetical persons. Notice that the 7-point scales have been scaled $+3$ to -3. Hence, a score of $+3$ for the importance scales means the person evaluates a particular attribute as extremely important, while a score of $+3$ for the belief statements indicates the person believes that it is extremely likely that he or she will receive the particular attribute if Brand X is used.

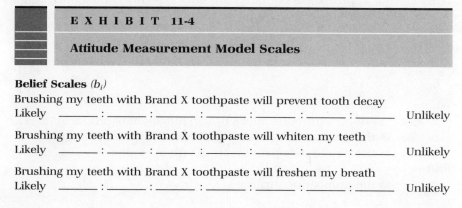

E X H I B I T 11-4

Attitude Measurement Model Scales

Belief Scales (b_i)

Brushing my teeth with Brand X toothpaste will prevent tooth decay

Likely _____ : _____ : _____ : _____ : _____ : _____ : _____ Unlikely

Brushing my teeth with Brand X toothpaste will whiten my teeth

Likely _____ : _____ : _____ : _____ : _____ : _____ : _____ Unlikely

Brushing my teeth with Brand X toothpaste will freshen my breath

Likely _____ : _____ : _____ : _____ : _____ : _____ : _____ Unlikely

Importance Scales (w_i)

When selecting a brand of toothpaste how important, to you, are the following characteristics of toothpaste:

	Important							Unimportant
Decay prevention	_____ : _____ : _____ : _____ : _____ : _____ : _____
Whitening ability	_____ : _____ : _____ : _____ : _____ : _____ : _____
Breath freshener	_____ : _____ : _____ : _____ : _____ : _____ : _____

Ideal Scale

For each of the following characteristics please indicate how much of each your ideal brand would have:

	A lot							A little
Decay prevention	_____ : _____ : _____ : _____ : _____ : _____ : _____
Whitening ability	_____ : _____ : _____ : _____ : _____ : _____ : _____
Breath freshener	_____ : _____ : _____ : _____ : _____ : _____ : _____

The compositional model described in the preceding example requires that the consumer give self-explicated belief and importance weights. In using compositional approaches, several issues should be considered. First, because of the compensatory nature of the model, two consumers can differ in the relative importance they attach to each salient attribute and can hold different beliefs about the attributes possessed by a brand and yet still have the same attitude score; in other

T A B L E   11-3
Attitude Measurement Model Data

	Person	
	1	2
Importance Scales		
1	+3	+3
2	+1	+3
3	+3	−2
Belief Scales		
1	+2	+1
2	+3	+2
3	+3	+3

Attitude toward Brand A

Person 1 $(3 \times 2) + (1 \times 3) + (3 \times 3) = 18$
Person 2 $(3 \times 1) + (3 \times 2) + (-2 \times 3) = 3$

words, the same "attitude" can be arrived at in many different ways. Thus, aggregating consumer responses may be difficult and even misleading. Second, an attribute rated as important may not be deterministic in the sense that it differentiates one brand or product from another. Consider, for example, the attribute of safety in automobiles. This attribute is likely to be rated as extremely important, but it probably does not sufficiently differentiate competing makes. Third, the tacit assumption in compositional models is that consumers know the reasons why one product or brand is preferred to another and can accurately verbalize these reasons. Finally, you should recognize that attributes may take on different meanings and importances depending on the stage in the purchase decision process and the purchase context.

Decompositional Models

Multiattribute compositional models for attitudes rest on three basic premises: (1) the researcher can identify the characteristics or attributes that consumers use in evaluating products or brands; (2) consumers know why they prefer one product or brand to another and can accurately express these reasons; and (3) the researcher can combine attribute rating assessments to accurately describe the consumer's overall judgment toward each product or brand. **Decompositional models** do not use consumers' ratings of product attributes but instead use overall evaluative judgments as the basic input. In other words, a respondent's overall evaluation of an object is "decomposed" into its components. We now discuss and illustrate two types of decompositional approaches that use overall judgments instead of set criteria to make inferences about product/brand attributes. Note that these very attributes were presumably used to form the initial evaluation and judgment.

Perceptual Mapping. Perceptual mapping attempts to uncover how consumers evaluate a set of competing products or brands by identifying the relevant dimensions along which the products or brands are being compared. A popular tool for constructing perceptual maps is **multidimensional scaling (MDS)**. MDS investigates consumers' evaluations of products or brands without the use of set criteria.[4]

MDS is a mathematical tool that enables us to represent the proximities between objects spatially as on a map. By **proximities** we mean any set of numbers that express the amount of similarity or difference between pairs of objects. In most of our applications, the objects will be products or brands. MDS procedures provide information on the perceived relationships among objects when the underlying dimensions of evaluation are not known. Thus, MDS attempts to map the objects in a space such that their relative positions in the space reflect the degree of perceived proximity (similarity) between them.

*Decompositional
models* Models that use
overall evaluative
judgments instead of set
criteria to make
inferences about product/
brand attributes that
presumably were
themselves used to form
the overall evaluative
judgments.

*Multidimensional scaling
(MDS)* Scaling technique
that attempts to uncover
how consumers perceive
the relationships among
products or brands by
identifying the relevant
dimensions along which
products or brands are
compared. MDS is a
mathematical tool that
enables us to represent
the proximities between
objects spatially as in a
map.

Proximities Any set of
numbers that express the
amount of similarity or
difference between pairs
of objects.

---

[4]Parts of the following discussion were adopted from W. R. Dillon and M. Goldstein, *Multivariate Analysis: Method and Application* (New York: John Wiley, 1984), Chapter 4.

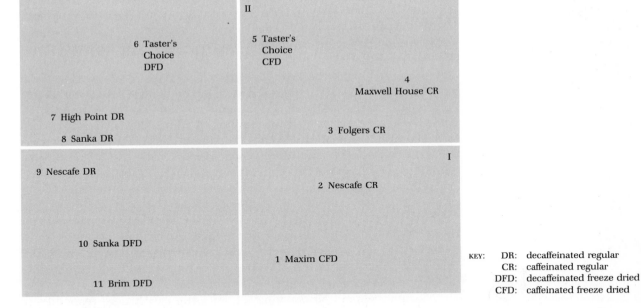

Figure 11-2

Two-dimensional map of eleven brands of coffee.

Perhaps the best way of understanding what MDS does is to consider the following problem. Suppose you are presented with a map of the United States and are asked to construct a table of intercity distances. Using a rule and the scale of the map, you find this to be a rather straightforward exercise. However, now reverse the problem: You are given a set of distances, such as those typically found in a table at the bottom of a map, and are asked to re-create the map itself. We all admit that this is a far more difficult exercise. MDS essentially is a method for solving this reverse problem.

In many marketing applications, the proximities represent consumers' perceptions of the similarity (dissimilarity) among a set of brands, and the resulting perceptual map graphically portrays the consumers' perceptions. For example, Figure 11-2 shows the two-dimensional map constructed from the similarity ratings for a set of eleven brands of coffee. This map presents the position of each brand in a reduced two-dimensional space. The two-dimensional configuration of coffee brands shown represents the terminal reduced space (final) solution. It was obtained after numerous trials. In other words, MDS procedures do not immediately achieve a terminal solution. Rather, a number of trials are initiated from a starting configuration; at each trial the configuration of objects in the (reduced) space is altered to improve the match between the points

331

in space and the original similarity values. The reduced spaced is evaluated on the basis of a measure of lack-of-fit, small values of which indicate little error between the fitted distances and the original proximity values from which the space was derived. The solution is called terminal when the improvement in fit after another trial does not exceed a predetermined value.

Interpretation of the space is fairly clear. The first dimension (axis) separates caffeinated from decaffeinated brands of coffee. Maxwell House, Folgers and Nescafe CR are on one end of dimension I, whereas High Point, Sanka, and Nescafe DR are on the other end. Dimension II appears to distinguish Taster's Choice caffeinated and decaffeinated freeze-dried coffee from the other brands of freeze-dried coffee. It is important to point out the interpretation of the dimensions is, in large part, very much an art, closely tied to the researcher's experience and knowledge of the properties of the products/brands being evaluated.

Researchers obtain the proximity values (similarity or dissimilarity values), which are the basic input for MDS analysis by asking respondents for (1) similarity judgments among all pairs of objects and/or (2) ratings of objects based on adjective descriptors. The first type of data produce *direct similarities*, the second, *derived similarities.*

Direct similarities The case where respondents are presented with object pairs and asked to judge their similarity.

The term **direct similarities** refers to the case where respondents are presented with object pairs and asked to judge their similarity. Use of direct-similarity judgments avoids the problems associated with adjective descriptors (such as attributes, features, and characteristics). Such descriptors are highly subjective and—since it is unlikely that all aspects of the differences in the objects can be described with them—often conceptually incomplete.

Similarity judgments can be recorded in several different ways, including:

Line marking Similarity judgments recorded by making a mark on a 5-inch line anchored by the phrases "Exact same" and "Completely different."

1. **Line Marking.** On a separate sheet of paper for each judgment, the respondent marks a 5-inch line anchored by the phrases "Exact same" and "Completely different":

Exact same _____ Completely different

The judgments as measured from the left-hand end of the scale indicate dissimilarity—the larger the number, the more dissimilar is the pair. Judgments can be coded from 0 to 127 (millimeters) or 0 to 100 (1/20 inch).

Sorting Procedure that involves presenting the respondent with the total stimulus set and asking him or her to sort the set into groups of like objects.

2. **Sorting.** The respondent sorts the total stimulus set (brands) into groups of like objects. The number of groups can be set by the researcher or can be determined by the sorter. After the respondent finishes the sort, the researcher records the allotment of the objects. A square (stimulus by stimulus) matrix is then constructed for each respondent, and entries are coded 0 if a stimulus pair is allocated to the same group and 1 if it is allocated to different groups. Summing the matrices across respondents yields the similarity judgments.

3. **Conditional Rank Orders.** The conditional rank-order method takes each object in turn as a standard for comparison. Each respondent is asked to rank the remaining objects in order of their similarity to this standard. The similarity-data matrix is constructed so that each row shows the similarity or dissimilarity with respect to the standard.

Conditional rank orders Procedure that takes each object in turn as a standard for comparison. Each respondent is asked to rank the remaining objects in order of their similarity to this standard.

Clearly the ease or difficulty of collecting direct similarity data is determined in large part by the number of objects. The more objects, the more comparisons. With $n = 7$ objects there are 21 pairs, with $n = 20$ objects there are 190 pairs. The number of pairs for a given number (n) of objects is $n(n - 1)/2$.

Incomplete data designs can overcome problems in comparing many objects. Here judgment pairs are randomly assigned to a respondent. For example, suppose we wish to compare 25 objects, requiring 300 similarity judgments. We can use three times as many respondents as intended and have each respondent make 100 judgments, where the judgment pairs have been randomly assigned.

The term **derived similarities** originates from the fact that the similarity data are constructed or *derived* from the respondent's ratings of each object. The respondent is presented with each object and asked to evaluate it based on adjective descriptors. Exhibit 11-5 shows a set of adjectives that could be used in evaluating cigarettes. Usually, the respondent is asked to indicate how well the adjective describes the object being evaluated—say, by assigning a number between 1 (describes the stimulus very well) and 100 (does not describe the stimulus at all).

Derived similarities Similarity data constructed or derived from the respondent's ratings of each stimulus on a set of verbal descriptors. The respondent is presented with each object and asked to evaluate it on a number of adjectives.

The use of adjective-rating data presumes that the selected set of adjectives provides a conceptually complete list of verbal descriptors to account for the major sources of between-object differences. A recommended practice is to run focus group interviews (Chapter 5) prior to the experiment to identify the salient dimensions of comparison.

E X H I B I T   11-5

Adjective Descriptors for Cigarettes

A cigarette made especially for women
For friendly sociable people
Has a satisfying taste
Has a smooth easy draw
For adventurous people
Low in tar and nicotine
Has a strong taste
Has a rich full-bodied tobacco flavor
Tastes good after a meal
Has a fresh cool taste
For stylish sophisticated people

Typically, each subject would be asked to indicate the extent to which each adjective describes the stimulus being evaluated—say, by assigning a number between 1 (describes the stimulus very well) and 100 (does not describe the stimulus at all).

Once the data have been collected, proximity values can be computed by using distance-type measures. A commonly used distance measure is the Euclidean distance, defined by

$$d_{ij} = \sqrt{\left\{ \sum_{k=1}^{p} (X_{ik} - X_{jk})^2 \right\}} \qquad (11\text{-}3)$$

where d_{ij} denotes the distance between objects i and j and X_{ik} and X_{jk} represent the response on the kth adjective descriptor, $k = 1, 2, \ldots, p$, for the ith and jth object, respectively.

One approach to interpreting the "map" derived from MDS is to examine the position of objects in the space. The first step is to look at the properties of objects occupying extreme positions in the derived space and attempt to identify an attribute or property that can explain their relative positions in the space. Next, look to see whether objects cluster together in the derived space and again attempt to identify an attribute or property that can explain the cluster.

E X A M P L E

Consider the reduced space shown in Figure 11-3. The derived cola drink space shown in the figure was based on respondents' ratings of ten cola drinks on the following thirteen adjective descriptors:

- Good—Bad
- Strong—Weak
- Sweet—Not sweet
- Bitter—Not bitter
- Sour—Not sour
- Fruity—Not fruity
- Spicy—Not spicy
- Coats mouth—Does not coat mouth
- Sharp—Not sharp
- Puckers mouth—Does not pucker mouth
- Fresh—Stale
- Chemical—Not chemical
- Complex—Simple

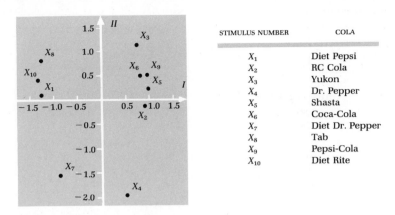

STIMULUS NUMBER	COLA
X_1	Diet Pepsi
X_2	RC Cola
X_3	Yukon
X_4	Dr. Pepper
X_5	Shasta
X_6	Coca-Cola
X_7	Diet Dr. Pepper
X_8	Tab
X_9	Pepsi-Cola
X_{10}	Diet Rite

Figure 11-3

Cola drink space.

Note that diet Pepsi, Tab, and Diet Rite are positioned on the (extreme) left side of dimension I, while the nondiet brands, RC Cola, Yukon, Dr. Pepper, Shasta, Coca-Cola, and Pepsi-Cola are positioned on the right side of the origin. Thus dimension I appears to be based on a diet/nondiet evaluation. Note that Dr. Pepper and Diet Dr. Pepper are located in the extreme lower half of dimension II. Thus, it appears to be reflecting a cherry-cola/regular cola evaluation.

Conjoint Analysis. In compositional models the respondent's self-explicated ratings are used to arrive at his or her overall judgment of a product or brand. In contrast, **conjoint analysis** is based upon a decompositional approach in which respondents react to various products, brands, concepts, and so forth in terms of overall preference. The objects being evaluated reflect a predetermined combination of attributes in a systematic way.[5] Conjoint analysis aims to find a set of weights for the individual attributes that, when combined, perhaps via an additive compositional rule, are most consistent with the respondents' overall evaluations (preferences). The term *decompositional* reflects the fact that respondents' overall evaluations are, in some sense, decomposed into their constituent parts. The term *conjoint* indicates that respondents rate the

Conjoint analysis
Decompositional approach in which respondents react to various products, brands, concepts, in terms of overall preference, where the various objects being evaluated reflect a predetermined combination of attributes in some systematic way.

[5]A pioneer in the development and use of conjoint analysis is Professor Paul Green at the Wharton School, University of Pennsylvania. For a more comprehensive introduction to conjoint analysis see P. E. Green and V. Rao, "Conjoint Measurement for Qualifying Judgmental Data," *Journal of Marketing Research*, 8 (1971), 355–363; P. E. Green and Y. Wind, *Multiattribute Decisions in Marketing: A Measurement Approach*, (Hinsdale, Ill.: Dryden Press, 1973), P. E. Green and Y. Wind, "New Way to Measure Consumer's Judgments," *Harvard Business Review*, 53(1975), 107–17.

TABLE 11-4

Packaged Soup Attributes

Attribute (factor)	Description (level)
Flavor	Onion
	Chicken noodle
	Country vegetable
Calories	80
	100
	140
Salt-freeness	Yes
	No
Price	1.19
	1.49

relative value of things taken jointly that might not be measurable taken one at a time.[6]

Suppose that a consumer package-goods company is concerned with consumer reactions to packaged soup mixes. Management interest centers on four attributes presumed to influence consumer preference:

1. Flavor
2. Calories (8 oz.)
3. Salt-freeness
4. Price

Under study are three alternative flavors, three alternative caloric levels, two alternatives involving salt-freeness, and two price alternatives. Table 11-4 describes the various alternatives. We will frequently refer to the attributes as *factors* and the specific values that they take on as *levels;* thus, we have two three-level factors and two two-level factors. These are in total $3 \times 3 \times 2 \times 2 = 36$ alternative product offerings. Table 11-5 describes each of the thirty-six product alternatives.

In conjoint analysis the respondent is asked to react to a product alternative in terms of an overall evaluation. The overall evaluation is generally a preference rating. For example, the respondent may be asked to rank the alternative products by overall preference; or the respondent may be asked to indicate his or her preference (from "least liked" to "most liked") for each alternative product on a 9-point scale. The last column in Table 11-5 shows one hypothetical respondent's actual rating of the thirty-six packaged soup alternatives, where the number 1 indicates "least liked" and the number 9 indicates "most liked." These data are used to compute the weight (that is, the *utility*) of each attribute, which indicates how influential each is in shaping the consumer's overall evaluations.

[6]R. M. Johnson, "Trade-Off Analysis of Consumer Values," *Journal of Marketing Research,* 11 (1974), 121–127.

TABLE 11-5
Packaged Soup Alternatives

Packaged soup alternative	Flavor	Calories	Salt-freeness	Price	Rating*
1	Onion	80	Yes	$1.19	9
2	Onion	80	Yes	1.49	8
3	Onion	80	No	1.19	6
4	Onion	80	No	1.49	6
5	Onion	100	Yes	1.19	7
6	Onion	100	Yes	1.49	6
7	Onion	100	No	1.19	5
8	Onion	100	No	1.49	5
9	Onion	140	Yes	1.19	7
10	Onion	140	Yes	1.49	6
11	Onion	140	No	1.19	5
12	Onion	140	No	1.49	5
13	Chicken noodle	80	Yes	1.19	7
14	Chicken noodle	80	Yes	1.49	6
15	Chicken noodle	80	No	1.19	2
16	Chicken noodle	80	No	1.49	2
17	Chicken noodle	100	Yes	1.19	3
18	Chicken noodle	100	Yes	1.49	3
19	Chicken noodle	100	No	1.19	2
20	Chicken noodle	100	No	1.49	1
21	Chicken noodle	140	Yes	1.19	2
22	Chicken noodle	140	Yes	1.49	2
23	Chicken noodle	140	No	1.19	2
24	Chicken noodle	140	No	1.49	1
25	Country vegetable	80	Yes	1.19	9
26	Country vegetable	80	Yes	1.49	8
27	Country vegetable	80	No	1.19	7
28	Country vegetable	80	No	1.49	6
29	Counury vegetable	100	Yes	1.19	8
30	Country vegetable	100	Yes	1.49	7
31	Country vegetable	100	No	1.19	6
32	Country vegetable	100	No	1.49	5
33	Country vegetable	140	Yes	1.19	6
34	Country vegetable	140	Yes	1.49	5
35	Country vegetable	140	No	1.19	5
36	Country vegetable	140	No	1.49	4

*1 = least liked; 9 = most liked.

Two basic data-collection procedures are used in conjoint analysis: the *tradeoff procedure* and the *full-profile approach*. In the **trade-off procedure,** also commonly referred to as the *two-factor-at-a-time procedure,* the respondent is asked to consider two attributes at a time.[7] The respondent's task is to rank the various combinations of each pair of attribute descriptors from most preferred to least preferred. Exhibit 11-6,

[7] Ibid.

Tradeoff procedure
Technique where the respondent is asked to consider two attributes at a time—to rank the various combinations of each pair of attribute descriptors from a most preferred to least preferred.

Part A, shows how this procedure is applied to consumer evaluations of packaged soup alternatives.

The trade-off procedure simplifies both implementation and information processing. Because attribute descriptors are paired and presented two at a time, this approach is simple to apply, lends itself to mail-questionnaire format, and reduces respondent information overload. However, the trade-off approach is not without limitations. First, rating descriptors two at a time can be confusing, for—if attributes tend to be correlated, which is a reasonable assumption in most cases—respondents may be unclear about what to assume about a particular descriptor not included in the pair being evaluated. For example, low-calorie packaged soup mixes may also apply to health/weight-conscious consumers by offering salt-freeness. Thus, in assigning a rank order to the pairing "80 calories and $1.19," the perceived relation between calories and salt-freeness could produce an evaluation that lacks clear meaning. Second, with this approach, the respondent must make a relatively large number of—albeit simpler—judgments. Even when procedures are used to reduce the number of two-way tables, the total number of judgements remains large. Third, respondents can easily adopt patterned responses, such as focusing on only one attribute before considering the others.[8] Fourth, this approach is particularly well-suited to products whose essence can be sufficiently captured by a verbal description. If an important attribute is color or size or shape, for example, then this approach may not be the best choice.

E X H I B I T   11-6

Two Alternative Data Collection Procedures

A. Two at a Time

What is more important to you: There are times when we have to give up one thing to get something else. We have a scale that will make it possible for you to tell us your preference in certain circumstances—for example, calories versus price. Please read the example below which explains how the scale works—and then tell us the order of your preference by writing in the numbers from 1 to 6 for each of the six questions that follow the example.

Example: Calories versus Price

Procedure:

Simply write the number 1 in the combination that represents your first choice. In one of the remaining blank squares, write the number 2 for your second choice. Then write the number 3 for your third choice, and so on from 1 to 6.

---

[8]R. M. Johnson, "Beyond Conjoint Measurement: A Method of Pairwise Tradeoff Analysis," in (ed.), *Advances in Consumer Research*, vol. III, ed. B. B. Anderson Proceedings of Association for Consumer Research, Sixth Annual Conference, 1976, 353–358.

Step 1

Price	Calories		
	80	100	140
$1.19	1		
$1.49			

Step 1 (Explanation)

You would rather pay the least ($1.19) and get the lowest caloric packaged soup alternative. Your first choice (1) is in the box as shown.

Step 2

Price	Calories		
	80	100	140
$1.19	1		
$1.49	2		

Step 2 (Explanation)

Your second choice is that you rather pay $1.49 and get the lowest caloric packaged soup alternative.

Step 3

Price	Calories		
	80	100	140
1.19	1	3	
1.49	2		

Step 3 (Explanation)

Your third choice is that you would rather pay $1.19 and get the next lowest caloric package soup alternative.

Final judgments

Price	Calories		
	80	100	140
$1.19	1	3	5
$1.49	2	4	6

This shows a sample order of preference for all possible combinations. Of course, your preferences could be different.

B. Full Profile (Stimulus Card)

Flavor
    Onion
Calories
    80
Salt-freeness
    Yes
Price
    $1.19
Overall Rating _____

Full profile procedure
Technique that simultaneously presents the respondent with a complete set of attribute descriptors. A stimulus card presents respondents with an attribute descriptor for each attribute included in the study; and respondents are asked for an evaluation of the product alternative defined by the selected attribute descriptors appearing on the card.

The alternative approach, the **full profile procedure,** simultaneously presents the respondent with a complete set of attribute descriptors. A sample "stimulus card" for a packaged soup alternative is shown in Exhibit 11-6, Part B. Notice that the stimulus card presents the respondent with a descriptor for each attribute included in the study. Respondents are asked for an evaluation of the product alternative defined by the selected descriptors on the card.

The principal advantage of the full-profile approach is its realism. Respondents are forced to consider attributes simultaneously, as opposed to two at a time. This feature is particularly important when attributes are correlated—by defining the levels of each attribute, potential correlations between actual products or brands are taken into account. It has the disadvantage of making the respondent's task difficult because several attributes must be considered at once. Note that while the two-at-a-time approach provides only a set of rank-orders, the full-profile procedure can employ either a rank-order or rating (that is, a nine-point equal-appearing scale ranging from "least liked" to "most-liked") format.

Several additional issues warrant discussion. First, note that the number of two-way tables, in the case of the trade-off procedure, and the number of stimulus cards, in the case of the full-profile approach, can be greatly reduced by applying procedures that require the respondent to rate (or rank) far fewer combinations.[9] For example, in a full-profile design with as many as 256 distinct combinations, a respondent may be required to rate (or rank) as few as eight stimulus cards. However, if attributes are correlated in actual products or brands, these types of procedures can produce profiles that may be unrealistic or even unbelievable. Second, the range of variation of attribute levels and interattribute correlation need to be seriously considered. Larger ranges for attribute levels will, all else the same, improve the accuracy in estimation of individual utilities, but large ranges in attributes may produce profiles that are not believable.

Utility scale values
Ratings that indicate how influential each attribute level is in the consumer's overall evaluations.

There are various approaches to computing the **utility scale value** of each attribute. These utilities indicate how influential each attribute level is in shaping the consumer's overall evaluation. Depending on the procedure chosen, either the rank-ordered preference data or the preference-rating data for each respondent constitutes the basic input. Individual utility scale values for each attribute level can be estimated at the individual or aggregate sample level; that is, for each respondent a set of attribute-level utilities is estimated, and/or at the aggregate level attribute level utilities are estimated for the entire (or some portion of the entire) sample of respondents. In either case, the utility scale values for each attribute level are chosen so that when they are combined (added together), the total utility of each combination will correspond as closely as possible to the original rank orders or preference ratings.

As we indicated above, techniques for estimating utility scale values

[9]P. E. Green, "On the Design of Choice Experiments Involving Multifactor Alternatives," *Journal of Consumer Research* 1 (1974), 61–68.

340

differ depending upon whether the input data are assumed to be ordinal (rank order only) or interval (ratings). Among the methods that treat the preference data as at most ordinal-scaled are MONANOVA,[10] PREFMAP,[11] Johnson's nonmetric trade-off procedure[12] and LINMAP.[13] The most popular method when the preference data are assumed to be interval-scaled is ordinary least squares (OLS) regression,[14] which we discuss in Chapter 16. The general consensus appears to be that these methods vary little in terms of their predictive validities.[15]

EXAMPLE

To derive utilities for the attributes requires that some sort of coding scheme, quantifies the profiles that are evaluated. One relatively easy way to do this is to use what are called *dummy variables*. Dummy variables indicate the presence or absence of a particular attribute. More specifically, consider the following coding scheme: Let

$$D_1 = \begin{cases} 1, \text{ if the packaged soup alternative under evaluation is onion} \\ 0, \text{ if otherwise} \end{cases}$$

$$D_2 = \begin{cases} 1, \text{ if the packaged soup alternative under evaluation is chicken} \\ \text{noodle} \\ 0, \text{ if otherwise} \end{cases}$$

$$D_3 = \begin{cases} 1, \text{ if the packaged soup alternative under evaluation is 80 calories} \\ 0, \text{ if otherwise} \end{cases}$$

$$D_4 = \begin{cases} 1, \text{ if the packaged soup alternative under evaluation is 100 calories} \\ 0, \text{ if otherwise} \end{cases}$$

$$D_5 = \begin{cases} 1, \text{ if the packaged soup alternative under evaluation is salt-free} \\ 0, \text{ if otherwise} \end{cases}$$

$$D_6 = \begin{cases} 1, \text{ if the packaged soup alternative under evaluation is priced at \$1.19} \\ 0, \text{ if otherwise} \end{cases}$$

[10] J. B. Kruskal, "Analysis of Factorial Experiments by Estimating Monotone Transformations of the Data," *Journal of the Royal Statistical Society*, Series B, 27 (1965), 251–263.

[11] J. D. Carroll, "Individual Differences in Multidimensional Scaling," in R. N. Shepard *Multidimensional Scaling: Theory and Applications in Behavioral Sciences*, vol. I, ed. R. N. Shepard et al. (New York: Seminar Press, 1972), 105–155.

[12] R. J. Johnson, "Varieties of Conjoint Measurement," Working Paper, Market Facts, Inc., Chicago (1973).

[13] See V. Srinivasau and A. D. Shocker, "Linear Programming Techniques for Multidimensional Analysis of Preferences," Psychometrika, 38 (1973), 337–369; V. Srinivasau and A. D. Shocker, "LINMAP Version IV—User's Manual." (Nashville, TN: Vanderbilt University, 1981).

[14] J. Johnston. *Econometric Methods*, 2nd ed. (New York: McGraw-Hill, 1972).

[15] See, for example, P. Cattin and D. R. Wittink, "A Monte-Carlo Study of Metric and Nonmetric Estimation Methods for Multiattribute Models," Research Paper No. 341, Graduate School of Business, Stanford University, 1976; F. J. Carmone, P. E. Green and A. K. Jain, "The Robustness of Conjoint Analysis: Some Monte Carlo Results," *Journal of Marketing Research*, 15 (1978), 300–303.

For example, in the case of the first packaged soup alternative described in Table 11-5 we have

T A B L E   11-6

Utility Coefficients

Attribute	Utility Coefficient
Flavor	
Onion	3.50
Chicken noodle	0
Country vegetable	3.66
Calories	
80	2.03
100	.46
140	0
Salt-freeness	
Yes	1.84
No	0
Price	
$1.19	.67
$1.49	0

Packaged soup alternative 1:

- Onion
- 80 calories
- Salt-free
- $1.19

so that

$$D_1 = 1 \qquad D_4 = 0$$

$$D_2 = 0 \qquad D_5 = 1$$

$$D_3 = 1 \qquad D_6 = 1$$

In other words, this particular packaged soup alternative can be described by the string (1,0,1,0,1,1). You have probably noted that we did not create a dummy variable for each level of an attribute. To avoid computational redundancies, we need only create $k - 1$ dummy variables for a variable having k levels.[16] Thus, we have defined two dummy variables for flavor (D_1 and D_2), two dummy variables for calories (D_3 and D_4), one dummy variable for salt-freeness (D_5), and one dummy variable for price (D_6).

Note also that the string (0,0,0,0,0,0) corresponds to the packaged soup alternative:

[16]To see why we need create only $k - 1$ dummy variables for an attribute having k levels, consider the following: The flavor attribute has three levels—onion, chicken noodle, and country vegetable. Let us specify one dummy variable for each level. Let the dummy variables be denoted by D_1, D_2, and D_3, where

$D_1 = 1$ if onion $D_2 = 1$ if chicken noodle $D_3 = 1$ if country vegetable
     0 if otherwise   0 if otherwise   0 if otherwise

Consider now each flavor alternative and its corresponding dummy variable codes:

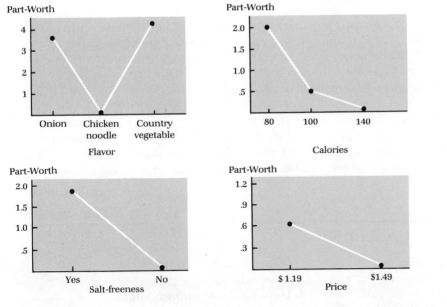

Figure 11-4

Graphical representation of utility coefficients.

- Country Vegetable
- 140 calories
- Salt
- $1.49

The level of the attribute assigned to the value zero is called the *base category* and is completely arbitrary; in other words, results are not affected by which attribute level is assigned the zero value.

An estimated utility coefficient could be derived for each attribute level based upon the preference ratings and the dummy variables. Hypothetical utilities for the four packaged soup attributes are given in Table 11-6. According to these utilities, the least preferred packaged soup alternative would be

- Chicken noodle
- 140 calories
- Salt
- $1.49

Figure 11-4 shows a graphical representation.

	D_1	D_2	D_3
Onion	1	0	0
Chicken noodle	0	1	0
Country vegetable	0	0	1

The reason why the third dummy variable (D_3) is not needed is because once we observe that $D_1 = 0$ and $D_2 = 0$, it must be that the packaged soup alternative is country vegetable (that is, D_3 must equal 1).

Summary

In this chapter we have considered the measurement and scaling of attitude. Though amorphous, attitudes play a central role in our understanding and anticipation of consumer behavior and, thus, are important to many marketing research investigations. Our emphasis has been on issues and problems that surface when measuring attitude and its constituent components. Among other things, we described how attitude is linked to behavior, discussed and illustrated the major scaling techniques used to measure attitude, and introduced two popular attitude-measurement models. The techniques we have described allow us to act as if attitude is truly measurable—they make marketing research possible.

Key Concepts

Attitude

Cognitions

Affect

Behavioral intentions

Affect referral

Likert scales

Semantic differential

Compositional models

Compensatory models

Multi-attribute attitude models

Decompositional models

Multidimensional scaling (MDS)

Conjoint analysis

Review Questions

1. Explain the concept of an attitude.
2. Describe the major types of scaling techniques that have been employed to measure a person's overall evaluation of an object.
3. Discuss the distinction between compositional and decompositional attitude measurement models.
4. Describe the primary compositional attitude measurement models.
5. Describe the primary decompositional attitude measurement models.

Questionnaire Design and Field Execution

- Explain the importance of questionnaire design and field execution.
- Discuss the four basic activities involved in question design: preliminary considerations, asking questions, constructing the questionnaire, and pretesting the questionnaire.
- Describe who conducts the fieldwork.
- Describe the activities and elements in fielding the study.
- Briefly discuss design and field considerations when conducting international marketing research.

Introduction

Two critical elements in a survey research study are questionnaire construction and field execution. A questionnaire is simply a data-collection instrument that sets out in a formal way the questions designed to elicit the desired information. The questionnaire continues the research process that began with identification of the management problem, specification of the information needed to solve this problem, selection of an appropriate method for collecting the necessary data, and identification of the target population of individuals who can provide the needed information. As we discussed in Chapter 5, a questionnaire can be administered with the aid of a computer, by means of the telephone, by a personal interviewer, or by mail; and although we associated questionnaires with survey research projects, they can be used in experimental designs as well (Chapter 6). Questionnaires can be used to collect information on a diverse set of topics. In Chapters 10 and 11 we introduced measurement scales capable of collecting information on product ratings, attitudes and opinions, purchase intentions, and behaviors. In this chapter we focus first on design issues—how scales should be worded in light of the specific objectives of the study and the target group of respondents who will be questioned. Then we focus on the field-execution phase. While the marketing problem may appear well-defined in terms of hypotheses, information needs, and the appropriate target population, effective operationalization of these components in the data-collection phase is needed to achieve valid and reliable results.

QUESTIONNAIRE DESIGN

It is an understatement to say that proper questionnaire design is of critical importance. Faulty questionnaire design is a major contributor to *nonsampling errors* and specifically to *response errors* (Chapter 7). Response errors occur because respondents do not give accurate answers to questions that have been asked, and many of the factors that lead a respondent to give inaccurate responses are traced directly to improper questionnaire design and construction. For example, the format of the question, the content of a question, or the organization of the questions can all induce a respondent to give an inaccurate response. As we indicated, response errors are particularly important since evidence indicates that nonsampling errors are a much larger part of the total survey error than are sampling errors.

By the time the researcher arrives at the questionnaire design stage of a given study, the marketing problem should already have been translated into a set of appropriate research questions. Next, these questions must be translated into the language of the respondent and then arranged in a questionnaire in a valid, logical fashion that will produce meaningful results.[1] Hence, we can view questionnaire design in terms of four interrelated activities:

1. Preliminary considerations
2. Asking questions
3. Constructing the questionnaire
4. Pretesting the questionnaire

PRELIMINARY CONSIDERATIONS

Before you can even start to consider how questions should be asked, you must translate the marketing problem into a set of research questions that identify (1) exactly what information is required, (2) exactly who are the appropriate target respondents, and (3) what data-collection method will be used to survey these respondents. The importance of these preliminary considerations cannot be overstated and we have devoted Chapters 2, 5, and 7 specifically to them.

---

[1] An excellent source for a detailed treatment of questionnaire design and construction issues is D. A. Dillman, *Mail and Telephone Surveys* (New York: John Wiley & Sons, 1978).

ASKING QUESTIONS

To the naive researcher, building good questions seems like a simple task: After all, each of us is always asking questions. However, the responses we get are often based on how the questions are constructed. Seemingly small changes in wording can cause large differences in responses. Unfortunately, the formulation of the questionnaire is all too often thought to be the easiest part of designing a survey. Question wording is a crucial element in maximizing the validity of survey data. The importance of the precise wording of questions is exemplified by the following well-known example:[2] Two priests, a Dominican and a Jesuit, are discussing whether it is a sin to smoke and pray at the same time. After failing to reach a conclusion, each goes off to consult his respective superior. The next week they meet again. The Dominican says, "Well, what did your superior say?" The Jesuit responds, "He said it was all right." "That's funny," the Dominican replies, "my superior said it was a sin." Jesuit: "What did you ask him?" Reply: "I asked him if it was all right to smoke while praying." "Oh," says the Jesuit, "I asked my superior if it was all right to pray while smoking."

General Guidelines

When you construct a questionnaire a general rule is to always ask yourself, "Why am I asking this question?" You must be able to explain how each survey question is closely related to the research question that underlies management's problem.

Three general guidelines help in devising a good questionnaire.

1. Write specific questions only after you have thoroughly thought through your research questions. Write the research questions down.
2. When you are working on the questionnaire, constantly refer to your research questions.
3. For each question you write, explain how the information obtained from responses will help in answering your research questions.

Satisfactory questions may already exist. Before you attempt to create new questions, search for questions on the same topic that may have been asked by other researchers in other studies. Most questionnaires contain some questions that have been used before; in fact, even some new questions probably have been adapted from questions used in the past. The point is that the repetition of questions is not only permitted

---

[2]Adapted from Seymour Sudman and Norman M. Bradburn, *Asking Questions* (San Francisco: Jossey-Bass Publishers, 1983).

but also encouraged in survey research and in social science in general.[3] Repeating questions that have demonstrated acceptable levels of reliability and validity can allow you to (1) reduce the time needed for testing, (2) compare results across a number of studies, and (3) establish response reliabilities for the study at hand.

Basic Principles

A number of specific considerations should be kept in mind when asking questions; the following basic principles form what could be called the "art" of asking questions.

Principle 1: Be Clear and Precise. The question should be understandable to both researcher and respondent, and should allow responses consistent with the desired level of measurement and response options that will afford actionable results. For example, consider the following two questions intended to identify volume of coffee consumption:

(A) How many cups of coffee do you drink in a typical work day?

———————
(WRITE IN NUMBER)

(B) How frequently do you drink coffee? *(Record choice below.)*

Extremely often	1
Very often	2
Not too often	3
Never	4

Note that question B is not very precise. It neither specifies the consumption period—that is, daily, weekly or monthly consumption, nor does it result in a precise measure of coffee consumption. Question B yields responses that have at best ordinal properties; in fact, one could argue that such a question would yield nominal data since it may not be possible to legitimately make comparisons across respondents—each response category may imply very different consumption frequencies to each respondent. In contrast, question A yields responses representing consumption rate, in terms of cups of coffee consumed, having ratio-scaled properties.

Principle 2: Response Choices Should Not Overlap. Along with the tenets of clarity and precision goes the idea of **mutual exclusivity.** What this means is that the response choices to a question should not overlap with one another. Consider the following question:

Mutual exclusivity
Condition where the response choices to a question do not overlap with one another.

———————
[3]Normally no permission from the originator of the question is required or expected, although you may want to communicate with the originator to find out whether there were difficulties with the question not reported in the publisher's source. For questionnaires that have been copyrighted, permission from the publisher is required.

Which of the following categories best describes your total household income before taxes in 1986? *(Circle one answer only.)*

Less than $10,000	1
$10,000–$15,000	2
$15,000–$25,000	3
$25,000 or higher	4

As you may have noticed, it is possible for individuals who live in households with incomes of exactly $15,000 or $25,000 to choose two response categories. Choices 2 and 3 should have been written as $10,000–$14,999 and $15,000–$24,999. Without this mutual exclusivity, it is difficult to say where the "true" response lies.

Principle 3: Use Natural and Familiar Language. Consider who makes up your sample when constructing your questions. Phrase questions in the colloquial language of your respondent group. Not only do different ethnic and social groups express their thoughts differently, but so do people living in different regions within the same country. Think about a sandwich prepared on a large loaf of bread: This is variously referred to as a "grinder," "hoagie," "hero," and "submarine" in different parts of the country. We don't mean to imply that the intent is to be chatty. Your language should always mean what you intend and should convey the intended meaning to the respondents in a clear and precise fashion.

The familiarity of language has also been shown to influence respondents' willingness to give accurate responses to threatening questions.[4] Threatening questions ask respondents to report on illegal or contrary-to-norm behaviors or conditions not generally discussed in public without tension. Response effects to such questions can be quite severe and can result in (1) the overstatement of desirable behavior (for example, voting) and (2) the understatement of behaviors perceived as being socially unacceptable (for example, alcohol or drug abuse). One study showed that response effects due to threatening questions can be decreased by allowing the respondents to select their own words for describing the threatening behavior under study.[5] One of the threatening behaviors investigated was intoxication.

E X A M P L E

The standard question for intoxication read:

In the past year, how often did you become intoxicated while drinking any kind of alcoholic beverage?

[4] Ed Blair, Seymour Sudman, Norman M. Bradburn, and Carol Stocking, "How to Ask Questions About Drinking and Sex: Response Effects in Measuring Consumer Behavior," *Journal of Marketing Research*, August 1977, 316–21.
[5] *Ibid.*, 318.

Respondents were handed a card containing the following response categories:

- Never
- Once a year or less
- Every few months
- Once a month
- Every few weeks
- Once a week
- Several times a week
- Daily

The alternative procedure allowed respondents to first provide their own word for intoxication through the following question:

> Sometimes people drink a little too much beer, wine, or whiskey so that they act different from usual. What word do you think we should use to describe people when they get that way, so that you will know what we mean and feel comfortable talking about it?

The intoxication question then read:

> Occasionally, people drink on an empty stomach or drink a little too much and become (respondent's word). In the past year, how often did you become (respondent's word) while drinking any kind of alcoholic beverage?

No response categories were offered for either item.

Other techniques have been used to improve response accuracy for threatening questions. For example, as we indicated in Chapter 10, *unbalanced scales* that include additional categories on the heavy end have been used in collecting data on alcohol consumption.

Principle 4: Do Not Use Words or Phrases That Show Bias. Biased or leading words or phrases are emotionally charged and suggest an automatic sentiment of approval or disapproval. **Loaded questions,** as they are called, suggest what the answer should be or indicate the researcher's position on the issue under study. In both instances, the respondent is not given a fair chance to express his or her own opinion and a consistent measurement error is introduced that would not exist if neutral phrasing were used.

Loaded questions
Questions that suggest
what the answer should
be or indicate the
researcher's position on
the issue under study.

E X A M P L E

Leading questions can take a variety of forms. Consider the question:

What did you dislike about the product you just tried?

The respondent is not given a "way out" if he or she found nothing to dislike. A more suitable way to ask this question would be to first ask:

Did you dislike any aspects of the product you just tried?

_____ Yes   _____ No

Certain words and phrases can also induce bias. For example:

Do you think Johnson and Johnson did everything possible in its handling of the Tylenol poisoning situation?

This is a leading question since the use of the phrase *everything possible* can produce biased responses. The issue is whether Johnson and Johnson acted *reasonably* in its handling of the Tylenol poisoning situation.

Another type of bias can occur when a respondent is required to rate a series of objects (such as brands of toothpaste) on the same set of characteristics. **Order bias** can be particularly troublesome in concept and product testing. Research has shown that the rating of objects may be related to the order in which they were presented for evaluation; in other words, brands receive different ratings depending on whether they were shown first, second, third, and so on.

Order bias Condition where brands receive different ratings depending on whether they were shown first, second, third, etc.

E X A M P L E

Shown below are the relative overall brand ratings of 60 respondents who evaluated three brands of analgesics (Bufferin, Excedrin and Tylenol) where the order of rating was varied. For each of the six possible pairings each brand was evaluated monadically. Scores were normed to sum to 100 for interpretation purposes.

Tylenol	10	Tylenol	15	Bufferin	30
Bufferin	60	Bufferin	55	Tylenol	10
Excedrin	30	Excedrin	30	Excedrin	60
Bufferin	35	Excedrin	25	Excedrin	35
Excedrin	30	Tylenol	5	Bufferin	35
Tylenol	35	Bufferin	70	Tylenol	30

It is clear from the preference ratings that the brand rated immediately following Tylenol received relatively higher scores. Thus the order in which the brands of analgesics were presented to the respondent may have affected the ratings given.

In order to control for this kind of order bias, both the order of object presentation and attribute presentation should be varied ("rotated") across respondents. Rotating objects and/or attributes across respondents minimizes the chance that systematic order effects will be misinterpreted because any biases are now randomly (uniformly) distributed.

**Double-barreled
questions** Questions in
which two opinions are
joined together.

Principle 5: Avoid Double-Barreled Questions. Questions in which two opinions are joined together are called double-barreled. With these questions, the respondent must answer two questions at once even though his or her opinions about the two may diverge. Consider, for example, the following question:

> Do you believe that McDonalds has fast and courteous service?

Here conjoined are questions about two different attitude objects, speed and courteous service.

Principle 6: State Explicit Alternatives. The presence or absence of an explicitly stated alternative can have dramatic effects on responses. Consider for example, the following two forms of a question asked in a "Pasta-in-a-Jar" concept test:

> Version A: Would you buy pasta-in-a-jar if available in a store where you normally shop?

> Version B: If pasta-in-a-jar and the canned pasta product that you are currently using were both available in the store where you normally shop, would you
>
> > (a) buy only the canned pasta product?
> > (b) buy only the pasta-in-a-jar product?
> > (c) buy both products?

The stated alternatives provide a context for interpreting the reaction to this new concept for Version B. In Version A, 42 percent of the respondents indicated that they would buy the new pasta-in-a-jar product. When specific alternatives were added (Version B) the number of respondents indicating that they would buy only the new pasta-in-a-jar product dropped to 24 percent. *You get a much too high reading off question A*

Principle 7: Questions Should Meet Criteria of Validity and Reliability. The issues of whether or not we are truly measuring what we are attempting to measure and whether or not we can replicate these responses at a later point in time should certainly be considered in question building (see Chapter 9). You should not assume that the same questioning approach will work similarly well for all product/service categories and all interviewing methods.

The validity and reliability of data can be severely compromised if respondents cannot accurately answer the questions asked. Two aspects of questions might make it impossible for a respondent to answer:

1. *Relevance.* It is possible to ask respondents questions on topics about which they are uninformed; in other words, the question is not relevant because the respondent has never been exposed to the answer—that is, the respondent lacks experience. An all-too-common example is to ask a respondent's opinion, in general or on spe-

cific performance characteristics, about a product, brand, store, or service that he or she has never heard of or has never consumed. Furthermore, respondents typically do not indicate their lack of knowledge—thereby compromising validity. The problem of relevance can be minimized by (1) selecting the proper target populations and (2) allowing the respondent to indicate his or her lack of knowledge by direct questioning or by including a "don't know" category on the scaling instrument.

2. *Memory.* In many instances a respondent is asked a question about something that has occurred in the past and may have forgotten the answer. Forgetting can cause three types of response effects: omission, telescoping, and creation.[6] **Omission** occurs when a respondent cannot recall that an event has occurred; **telescoping** occurs when a respondent compresses time or remembers an event as occurring more recently than it actually occurred (for example, in the case of a respondent indicating visits to a particular store twice in the last week although one of the visits occurred ten days ago); **creation** occurs when a respondent recalls an event that did not actually occur. It is reasonable to expect that **unaided questions,** ones that do not provide any clues to the answer, can result in an understatement of specific events. On the other hand, **aided questions,** ones that provide clues that potentially help the respondent recall more accurately, can increase telescoping and creation. Response effects due to memory factors can be diminished by (1) asking respondents questions only about *important* events that occurred within the last few days[7] and (2) informing respondents that the aided-recall questions to be asked contain some bogus items.[8]

Omission Interviewing condition that occurs when a respondent cannot recall that an event has occurred.
Telescoping Condition that occurs when a respondent compresses time, or remembers an event as occurring more recently than it actually occurred.
Creation Situation where a respondent recalls an event that did not actually occur.
Unaided questions Questions that do not provide any clues to the answer.
Aided questions Questions that provide clues to potentially help the respondent recall more accurately.

CONSTRUCTING THE QUESTIONNAIRE

Now that we've discussed principles of good question design, we will present some suggestions for arranging the questions in a form that provides meaningful results in a cost- and time-efficient manner. Several important issues need to be considered when constructing a questionnaire.

Response Formats

Two general types of response formats can be used in constructing a questionnaire: *open-ended* and *itemized* (closed-ended).

[6]Seymour Sudman and Norman M. Bradburn, "Effects of Time and Memory Factors on Response in Surveys," *Journal of the American Statistical Association,* December 1973, 805–15.
[7]Yoram Wind and David Lerner, "On the Measurement of Purchase Data: Surveys Versus Purchase Diary," *Journal of Marketing Research,* May 1970, 254–55.
[8]Daniel Starch, *Measuring Advertising Readership and Results,* New York: McGraw-Hill Book Company, 1966, 20.

Open-Ended Questions. With an open-ended question format the respondent is free to choose any response deemed appropriate, within the limits implied by the question. For example, the question series

What did the commercial say?

_____

_____

_____

_____

_____

What did the commercial show?

_____

_____

_____

_____

_____

What did you like about the commercial you just saw?

_____

_____

_____

_____

_____

allow the respondent to choose his or her own words in describing the commercial.

Not all studies include open-ended questions. However, when they are included, their primary purpose is to obtain the respondent's own verbalization of, comprehension of, and reaction to stimuli. The stimuli may cover a broad range (such as ads, commercials, packages, products, concepts). Therefore, it is impossible to set rules for every possible situation in which open-ended questions might be used or set rules for the processing of the open-ended questions. However, there are several good reasons for asking open-ended questions.

1. Open-ended questions may be used to check and/or corroborate the results of the quantitative or closed-ended questions. Along these same lines, open-ended questions also may be used to find a wider range of response and reaction than is included in the quantitative or structured questions.

2. Open-ended questions may be used to obtain direct comparisons and more specific areas of preference and rejection when two or more stimuli (e.g., products or concepts) are involved in a test.

3. Open-ended questions may be used to determine whether a particular communication vehicle (e.g., commercial or concept) conveys its intended objectives.

4. Open-ended questions may be used to determine respondents' affective reactions or feelings as a result of exposure to a stimulus (e.g., commercial, concept, package, product, or ad).

354

There are several drawbacks to using open-ended questions. First, they are not very well suited for self-administered questionnaires, simply because most respondents will not write elaborate answers. Second, answers to open-ended questions may be a more direct result of the respondent's ability to articulate than a measure of the respondent's knowledge or interest in the issue being investigated. Third, interviewer bias can be a serious problem with the use of open-ended questions (see Chapter 5). Finally, open-ended questions must eventually be coded or categorized for analysis purposes, and this is often a tedious task laden with ambiguities (see Chapter 13). An alternative is called **precoding.** Here the respondent is presented with an open-ended question such as

What brand of shampoo did you last purchase?

After the respondent has indicated the brand last purchased, the interviewer checks off that brand on a list that contains the most popular brands in the product category. As such, this type of open-ended question is treated from the viewpoint of the interviewer as an itemized question.

Precoding Procedure of assigning a code number to every possible response to an open-ended question.

E X A M P L E

Precoded

Q. What brands of toothpaste have you ever heard of? *(Do not read list. Record below.)* Any others?

Unaided

Aim 1
Aqua-Fresh 2
Colgate 3
Crest 4
Gleem 5
Pepsodent 6
Topol 7
Others (please specify) _____
_____
_____

Uncoded

Q. What brands of toothpaste have you ever heard of? *(Record responses verbatim on lines provided below.)*

_____   _____
_____   _____
_____   _____

Harder on the interviewer

Itemized (Closed-Ended) Questions. With an itemized-question format the respondent is provided with numbers and/or predetermined descriptions and is asked to select the one that best describes his or her feelings.

Itemized (closed-ended) questions Format where the respondent is provided with numbers and/or predetermined descriptions and is asked to select the one that best describes his or her feelings.

Exhibit 12-1 presents several examples. Itemized questions can take on many different formats. Recall that in Chapter 10 we discussed in some detail several issues related to itemized-question formats: namely, (1) the number of response alternatives (such as multiple-choice or dichotomous), (2) the nature and degree of verbal description, (3) the number of favorable and unfavorable categories, (4) the presence of a neutral position, and (5) the forced or nonforced nature of the scale.

E X H I B I T 12-1

Structured Response Alternatives

Response alternatives to a "purchase intent" question:

Balanced with Neutral Position

Definitely would buy
Probably would buy
Might or might not buy
Probably would not buy
Definitely would not buy

Balanced Without Neutral Position

Definitely would buy
Probably would buy
Probably would not buy
Definitely would not buy

Balanced, Non Forced

Definitely would buy
Probably would buy
Don't know/no answer
Probably would not buy
Definitely would not buy

Balanced, Graphic Rating

(Place an "X" in a position on the line that indicates your likelihood of buying Product X.)

Would _____Would
not buy   Might or   buy
                        might not buy

Dichotomous

Would buy
Would not buy

Unbalanced

Definitely would buy
Probably would buy
Might or might not buy
Would not buy

The obvious advantages of itemized-question formats relate to their ease of use in the field: their ability to reduce interviewer bias (and specifically bias due to differences in how articulate respondents are); and, finally, the relatively simple approach required with respect to coding and tabulation. To be effective, however, itemized-question formats require a substantial amount of effort, particularly with respect to pretesting. The use of itemized-question formats presumes that the predetermined set of response categories adequately reflects all of the possible and relevant responses at the appropriate level of precision, and that it will not produce distortions in the data.

Logical Flow

To respondents, questionnaires should appear as logical, carefully-thought-out examinations. In everyday life, we are generally asked about what we have done and then about the details surrounding a given occurrence before we go on to talk about another unrelated situation. This is also the typical flow in marketing research surveys—there is a progression from evaluative to diagnostic questioning or vice versa and then on to classification questions. For example, in a product concept test, we might ask consumers the following array of questions after they have read about a new product idea:

- EVALUATIVE
    Purchase intent
- DIAGNOSTIC
    Reasons for expressed level of purchase intent
    Uniqueness (of idea)
    Believability (of idea)
    Importance of main benefit
    Expected frequency of usage
    Ratings on a series of product benefits
- CLASSIFICATION
    Age
    Marital status
    Family size
    Education
    Occupation
    Income

There are several issues to consider when developing the flow of the questionnaire.[9]

Introducing the Questionnaire. Many respondents will have some initial suspicions or fears concerning why they are being interviewed. The introduction must make clear the purpose of the study. It need not be

---

[9]Parts of the following discussion were adapted from Sudman and Bradburn, *Asking Questions*, 208–228.

long and complicated, however. Instead, the first several questions should indicate the nature and purpose of the study.

In personal interviews, for example, respondents should identify themselves and the organization(s) they represent and should immediately give a one- or two-sentence description of the purpose of the study. On the other hand, in mail surveys the nature and purpose of the study is given in the cover letter that accompanies the questionnaire. The major points that should be covered include[10]

- What the study is about and its social usefulness
- Why the respondent is important
- Promise of confidentiality and explanation of identification number appearing on the questionnaire
- Reward for participation
- What to do if questions arise
- Thank you

These points should be covered in less than one page.

The First Questions. At all costs, bad initial impressions must be avoided. The opening questions should be easy and nonthreatening and, if possible, significant to the respondent. Some survey researchers suggest opening with a question that is easy and of interest to the respondent even if it is not relevant to the study at hand—for instance, a question about movie-going behavior.

In personal interviews it is common to begin with a fairly general open-ended attitude question concerning the topic of the study. This forces the respondent to focus on the relevant topic and gives the respondent the opportunity to reveal those views that he or she feels are most salient. On the other hand, in mail and other self-administered questionnaires the practice is to start with a simple closed-ended question.

Demographic Questions. Since most demographic questions are perceived as personal and even threatening by a least some respondents, they are generally asked at the end of the questionnaire. Obviously, a refusal to answer the income question will not affect responses to other questions if income is the last question in the questionnaire.

Funnel sequence The procedure of asking the most general (or unrestricted) question about the topic under study first, followed by successively more restricted questions.

Funnel and Inverted-Funnel Sequences. Typically the **funnel sequence** is followed when the respondent is assumed to have some ideas about a topic. By funnel sequence is meant the procedure of asking the most general (or unrestricted) question about the topic under study first, followed by successively more restricted questions. This approach prevents early questions from conditioning or biasing responses to questions

---

[10]A careful discussion of these points can be found in D. Dillman, *Mail and Telephone Surveys: The Total Design Method* (New York: John Wiley & Sons, 1978).

that come later. For example, the following series of questions illustrates the funnel sequence used to determine what the respondent thinks about a new-product concept and his or her reactions to specific end-benefit claims.

1. What is your overall reaction to the new-product concept?
2. Did you find anything hard to believe about the new-product concept?
3. *(If yes)* What did you find hard to believe?
4. Did you find *(specific idea)* hard to believe?

The funnel-sequence technique can prove useful when one wants to ascertain something about the respondent's frame of reference.

In other instances, an **inverted-funnel sequence** is useful. With this technique, the sequence is inverted in the sense that the questioning begins with specific questions and concludes with the respondent answering the general question. The approach compels respondents to consider certain specific points in reaching their evaluations. This approach is also useful when the interviewer wishes to ensure that all respondents base their evaluations on similar specific factors. The inverted-funnel sequence approach appears most useful for low-salience topics—that is, topics in which the respondent is without strong feelings or on which he or she has not formulated a point of view.

Inverted funnel sequence Sequence inverted in the sense that the questioning begins with specific questions and concludes with the respondent answering the general question.

Note that the funnel-sequence approach is only applicable to personal or telephone interviews. In mail and other self-administered questionnaires the respondent will typically look over the entire questionnaire before starting to answer. In contrast, however, the inverted-funnel sequence approach can be used in mail questionnaires as well as in personal interviews.

Changing Topics. The questionnaire frequently contains questions that deal with more than one topic. In such instances, all of the questions that deal with one topic should be listed together before a new topic begins. In addition, when switching topics use a transitional phrase to help respondents switch their train of thought.

Filter Questions. A question that is asked to determine which branching question, if any, will be asked is referred to as a **filter question.** These questions are asked to ensure that all possible contingencies are covered and to reduce the chance of interviewer or respondent error and encourage complete responses.

Filter question A question that is asked to determine which branching question, if any, will be asked.

Skip patterns in a questionnaire can become quite complicated. In many instances the appropriate skip pattern is based on several questions. A simple procedure to account for all contingencies is to make a flow chart of the logical possibilities and then to prepare the filter question and instructions based upon the flow chart. A flow chart used in a market study for a new brand is shown in the following example.

EXAMPLE

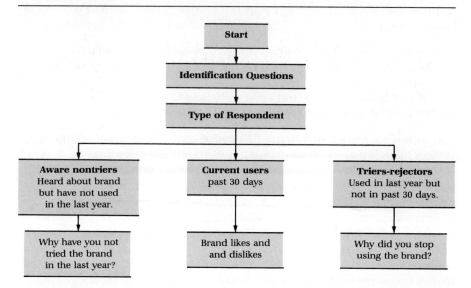

In this instance, answers to awareness and usage questions are used to ensure that all segments of the sample fall into one and only one question sequence.

Placement of filter questions is important, and two guidelines should be followed. First, if only a single filter is used, it should be placed just before, or as close as possible, to its corresponding branching question. Avoid having the interviewer flip back and forth in the questionnaire. Second, if multiple filter questions are required, they should all be asked before proceeding to more detailed questions; if not, the respondent may discover that detailed questions can be avoided by giving certain answers to the filtering questions.

Exhibit 12-2 provides a checklist of the major points to be considered when planning the flow of the questionnaire.

EXHIBIT 12-2

**Checklist of Major Points to Consider When Planning
the Flow of the Questionnaire**

1. Start with easy, salient, nonthreatening, but necessary questions. Put the more difficult or threatening questions near the end of the questionnaire. Never start a mail questionnaire with an open question that requires a great deal of writing.

2. Since some demographic questions are threatening, put these questions at the end of the interview. If at all possible, avoid asking demographic questions first.

3. For personal interviews use funneling procedures to minimize order effects. Start with the more general questions and move to more specific questions. For low-salience topics, however, it may be necessary to ask questions on specific dimensions of the topic before asking for a summary view.

4. If questions deal with more than one topic, complete questions on a single topic before moving on to a new topic.

5. When switching topics, use a transitional phrase to make it easier for respondents to switch their trains of thought.

6. To ensure that all contingencies are covered, make a flow chart for filter questions. Filter questions should not require extensive page flipping by the interviewer or respondent or require remembering answers to earlier questions.

7. If multiple filter questions are to be asked, try to ask all of them before asking the more detailed questions. Otherwise, respondents may learn how to avoid answering detailed questions.

Source: S. Sudman and N. M. Bradburn, *Asking Questions* (San Francisco: Jossey-Bass Publishers, 1983), 207–208.

Layout Considerations[11]

Keep in mind that other people must deal with the questionnaire. Designing the physical format of the questionnaire in a complex manner will complicate not only the lives of the interviewer and respondent, but also those of the data-processing personnel when they try to unravel the mess.

Use of Booklets. There are at least four reasons to recommend the use of a booklet format in questionnaires: (1) booklets prevent pages from being lost or misplaced, (2) booklets allow the interviewer or respondent to turn pages more easily, (3) booklets allow the use of double-page format for questions, and (4) booklets look more professional and are easy to follow when used in self-administered interviews.

Appearance of Self-Administered Questionnaires. Appearance can have a dramatic effect on cooperation in mail and other self-administered questionnaires (see Chapter 5). As a general rule, the questionnaire should look as easy to read and answer as possible to the respondent and should have a professional appearance. The date, title of the study, and name of the organization conducting the study should appear on the first page of the questionnaire.

Use of Blank Space and Typeface. A tendency of beginners when designing a questionnaire is to crowd questions together in hope of making

[11]Parts of the following discussion were adapted from Sudman and Bradburn, *Asking Questions*, 208–228.

the questionnaire look shorter. Crowded questions with little blank space between them often give the impression of an overly complex questionnaire. The respondent's perception of the difficulty of the task is extremely important in determining cooperation rates, especially in self-administered questionnaires. Less-crowded questionnaires with ample blank spaces look easier and generally result in higher cooperation rates along with fewer response errors by interviewers or respondents. Along these same lines, the type should be sufficiently large and clear to cause no strain in reading—avoid photo-reducing the questionnaire whenever possible.

Color Coding. Although color has been found not to influence response rates to questionnaires (see Chapter 5), and it is not easier for interviewers to use, color coding can help in some respects. Printing questionnaires on different colored paper can be used to distinguish groups of surveys to be used with certain groups of respondents (for example, those who used a particular product in a test involving a number of products, those belonging to a specific subsample group—heavy versus light users, and so forth).

more for person administering [handwritten note in margin]

Question Numbering. There are at least two good reasons for numbering the questions in a questionnaire. First, numbering questions may help alert the interviewer or respondent that a question has unintentionally been skipped. Second, numbering questions provides an identifiable system that can prove useful in developing interviewer instructions, especially with regard to appropriate skip patterns.

Fitting Questions on a Page. Splitting a question, including any of its response categories, is never recommended. With split questions the interviewer or respondent is likely to assume that the question has ended at the end of a page. The result will be answers based upon incomplete and potentially misleading questions. In addition, one should generally avoid splitting a series of related questions.

Interviewer Instructions. Directions for individual questions should be placed as near as possible to the questions—usually just before or just after the question, depending on the nature of the direction. If the instructions deal with how the respondent should answer or how the question should be administered, then they should be placed before the question. If, on the other hand, the instructions relate to how the answers should be recorded or how the interviewer should probe, then they should be placed after the question. In order to distinguish instructions from questions, distinctive type (such as capitals or italics) is commonly used. The objective is simply to avoid having interviewers mistakenly read directions to respondents as part of the question.

Response Category Formats. Exhibit 12-3 presents a series of demographic questions as they are often formatted by the beginning questionnaire designer. First, notice that the page looks crowded and confusing.

Moreover, the respondent may be confused about whether the blank line is to be used with the response category before it or after it. This confusion can lead to response errors.

EXHIBIT 12-3

Unacceptable Formats of Commonly Asked Survey Questions

Q-22 Your sex: _____Male _____Female

Q-23 Your present marital status: _____Never married _____Married
_____Separated _____Widowed

Q-24 Number of children you have in each age group: _____Under five years
_____5–13 _____14–18 _____19–25 and over

Q-25 Your present age: _____

Q-26 Do you own (or are you buying) your own home? _____No _____Yes

Q-27 Did you serve in the armed forces? _____No _____Yes
(Year entered _____year discharged _____)

Q-28 Are you presently: _____Employed _____Unemployed _____Retired
_____Full-time homemaker

Q-29 Please describe the usual occupation of the principal wage
earner in your household, including title, kind of work, and
kind of company or business. (If retired, describe the usual
occupation before retirement.)

Q-30 What was your approximate net family income, from all sources,
before taxes, in 1970?

Less than $3,000_____	10,000 to 12,999_____	20,000 to 24,999_____
3,000 to 4,999_____	13,000 to 15,999_____	25,000 to 30,000_____
5,000 to 6,999_____	16,000 to 19,999_____	Over $30,000_____
7,000 to 9,999_____		

Q-31 What is the highest level of education that you have completed?

No formal education_____	_____Some college
Some grade school_____	_____Completed college . . .
Completed grade school_____	major_____
Some high school_____	_____Some graduate work
Completed high school_____	A graduate degree. . . degree and
	major_____

Q-32 What is your religious preference? _____Protestant denomination
_____Jewish _____Catholic _____Other _____Specify _____None

Q-33 How frequently did you attend religious services in a place of worship
during the past year: _____Regularly _____Occasionally
_____Only on special days _____Not at all

Q-34 Which do you consider yourself to be? _____Republican _____Democrat
_____Independent _____Other _____Specify

Q-35 Which of these best describes your usual stand on political
issues? _____Conservative _____Liberal _____Middle of the road
_____Radical

Source: D. Dillman, *Mail and Telephone Surveys* (John Wiley & Sons, 1978), 134.

Another tendency of beginning questionnaire designers is to place category headings in a sideways format—done frequently in order to conserve space. Exhibit 12-4 illustrates this type of formatting. Sideways formatting requires continuous shifting of the page or the flexibility of a

E X H I B I T 12-4

Unacceptable Format of Series Questions

Much has been said about the quality of life offered by various sizes of cities. We would like to know how you feel. First, please show which city size is best for each of the characteristics by putting an "X" in the appropriate column by each item. Second, please look back over the list and show which three of these characteristics would be most important to you if you were selecting a new community in which to live by ranking them from 1 (most important) to 3 (third most important).

	City below 10,000 people	City of 10,000 to 49,999 people	City of 50,000 to 149,999 people	City of 150,000 people or over
Equality of opportunities for all residents, regardless of race				
Place in which to raise children				
Community spirit and pride				
General mental health of residents				
Adequacy of medical care				
Protection of individual freedom and privacy				
Friendliness of people to each other				
Adequacy of police protection				
General satisfaction of residents				
Respect for law and order				
Lowest costs for public services (Like water, sewer, and police)				
Recreational and entertainment opportunities				

Source: From D. Dillman, *Mail and Telephone Surveys*, (John Wiley & Sons, 1978), 139.

contortionist in order to read the category headings, and so it is not recommended. A better format would be to give more space to the category headings:

City Below 10,000 people	City of 10,000 to 49,999 people	City of 50,000 to 150,000 people	City over 150,000 people

The generally accepted standard is to use vertical answer formats for individual questions, which means that the interviewer or respondent will be reading down a single column.

Another formatting strategy is to use *grids*. Grids can be used when there are a number of simultaneous questions that use the same set of response categories (for example, What brands of toothpaste have you ever heard of? Which brand or brands of toothpaste have you used in the past 30 days? Which *one* brand do you use most often?). Simply include an instruction for the interviewer or respondent to record in the appropriate column. Exhibit 12-5 presents an illustrative prototype.

Skip Instructions. Skip instructions are communicated to interviewers or respondents by two methods: verbal instructions or arrows that point to the next question. Both methods are acceptable.

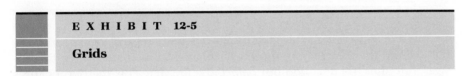

E X H I B I T   12-5

Grids

Fragrances

5a. *(Hand respondent card A)* Listed on this card are several brands of fragrances. Would you please tell me which of these brands you have personally used in the past 3 months? *(Circle all mentioned below in column 5a.)*

5b. Which brands, if any, have you personally used in the past month? *(Circle all mentioned below in column 5b.)*

5c. Now, which one of these brands would you say you personally use most often? *(Circle one below in column 5c.)*

	(5a) Past 3 Months	(5b) Past Month	(5c) Most Often
Arpege	1 (20)	1 (23)	1 (26)
Aviance	2	2	2
Avon (all)	3	3	3
Babe	4	4	4
Cachet	5	5	5
Chanel #5	6	6	6
Chantilly	7	7	7
Charlie	8	8	8
Emeraude	9	9	9

Estee	1 (21)	1 (24)	1 (27)
Farouche	2	2	2
Intimate	3	3	3
Jean Nate	4	4	4
Je Reviens	5	5	5
Jontue	6	6	6
Joy	7	7	7
L'Air du Temps	8	8	8
Masumi	9	9	9
My Sin	1 (22)	1 (25)	1 (28)
Norell	2	2	2
Nuance	3	3	3
Rive Gauche	4	4	4
Shalimar	5	5	5
Tabu	6	6	6
Tigress	7	7	7
White Shoulders	8	8	8
Windsong	9	9	9
Youth Dew	0	0	0
Other (specify)			
_____	X	X	X
_____			
_____			

(Take Back Card "A")

Several guidelines should be followed with regard to skip instructions. First, the instruction should be placed immediately after the answer, not after the question but *before* the answer. This method ensures that the interviewer or respondent will not forget or ignore the instructions. Second, do not place the skip instruction only at the beginning of a subsequent question when there have been questions in between. For example, the instructions

> *If the respondent answered yes to Q.10, ask Q.15*
> *otherwise skip to Q.12*

placed at the beginning of Question 15 would require the interviewer to look back and locate the respondent's answer to Question 10. Any backward flow is to be avoided. In this case the skip instructions should be placed after the response to the filter question with the appropriate response categories placed before the follow-up question.

E X A M P L E

Q.4   Have you heard of brand X?
      Yes (*ask A*)   33-1
      No (*skip to Q.5*)   -2
      Not sure (*skip to Q.5*)   -3

If Yes
    A. Have you used brand X in the last 30 days?
        Yes (*skip to Q.6*)   34-1
        No   -2
    B. Have you used brand X in the last 6 months?
        Yes (*skip to Q.6*)   35-1
        No   -2

Finally note that skip instructions should always be worded positively, not negatively, to reduce the chance of interviewer error.

Preparation for Data Processing. The raw data—that is, each respondent's answers to the questions asked—are contained on the questionnaire. In order for the data to be analyzed, numerical values and/or alphanumeric symbols must be assigned to each response in such a way that they can be read by a computer (mainframe, minicomputer, or personal computer). In most, if not all, commercial marketing research studies, the amount of data collected is so voluminous as to preclude hand tabulation. Two essential terms need to be defined before we continue with our discussion of advance procedures for data processing.

■ **Case.** The term *case* refers to the unit of analysis for the study; in other words, a case is that thing, object, person, or whatever, that supplied the answers to the questions asked. The respondent is the most common unit of analysis in commercial marketing research studies, and so each respondent would constitute a case. The total number of cases equals the sample size.

Case The unit of analysis for the study.

■ **Record.** A *record* refers to a string of coded data in machine-readable format. It has become customary to view a record as consisting of 80 field positions where each field position (or series of field positions) contains the coded responses for a specific question. The reason for this is that historically the standard way of transferring the raw data from the questionnaire to a computer was with the use of a computer card consisting of 80 vertical columns. The data were put on the card by a keypunch machine, which literally punched holes within the columns. Most academic computer centers removed keypunch machines some years ago. Data are entered directly into computer memory via on-line CRT work stations. However, most tab houses still find it easier to first have the data punched onto cards and then create a magnetic tape. Once the tape is created, it is loaded into computer memory and the cards are then discarded. For ease of discussion we will continue to view a record as consisting of 80 field positions. As we will illustrate shortly, one or more field positions (columns) are assigned to a variable (question) and then a numerical value or alphanumeric symbol is assigned to that field position to represent the elicited response. If the data take up more than 80 field positions (columns) then another

Record A string of coded data in a machine-readable format.

record is utilized; if the data exhaust the next 80 field positions (columns) then yet another record is utilized, and so on until all of the data has been recorded. Thus, a case can consist of one or many records, depending on the number of questions asked, and together the number of cases and the number of records per case define the data set.

It is important to consider how the data will be processed and analyzed when constructing the questionnaire. If processing and analysis of the data are considered after the interviewing is complete, uncorrectable problems are likely to surface. Experienced researchers generally do as much preparation as possible for data processing before the questionnaire is printed. Advance preparation undoubtedly saves substantial amounts of time and money and can eliminate questions that may not provide the needed information.

Precoding of closed-ended questions and precolumning of the entire questionnaire are the two principal activities in preparing the data for processing. Precoding involves assigning a code number to every possible response to a closed-ended question. Precolumning involves assigning each response category or other identifying information contained in the questionnaire to a specific location on a computer card or magnetic tape. The precoding activity involves designating a coding scheme prior to undertaking fieldwork, and the actual codes as well as field position are printed on the questionnaire. You may have noted that in many of the examples and exhibits previously used in this chapter we have used precodes.

E X A M P L E

Consider following question concerning natural-cereal brand usage.

	Yes	No
Frozen waffles	1/8[ ]-1	[ ]-2
Instant coffee	1/9[ ]-1	[ ]-2
Frozen orange juice	1/10[ ]-1	[ ]-2
Cold cereal	1/11[ ]-1	[ ]-2

The number to the left of the slash (/) denotes the record number (or card number); the number to the left of the box ([   ]) designates the field position that the response will appear in; the number to the right of the box ([   ]) gives the appropriate code; the box ([   ]) itself is used by the interviewer to record the elicited response. The same approach is used to code responses that do not fall into categories; for example, a respondent's consumption of natural and/or cold cereal brands might be requested and coded as follows:

> How many 13 oz. boxes of natural and/or cold cereal does your
> family consume in a typical month?
>
> ————2/20–21

Here the number 2 to the left of the slash (/) indicates that this response will

Figure 12-1

Computer card showing how answers are recorded.

appear on the second record (card) for each respondent; the numbers 20–21 to the right of the slash (/) indicate that the response to this question should be entered into the twentieth and twenty-first field positions (or columns of the card). Note two points: first, by reserving two spaces for the response, the largest response that can be recorded is 99; second, if the response is 9 or less only the twenty-first field position (or column) will be used. In other words, the entered response is right-justified. Figure 12-1 illustrates how the first three respondents' answers to these two questions would be entered into the computer and/or appear on a computer card.

We see that the first three field positions (or columns) are dedicated to a case identification number, which indicates the respondent; field position (or column) number 6 indicates the record (or card) number; field positions (columns) 8–11 are reserved for responses to question number 5 where a 1 indicates that the product has been consumed in the past month and a 2 indicates that it has not; field positions (or columns) 20–21 are reserved for the number of boxes of cold cereal consumed in a typical month. Thus, examining the data we see that respondent 001 has eaten frozen waffles, frozen orange juice and cold cereal, but not instant coffee, and consumes five boxes of cold cereal in a typical month.

Several other points warrant some discussion. First, "don't know" or "not applicable" response categories are also precoded with a predesignated number such as "9." Second, missing data are generally at this juncture left blank. We will discuss how missing data can be handled in Chapter 13. Third, special consideration should be given to items that will be combined to form an overall scale. Recall our discussion of summated scales in Chapter 10, and in particular the discussion of attitude measurement and scaling in Chapter 11. Because the numerical codes for the response categories are to be added up, it is vital that the codes be scaled in the same direction for all the questions that will be combined. If, for example, there are two items, each with three response categories, and the most favorable response category in Question 1 is coded 1 and the corresponding response category in Question 2 is coded 3, the two items cannot be added unless one set of categories is recoded so that it is in the proper order. Fourth, open-ended questions cannot, in general, be precoded. Issues surfacing with open-ended questions will also be discussed in Chapter 13. Finally, if computer-assisted interviewing or CATI systems are used, no precolumning of the questionnaire will be necessary since responses are entered into the computer directly. Note, however, that the same kind of thinking must be done by the researcher in preparing the computer program for a computer-assisted or CATI interview. Later in this chapter we provide a brief overview of three popular computer-assisted systems for electronic questionnaire design.

Exhibit 12-6 provides a checklist of the major points to be considered when designing the format of the questionnaire. In addition, Exhibit 12-7 presents a questionnaire used in a recent brand personality study; its construction reflects many of the points raised in this section.

E X H I B I T 12-6

Checklist of Major Points to Consider in Laying Out the Questionnaire

1. Use booklet format for ease in reading and turning pages and to prevent lost pages.
2. A mail or self-administered questionnaire should look easy to answer and professionally designed and printed. A date, title of the study, and the name of the organization conducting the study should appear on the first page of the questionnaire.
3. Do not crowd questions. Be sure that sufficient space is left for open-ended questions, since the answer will not be longer than the space provided.
4. Use sufficiently large and clear type so that there is no strain in reading.
5. Colored covers or sections of the questionnaire may be helpful to interviewers when multiple forms are used or for complex skipping patterns.
6. Each question should be numbered, and subparts of a question should be lettered to prevent questions from being omitted in error and to facilitate the use of skip instructions. Indent subparts of questions.
7. Do not split a question between two pages, since interviewers or respondents may think that the question is completed at the end of a page.
8. Provide directions and probes for specific questions at appropriate places in the questionnaire; identify these directions with distinctive type, such as capitals or italics.
9. Use vertical answer formats for individual questions.

10. Place skip instructions immediately after the answer.

11. Precode all closed-ended questions to facilitate data processing and to ensure that all the data are in proper form for analysis.

12. Precolumn the questionnaire.

Source: S. Sudman and N. M. Bradburn, *Asking Questions* (San Francisco: Jossey-Bass Publishers, 1983), 290–210.

E X H I B I T   12-7

Questionnaire

Ice Cream Brand Personality Study   Card 2

1. People we have spoken to use different words to describe their idea of an ideal product. We would like to get your impressions of what your ideal packaged ice cream would be like. By ideal we mean the best possible packaged ice cream you can imagine ever eating at home. I am going to show you a list of words. *(Place yellow ideal rating pages in front of respondent.)* I would like you to read through this list and consider the words that you feel describe your ideal packaged ice cream. You can do this by using a scale from 7 to 1, where "7" means *"definitely applies"* and "1" means *"does not apply at all."* You may use any number from 7 to 1, but just remember that the higher the number the more you feel it applies, and the lower the number the less you feel it applies. Starting with the first word, write in the number from 7 to 1 that indicates how much the word describes your ideal packaged ice cream. *(Show respondent where to write in answer.)* Then go on to the next word. Of course there are no right or wrong answers to this question; we are just interested in your opinions. We have found that it is best to work quickly and to use your initial impressions. *(Make sure respondent understands what she is to do. When respondent has finished, take back rating pages. Check to make sure one number from 1 to 7 has been filled in for all words.)*

2a. Earlier, when you were checking the words that describe your ideal packaged ice cream, were you thinking about a particular brand?

      Yes   1   *(Ask Q.2b)*   (2/65)

      No   2   *(Skip to Q.3)*

2b. What brand was that? _____(2/66–67)

To determine brands to be asked about in Q.3–Q5:
  Refer to screener grid Q.F
    *Starting with X'D brand write in the names of **ALL BRANDS CIRCLED** in Q.F, on the lines provided at the top of **both** blue rating pages.*
(Show respondent commercials.)

371

Yellow Rating Scale
*Ideal Packaged Ice Cream—The Best Ice Cream
You Can Imagine Ever Eating At Home*

Rating Scale	Definitely Applies						Does Not Apply At All	
	7	6	5	4	3	2	1	
Classic	7	6	5	4	3	2	1	(2/39)
Serious	7	6	5	4	3	2	1	(2/40)
Blue collar	7	6	5	4	3	2	1	(2/41)
Warmhearted	7	6	5	4	3	2	1	(2/42)
Timid	7	6	5	4	3	2	1	(2/43)
Commonplace	7	6	5	4	3	2	1	(2/44)
Opinionated	7	6	5	4	3	2	1	(2/45)
High class	7	6	5	4	3	2	1	(2/46)
Active	7	6	5	4	3	2	1	(2/47)
Earthy	7	6	5	4	3	2	1	(2/48)
All American	7	6	5	4	3	2	1	(2/49)
Erotic	7	6	5	4	3	2	1	(2/50)
Humorous	7	6	5	4	3	2	1	(2/51)
Childish	7	6	5	4	3	2	1	(2/52)
Realistic	7	6	5	4	3	2	1	(2/53)
Adaptable	7	6	5	4	3	2	1	(2/54)
Sociable	7	6	5	4	3	2	1	(2/55)
Lower class	7	6	5	4	3	2	1	(2/56)
Sensible	7	6	5	4	3	2	1	(2/57)
Suburban	7	6	5	4	3	2	1	(2/58)
Hardworking	7	6	5	4	3	2	1	(2/59)
Leader	7	6	5	4	3	2	1	(2/60)
Careful	7	6	5	4	3	2	1	(2/61)
Traditional	7	6	5	4	3	2	1	(2/62)
Aloof	7	6	5	4	3	2	1	(2/63)
Generous	7	6	5	4	3	2	1	(2/64)

Card 3–5

3–5. People we have spoken to have also used different words to describe different brands of products. For example, thinking about makes of cars, a person may feel that the description "youthful" describes a Jeep but does not describe a Buick.

We would like to get your impressions of different brands of packaged ice creams. I am again going to show you a list of words. *(Place blue brand rating pages in front of respondent.)*

For each of the descriptive words listed down the side of the page, write in the number from 7–1 that best describes how much you feel that word describes each of the ice creams.

Blue Rating Form

Definitely Applies					Does Not Apply At All	
7	6	5	4	3	2	1

	(Brand of packaged ice cream) (3/31–32)	(Brand of packaged ice cream) (4/31–32)	(Brand of packaged ice cream) (5/31–32)
Classic	_____ (3/33)	_____ (4/33)	_____ (5/33)
Serious	_____ (3/34)	_____ (4/34)	_____ (5/34)
Blue collar	_____ (3/35)	_____ (4/35)	_____ (5/35)
Warmhearted	_____ (3/36)	_____ (4/36)	_____ (5/36)
Timid	_____ (3/37)	_____ (4/37)	_____ (5/37)
Commonplace	_____ (3/38)	_____ (4/38)	_____ (5/38)
Opinionated	_____ (3/39)	_____ (4/39)	_____ (5/39)
High class	_____ (3/40)	_____ (4/40)	_____(5/40)
Active	_____ (3/41)	_____ (4/41)	_____ (5/41)
Earthy	_____ (3/42)	_____ (4/42)	_____ (5/42)
All American	_____ (3/43)	_____ (4/43)	_____ (5/43)
Erotic	_____ (3/44)	_____ (4/44)	_____ (5/44)
Humorous	_____ (3/45)	_____ (4/45)	_____ (5/45)
Childish	_____ (3/46)	_____ (4/46)	_____ (5/46)
Realistic	_____ (3/47)	_____ (4/47)	_____ (5/47)
Adaptable	_____ (3/48)	_____ (4/48)	_____ (5/48)
Sociable	_____ (3/49)	_____ (4/49)	_____(5/49)
Lower class	_____ (3/50)	_____ (4/50)	_____ (5/50)
Sensible	_____ (3/51)	_____ (4/51)	_____ (5/51)
Suburban	_____ (3/52)	_____(4/52)	_____ (5/52)
Hardworking	_____ (3/53)	_____ (4/53)	_____ (5/53)
Leader	_____ (3/54)	_____ (4/54)	_____ (5/54)
Careful	_____ (3/55)	_____ (4/55)	_____ (5/55)
Traditional	_____ (3/56)	_____ (4/56)	_____ (5/56)
Aloof	_____ (3/57)	_____ (4/57)	_____ (5/57)
Generous	_____ (3/58)	_____ (4/58)	_____ (5/58)

Card 6

Now, just a few questions for classification purposes only.

6a. How many containers of ice cream have you bought to be eaten at home in the past 30 days? *(Record exact #. Record zero for none.* If **none** skip to Q.7.)

TOTAL # Containers _____ (6/10–11)
(Ask Q.6b for each container size listed below)

6b. Of the (Insert # containers from Q.6a) containers you bought how many were (Insert size)? (Record exact #. Record zero for none. Repeat for each size listed.)

Pints	_____	(6/12–13)
Quarts	_____	(6/14–15)
½ Gallons	_____	(6/16–17)
Gallons	_____	(6/18–19)

(Total should add to number in Q.6a.)

373

7. Are you . . .? (Read list)

Married	1 (6/20)
Single	2
Widowed	3
Separated	4
Divorced	5
(Do not read) Refused	x

8. Are you currently . . .? *(Read list.)*

Employed full-time	1 (6/21)
Employed part-time	2
Not employed outside the home, or	3
(Do not read) Refused	4

9a. Including yourself, how many persons are there in your household?

One	1 (6/22)	(SKIP TO Q.10)
Two	2	
Three	3	
Four	4	(ASK Q.9b)
Five	5	
Six or more	6	

9b. How many children under 18 years old?

Under 18: _____(6/23–24)

10. What was the last grade of school *you* completed? *(Do **not** read list.)*

No formal schooling	1 (6/25)
Completed grammar school	2
Some high school	3
Graduated high school	4
Some college	5
Graduated college	6
Refused	y

(Refer to Q.7, if "married", ask Q.11. Otherwise, skip to Q.12)

11. Is your husband currently . . .? *(Read list.)*

Employed full-time	1 (6/26)
Employed part-time	2
Not employed, or	3
(Do not read) Refused	x

(Hand respondent card 12)

12. Which letter on this card best describes your annual household income before taxes?

A. Under $10,000	1 (6/27)
B. $10,000 to $14,999	2
C. $15,000 to $24,999	3
D. $25,000 to $34,999	4

E. $35,000 to $49,999   5
F. $50,000 to $74,999   6
G. $75,000 or more   7
    Refused   x

(Take back card 14)

THANK RESPONDENT FOR PARTICIPATION! BE SURE TO:

RECORD ALL INFORMATION IN BOX AT TOP OF SCREENER.

STAPLE IN THIS ORDER:
  Screener
  Main Questionnaire
  Yellow ideal rating pages
  Blue brand rating pages.

PRETESTING THE QUESTIONNAIRE

In discussing itemized-question formats, we indicated that their effective use undoubtedly requires substantial effort on the part of the researcher—since the appropriate set of response categories needs to be determined, generally by conducting pretests. Pretests are indispensable in developing good questionnaires. A thorough pretest examines the potential for both respondent and interviewer error. We now discuss five types of decisions involved in pretesting.[12]

1. *What items should be pretested?* All aspects, including layout, question sequence, word meaning, question difficulty, branching instructions, and so on should be part of the pretest.

2. *How should the pretest be conducted?* To whatever extent possible the pretest should involve administering the questionnaire in an environment and context identical to the one that will be used in the final survey. An essential feature of conducting the pretest involves **debriefing** and/or **protocol analysis.** Debriefing takes place after a respondent has completed the questionnaire; it involves asking respondents to explain their answers, to state the meaning of each question, and to describe any problems they had with answering or completing the questionnaire. In protocol analysis the respondent is asked to "think aloud" while completing the questionnaire.

Debriefing Procedure of asking respondents to explain their answers, to state the meaning of each question, and to describe any problems they had with answering or completing the questionnaire.
Protocol analysis Procedure where the respondent "thinks aloud" while completing the questionnaire.

[12]The following discussion is based on Shelby D. Hunt, Richard D. Sparkman, Jr., and James Wilcox, "The Pretest in Survey Research: Issues and Preliminary Findings," *Journal of Marketing Research,* May 1982, 269–73.

3. *Who should conduct the pretest?* With telephone and personal pretest interviews, a number of parties should participate. First, the project director and/or person responsible for developing the questionnaire should complete several pretests. The majority of the pretest interviews should be conducted by regular staff interviewers. It is a good idea to assign both very experienced and relatively new interviewers to do the pretest interviews.

4. *Who should be the respondents in the pretest?* The respondents included in the pretest should be as similar as possible to the target population in terms of familiarity with the topic, attitude and behaviors with the topic, general background characterisitics, and so on. This is absolutely critical to performing a pretest.

5. *How large a sample is required for the pretest?* Unfortunately there is no one answer to this question. To a large degree it depends on how varied is the target population. With a heterogeneous target population a larger pretest sample will be required in order to satisfy the conditions specified under Question 4. In addition, with complex questionnaires it is good advice to use a large pretest sample.

Pretesting questionnaires should be taken seriously. As has been said, "No amount of intellectual exercise can substitute for testing an instrument designed to communicate with ordinary people."[13]

ELECTRONIC QUESTIONNAIRE DESIGN

As we indicated in Chapter 5, computer-assisted interviewing is fast becoming a dominant force in collecting data from respondents. Various systems for developing computer-aided questionnaires for gathering survey data have recently become available. These systems allow the user to design the logic and flow of the questionnaire. We briefly review three computer programs for developing and implementing computer-aided questionnaires.[14]

Electronic Questionnaire Design and Analysis with CAPPA, by Paul E. Green, K. Kedia, and Rishiyur S. Nikhil (Palo Alto, Calif.: The Scientific Press, 1985). *CAPPA* allows the user to construct a questionnaire, computerize the data collection, and analyze the data. The core of *CAPPA* is a command file. The command file, developed by the user, specifies presentation and question-type options. It is created with the aid of the user's own word processor. The command file includes options for item randomization, branching, forced response, help files, and fifteen question types (such as open-end rank, integer-scale, constant-sum). The questionnaire is constructed by designating the question number, type,

[13]Charles H. Backstrom and G. D. Hursch, *Survey Research*, Evanston, Ill.: Northwestern University Press, 1963.

[14]Parts of the following material was taken from an article by Scott M. Smith appearing in the *Journal of Marketing Research*, February 1986, 83–85.

and options. In addition, the user can enter text for instructions to the subject and possible answers. *CAPPA* automatically formats the question for the screen. The user may specify any of 64 color combinations for the background and foreground of the input text.

Ci2 System, Richard M. Johnson (Ketchum, Idaho: Sawtooth Software, Inc., 1985). System is an integrated questionnaire-design and data-collection system that allows the user to develop virtually any type of question or scale. *Ci2* is well documented and menu driven. It includes an editor for question construction, a command language for designing questionnaire logic and flow, and programs for integrating the questionnaire and logic files, printing questions, and summarizing data files.

ATHENA, CRC Information Systems, Inc. (New York, New York, 1986). ATHENA is a powerful, practical computer-assisted telephone interviewing system that runs on multi-user IBM PC/AT's (or look-alike micros) and on mini-computers made by many different manufacturers. It is completely menu-driven and interactive. Questionnaires are written in conversational language in response to prompts by the system. The system is powerful enough to handle massive, complex jobs involving multidimensional and hierarchial quotas and many different permutations of the questionnaire. In addition, it has the ability to (1) handle manually entered or tape sample telephone numbers, (2) integrate respondent information from previous waves into the current questionnaire, (3) access information associated with telephone numbers, such as zip codes or census data, if available, (4) set up an automatic system for call-backs, and (5) backtrack within the questionnaire.

FIELD EXECUTION

Probably the single most important part of the marketing research process is the data-collection phase. Although the design and analysis stages are vital to the solution of a particular research problem, poor instruction and control of the data-gathering process in the field can lead to invalid information and conclusions. We now discuss how the data-collection (fieldwork) process actually works and describe procedures used to ensure that the quality of the information gathered is maintained.

Who Conducts Fieldwork?

You may recall from Chapter 1 our discussion of the three key players in the commercial marketing research business: corporations (manufacturers, service industry, and the like), advertising agencies, and research suppliers. It is typical for the corporation and ad agency to contract for a particular study, while the research supplier helps to design, execute, and analyze the study. The "execution" role of the supplier includes the important aspect of data gathering.

The data-collection function at a supplier falls under the responsibility of the field department. This group is typically headed by a person with the title of "director" or "vice president—field operations." This individual makes sure that quality and cost efficiency are maintained for all studies passing through the department. Generally, the department staffed with a number of "field supervisors" (who are responsible for day-to-day planning and control of specific studies), "samplers" (who purchase or establish samples first-hand), and people who provide clerical support in shipping studies to actual internal and/or external interviewing sites and checking the questionnaires in after data collection has been completed.

Depending upon the size and staffing ability of the supplier, data may be collected either within or outside the organization. It is fairly typical these days for medium- and large-size research firms to have their own internal WATS telephone-interviewing capabilities, while some companies such as Market Facts M/A/R/C have internal capabilities for conducting full-scale mall-intercept studies. Internal fieldwork operations provide suppliers who have them with a competitive advantage: it usually means cost-efficiency and better quality control to prospective clients.

For those suppliers not possessing their own means of data collection, their fieldwork must be subcontracted to one or more of thousands of independently owned and operated interviewing services. Many of these relatively small companies operate central location personal and/or telephone-interviewing facilities in one or more markets throughout the country. These independent agencies usually only conduct central-location personal and telephone interviews, with an ever-decreasing number conducting personal in-home (door-to-door) interviews.

Fielding a Study

The fielding of a study actually begins in the "proposal" stage of the research process (described in Chapter 2). At the time the proposal is being prepared the project director discusses the research problem and a possible research method with the field director. Specifically the target audience, sampling, and interviewing methods are determined. When all of the study specifications have been determined, the field director prepares cost and timing estimates for conducting data collection. The sequence of activities in fielding a study is:

1. Initial cost estimates
2. "Alerting" the study
3. Field instructions
4. Briefing
5. Data collection
6. Evaluation of fieldwork quality

Cost Estimates. Estimating cost and timing for conducting the fieldwork in a study is more likely classified as art than science. Having a "feel" for what it takes to collect the required number of interviews using a specific research approach comes with years of experience and really cannot be estimated with "hard and fast" rules. While there is no truly accurate estimation formula, there are a number of parameters you can consider when selecting specific sampling/interviewing methods.

In general, regardless of the method chosen, two factors determine the cost in the fieldwork: (1) incidence of qualified respondents and (2) questionnaire length. Most studies require that respondents have specific characteristics in order to be interviewed. For example, a cola taste-test may require a sample of men and women who have had a least two glasses of a carbonated cola beverage in the past week. This group of individuals may only account for 35 percent of the population (an incidence of 35 percent). In other words, if I talk to (or "screen") 100 people, only 35 people will qualify. Recall that we illustrated how to determine the number of contacts needed in Chapter 7. As a general rule, the lower the incidence, the greater the number of people who have to be screened for qualification, and the greater the number of *screening hours*.

The other key variable is questionnaire length. Interviewing hours are directly related to the amount of time it takes to administer the questionnaire to a qualified respondent. However, when questionnaire length goes beyond 15–20 minutes, other costs are incurred. With leisure time becoming more and more valuable to individuals, there is less willingness to participate in longer interviews. This factor results in lower cooperation rates for longer questionnaires—hence, more screening and the use of incentives to increase production rates.

The effects of incidence and questionnaire length are compounded by supervisory costs. Each interviewing supplier, whether inside or outside of the company, has supervisors and other staff responsible for training and supervising the interviewers. These supervisor costs are usually charged by adding a percentage (about 50–60 percent) to the cost of interviewing.

In addition to the general factors mentioned above, other costs can be incurred based on the type of interviewing method used. Exhibit 12-8 summarizes potential costs associated with some of the more popular methods. Other factors such as time of day of the interview, sample administration and control, and the need for specially trained interviewers, can also affect the cost of data collection.

"Alerting" the Study. With a "ballpark" cost estimate and expected study specifications in hand, the field director now goes through the process of subcontracting the data collection to one or more field services, whether they be internal or external to the research supplier. This process sounds a lot easier than it actually is. Although a cost estimate is constructed internally, the budgeted amount must now be negotiated with the various services, usually through an oral agreement arranged by

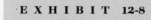

E X H I B I T 12-8

**Potential Costs Associated with Three Popular
Interviewing Methods**

Central location (WATS telephone)	Central location (Mall intercept)	Personal in-home (door-to-door)
Telephone charges	Location rental	Travel time
CRT terminal costs	Equipment rental (VCR, displays, refrigeration, etc.)	Mileage
	Supplies (cups, utensils, etc.)	
	Storage (product)	

telephone. It is a real challenge for the field director to bring the study in under budget given the variation of data-collection costs from market to market. Using good interpersonal skills, the successful field director manages to accomplish the task of obtaining quality work in a cost-efficient manner.

Now that agreement has been reached on the key parameters of the study relating to sampling technique, questionnaire length, incidence, cost and timing, an individual in the field department, usually called a field supervisor, sets out to prepare field instructions.

Field Instructions. Issuing field instructions to the party (parties) conducting the fieldwork is an attempt by the supplier to formalize the orally-agreed-to contract for services. Without mentioning the agreed upon cost-per-interview, the instructions generally specify what is considered acceptable interviewing techniques, what can be expected from the field service operator or designated representative, and how the specific interview at hand is to be administered by the interviewers themselves. These instructions are broken down into three common types: general, supervisor, and interviewer.

The general instructions reiterate to interviewers what is acceptable in both a technical and ethical sense. They may include direction on how to screen respondents by asking questions as they are stated, rather than in a manner that heightens the chance of finding a qualified respondent, and how to ask open-ended questions using the proper "probing" method. The reinforcement of good technique helps to insure the quality of the data-collection effort.

The second set of instructions is addressed to the interviewing supervisor. This letter provides the field operators with guidance in the planning, organization, and control of the fieldwork for which they are responsible. To begin with, it contains a "packing list" or itemization of all materials shipped that will be used by the interviewers, such as questionnaires, display materials, report forms, product, and so forth. Another section provides for the organization and control of the sample being utilized within the study; for example, it answers such questions as:

- Who is a qualified respondent?
- How should quota groups be filled?
- How do I keep track of the incidence of the groups that we are interviewing, and how and when are the key figures to be reported back to the supplier?
- When and where should the sample be selected?

A third portion of the supervisor instructions describes the interviewing procedure itself, as it is to be conveyed to the interviewers at the briefing. Finally, the agreed-upon work schedule is confirmed and billing instructions are provided.

The interviewer instructions constitute what is probably the key to valid and reliable data generation. This guide specifies detailed sample selection and questionnaire administration procedures on a question-by-question basis. It should provide direction for interviewers so that the fieldwork is conducted in a consistent fashion by all who are involved.

Briefing. Having received the necessary materials and instructions from the supplier, the field operator holds a meeting of all interviewers taking part in the study; this is often called a *briefing*. At this session, usually 2–3 hours in length, the field service supervisor makes clear what is expected of each interviewer working on the study. The field instructions are reviewed, and each interviewer gets a chance to administer the questionnaire in order to make it easier when actually meeting with respondents. The briefing is typically held on the same day as interviewing begins so as to keep the instructions clear in the interviewers' minds.

Data Collection. Obviously, the most critical portion of the fielding of a study is the actual data that will be used in the analysis of the marketing problem. If quality data are not provided in a timely manner, the marketing research effort is a waste of money.

The length of time needed for data collection may vary from a number of days to a number of months depending upon the incidence of or difficulty in finding the group under study, the length of interview, the sample size, and the number of interviewers working on the study. It typically takes under two weeks to complete.

The quality of fieldwork is enhanced through good communication between the supplier's field department and its "subcontractors"—that is, the field services. This process begins with the initial telephone alert, continues with good written instructions by the supplier and daily progress reporting by the service, and concludes with the suppliers' feedback of an independent validation report.

Evaluation of Fieldwork Quality. At the completion of the data-collection phase, the interviewer's work is scrutinized in at least two ways: *check-in* and *validation*. The completed work from a particular field service is usually checked in by one of the field supervisors at the supplier—the **check-in** process. At the lowest level of examination, the questionnaires are counted to make sure that the necessary quotas (or cells) have been completed properly. After this basic enumeration procedure has been conducted, the questionnaires usually undergo further checking in specific areas relating to complicated screening questions, skip patterns, open-ended question probing, and so on. Further details on check-in procedures will be discussed in Chapter 13.

The second important quality check on fieldwork is in making sure that the interview has actually taken place—the **validation** process. Between 10 and 20 percent of all respondents "reportedly" interviewed are recontacted by telephone and asked a few questions to verify that the interview did take place. These questions may involve qualifying criteria (such as, specific product usage) and questions generally related to the study (such as "Do you remember trying two cola soft drinks?"). When respondents cannot satisfactorily answer these questions, the interviews that they supposedly had taken part in are often declared "invalid" and not processed. Should more than one invalid questionnaire be traced to a given interviewer, it is often the practice to discard all of that interviewer's work.

INTERNATIONAL CONSIDERATIONS

In closing this chapter it is worthwhile to briefly comment on the problems in foreign primary data collection. In large measure, such problems are different from those in the United States only in degree. The success of a survey, be it internationally or nationally based, rests on the ability of the researcher to ask the right questions in a manner that increases the likelihood that the respondent will provide the desired information.

Several considerations should be made when conducting a marketing research study abroad.[15]

Unwillingness to Respond. In certain countries it is necessary to enlist the aid of locally prominent individuals to gain the cooperation of the community. A thorough understanding of the culture is necessary if satisfactory response rates are to be obtained. In some cultures a female will not consent to an interview by a male or any stranger. In other cultures men will be reticent to discuss such topics as personal hygiene or preferences in clothing because they feel it would be beneath their dignity—and most definitely not in the presence of a female interviewer.

[15]For further discussion of the following considerations see S. P. Douglas and S. Craig. *International Marketing Research* (Englewood Cliffs, N.J., Prentice-Hall, Inc. 1983) or P. C. Cateora. *International Marketing* 5th edition (Homewood, Ill.: Richard D. Irwin, Inc., 1983) Chapter 9.

The inability of the respondent to articulate the answer to a question should be seriously considered when conducting marketing research in foreign countries. In particular, the issue of *relevance*, discussed earlier in this chapter, is an important factor. It is difficult, if not impossible, for respondents to answer questions concerning goods and services that have never been available, are not in common use within the community, or whose use is not well understood.

Sampling and Fielding the Survey. In many countries telephone directories, census tract and block data, and detailed socioeconomic characteristics of the target population are just not available or, if available, may be uselessly dated. This adversely affects one's ability to draw nonprobability as well as probability designs and to conduct personal interviews of any variety. For example, without age distributions for the target population, it is difficult for the marketing researcher to set representative age quotas. Moreover, in certain cultures, convenient samples are doomed to failure. In Saudi Arabia, for instance, due to the practice of Purdah, shopping mall interviews produce all-male samples.[16]

Inadequate mailing lists and poor postal and telephone services can make marketing research in foreign countries extremely difficult. In many countries it is common to find that only a very small percentage of the population has telephones, and an alarmingly large percentage of the telephone lines (over fifty percent) may be out of service at the same time.[17] Mail surveys suffer from similar problems. Delays of weeks in delivery are common, and, in certain countries, expected response rates are lowered considerably because the questionnaire can be mailed back only at a post office.

Comprehension and Language. One of the primary difficulties in conducting marketing research abroad is that of language differences. Idioms and the difficulty of exact translation create problems in question construction and in interpreting the answers. Another problem is literacy. In some countries, written questionnaires are useless because of low literacy rates. Different dialects and languages can make a national survey extremely difficult and impractical. India, for example, has fourteen official languages and many more unofficial ones.

An obvious solution to the semantic problem is to have questionnaires prepared or reviewed by someone fluent in the native language. One variation is to have material translated from one language into another language and then have a third party translate it back into the original language. This is called **back translation.**

Back translation
Procedure in which material is translated from one language into another language and then translated back into the original language.

---

[16] David C. Pring, "American Firms Rely on Multinational Research Suppliers to Solve Marketing Problems Overseas," *Marketing News*, May 15, 1981, sect. 2, 2.

[17] "Cairo's Telephone System Improves," *World Business Weekly*, February 16, 1981, 19.

Researchers must always verify that the right questions are being asked. For instance, a *Reader's Digest* study of consumer behavior in Western Europe reported that France and West Germany consumed more spaghetti than Italy did. The question asked about branded and packaged spaghetti but did not ask about spaghetti purchased in bulk. Since most Italians purchase bulk spaghetti rather than branded or packaged spaghetti, their consumption was underestimated. If the goal of the research was to estimate packaged and branded spaghetti consumption, the results would have been correct. On the other hand, if the goal of the research was to estimate total spaghetti consumption, the results would have been incorrect.[18]

Summary

Questionnaire design and field execution are critical elements in survey research. Knowing how to properly ask a set of questions, how to effectively construct a questionnaire, and how to implement a field study is necessary to ensure that the desired information will be collected as efficiently as possible, whether in an internationally or nationally based study.

Key Concepts

Asking questions
Response formats
Questionnaire flow
Skip instructions
Preparation for data processing
Pretesting
Electronic questionnaire design
Fieldwork
International considerations

Review Questions

1. Describe the basic principles involved when asking questions.
2. Why should open-ended questions be asked?

---

[18]Charles S. Mayer, "The Lessons of Multinational Research," *Business Horizons*, December 1978, 11.

3. What are the critical elements to consider wh[...] of a questionnaire?
4. What are the major points to consider in laying out [...] naire?
5. Briefly describe the sequence of activities in fielding a study.

...ES FOR PART IV

...Makers Use "Image" Map
...Position Products:
...act Study

WALL STREET JOURNAL

Exasper... the growing similarity of cars on the road, a former Detroit auto executive recently remarked that if all of today's models were lined up end to end, even the top officers of the Big Three car makers would have a hard time telling them apart at a respectable distance.

The comment addresses an increasing challenge for automotive stylists and marketers. As fuel-efficiency requirements have narrowed design and performance characteristics for cars, the auto companies have had to turn to more subtle ways of drawing distinctions between different models. An example of how that is done is the "brand image" map shown below [Figure 1].

The map, created by the marketing department at Chrysler Corp., shows how car makers try to calculate differences between their products these days. "With size less a dominant factor, it's no longer that easy to know what any single product represents in the minds of consumers," says R. N. Harper Jr., manager of product marketing plans and research at the No. 3 car maker.

Marketing maps have been in use for some time at consumer-goods companies that sell near-generic items like cigarettes and dog food. But only recently have they become a valuable tool for "positioning" automobiles.

According to Mr. Harper, Chrysler draws up a series of such maps about three times a year, using responses to customer surveys. The surveys ask owners of different makes to rank their autos on a scale of one to 10 for such qualities as "youthfulness," "luxury," and "practicality."

Source: The Wall Street Journal, 22 March 1984, 31.

The answers are then worked into a mathematical score for each model and plotted on a graph that shows broad criteria for evaluating customer appeal.

The illustration below uses the technique to measure the images of the major divisions of U.S. auto makers, plus a few import companies. Using it, Chrysler would conclude, for instance, that the position of its Plymouth division in the lower left-hand quadrant means that cars carrying the Plymouth name generally have a practical, though somewhat stodgy, image. The Chrysler nameplate, by contrast, is perceived as more luxurious—though not nearly as luxurious as its principal competitors— Cadillac and Lincoln.

The map has other strategic significance, as well. By plotting on the map strong areas of customer demand, an auto maker can calculate whether its cars are on target. It can also tell from the concentration of

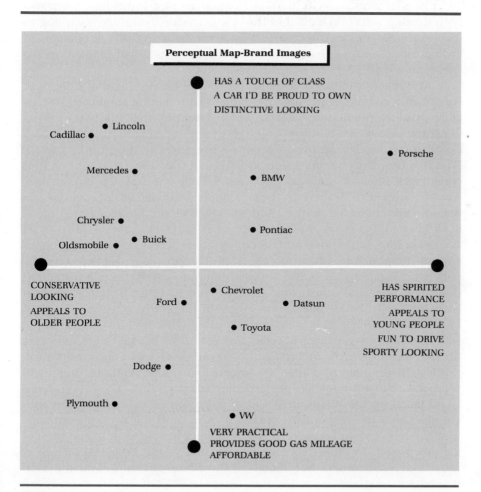

Perceptual Map-Brand Images

Figure 1

387

dots representing competing models how much opposition it is likely to get in a specific territory on the map. Presumably, cars higher up on the graph should also fetch a higher price than models ranked toward the bottom, where the stress is on economy and practicality.

After viewing the results for its divisions, Chrysler concluded that Plymouth, Dodge, and Chrysler all needed to present a more youthful image. It also decided that Plymouth and Dodge needed to move up sharply on the luxury scale.

Similarly, General Motors Corp. might find after looking at the map that its Chevrolet division, traditionally for entry-level buyers, ought to move down in practicality and more to the right in youthfulness. Another problem for GM on the map: the close proximity of its Buick and Oldsmobile divisions, almost on top of each other in the upper left-hand quadrant. That would suggest the two divisions are waging a marketing war more against each other than the competition.

Chrysler also uses its marketing map to plot individual models—both those it sells currently and those it plans for the future. By trying to move a model into an unoccupied space on the map through changes in styling, price or advertising, the company believes it can better hope to carve out a distinctive niche in the market.

"The real advantage of the map," says Mr. Harper, "is that it looks at cars from a consumer perspective while also retaining some sort of tangible product orientation." He says, for example, that his bosses were delighted when, on a recent map, Chrysler's forthcoming Lancer and Commander models showed up on the map next to the Honda Accord. (The two new Chrysler compacts are due out this fall.) "That told us that consumers think of our two new cars exactly the way we hoped they would," says Mr. Harper. "It was tangible evidence of where the car would compete in the market. And frankly, that can be hard to get these days."

A leading automobile manufacturer was interested in developing an "image" map for the subcompact market. The procedure agreed upon for collecting subcompact brand images differed slightly from the method described above. At most, four ratings were to be collected from each respondent. To be eligible for inclusion in the study, a respondent had to (1) have purchased a subcompact automobile within the last three years, (2) have been under 45 years of age, and (3) belong to a household, no member of which, including the respondent, was employed within the last three years by either an advertising, public relations, manufacturer/dealer of automobiles, or marketing research firm. The ratings were to be taken on the respondent's *ideal* subcompact automobile, the subcompact that the respondent *currently owns,* and the two subcompacts that the respondent *considered* when making his or her last purchase of a subcompact. In other words, a respondent would be asked to rate at most four subcompact automobiles. The dominant entries in the subcompact market are:

Pontiac Sunbird   Honda Accord
Chevrolet Cavalier   Toyota Celica
Oldsmobile Firenza   Toyota Corolla
Buick Skyhawk   Ford Tempo
Honda Civic   Nissan 200SX

Each automobile was to be rated on a set of 20 attributes. The attributes derived from focus group interviews are listed below.

Sensible	Independent	High performance
Comfortable	Contemporary	Practical
Dependable	Mature	Down-to-earth
Luxurious	Classic	Youthful
Exciting	Affordable	Efficient
Adventurous	Sporty	Economical
Fashionable	Family-oriented	

Rate 20 attributes for as many as 4 autos

The automobile manufacturer was also interested in understanding the trade-offs subcompact car purchasers make with respect to attributes such as

Economy
High performance
Ease in driving
Dependability

Standard demographic data were also to be collected.

Questions

DD   50 pts Due next Monday

1. The questionnaire developed by the marketing research group is shown in Exhibit 1. Based upon what you know about designing a questionnaire, discuss the following issues:
   - Is the questionnaire going to provide the necessary data?
   - Are there any problems with how the questions are asked?
   - Are there any problems with how the questions are constructed?
2. How can the questionnaire be improved? Develop a "better" questionnaire.
3. Prepare a set of interviewer instructions for your questionnaire.

EXHIBIT 1A

Survey of Subcompact Owners

Screener

Respondent's Full Name: _____

Address: _____

City: _____ State: _____ Zip Code: ____

Telephone Number: (____)_____

Interviewed by: _____ Date: _____

Hello, I'm _____ from _____.
We're conducting a study of automobile purchases, and I'd like to ask [*name
from listing*] a few questions about his/her selection of [*car make and model and
year*].

1. Are you or any member of your household employed by . . .?

An advertising or public relations firm	A
A manufacturer or dealer of automobiles, or	B
A marketing research company	C

[*If "yes" to any, terminate and circle next highest number:* 01 02 03 04 05 06 07 08
09 10 11 12 13 14 15. *Re-use screener.*]

2. Which of the following groups includes your age?

18–24	1
25–34	2
35–~~45~~ 44	3
~~45~~ or above	4 [*If 4, terminate and circle next highest number:* 01 02

03 04 05 06 07 08 09 10 11 12 13 14 15. *Re-use screener.*]

3. Are you . . .? [*Read list*]

Married	1
Single	2
Divorced	3
Separated	4
Widowed	5
[*Do not read*] *Refused*	y

4. What was the last grade of school *you* completed? [*Do not read list*]

No formal schooling	1
Completed grammar school	2
Some high school	3
Graduated high school	4
Some college	5
Graduated college	6
Refused	y

5. Is your annual household income before taxes . . .? [*Read list*]

Under $15,000	1
Between $15,000 and $24,999	2
Between $25,000 and $34,999	3
Between $35,000 and $49,999	4
$50,000 or more	5
[*Do not read*] Refused	6

6. Could you tell me the make, model, and year of your last car?

_____ _____ ____

7. Was ~~your previous~~ car new or used when you purchased it? *[handwritten: this]*

[handwritten: No]   New

      Used

[handwritten: No]

8. Do you still own ~~your previous~~ car? *[handwritten: this]*

      Yes

      No

9. Including yourself, how many persons are there in your household?

One	1
Two	2
Three	3
Four	4
Five	5
Six or more	6

[handwritten brace: Put under #3]

10. How many are over the age of seventeen?

      Number over 17 _____

11. Are there any other cars currently owned by members of your household?

      Yes

      No

12. Could you tell me their Makes, Models, and Years?

_____   _____   _____

_____   _____   _____

13. [If respondent still owns ~~previous~~ car or if other cars are owned by household members, ask:] Would you consider your [*name of car from listing*] your main or second car?

      Main

      Second

14. From the following list of options, would you tell me which ones you purchased? [*For each "no," ask:*] Did you consider purchasing the option?

Air conditioning	Yes	Considered	*[handwritten: Don't use]*
Automatic transmission	Yes	Considered	
Special radio or cassette	Yes	Considered	
Sunroof	Yes	Considered	
Special wheels	Yes	Considered	
Turbocharger	Yes	Considered	
Power steering	Yes	Considered	
Dual mirrors	Yes	Considered	
Tinted glass	Yes	Considered	

15. Could you tell me which of the following features were major factors and which were minor factors in your choice of your [*car name from listing*]?

      Economy

      Easy to drive

      High performance

      Dependability

[handwritten: Want to know trade-off]

391

16. Which of the following words describe your ideal car? [On "A" forms, start at top of list; on "B" forms, start at bottom of list]

1	Sensible	____
2	Comfortable	____
3	Dependable	____
4	Luxurious	____
5	Exciting	____
6	Adventurous	____
7	Fashionable	____
8	Independent	____
9	Contemporary	____
10	Generous	____
11	Mature	____
12	Classic	____
13	Affordable	____
14	Sporty	____
15	Family-oriented	____
16	Careful	____
17	Performance	____
18	Necessity	____
19	Practical	____
20	Down-to-earth	____
21	Youthful	____
22	Efficient	____

[handwritten: only deals w/ the ideal car]

Case 2: Thwack! Smack! Sounds Thrill Makers of Hunt's Ketchup

By Betsy Morris
Staff Reporter of *THE WALL STREET JOURNAL*

For 20 years, the makers of Hunt's ketchup have been seeing red as their product played the patsy in those relentless commercials by Heinz.

First, they watched as their own brand sopped out onto paper napkins, bleeding puddles that were always bigger and runnier than Heinz's. Then they watched as their ketchup cascaded out of bottles, oozed through coffee filters, dribbled down plates.

Each time the Hunt's gushed all too readily down one side of the television screen, Heinz inched ever so slowly down the other, underscoring its claim as "the slowest ketchup in the West" and "the taste that's worth the wait."

Though Hunt's wasn't often identified by name, its producers took the whole thing quite personally. "God, it made me angry," says Frederick

Source: The Wall Street Journal, 27 April 1984, 1.

B. Rentschler, president and chief executive of Swift/Hunt-Wesson Inc., the Esmark Inc. unit that makes Hunt's. "I winced every time I heard of those."

But as it says in the Heinz commercial, good things come to those who wait. After years of trying, Hunt-Wesson has finally succeeded in concocting a ketchup as thick, rich, and hard to shake out of the bottle as Heinz. In advertisements that began last fall, country-and-western singer Roy Clark boasts: "You can't buy a thicker ketchup (than Hunt's), so why pay more for Heinz?" The long-running Heinz ads have quietly disappeared.

Question

1. Design a questionnaire to determine (1) consumers' attitudes toward the new reformulated thicker Hunt's ketchup, (2) whether consumers prefer the new reformulation to the old standard and (3) whether they prefer it to the market leader, Heinz. Also of interest to management is the question of whether segments exist that exhibit differential preference for the new entry. A final issue of some concern centers on whether there exists other unmet end-benefits that Hunt can capitalize on in future product reformulation.

Case 3: S&L's Pushing to End Homebuyers' Preference for Fixed-Rate Loans

By Timothy D. Schellhardt and Christopher Conte
Staff Reporters of THE WALL STREET JOURNAL

Washington—The savings and loan industry is beginning a new effort to end America's love affair with the fixed-rate mortgage.

Many thrift institutions were nearly ruined in the past few years by heavy holdings in cheap, fixed-rate, 30-year home loans, and they are dismayed by a recent resurgence of the mortgages, the traditional mainstay of home finance. With the help of sympathetic regulators, S&Ls are trying anew to wed home buyers to adjustable-rate mortgages, which fluctuate with market rates. (S&Ls are the nation's major home-mortgage lenders, with about 40% of the market.)

Large West Coast S&Ls are spearheading the effort. They are trying to redirect the efforts of the government-controlled Federal Home Mortgage Corp. away from its historical preoccupation with fixed-rate loans.

Source: The Wall Street Journal, 1 July 1983, 17.

"Fixed-rate mortgages are out of the question," asserts Leonard Shane, chairman of Mercury Savings Association of Huntington Beach, Calif., and head of the U.S. League of Savings Institutions. "There's no way fixed-rate mortgages will survive."

The S&Ls' chief ally is Edwin Gray, a former California S&L executive and the new chairman of both the Federal Home Loan Bank Board and the mortgage corporation, which is affiliated with the Bank Board. He has made promoting variable-rate mortgages a cornerstone of his first few months in office.

Homebuyers' Preference

The industry's trouble is that some 70% of all home buyers prefer fixed-rate mortgages, according to a recent Louis Harris Poll and Bank Board statistics on mortgage originations. Sensing the public mood, Congress has made it clear that it wants government-sponsored housing corporations to support a "viable fixed-rate mortgage market."

"Consumers have simply made up their minds they don't like adjustable-rate mortgages," says Michael Sumichrast, chief economist of the National Association of Home Builders. "How are you going to fight it?"

Adjustable-rate mortgages came into widespread use a few years ago when interest rates soared, and many lenders became reluctant to make fixed-rate home loans. But as mortgage rates dropped, home buyers showed a preference for fixed-rate loans, including government-backed mortgages, which come only with fixed rates.

In addition, some new investors in the increasingly important secondary, or resale, mortgage market also have shown a preference for fixed-rate mortgages. Such investors as pension funds and insurance companies actively seek long-term loans that allow them to project their returns many years into the future.

Mr. Gray and industry people are concentrating their lobbying efforts on the mortgage corporation, known as Freddie Mac. Historically, it has bought mostly fixed-rate loans from mortgage originators and sold them, packaged as securities, to investors.

Prodded by its chairman, Mr. Gray, Freddie Mac is launching a national "educational" campaign to promote adjustable-rate mortgages. Besides touting the advantages of so-called ARMs in national advertisements aimed at home lenders, the corporation plans to train S&L officials to design and market them.

The corporation has also started a national study to determine what type of adjustable-rate mortgage will appeal to the public, and it has agreed to become more aggressive in buying different kinds of variable-rate loans from mortgage originators. Mr. Shane says the corporation has promised to buy at least $100 million of the mortgages by year-end, up from $49.6 million last year.

To Mr. Gray, the rationale for switching to adjustable-rate mortgages is obvious. He warns S&L officials to avoid the danger that threatened their industry during the past several years—financing long-term, fixed-rate loans with volatile short-term deposits. Variable-rate loans, he says, enable institutions to match their income and their costs, thus insulating them from volatile interest rates.

"For the savings and loan business, the long-term, fixed-rate mortgage that stays on your books represents the closest thing I can think of to financial arsenic," he recently told Texas S&L officials. "The only known real antidote is the ARM."

Mr. Gray's advice apparently is having some effect. According to a U.S. League survey, 40% of the nation's thrifts aren't making fixed-rate loans, and banking industry officials say that an even higher percentage of banks may have stopped offering them. However, other S&Ls, banks and mortgage bankers are taking up the slack and making the fixed-rate loans. And, according to an industry economist, "a lot more retain them in their own portfolios than admit they do."

The advantage of adjustable-rate mortgages for consumers, their backers argue, are that the rate can decline and, unlike most fixed-rate mortgages made these days, changeable-rate loans can usually be assumed by a new buyer.

Many home buyers, however, see variable-rate mortgages as merely a device to transfer interest-rate risks to them and away from lenders. Says Maurice Mann, vice chairman of Warburg, Paribas, Becker Inc.: "As long as people expect inflation, it's going to be very hard to get them away from fixed-rate mortgages."

Proponents of variable-rate mortgages complain that S&Ls haven't been competitive enough in setting rates on the adjustable loans. They contend that variable-rate loans could be offered profitably at very attractive rates but that such loans are generally being made at only a percentage point or two below the rate on fixed-rate loans. Many consumers aren't willing to take on the added risk associated with a floating rate loan for such a small rate advantage.

Capital-Market Investors

The biggest problem for the variable-rate loans may be that many investors in the capital markets like fixed-rate loans. Their main concern with mortgages is that they are often paid off before maturity, and clever underwriters are developing techniques to package fixed-rate mortgages for sale to such investors in ways that provide protection against such early retirement.

Much to the chagrin of fixed-rate opponents, Freddie Mac recently offered $1 billion in securities backed by long-term loans with features that provided some call-protection. The combination proved highly popular, and undoubtedly will be used again.

"There's always going to be a fixed-rate mortgage as long as there's a secondary market," says Jay Connolly, a vice president at Salomon Brothers, the investment-banking firm.

Mr. Shane argues that capital markets won't provide enough funds to meet total housing demand. But Mr. Mann counters that the secondary market "has an unlimited absorptive capacity" for mortgages.

Despite the pressure from S&Ls, most housing analysts say it's up to the industry to lure consumers away from fixed-rate mortgages. "The best we can do is keep a solid, fixed-rate program going and ascertain the best ARM product we can," concludes Lee Holmes, senior vice president for Freddie Mac. Adds Mr. Connolly: "It all boils down to the final product and whether consumers see it as desirable."

Questions

1. Discuss the measurement and scaling issues that should be considered when developing an attitudinal study on ARMs.
2. Fixed-rate loans change over time; for example in 1986 fixed rates were in the 10–11 percent range. Do consumers' attitudes toward fixed-rate loans vis-á-vis ARMs change with the absolute level of fixed rates? If so, how do S&L's account for this situational effect in measuring attitudes?
3. Using an attitudinal framework, how would you answer the question proposed by Mr. Connolly: "It all boils down to the final product and whether consumers see it as desirable."

Case 4: Consumer Attitudes and Perceptions Toward Seafood When Eating Out: Measurement Development

In Part II, Case Study 2, we introduced the preliminary phase of a study focusing on consumers' attitudes and perceptions toward seafood—in particular, nontraditional species—when eating out. The following describes the results from the focus group interviews.

Eating Fish in Restaurants

Fish was seldom consumed at home. Participants objected to the residual odor after its preparation.

Those who do prepare fish at home emphasize the ease with which it can be prepared.

■ "I like to eat foods I don't eat at home—my daughter is allergic to fish so we don't eat it at home."

Source: Materials for this case were supplied by Dr. Robert C. Lewis of the Department of Hotel and Restaurant Administration, University of Massachusetts.

- "I like to eat fish when it's been cooked by someone else."
- "We never cook fish at home, but we love seafood so we go out."
- "I don't like the smell of fish at home—when I go out that's my chance to have fish."
- "No one else in the house eats fish, so I get it when I go out."
- "I eat it more away from home because of the odor."
- "Fish out is a treat."
- "It's always a treat to have fish at home."
- "I don't think I've ever left home thinking about having a super fish meal. The only time I've done that is when I'm on vacation, down on the Cape or something."
- "Preparation of good fresh fish is quickly done at home—under the broiler—it's easy—so I order more difficult things when I go out."

Several participants established a linkage between trust in the knowledge of the restaurant staff and their willingness to try new dishes.

- "The better the restaurant—the more trust I have in the waiter and the more willing I am to try."
- "I'd have more trust in a more expensive restaurant—they pay their help better to be more informed."
- "If you've eaten in a restaurant before you know how they cook."

Trust in the freshness of fish was also an issue.

- "I'll eat fish only in a restaurant that specializes—otherwise I feel it's not fresh—probably frozen."
- "I wouldn't ask them—they don't know."
- "If you're at the shore and you don't order seafood you're foolish."

Some respondents were purists who preferred their fish broiled with butter and lemon, while others either had a favorite sauce or were willing to try new methods of preparation.

- "I don't like anything fried."
- "I like fish in a casserole."
- "Broiled or baked is always dry."
- "No bread crumbs—I like to see the fish."
- "It depends on the texture—is it flaky and moist or like rubber?"
- "If they're going to charge a big price I would hope they would do something to it."
- "I choose the fish first, then the method of preparation."

Some participants had tried a range of sauces and enjoyed them, while others had not.

Pro
- "Dill sauces"
- "Newburgh"
- "Ginger sauce"
- "Nothing too overpowering"
- "I had a good white wine cheese sauce—it was excellent."

397

Con

- "Never had any."
- "Don't like sauces—just butter."
- "Sauce could kill a good piece of fish—I like just lemon."
- "When I'm eating fish for health and weight, I stick to vegetables—no bread, no potatoes. I'd be defeating the purpose with a sauce."

Barriers to Fish Consumption

Some participants did not prepare fish at home because of the work involved in cleaning and deboning fish.

- "I don't like really strong fish."
- "I don't like the odor or a fishy taste."
- "I don't like bones—that's why I usually get schrod."
- "I don't like bones—I don't like to be surprised."
- "The skin is usually chewy and slimy."
- "I fish a lot—to get rid of bones it depends on the size of the fish and how you fillet it."

The discussion of odor led to some mention of freshness in several groups.

- "Fresh fish doesn't smell."
- "I get fish on the Cape—it has no odor."
- "Fresh-caught fish has no smell."
- "Supermarket fish smells when you cook it."
- "When you buy fish you can see how fresh it is."
- "Oh, you can taste the difference."
- "In most big restaurants it's easy to get fresh fish."
- "If I'm in another part of the country I won't order fish."

Reactions to Specific Fish

None of the fish named as favorites could be considered nontraditional. Schrod and swordfish were named most often.

- "I like schrod—there's an occasional bone but it's not too bad."
- "I'd go for swordfish if you want a meatier fish."
- "I go deep sea fishing—I like flounder."
- "I like schrod—it's tender and moist."
- "Swordfish is my favorite—it's meatier, solid, chewy."
- "Swordfish has more flavor—almost sweet."
- "Salmon for one—I love the color—I was brought up on it."
- "Schrod—it's light, not oily, juicy."
- "I like schrod—the taste isn't fishy, it's flaky."
- "I like white fish that are sweet."
- "Fillet of sole, sometimes schrod."
- "I like swordfish or salmon for the taste and texture."

- "Haddock—flavorful but mild."
- "Haddock—out of habit."
- "Haddock—a nice piece of fish, not too gamy."
- "I like salmon with hollandaise sauce."

PART IV

Case Studies

Attitudes Toward Nontraditional Fish

Of those people who were reluctant to try new fish, the monetary risk was occasionally mentioned as a reason.

- "I don't want to pay $8 or $9 for something I might not like."
- "If you're going to spend $10 or $15, why try something you don't know you're going to like when there are so many good things on the menu?"

For an overwhelming majority of participants, the name of the fish caused considerable reaction. Some reactions to specific fish are listed below:

Shark
- "I think it sounds unappetizing—*Jaws*—it bothers me to be deceived."
- "I suppose I would try it if I was in one of those moods to try something new."
Tilefish
- "Makes me think of Spanish or Italian tiles."
Monkfish
- "Doesn't sound tempting."
Skate
- "I think they ought to change the name—it sounds sharp."

In each of the groups there were participants who were eager to try new types of seafood or new methods of preparation and others who liked to play it safe.

- "I'll try something new if the ingredients look good."
- "I wouldn't order something I'd never had—a lot of fish is too strong."
- "I might taste someone else's."
- "If there is something in it that I know I like—otherwise I wouldn't risk it."
- "I tried shark—it was really tasty—my dad came back from San Francisco and he was raving about it."

Participants were asked what they thought of specific seafoods named by the moderator. In some cases they reacted to the fish based on having tasted it, while in other cases they reacted to the name or its reputation. Some specific reactions are listed below:

Cod
- "Cod is a wormy fish."

399

Flounder

- "Flounder is a bottom feeder."

Pollock

- "I liked it; I've cooked it—it has a stronger flavor than schrod—it's a cheaper fish."

Whitefish

- "The only way I've had it was smoked—smoked was greasy."
- "It sounds like it's related to schrod or haddock."
- "Yes, sounds like schrod."

Mackerel

- "That's ok; it's a fish, not a predator."
- "You see them all the time in the grocery store."

Less well-known seafoods were greeted with a degree of suspicion. It may be inferred that the most common consumers' attitude is that if a species is underutilized there must be a reason.

Shark

- "Most people have probably eaten shark and didn't realize it—it sometimes passes for swordfish or scallops."
- "Don't tell me it's shark—I don't want to know."
- "I couldn't try shark—I don't know why—I just couldn't."

Butterfish

- "None would get my interest."
- "Maybe it's like sole or schrod."
- "It would be something I would ask about."
- "I would have to know what it tasted like."
- "I would try it if it were boneless, white."

Monkfish

- "They're the ugliest things in the world."

Skate

- "That doesn't sound good."
- "You know those perfectly round scallops, those are mostly skate, sometimes shark."
- "They look like rays."
- "If you saw one after you'd caught one you'd probably never eat it."

Eel

- "I liked it."
- "No—I've caught one—they're slimy things."
- "No way I'd try it."
- "I've tried it—I didn't like the texture."
- "Definitely out—that's like a snake."
- "It tastes like salmon."
- "It's oily."
- "I've had it in a tomato and onion sauce—it's really not bad."

Squid

- "Definitely no."
- "I had it—didn't like it—nothing to do with the taste—it's the way they look."
- "My wife's family had it every Christmas—I've made it through all these years without trying it."
- "I think of those things as reptiles."
- "I would be more willing to try some of these exotic names if I was on vacation in a place where that might be the main food."

Questions

1. How can the results of the focus group session help in developing a questionnaire dealing with consumers' attitudes and perceptions toward nontraditional fish when eating out?
2. Prepare an outline of the questionnaire you would use to measure consumers' attitudes and perceptions toward nontraditional fish when eating out.
3. Based upon the information provided above and your answer to question 2, develop a set of measurement scales to measure consumers' attitudes and perceptions toward nontraditional fish when eating out.

PART V

DATA PROCESSING AND ANALYSIS

Having decided what information is needed to solve the marketing problem at hand—how to acquire the necessary data, who should be in the sample, what questions to ask, and how to construct the questionnaire—we now turn to analysis and interpretation. Specifically, in Chapter 13 we discuss the activities necessary to prepare the raw data collection forms for analysis; in Chapter 14 various methods for summarizing data are presented. These procedures are extremely useful in acquiring an understanding of the nature of a set of data. Chapter 15 discusses procedures for testing hypotheses concerning means and proportions. These procedures allow us to make inferences from the data collected (i.e., the sample) to the target population of interest. Finally, in Chapter 16 we take up the important topic of correlation and regression analysis. These procedures allow us to investigate the relationships among a set of variables with a view toward explaining the phenomena under study.

An appendix which discusses several of the more popular multivariate data analysis procedures is also provided. Multivariate analysis deals with the *simultaneous* relationships among three or more variables, as opposed to the analysis of a single variable, or the analysis of pairwise relationship between two variables. Over the past decade multivariate data analysis techniques have seen wider acceptance and use in almost all fields of inquiry, due in large measure to the advent of high speed, large storage capacity computers and easy-to-use software packages for implementing multivariate analyses. Though it is beyond the scope of this text to discuss multivariate data analysis methods in great detail, the appendix should nevertheless provide an adequate introduction to this class of procedures. In addition Chapter 17, Part VI, applies several of these procedures in the context of product positioning, market segmentation and market structure analysis.

Data Processing and Tabulation

CHAPTER OBJECTIVES

- Explain the functions necessary to transform the information contained in the questionnaires into a form that allows the data to be analyzed.
- Describe the procedures for checking in questionnaires.
- Describe the process of editing.
- Define basic concepts and terms relating to how the raw data are put into a machine-readable form.
- Explain coding practices for open-ended questions.
- Discuss code sheet building.
- Describe the processes involved in transcribing raw data onto magnetic tape or disk or directly into the computer.
- Describe sample balancing, a procedure for statistically adjusting the data prior to analysis.
- Discuss how sample tables and banners are specified.
- Discuss several typical scale transformations that render the data comparable across respondents or items.

Introduction

We now turn to discuss data-analysis issues. The first step in data analysis is to transform the information contained in the validated questionnaires into a form that allows the data to be analyzed, efficiently and accurately. This chapter describes the activities necessary to prepare the **raw data** collection forms for data analysis. Only after we understand what must be done to get the questionnaires into a form that allows analysis of the data they contain can we turn our attention to how the data are analyzed.

The functions described in this chapter serve two purposes. First, they establish, as far as possible, uniformity in the processing of data. Among other things, this uniformity allows comparisons to be made

Raw data Respondent's answers to questions as they are contained on the questionnaire.

404

across similar tests of different product categories. Second, they establish the rules and/or guidelines for the various steps in processing the data. The major steps in processing the data are

- check-in
- editing
- coding
- transcription and cleaning
- statistical adjustment
- data transformations
- tabulation specifications

Our discussion of data processing will describe each step.

CHECK-IN

The **check-in procedure** involves checking a job in from the field. Involved are (1) a check of all questionnaires for completeness and interviewing quality and (2) a count of usable questionnaires by required quota and/or cell groups, according to study design.

Check-in procedure
Initial step in data processing; involves a check of all questionnaires for completeness and interviewing quality and a count of usable questionnaires by required quota and/or use groups as per study design.

Checking for Acceptable Questionnaires. After a questionnaire is received from the field, it must be inspected to determine whether it is acceptable for use in the study. Several problems relating to completeness and interviewing quality can cause a questionnaire to be excluded:

1. Portions of the questionnaire, or key questions, are left unanswered.
2. There is evidence that the respondent did not understand the instructions for filling out the questionnaire and/or did not take the task seriously. For example, in the former instance, it may be obvious that skip patterns were not followed properly; in the latter instance, the answers to the questions may show very little variance, say, all 1s or all 7s on a series of 7-point rating items.
3. The returned questionnaire may be physically incomplete, having a page or several pages missing.
4. The questionnaire may have been filled out by someone who should have been screened out of the sample—that is, someone who does not qualify for the target population.
5. The questionnaire may have been completed properly but returned after a preestablished cutoff date.

[handwritten margin note: Very hard to determine]

Notes should be maintained on the quality of the fieldwork throughout the check-in process, as well as during subsequent processing functions, for feedback to local supervisors.

Counting the Questionnaires. The marketing research proposal specifies the sampling requirements. A count of usable questionnaires by required quota and/or cell groups must be maintained to detect any problems in adhering to the study design. Shortages must be identified and a replacement action determined while the study is still in the field. Acceptable attrition levels should be established in advance. The local supervisor should forward returned questionnaires to the research firm so that check-in editing and code building can start as soon as possible, as opposed to holding them until all of the fieldwork is completed.

EDITING

Editing process Review of the questionnaires for maximum accuracy and precision.

    The **editing process** involves reviewing the questionnaires for maximum accuracy and precision. Editing may be done by hand and/or on a machine as part of the cleaning process. Whether done by hand or by machine, written instructions are required to ensure that the editing is done consistently. Typically, abbreviations are used in writing the field and hand-editing instructions. The following example shows typical instructions and what they mean for one question from a carbonated soft drink survey.

E X A M P L E

P #	Q #	CARD/COL (2 digits)	Condition
2 [page no. 2]	6 [question no. 6]	112 [When transferring to a computer card, the response to this question will appear in card 1 column 12.]	If blue Q'RE MB 112/1–7 [If the response is any of the seven diet carbonated soft drinks listed under question no. 6, then respondent will receive a blue questionnaire and one of the 1–7 boxes must be (MB) checked.]
			If yellow Q'RE MB 112/8 and (113/1-y or 114/1–5, 9, 0) [If response is not any one of the seven diet soft drink brands listed under question no. 6, then the 8-box must be checked and respondent should receive a yellow questionnaire. In such cases, if the respondent indicated another carbonated soft drink a 1 will appear

in card 1 column 13, indicating a yes, and the actual brands mentioned will be coded 1–5; a 9 indicates that other than a carbonated soft drink was mentioned; a 0 indicates that no other brand was mentioned, that is, card 1 column 14 is blank.]

Notice that part of the editing instructions involve coding. We have discussed how closed-ended questions are precoded in Chapter 12 and will soon discuss coding of open-ended questions.

Obviously, the extent to which the editing is consistent depends in large measure on the number of persons responsible for the editing function. In a small study one person may do all editing, and consistency is likely to be high. In the case of a large study, more than one person probably will be involved in the editing process and consequently consistency checks must be instituted.

As we indicated, response consistency and accuracy are the primary concerns in editing. Editing instructions are written to include as complete a check as possible for consistency. When two answers are inconsistent—for example, the respondent indicates no familiarity with the test brand, but also indicates that the brand was purchased on the last shopping trip—it may be possible to determine which, if either, of the two is correct. When this is not possible, both answers should be discarded. With respect to accuracy the person responsible for editing concentrates on signs of interviewer bias or cheating; for example, common patterns of responses across different questionnaires for the same interviewer or recorder can signal potential problems. Finally, in addition to accuracy and consistency the person conducting the editing function is also concerned with (1) response legibility, (2) response clarity, and (3) response completeness. In all cases the person doing the editing follows the editing instructions in correcting any ambiguities, or, if possible, consults the interviewer or recorder.

CODING PROCEDURES

Put simply, **coding** involves assigning a numerical value (code) or alphanumeric symbol to represent (1) a specific response to a specific question and (2) the column position that the designated code or symbol will occupy on a data record. The coding process entails several different

Coding Assignment of a numerical value (code) or alphanumerical symbol to represent a specific response to a specific question along with the column position that the designated code or symbol will occupy on a data record.

Precoding Coding specifications designated prior to fieldwork.

Postcoding Coding specifications designated after the questionnaires have been returned from the field.

activities. For certain types of question formats (such as closed-ended questions), the coding specifications are designated before fieldwork begins (**precoding**). We have discussed precoding activities in some detail in Chapter 12. Open-ended questions are much more likely to have the coding specifications designated after the questionnaires have been returned from the field (**postcoding**), although in certain instances a coding scheme for such questions can be developed before the completion of the fieldwork.

Open-Ended Questions

As we indicated in Chapter 12 not all studies include open-ended questions. When they are included, however, their primary purpose is to obtain the respondent's own verbalization of, comprehension of, and reaction to stimuli. Consequently, coding open-ended responses can be difficult, and explicit instructions are necessary to insure consistency among coders. The initial work of all coders is usually checked until it is clear that each coder thoroughly understands the codes. Continuing spot checks are also routinely made.

As a general rule, the construction of codes for open-ended questions must proceed with the defined study objectives in mind. In Chapter 12 we discussed situations when open-ended questions may be used. The following list provides some general guidelines on how codes should be built.[1]

1. Check prior studies or structured questions within the same study to help build codes to meet the objectives of the specific open-ended questions. For example, (1) codes should include a repetition of the specific attributes the structured question is designed to measure so as to check the results of those questions; and/or (2) codes from a prior study should be used when we want to track changes in specific open-ended questions.

2. Be sure to cover critical issues even if no one mentioned them. For example, in a test of two commercials involving alternative communication objectives, codes should be developed which include each communication objective regardless of whether respondents actually played them back. In certain instances it is extremely important to know that no one mentioned a particular response. Consider, for instance, the situation of investigating deception in advertising.

3. If open-ended questions are used to obtain direct comparisons and more specific areas of preference and rejection when two or more products or concepts are involved in a test, the codes constructed must correctly reflect all the thoughts and reactions of the respondent to the preferred/not-preferred products or concepts.

[1]Parts of this material were adapted from J. Pope, *Practical Marketing Research* (New York: AMACOM, 1981), 89–90.

4. When open-ended questions are used to determine respondent's affective reactions or feelings as a result of exposure to a stimulus (such as a commercial, concept, package, product, or ad), the codes must be inclusive; that is, built to reflect all of the respondent's reactions or feelings, whether they be totally negative, totally positive, or a combination of both.

Most codes, regardless of the objectives, require what are called **nets,** basic category headings. These category headings group different ways of expressing a basic idea. Examples of such group headings are:

Nets Basic category headings.

Efficacy: Relieves headache pain
Fast relief
Long lasting relief
Extra strength relief

Aroma: Smells like an imported cigar
Smells like an expensive cigar
Smells good

There are two reasons to have category headings. First, category headings help to organize responses relating to one idea. Second, and perhaps more importantly, category headings determine how many *respondents* made comments related to the category as opposed to how many *responses* were made. For this purpose it is necessary to net responses relating to the category. For example, if taste were an objective of an ad or commercial, you would want to know how many people expressed an idea related to taste. Without a net of the category a table might look like this:

Efficacy

Relieves headache pain	50
Fast relief	35
Long lasting relief	12
Extra strength relief	26

There are, in fact, 123 references to efficacy. Those 123 references could have been made by as many as 123 people (if each person only referred to efficacy once) or as few as 50 people, all of whom mentioned headache relief and/or another phrase as well. It is almost a certainty that the total number of people is somewhere between 50 and 123 because neither of the extremes described is likely to happen. Thus, one must obtain a net count of people who made one or more references to efficacy. These nets can be accomplished in the actual coding or by machine.

Code Sheets

Code sheets instruct the coders on how to handle each question.

Code Sheet Building. When codes are defined, a listing of all types of responses being assigned to each code should be made on the code sheet. A listing of all responses will enable coders to know the specific responses that apply to specific codes; that is, responses such as, "is dietetic," "has less calories," "good for people watching their weight," all go into "low calorie" code. In addition, all codes are to reflect the totality of the actual response. A code list that includes the totality of responses will eliminate *incorrect* and misleading key-word coding. Consider the following illustrations of incorrect key-word coding:

> **Response:** "No beer is better than Bud"
> **Incorrectly Coded:** Prefer Budweiser
> **Response:** "Can pay off in monthly installments"
> **Incorrectly Coded:** Economical
> **Response:** "Is sugar-free"
> **Incorrectly Coded:** Dislike taste

Coders must keep a list of "all other" mentions within *each* category heading not covered by specific codes within the category heading. Typically each response is listed by questionnaire number. A tabulation is required of the number of times each separate "all other" mention is made. When a specific response is mentioned by, say, 5 percent or more respondents, the "all other" mention is a specific code.

Abbreviations of the code definitions in the final summary or computer tables are not allowed when such abbreviations in any way alter or do not entirely reflect the *meaning* of the code definition. An example of abbreviation where meaning is changed follows:

- *Code on code sheet*—"Leaves hair manageable, no tangles, no need for cream rinse"
- *Code incorrectly reported on table with abbreviation*—"No need for cream rinse"

Code Sheet Formats. The code sheet consists of the following elements:

1. *Heading.* The heading identifies the study, the particular question, and the card and column numbers in the data record.
2. *Column identification.* Each applicable column is to be listed on the left-hand side of the page with the appropriate punches, and all columns used to code the questions are to be listed at the top of the page.
3. *Coding instructions.* Limitations/restrictions and required multiple codes are to be stated next to each code where applicable.
4. *Special instructions.* Instructions for the use of "borrowed columns"

or use of columns out of sequence are to be written at the bottom of the appropriate code sheet.

5. *Standard requirement.* On all questions (close-ended and open-ended) use x = don't know; y = no answer. These codes must be in the last column of the field used for that question.

A prototypical code sheet is displayed in Exhibit 13-1.

EXHIBIT 13-1

Prototypical Code Sheet

Study # _____562_____

Subject/objective of question(s): Carbonated soft drinks—selected brands used in past 3 months

Page(s) of questionnaire: __2 of screener__

Question(s): _____7_____

What other brands of carbonated soft drinks have you yourself drunk during the past three months?

Cols. ____25–26____

Card _____1_____

Col. 25 –1 Dr. Pepper
         –2 Coke
         –3 Classic Coca-Cola
         –4 7-up
         –5 Sprite
         –6 Slice
         –7 Pepsi
         –8 Cherry Coca-Cola
         –9 Fanta
         –0 C & C Cola
         –x RC Cola
         –y Mountain Dew

Col. 26 –1 Diet Coke
         –2 Tab
         –3 Diet Pepsi
         –4 Diet 7-up
         –5 Diet Sprite
         –6 Diet Slice
         –7
         –8
         –9 Brand names, non-specific carbonated soft drinks
         –0 All other carbonated soft drinks
         –x Don't know
         –y No answer

TRANSFERRING THE DATA

The next phase in data processing involves physically transferring the data from the questionnaires onto magnetic tape or disk or directly into the computer via CRT entry. With CATI and computer-assisted systems there is no need to transfer the data since data are put into computer memory at time of collection. As we indicated in Chapter 12, tab houses typically key punch the data first and then transfer to magnetic tape. Two other methods are available for transferring the data. The first utilizes **mark-sensed questionnaires** that require answers to be recorded with a special pencil in an area coded specifically for that answer and machine-readable. The second is **optical scanning,** which involves direct machine reading of the numerical values or alphanumeric codes and transcription onto cards, magnetic tape, or disk.

Mark-sensed questionnaire Format that requires answers to be recorded with a special pencil in an area coded specifically for that answer and which can be read by a machine.

Optical scanning Direct machine reading of numerical values or alphanumeric codes and transcription onto cards, magnetic tape, or disk.

Verification

As we indicated most tab houses use key-punching services. Key punching is relatively fast and inexpensive—an experienced keypunch operator can complete about 100 cards per hour at a cost of 20–25 cents per card. Experienced keypunch operators do not make many errors. There are no standard requirements for keypunch **verification.** Verification is possible with use of a verifier machine and a second operator. The second operator essentially repunches the data from the original questionnaire, and this card is compared with the original card. If the two cards match, nothing happens; if they do not match, the questionnaire is singled out and put aside for reentry. A similar procedure is available for data stored on magnetic tape or disk. This type of verification generally doubles both the time and cost of data entry.

Verification Procedures aimed at ensuring that data from the original questionnaires have been accurately transcribed onto computer cards, magnetic tape or disk.

With CATI or computer-assisted systems the data entry is automatic. However, because data entry occurs at the time the information is recorded, a different approach to verification is needed. First, the system should allow a mistake to be corrected before it becomes part of the data file. Second, it is often desirable to let the interviewer (CATI) or respondent (computer-assisted) see the recorded answer on the screen and then have the respondent verify or contradict the response. If the answer is verified the next question is repeated; if the answer is contradicted the question is asked again.

Cleaning

The data must be completely cleaned prior to final tabulating. **Cleaning** includes a check of all internal consistencies, all possible codes, and all impossible punch codes.

Cleaning A check of all internal consistencies, all possible codes, and all impossible punches.

Multipunches. Consider the cleaning instructions for question number 7 shown in the example below.

E X A M P L E

Q#	BASE	Card #	Col. #	Type / Legal Punches	Notes
7	TR	1	25	MP(1-y)	If not 12/1-7, MB12/8 and
			26	MP(1-5, 9, 0, x, y)	MB(13/(1-9, 0, x, y) or 14/(1-5, 9, 0, x, y)

The base for this question is all respondents (TR); answers to this question should appear on card number 1 and in columns 25 and 26. For column 25 the legitimate codes are 1, 2, 3, 4, 5, 6, 7, 8, 9, 0, x, y; for column 26 the legitimate codes are 1, 2, 3, 4, 5, 9, 0, x, y. (See also Exhibit 13-1). Because this question involves multiple responses—a respondent can have eaten more than one brand of cold cereal in the past month—the instructions are to have these columns multipunched (MP). A computer card has twelve spaces available for punches within each vertical column. Ten of the spaces are reserved for numerical values 0, 1, 2, 3, 4, 5, 6, 7, 8, 9 running from the top to the bottom of each column. Above the zero space there are the two remaining spaces that can be punched. With single punching, each column of a computer card has only one numeric punch (0-9). With multiple punching the keypunch machine punches holes into more than one space for a given column. For example, if a respondent indicates that he or she has drunk Dr. Pepper, Sprite, Slice and Fanta during the past month, then in column 25 there are punches in those spaces designated for the numerical values 1, 5, 6, and 9. When multiple punches are used, a special program spreads the data when it is transferred onto magnetic tape or disk. Thus, each possible brand of carbonated soft drink would be assigned to a column and a 1 or 0 would indicate whether it was or was not drunk during the past three months. Obviously, multipunches can be avoided altogether by precoding the question in this way. We recommend that you do not use multipunches, since without special computer programs the data will not be be able to be accessed. However, if the supplier insists on using multipunches make sure the data are spread when they are transferred onto magnetic tape or disk. Finally, the cleaning instructions also indicate that if in column 12 space positions 1–7 do not have any punches, then space position 8 should be punched and columns 25 or 26 must be punched; for column 25 the legitimate codes are 1–9, 0, x, y and for column 26 the legitimate codes are 1–5, 9, 0, x, y.

Frequency Distribution. Another step in the process of cleaning the data for final analysis is to obtain various summary statistical information on each question taken separately. Typically the initial step is to tabulate

Frequency distribution
The number of respondents who chose each alternative answer as well as the percentage and cumulative percentage of respondents answering.

413

responses on a question-by-question basis. The frequency distribution of each question shows the number of respondents who chose each alternative answer as well as the percentage and cumulative percentage of respondents answering. Consider, for example, the frequency distribution shown in Table 13-1. The table gives the frequency distribution for 300 respondents who were asked:

Last year what was your total taxable income?

Under $5,000 . . . . 1/22 [	]–1
$5,000–$9,999 . . . . [	]–2
$10,000–$14,999 . . . . [	]–3
$15,000–$19,999 . . . . [	]–4
$20,000–$24,999 . . . . [	]–5
$25,000–$34,999 . . . . [	]–6
$35,000–$49,999 . . . . [	]–7
$50,000 and over . . . . [	]–8
No answer . . . . [	]–9

The first column in Table 13-1 is the category label or level of the variable. The second column refers to the number assigned to each level as dictated by the precoding process. The third column displays the actual number of respondents checking a particular category; for example, 15 people in the sample reported income less than $5,000. The fourth column displays the percent of the total sample represented by each category; for example, 50 people reported income in the category $10,000 to $14,999 which represents 16.7 percent of the 300 people. The fifth column gives the adjusted percentage after removing those people who did not respond to this question. Notice that 15 people or 5 percent did not answer the question on income. We will discuss how to handle missing responses later. The last column presents the adjusted cumulative frequencies; for example, 33.3 percent of the sample reported income of $14,999 or less (95/285 = .333). Frequency distributions can help in isolating illegal responses or missing data and give an initial glimpse at the data.

Missing Responses. The final step in the cleaning process involves deciding what to do with missing responses. After isolating the questions for which missing responses have occurred, perhaps through frequency distributions or by obtaining a column-by-column count of the responses to each question, a decision must be made regarding how to specifically treat questions that some respondents did not answer. There are several possible strategies to consider.

Leaving them blank
Procedure whereby missing data are recorded as blanks.

1. **Leaving them blank** is an acceptable practice for certain types of analyses. For example, blanks can be adjusted for when presenting simple tabulations (or cross-tabulations—see Chapter 14) by simply adjusting percentages and cumulative percentages for the percent-

Frequency Distribution for Income Categories

Category label	Code	Number	Percentage	Adjusted percentage	Adjusted cumulative percentage
Under $5,000	1	15	5.0	5.3	5.3
$5,000–$9,999	2	30	10.0	10.5	15.8
$10,000–$14,999	3	50	16.7	17.5	33.3
$15,000–$19,999	4	60	20.0	21.1	54.4
$20,000–$24,999	5	80	26.7	28.1	82.5
$25,000–$34,999	6	30	10.0	10.5	93.0
$35,000–$49,999	7	15	5.0	5.3	98.1
$50,000 and over	8	5	1.6	1.8	100.0
No Answer	9	15	5.0	—	
Total		300	100.0		

age of missing responses. Table 13-1 presents the adjusted cumulative percentages. For other types of analyses (such as regression analysis—see Chapter 16) blanks can be problematic.

2. **With casewise deletion** any case (respondent) is removed if *any* of his or her responses are identified as missing. The obvious problem is that much of the available sample can be thrown away.

3. **In pairwise deletion** all of the available nonmissing data are used for each calculation. For example, consider a respondent who did not answer the income question but provided complete answers to all other questions. This respondent's data would be included in all calculations except those involving the income variable. For a correlation coefficient (see Chapter 16) this approach would mean that all observations that have complete information on both variables would be used; in other words, all respondents who did not provide complete information on both variables would be deleted. This approach works well for large samples having relatively few missing responses and where there is no reason to believe that missing responses follow a systematic pattern across certain questions.

4. **The mean response** approach involves replacing a missing response with a constant—typically the mean response to the question. Under this approach the mean of the variable remains unchanged and there is usually very little effect on other statistics, such as correlations (see Chapter 16).

5. **With the imputed response** approach the respondent's answers to other questions asked are used to impute or deduce an appropriate response to the missing question. For example, based on the educational level attained, we might fill in missing income data by estimating the relationship between income and education for all respondents who have answered both questions or by replacing the

Casewise deletion
Strategy for missing responses where any case, respondent, is removed if *any* of his or her reponses are identified as missing.
Pairwise deletion
Strategy for missing responses that involves using all of the available nonmissing data for each calculation.
Mean response
Approach to missing responses that involves replacing a missing response with a constant—the mean, median or mode response to the question depending on the measurement scale used.
Imputed response
Approach to missing responses where the respondent's answers to other questions asked are used to impute or deduce an appropriate response to the missing question.

missing response with the mean income level of all respondents having the same education level as the respondent who did not provide income data. This approach can be very risky since it can introduce considerable research bias into the results.

STATISTICALLY ADJUSTING THE DATA

When nonprobability sampling techniques are used, the sample frequently is not representative of the general population; the same can be true with probability samples because of nonsampling errors. In such cases we may want to weight the sample to match the general population on specific characteristics before tabulating other variables to estimate their population distributions. For example, we may want to weight a sample of people to match census data on age and sex before tabulating a third characteristic—say, education. This type of procedure is frequently used in market and segmentation studies where the percentage of users of each brand are weighted up or down to agree with actual market-share data. This procedure is called **sample balancing** and typically is done before transforming the data and specifying tabulation requirements.

Sample balancing
Procedure where the sample is weighted to match the general population on specific characteristics before tabulating other variables to estimate their population distribution.

Logic Behind Sample Balancing

To understand the logic behind sample balancing, consider the (hypothetical) sample 3 × 2 cross-tabulated data shown in Table 13-2. Note that we refer to this table as a 3 × 2 cross-classification table because there are two variables, age and sex, where age has three levels (young, middle, and old) and sex has two levels (men and women). The elements appearing in the six cells of the table are frequency counts, which reflect the number of sampled individuals having a specific age and sex composition—that is, the number of observations falling in the cell defined by an age (row) and sex (column) descriptor. For example, there are 10 young men in the sample, 30 middle-aged men, and 40 old men. Notice that the age and sex marginal totals are also given. By "marginal" we simply mean the total number of observations having a common characteristic with respect to age and with respect to sex. For example, with respect to age, there are 40 persons in the sample who are young; 70 who are middle-aged; 90 who are old. With respect to sex there are 80 men in the sample and 120 women.

To illustrate the concept of sample balancing, suppose that we want to match this sample to a "control" sample of 2,000 observations that are known to be representative of the population distribution with respect to age and sex. We will refer to this sample as the **control population.** The control population 3 × 2 cross-classification is shown above in Table 13-3.

Control population
Sample known to be representative of the population distribution with respect to the variables of interest.

TABLE 13-2
Sample 3 × 2 Cross-tabulated Data

	Sex		
Age	Men	Women	Marginal
Young	10	30	40
Middle	30	40	70
Old	40	50	90
Marginal	80	120	200

TABLE 13-3
Control Population 3 × 2 Cross-classification

	Sex		
Age	Men	Women	Marginal
Young	200	400	600
Middle	420	380	800
Old	340	260	600
Marginal	960	1,040	2,000

At this point let us introduce some general notation. The six cells in Tables 13-2 and 13-3 are characterized by two variables that we will denote by A and B, where A (age) assumes three levels, A_1, A_2, A_3 and B (sex) assumes two levels, B_1, B_2. The individual frequency counts in the sample table will be denoted by n_{ij}, *where* n_{ij} gives the number of sample observations in the cell defined by row A_i and column B_j, $i = 1, 2, 3$ and $j = 1, 2$. The individual frequency counts in the control population table will be denoted by N_{ij}, where N_{ij} gives the number of control population observations in the cell defined by row A_i and column B_j, $i = 1, 2, 3$ and $j = 1, 2$. Thus

$$n_{11} = 10 \qquad N_{11} = 200$$
$$n_{21} = 30 \qquad N_{21} = 420$$
$$n_{31} = 40 \qquad N_{31} = 340$$
$$n_{12} = 30 \qquad N_{12} = 400$$
$$n_{22} = 40 \qquad N_{22} = 380$$
$$n_{32} = 50 \qquad N_{32} = 260$$

By using a "+" we can denote the respective marginal totals in each table. (Recall that we used this notation in discussing treatment effects in Chapter 6.) The number of sample observations all having the common characteristic A_1 is denoted by n_{1+}, the number with A_2 by n_{2+}, and the number with A_3 by n_{3+}. In the control population table, the number of control population observations all having the common characteristic A_1 is denoted by N_{1+}, the number with A_2 by N_{2+}, and the number with A_3 by N_{3+}. Similarly, we can define n_{+1}, n_{+2}, and N_{+1} and N_{+2}. The situation is shown in Figure 13-1 which presents parallel tables for the sample and for the control population.

Cell Matching

One method used in marketing research to statistically adjust data is **cell-matching.** As the name implies, cell-matching involves adjusting

Cell matching Sample balancing procedure that involves adjusting each cell individually to match the corresponding population frequency.

417

System for notation for cell frequencies and marginal totals

Sample

		B: $j = 1$	2	
A	$i = 1$	n_{11}	n_{12}	n_{1+}
	$= 2$	n_{21}	n_{22}	n_{2+}
	$= 3$	n_{31}	n_{32}	n_{3+}
		n_{+1}	n_{+2}	

Control population

		B: $j = 1$	2	
A	$i = 1$	N_{11}	N_{12}	N_{1+}
	$= 2$	N_{21}	N_{22}	N_{2+}
	$= 3$	N_{31}	N_{32}	N_{3+}
		N_{+1}	N_{+2}	

$$n_{1+} = n_{11} + n_{12} \qquad N_{1+} = N_{11} + N_{12}$$
$$n_{2+} = n_{21} + n_{22} \qquad N_{2+} = N_{21} + N_{22}$$
$$n_{3+} = n_{31} + n_{32} \qquad N_{3+} = N_{31} + N_{32}$$

$$n_{+1} = n_{11} + n_{21} + n_{31} \qquad N_{+1} = N_{11} + N_{21} + N_{31}$$
$$n_{+2} = n_{12} + n_{22} + n_{32} \qquad N_{+2} = N_{12} + N_{22} + N_{32}$$
$$n_{++} = n_{1+} + n_{2+} + n_{3+} \qquad N_{++} = N_{1+} + N_{2+} + N_{3+}$$
$$n_{++} = n_{+1} + n_{+2} \qquad N_{++} = N_{+1} + N_{+2}$$

Figure 13-1

System of notation for cell frequencies and marginal totals.

each cell individually; in other words, one can simply weight each cell up or down to the corresponding population frequency, where the weighting factors for each cell are given by N_{ij}/n_{ij} as shown in Table 13-4. Multiplying each observed sample cell count (Table 13-2) by the respective weighting factor yields the adjusted table, Table 13-5, which matches the control population table, within rounding.[2]

Cell-matching is appropriate when (1) there are only two variables; (2) the observed sample cell frequences are relatively close to the control population or census to begin with; and (3) the control population or census cell frequencies are known.

Marginal Matching

Marginal matching
Sample balancing procedure that involves matching the sample to control population or census on each of the variables separately.

The method of **marginal matching** is another way to insure that the sample will match the control population or census. However, in contrast to cell-matching, marginal matching involves matching the sample to control population or census on each of the variables separately; that is, on each of the marginal distributions. Though marginal matching

[2]In commercial marketing research, the practice is to adjust each cell to match population proportions, as opposed to frequencies.

TABLE 13-4		
Weighting Factors for Table 13-2 and 13-3		

		Sex	
		Men	Women
Age	Young	20.00	13.33
	Middle	14.00	9.50
	Old	8.50	5.20

TABLE 13-5			
Adjusted Table for Sample Shown in Table 13-2.			

		Sex		Age Marginal
		Men	Women	
Age	Young	200	399.9	599.9
	Middle	420	380	800
	Old	340	260	600
Sex	Marginal	960	1039.9	1999.9

will generally bring the sample closer to the control population or census on cells as well as marginals, the adjusted cell frequencies will not necessarily be exactly the same as their control population or census counterparts; only the marginal distributions will be in agreement. The premise underlying this approach is that by only matching on marginal distributions, the sample has been improved for the purpose of estimating the distributions of sampling variables—which is the objective of the survey. Sample balancing by marginal matching involves the minimum amount of weighting necessary to match the sample to the control population or census separately or "marginally" on variables presumed to be correlated with survey objectives that are known (in the control population or census).

Sample balancing with marginal matching involves an iterative procedure, called *the method of iterative proportions*.[3] Though conceptually this method is quite straightforward, it does involve considerable amount of computation. In fact it was hardly practical until the advent of electronic digital computers that can perform the large number of computations needed at rapid speed. There is a general-purpose computer program available today for balancing a relatively large number of variables.[4]

DATA TRANSFORMATIONS

Frequently, the researcher will want to transform the raw data prior to specifying the tabulations to be performed and the final analysis. Two broad types of transformations are routinely performed: variable (re)specifications and scale transformations.

[3]W. E. Deming, *Statistical Adjustment of Data* (New York: John Wiley & Sons, 1943).
[4]A flexible sample balancing program is available from MarketMath, Inc., 1860 Broadway, New York, N.Y. 10023.

Variable (re)specification
Transformation of data
that creates new variables
and/or collapses the
categories of existing
variables in order to
respecify a variable into a
form consistent with the
aims of the study.

Variable (Re)specification

The two most frequent types of **variable (re)specification** relate to creating new variables and/or collapsing the categories of existing variables. For example, certain variables of interest are multidimensional, a linear composite of several other variables. Social class, for instance, is generally thought to be a weighted average of a person's education, occupational status, and income; thus prior to tabulation a social class variable would be created as follows:

Social Class = a (Education) + b (Occupation) + c (Income)

where the constants a, b, and c reflect the relative weights of each component, which would be set by the researcher according to the specific definition of social class being used. (Recall we used weighting factors in calculating the BPI index in Chapter 3.)

In other instances the researcher may want to collapse or combine certain response categories prior to tabulation—to respecify a variable into a form consistent with the aims of the study. For example, in a segmentation study the basis for segments could be usage, where the original usage variable having, say, twelve response categories has been collapsed into three categories according to a specific definition of *light*, *moderate*, and *heavy* usage. It must be emphasized that the relationship between two or more variables will change after one or more of the variables has been collapsed. That is, in general, collapsing or combining response categories will alter relationships. We discuss this issue further in Chapter 16.

Scale Transformations

Frequently, to make comparisons across respondents and/or scale items, the data are transformed by one of a number of simple arithmetic operations. Consider, for example, Table 13-6, which gives data for ten respondents on three attitude measurement scales—a four-item semantic scale, a three-item Likert scale, and a continuous rating scale. Table 13-6 is actually a data matrix consisting of 10 rows and 8 columns. In the discussion to follow we will refer to an element (score) in the table by the symbol X_{ij}, where i denotes the respondent (row) and j denotes the measurement scale (column). Table 13-6 clearly shows that the units of measurement for the three types of measurement scales vary in the extreme. Thus, while one can make statements about the scores on any one measurement scale, it is not meaningful to make comparisons across the measurement scales for any one respondent. In other words, if we are interested in how a respondent's scores on the semantic measurement scales compares with his or her score on the continuous rating scale, we must not only note the two scores for the respondents but must also observe the scores on these two measurement scales for *all* respondents in the sample. By direct observation, the row order in Table

Original Data for Three Attitude Scales

Subject	Semantic differential (four-item)				Likert Scale (three-item)			Continuous rating scale
	SD$_1$	SD$_2$	SD$_3$	SD$_4$	LK$_1$	LK$_2$	LK$_3$	CON
1	7	7	6	7	5	5	5	95
2	6	6	7	5	4	5	5	85
3	3	2	2	3	1	1	1	30
4	5	7	6	7	5	4	5	40
5	4	6	5	5	3	4	5	70
6	1	1	2	1	. 1	2	1	20
7	4	6	5	4	3	4	3	60
8	6	6	7	6	5	4	4	80
9	3	5	4	3	2	2	3	55
10	4	3	5	4	2	3	3	45

13-6 is meaningless and we may want to convert the data to a more useful form for comparative purposes.

There are two popular **scale transformation** procedures. Each of these transformations affect the data in different ways.

Normalization. This involves transforming each column of the data matrix by dividing each element by the square root of the sum of the squared elements. Normalizing the variables scales the data so that the sum of their squares equals unity. Letting $X_{N(ij)}$ denote the normalized value for the ith individual on the jth scale item we can write

$$X_{N(ij)} = X_{ij}/\sqrt{(\Sigma_i X_{ij}^2)} \qquad (13\text{-}1)$$

To normalize the data matrix, each item is divided by the square root of the sum of the squared elements. For example, the sum of the squared elements for the first semantic differential in Table 13-6 is

$$7^2 + 6^2 + 3^2 + 5^2 + 4^2 + 1^2 + 4^2 + 6^2 + 3^2 + 4^2 = 213$$

Hence, we would divide each element by $\sqrt{213} = 14.595$. That is, the normalized values for subject 1 on the first semantic differential scale would be:

$$\frac{7}{14.595} = 0.480$$

Table 13-7 presents the normalized data.

Scaling a data matrix by normalizing the columns (scales) will mean that the sum of the squared (transformed) elements in a column (scale) equals one. If the original data units from scale to scale are noncomparable, normalizing the columns (scales) will make the data comparable

Scale transformations Procedures for transforming data by one of a number of simple arithmetic operations to make comparisons across respondents and/or scale items.

Transformed Data

	Normalization							
	Semantic differential				Likert scale			Continuous rating scale
Subject	SD_1	SD_2	SD_3	SD_4	LK_1	LK_2	LK_3	CON
1	.480	.418	.366	.457	.458	.435	.415	.480
2	.411	.358	.427	.326	.367	.435	.415	.430
3	.206	.199	.122	.196	.092	.087	.083	.152
4	.342	.418	.366	.457	.458	.348	.415	.202
5	.274	.358	.305	.326	.275	.348	.415	.354
6	.069	.060	.122	.065	.092	.174	.083	.101
7	.274	.358	.305	.261	.275	.348	.249	.303
8	.411	.358	.427	.391	.458	.348	.332	.405
9	.206	.298	.244	.196	.183	.174	.249	.278
10	.274	.179	.305	.261	.183	.261	.249	.228

	Standardization							
	Semantic differential				Likert scale			Continuous rating scale
Subject	SD_1	SD_2	SD_3	SD_4	LK_1	LK_2	LK_3	CON
1	1.53	.99	.61	1.32	1.19	1.19	.95	1.50
2	0.96	.52	1.17	.26	.56	1.19	.95	1.10
3	−0.74	−1.36	−1.62	−.79	−1.32	−1.78	−1.58	−1.14
4	.40	.99	.61	1.32	1.19	.44	.95	−.73
5	−0.17	.52	.06	.26	−0.06	.44	.95	.49
6	−1.87	−1.83	−1.62	−1.84	−1.31	−1.04	−1.58	−1.54
7	−0.17	.52	.06	−.26	−0.06	.44	−.32	.08
8	0.96	.52	1.17	.79	1.19	.44	.32	.89
9	−0.74	.05	−.50	−.79	−.69	−1.04	−.32	−.12
10	−0.17	−.89	.06	−.26	−.69	−.30	−.32	−.53

(see Table 13-7). It does so by equating scale magnitudes, but without equating the means and standard deviations between the scales.

Standardization. The standarization transformation subtracts the mean of the data for a variable from the original data and then divides by the standard deviation. Letting $X_{S(ij)}$ denote the standardized value for the ith individual on the jth scale item we can write

$$X_{S(ij)} = (X_{ij} - \overline{X}_{+j}) / s_{x(j)} \tag{13-2}$$

where $\overline{X}_{+j}$ denotes the jth column (scaled) mean, and

$$s_{x(j)} = \sum (X_{ij} - \overline{X}_{+j})^2 / (n - 1) \qquad (13\text{-}3)$$

is the standard deviation of the jth scale item.

The most common data transformation in practice is standardization. To standardize a data matrix, we first subtract the column mean for the variable and then divide by the respective standard deviations. The columns will sum to zero; however, now each variable will have a variance of 1.

The standardized values for the items of the three scales are reported in Table 13-7. Notice that, within rounding error, the mean of each scale is now 0 and each scale has a variance of 1.

The effect of standardization is to reduce the data to common units of deviation around the mean. Thus, standardized data are expressed in *standard score units.* This allows comparison not only of data that have different units, but also of data on the different measurement scales (see Table 13-7).

TABLE SPECIFICATIONS

The final phase in the data-processing function is to determine *tabulation specifications*—specifying what tables will be required. The tab house is given sample tables and banner specifications including column and punch specifications. Tables 13-8 and 13-9 are examples. Table 13-8 presents **banner** specifications. The banner spans the columns of the cross-tab. It represents all of the subgroups being used in the analysis.

Banner The variables that span the columns of the cross-tab; generally represents the subgroups being used in the analysis.

T A B L E 13-8
Banner Specifications

Banner # _____ A _____

Study # _____
Supplier name _____
Tab house _____

| Alphabetic heading | Concept A | | | | | Concept B | | | | |
	Total	Cola user	Other soft drink user	Heavy cola user	Light cola user	Total	Cola user	Other soft drink user	Heavy cola user	Light cola user
Card	1	1	1	2	2	1	1	1	2	2
Column(s)	1–3	25	25	15	15	1–3	25	25	15	15
Punch Designation	101–189	3	8	4–8	1–3	201–289	3	8	4–8	1–3

423

T A B L E 13-9
Tabulating Specifications

Supplier Name _____

Supplier # _____

Study # _____

Table #	Table title	Question number	Base	Base description	Card column number	Stub Code bk/ q'naire	Stub See below	Cross-tab	Special instructions
1	Overall rating of carbonated soft drink based on concept seen	Placement 8	All	Total respondents	Col. 15		X	Banner "A"	Mean rating Standard error

Stub (rows of cross-tab)

Excellent/very good (5,4)

Excellent (5)

Very good (4)

Good (3)

Fair/poor (2,1)

Fair (2)

Poor (1)

Don't know/no answer

Each of the subgroups is called a banner point and is defined by responses found in the questionnaire. Typically, commercial cross-tabulation packages allow for up to 20 banner points per table. For example, from Table 13-8 we see that Banner A has 10 banner points, five for each concept seen.

Table 13-9 presents the tabulating specifications. The specifications for any given table involve defining its title, the total base of respondents, column position of question to be analyzed, question response format (**stub**), banner specifications, and any special instructions (such as means or standard deviations). Note that the stub relates to the formations of responses to the question being analyzed. For example, the first table involves respondents' overall ratings of carbonated soft drinks (based on the concept seen). These ratings (the stubs excellent to poor) will be cross-classified with user type as defined in Banner "A" specifications and means and standard deviations will be computed.

Stub Delineates the response formats to be used in the cross-tab. Stubs make up the rows of the cross-tab.

Summary

After the data from a survey have been collected, they must be prepared for analysis. Analysis usually requires that invalid responses be deleted, that inconsistencies be found, that the data be coded and transcribed to machine-readable form, that missing data be accounted for, that comparisons can be made across categories, that the sample be weighted to match the general population, and that data be transformed. These requirements are met through check-in, editing, coding, verification, and cleaning procedures—as well as through statistical adjustments of the data, data transformation, and tabulation specifications.

Key Concepts

Check-in   *Scale Transformations*
Editing   *Table Specifications*
Coding   *Banner*
Transforming Data   *Stubs*
Sample Balancing

Review Questions

1. Describe the activities involved in checking a job in from the field.
2. Discuss the coding process and the distinction between precodes and postcodes.
3. Describe the activities involved in transferring the data onto magnetic tape or disk or directly into the computer via CRT entry.
4. Why is it necessary to sometimes statistically adjust the data? Discuss the logic behind this approach.
5. Under what circumstances would the researcher want to transform the raw data prior to specifying the tabulations to the performed and the final analysis?

Preliminary Data Analysis

CHAPTER OBJECTIVES

- Describe the various methods for summarizing data.
- Explain how cross-tabulations and descriptive statistics, measures of central tendency and measures of variability, can be used to understand the nature of a set of data.
- Demonstrate how to graphically represent the data and the pitfalls to avoid so that the data is not badly displayed.

Introduction

Once the data have been prepared for processing, the researcher will undoubtedly want to display the information in summary format. With large quantities of data it is essential to have efficient methods for summary and display. The common practice is to use cross-tabulations and various descriptive statistics such as means, medians, and standard deviations. When many variables or subgroups of respondents are involved, graphs are frequently used.

In Chapter 14, we focus on methods for summarizing and displaying data to set the stage for more detailed discussions of data analysis in Chapters 15 and 16. Here we discuss and illustrate cross-tabulations, various descriptive statistics, and methods for displaying data graphically. The various methods and techniques considered provide a means of inspecting the data before testing formal research hypotheses related to the specific objectives of the study. They allow us to understand the nature of the data collected and consequently give a preliminary glimpse of what to expect.

Cross-tabulation
Common method for describing frequency distributions of two variables simultaneously.

DATA SUMMARY METHODS

Cross-tabulations

Cross-tabulations represent an extension of the frequency distributions presented in Chapter 13. Frequency distributions summarize data by tabulating the number, and corresponding percentage, of respondents reporting a particular response—for example, the number and percent of male and female respondents. Cross-tabulation is a common method of describing more than one variable at a time. Here the levels of one variable are cross-classified with the levels of another variable. The resulting table provides the bivariate (two variables at one time) frequency distribution. These tables are also frequently referred to as contingency tables.

To set the stage for our discussion we use data collected from 500 respondents who participated in a hamburger image study. Respondents, aged 18–34 and 35 years or older, provided ratings on three items using a seven point agree-disagree rating format. To be more specific, each respondent rated a popular fast-food hamburger according to the scale shown in the example.

E X A M P L E

---

1. Tastes like a backyard burger

   (1)   (2)   (3)   (4)   (5)   (6)   (7)

2. A fun-sounding name

   (1)   (2)   (3)   (4)   (5)   (6)   (7)

3. Appeals mostly to kids

   (1)   (2)   (3)   (4)   (5)   (6)   (7)

The numbers on the scale correspond to:

1—Definitely disagree
2—Strongly disagree
3—Disagree
4—Neither disagree nor agree
5—Agree
6—Strongly agree
7—Definitely agree

In addition, respondents were also asked how frequently they visit (eat at) a fast food restaurant:

On average, how many times do you eat at a fast food restaurant in a typical week?

Once a week or less	_____	−1
2–3 times a week	_____	−2
4 or more times a week	_____	−3

TABLE 14-1
Cross-classification of Item 1 by Usage

Item 1: "Tastes like a backyard burger"	Usage			Row total
	Light	Average	Heavy	
Definitely disagree	34	51	56	141
Strongly disagree	35	36	27	98
Disagree	36	32	29	97
Neither disagree nor agree	31	26	13	70
Agree	12	12	5	29
Strongly agree	14	23	20	57
Definitely agree	3	2	3	8
Column total	165	182	153	500

Based on their responses to these questions, each respondent was categorized as being a light (1 visit or less per week), average (2–3 visits per week) or heavy (4 or more visits per week) user.

Table 14-1 presents the cross-classification of responses to item 1: "Tastes like a backyard burger" and usage (light, average, and heavy). The column and row totals give the marginal counts and frequencies for each variable. From the table we see that 165 out of the 500 respondents were light users, 182 were average users, and 153 were heavy users; 141 out of the 500 respondents indicated that they definitely disagree with item 1, 98 indicated they strongly disagree, 97 indicated they disagree, 70 indicated that they neither disagree nor agree, 29 indicated they agree, 57 indicated that they strongly agree, and 8 indicated that they definitely agree with item 1. Row and column marginal totals provide the same information as the single variable frequency distributions discussed in Chapter 13.

The individual row-column elements, however, provide additional information. Specifically, the individual row-column elements provide information on the joint relationship between the two variables making up the cross-tabulation. For example, of the 8 respondents who indicated that they definitely agree with item 1, 3 are heavy users. To facilitate interpretation, the raw counts (individual row-column elements) are usually converted to percentages. Table 14-2 presents the output obtained from the widely used statistical software package, SPSS—Statistical Package for the Social Sciences.[1] Notice that in each of the cells, 4 numbers are reported. The first number is the actual count, the second number is row percentage, the third number is the column percentage and the fourth number is the total percentage.

[1]N. H. Nie, C. H. Hull, J. G. Jenkins, K. Steinbrenner, and D. H. Beent, *Statistical Package for the Social Sciences* (New York: McGraw-Hill).

SPSS Cross-tabulation

COUNT ROW PCT COL PCT TOT PCT	USAGE			
	Light 1.	Average 2.	Heavy 3.	ROW TOTAL
ITEM1 1.	34 24.1 20.6 6.8	51 36.2 29.0 10.2	56 39.7 36.6 11.2	141 28.2
2.	35 35.7 21.2 7.0	36 36.7 19.8 7.2	27 27.6 17.6 5.4	98 19.6
3.	36 37.1 21.8 7.2	32 33.0 17.6 6.4	29 29.9 19.0 5.8	97 19.4
4.	31 44.3 18.8 6.2	26 37.1 14.3 5.2	13 18.6 8.5 2.6	70 14.0
5.	12 41.4 7.3 2.4	12 41.4 6.6 2.4	5 17.2 3.3 1.0	29 5.8
6.	14 24.6 8.5 2.8	23 40.3 12.6 4.6	20 35.1 13.1 4.0	57 11.4
7.	3 37.5 1.8 .6	2 25.0 1.1 .4	3 37.5 2.0 .6	8 1.6
COLUMN TOTAL	165 33.0	182 36.4	153 30.6	500 100.0

For example, consider the cell that corresponds to row seven (definitely agree) and column three (heavy users). The first number (3) indicates that of the 500 respondents surveyed, three were heavy users and definitely agreed with the statement. The second number (37.5) is the row percentage. Of the eight responding that they "definitely agree" with item 1, three were heavy users and thus 3/8 = 37.5 percent; in other words, 37.5 percent of the respondents indicating definitely agree were heavy users. Now the third number is the column percentage which gives the percentage of heavy users who definitely agree with item 1. From the table we see that 2 percent of the heavy users definitely agree with item

430

T A B L E 14-3
Cross-tabulation: Banner and Stub

		Total Sample	Cross-section							
			Usage			Age		Usual visit		
			Light	Avg	Heavy	18–34	35+	Breakfast	Lunch	Dinner
		500	165	182	153	202	298	130	230	140
		100.0	100.0	100.0	100.0	100.0	100.0	100.0	100.0	100.0
Tastes like a backyard burger										
Definitely disagree	(1)	137	34	51	56	67	74	41	52	44
		27.4	20.6	28.02	36.6	33.2	24.8	31.5	22.6	31.4
	(2)	98	35	36	27	37	61	24	43	31
		19.6	21.2	19.8	17.6	18.3	20.5	18.5	18.7	22.1
	(3)	98	36	32	29	44	56	24	50	24
		19.6	21.8	17.6	19.0	21.8	18.8	18.5	21.7	17.1
	(4)	71	31	26	13	22	51	17	36	18
		14.2	18.8	414.3	8.5	10.9	17.1	13.1	15.7	12.9
	(5)	30	12	12	5	9	21	6	16	8
		6.0	7.3	6.6	3.3	4.5	7.0	4.6	7.0	5.7
	(6)	58	14	23	20	21	32	16	28	14
		11.6	8.5	12.6	13.1	10.4	10.7	12.3	12.2	10.0
Definitely agree		8	3	2	3	2	3	2	5	1
	(7)	1.6	1.8	1.1	2.0	1.0	1.0	1.5	2.2	0.7

1. Finally, the fourth number appearing in each cell is the total percentage obtained by dividing each cell count by the total sample size (3/500 = .6 percent).

Several points warrant further discussion. First, the cross-tabulations shown in Tables 14-1 and 14-2 are in a different format from that typically used in commercial marketing research. Recall from previous discussions, and in particular Chapter 13, that the cross-tabulations used in commercial marketing research are defined in terms of banner points and stubs. The banner, consisting of at most twenty individual banner points, defines the column headings, and the response variable, the stub, defines the row headings. Table 14-3 shows the cross-tabulation of item 1 with 9 banner points. Specifically, responses to the question "Tastes like a backyard burger" are cross-classified first by the total sample (column 1) then by usage (light, average, and heavy), then by age (18–34 years of age, 35 years of age or older), then by usual time of visit (breakfast, lunch, dinner). For each cell in the table, two numbers are provided. The first number represents the actual count and the second number represents the column percentage.

Second, though cross-tabulations provide an efficient way to summarize the data, it must be kept in mind that they provide information only on bivariate (two variables at a time) relationships—no information is provided on three or more variables taken simultaneously. Finally, note that although cross-tabulations can provide a lot of information in a condensed form, they are not an efficient way to search for results. With 50 variables there are 1,225 possible two-way cross-tabs to examine—clearly an unwieldy number. Thus cross-tabulations are an extremely useful tool in the initial examination of the nature of the data, but are not particularly well-suited to searching for relationships among many variables.

Descriptive Statistics

Descriptive statistics summarize data by presenting the most likely response to a question (the mean) and the variability in responses (the standard deviation) with a single number. Consequently, descriptive statistics are useful in making across-group comparisons. The descriptive statistics that we discuss are measures of central tendency (mean, median, and mode) and measures of dispersion (standard deviation and the interquartile range).

Measures of Central Tendency

Mode Most frequently occuring response.

1. **Mode.** The mode represents the most frequently occuring value. If we graph the distribution, the highest peak is the mode. The mode is a good measure of central tendency when the variable of interest is categorical or categorized into a number of classes.

Median Value halfway between the highest and lowest values.

2. **Median.** The median is that value which is exactly halfway between the highest and lowest values. When the variable of interest is considered to be a continuous variable (such as age), but has been collected using a number of discrete categories (for example, 18–24, 25–34), the calculation of the median (50th percentile) or any percentile, is a little different. The calculation for any percentile is

$$V_c = \ell_b + \left[\frac{C - CP_b}{P_c} \right] w \qquad (14\text{-}1)$$

where

V_c = the value of the corresponding percentile

ℓ_b = the lower boundary of intervals in which the centile falls

C = percentile in question

CP_b = cumulative percentage for categories below the category in which centile falls

P_c = proportion for the category in which the centile falls

w = width of the interval

"Tastes like a backyard burger"

Category	Code	Number	Percent	Cumulative percent
Definitely disagree	1	141	28.2	28.2
Strongly disagree	2	98	19.6	47.8
Disagree	3	97	19.4	67.2
Neither disagree nor agree	4	70	14.0	81.2
Agree	5	29	5.8	87.0
Strongly agree	6	57	11.4	98.4
Definitely agree	7	8	1.6	100.0

For example, consider the frequency distribution for item 1, "Tastes like a backyard burger", shown in Table 14-4. The values range from 1 to 7. If we let $w = 1$ (the width of the categories) we can say that a value's range is $\pm$ .5 of the scale value. That is, the lower boundary for code 2 is 1.5 and the upper boundary is 2.5. Let's say we are interested in calculating the median value for item 1. We can see from the cumulative percent column that 50 percent of the sample is in category 3, "disagree". Now CP_b is the cumulative percentage for the category below the category in which V_c falls, which in this case is $CP_b = .478$. The percent of the category in which the median falls is 19.4 percent; therefore $P_c = .194$. Lastly, with $w = 1$ the lower boundary is 2.5. Consequently, $V_{.50}$ from equation (14-1) is

$$V_{.50} = 2.5 + \left[\frac{.50 - .478}{.194} \right] 1$$
$$= 2.6$$

This method for finding the median is recommended even when the raw data are available.[2] Furthermore, the same calculations can be used to determine the 25th and 75th percentiles, which are necessary to determine the interquartile range.

3. **Mean.** The mean is by far the most frequently used measure of central tendency. Letting, as is customary $\bar{X}$ denote the mean, we have

Mean The average value.

$$\bar{X} = \sum_{i=1}^{n} X_i/n \tag{14-2}$$

[2]William L. Hays, *Statistics for the Social Sciences*, 2nd ed. (New York: Holt, Rinehart and Winston, 1973), 217–219.

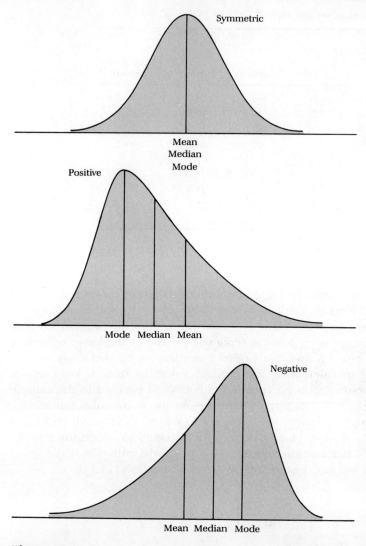

Figure 14-1

Relationship between central tendency and the symmetry of a distribution.

That is, we simply add all of the values that a variable takes on and then divide by the sample size. In other words, the mean is simply the average value of a variable.

The similarity (or dissimilarity) among the different measures of central tendency provides important information on the symmetry (or asymmetry) of the responses. Figure 14-1 compares these three measures of central tendency for two common types of distribution: **symmetric** and

Symmetric distribution
Distribution where values on either side of the center of the distribution are the same.

434

Item 2: "A fun-sounding name"   Item 3: "Appeals mostly to kids"

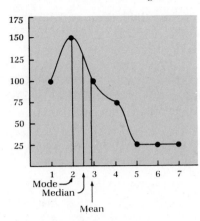
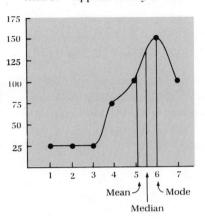

Figure 14-2

Distribution of hamburger-image-study items.

skewed distributions. Notice that, on the one hand, when the distribution is symmetric, all the measures of central tendency are equal; on the other hand, when the distribution is asymmetric, they differ. It follows that by comparing the mode, median, and mean of the distribution of responses, we can get a rough idea of its shape, especially with respect to its symmetry or lack thereof. When a distribution is asymmetric we refer to the distribution as being skewed. Figure 14-1 presents two asymmetric or skewed distributions. Notice that when the distribution is negatively skewed the median is greater than the mean, whereas when the distribution is positively skewed the mean is greater than the median.

Figure 14-2 presents the plot of the distribution for each of the two items asked in the hamburger image study that we have been discussing. Notice that for item 2, "A fun-sounding name", and item 3, "Appeals mostly to kids", the three measures of central tendency assume different values. Hence, the evidence indicates that item 2 is positively skewed (mode > mean > median); and item 3 is negatively skewed (mode > median > mean).

Measures of Variability. Measures of variability reflect the amount of dispersion or "spread" in the data. Two sets of data may differ in both central tendency and dispersion; or two sets of data may have the same central tendency but differ greatly with respect to dispersion. Three of

Skewed distribution
Distribution where one tail is fat, while the other is thin.

435

the more commonly used measures of variability are the range, the standard deviation (or variance), and the interquartile range.

1. **Range.** The range is the difference between the largest and smallest observations in a set of data. That is,

$$\text{Range} = X_{\text{largest}} - X_{\text{smallest}} \tag{14-3}$$

The range measures the "total spread" in a data set. Though simple and easily calculated, the range suffers to the extent that it does not take into account how the data are distributed between the largest and smallest values.

2. **Standard deviation.** The standard deviation of a variable, X, denoted as s_x, can be calculated by using the following formula:[3]

$$s_x = \sum_{i=1}^{n} \sqrt{\frac{(X_i - \overline{X})^2}{n-1}} \tag{14-4}$$

where

n = total sample size

X_i = value of the ith respondent on the variable of interest

$\overline{X}$ = mean of the variable of interest

Recall that we discussed the standard deviation in relation to sampling precision in Chapter 7. The smaller the standard deviation, the more the observations cluster around the mean, and thus, in such cases, we would say that the data exhibit little variability. The square of the standard deviation gives the *variance* of the variable.

3. **Interquartile range.** In order to calculate the interquartile range, we must first compute the 25th and 75th percentiles, commonly referred to as hinges. The 25th percentile is the response category that contains at least 25 percent of the responses, while the 75th percentile is the response category that contains 75 percent of the responses. The interquartile range is simply the difference between the 75th and 25th percentiles. That is,

$$\text{Interquartile Range} = V_{.75} - V_{.25}$$

To illustrate, consider the frequency distribution for item 1 shown in Table 14-4. From equation (14-1) the 25th percentile (that is $C = .25$) is

$$V_{.25} = .5 + \left(\frac{.25 - .0}{.282} \right) 1$$

$$= 1.38$$

---

[3] From the definition of σ^2 and properties of the expected value it can be shown that $E(s^2) = \dfrac{n-1}{n}\sigma^2$. Hence, s^2 is a biased estimator of σ^2, if we divide by n, but it is an unbiased estimator when we divide by $n-1$. For a complete discussion of this relationship, see Paul G. Hoel, *Introduction to Mathematical Statistics*, 3rd ed. (New York: John Wiley & Sons, 1962), 229.

The 75th percentile is

$$V_{.75} = 3.5 + \left(\frac{.75 - .672}{.14} \right) 1 = 4.06$$

Thus, the interquartile range is

$$V_{.75} - V_{.25} = 4.06 - 1.38 = 2.68$$

In the following example, we use data collected from forty-two respondents (undergraduate students) who were asked to answer a series of questions dealing with their fast-food consumption experiences. The data were collected via computer-assisted interviewing under a telephone interviewing format. Exhibit 14-1 presents the questionnaire and Table 14-5 the raw data.

E X H I B I T   14-1

Questionnaire: Fast Food Consumption Experiences

1. Have you yourself bought food from a fast-food restaurant in the past month?

   1 – Yes   (3)
   2 – No

2. At which fast-food restaurant did you eat last?

   1 – Burger King   (4)
   2 – Jack-in-the-Box
   3 – Kentucky Fried Chicken
   4 – McDonald's
   5 – Wendy's
   6 – White Castle
   7 – Other

3. What other fast-food restaurants have you ever eaten at?

   1 – Burger King   (5)
   2 – Jack-in-the-Box   (6)
   3 – Kentucky Fried Chicken   (7)
   4 – McDonald's   (8)
   5 – Wendy's   (9)
   6 – White Castle   (10)

4. Have you ever heard of a fast-food restaurant called . . . *(Insert restaurants not checked in Q2 or Q3)?*

   1 – Yes   (11-16)
   2 – No

CARD 1
ID *01*   (1-2)

5. Which fast-food restaurant do you go to most often?

   1 – Burger King   (17)
   2 – Jack-in-the-Box
   3 – Kentucky Fried Chicken
   4 – McDonald's
   5 – Wendy's
   6 – White Castle

6. Have you seen or heard any advertising for fast-food restaurants lately?

   1 – Yes   (18)
   2 – No

7. Which fast-food restaurants have you seen advertised?

   1 – Burger King
   2 – Jack-in-the-Box   (19-24)
   3 – Kentucky Fried Chicken
   4 – McDonald's
   5 – Wendy's
   6 – White Castle

8. Did you like the advertising for *(first mention to Q7)?* _____

   1 – Yes   (25)
   2 – No

437

9. Would you say that *(response to Q5)* is excellent, very good, good, fair, or poor on fast service:

1 – Excellent
2 – Very Good   (26)
3 – Good
4 – Fair
5 – Poor

10. Would you say that *(response to Q5)* is excellent, very good, good, fair, or poor on cleanliness:

1 – Excellent   (27)
2 – Very Good
3 – Good
4 – Fair
5 – Poor

11. Would you say that *(response to Q5)* is excellent, very good, good, fair, or poor on good location:

1 – Excellent   (28)
2 – Very Good
3 – Good
4 – Fair
5 – Poor

12. Would you say that *(response to Q5)* is excellent, very good, good, fair, or poor on selection of menu items:

1 – Excellent   (29)
2 – Very Good
3 – Good
4 – Fair
5 – Poor

13. Would you say that *(response to Q5)* is excellent, very good, good, fair or poor on hours of operation:

1 – Excellent   (30)
2 – Very Good
3 – Good
4 – Fair
5 – Poor

14. Would you say that *(response to Q5)* is excellent, very good, good, fair, or poor on quality food:

1 – Excellent   (31)
2 – Very Good
3 – Good
4 – Fair
5 – Poor

15. Would you say that *(response to Q5)* is excellent, very good, good, fair, or poor on value for the money:

1 – Excellent   (32)
2 – Very Good
3 – Good
4 – Fair
5 – Poor

16. Do you live

1 – On campus   (33)
2 – Off campus

17. Do you own a car?

1 – Yes   (34)
2 – No

18. Do you work while at school?

1 – Yes   (35)
2 – No

19. In a typical week, how often do you eat a meal (breakfast/lunch/dinner) at a fast food restaurant?

1 – Rarely   (36)
2 – One to three times
3 – More than three

20. Which meal do you mostly eat at a fast food restaurant?

1 – Breakfast   (37)
2 – Lunch
3 – Dinner

T A B L E   14-5
Raw Data: Fast-Food Consumption Experiences

```
 12 1       0    031   111   2132213321211
 2151 11    1    0411  111   2222223212232
 3241 1 1   1    0411   11   2123233421222
 4141 111   1    04211111   1443333311122
 521  111   1    011    11    334323321222
 614111 1        1411  111   2221323211231
 7141 1 1   1    1111  111   2232222321122
 824      1        62        115555555521212
 9141 1 1   0    041   111   2121222212121
1011   111  1    01111111   2244223122132
1111   111  1    0111  111   2322323211233
12141 1 1   1    0111  111   1221243311232
13131   11  0    1111  11112224333421121
141411   1     1 14111111   2131224221222
15141 1 1   1    14111111   2342433211233
1611   111  1    1411  111   1422343321122
1711   1111 1    111   11112222223321222
18151 11    1    1111111112231324211231
1911   1111 1    111   11112121323221123
202611111        511   11111223121121222
2111 11111       111   11112333333321221
2211   1111 1    411   111   1232213311221
23241 1 1   1    421   111   1423234421123
24141 1 1   1    0111  111   1232433222222
25141 1 1   1    0411  111   1322322221231
26141 1 1   1    0411  111   1222223312131
27141 1 1   1    1411  111   2222222222223
2814111 1        1411  111   2232224322122
29131   11  1    1411   11    2322333311121
3011   111  1    1111  111   2133222311123
31151 11    1    1121   11    2332334321131
3214111 11       411   11112122233221223
33141 111   1    1411  1111   221212211231
34141 1 11  1    411    11    2223232311132
3511   1111 1    111111112333324321233
3611   111  1    0111  111   2222313421122
37141 1 1   1    0411  111   2232323212221
38151   1   11   0111  111   1232324322132
39141 1 1   1    0111        1222322321123
40141     1  01   0411  111   1332332211221
411  11111        091    1   2333433321112
4214111          11411  111   1233443322123
```

E X A M P L E

To better understand the nature of the data collected in the fast-food image study, management was interested in generating the following tables:

Table no.	Title	Question no. (card/column)	Banner		
1(14-6)	Visit most often Burger King and McDonald's by time of visit	5(1/17-1,-4)	A: Time of visit (1/37)		
2(14-7)	"McDonald's has a good location" McDonald's used most often	11(1/28)	B: McDonald visit most often (1/17-4) Total Housing (1/33) Car (1/34) Work (1/35)		
3(14-8)	Mean ratings on specific attributes—Burger King vs. McDonald's	9-15 (1/26 . . . 32)	C: Burger King visit most often (1/17-1) McDonald's visit most often (1/17-4)		
4(14-9)	Mean ratings on specific attributes—Burger King and McDonald's visit most often by time of visit	9-15 (1/26 . . . 32)	D: Burger King visit most often (1/17-1) Total		
			Visit breakfast (1/37-1) Visit lunch (1/37-2) Visit dinner (1/37-3)		
			McDonald's visit most often (1/17-4) Total		
			Visit breakfast (1/37-1) Visit lunch (1/37-2) Visit dinner (1/37-3)		

Tables 14-6 through 14-9 present the summary information.

GRAPHIC REPRESENTATIONS OF DATA

We are all familiar with the saying "one picture is worth a thousand words." Data graphs are a valuable means of summarizing and displaying data. However, depending on how the graphs are constructed, they can be very misleading. The quality of data display can deteriorate if the

T A B L E 14-6

Visit Most Often Burger King and McDonald's by Time of Visit*

```
                                         TIME OF VISIT

          COUNT     I
VISIT     ROW PCT   I   BREAKFAST         LUNCH            DINNER          ROW
MOST      COL PCT   I                                                      TOTAL
OFTEN     TOT PCT   I            1.I              2.I              3.I
        ------------I-------------I----------------I----------------I
             1.     I      4      I       8        I       5        I      17
        Burger King I    23.5     I     47.1       I     29.4       I    44.7
                    I    30.8     I     53.3       I     50.0       I
                    I    10.5     I     21.1       I     13.2       I
        ------------I-------------I----------------I----------------I
             2.     I      9      I       7        I       5        I      21
        McDonald's  I    42.9     I     33.3       I     23.8       I    55.3
                    I    69.2     I     46.7       I     50.0       I
                    I    23.7     I     18.4       I     13.2       I
        ------------I-------------I----------------I----------------I
          COLUMN           13             15               10              38
          TOTAL          34.2           39.5             26.3           100.0
```

*Output taken directly from SPSS

T A B L E 14-7

"McDonald's Has a Good Location"—McDonald's Visited Most Often

McDonald's has a good location		Total	Housing		Own Car		Work	
			Off-campus	On-campus	Yes	No	Yes	No
Excellent	(1)	4	3	1	3	1	1	3
		(19.0)	(25.0)	(11.1)	(21.4)	(14.3)	(11.1)	(25.0)
	(2)	12	7	5	7	5	4	8
		(57.1)	(58.3)	(55.6)	(50.0)	(71.4)	(44.4)	(66.7)
	(3)	5	2	3	4	1	4	1
		(23.8)	(16.7)	(33.3)	(28.6)	(14.3)	(44.4)	(8.3)
	(4)	0	0	0	0	0	0	0
		(0.0)	(0.0)	(0.0)	(0.0)	(0.0)	(0.0)	(0.0)
Poor	(5)	0	0	0	0	0	0	0
		(0.0)	(0.0)	(0.0)	(0.0)	(0.0)	(0.0)	(0.0)
No Answer		0	0	0	0	0	0	0
		(0.0)	(0.0)	(0.0)	(0.0)	(0.0)	(0.0)	(0.0)
Total Respondents		21	12	9	14	7	9	12
		(100.0)	(57.1)	(42.9)	(66.7)	(33.3)	(42.9)	(57.1)

TABLE 14-8

**Mean Ratings on Specific Attributes—
Burger King vs. McDonald's**

	Visit Most Often	
Attributes	Burger King	McDonald's
Service	2.18	2.29
Cleanliness	2.65	2.48
Location	2.35	2.05
Menu	2.76	2.52
Hours	2.29	2.48
Quality	2.88	2.86
Value	2.76	2.57

TABLE 14-9

**Mean Ratings on Specific Attributes—Burger King and McDonald's: Visited Most Often by
Time of Visit**

Attribute	Burger King				McDonald's			
	Total	Breakfast	Lunch	Dinner	Total	Breakfast	Lunch	Dinner
Service	2.2	2.5	2.1	2.0	2.3	2.2	2.3	2.4
Cleanliness	2.6	2.8	2.8	2.4	2.5	2.3	2.6	2.6
Location	2.4	2.5	2.4	2.2	2.0	1.7	2.3	2.4
Menu	2.8	3.0	2.6	2.8	2.5	2.6	2.3	2.8
Hours	2.3	2.8	2.3	2.0	2.5	2.0	2.7	3.0
Quality	2.9	2.8	3.0	2.8	2.9	2.6	3.1	3.0
Value	2.8	3.0	2.8	2.6	2.6	2.3	2.9	2.6

wrong procedures are followed.[4] Depending on how we construct the data graphs we can hide differences or create differences. For example, consider Figure 14-3, which shows the number of public and private elementary schools for selected years 1929–1970. Looking at the graph we would conclude that the number of public schools has dropped substantially, but the number of private schools has remained about the same for the period of study. Now certainly we would expect that the number of private schools is only a small percentage of elementary schools. Hence, when we plot the number of private schools in thousands of schools ranging from 0 to 400, any fluctuations are hidden by the scale. Consider Figure 14-4, which plots the number of private schools in thousands, but from 0 to 15. Here we see a different picture from that por-

[4]Howard Wainer, "How to Display Data Badly," *The American Statistician*, May 1984, 137–147.

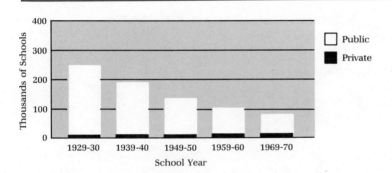

Figure 14-3

Poorly designed bar graph, showing public and private elementary schools, 1929–1970, where the variation in number of private schools is obscured by scale. From Howard Wainer, "How to Display Data Badly," *The American Statistician*, May 1984, 139.

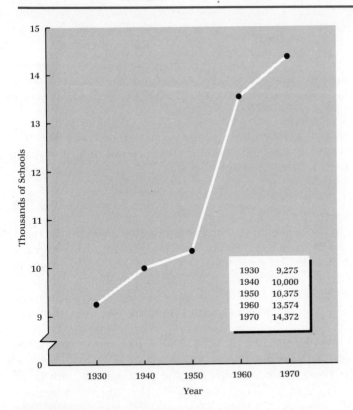

1930	9,275
1940	10,000
1950	10,375
1960	13,574
1970	14,372

Figure 14-4

Line graph showing number of private elementary schools, 1930–1970; unlike Figure 14-3, this graph shows a large increase. From Howard Wainer, "How to Display Data Badly," *The American Statistician*, May 1984, 140.

443

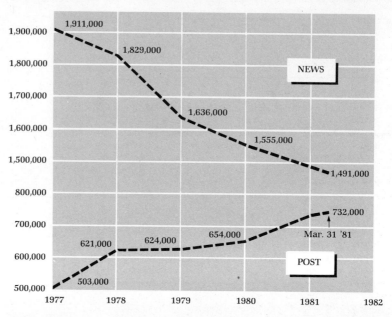

Figure 14-5

Line graph with change of scale. From Howard Wainer, "How to Display Data Badly," *The American Statistician*, May 1984, 141.

trayed in Figure 14-3. The magnitude of the scale is determined by the person creating the graph; thus, you should take care not to let the magnitude of the scale hide fluctuations when they exist, or create fluctuations when they don't exist.

Consider next Figure 14-5. Looking at the graph it appears that the *Post* has caught up to the *Daily News* in terms of circulation. However, notice the change in the scale at 800,000. Previously, the scale points have been changing at intervals of 100,000, but now (at 800,000) they jump up by 700,000. Hence, the difference in circulation appears smaller than it actually is. While it is true that one can *see* the circulation numbers 1,491,000 for the *Daily News* and 732,000 for the *Post*, the crucial question is, as a reader of the graph, did you use the numbers or lines to make your interpretation?

In the rest of this chapter, we present some of the more commonly used data graphics—namely, bar charts, line charts, pie charts, and box and Whisker plots. There are numerous graphic packages for both large mainframe computers and personal computers. The graphs illustrated here were originally constructed using *Chartmaster*™ and SYSDAT.™ In Chapter 23, which discusses how research results should be presented, examples of bar charts and pie charts using a spreadsheet program called *Lotus 123* are also illustrated.

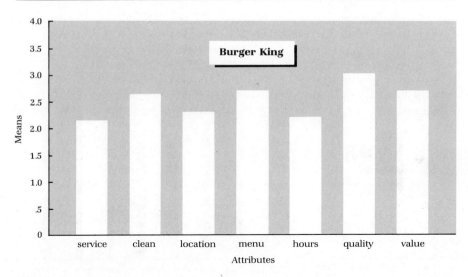

Figure 14-6

Bar graph.

Bar Charts

In the fast-food restaurant survey, students responded to seven attributes for the restaurant they visited most often. If the management of, for example, Burger King were interested in comparing mean responses to seven attributes, they could construct a bar chart like the one shown in Figure 14-6.

The vertical axis scales the mean values, and the seven attributes are spread along the horizontal axis. Consequently, the higher the bar, the greater the mean value for that attribute. However, we must remember that 1 = Excellent—therefore, the smaller the mean, the better the perception. From the figure we can see that the attribute "quality of food" had the greatest mean value and consequently received the poorest rating. Notice also that there are only small differences in the heights of the bars; this difference indicates small variation in the mean values for the different attributes.

Bar charts are also useful for comparing responses across groups. For example, assume management wanted to compare the mean attribute responses by time of visit (breakfast, lunch, dinner). In this case, a clustered bar chart or a stacked bar chart could be used. Figure 14-7 provides examples of these bar charts. In Figure 14-7 graph (a) is a stacked bar chart. Notice that the three groups (breakfast, lunch, dinner) are stacked on each other for each attribute. Alternatively, graph (b) is a clustered bar chart; notice that all three groups are graphed for each attribute.

445

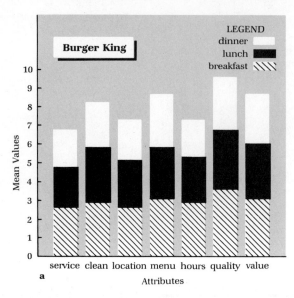

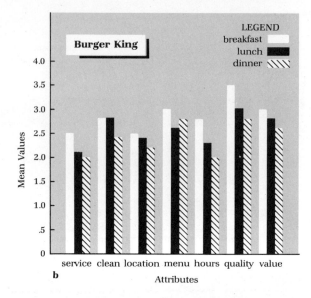

Figure 14-7

Stacked and clustered bar charts.

Line Charts

In a bar chart, the height of a particular bar represents the mean value for that attribute. If we connect the tops of the bars, we have a line chart. Figure 14-8 presents a line chart for the data graphed in Figure 14-7.

Pie Charts

Pie charts are alternative methods for presenting frequency distributions. The larger the slice of the pie, the greater is the frequency. Figure 14-9 is a pie chart of the times of visit (breakfast, lunch and dinner) for those respondents who visit Burger King most often.

Box and Whisker Plots

Box and whisker plots A graphic technique that provides information about central tendency, variability, and shape of distribution.

A **box and whisker plot** is a very useful graphic technique. These plots provide information about central tendency, variability, and shape of a distribution of responses. In addition, box and whisker plots are very useful for comparing responses across several variables and/or groups.

Consider Figure 14-10, which shows a hypothetical box and whisker plot. Inside the box the "+" indicates the mean value, and the line that divides the box indicates the median. The box itself extends from the 25th percentile to the 75th percentile; that is, the interquartile range. The

446

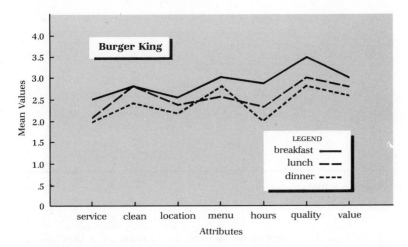

Figure 14-8

Line chart.

horizontal lines extending from the box are called whiskers. The whiskers show the minimum and maximum responses. However, when the minimum or maximum value represents only a small percentage, this value is represented by a symbol (such as 0 or *) and the whisker extends only the length of the box. For example, suppose we measure intention to purchase a brand on an eleven-point scale, where 1 indicates "no intention" and 11 indicates "definitely will buy." Say that out of 100 people only one person marks "no intention." Hence, the minimum value is 1

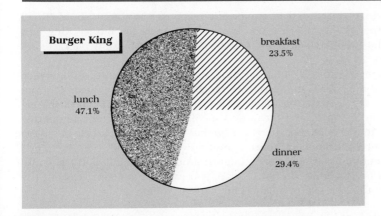

Figure 14-9

Pie chart.

447

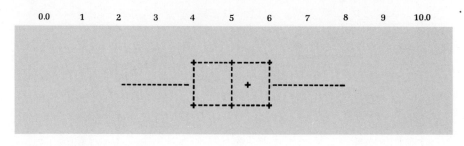

Figure 14-10

Hypothetical box and whisker plot.

percent. In this case, this observation would be shown by a designated symbol and the whisker could extend only as far as the interquartile range.[5]

Thus a box and whisker plot conveys information concerning central tendency (the mean and the median) and variability (the range and interquartile range). One can also assess the degree of skewness (or asymmetry) in the data by examining the relative position of the whiskers and by noting the location and number of outliers (extreme values) at each end of the scale.[6] Finally, by stacking or placing box plots side by side, we can easily compare responses across variables and/or groups.

E X A M P L E

Assume we are interested in comparing responses to the attribute "Good value for the money" in the fast-food restaurant survey for Burger King and McDonald's. The grouped box plots, using SYSDAT™ PC-software package, are shown in Figure 14-11.

In this example, group 1 is Burger King and group 2 is McDonald's. Notice for group one, Burger King, the responses range from 1 to 4, the mean and median are 3 and the interquartile range is from 2 to 3. For McDonald's the responses range from 2 to 4, the mean and median are 2, and the interquartile range is from 2 to 3. Notice that there is a symbol "()" appearing in the box plots that we have not yet discussed. These parentheses are referred to as "notches" and define a simultaneous confidence interval around the median. If the confidence intervals of two boxes do not overlap, you can be confident at about the 95 percent level that the two population medians are different.[7]

---

[5]"Graphic Displays of Data: Box and Whisker Plots," a report from Market Facts, Inc.
[6]Ibid.
[7]SYSDAT manual, 1984, 73.

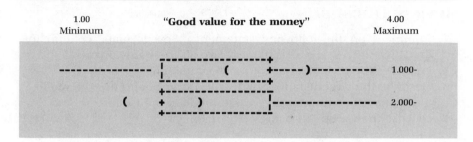

Figure 14-11

Grouped box and whisker plots.

Summary

This chapter has focused on methods for summarizing and displaying data. These include cross-tabulations, various descriptive statistics, and graphs. These methods provide us with a vehicle for inspecting the data before we test formal research hypotheses related to specific study objectives. As such, they allow us to come to better understand the nature of the data collected and give us a preliminary glimpse of what to expect.

Key Concepts

Cross-Tabulation
Measures of Central Tendency
Mean
Median
Mode
Measures of Variability
Range

Standard Deviation
Interquartile Range
Bar Charts
Line Charts
Pie Charts
Box & Whisker Plots

Review Questions

1. Comment on the following statement: "Row formats, column formats, who cares; cross-tabulations are all the same anyway!"
2. What are the caveats in using cross-tabulations?
3. Describe the circumstances that would lead one to use the mode as a measure of central tendency; the median; the mean.
4. Discuss the various measures of variability.

Data Analysis: Hypothesis Testing

CHAPTER OBJECTIVES

- Describe the procedure for testing hypotheses.
- Use hypothesis tests to test specific ideas concerning means and proportions obtained from samples.
- Explore the difference between statistical significance and practical importance.

Introduction

In Chapter 13 various methods for scale transformations, data description, and sample balancing were presented. And in Chapter 14 we discussed and illustrated various data analysis and graphing techniques that can provide a preliminary glimpse of the data. These techniques can provide suitable information for many of the marketing manager's needs. However, in some cases, the manager may want to test whether the collected data support some prespecified notion. In this chapter we present methods for testing whether or not the data support specific notions. These methods are called hypothesis tests. First, we present a general discussion of hypothesis testing. Then we move on to present many of the most commonly used hypothesis tests. The chapter closes with a discussion of statistical significance and its relationship to managerial relevance.

HYPOTHESIS TESTING PROCEDURES

We begin our discussion of data analysis by describing procedures for testing hypotheses. A **hypothesis** is an assumption or guess the researcher or manager makes about some characteristic of the population being sampled.[1] Throughout this book and especially in Chapter 6, we

Hypothesis An assumption or guess the researcher or manager has about some characteristic of the population being sampled.

[1]Charles R. Hicks, *Fundamental Concepts in the Design of Experiments*, 2nd ed. (Holt, Rinehart and Winston, 1973).

have provided examples of marketing research proposals, which typically contain an action standard. For example, in Exhibit 6-5, the action standard states that in order to be judged successful, the percentage of unaided and aided recall must be statistically significant from the norm.

Rarely will the sample data yield a value equal to the action standard. Hence, the manager is faced with the question: Is the percentage of recall obtained from the sample different enough from the norm to conclude that we have better (worse) than average copy? Hypothesis testing is directed at answering such questions.

For example, a sales manager might assume that on average all sales orders are received by retailers four days after the salesperson has called in the order. To investigate this hypothesis empirically, the sales manager draws a random sample of invoices and records the number of days between the retailer's placing the order and the retailer's receiving the shipment. Suppose that the data indicate that it takes 4.7 days on average for a retailer to receive the shipment. Now, what should the sales manager conclude about the stated hypothesis? That is: Is the hypothesis correct or incorrect? Clearly, the sample value of order-fulfillment time (4.7 days) is different from the hypothesized value (4.0 days). However, the question that hypothesis testing addresses is: Are the two values different enough for us to conclude that our hypothesis is incorrect? Or stated somewhat differently, is the value 4.7 close enough to 4.0 to lead us to believe that the mean time it takes to receive a shipment in the population is actually 4.0 days?

In hypothesis testing we determine whether a hypothesis concerning a population characteristic is tenable. Using our example, the sales manager's hypothesis is that the population average (μ) of order fulfillment time is 4.0 days. A **statistical hypothesis test** determines the probability of observing a sample mean of 4.7 days if indeed the population mean (or hypothesized mean) is 4.0 days. In other words, if the hypothesis is true ($\mu = 4.0$), how likely is it that we should observe a sample with a mean value of 4.7 days?

Statistical hypothesis test Test that determines the probability of observing a sample mean of $\overline{X}$ if indeed the population mean (or hypothesized mean) is μ.

Essentially, there are two explanations for observing a difference between the hypothesized value and the sample value: (1) the hypothesis is true, and the difference we observe is simply due to sampling error; or (2) the hypothesis is false and the true mean is some other value. As we will see, hypothesis testing consists of using sample data to determine which explanation is more probable.

Steps in Hypothesis Testing

Hypothesis testing involves a series of steps. First, we must specify our hypothesis. Second, we must choose an appropriate statistical method for testing the hypothesis. And third, we must construct a decision rule that indicates whether or not we should reject the hypothesis.

Step 1: Stating the Hypothesis. Hypotheses are stated using two forms: (1) a **null hypothesis** *(HO:)* and (2) an **alternative hypothesis** *(HA:)*. The null hypothesis is the hypothesis that is tested. For example, the sales manager in the previously described scenario would formulate the null hypothesis as:

HO: μ = 4 days

The alternative hypothesis *(HA:)* is simply a competing hypothesis to the null. An alternative hypothesis can be either directional or nondirectional. For example, we could specify the alternative hypothesis as

HA: $\mu \neq$ 4 days

Here we are specifying no direction to the competing hypothesis; if we decide HO is not true, μ can be greater than or less than the hypothesized value of 4 days. Conversely, we could specify a direction to the alternative hypothesis. For example, if the sales manager actually believed that the population average of fulfillment time is less than or equal to 4.0 days, then

HO: $\mu \leq$ 4.0

HA: $\mu >$ 4.0

When the alternative hypothesis is directional, we have a **one-tail hypothesis test,** whereas when the alternative hypothesis is nondirectional we have a **two-tail hypothesis test.** We will return to the issue of one-tail versus two-tail hypothesis tests shortly.

Notice that whether we specify a nondirectional or directional alternative hypothesis, the null and alternative hypotheses are in competition concerning a particular assumption about the population. Consequently, both cannot be true. This is the essence of hypothesis testing. We use sample evidence to determine which of the two hypotheses is more probable.

Step 2: Choosing a Test Statistic. Each hypothesis test has an accompanying test statistic *(TS)*. For example, if we want to test the null hypothesis, HO: μ = 4 days, we could use either a Z-test or a t-test. As you might recall from your basic statistics course, the t-distribution is recommended for situations in which the sample size *(n)* is less than thirty. In contrast, the Z-distribution is used when the sample size exceeds 30. Though this rule generally applies, let us try to understand the reasons and assumptions underlying its use.

To do so we need to make use of the sampling distribution. When the sample size is large, the shape of the sampling distribution is normal. In such cases, the mean of the sampling distribution is equal to the mean of the population with variance given by $\sigma_{\bar{x}}^2 = \sigma^2/n$. When constructing confidence intervals we substituted s^2 for σ^2, where s^2 is the unbiased estimate of

Null hypothesis The hypothesis that is tested.
Alternative hypothesis A competing hypothesis to the null.

One-tail hypothesis test Test used when the alternative hypothesis is directional—the entire region of rejection is in one tail of the distribution.
Two-tail hypothesis test Test used when the alternative hypothesis is nondirectional—the region of rejection is in both tails of the distribution.

453

σ^2. Now the estimated variance of the mean, $s_{\bar{x}}^2 = s^2/n$, will most likely not equal $\sigma_{\bar{x}}^2 = \sigma^2/n$; however, when the sample size is large this is not a major concern because the sample-based estimate s^2 becomes more precise in the sense of being close to the population value σ^2.

When testing the hypotheses about μ, or alternatively, in making inferences about μ, we utilize standardized scores, or Z-values[2] given by

$$Z = \frac{\bar{X} - E(\bar{X})}{\sigma_{\bar{x}}} \tag{15-1}$$

However, to utilize the standard scores or Z-values shown we need to know the population standard error, $\sigma_{\bar{x}}$, or equivalently the population variance σ^2, since $\sigma_{\bar{x}} = \sqrt{\sigma^2/n}$, but such information is rarely, if ever, known. A way to circumvent this problem is to substitute s^2 for σ^2; however, if we do this the explicit assumption is that the sample size is large enough to provide a value of s^2 that is close to the true value of σ^2. Thus, the Z-test statistic shown in equation (15-1) is the appropriate test statistic to use when either the population variance σ^2 is known, or the sample is large enough for us to believe that s^2 is a precise estimate of σ^2, and therefore $s_{\bar{x}}$ can be substituted for $\sigma_{\bar{x}}$ in equation (15-1). In cases where the available sample is not sufficiently large to let us believe that s^2 is reasonably close to σ^2, the appropriate test statistic utilized is not the standardized score given in equation (15-1). Instead, the appropriate test statistic is given by

$$t = \frac{\bar{X} - E(\bar{X})}{\hat{\sigma}_{\bar{x}}} \tag{15-2}$$

which is called the t-test statistic. Though the t-test statistic bears a close resemblance to the Z-test statistic, there is a difference. Specifically, in comparing equations (15-1) and (15-2) we can see that the denominators are not the same. The denominator of the Z-test statistic (equation 15-1), is a constant, whereas the denominator of the t-test statistic (equation 15-2) is a random variable, which is reflected by the "^" over $\sigma_{\bar{x}}$. In other words, when using the t-test statistic we need to *estimate* $\sigma_{\bar{x}}$, the standard error of the mean, as well as $\bar{X}$, the mean, itself. However, in a strict sense, we can use the t-test statistic only if the distribution of X_i is normal. If the population distribution of X_i is not normal, the estimates of the mean and the variance of the mean are not statistically independent. In cases where normality of X_i is not satisfied it is extremely difficult to specify the exact distribution of the t-test statistic.[3]

Step 3: Constructing a Decision Rule. Sample data are used to obtain a calculated value of the test statistic. For example, if the sample mean (4.7 days) was based on a sample of 25 we would use the t-test statistic.

[2]William L. Hays, *Statistics for the Social Sciences*, 2nd ed. (Holt, Rinehart and Winston, 1973), 392.
[3]Ibid.

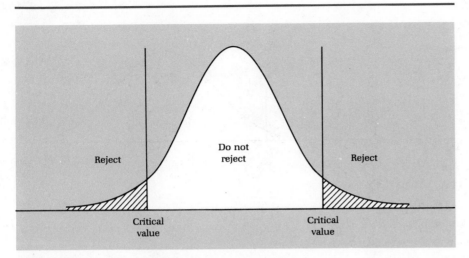

Figure 15-1

Two-tail region of rejection.

Now, if the standard deviation for our sample of 25 was, say 2.0, our calculated t-value (t_c) would be:

$$t_c = \frac{\overline{X} - \mu}{s/\sqrt{n}} \qquad (15\text{-}3)$$

$$= \frac{4.7 - 4.0}{2/\sqrt{25}}$$

$$= 1.75$$

We must now decide whether the value of the test statistic is large enough to warrant rejection of our hypothesis. To do so we establish a **region of rejection.** Basically, this region of rejection is a cut point, often referred to as a critical value. Consider Figure 15-1, which illustrates the rejection region for a two-tail test. If the calculated value of the test statistic falls in the shaded area we reject the null hypothesis.

To better understand the rationale underlying the use of the region of rejection in hypothesis testing let us once again consider the t-distribution, though the same results hold for the Z-distribution. The formula for the t-distribution shown in (15-2) is

$$t = \frac{\overline{X} - E(\overline{X})}{\hat{\sigma}_{\overline{X}}} \qquad (15\text{-}4)$$

or, equivalently

$$t = \frac{\overline{X} - \mu}{s/\sqrt{n}} \qquad (15\text{-}5)$$

Region of rejection A cut point often referred to as a critical value; if the value of the test statistic falls to the right or the left of this critical value we reject the null hypothesis.

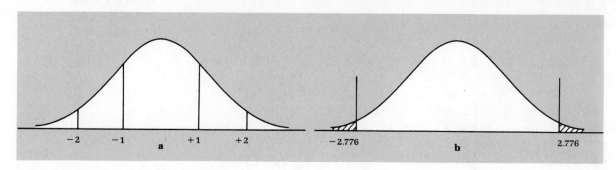

Figure 15-2

Critical regions for *t*-distribution for *n* = 5.

Hence, if we want the sampling distribution of *t* when the null hypothesis is true (when the mean is μ), then we would derive the frequency distribution for the values calculated from (15-2) for all samples of size *n*.

Figure 15-2, Part **a** presents the distribution when the sample size (*n*) equals 5. We can interpret the distribution as follows: If the null hypothesis is true, it is highly probable you will get a calculated value of *t* in the range −1 to 1. However, it is unlikely you will get a calculated value less than −2 or greater than 2, if the null hypothesis is true. Because this is a density function we can determine the probability of observing a specific value of *t* given that the null hypothesis is true. This value is our critical value. The shaded areas in Figure 15-2, Part **b** represent .025 percent of the distribution. Hence, if our calculated test statistic was less than −2.776 or greater than 2.776 we would reject our null hypothesis and be confident of making the right decision in 95 out of 100 cases based upon the sample data. Hypothesis tests are based on sample data; consequently, we never reject or fail to reject a hypothesis with certainty. The decision to reject or not reject the null is always subject to error.

Inspecting Table 3 of the Statistical Appendix gives us the tabled critical *t*-values. Notice that for a specified level of α, the region of rejection changes for different degrees of freedom, denoted by *df*, where *df* = *n* − 1. Unlike the *Z*-distribution, the *t*-distribution is actually a family of distributions. The sampling distribution of the *t*-test statistic depends on the estimate of $\sigma_{\bar{x}}$, which changes as the sample size is varied. Consequently, to determine the region of rejection for a *t*-test statistic we need to specify both the confidence level (1 − α/2) and the degrees of freedom (*df*).

The significance level for a statistical test is specified as 1 − α, or 1 − α/2, the difference being whether we want to conduct a one-tailed

$(1 - \alpha)$ hypothesis test or a two-tailed $(1 - \alpha/2)$ hypothesis test. For example, if the sales manager wanted to test the hypothesis that delivery time was less than the hypothesized value of 4.0, then he or she would use a one-tail test. That is, the entire region of rejection would be in the left-hand tail of the distribution. Consequently, when specifying the tabled value of a test statistic we use two subscripts: the first refers to the confidence level of the hypothesis test, and the second refers to the degrees of freedom. When we wish to use a one-tail test the first subscript is denoted as $1 - \alpha$, whereas if we wish to utilize a two-tail test the first subscript will be denoted as $(1 - \alpha/2)$. For example, $t_{(1 - \alpha;\, df)}$ refers to a one-tail t-test with a given level of degrees of freedom (df), while $t_{(1 - \alpha/2;\, df)}$ refers to a two-tail t-test with a given level of degrees of freedom (df).

Basically the decision rule is to reject the null hypothesis if the calculated value of the test statistic falls in the region of rejection and to fail to reject the null hypothesis if the calculated value of the test statistic does not fall in the region of rejection. Letting TS_c be the calculated value of the test statistic and TS_t be the tabulated value of the test statistic for some specified α level, we reject *HO:* if

$$TS_c > TS_t \text{ or } -TS_c < -TS_t$$

Thus the decision rule is simply to reject the null hypothesis if the value of TS_c lies in the region of rejection as established by the critical values of TS_t.

EXAMPLE

Returning to the example we used to explain the steps in hypothesis testing, suppose we wanted to test the hypothesis that the population mean was 4.0 days. The sample of $n = 25$ elements from the population has a sample mean of 4.7 with a standard deviation of 1.1. The null and alternative hypotheses are:

HO: $\mu = 4.0$

HA: $\mu \neq 4.0$

To test this hypothesis we use the t-test statistic

$$t = \frac{\overline{X} - \mu}{s/\sqrt{n}} \tag{15-6}$$

where in this case $\overline{X}$ is the sample mean (4.7) and μ is the assumed population parameter (mean) equal to 4.0. Now the calculated t-value is

$$t_c = \frac{4.7 - 4.0}{1.1/\sqrt{25}} = 3.18$$

Given that the null hypothesis is true, the shaded areas of Figure 15-3 indicate that for $df = 25 - 1$, 95 percent of the t-values calculated lie between the region -2.064 and $+2.064$, and these values constitute the region of rejection. Hence,

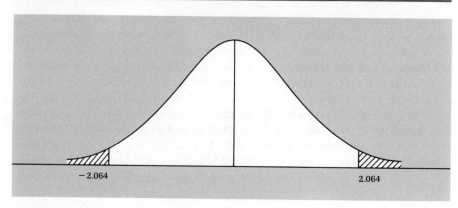

Figure 15-3

Region of rejection for *t*-test statistic for α = .05 and *df* = 24.

with a calculated value of 3.18 we would reject the null hypothesis, since the test statistic does fall within the region of rejection. The distribution shown in Figure 15-3 gives the *t*-values we would expect if the true mean of the population was the hypothesized value 4.0. Hence, what we are rejecting is the likelihood of observing a mean value of 4.7 (with a standard deviation of 1.1 based on a sample size of 25) coming from a population distribution where the population mean parameter is 4.0.

Error Types

Hypothesis testing is subject to two types of error, customarily referred to as Type I and Type II error. Suppose we specify a null hypothesis and, based on the sample data, we reject the null hypothesis. We may have reached a wrong conclusion simply because the observed difference between the sampled value and the hypothesized population value is due to sampling error. That is, the sample data actually come from a population whose mean is equal to the (null) hypothesized value but—because of sampling fluctuation—this particular value of $\overline{X}$ differs from μ. **Type I error** occurs when the null hypothesis is in fact true, but is nevertheless rejected on the basis of the sample data. The researcher sets the tolerance of committing Type I error. The likelihood of committing Type I error is called the **alpha (α) level.** Hence 1 − α is the probability of making a correct decision if we fail to reject the null hypothesis *(HO:)*, when in fact it is true.

On the other hand, we could fail to reject the null hypothesis *(HO:)* when in fact the alternative *(HA:)* is true. This is referred to as **Type II or beta (β) error.** Hence 1 − β, which is called the **power of the test,** reflects the probability of making a correct decision of rejecting the null

Type I error Situation occurring when the null hypothesis is in fact true, but is nevertheless rejected on the basis of the sample data.
Alpha (α) level The likelihood of committing Type I error.
Type II or beta (β) error Situation occurring when we fail to reject the null hypothesis *(HO:)* when in fact the alternative *(HA:)* is true.
Power of the test (1 − β) The probability of making a correct decision of rejecting the null hypothesis *(HO:)* when in fact it is false.

458

T A B L E 15-1

Errors in Hypothesis Testing

Decision based on sample	Actual value for population	
	HO: true	*HO:* false
Reject *HO:*	Type I error (α)	$1 - \beta$
Fail to reject *HO:*	$1 - \alpha$	(β) Type II error

hypothesis *(HO:)* when in fact it is false. Consequently, α and β represent probabilities of error concerning whether or not we reject the null hypothesis, given that the null hypothesis is actually true or false. That is,

$$\alpha = \text{Pr (reject } HO:) \text{—} HO: \text{ true}$$

$$\beta = \text{Pr (not reject } HO:) \text{—} HO: \text{ not true and}$$

$$1 - \beta = \text{Power} = \text{Pr (reject } HO:) \text{—} HO: \text{ not true}$$

When we reject or fail to reject a null hypothesis our decision is never made with certainty. Consequently, there is a probability that our decision is correct and there is a probability that our decision is not correct. The probabilities of making a correct decision are $(1 - \alpha)$ and $(1 - \beta)$. The probabilities of making an incorrect decision are α (Type I) and β (Type II). These probabilities are shown in Table 15-1. As we mentioned previously, the level of α is at the discretion of the researcher. However, the determination of β is more complicated, as the following example demonstrates.

E X A M P L E

A sales manager believes that the top salespeople make on average 20 calls per month on new accounts. To test this hypothesis the manager decides to take a random sample of 30 salespeople who have exceeded company sales quotas for the past four quarters. The results indicate that for the sample of 30 salespeople on average they made 18 calls per month with a standard deviation of 5 calls. The sales manager wants to test the hypothesis with an α level of .05. The test statistic would be

$$Z_c = \frac{\overline{X} - \mu}{s/\sqrt{n}}$$

$$= \frac{18 - 20}{5/\sqrt{30}}$$

$$= -2.19$$

The critical value for a two-tail test at $\alpha = .05$ is ± 1.64. Since the calculated value of Z_c (-2.19) is less than the critical value -1.64, we would reject the null

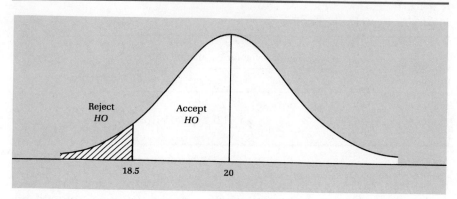

Figure 15-4

Critical region for hypothesis test with $\mu = 20$.

hypothesis. Let us now calculate the mean value that corresponds to the dividing line of the $\alpha = .05$ criterion of the two-tail test. Since $Z_c = -1.64$, $n = 30$, $s = 5$, and $\mu = 20$ we have

$$-1.64 = \frac{\overline{X} - 20}{5/\sqrt{30}},$$

or

$$\overline{X} = 20 - 1.64(5/\sqrt{30})$$
$$= 18.50$$

This relationship is shown in Figure 15-4. Hence a mean value of greater than 18.5 would lead us to accept *(HO:)*, whereas a mean value of less than or equal to 18.5 would lead us to reject *(HO:)*.

To calculate β we must specify some value for the alternative hypothesis *(HA:)*.[4] One alternative we could specify would be the sample mean value of 18.5. To calculate the β error we first substitute this value of *(HA:)* into the Z formula, whereby we get

$$Z_c = \frac{18.5 - 18}{5/\sqrt{30}}$$
$$= .5477$$

From Table 2 of the Statistical Appendix we find that the probability of Type II error (β) is $.5000 - .2088 = .2912$. Hence the power of the test is $1 - .2912$ or .71.

Now suppose instead of testing the hypothesis at $\alpha = .05$ we had previously decided to test the hypothesis at $\alpha = .01$. The mean value associated with this critical value is

$$\overline{X} = 20 - 2.33(5/\sqrt{30})$$
$$= 17.87$$

[4]Example taken from John E. Freund, *Statistics as a First Course*, 2nd ed. (Prentice-Hall, 1976), 240–241.

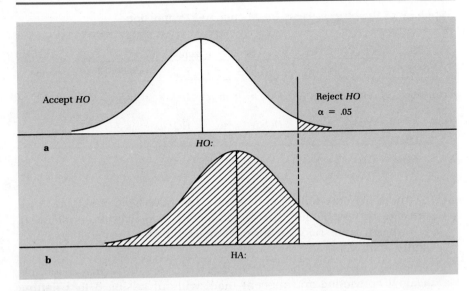

Figure 15-5

Relation between α and β error.

The corresponding value of β, again assuming $\mu = 18$, is obtained from first computing

$$Z_c = \frac{17.87 - 18}{5/\sqrt{30}}$$

$$= -.1424$$

and then consulting Table 2 of the Statistical Appendix, where we find that $\beta = .5000 - .0557 = .44$. The power of the test is $1 - .44 = .56$. Notice that by decreasing α we increase β. This relationship is shown in Figure 15-5. The shaded portion in Figure 15-5, Part **a,** is the α error while the shaded portion of 15-5, Part **b,** is the β error. Notice that if we decrease α, by moving the critical value point to the right in 15-5, Part **a,** we must necessarily increase β.

For an alternative explanation of the tradeoffs between α error and β error consider this analogy to jurisprudence:

> In a murder trial, the jury is being asked to decide between *HO:*, the hypothesis that the accused is innocent, and the alternative *HA:,* that he is guilty. A type I error is committed if an innocent man is condemned, while a type II error occurs if a guilty man is set free. The judge's admonition to the jury that "guilt must be proved beyond a reasonable doubt" means that α should be kept very small.
>
> There have been many legal reforms (for example, limiting the power

T A B L E 15-2

Typology of Hypothesis Tests for Means and Proportions

Type of test	Number of samples		
	One	Two	More than two
Proportion	$HO: \pi = \pi^*$	$HO: \pi_1 = \pi_2$	$HO: \pi_1 = \pi_2 = \cdots = \pi_K$
Mean	$HO: \mu = \mu^*$	$HO: \mu_1 = \mu_2$	$HO: \mu_1 = \mu_2 = \cdots = \mu_K$

of the police to obtain a confession) that have been designed to reduce α, the probability that an innocent man will be condemned. But these same reforms have increased β, the probability that a guilty man will evade punishment.

There is no way of pushing α down to zero (insuring absolutely against convicting an innocent man) without raising β to 1 (letting every defendant go free).[5]

The only way to simultaneously decrease both α and β would be, in our legal analogy, to collect more evidence. In research, we can collect more evidence by increasing our sample size.

HYPOTHESIS TESTS

In this chapter we present several of the most widely used hypothesis tests. We describe tests for proportions and means, for hypotheses that relate to one or more than one independent sample or related samples. Table 15-2 presents the typology of the hypothesis tests to be discussed. Although each of the hypothesis tests invokes different test statistics, all involve the following ingredients:

1. *HO:* Null hypothesis
2. *HA:* Alternative hypothesis
3. *TS_c:* Calculated test statistic
4. *TS_t:* Tabulated value of test statistic
5. *DR:* Decision rule concerning rejection of the null

The distributions used in this chapter for comparing the TS_c to TS_t are the Z-distribution, the t-distribution, the F-distribution, and chi-square (χ^2) distribution. The tabled values for these distributions appear in Tables 2, 3, 4, and 5 of the Statistical Appendix, respectively.

[5]Thomas H. Wonnacott and Ronald J. Wonnacott, *Introductory Statistics for Business and Economics,* 2nd ed. (John Wiley & Sons, 1977), 259–260.

Before presenting the specific hypothesis tests we need to explain the distinction between independent and related samples.

Independent Versus Related Samples

In some cases the researcher might want to test the hypothesis that a parameter in one population is equal to the parameter in another population. The appropriate test statistic depends on whether the samples are independent or related. By **independent samples** we mean that the measurement of the variable of interest in one sample in no way affects the measurement of the variable in the other sample. It does not mean that we have two different surveys, although we could. By **related samples** we mean that the measurement of the variable of interest in one sample can influence the measurement of the variable in some other sample.

For example, in a mail survey we might collect information relating to frequency of eating fast food for lunch and in addition collect information on the gender of the respondent. Now suppose we want to test the hypothesis of no difference in the incidence of fast-food consumption (at lunch time) between males and females. In this case, a test statistic that assumes independent samples is appropriate, since in no way would a male's response affect or alter the way a female responds, and vice versa.

Alternatively, suppose we want to determine the effect of a cents-off promotion to retailers on the amount of shelf space given to the product. To determine this effect we draw a random sample of retailers and measure shelf space for a four-week period. At the end of the four weeks we introduce the promotion and measure shelf space for the next four-week period. Note that these samples are not independent. The measurement of shelf space in the second four-week period can be, and most likely is, affected by the actions of the retailers in the first four-week period. This influence on the variable of interest must be taken into consideration when performing the test; in other words, to test the hypothesis of no difference between pre- and post-tests on shelf space, we would have to use a test statistic appropriate for related samples.

With the distinction between independent and related samples behind us, we now turn to specific kinds of hypothesis tests.

Independent samples The measurement of the variable of interest in one sample in no way affects the measurement of the variable in the other sample.

Related samples The measurement of the variable of interest in one sample can affect the measurement of the variable in some other sample.

TESTS OF PROPORTIONS

One-Sample Test

To test the hypothesis that a proportion is equal to some prespecified value we use a **one-sample proportion test.** The appropriate test statistic is:[6]

[6]We provide the *Z*-test; however, we could substitute the sample estimate of the population variance and use a *t*-test.

One-sample proportion test Test of the hypothesis that a proportion is equal to some prespecified value.

$$Z_c = \frac{p - \pi^*}{\sqrt{\dfrac{\pi^*(1 - \pi^*)}{n}}}$$

(15-7)

where

p = the sample proportion

π^* = the prespecified population proportion

n = the sample size

The steps to test this hypothesis are:

HO: $\pi = \pi^*$

HA: $\pi \neq \pi^*$

TS_c: $Z_c = (p - \pi^*)/\sqrt{\pi^*(1 - \pi^*)/n}$

TS_t: $Z_{t(1 - \alpha/2)}$

DR: Reject *HO:* if $Z_c > Z_{t(1 - \alpha/2)}$, or $-Z_c < -Z_{t(1 - \alpha/2)}$

E X A M P L E

In geographical areas similar to the one where the fast-food study described in Chapter 14 was conducted, market data indicated that Burger King captured 30 percent of the student market. The sample results indicated that 17 of the 42 students (40 percent) reported visiting Burger King most often. Management wanted to determine if the 40 percent was statistically significantly greater than the market figure of 30 percent. To test this hypothesis we use a one-sample proportion test.

Following the standard procedure we have

HO: $\pi^* \leq .30$

HA: $\pi^* > .30$

TS_c: $Z_c = p - \pi^*/\sqrt{\pi^*(1 - \pi^*)/n}$

TS_t: $Z_{t(1 - \alpha)}$

DR: Reject *HO:* if $TS_c > TS_t$ or $-TS_c < -TS_t$

The calculated test statistic (Z_c) is

$$Z_c = \frac{.40 - .30}{\sqrt{\dfrac{(.30)(.70)}{42}}}$$

$$= 1.41$$

Letting $\alpha = .05$ we have, from Table 2 of the Statistical Appendix, a value of 1.65 for Z_t.

Since the calculated Z-value does not exceed the tabled Z-value we fail to reject our null hypothesis. That is, the observed difference between the market standard (30 percent) and the sample proportion (40 percent) is not statistically significant. We can estimate a 95 percent confidence interval for the percentage of students visiting Burger King most often as:

$$p \pm (Z_{1 - \alpha/2})s_{\bar{p}}$$ (15-8)

where

$$s_{\bar{p}} = \sqrt{\frac{p(1 - p)}{n}}$$ (15-9)

From our data (15-8) evaluates to

$$.40 \pm (1.96) \sqrt{\frac{(.4)(.6)}{42}}$$

so that

$$.25 \leq \pi \leq .55$$

Notice that the confidence interval contains the market average of 30 percent.

Two-Independent-Sample Test

In certain cases we want to test whether the observed proportion in one sample is equal to the observed proportion in another sample (the **two-independent-sample test**). The appropriate test statistic is

$$Z_c = \frac{p_1 - p_2}{s_{\bar{p}_1 - \bar{p}_2}}$$ (15-10)

Two-independent-sample test Test whether the observed proportion (mean) in one sample is equal to the observed proportion (mean) in another sample.

The numerator in (15-10) is simply the difference between the proportions for the two samples. The denominator in (15-10) is the standard error of the difference in the two sample proportions and is calculated as:

$$s_{\bar{p}_1 - \bar{p}_2} = \sqrt{\left[p^*(1-p^*) \right]\left[\frac{1}{n_1} + \frac{1}{n_2} \right]}$$ (15-11)

where

$$p^* = \frac{n_1 p_1 + n_2 p_2}{n_1 + n_2}$$

p_1 = the proportion in sample one

p_2 = the proportion in sample two

n_1 = the size of sample one

n_2 = the size of sample two

The steps to test this hypothesis are

HO: $\pi_1 = \pi_2$

HA: $\pi_1 \neq \pi_2$

TS$_c$: $Z_c = (p_1 - p_2)/(s_{\bar{p}_1 - \bar{p}_2})$

TS$_t$: $Z_{t(1 - \alpha/2)}$

DR: Reject *HO:* if $Z_c > Z_{t(1 - \alpha/2)}$ or $-Z_c < -Z_{t(1 - \alpha/2)}$

E X A M P L E

Of the 42 students sampled in the fast-food study discussed in Chapter 14, 16 (38.1 percent) lived on campus while 26 (61.9 percent) lived off campus. Management wanted to determine if any statistical difference existed between students living on campus and students living off campus who choose Burger King as the fast-food restaurant to visit most often. To test this hypothesis a two-sample proportion test was used. Following our standard procedure we have:

$HO: \pi_1 = \pi_2$

$HA: \pi_1 \neq \pi_2$

$TS_c: t_c = (p_1 - p_2)/(s_{\bar{p}_1 - \bar{p}_2})$

$TS_t: t_{t(1 - \alpha/2; df = n_1 + n_2 - 2)}$

DR: Reject HO: if $TS_c > TS_t$ or $-TS_c \leq TS_t$

To calculate the test statistic we must first determine the proportion of students visiting Burger King in the two groups (on- versus off-campus housing). Four, or 25 percent, of the 16 students living on campus reported going to Burger King most often, whereas 13, or 50 percent, of the 26 students living off campus reported going to Burger King most often. Arbitrarily, letting those students living on campus be group one and the students living off campus be group two, we have

$n_1 = 16 \qquad n_2 = 26$

$p_1 = .25 \qquad p_2 = .50$

Consequently, the calculated test statistic (t_c) is

$$t_c = \frac{.25 - .50}{\sqrt{(.40)(.60)\left(\frac{1}{16} + \frac{1}{26}\right)}}$$

$$= -1.606$$

Letting $\alpha = .05$ we have from Table 3 of the Statistical Appendix, $t_t = \pm 2.021$. Since t_c is not greater than t_t we fail to reject our null hypothesis. Hence, we would conclude that the percentage of students going to Burger King is not greater for those living off campus than for those students living on campus. This at first may appear somewhat surprising since $p_1 = .25$ and $p_2 = .50$, and more than three times as many students living off campus visit Burger King (13 students) than those living on campus (4 students). The reason for this apparent anomaly relates to the basis of statistical testing, namely variance and sample size. Note in this sample the pooled variance is relatively large and the sample sizes are relatively small. We discuss this issue further in the final section of this chapter.

More Than Two Independent Samples

When we have more than two groups and are interested in testing a hypothesis of equality of proportions for some variable of interest among the groups, we must use a test statistic other than the Z- or t-test statistic. The test statistic most frequently used in this situation is the Pearson chi-square statistic. In essence, the **chi-square test statistic** measures the *goodness of fit* between the numbers observed in the sample and the numbers we should have seen in the sample if the null hypothesis is true. The chi-square test statistic (χ^2) is calculated as

$$\chi_c^2 = \sum_{i=1}^{K} \frac{(O_i - E_i)^2}{E_i} \tag{15-12}$$

Chi-square test statistic Measure of the goodness of fit between the numbers observed in the sample and the numbers we should have seen in the sample given the null hypothesis is true.

where

O_i = the observed value in the ith sample

E_i = the expected value in the ith sample, given that the null hypothesis is true

K = the number of sample groups being tested

Like the t-distribution, the chi-square distribution is a family of distributions. Consequently, to determine the region of rejection we must specify the degrees of freedom *(df)* in addition to a significance level $(1 - \alpha)$. With this application of the chi-square test statistic, the number of degrees of freedom is equal to the number of groups (independent samples) minus one. Thus, the degrees of freedom are[7]

$$df = K - 1 \tag{15-13}$$

EXAMPLE

Management was interested in determining if students were more likely to go to Burger King for breakfast, lunch, or dinner. To test statistically the hypotheses of equal usage for the three time periods, a $K = 3$ independent sample hypothesis test was used. The test is

HO: $\pi_1 = \pi_2 = \pi_3$

HA: Not all π_i are equal

TS$_c$: $\chi_c^2 = \sum_{i=1}^{K}(O_i - E_i)^2/E_i$

TS$_t$: $\chi_{t(1 - \alpha; df = K - 1)}^2$

DR: Reject *HO:* if $TS_c > TS_t$

Of the 17 respondents indicating going to Burger King most often, 4 reported primarily going for breakfast, 8 reported going for lunch, and 5 reported going for dinner. If the null hypothesis were true we would expect equal usage over the three time periods; hence $E_i = 17/3 = 5.67$. The chi-square test statistic is

$$\chi_c^2 = (4 - 5.67)^2/5.67 + (8 - 5.67)^2/5.67 + (5 - 5.67)^2/5.67$$

$$= 1.53$$

[7]The chi-square test statistic is widely used for testing for independence of variables constituting a contingency table having *I*-rows and *J*-columns. Here the degrees of freedom are equal to $(I - 1)(J - 1)$. This application of the Pearson chi-square statistic is demonstrated in Chapter 16.

The tabled value of chi-square with $\alpha = .05$ and $df = 3 - 1 = 2$ is, from Table 5 of the Statistical Appendix, 5.99. Since our calculated test statistic (1.53) is not greater than our tabled test statistic (5.99) we fail to reject the null hypothesis.

TESTS OF MEANS

One-Sample Test

Here we want to test if a sample mean is equal to, greater than, or less than some hypothesized mean value of a particular population. The test statistic, assuming a sample size of $n \geq 30$, is

$$Z = \frac{\overline{X} - \mu^*}{s/\sqrt{n}} \tag{15-14}$$

The steps for testing the hypothesis are:

HO: $\mu = \mu^*$

HA: $\mu \neq \mu^*$

TS$_c$: $Z_c = \dfrac{\overline{X} - \mu^*}{s/\sqrt{n}}$

TS$_t$: $Z_{t(1-\alpha/2)}$

DR: Reject *HO:* if $Z_c > Z_{t(1-\alpha/2)}$ or $-Z_c < -Z_{t(1-\alpha/2)}$

E X A M P L E

McDonald's has been conducting consumer surveys for many years. Over this time span, the ratings of McDonald's on various attributes, some of which were included in the fast-food survey previously described, have been averaged to form attribute norms. For example, over the years McDonald's norm on "service" is 2.6. A natural question arising out of the fast-food survey was whether students' perception of McDonald's service was statistically different from the norm. To test the hypothesis, a single sample test concerning the mean was used. Since our sample size is less than thirty, and only 21 students reported on McDonald's, the significance test uses the *t*-distribution. With this in mind our procedure is

HO: $\mu = 2.6$

HA: $\mu \neq 2.6$

TS$_c$: $t_c = \dfrac{\overline{X} - \mu^*}{s/\sqrt{n}}$

TS$_t$: $t_{t(1-\alpha/2;\ df=n-1)}$

DR: Reject *HO:* if $TS_c > TS_t$ or $-TS_c \leq TS_t$

The sample mean for the service attribute was 2.29, with a standard deviation of .956. Therefore, the test statistic (t_c) is

$$t_c = \frac{2.29 - 2.6}{.956/\sqrt{21}} = -1.49$$

The degrees of freedom for the single mean test are $df = n - 1$, which in our sample is $21 - 1 = 20$. Consequently, with $\alpha = .05$ and $df = 20$, the tabled t-value for a two-tail test is 2.086. We would fail to reject our null hypothesis and conclude that for this student sample, service was not perceived as statistically different from the norm.

Two-Independent-Sample Test

Suppose that we want to test whether the observed means from two independent samples differ enough for us to conclude that the populations are statistically different with respect to their means. The most commonly used approach to test this hypothesis is the t-test. Note, however, that with large samples in each group or known variance we could use the Z-test statistic. The calculations are the same. The only difference is whether we utilize a Z- or t-distribution to establish the critical value.

The appropriate hypothesis test is:

$HO: \mu_1 = \mu_2$

$HA: \mu_1 \neq \mu_2$

$TS_c: t_c = \overline{X}_1 - \overline{X}_2/s_{\overline{x}_1 - \overline{x}_2}$

$TS_t: t_{t(1 - \alpha/2;\ df\ =\ n_1 + n_2 - 2)}$

$DR:$ Reject $HO:$ if $t_c > t_{t(1 - \alpha/2;\ df\ =\ n_1 + n_2 - 2)}$ or

$\qquad\qquad -t_c < -t_{t(1 - \alpha/2;\ df\ =\ n_1 + n_2 - 2)}$

Because we are using a t-test statistic we must assume that the two populations are normally distributed and that the samples are independent. The denominator of the t-test $(s_{\overline{x}_1 - \overline{x}_2})$ is the standard error of the difference in the means. It is calculated as

$$s_{\overline{x}_1 - \overline{x}_2} = \sqrt{s_p^2 \left(\frac{1}{n_1} + \frac{1}{n_2} \right)} \qquad\qquad (15\text{-}15)$$

where s_p^2 is the pooled variance given by

$$s_p^2 = \frac{\sum\limits_{i=1}^{n_1}(X_{1i} - \overline{X}_1)^2 + \sum\limits_{i=1}^{n_2}(X_{2i} - \overline{X}_2)^2}{n_1 + n_2 - 2} \qquad\qquad (15\text{-}16)$$

The calculation of the pooled variance can be simplified if we know the variance of each mean. Specifically, if we know the variance of $\overline{X}_i$, we can easily calculate $\sum (X_i - \overline{X})^2$ by the following relationships. Since

$$s^2 = \sum_{i=1}^{n} (X_i - \bar{X})^2/(n - 1) \tag{15-17}$$

we have by simple manipulation

$$\sum_{i=1}^{n} (X_i - \bar{X})^2 = (n - 1)s^2 \tag{15-18}$$

Homoscedasticity In the population the variance of the variable being tested is the same in all samples.

The pooled variance t-test statistic discussed above requires the assumption of **homoscedasticity.** Homoscedasticity simply means that in the population the variance of the variable being tested is the same in all samples. Hence, in the case of two samples we are hypothesizing

$$HO: \sigma_1^2 = \sigma_2^2$$

To test this hypothesis we use an F-test. The F-distribution, like the t- and χ^2 distributions, is a family of distributions. Consequently we must specify the degrees of freedom to determine the region of rejection. Note that the larger of the two variances is always placed in the numerator. To determine the tabulated value of the F-distribution, in addition to the confidence level $(1 - \alpha)$, we need two measures of the degrees of freedom for the test: the numerator and the denominator degrees of freedom. The test shown here is the ratio of the variance from one group divided by the variance of another group. Letting i reference one group and j the other, the TS_c is $F = s_i^2/s_j^2$ with degrees of freedom for the numerator equal to $n_i - 1$ and the degrees of freedom for the denominator equal to $n_j - 1$. The appropriate hypothesis test is:

$$HO: \sigma_1^2 = \sigma_2^2$$
$$HA: \sigma_1^2 \neq \sigma_2^2$$
$$TS_c: F_c = \sigma_1^2/\sigma_2^2$$
$$TS_t: F_{t(1-\alpha;\ df\ =\ n_1-1,\ n_2-1)}$$
$$DR: \text{Reject } HO: \text{ if } F_c > F_{t(1-\alpha;\ df\ =\ n_1-1,\ n_2-1)}$$

If we do not reject this hypothesis we simply use the pooled variance t-test statistic. However, if we do reject the hypothesis we can use a separate variance t-test. The standard error of the difference $s_{\bar{x}_1-\bar{x}_2}$ for a separate variance t-test is

$$s_{\bar{x}_1-\bar{x}_2} = \sqrt{\frac{s_1^2}{n_1} + \frac{s_2^2}{n_2}} \tag{15-19}$$

Hence, we must first test for homogeneity of variance to decide which t-test to use. We should note that if homogeneity of variance is rejected and separate variance estimates are used then the degrees of freedom associated with the test statistic can be approximated by $n_1 + n_2 - 1$.

470

E X A M P L E

Management wanted to determine if there was any statistically significant difference in the ratings for convenience of location between those respondents that chose Burger King versus McDonald's to go to most often. To test the hypothesis a *t*-test between means was used. First, an *F*-test was used to test the assumption of equal variances. The procedure is:

$HO: \sigma_1^2 = \sigma_2^2$

$HA: \sigma_1^2 \neq \sigma_2^2$

$TS_c: F_c = s_1^2/s_2^2$

$TS_t: F_{t(1-\alpha; df = n_1-1, n_2-2)}$

DR: Reject *HO*: if $TS_c > TS_t$

The standard deviations are .669 and .996 for McDonald's and Burger King, respectively. With these values, our calculated *F* is

$F_c = (.996)^2/(.669)^2$

$= 2.22$

The sample sizes are 17 for Burger King and 21 for McDonald's. Since the variance for Burger King is in the numerator of the *F* statistic, the degrees of freedom are $17 - 1 = 16$ for the numerator and $21 - 1 = 20$ for the denominator. Letting $\alpha = .05$ our tabled value for F_t is from Table 4 of the Statistical Appendix is between 2.20 and 2.12. Notice that we must extrapolate between 15 and 20 degrees of freedom in the numerator. Hence our $F_t \simeq 2.15$. Therefore we reject the null hypothesis and use the separate variance estimate for our *t*-test.

Letting Burger King be group one, the sample results are:

$n_1 = 17 \qquad n_2 = 21$

$\overline{X}_1 = 2.35 \qquad \overline{X}_2 = 2.05$

$s_1 = .996 \qquad s_2 = .669$

The hypothesis test using our standard procedure is

$HO: \mu_1 = \mu_2$

$HA: \mu_1 \neq \mu_2$

$TS_c: t_c = \dfrac{\overline{X}_1 - \overline{X}_2}{\sqrt{\dfrac{s_1^2}{n_1} + \dfrac{s_2^2}{n_2}}}$

$TS_t: t_{t(1-\alpha; df = n_1+n_2-2)}$

DR: Reject *HO*: if $TS_c > TS_t$ or $-TS_c < -TS_t$

Using the reported sample results

$t_c = \dfrac{2.35 - 2.05}{\sqrt{\dfrac{.992}{17} + \dfrac{.448}{21}}}$

$= 1.06$

471

The tabled value of t with $\alpha = .05$ and $21 + 17 - 2 = 36$ degrees of freedom is between 2.042 and 2.021. Notice that the reported degrees of freedom are 30 and then 40. Hence by interpolation the value is $\simeq 2.05$.

We fail to reject the null hypothesis since TS_c is not greater than TS_t and conclude there is no difference in the perception of convenience, by location, between Burger King and McDonald's for the student sample.

More Than Two Independent Samples

Analysis of variance (ANOVA) A way to test hypotheses of no differences among means for more than two independent samples. ANOVA is applicable whenever we have interval measurement on k independent groups.

When we want to test hypotheses of no differences among means for more than two independent samples we use a statistical technique called **analysis of variance (ANOVA).** The hypothesis to be tested is

$$HO: \mu_1 = \mu_2 = \mu_3 = \ldots = \mu_K$$

That is, the means for the K samples are statistically equivalent. Analysis of variance is applicable whenever we have interval measurement on K independent groups. Most applications of ANOVA are in the analysis of data resulting from experimental design. In Chapter 6 we presented an example of a study where the objective was to measure the effects of different advertising executions on aided 24-hour day-after recall scores. The data for the study were presented in Table 6-2 and, for convenience, are reproduced in Table 15-3. Here we develop the basic one-way ANOVA design. Appendices 15A and 15B present extensions of this basic design.

In the example y_{ij} denoted the 24-hour day-after recall score for the ith respondent who saw the jth treatment condition; $\bar{y}_{+j}$ was the mean recall score and $\bar{y}_{++}$ was the overall mean. Hence, the quantity $(y_{ij} - \bar{y}_{++})$ gives the deviation of the ith respondent in the jth treatment from the overall or grand mean. Now it can be shown that if we were to square this quantity and sum the squared deviations, the following formula holds:

$$\sum_i \sum_j (y_{ij} - \bar{y}_{++})^2 = \sum_j n_j(\bar{y}_{+j} - \bar{y}_{++})^2 + \sum_i \sum_j (y_{ij} - \bar{y}_{+j})^2 \qquad (15\text{-}20)$$

T A B L E   15-3
Day-After Recall Scores

	Ad 1	Ad 2	Ad 3	Ad 4	Ad 5
	0	3	5	9	7
	1	2	7	10	8
	2	1	4	10	8
	1	2	4	7	5
Total	4	8	20	36	28
$\bar{y}_{+j}$	1	2	5	9	7

T A B L E 15-4

Calculations for Total Sum of Squares and Within Sum of Squares for Data Shown in Table 15-3

i	j	Total	Within
		y_{ij}	
1	1	$(0 - 4.8)^2 = 23.04$	$(0 - 1)^2 = 1$
2	1	$(1 - 4.8)^2 = 14.44$	$(1 - 1)^2 = 0$
3	1	$(2 - 4.8)^2 = 7.84$	$(2 - 1)^2 = 1$
4	1	$(1 - 4.8)^2 = 14.44$	$(1 - 1)^2 = 0$
1	2	$(3 - 4.8)^2 = 3.24$	$(3 - 2)^2 = 1$
2	2	$(2 - 4.8)^2 = 7.84$	$(2 - 2)^2 = 0$
3	2	$(1 - 4.8)^2 = 14.44$	$(1 - 2)^2 = 1$
4	2	$(2 - 4.8)^2 = 7.84$	$(2 - 2)^2 = 0$
1	3	$(5 - 4.8)^2 = 0.04$	$(5 - 5)^2 = 0$
2	3	$(7 - 4.8)^2 = 4.84$	$(7 - 5)^2 = 4$
3	3	$(4 - 4.8)^2 = 0.64$	$(4 - 5)^2 = 1$
4	3	$(4 - 4.8)^2 = 0.64$	$(4 - 5)^2 = 1$
1	4	$(9 - 4.8)^2 = 17.64$	$(9 - 9)^2 = 0$
2	4	$(10 - 4.8)^2 = 27.04$	$(10 - 9)^2 = 1$
3	4	$(10 - 4.8)^2 = 27.04$	$(10 - 9)^2 = 1$
4	4	$(7 - 4.8)^2 = 4.84$	$(7 - 9)^2 = 4$
1	5	$(7 - 4.8)^2 = 4.84$	$(7 - 7)^2 = 0$
2	5	$(8 - 4.8)^2 = 10.24$	$(8 - 7)^2 = 1$
3	5	$(8 - 4.8)^2 = 10.24$	$(8 - 7)^2 = 1$
4	5	$(5 - 4.8)^2 = 0.04$	$(5 - 7)^2 = 4$
		$\sum_i \sum_j (y_{ij} - \bar{y}_{++})^2 = 201.2$	$\sum_i \sum_j (y_{ij} - \bar{y}_{+j})^2 = 22$

Between sum of squares

$$n_j \sum_j (\bar{y}_{+j} - \bar{y}_{++})^2 = 40[(1 - 4.8)^2 + (2 - 4.8)^2 + (5 - 4.8)^2$$

$$+ (9 - 4.8)^2 + (7 - 4.8)^2] = 179.2$$

Notice that we can also get the between sum of squares by subtraction

Total variation = Between variation + Within variation

201.2 = Between + 22

Between = 201.2 − 22

= 179.2

The term on the left-hand side of the equation is called the *total sum of squares (TSS)*. The first term on the right hand side of the equation is called the *between sum of squares (BSS)* and the second term on the right is called the *within* or *error sum squares (WSS)*. We will discuss the between and the within sum squares soon but first let us demonstrate how to calculate these quantities. The calculations are presented in Table 15-4.

Formula (15-20) is referred to as "the fundamental equation of analysis of variance."[8] The total sum of squared deviations from the overall mean is decomposed into the sum of squared deviations between treatment means and the overall mean, and the sum of squared deviations within a treatment. Recall from Chapter 6 that in discussing experimental effects the model used to express individual recall scores [equation (6-1)] was

$$y_{ij} = \bar{y}_{++} + T_j + e_{ij} \tag{15-21}$$

where

$$\bar{y}_{++} = \text{the overall mean}$$
$$T_j = \text{the effect of the } j\text{th exposure}$$
$$e_{ij} = \text{an error term}$$

Note the similarity between this formula and the fundamental equation of analysis of variance. In ANOVA, T_j is the effect of the jth treatment. We might ask why any one group has recall scores that are greater than (less than) the overall average. Notice that if no group is very different from the overall average, then

$$\mu_1 = \mu_2 = \mu_3 = \mu_4 = \mu_5$$

which is exactly the hypothesis that is being subjected to testing. The within group or error sum of squares represents the variation in respondents' recall scores for people who have seen the same treatment ad. Given that these people were randomly assigned to the treatment, any difference in their scores must be due to a unique reaction to the ad and is therefore called unexplained variation; that is, we cannot explain the variation due to exposure to a particular ad (within treatment). However, the between-group variation represents differences in recall scores for groups that were exposed to different treatments. Hence, we say we can explain the difference in group scores as a function of exposure to a particular treatment. As shown in (15-20) the **total variation** is equal to the sum of **between-group variation** plus **within-group variation;** consequently, the larger the between sum of squares the smaller the within sum of squares.

To test the hypothesis of no difference in group means

$$HO: \mu_1 = \mu_2 = \mu_3 = \mu_4 = \mu_5$$

we examine the ratio of between- to within-sum of squares.

Table 15-5 presents the typical analysis of variance table. To test the hypothesis of equality of group means we use an F-test with $k - 1$ degrees of freedom in the numerator and $n - k$ degrees of freedom in the denominator, where k is the number of treatment means tested. Note that for the F-test to be strictly valid, the variances must be the same in each sample (that is, the assumption of homoscedasticity is required).

Total variation Sum of between variation plus within variation.

Between group variation
Between-group differences in scores for groups that were exposed to different treatments—represents "explained" variation.

Within-group variation
Within-group sum of squares; reflects differences in scores for respondents in the same group—represents "unexplained" variation.

[8]Charles R. Hicks, *Fundamental Concepts in the Design of Experiments*, 2nd ed. (Holt, Rinehart and Winston, 1964), 28.

T A B L E 15-5

Analysis of Variance Table

Source	Sum of squares	Degrees of freedom	Mean sum of squares	F
Between (BSS)	$\sum_j n_{j1}\bar{y}_{+j} - \bar{y}_{++})^2$	$K - 1$	$BSS/K - 1$	$BSS/(K - 1)$
Within (WSS)	$\sum_i \sum_j (y_{ij} - \bar{y}_{+j})^2$	$n - K$	$WSS/n - K$	$WSS/(n - K)$
Total (TSS)	$\sum_i \sum_j (y_{ij} - \bar{y}_{++})^2$	$n - 1$		

E X A M P L E

We have already calculated the *TSS*, *BSS*, and the *WSS* for the recall data shown in Table 15-3 (see Table 15-4). With $k = 5$ treatment groups the hypothesis testing procedures can be described as follows:

HO: $\mu_1 = \mu_2 = \mu_3 = \mu_4 = \mu_5$

HA: not all μ_k are equal

TS$_c$: $F_c = (BSS/(K - 1))/(WSS/(n - K))$

TS$_t$: $F_{t(1 - .05;\ df = 5-1,\ 20-5)}$

DR: Reject *HO:* if $F_c > F_t$

From Table 15-4 we find that

$$F_c = \frac{BSS/(K - 1)}{WSS/(n - K)}$$

$$= \frac{179.2/4}{22/15} = 30.55$$

The ANOVA table is presented in Table 15-6. At $\alpha = .05$ and with 4 degrees of freedom in the numerator and 15 degrees of freedom in the denominator, the critical *F*-value is 3.06. Since $F_c(30.55) > F_t(3.06)$ we reject the hypothesis.

T A B L E 15-6

ANOVA Table for Data Shown in Table 15-3

Source	Sum of squares	Degrees of freedom	MSS	F
Between	179.2	$5 - 1 = 4$	44.8	30.55
Within	22	$20 - 5 = 15$	1.467	
Total	201.2	19		

In the two-group case the alternative hypothesis *(HA:)* simply states, for a two-tail test, that the groups are not equal. Hence, if our hypothesis test indicates that we should reject the null we know that μ_1 is statistically different (from) μ_2. However, when we have more than two groups, the alternative hypothesis states that not all of the group means are equal. Some of the means may not be statistically significantly different. That is, in our example of day-after recall scores, we could find that some of the treatment ads are different whereas some are not. Therefore, having concluded, by rejecting the null, that there is a statistically significant difference in the treatment ads, interest then centers on determining which of the means are different. To answer this question we select a method of **a posteriori comparisons.**

A posteriori
comparisons Techniques
used to determine which
of the means are
statistically different once
the null hypothesis is
rejected.

A Posteriori Comparisons. If we reject the null hypothesis

$$HO:\ \mu_1 = \mu_2 = \mu_3 = \ldots = \mu_K$$

interest then centers on determining which of the means are statistically different. It would seem intuitive to calculate a *t-* or *Z*-test statistic since we now want to compare two means. However, the problem with this approach is that the α level is affected by the number of tests we perform since the tests are not independent. To test each pair of means, with $K = 5$, we would have to perform $[5(4)/2] = 10$ separate *t-* or *Z*-tests. The corresponding tabled values of *t* or *Z* would not reflect the appropriate α level. That is, we may think we have set $\alpha = .05$; however, the actual level of α is greater than $\alpha = .05$ and increases with the number of comparisons we make. For this reason we utilize a posteriori comparisons. These techniques specifically account for the number of comparisons to be made and hold α constant at the level specified by the researcher. There are a variety of a posteriori comparison methods. One popular method is the Newman-Keuls comparison procedure.[9]

Related Sample Tests

Previously we stated that when we have more than one sample the assumption is that the samples are independent. That is, measurement in one sample does not in any way affect measurement in another sample. In some instances this assumption is not met. Consider the following example.

E X A M P L E

To determine how much attitude toward a brand changes as a result of exposure to a particular commercial, subjects were pretested to measure existing attitudes. Next, they were exposed to an ad, and post-exposure attitude scores were obtained. The experimental results are shown in Table 15-7.

[9]See Hicks, for further details on a posteriori comparisons.

TABLE 15-7

Before-After Experimental Results

Subject	Pre-exposure attitudes (A_1)	Post-exposure attitudes (A_2)	Attitude change (d_i)
1	50	53	3
2	25	27	2
3	30	38	8
4	50	55	5
5	60	61	1
6	80	85	5
7	45	45	0
8	30	31	1
9	65	72	7
10	70	78	8

Now assume we ignore the fact that the samples are related. We would test the hypothesis of no attitude change as:

HO: $\mu_{A_1} = \mu_{A_2}$

HA: $\mu_{A_1} \neq \mu_{A_2}$

TS_c: $t_c = \dfrac{\overline{X}_{A1} - \overline{X}_{A2}}{\sqrt{s_p^2\left(\dfrac{1}{n_1} + \dfrac{1}{n_2}\right)}}$

TS_t: $t_t = t_{(1-\alpha;\, df = n_1 + n_2 - 2)}$

DR: Reject HO: if $T_c > TS_t$ or $-T_c < -TS_t$

The test statistic is

$$t_c = \frac{50.5 - 54.5}{8.55}$$

$$= -.468$$

Since $t_{(.95;18)} = 1.729$ we fail to reject our null hypothesis and conclude that the ad had no impact on attitude change. However, notice from the attitude change column shown in Table 15-7 that in all cases except one (subject 7), post-exposure attitude was higher or more favorable than pre-exposure attitude. When we take into account the fact that the samples are related, the hypothesis does not change but the test statistic does. The t-test statistic for a related sample is

$$TS_c = \frac{\Sigma d_i/n}{s_d/\sqrt{n}} \tag{15-22}$$

where

d_i = the difference in the scores, or in this case the attitude change

s_d = the standard deviation of the differences

n = sample size

From the data in Table 15-7 the test statistic is

$$TS_c = \frac{4.0}{3.02/\sqrt{10}}$$

$$= 4.19$$

The region of rejection is $t_{(1-\alpha/2; \, df=n-1)}$ which, with $n = 10$ and the α level at .05, is equal to 2.26. Hence, we now reject our null hypothesis and conclude that the ad does have a statistically significant impact on attitudes.

STATISTICAL SIGNIFICANCE

Statistically significant finding Indication that our notions (hypotheses) about a population are likely given the sample evidence.

A **statistically significant finding** means that our notions (hypotheses) about a population are likely given the sample evidence. We must remember that when we are conducting hypothesis tests we are dealing with samples and not populations. Whenever we sample we have the possibility of sampling error. Hence the difference between what we hypothesize and what we observe may be due to sampling error or to the fact that our notions are incorrect. A statistically significant finding means that the difference is not, at some specified level of error (α), due to sampling error. Hence, the level of statistical significance should be related to sample size, and it is.

However, the relevance of the research finding to managerial decision making is a totally separate issue. "Statistical significance is a statement about the likelihood of the observed result, nothing else. It does not guarantee that something important, or even meaningful, has been found."[10]

For example, assume you were faced with the decision of choosing between two vacation spots to go to for spring break, and an important factor in your decision is the average price for a hotel room. If we told you, because we know the actual average price, that the average price for one spot was $50.00 and the average price for another was $50.50, would this help you make your decision? That is, how relevant is the difference? Depending on the sample size, the difference may be statistically significant.

Consider the situation where an advertising manager is copy testing a print ad for day-after recall. The norm for brand recognition for this type of ad is 30 percent; that is, 30 percent of the people questioned report having seen the brand advertised. Results of a survey indicate that 37 percent of the people questioned report having seen this particular ad. To test the hypothesis of no difference between the sample results and the norm we would use a one-sample proportion test. The calculated Z-values for different sample sizes are shown on the next page.

[10] Hays, 384.

Sample Size	Z-calculated
30	.84
50	1.08
100	1.53
200	2.16
500	3.42

From our previous discussions we know that at $\alpha = .05$ the tabled value (Z_t) is 1.96. Hence, if we had a sample size of 30, 50, or 100 we would not reject the null hypothesis, whereas if we had a sample size of 200 or more, we would reject the null. The reason is that with the smaller sample sizes, the difference we observe (.30 versus .37) could very likely be due to sampling error. However, with sample sizes in excess of two hundred we have confidence that the difference is not due to sampling error. Another way to look at this issue is to construct a 95 percent confidence interval for samples of size 100 and 500.

Sample Size	Confidence Interval
100	$.28 \leq \pi \leq .46$
500	$.33 \leq \pi \leq .41$

Notice that with the sample of 500 we would expect to obtain a mean recall score for this ad not less than 33 percent in 95 of 100 trial samples; hence, we can safely conclude that it scores better than the norm. However, with a sample size of 100 it is inconclusive that the population recall score for this ad would be different from the norm since in 95 out of the 100 trial samples we would expect to find mean recall scores between 28 percent and 46 percent.

Before concluding this chapter we warn the reader of a problem concerning statistical significance when a number of statistical tests are conducted on the same variable from the same sample. For example, consider the case where a researcher is interested in testing for differences between groups on top-box intention scores and the groups are: gender at two levels, income at two levels, and age at two levels. Here the researcher might perform three 2-group tests of differences in proportions. A problem arises in choosing the critical value. If we set α at .05 and choose a critical value from Table 2, 3, 4, or 5 in the Statistical Appendix this critical value does not reflect the fact that we are conducting more than one statistical test. Consequently, the significance level will be less than the desired 95 percent level. The researcher faced with this situation should use tabled values that account for multiple tests.[11]

[11] The interested reader should begin by consulting Mitchell Dayton and William D. Schafer, "Extended Tables of *t* and Chi-Square for Bonferoni Tests with Unequal Error Allocation," *Journal of the American Statistical Association* 68 (March 1973), 78–83.

Summary

In most marketing research proposals an action standard is specified. In this chapter we discussed various methods for testing the difference between hypothesized values (in some cases the specified action standards) and the observed sample values. In many cases these hypotheses are notions or guesses that management has concerning their markets. Using the sample information and the procedure for testing hypotheses allows the researcher to tell management how probable the guesses are.

Key Concepts

Hypothesis Testing	*Tests of Proportions*
Type I and Type II Error Rates	*Tests of Means*
Independent Versus Related Samples	*Statistical Significance*

Review Questions

1. When the calculated test statistics falls in the region of rejection the null hypothesis is rejected.
   a. How do we establish the region of rejection?
   b. In your own words, what does it mean when a TS_c lies in the region of rejection?
2. Discuss the difference between Type I and Type II errors.
3. Explain why not all statistically significant findings are of managerial relevance.
4. Assume that we have ANOVA with three groups and we reject the null hypothesis that $\mu_1 = \mu_2 = \mu_3$. What problems arise if we perform all possible t-tests between the group means? How can these problems be corrected?
5. Discuss the relationship between sample size and statistical significance.

Analysis of Variance with More Than One Treatment Condition

In Chapter 15 analysis of variance is used to test different treatment conditions for differences in mean scores for a criterion variable. The criterion variable (y_{ij}), the response for the ith person in the jth treatment, is modeled as

$$y_{ij} = \bar{y}_{++} + T_j + e_{ij} \tag{15A-1}$$

where

$\bar{y}_{++}$ = an overall mean
T_j = the effect of the jth treatment condition
e_{ij} = the error term

The total sums of squares *(TSS)* or $\Sigma\Sigma(y_{ij} - \bar{y}_{++})^2$, the difference between a person's score on the criterion variable and the overall mean,

consists of two parts: (1) between sums of squares $\left[\sum_{j=1}^{J} n_j (\bar{y}_{+j} - \bar{y}_{++})^2 \right]$

and (2) within sums of squares $\left[\sum_{i=1}^{n} \sum_{j=1}^{J} (y_{ij} - \bar{y}_{+j})^2 \right]$.

The between sums of squares *(BSS)* represent that part of the total sums of squares due to the treatment conditions (that is, explained variation), whereas the within sums of squares *(WSS)* represent that part of the total sums of squares not due to the treatments (that is, unexplained variation).

To test the null hypothesis of equality of treatment means, an *F*-test calculated as

$$F_c = \frac{BSS/df}{WSS/df} \tag{15A-2}$$

is used. Hence, the more variation due to differences in treatment means *(BSS)*, the more likely it is that the null hypothesis will be rejected.

In some cases the experimental design has more than one treatment condition. Consider the example of the completely randomized factorial design introduced in Chapter 6. Subjects are exposed to a color-of-package treatment condition and a brand-price treatment condition. Letting

481

C_i be the effect of the ith color and P_j be the effect of the jth price, the model becomes

$$y_{ijk} = \bar{y}_{+++} + C_i + P_j + CP_{ij} + e_{ijk} \qquad (15A\text{-}3)$$

Note that to be consistent with standard notation we now subscript individuals by k. The total variation for the score on the criterion variable for the kth person in the ith, jth treatment from the overall mean $(\bar{Y}_{+++})$ can be decomposed into the variation due to the ith treatment condition, the variation due to the jth treatment condition, the interaction between the ith and jth treatment conditions, and the error or unexplained variation e_{ijk}. That is,

$$\sum_i^I \sum_j^J \sum_k^K (y_{ijk} - \bar{y}_{+++})^2$$

$$= nJ\sum_i (\bar{y}_{i++} - \bar{y}_{+++})^2 + nI\sum_j (\bar{y}_{+j+} - \bar{y}_{+++})^2 \quad (15A\text{-}4)$$

$$+ n\sum_i \sum_j (\bar{y}_{ij+} - \bar{y}_{i++} - \bar{y}_{+j+} + \bar{y}_{+++})^2$$

$$+ \sum_i \sum_j \sum_k (y_{ijk} - \bar{y}_{ij+})^2$$

where

$$\sum_i \sum_j \sum_k (y_{ijk} - \bar{y}_{+++})^2 = \text{total sum of squares (SST),}$$

$$nJ\sum_i (\bar{y}_{i++} - \bar{y}_{+++})^2 = \text{sum of squares due to the } I \text{ color-of-package treatment conditions (SSC),}$$

$$nI\sum_j (\bar{y}_{+j+} - \bar{y}_{+++})^2 = \text{sum of squares due to the } J \text{ brand-price treatment conditions (SSP),}$$

$$n\sum_i \sum_j (\bar{y}_{ij+} - \bar{y}_{i++} - \bar{y}_{+j+} + \bar{y}_{+++})^2 = \text{sum of squares due to the interaction of color-of-package and brand-price treatment conditions (SSCP), and}$$

$$\sum_i \sum_j \sum_k (y_{ijk} - \bar{y}_{ij+})^2 = \text{error sum of squares (SSE)}$$

Now, SSC and SSP are the main effects of color and price, which are interpreted in the same manner as the main effect of a commercial on recall scores shown in Chapter 15. However, now we have an effect due to the interaction of color and price (SSCP). Before proceeding to an example demonstrating the calculation of these effects and subsequent hypothesis tests, let's first take a look at the interaction effect.

Figure 15A-1 presents the plots of the treatment means shown in Table 15-A1. Remember that in Chapter 6 we said an interaction was present when the factor level lines were not parallel. Consider panel **a** of

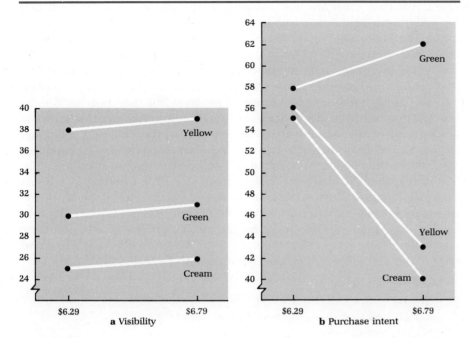

Figure 15A-1

Plot of treatment means.

Figure 15A-1. Here we have three factor level lines. Notice that at either price level, yellow is always the most visible, cream the least visible, and green almost equidistant between the two. Hence given statistical significance for the color factor, yellow is the most significant regardless of price. Now consider panel **b** of Figure 15A-1. At the price level of $6.29 all colors generate about the same purchase-intent scores; however, at the $6.79 price level purchase-intent scores for yellow and cream decrease considerably, whereas purchase-intent scores for green actually increase.

T A B L E 15A-1
Treatment Means

	Visibility				Purchase intent		
	Price		Color		Price		Color
Package color	$6.29	$6.79	treatment mean	Package color	$6.29	$6.79	treatment mean
Cream	25	26	25.5	Cream	55	40	47.5
Green	38	39	38.5	Green	58	62	60
Yellow	30	31	30.5	Yellow	56	43	49.5
Price treatment mean	31	32	31.5	Price treatment mean	56.3	48.3	52.3

The factor level lines are not parallel which indicates interaction. It can be said that a significant interaction renders main effects tenuous. To understand the meaning of this statement assume that the main effect of color on purchase-intent scores is significant. Simply looking at the means for the main effect of color (see Table 15A-1) we would conclude that green produces the best purchase-intent scores. However, notice that this is true for the $6.79 brand-price level but may not be true for the $6.29 brand-price level; that is, at this level the treatment means may not be statistically significantly different. Hence, the choice of color depends on the level of price, and this is what is meant by a significant interaction; the effects of one factor depend on the level of another factor.

In the one-way analysis of variance presented in Chapter 15, we test the null hypothesis of equality of treatment means for the levels of the treatment condition. When we have a two-factor design we test a hypothesis for the equality of treatment means for each of the factors and their interaction. Letting C_i be the effect for color, P_j be the effect for price and CP_{ij} be the interaction effect, the hypotheses to be tested are

1. Main effect of color
   HO: $C_1 = C_2 = \cdots = C_I = 0$
   HA: Not all $C_i = 0$
2. Main effect of price
   HO: $P_1 = P_2 = \cdots = P_J = 0$
   HA: Not all $P_j = 0$
3. Interaction of color and price
   HO: $CP_{11} = CP_{12} = \cdots = CP_{IJ} = 0$
   HA: Not all $CP_{ij} = 0$

We again use an *F*-test to statistically test these hypotheses. The formula for the appropriate *F*-test for each hypothesis is shown in Table 15A-2.

T A B L E 15A-2
Analysis of Variance Table—Two Factor Design

Source	SS	df	MS	F_c
Factor C (SSC)	$nJ\sum_i (\bar{y}_{i++} - \bar{y}_{+++})^2$	$I - 1$	$SSC/(I - 1)$	$\dfrac{SSC/(I - 1)}{ESS/IJ(n - 1)}$
Factor P (SSP)	$nI\sum_j (\bar{y}_{+j+} - \bar{y}_{+++})^2$	$J - 1$	$SSP/(J - 1)$	$\dfrac{SSP/(J - 1)}{ESS/IJ(n - 1)}$
Interaction (SSCP)	$n\sum_i \sum_j (\bar{y}_{ij+} - \bar{y}_{i++} - \bar{y}_{+j+} + \bar{y}_{+++})^2$	$(I - 1)(J - 1)$	$\dfrac{SSCP}{(I - 1)(J - 1)}$	$\dfrac{SSCP/(I - 1)(J - 1)}{ESS/IJ(n - 1)}$
Error (ESS)	$\sum_i \sum_j \sum_k (y_{ijk} - \bar{y}_{ij+})^2$	$IJ(n - 1)$	$\dfrac{ESS}{IJ(n - 1)}$	
Total	$\sum_i \sum_j \sum_k (y_{ijk} - \bar{y}_{+++})^2$	$nIJ - 1$		

Analysis of Variance—Visibility Scores

Source	SS	df	MS
Color *(SSC)*	8,600	2	4300.00
Price *(SSP)*	75	1	75.00
Color × Price *(SSCP)*	0	2	0.00
Error *(ESS)*	98,223	294	334.09
Total *(TSS)*	106,898	299	

$TSS = 106{,}898$

$$SSC = nJ \sum_i (\bar{y}_{i++} - \bar{y}_{+++})^2 = (50)(2)\,[(25.5 - 31.5)^2$$
$$+ (38.5 - 31.5)^2$$
$$+ (30.5 - 31.5)^2]$$
$$= 100\,(36 + 49 + 1)$$
$$= 8{,}600$$

$$SSP = nI \sum_j (\bar{y}_{+j+} - \bar{y}_{+++})^2 = (50)(3)\,[(31 - 31.5)^2$$
$$+ (32 - 31.5)^2]$$
$$= 150\,(.25 + .25)$$
$$= 75$$

$$SSCP = n \sum_i \sum_j (\bar{y}_{ij+} - \bar{y}_{i++} - \bar{y}_{+j+} + \bar{y}_{+++})^2 = 50\,[(25 - 31 - 25.5 + 31.5)^2$$
$$+ (38 - 31 - 38.5 + 31.5)^2$$
$$+ (30 - 31 - 30.5 + 31.5)^2$$
$$+ (26 - 32 - 25.5 + 31.5)^2$$
$$+ (39 - 32 - 38.5 + 31.5)^2$$
$$+ (31 - 32 - 30.5 + 31.5)^2]$$
$$= 50\,(0 + 0 + 0 + 0 + 0 + 0)$$
$$= 0$$

$ESS = $ (by subtraction) $= 106{,}898 - 8{,}600 - 75 - 0 = 98{,}223$

We first test for the effects of color and price on visibility scores. The analysis of variance table, including calculations of the sum of squares, is presented in Table 15A-3. Notice that the sum of squares for the interaction term *(SSCP)* is zero, which reflects the parallelism of the treatment level lines shown in Figure 15A-1.

The calculated *F*-value for the color treatment conditions is 12.87

$$F = \frac{8600/2}{98223/294}$$

which allows rejection of the null hypothesis of the $\alpha = .05$ level. The calculated *F*-value for the price treatment conditions is .22

$$F = \frac{75/1}{98223/294}$$

consequently, the null hypothesis is not rejected and we would conclude that with respect to visibility only the color of package had a statistically significant effect.

Analysis of Variance Table—Purchase-Intent Scores

Source	SS	df	MS
Color *(SSC)*	9,017	2	4,508.50
Price *(SSP)*	4,800	1	4,800.00
Color × price *(SSCP)*	5,450	2	2,725.00
Error *(ESS)*	123,626	294	420.50
Total *(TSS)*	142,893	299	

$TSS = 142,893$

$SSC = (50)(2) [(47.5 - 52.3)^2 + (60 - 52.3)^2 + (49.5 - 52.3)^2]$
$\quad = 9,017$

$SSP = (50)(3) [(56.3 - 52.3)^2 + (48.3 - 52.3)^2]$
$\quad = 4,800$

$SSCP = (50) [(55 - 56.3 - 47.5 + 52.3)^2 + (58 - 56.3 - 60 + 52.3)^2 + (56 - 56.3 - 49.5 + 52.3)^2$
$\quad + (40 - 48.3 - 47.5 + 52.3)^2 + (62 - 48.3 - 60 + 52.3)^2 + (43 - 48.3 - 49.5 + 52.3)^2]$
$\quad = 5,450$

$ESS = \text{(by subtraction)} = 142,893 - 9,017 - 4,800 - 5,450 = 123,626$

Let's now turn to the purchase-intent scores. Table 15A-4 presents the analysis of variance table, including the calculations of the sum of squares.

With a calculated *F*-value of 6.48 $(F_C = \dfrac{5450/2}{123626/294})$, the null hypothesis of no interaction is rejected at the $\alpha = .05$ level (critical value of $F_{(1 - .05; 2,294)}$ is approximately 3.00 from Table 4 of the statistical appendix). In addition, the null hypothesis is rejected at $\alpha = .05$ for both of the main effects. Ignoring the significant interaction we conclude that the price of $6.29 and the color green produce the greatest purchase-intent scores. However, notice from Figure 15A-1 that if we choose the price level of $6.29 there is not much difference in purchase-intent scores for the three different colors. With a significant interaction we must assess differences in treatment conditions at each level of the other treatment condition. These tests are called tests of simple main effects and the interested reader is referred to Winer.[1] Basically what is involved is testing for differences among the color-package treatment conditions at the $6.29 brand-price level and then at the $6.79 brand-price level, or alternatively testing for differences in the brand-price treatment levels at each of the three color-package treatment conditions. Remember that significant interactions render main effects tenuous. Hence, whenever we have more than one treatment condition and a significant interaction term, care must be exercised in the interpretation of main effects.

[1] B. J. Winer, *Statistical Principles in Experimental Design* (New York: McGraw-Hill, 1971).

Analysis of Covariance

15B

In Chapter 6 we discussed concepts and issues related to experimental designs. In the course of the discussion we indicated that one method of controlling for extraneous sources of variation due to factors other than the variable that has been manipulated is via *statistical control*. In essence, statistical control involves purging the effect of the extraneous causal factor from the criterion measure. *Analysis of covariance* (ANCOVA) attempts to increase the precision of an experiment by removing possible sources of variance in the criterion variable that are attributable to factors not controlled for by the researcher. As we will see, these influences are removed statistically and by so doing the error variance can be decreased—resulting in more sensitive (that is, precise) experiments.

THE ANCOVA MODEL

Recall from Chapters 6 and 15 that the traditional ANOVA model is

$$y_{ij} = \bar{y}_{++} + T_j + e_{ij} \tag{15B-1}$$

where $\bar{y}_{++}$ denotes the overall mean response and T_j $(j = 1, 2, \ldots, K)$ denotes the differential effect of the Kth treatment condition on the criterion measure. As before e_{ij} denotes the error term.

Suppose now that in addition to the manipulated variable the researcher suspects that another extraneous factor has influenced the observed measures on the criterion variable. We refer to this other extraneous factor as the *covariate*. In ANCOVA the traditional ANOVA model is augmented in such a way as to account for the variation in the criterion variable that is due to the covariate. Specifically, we introduce another term, denoted as X_{ij}, representing the covariate and express the model shown in equation (15B-1) as

$$y_{ij} = \bar{y}_{++} + T_j + c(X_{ij} - \bar{X}_{++}) + e_{ij} \tag{15B-2}$$

The variable X_{ij} denotes the value of the covariate for the ith individual in the jth treatment condition; c denotes the coefficient representing the average effect of a unit change in the covariate on the criterion variable, and $\overline{X}_{++}$ is the overall mean of the covariate. (In Chapter 16 this effect (c) is known as a *regression coefficient*.) Verbally, the algebraic model shown in equation (15B-2) can be expressed as

$$\begin{pmatrix} \text{Observed value} \\ \text{of dependent} \\ \text{variable} \end{pmatrix} = (\text{constant}) + \begin{pmatrix} \text{effect of} \\ \text{treatment} \\ \text{condition} \end{pmatrix} + \begin{pmatrix} \text{effect} \\ \text{of} \\ \text{covariate} \end{pmatrix} + \begin{pmatrix} \text{error} \\ \text{term} \end{pmatrix}$$

To better understand how ANCOVA works we can compare the error term with that obtained under the basic ANOVA model. We can view $c(X_{ij} - \overline{X}_{++})$ as representing that part of y_{ij} that is accounted for by changes in the covariate (X), while e_{ij} is the *residual* error that still remains. Letting e^*_{ij} denote the error term under ANCOVA and e_{ij} denote the error term under ANOVA we can write

$$e_{ij} = e^*_{ij} + c(X_{ij} - \overline{X}_{++})$$

Under the assumption that the e_{ij} and $c(X_{ij} - \overline{X}_{++})$ are independent we have

$$\text{Var}(e_{ij}) = \text{Var}(e^*_{ij}) + \text{Var (due to } X)$$

Thus, the variance of the error term after covariance adjustment is no more than the variance of the error term under the standard ANOVA model ignoring the variance due to the covariate (X).

SUM OF SQUARES AND TESTING

From equation (15B-2) it is apparent that the criterion variable may be adjusted for the covariate as follows

$$y_{ij(adj)} = y_{ij} - c(X_{ij} - \overline{X}_{++}) \tag{15B-3}$$

where $y_{ij(adj)}$ denotes the value of the criterion variable adjusted for the covariate. In covariance analysis we are still concerned with testing the hypothesis that the treatment condition means are equal. Thus, based upon the preceding discussion and equation (15B-3), it would appear that we could accomplish this by conducting an analysis of variance on the adjusted scores $y_{ij(adj)}$. However, unless the coefficient c is known, which rarely is the case, this is not the recommended approach. The problem is that c in most cases must be estimated from the sample by using data from all of the treatment conditions. Because the adjusted treatment condition means are not independent of each other the F-test for testing the equality of treatment condition means is not strictly valid. Another approach must therefore be followed.

Formulas for Computing Unadjusted Sum of Squares and Cross-Products

Total:

$$TSS(y) = \sum_{j=1}^{K} \sum_{i=1}^{nj} (y_{ij} - \bar{y}_{++})^2 = \sum_{j=1}^{K} \sum_{i=1}^{nj} y_{ij}^2 - \left(\sum_{j=1}^{K} \sum_{i=1}^{nj} y_{ij} \right)^2 \Big/ n$$

$$TSS(X) = \sum_{j=1}^{K} \sum_{i=1}^{nj} (X_{ij} - \bar{X}_{++})^2 = \sum_{j=1}^{K} \sum_{i=1}^{nj} X_{ij}^2 - \left(\sum_{j=1}^{K} \sum_{i=1}^{nj} X_{ij} \right)^2 \Big/ n$$

$$TSS(yX) = \sum_{j=1}^{K} \sum_{i=1}^{nj} (y_{ij} - \bar{y}_{++})(X_{ij} - \bar{X}_{++})$$

$$= \sum_{j=1}^{K} \sum_{i=1}^{nj} y_{ij}X_{ij} - \left(\sum_{j=1}^{K} \sum_{i=1}^{nj} y_{ij} \sum_{j=1}^{K} \sum_{i=1}^{nj} X_{ij} \right) \Big/ n$$

Between:

$$BSS(y) = \sum_{j=1}^{K} n_j(\bar{y}_{+j} - \bar{y}_{++})^2$$

$$BSS(X) = \sum_{j=1}^{K} n_j(\bar{X}_{+j} - \bar{X}_{++})^2$$

$$BSS(yX) = \sum_{j=1}^{K} n_j(\bar{y}_{+j} - \bar{y}_{++})(\bar{X}_{+j} - \bar{X}_{++})$$

Within:

$$WSS(y) = \sum_{j=1}^{K} \sum_{i=1}^{nj} (y_{ij} - \bar{y}_{+j})^2$$

$$WSS(X) = \sum_{j=1}^{K} \sum_{i=1}^{nj} (X_{ij} - \bar{X}_{+j})^2$$

$$WSS(yX) = \sum_{j=1}^{K} \sum_{i=1}^{nj} (y_{ij} - \bar{y}_{+j})(X_{ij} - \bar{X}_{+j}) = \sum_{j=1}^{K} \sum_{i=1}^{nj} y_{ij}X_{ij} - \frac{n}{K} \left(\sum_{j=1}^{K} y_{+j}\bar{X}_{+j} \right)$$

The first step is to develop the necessary sum of squares. Let

$TSS(\cdot)$ = Total sum of squares for factor $(\cdot)$

$BSS(\cdot)$ = Between sum of squares for factor $(\cdot)$

$WSS(\cdot)$ = Within sum of squares for factor $(\cdot)$

Table 15B-1 shows the necessary formulas for computing the unadjusted sum of squares and cross products. (By *cross products* we simply mean the yX effect.)

To perform the ANCOVA test we need to adjust these sums of squares. In essence the adjustment removes the effect of the covariate from the total, between, and within sum of squares for the criterion variable y. These are shown on the following page.

$$TSS(y_{adj}) = TSS(y) - \left(\frac{TSS(yX)^2}{TSS(X)}\right)$$

$$WSS(y_{adj}) = WSS(y) - \left(\frac{WSS(yX)^2}{WSS(X)}\right)$$

$$BSS(y_{adj}) = TSS(y_{adj}) - WSS(y_{adj})$$

The hypothesis testing procedure follows the standard format.

$HO:\ \mu_1 = \mu_2 = \ldots = \mu_K$

$HA:$ not all μ_K are equal

$$TS_c:\ F_c = \frac{BSS(y_{adj})/(K - 1)}{(WSS(y_{adj})/(n - K - 1)}$$

$TS_t:\ F_t(1 - \alpha; K - 1, n - K - 1)$

$DR:$ Reject $HO:$ if $F_c > F_{t(1-\alpha;\ K-1,\ n-K-1)}$

Note that the degrees of freedom associated with the adjusted within sum of squares is $(n - K - 1)$. One additional degree of freedom is lost because of the estimation of the within-treatment effect $WSS(yX)^2/WSS(X)$.

Table 15B-2 shows data on pre- and post-exposure attitude scores for twelve respondents who participated in a three-cell *before-after* advertising execution test. Table 15B-3 shows summary computational details and the resulting ANOVA table, ignoring the covariate, which in this

T A B L E 15B-2
Pre- and Post-Attitude Scores for Three-Cell Before-After Advertising Execution Test

Respondent	Pre-exposure attitude score (y)	Post-exposure attitude score covariate (X)
1	6	6
2	7	6
3	8	8
4	5	5
Cell 1	$\bar{y}_{+1} = 6.5$	$\bar{X}_{+1} = 6.25$
5	7	5
6	5	3
7	4	2
8	6	4
Cell 2	$\bar{y}_{+2} = 5.5$	$\bar{X}_{+2} = 3.5$
9	8	10
10	7	9
11	6	8
12	9	11
Cell 3	$\bar{y}_{+3} = 7.5$	$\bar{X}_{+3} = 9.5$
	$\bar{y}_{++} = 6.5$	$\bar{X}_{++} = 6.42$

T A B L E 15B-3
Summary Computations and ANOVA Table

Source	SS	df	MSS	F_c
Between	$BSS = 8$	$K - 1 = 2$	$\dfrac{BSS}{(K - 1)} = 4$	$\dfrac{4}{1.67} = 2.4$
Within	$WSS = 15$	$n - K = 9$	$\dfrac{WSS}{(n - K)} = 1.67$	
Total	$TSS = 23$	$n - 1 = 11$		

$$BSS = \sum_{j=1}^{K} n_j(\bar{y}_{+j} - \bar{y}_{++})^2 = [4(6.5 - 6.5)^2 + 4(5.5 - 6.5)^2 + 4(7.5 - 6.5)^2]$$
$$= 8$$

$$WSS = \sum_{j=1}^{K}\sum_{i=1}^{nj} (y_{ij} - \bar{y}_{+j})^2 = (6 - 6.5)^2 + (7 - 6.5)^2 + \cdots + (6 - 7.5)^2$$
$$+ (9 - 7.5)^2$$
$$= 15$$

$$TSS = \sum_{j=1}^{K}\sum_{i=1}^{nj} (y_{ij} - \bar{y}_{++})^2 = (6 - 6.5)^2 + (7 - 6.5)^2 + \cdots + (6 - 6.5)^2$$
$$+ (9 - 6.5)^2$$
$$= 23$$

case is the pre-exposure attitude score. From the table we would conclude the three cells are not different—that is, the three advertising executions come from the same population and therefore their post-exposure mean attitude scores are the same.

The ANCOVA test is carried out in Table 15B-4. Note that the adjusted treatment condition mean sum of squares is 5.17 and the adjusted within-treatment condition mean sum of squares is 0.77. The associated F ratio of 26.98, with 2 and 8 degrees of freedom, is highly significant at the .05 level. Thus, in contrast to the ANOVA results, we conclude that the three advertising executions differ once the influence of the covariate is removed.

CONCLUSION

In the preceding example covariance adjustment led to an increase in precision; after adjustment the treatment conditions were found to be significant. However, it is possible for covariance analysis to lead to a decrease in precision. If the covariate is highly related to the manipulated variable (treatment conditions) and *not* highly related to the criterion variable, then covariance adjustment can remove a large part of the treatment effect, thereby reducing precision. In such cases partialing out the covariate is not appropriate.

Summary Calculations and ANCOVA Table

Source	SS	df	MSS	F_c
Between	BSS = 5.17	$K - 1 = 2$	$\dfrac{BSS}{(K-1)} = 2.59$	$\dfrac{2.59}{.096} = 26.98$
Within	WSS = 0.77	$n - K - 1 = 8$	$\dfrac{WSS}{(n-K-2)} = .096$	
Total	TSS = 5.94	$n - 2 = 10$		

Preliminary calculations	Cell 1	Cell 2	Cell 3	Total
n_j	4	4	4	12
Σy	26	22	30	78
ΣX	25	14	38	77
Σy^2	174	126	230	530
ΣyX	167	82	290	539
ΣX^2	161	54	366	581

$$TSS(y) = \sum_{j=1}^{K} \sum_{i=1}^{n_j} (y_{ij} - \bar{y}_{++})^2 = \sum_{j=1}^{K} \sum_{i=1}^{n_j} y_{ij}^2 - \left(\sum_{j=1}^{K} \sum_{i=1}^{n_j} y_{ij}\right)^2 \bigg/ n$$

$$= 530 - (78)^2/12 = 23$$

$$TSS(X) = \sum_{j=1}^{K} \sum_{i=1}^{n_j} (X_{ij} - \bar{X}_{++})^2 = \sum_{j=1}^{K} \sum_{i=1}^{n_j} X_{ij}^2 - \left(\sum_{j=1}^{K} \sum_{i=1}^{n_j} X_{ij}\right)^2 \bigg/ n$$

$$= 581 - (77)^2/12 = 86.92$$

$$TSS(yX) = \sum_{j=1}^{K} \sum_{i=1}^{n_j} y_{ij} X_{ij} - \left(\sum_{j=1}^{K} \sum_{i=1}^{n_j} y_{ij} \sum_{j=1}^{K} \sum_{i=1}^{n_j} X_{ij}\right) \bigg/ n$$

$$= 539 - (78)(77)/12 = 38.5$$

$$WSS(X) = \sum_{j=1}^{K} \sum_{i=1}^{n_j} (X_{ij} - \bar{X}_{+j})^2 = (6 - 6.25)^2 + (6 - 6.25)^2 + \cdots + (8 - 9.5)^2 + (11 - 9.5)^2$$

$$= 14.77$$

$$WSS(yX) = \sum_{j=1}^{K} \sum_{i=1}^{n_j} (y_{ij} - \bar{y}_{+j})(X_{ij} - \bar{X}_{+j}) = \sum_{j=1}^{K} \sum_{i=1}^{n_j} y_{ij} X_{ij} - \frac{n}{K}\left(\sum_{j=1}^{K} \bar{y}_{+j} \bar{X}_{+j}\right)$$

$$= 539 - 4\,[(6.5)(6.25) + (5.5)(3.5) + (6.5)(6.42)]$$
$$= 539 - 524.5 = 14.5$$

$$TSS(y_{adj}) = TSS(y) - \frac{TSS(yX)^2}{TSS(X)}$$

$$= 23 - \frac{(38.5)^2}{86.92} = 5.94$$

$$WSS(y_{adj}) = WSS(y) - \frac{WSS(yX)^2}{TSS(X)}$$

$$= 15 - \frac{(14.5)^2}{14.77} = .77$$

$$BSS(y_{adj}) = TSS(y_{adj}) - WSS(y_{adj})$$
$$= 5.17$$

Measures of Association and Regression Analysis

CHAPTER OBJECTIVES

- Present the notion of covariation between two random variables.
- Demonstrate the calculation of correlation coefficients for variables measured on interval, ordinal, or nominal scales.
- Use simple regression analysis to predict values of one variable given a value for another variable.
- Describe multiple regression analysis.
- Explain the effects of multicollinearity on the estimation of regression coefficients.
- Provide statistical tests for regression coefficients.
- Describe the assumptions underlying regression analysis.

Introduction

Chapter 15 focused on data-analysis methods and tests of hypotheses that considered only one variable at a time. Although these methods did allow for group differences to be tested, the hypotheses were formulated in terms of a single variable.

In this chapter we again formulate and test hypotheses; however, we concentrate on investigating the relationships between two random variables. We use the term random variable to indicate that the variation in a variable is not controlled by the researcher.

•In Chapter 9 we discussed the different scales of measurement: nominal, ordinal, interval, and ratio. The method used to calculate the correlation between two variables depends on the scale used to measure the variables. Thus, in this chapter we discuss methods for calculating the correlation when both variables adhere to either a nominal, ordinal, or interval scale; in addition, we investigate methods of calculating the correlation between variables measured on (two) different scales.

When two variables are correlated there is a systematic relationship between the values assumed by one variable and the values assumed by the other variable. In some cases we may wish to predict or explain the variation in one variable on the basis of some other variable or a set of variables. When this is the objective of the analysis we can use a statistical technique called *regression analysis.* After we present methods for calculating correlation coefficients, we present simple (one dependent and one independent variable) regression analysis and multiple (one dependent and more than one independent variable) regression analysis.

ASSOCIATION BETWEEN VARIABLES

Covariation A systematic relationship between the level of one variable and the level of some other variable.

Before we investigate specific measures of correlation we need to understand what is meant by **covariation.** If two variables covary then there is a systematic relationship between the level of one variable and the level of some other variable.

E X A M P L E

Scatter diagram A bivariate plot of two variables.

Columns 2 and 3 of Table 16-1 present hypothetical data on size of sales force and market coverage. Inspection of the data provides support for association between the two variables. Notice that those firms with a large sales force also tend to have high market coverage, whereas firms with a small sales force tend to have low market coverage. Figure 16-1, part **a** displays the bivariate plot of these two variables. These plots are typically called **scatter diagrams** and are useful for visually inspecting the association, if any, between two variables. The numbers in parentheses refer to the firms listed in Table 16-1.

T A B L E   16-1
Hypothetical Data Used for Measuring Covariation

(1) Firm	(2) Sales force	(3) Market coverage (%)	(4) Out-of-stock items	(5) Average dollar sale	(6) Turnover ratio
1	100	10	30	30	30
2	200	30	17	40	35
3	400	30	15	35	25
4	300	50	19	25	30
5	500	50	13	45	15
6	500	60	10	35	15
7	600	70	11	40	20
8	100	20	22	50	40
9	800	80	10	35	25
10	700	50	9	30	15
11	1000	80	3	35	40
12	700	60	12	45	20
13	800	70	2	45	30
14	900	90	2	40	30
15	1000	90	5	50	45

The type of association shown in Figure 16-1, part **a** is called **direct or positive assocation,** since as the value of one variable increases (decreases) there is a tendency for the value of the other variable to increase (decrease). It is also possible to observe an **inverse or negative association** between two variables. The term negative association is used

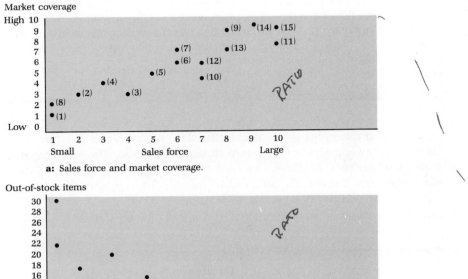

a: Sales force and market coverage.

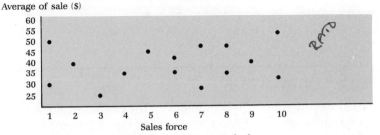

b: Sales force and out-of-stock data.

c: Sales force and average dollar amount of sale.

Figure 16-1

Scatter diagram for data in Table 16-1. Number in parentheses refers to firm number, Table 1.

495

whenever the value of one variable increases (decreases) and the value of the other variable decreases (increases). Note that the terms positive and negative are not subject to value judgments; that is, positive relationships are not "good" and negative relationships are not "bad."

E X A M P L E

Columns 2 and 4 of Table 16-1 present data for the size of the sales force and items out-of-stock for the same 15 firms. The scatter diagram for these data is displayed in Figure 16-1, part **b**. In contrast to the relationship shown in part **a** of this figure, there is an inverse relationship between size of sales force and out-of-stock; that is, companies with small sales forces were more likely to be out-of-stock.

Our two examples demonstrate the case where an association, positive or negative, exists between two variables. However, there are circumstances when two variables may not be associated. By **no association** we mean that there is no systematic relationship between the level of one variable and the level of another variable. In other words, the variation in one variable is independent of the variation in the other variable.

No or zero association A situation in which there is no systematic relationship between the level of one variable and the level of another variable.

E X A M P L E

Consider columns 2 and 5 of Table 16-1 which give information on the size of sales force for the 15 firms and the corresponding average dollar amount of a sale. The scatter diagram for the data is shown in Figure 16-1, part **c.** Note that smaller firms have *both* large and small average dollar sales and the same is true for larger firms—larger firms also have *both* large and small average dollar sales. Hence, there is no systematic relationship between size of sales force and the level of the other variable (average dollar sale).

MEASURES OF CORRELATION

The method or procedure used to measure the degree of association between two variables ultimately depends on the measurement scale to which the variables refer.

Interval or Ratio-Scaled Variables

The most commonly used measure of correlation was developed by Carl Pearson in the early 1900s and is referred to as the **Pearson prod-**

uct moment correlation, or simply as the product moment correlation between two variables. Denoting the variables as X_i and y_i and their corresponding linear correlation as r_{xy}, the formula for computing the sample-based product moment correlation is

Pearson product moment correlation
Measure of the linear association between two interval or ratio scaled variables.

$$r_{xy} = \frac{\sum_{i=1}^{n}[(X_i - \bar{X})(y_i - \bar{y})]/n - 1}{\sqrt{\dfrac{\sum_{i=1}^{n}(X_i - \bar{X})^2}{n - 1}} \sqrt{\dfrac{\sum_{i=1}^{n}(y_i - \bar{y})^2}{n - 1}}} \qquad (16\text{-}1)$$

The denominator of formula (16-1) should look familiar; it is simply the product of the standard deviation of X_i and y_i. Covariance measures the degree to which two variables covary—that is, the extent to which the variables display some degree of positive or negative association.

Computation shows that the covariance between sales force (y_i) and market coverage (X_i) is 99,800. However, does a covariance of 99,800 represent strong or weak association between the two variables? From equation (16-1) we can see that the larger the values of y_i and X_i, the larger will be the covariance because we are summing the product of $(X_i - \bar{X})(y_i - \bar{y})$. In other words, the covariance between two variables is affected by the units of measurement. To illustrate this notion let's multiply the sales force size for each firm shown in Table 16-1 by ten. Hence instead of 100 salespersons, firm 1 now has 1,000 salespersons, firm 2 now has 2,000 salespersons instead of 200 salespersons, and so forth. The covariance between the two variables is now 998,000; however, the basic relationship between the two variables has not changed. That is, the scatter diagram would be identical to Figure 16-1 with only the scale of the vertical axis changed. It is for this reason that we divide the covariance between y_i and X_i by the product of their standard deviations as shown in equation (16-1). Unlike the covariance between X_i and y_i, the correlation (r_{xy}) is bounded by the range -1 to $+1$, where -1 would represent perfect negative correlation, $+1$ represents perfect positive correlation, and zero represents no correlation. In the case of perfect positive or perfect negative correlation, all of the points in a scatter diagram would fall on a straight line. As the points deviate from a straight line the correlation decreases.

In Chapter 13 the standardization transformation was discussed. Letting X_i' be the standardized value associated with X_i and y_i' be the standardized value associated with y_i, where with

$$X_i' = (X_i - \bar{X})/s_x$$

and

$$y_i' = (y_i - \bar{y})/s_y$$

we know that $\bar{X}' = \bar{y}' = 0$ and $s_{x'} = s_{y'} = 1$.

497

Hence the correlation $(r_{x'y'})$ between the standardized variables $(X'$ and $y')$ is

$$r_{x'y'} = \frac{\sum\limits_{i=1}^{n} (X'_i - 0)(y'_i - 0)/(n - 1)}{\sqrt{1}\,\sqrt{1}}$$

$$= \sum\limits_{i=1}^{n} (X'_i y'_i)/n - 1 \tag{16-2}$$

Thus, we see that the covariance between two standardized variables is the correlation between the variables.

E X A M P L E

To illustrate the calculation of the product moment correlation let us return to the data shown in Table 16-1. Applying equation (16-1) we find

$$r_{xy} = \frac{99{,}800/14}{(305.19)(25.0)} = .93$$

The correlation r_{xy} is the sample-based correlation between X_i and y_i. It is an estimate of the population correlation (ρ_{xy}) between the two variables. If we want to statistically test the hypothesis of no correlation in the population between X_i and y_i (that is, $HO\!: \rho_{xy} = 0$), the procedure is[1]

$HO\!: \rho_{xy} = 0$

$HA\!: \rho_{xy} \neq 0$

$$TS_c\!: t_c = \frac{r_{xy}\sqrt{n - 2}}{\sqrt{1 - r_{xy}^2}}$$

$TS_t\!: t_{t(1-\alpha;\, df = n-2)}$

$DR\!:$ Reject $HO\!:$ if $TS_c > TS_t$ or $-TS_c < -TS_t$

E X A M P L E

The test of whether the correlation between size of sales force and market coverage is statistically different from zero proceeds as follows: With $r_{xy} = .93$ we find

$$t_c = \frac{.93\sqrt{13}}{\sqrt{.14}}$$

$$= 8.96$$

[1]John Neter, William Wasserman, and Michael J. Kuter, *Applied Linear Statistical Methods,* 2nd ed. (Homewood, Ill.: Richard D. Irwin, 1985), 501–503.

498

From Table 3 in the Statistical Appendix the region of rejection at $\alpha = .05$ and $df = n - 2 = 13$ is 2.160. Since the test statistic calculated (TS_c) exceeds the tabulated critical test statistic (TS_t), $TS_c > TS_t$, we reject the null hypothesis, concluding that sales force and market coverage are correlated.

As stated previously, the product moment correlation measures the linear association between two interval-scaled or ratio-scaled variables. If two variables exhibit nonlinear association, the product moment correlation will likely be close to zero; however, this does not mean that the variables are not associated. Consider, for example, the data in columns 2 and 6 of Table 16-1. Plotting these data shows a "U"-shaped pattern. In other words, both large and small firms have high turnover ratios of salespeople, and midsize firms have lower turnover ratios. Hence, as the size of a firm increases, the turnover ratio decreases until some point and then reverses itself and increases as the size of a firm increases. The (linear) product moment correlation is close to zero (.033), indicating little association between the variables. However, there is a fairly strong association between the variables, but it is not linear in character.

Ordinal Scales

As we discussed in Chapter 9, the mean is not the appropriate measure of central tendency when the data have ordinal-scale properties; consequently, we cannot use the product moment correlation. With variables having ordinal rank-order properties, the appropriate measure of correlation is **Spearman's rank-order correlation coefficient**, which we will denote simply as ρ_s (and r_s for the sample-based estimate).

Spearman's rank-order correlation coefficient Measure of linear association between variables that have ordinal scale properties.

The sample-based Spearman's rank-order correlation coefficient can be calculated from the following formula.[2]

$$r_s = 1 - 6 \sum_{i=1}^{n} \frac{d_i^2}{n(n^2 - 1)} \qquad (16\text{-}3)$$

where d_i represents the difference in ranking for the ith object, n is the number of objects ranked, and the number 6 appearing in the numerator is a constant needed to ensure that the sample-based estimate of the correlation coefficient is an unbiased estimate of its population counterpart. How formula (16-3) is applied will become clear in the following example.

[2]Robert L. Winkler and William L. Hays, *Statistical Probability: Inference and Decision,* 2nd ed. (New York: Holt, Rinehart and Winston, 1975), 867–870.

EXAMPLE

To illustrate the calculation of the rank-order correlation coefficient, consider the following example. An advertising agency was interested in the relationship between the copy-testing procedures of two copy-testing suppliers. Each of the copy-testing services evaluated copy on a number of dimensions (such as attention, recall, and persuasion) and produced a rank ordering of the copy that purportedly reflected the advertisement's overall effectiveness. The advertising agency needed to select one of the copy-testing services; however, a major concern centered on the consistency of the rank orderings produced by each of the copy-testing services and the internal rank ordering of ads within the advertising agency itself. To investigate this issue, the agency asked each supplier to copy-test ten ads and rank-order them with respect to overall performance. These rankings would be used to determine which, if any, of the suppliers' ranking was most associated with the agency's own ranking of the ten ads.

Table 16-2 contains the rankings for the agency and the two suppliers. To determine the correlation between the advertising agency's rank ordering and those of each testing service the difference in rank orderings (d_i) and the squared differences (d_i^2) must first be calculated. (The d_i's are shown in Table 16-2). Applying formula (16-3) the correlation between the rank orderings of the advertising agency and supplier 1 is

$$r_s = 1 - (6)(14)/10(10^2 - 1) = .92$$

and the correlation between the advertising agency and supplier 2 is

$$r_s = 1 - (6)(62)/10(10^2 - 1) = .62$$

TABLE 16-2
Ranking of Ads

Advertisement	Agency Ranking	Supplier 1		Supplier 2	
		Ranking	d_i	Rating	d_i
A	1	2	−1	3	−2
B	8	9	−1	5	3
C	5	6	−1	6	−1
D	2	1	1	1	1
E	4	3	1	8	−4
F	7	7	0	9	−2
G	10	10	0	7	3
H	9	8	1	10	−1
I	3	5	−2	4	−1
J	6	4	2	2	4

We can also perform a test of whether the rank-order correlation coefficient is statistically different from zero. The hypothesis and test statistic are described below and illustrated in the following example.

$HO: \rho_s = 0$

$HA: \rho_s \neq 0$

$$TS_c: t_c = \frac{r_s\sqrt{n-2}}{\sqrt{1-r_s^2}}$$

$TS_t: t_{t(1-\alpha; \, df = n-2)}$

DR: Reject HO: if $t_c > t_{t(1-\alpha; \, n-2)}$ or $-t_c < -t_{t(1-\alpha; \, n-2)}$

EXAMPLE

Let us return to the data on copy-testing services introduced in the previous example. From previous results, the test statistics can be computed as follows:

$t_{c_1} = .92\sqrt{8}/\sqrt{1 - .92^2} = 6.64$ (supplier 1)

$t_{c_2} = .62\sqrt{8}/\sqrt{1 - .62^2} = 2.24$ (supplier 2)

Hence, for $t_{t(.05;8)} = 2.306$ (see Table 3, in the Statistical Appendix) we reject the null hypothesis of no association between the advertising agency's rankings and those of supplier 1, in the population, but cannot reject the null hypothesis of no association between the rankings of the advertising agency and those of supplier 2 in the population. Consequently, the advertising agency would select supplier 1 to perform their copy testing because (1) the correlation between this supplier's rankings of ads and the advertising agency's own ranking was statistically significant, and (2) the correlation was strong.

Nominal Scales

When data adhere to a nominal scale the method of analysis typically consists of determining the number or proportion of observations for each level of the variable. For example, if we asked a sample of people what type of deodorant they prefer—such as spray, stick, or roll-on—to analyze the data we probably would determine the proportion of the people sampled who preferred each type of deodorant. When we have two variables that adhere to a nominal scale and we want to determine the level of association between the two variables, we first cross-classify the variables to form a contingency table of dimensions $I \times J$, where I is the number of levels of one variable (typically the variable constituting the rows) and J is the number of levels of the other variable (typically the variable constituting the columns).

The most widely used measures of association for nominal data are those based on the **chi-square statistic.**

Chi-square statistic A measure for the difference between what we observe from the sample and what we should have observed in the sample if the two variables were not associated.

Measures Based on Chi-Square Statistic. In Chapter 15, the chi-square statistic was defined as

$$\chi_c^2 = \sum_{k=1}^{K} (O_k - E_k)^2 / E_k \tag{16-4}$$

where

O_k = the observed count in the kth cell of the table

E_k = the expected count in the kth cell of the table

K = the number of cells in the table ($K = I \times J$)

The observed counts (O_k) are those formed from the cross-classification of the two variables. The expected counts (E_k) are those we would expect to observe if the null hypothesis were true. Letting ρ_n be the population correlation for two nominally scaled variables, the null hypothesis is

$HO: \rho_n = 0$

That is, the variables are independent.

Consider the case where we have two nominal variables: gender (female, male) and coffee preference (drip, instant). The cross-classification of these two variables produces a 2×2 contingency table having four cells, shown in Table 16-3. Here the n_{ij} represent the observed counts. For example, letting $i = j = 1$ we have cell n_{11}, which is the number of observations in the sample that are female and prefer drip coffee, whereas letting $i = 1$ and $j = 2$ we have n_{12}, which is the number of observations in the sample that are female and prefer instant coffee. The same interpretations hold for n_{21} and n_{22}. Notice that the totals for rows and columns use a "+" as a subscript. Recall this type of notation from Chapter 13. When the "+" is used for the j subscript (n_{i+}) it means that we are summing over j or the columns for the ith row. Hence, if we let $i = 1$ for n_{i+} we get n_{1+} or the total for the first row. Therefore, n_{i+} represent the totals for the rows and n_{+j} represent the totals for the columns. The total sample size (n) is expressed as n_{++}.

T A B L E   16-3

2×2 Contingency Table for Coffee Preference

	Table **a**				Table **b**		
	Preference				Preference		
Gender	Drip		Instant	Gender	Drip		Instant
Female	n_{11}	n_{12}	n_{1+}	Female	p_{11}	p_{12}	p_{1+}
Male	n_{21}	n_{22}	n_{2+}	Male	p_{21}	p_{22}	p_{2+}
	n_{+1}	n_{+2}	n_{++}		p_{+1}	p_{+2}	1

Dividing the observed counts (n_{ij}) by the total sample size (n_{++}) provides a corresponding probability table.[3] This table is shown in Table 16-3, part b. The numbers in the cells of the table are called joint probabilities. Hence p_{22} is the joint probability of a sample element being male and preferring instant coffee, whereas the numbers representing rows or column totals are called marginal probabilities. Consequently, p_{+1} is the probability of preferring drip coffee. Probability theory tells us that when two variables are independent their joint probability is equal to the product of their marginal probabilities. Hence the expected joint probabilities for the four cells given the null hypothesis of no association are calculated as

Cell (11) $= p_{1+} \times p_{+1}$
Cell (12) $= p_{1+} \times p_{+2}$
Cell (21) $= p_{2+} \times p_{+1}$
Cell (22) $= p_{2+} \times p_{+2}$

The expected values for each cell can be calculated by substituting the row or column totals for the row or column probabilities and dividing by the sample size (n_{++}). For example, the expected count for cell (11) would be:

Expected count cell (11) $= (n_{1+}n_{+1})/n_{++}$

The chi-square statistic provides us with a measure for the difference between what we observe from the sample (O_k) and what we should have observed in the sample (E_k) if the two variables were not associated—that is, assuming the null hypothesis is true.

So far we have considered only the case of a 2 × 2 table. Frequently either the rows, columns, or both have more than two levels. The calculations for the expected counts are the same for any size ($I \times J$) contingency table. The expected count for any cell is equal to the product of the corresponding row and column marginals divided by the total sample size. For example, if we had a 4 × 5 contingency table and wanted to calculate the expected count for the (2,3) cell, given the null hypothesis of independence, we would divide the product of the marginal totals for the second row and third column by the total sample size:

$(n_{2+}n_{+3})/n_{++}$

Once we have calculated the chi-square statistic (χ_c^2) we can use this value to calculate the correlation between the two variables. A variety of correlation coefficients have been proposed to measure the degree of association between two nominal variables based on the value of χ_c^2. However, some of the coefficients are only applicable for 2 × 2 tables and some of the coefficients have an upper limit less than one. Here we provide **Cramer's contingency coefficient (V)**, which is appropriate for any

---

[3] Stephen E. Fineberg, *The Analysis of Cross-Classified Categorical Data* (Boston: MIT Press, 1977), 11.

Cramer's contingency coefficient (V) Measure of the degree of association between nominal variables which is appropriate for any size contingency table.

size contingency table and in the case of perfect correlation $V = 1$, whereas $V = 0$ if the variables are independent.

Cramer's contingency coefficient (V) is calculated as:[4]

$$V = \sqrt{\frac{\chi_c^2/n}{q - 1}} \tag{16-5}$$

where

χ_c^2 = the calculated value of the chi-square statistic

n = the sample size

q = the smaller of I or J

In addition, we can use the chi-square statistic to statistically test the null hypothesis of no association. Following the standard procedure, the hypothesis test is:

HO: $\rho_n = 0$

HA: $\rho_n \neq 0$

$TS_c:\ \chi_c^2 = \sum_{k=1}^{K} (O_k - E_k)^2/E_k$

$TS_t:\ \chi_{t(1-\alpha;\ df\ =\ (I\ -\ 1)(J\ -1))}^2$

DR: Reject *HO:* if $\chi_c^2 > \chi_{t(1\ -\ \alpha;\ (I\ -\ 1)(J\ -\ 1))}^2$

Note that the degrees of freedom associated with the test statistic is

$$df = (I - 1)(J - 1) \tag{16-6}$$

E X A M P L E

A chain of grocery stores was interested in determining the level of association, if any, between coupon redemption (yes, no) and the time of week the shopping was done (weekday or weekend). The data from a sample of 100 were cross-classified and the observed counts are shown in Table 16-4, part **a**. The expected counts for the null hypothesis of no association are also provided in part **b** of the table.

The chi-square statistic (16-4), based on the observed and expected counts, is

$$\chi_c^2 = \sum_{k=1}^{K} \frac{(O_k - E_k)^2}{E_k}$$

$$= (5 - 13.5)^2/13.5 + (40 - 31.5)^2/31.5 + (25 - 16.5)^2/16.5$$
$$+ (30 - 38.5)^2/38.5$$

$$= 13.90$$

[4]Albert M. Liebetrau, *Measures of Association* (Beverly Hills: Sage Publications, 1983), 14.

TABLE 16-4

**Cross-Classification of Coupon Redemption
and Time of Shopping Trip**

Table **a**—Observed counts (O_k)
Time of shopping trip

Coupon redemption	Weekend	Weekday	
Yes	5	40	45
No	25	30	55
	30	70	100

Table **b**—Expected counts (E_k)
Time of shopping trip

Coupon redemption	Weekend	Weekday	
Yes	13.5	31.5	45
No	16.5	38.5	55
	30	70	100

$E_{11} = (n_{1+} \times n_{+1})/n_{++} = (45 \times 30)/100 = 13.5$
$E_{12} = (n_{1+} \times n_{+2})/n_{++} = (45 \times 70)/100 = 31.5$
$E_{26} = (n_{2+} \times n_{+1})/n_{++} = (55 \times 30)/100 = 16.5$
$E_{22} = (n_{2+} \times n_{+2})/n_{++} = (55 \times 70)/100 = 38.5$

We first use the value of χ_c^2 to test the null hypotheses of no association. With $I = 2$ and $J = 2$ we have $(2 - 1)(2 - 1)$ or 1 degree of freedom. The tabled test statistics $(\chi_{t(1-\alpha;\ df)}^2)$ for $\alpha = .05$ and 1 degree of freedom is, from Table 4 in the Statistical Appendix, 3.84.

Since $\chi_c^2(= 13.90) > \chi_t^2(= 3.84)$ we reject the null hypothesis of no association. The level of association, using Cramer's V, is

$$V = \sqrt{\frac{13.90/100}{2 - 1}} = .37$$

Mixed Scales

It is not uncommon for the marketing research analyst to be faced with the task of determining the correlation between two variables having different scale properties. We consider two specific situations.

**Point-biserial correlation
coefficient** Coefficient
that measures the
association between a
dichotomous variable and
an interval scaled variable.

Dichotomous and Interval-Scale Variables.[5] A frequently encountered data-analysis situation occurs when one variable has interval-scale properties and the other variable is dichotomous. In such cases the dichotomous variable is coded such that its level assumes the values zero or one; for example, in the case of gender, males = 1 and females = 0. (Note that it makes no difference if the assigned codes are males = 0 and females = 1.) The correlation coefficient used to measure the association between a dichotomous variable and an interval-scaled variable is called the **point-biserial correlation coefficient,** which we will denote as simply r_{PB}. The point biserial correlation can be computed by use of the Pearson product-moment correlation coefficient.

E X A M P L E

A regional telephone company wanted to estimate the average family expenditure on long-distance calls. The research supplier thought that a stratified sampling design should be used; however, the researchers were uncertain what specific factor to stratify the population on. Management suggested two variables: (1) home ownership (own versus rent) and (2) whether or not the family had lived out of state for at least six months in the last five years (yes or no). In Chapters 7 and 8 we mentioned that efficiencies gained through stratified sampling are a function of the correlation between the response variable (the variable estimated) and the stratifying variable (the classification variable). To assess the correlation between these two potential stratifying variables and monthly expenditure on long-distance calls, the research supplier conducted a pilot survey of 15 local families. The data from the pilot sample are presented in Table 16-5.

The two stratification variables are dichotomous; therefore, the point biserial correlation coefficient (r_{PB}) is the appropriate measure of association. There is a fairly strong association between living out of state for at least six months in the last five years and long-distance expenditures (r_{PB} = .66); however, there is less association between home ownership and long-distance expenditure (r_{PB} = .04). Thus, management would probably stratify based on whether a family lived out of state for at least six months in the last five years.

The algebraic sign of the point-biserial correlation coefficient is arbitrary in that the researcher determines which level of the dichotomous variable is coded 0 and which level is coded 1. If one switches the 0 and 1 codes for the respective categories of the dichotomous variable, then the algebraic sign attached to r_{PB} coefficient will change but its magnitude will not.

[5]When the dichotomous variable is actually a continuous variable that has been dichotomized, the appropriate correlation coefficient is the biserial correlation coefficient. See Warren S. Martin, "Effects of Scaling on the Correlation Coefficient: Additional Considerations," *Journal of Marketing Research*, May 1978, 304–308, for a presentation of the results of a mathematical simulation comparing the use of Pearson's product moment correlation where the biserial correlation is the appropriate measure.

T A B L E 16-5
Pilot Survey Data

Element	Long-distance phone bill	Home ownership	Move
1	2.50	own (0)	no (1)
2	25.75	own (0)	yes (0)
3	38.50	rent (1)	yes (0)
4	5.00	rent (1)	no (1)
5	15.50	own (0)	yes (0)
6	9.20	own (0)	no (1)
7	4.00	own (0)	no (1)
8	45.00	own (0)	yes (0)
9	10.90	rent (1)	no (1)
10	5.40	rent (1)	no (1)
11	12.75	rent (1)	no (1)
12	18.65	own (0)	yes (0)
13	23.40	rent (1)	no (1)
14	18.50	own (0)	no (1)
15	14.50	own (0)	yes (0)

To statistically test the significance of a point-biserial correlation coefficient we use the same procedure as for the Pearson product moment correlation coefficient; hence, the test statistic is

$$t_c = \frac{r_{PB}\sqrt{n-2}}{\sqrt{1 - r_{PB}^2}}$$ (16-7)

with $n - 2$ degrees of freedom.

E X A M P L E

Applying formula (16-7) for each of the two stratification variables introduced in the previous example yields the following results:

$$t_{c_1} = \frac{.04\sqrt{13}}{\sqrt{1 - .04^2}} = -.14 \text{ (home ownership)}$$

and

$$t_{c_2} = \frac{.66\sqrt{13}}{\sqrt{1 - .66^2}} = 3.17 \text{ (out-of-state)}$$

The region of rejection with $\alpha = .05$ and $df = n - 2 = 13$ is, from Table 3 in the Statistical Appendix, 2.160. Therefore, only the correlation between long-distance expenditure and living out of state for at least six months in the last five years is statistically significant.

In Chapter 15 we used a t-test statistic of the form (see equation 15-21)

$$t = \frac{\overline{X}_1 - \overline{X}_2}{\sqrt{s_p^2 \, (1/n_1 + 1/n_2)}}$$

in order to test for the statistical difference between two samples on some interval-scaled variable. The preceding examples of point-biserial correlation may appear to be similar to this test; in other words, we might simply ask, is there a statistically significant difference in average monthly long-distance expenditures between those families that have lived out of state for at least six months in the last five years and those families that have not? Though the t-test statistic can be used to evaluate this hypothesis, the test statistic does not provide information on the level of association between these variables. We can, however, convert the t-value calculated from the t-test statistic to a point-biserial correlation coefficient.[6] The appropriate conversion formula is

$$r_{PB} = \sqrt{\frac{t_c^2}{t_c^2 + df}} \tag{16-8}$$

E X A M P L E

Designate families that have lived out of state as group 1 members and all other families as group 2 members. Thus from Table 16-5 we have

$$n_1 = 6 \qquad\qquad n_2 = 9$$
$$\overline{X}_1 = 26.32 \qquad\qquad \overline{X}_2 = 10.18$$
$$s_{x_1} = 12.75 \qquad\qquad s_{x_2} = 7.06$$

Using the pooled variance formula (15-22) and the t-test statistic formula (equation 15-21), we find that

$$t = \frac{26.32 - 10.18}{\sqrt{93.20(1/6 + 1/9)}} = 3.17$$

[6]J. Welkowitz, R. B. Bower, and J. Cohen, *Introductory Statistics for the Social Sciences* (New York: Academic Press, 1976), 187.

The point-biserial correlation coefficient is, from formula (16-8),

$$r_{PB} = \sqrt{\frac{3.17^2}{3.17^2 + 13}} = .66$$

which agrees with the previous result.

Categorical and Interval-Scale Variables. In many situations, the marketing research analyst may be interested in the relationship between a categorical variable having more than two levels and an interval-scaled variable. In this case, there is no specific formula for calculating the correlation between such variables. One approach is to transform the interval-scaled variable into a smaller number of categories, cross-classify the transformed variable with the categorical variable, and then use a measure of correlation appropriate for contingency tables (such as Cramer's V). The number of categories formed for the continuous variable usually depends on sample size considerations. Of course, with large sample sizes the continuous variable can be broken down into a large number of categories or classes. However, if we designate a large number of classes for the continuous variable, then the resulting contingency table may be very sparse—that is, each cell of the table will have only a small number of observations, and many cells may even have no observed counts. It is difficult to handle contingency tables in which many of the cells have few or no observations. A generally accepted practice is to have five responses per cell. This suggestion (five observations per cell) is, however, only a guideline, and not a hard and fast rule.

E X A M P L E

A manufacturer of a super-premium brand of ice cream was interested in the association between total monthly consumption of ice cream and three categories of super-premium brand users: aware of brand and not used in last 30 days (1), unaware of brand (2), and users (3). A mall-intercept interview method was used to collect the data from a sample of 400 consumers who reported having consumed ice cream in the last 30 days. Monthly consumption of ice cream, for analysis purposes, was categorized into three levels: light (1), average (2), and heavy (3). Table 16-6 part **a** presents the cross-classification of the two variables. The expected counts given the null hypothesis of no association are provided in part **b** of the table.

To calculate Cramer's V (equation 16-5) we first must calculate the chi-square statistic. The value of the chi-square from equation (16-4) is

$$\chi_c^2 = (150 - 150)^2/150 + (125 - 112.5)^2/112.5 + (25 - 37.5)^2/37.5$$
$$+ (40 - 32.5)^2/32.5 + (20 - 24.38)^2/24.38 + (5 - 8.13)^2/8.13$$
$$+ (10 - 17.5)^2/17.5 + (5 - 13.13)^2/13.13 + (20 - 4.38)^2/4.38$$
$$= 73.23$$

From Table 4 in the Statistical Appendix the tabled value of the critical chi-square at $\alpha = .05$ with $(3 - 1)(3 - 1) = 4$ degrees of freedom is 9.49. Hence we reject the null hypothesis of no association and calculate the level of association using Cramer's V as

$$V = \sqrt{\frac{73.23/400}{3 - 1}}$$
$$= .30$$

Collapsing Variable Categories

When a continuous variable is artificially categorized or a categorical variable is collapsed to a smaller number of categories, the basic structure of the data has been changed and consequently the original association can be affected. However, there are no rules that allow us to know

T A B L E 16-6
Cross-Classification of Ice Cream Consumption by User Category

Part **a**: observed counts

Users	Consumption Light (1)	Average (2)	Heavy (3)	
Aware/not used (1)	150	125	25	300
Unaware (2)	40	20	5	65
Users (3)	10	5	20	35
	200	150	50	400

Part **b**: expected counts

Users	Consumption Light	Average	Heavy
Aware/not used	150.00[a]	112.50[b]	37.50[c]
Unaware	32.50[d]	24.38[e]	8.13[f]
Users	17.50[g]	13.13[h]	4.38[i]

[a] $E_{11} = (300 \times 200)/400 = 150$
[b] $E_{12} = (300 \times 150)/400 = 112.5$
[c] $E_{13} = (300 \times 50)/400 = 37.5$
[d] $E_{21} = (65 \times 200)/400 = 32.5$
[e] $E_{22} = (65 \times 150)/400 = 24.38$
[f] $E_{23} = (65 \times 50)/400 = 8.13$
[g] $E_{31} = (35 \times 200)/400 = 17.5$
[h] $E_{32} = (35 \times 150)/400 = 13.13$
[i] $E_{33} = (35 \times 50)/400 = 4.37$

T A B L E 16-7
Cross-Classification of Collapsed Variables

Users	Consumption 1	2	
1	150	150	300
2	50	50	100
	200	200	400

exactly the nature of the effect. The analyst must be aware that collapsing variables may mask or create structural relationships that did not exist in the original. The following example illustrates this point.

EXAMPLE

If we dichotomize the two variables in Table 16-6 by collapsing the third level into the second level, the resulting contingency table is shown in Table 16-7. The calculated chi-square statistic for these data is zero, as opposed to 73.23. Hence, in contrast to our previous conclusion, we now conclude that the variables are independent.

REGRESSION ANALYSIS

When two variables are correlated there is a systematic relationship between them. If the relationship is strong, then we may be able to predict the value of one variable given information concerning the value of the other variable. To be consistent with previous discussion, we will refer to the variable to be predicted as the **criterion** or **dependent variable** and the variable upon which the prediction is based as the **predictor** or **independent variable.** Although we use the terms dependent and independent variables, this does not imply causality; that is, we do not mean that the independent variable causes the dependent variable. In Chapter 6 (experimental design) we manipulated a variable (independent) while controlling all other potential causal factors and measured the effect of the manipulation on another variable, the dependent variable. In that case, we could conclude that the relationship was causal; in other words, the effect of the manipulation actually did cause the observed response. We now discuss a statistical technique called **regression analysis** that can be used for predicting the value of the dependent variable once the level of the independent variable has been set. Regression analysis determines how much of the variation in the dependent variable can be *explained* by the independent variable. Again, though the independent variable may explain the variation in the dependent variable, it does not necessarily imply causation.

Criterion or dependent variable The variable to be predicted.
Predictor or independent variable The variable upon which the prediction is based.

Regression analysis Procedure that determines how much of the variation in the dependent variable can be explained by the independent variable.

SIMPLE REGRESSION ANALYSIS

Regression analysis specifies a functional relationship between two or more variables. In the two-variable case, letting *y* represent the depen-

511

dent variable and X represent the independent variable, a functional relationship between X and y can be specified as simply

$$y = f(X) \tag{16-9}$$

Thus, given a value of X, denoted by X_i, we calculate a value of y for the given functional relationship. The most common functional specification is a linear, straight-line relationship of the form

$$f(X) = \beta_0 + \beta_1 X_i \tag{16-10}$$

In formula (16-10) β_0 represents the y-intercept. This is the point where the straight line crosses the y axis; that is, the value of y when $X_i = 0$. β_1 is the slope of the straight line (change in y for a unit change in X). If the algebraic sign of β_1 is positive, then the straight line will slope upward from left to right; if the algebraic sign of β_1 is negative, then the line will slope downward from left to right.

E X A M P L E

Consider the following data, which provides 5 values of X and 5 values of y.

X	y
0	4
2	8
4	12
6	16
8	20

The functional relationship between X and y is

$$y = 4 + 2X_i$$

This relationship is plotted in Figure 16-2. In this case, $\beta_0 = 4$ and $\beta_1 = 2$. Notice that the line crosses the y axis at 4; that is, y equals 4 when X_i equals 0. β_1 is the slope of the line which, in this case, is equal to the 2. The slope indicates the unit increase in y for a unit increase in X ($\Delta y / \Delta X = 4/2 = 2$). The line connecting the dots or points in Figure 16-2 is called the **regression line.**

Regression line A line fitted to the data that in some sense best captures the functional relationship.

The data points shown in Figure 16-2 form a straight line; consequently, the functional form $f(X) = \beta_0 + \beta_1 X_i$, where $\beta_0 = 4$ and $\beta_1 = 2$ fits the data perfectly. However, in practice, rarely, if ever, will the data points in a scatter diagram form a straight line. Consider, for example, Figure 16-3, which contains a scatter diagram for six values of X and y. Notice the plot of values suggests that there is a positive functional relationship between X and y (as X increases, y increases) but no one linear monotonic functional relationship ($y = \beta_0 + \beta_1 X_i$) will connect all of the dots. When this is the case, which it almost always is, we fit the one regression line to the data that best captures the functional relationship.

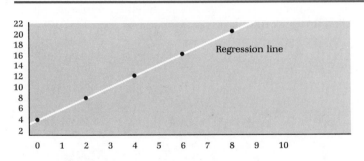

Figure 16-2

Plot of data given in Table 16-4.

In Figure 16-3 we have inserted a regression line. This choice for a regression line seems appropriate because it directly passes through two of the points and is equidistant from the other four points. The functional form of the regression line is

$$f(X) = \beta_0 + \beta_1 X_i = 10 + (1) X_i \tag{16-11}$$

In Table 16-8 we have calculated the predicted values of y for each X. Predicted values are denoted as $\hat{y}_i$. Notice in two cases that the actual value of y is equal to the predicted value, $\hat{y}$. In these cases, the regression line passes directly through the point. However, in the other four cases there is a difference between the predicted values and the actual values. This difference is called the **residual** and is typically denoted as ϵ_i. This

Residual An error term representing the difference between the actual and predicted values of the dependent variable.

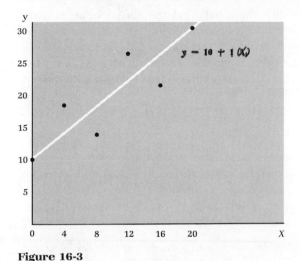

Figure 16-3

Scatter diagram and regression line for six values of X and y.

TABLE 16-8

Calculation of Predicted Values of *y*

Observation	X_i	Actual y_i	Predicted $\hat{y}_i$
1	0	10	10
2	4	18	14
3	8	14	18
4	12	26	22
5	16	22	26
6	20	30	30

$\hat{y}_1 = 10 + (1)(0) = 10$
$\hat{y}_2 = 10 + (1)(4) = 14$
$\hat{y}_3 = 10 + (1)(8) = 18$
$\hat{y}_4 = 10 + (1)(12) = 22$
$\hat{y}_5 = 10 + (1)(16) = 26$
$\hat{y}_6 = 10 + (1)(20) = 30$

residual is an error term representing the difference between y_i and $\hat{y}_i$ (the actual and predicted values of the dependent variable). The error term reflects the fact that rarely will all of the variations in y be explained by X—that is, there are other factors that influence the dependent variable. Note that in the case of y_1 and y_6 the residual equals zero; that is, the actual and predicted values are identical.

$$\epsilon_i = y_i - \hat{y}_i \tag{16-12}$$

Given that $\hat{y}_i$ is equal to $\beta_0 + \beta_1 X_i$, the regression formula becomes

$$y_i = \beta_0 + \beta_1 X_i + \epsilon_i \tag{16-13}$$

Since ϵ_i represents the difference between the actual value and the predicted value, we want estimates of β_0 and β_1 for which ϵ_i is at a minimum. This is a minimization problem and the technical details can be found, for the interested reader, in standard statistics texts.[7] Here we simply provide the formula for calculating the sample-based estimates of β_0 and β_1.

Estimator

To this point the regression formulas have used upper-case Greek letters to refer to population values, as is customary. Hereafter we use Roman letters to refer to sample-based estimates. Hence, we use b_0 and b_1 to refer to the sample-based estimates of β_0 and β_1, respectively. Following this convention, the sample-based regression formula is

[7]See, for example, Paul G. Hoel, *Introduction to Mathematical Statistics* (New York: John Wiley & Sons, 1962), 170.

$$y_i = b_0 + b_1 X_i + e_i \qquad (16\text{-}14)$$

The estimate of the slope, b_1, is calculated according to the following formula:

$$b_1 = \frac{\sum\limits_{i=1}^{n} (X_i - \bar{X})(y_i - \bar{y})}{\sum\limits_{i=1}^{n} (X_i - \hat{X})^2} \qquad (16\text{-}15)$$

The estimate of the intercept, b_0, is calculated according to the following formula:

$$b_0 = 1/n \, (\Sigma y_i - b_1 \, \Sigma X_i) \qquad (16\text{-}16)$$

The formulas for b_0 and b_1 will produce a regression line such that e_i is minimized. In other words, there is no other set of coefficients for b_0 and b_1 that would provide "better" estimates of y. These equations have a long history and are referred to as the **normal equations,** or the **ordinary least-squares (OLS)** estimates of β_0 and β_1. Before proceeding, it should be noted that the sum of e_i (Σe_i) will always equal zero. Hence, what we actually minimize is the square values of e_i (Σe_i^2). This is why this method is commonly called least-squares estimation.

Normal equations/ ordinary least-squares Formulas that produce a regression line such that Σe_i^2 is minimized.

E X A M P L E

Table 16-9 demonstrates how the least-squares estimates for β_0 and β_1 can be calculated for the data introduced in the previous example. Based on these calculations the least-squares estimates of the regression line is

$$y_i = 11.14 + .886X_i + e_i.$$

The least-squares predicted values of y_i are

$\hat{y}_1 = 11.14 + .886(0) = 11.14$

$\hat{y}_2 = 11.14 + .886(4) = 14.68$

$\hat{y}_3 = 11.14 + .886(8) = 18.23$

$\hat{y}_4 = 11.14 + .886(12) = 21.77$

$\hat{y}_5 = 11.14 + .886(16) = 25.32$

$\hat{y}_6 = 11.14 + .886(20) = 28.86$

In Table 16-10 we compare the least-squares estimates of y with the "eyeball" estimates of y (those given in Table 16-8 that intuitively appeared to fit the data). Notice that the sum of the squared residuals (Σe_i^2) is smaller for the least-squares estimates than for the "eyeball" estimates. As indicated earlier, the coefficient calculated from formulas (16-15) and (16-16) will *always* produce the regression line that minimizes the sum of the squared residuals.

T A B L E   16-9

Estimates of β_0 and β_1

Observation	X_i	$(X_i - \bar{X})$	$[(X_i - \bar{X})(y_i - \bar{y})]$	$(y_i - \bar{y})$	y_i	$(X_i - \bar{X})^2$	$(y_i - \bar{y})^2$
1	0	−10	100	−10	10	100	100
2	4	−6	12	−2	18	36	4
3	8	−2	12	−6	14	4	36
4	12	2	12	6	26	4	36
5	16	6	12	2	22	36	4
6	20	10	100	10	30	100	100
Sum	60	0	248	0	120	280	280

$$b_1 = \frac{\sum_{i=1}^{n}(X_i - \bar{X})(y_i - \bar{y})}{\sum_{i=1}^{n}(X_i - \bar{X})^2} = \frac{248}{280} = .886$$

$$b_0 = \frac{1}{n}(\Sigma y_i - b_1 \Sigma X_i) = \frac{1}{6}(120 - (.886)(60)) = 11.14$$

T A B L E   16-10

Comparisons of Least-Squares Estimates with "Eyeball" Estimates

Least squares				Eyeball			
y_i	$\hat{y}_i$	e_i	e_i^2	e_i^2	e_i	$\hat{y}_i$	y_i
10	11.14	−1.14	1.30	0	0	10	10
18	14.68	3.32	11.02	16	4	14	18
14	18.23	−4.23	17.89	16	−4	18	14
26	21.77	4.23	17.89	16	4	22	26
22	25.32	−3.32	11.02	16	−4	26	22
30	28.86	1.14	1.30	0	0	30	30
			60.42	64			

Evaluating Regression Results: r^2

In the previous section we demonstrated that $y_i = \hat{y}_i + e_i$ where $\hat{y}_i$ represents the portion of y_i explained by the regression equation and e_i represents the portion of y_i unexplained by the regression equation. It can be shown that the variation in y_i can be decomposed into two parts: *explained variation* and *unexplained variation*. It seems obvious that the smaller the unexplained variation, the better the fit of the regression line

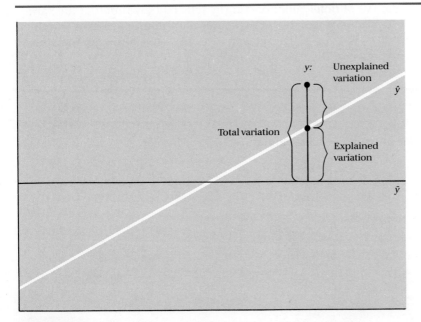

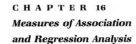
Figure 16-4

Relationship between explained, unexplained, and total variation of *y*.

to the points in the scatter diagram. The total variation in the dependent variable is given by:

$$\text{Total variation} = \sum_{i=1}^{n} (y_i - \bar{y})^2 \tag{16-17}$$

This total variation can be partitioned as follows:

$$\sum_{i=1}^{n} (y_i - \bar{y})^2 = \sum_{i=1}^{n} (\hat{y}_i - \bar{y})^2 + \sum_{i=1}^{n} (y_i - \hat{y}_i)^2 \tag{16-18}$$

Total   Explained   +   Unexplained
          variation   variation

The relationship of these quantities is displayed in Figure 16-4.

The ratio of explained to total variation is called the **coefficient of determination (r^2).**

$$r^2 = \frac{\text{Explained variation}}{\text{Total variation}} \tag{16-19}$$

The coefficient of determination is a measure of goodness-of-fit; however, it does not indicate the percentage of correct predictions or the likelihood of correctly predicting the value of *y* given a specific value of

Coefficient of determination (r^2) The ratio of explained to total variation.

517

X. The coefficient of determination simply tells us how much of the variation in the dependent variable is explained by the independent variable. The range of r^2 is 0 to 1. The closer r^2 is to 1 the stronger the linear relationship between the two variables.

E X A M P L E

The calculations of r^2 for the data previously introduced is shown below.

Total variation $\sum_i (y_i - \bar{y})^2$	=	Explained variation $\sum_i (\hat{y}_i - \bar{y})^2$	+	Unexplained variation $\sum_i (y_i - \hat{y}_i)^2$
$(10 - 20)^2 + (18 - 20)^2 +$ $(14 - 20)^2 + (26 - 20)^2 +$ $(22 - 20)^2 + (30 - 20)^2$		$(11.14 - 20)^2 + (14.68 - 20)^2 +$ $(18.23 - 20)^2 + (21.77 - 20)^2 +$ $(25.32 - 20)^2 + (28.86 - 20)^2$		$(10 - 11.14)^2 + (18 - 14.68)^2 +$ $(14 - 18.23)^2 + (26 - 21.77)^2 +$ $(22 - 25.32)^2 + (30 - 28.86)^2$
280	=	219.87	+	60.43

$$r^2 = \frac{\text{Explained variation}}{\text{Total variation}}$$

$$= \frac{219.87}{280.00} = .79$$

Thus, we conclude that 79 percent of the variation in y is explained by its linear relationship with X.

Predicting y_i

Let $Y_{(x=k)}$ denote the predicted value of y when $X = k$. Thus, the prediction equation is

$$y_{(x=k)} = b_0 + b_1 X_k \tag{16-20}$$

The estimated variance of $y_{(x=k)}$ is given as

$$s^2_{y(x=k)} = MSE[1/n + (X_k - \bar{X})^2/\sum(X_i - \bar{X})^2] \tag{16-21}$$

where MSE stands for *mean square error*, which is given by $\sum e_i^2/n - 2$. A $1 - \alpha/2$ confidence interval for $y_{(x=k)}$ is

$$y_{(x=k)} \pm t_{t(1-\alpha/2; \, df = n-2)} \, s_{y(x=k)} \tag{16-22}$$

E X A M P L E

Let us once again return to the data we have been using and consider predicting the value of y when $X = 18$. From previous results and formula (16-20), we have

$$y_{(18)} = 11.14 + .886(18) = 27.09$$

The estimated variance for $X = 18$ is, from equation (16-21),

$$s^2_{y(18)} = (60.43/4)[\frac{1}{6} + (18 - 10)^2/280] = 5.97$$

A 95 percent confidence interval is

$$y_{(18)} \pm (2.776) \, s_{y(18)}$$
$$27.09 \pm (2.776)(2.44)$$
$$20.31 \leq Y_{(18)} \leq 33.87$$

In other words, we are 95 percent confident that upon repeated sampling the true value of y is greater than or equal to 20.31 and less than or equal to 33.87 when X equals 18.

Statistical tests concerning the regression model are considered in the section that immediately follows. There we discuss the **multiple regression model** that considers the general case of more than one independent variable. In addition, we also discuss the assumptions underlying the regression model.

Multiple regression model Model that considers the general case of more than one independent variable.

MULTIPLE REGRESSION

The Model

In the previous example we attempted to explain the variation in a dependent variable using one independent variable. In many cases, however, interest centers on the relationship between a criterion variable and a set of independent variables. In such cases, the regression formula shown in equation (16-13) becomes

$$y_i = \beta_0 + \beta_1 X_{1i} + \beta_2 X_{2i} + \ldots + \beta_p X_{pi} + \epsilon_i \tag{16-23}$$

where

y_i = ith response for the criterion variable

X_{1i} = ith response for the first independent variable

X_{2i} = ith response for the second independent variable

X_{pi} = ith response for the pth independent variable

β_0 = model intercept

β_1 = regression coefficient for variable 1

β_2 = regression coefficient for variable 2

.
.
.

β_p = regression coefficient for variable p

ϵ_i = ith residual

Consistent with simple regression analysis (that is, one independent variable) we want estimates of the parameters $(\beta_0, \beta_1, \beta_2, \ldots, \beta_p)$ that minimize the sum of the squared residuals, $\Sigma e_i^2 = \Sigma(y_i - \hat{y}_i)^2$. The formula for these parameter estimates become exceedingly complex as the number of independent variables increase. Here we present the case of two independent variables and discuss interpretations and limitations of the model. However, all of the results apply to the case where there are more than two independent variables.

The estimates of the parameters are:

$$b_0 = \bar{y} - (\hat{b}_1 \bar{X}_{1i} + \hat{b}_2 \bar{X}_{2i}) \tag{16-24}$$

$$b_1 = \frac{\dfrac{\Sigma(X_{1i} - \bar{X}_1)(y_i - \bar{y})}{\Sigma(X_{1i} - \bar{X}_i)^2} - \sqrt{\dfrac{\Sigma(y_i - \bar{y})^2}{\Sigma(X_{1i} - \bar{X}_1)^2}}}{1 - r_{12}^2} r_{y2} r_{12} \tag{16-25}$$

$$b_2 = \frac{\dfrac{\Sigma(X_{2i} - \bar{X}_2)(y_i - \bar{y})}{\Sigma(X_{2i} - \bar{X}_2)^2} - \sqrt{\dfrac{\Sigma(y_i - \bar{y})^2}{\Sigma(X_{2i} - \bar{X}_2)^2}}}{1 - r_{12}^2} r_{y1} r_{12} \tag{16-26}$$

where

r_{y2} = the correlation between y and X_2

r_{y1} = the correlation between y and X_1

r_{12} = the correlation between X_1 and X_2

Notice that for both b_1 and b_2 the first expression in the numerator is equal to the estimate of the coefficient for the simple regression model shown in equation (16-15). The other terms in expressions (16-25) and (16-26) reflect the correlation between the independent variables themselves. Notice that if $r_{12} = 0$, then the estimates of b_1 and b_2 will be the same as if we regressed y on each independent variable separately. However, when the independent variables are correlated $(r_{12} \neq 0)$, the estimates of the coefficient will be different from those that would be obtained if each variable were regressed on each variable separately. When X_1 and X_2 are correlated the data are said to be multicollinear. As we will demonstrate, when **multicollinearity** is present interpretation of the regression coefficients can be misleading.

Multicollinearity Correlation among independent variables. Multicollinearity causes problems in interpreting the individual regression coefficients because the values are affected by the amount of association between the independent variables themselves.

Standardized Regression Coefficients

When the dependent variable is regressed on a number of independent variables, interest typically centers on comparing the importance of the independent variables. That is, which of the independent variables are the most important for predicting values of the dependent variable?

Since a regression coefficient for an independent variable reflects the

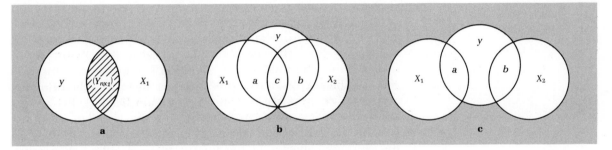

Figure 16-5

Venn diagram.

unit change in y for a unit change in the independent variable X the calculated regression coefficients should reflect variable importance. However, it is usually difficult to compare regression coefficients when the variables are measured in different units. Standardized regression coefficients, often called beta coefficients, are used to facilitate these comparisons.[8]

The standardized regression coefficient (b'_k) for a variable (X_k) is

$$b'_{x_k} = b_{x_k} \, (s_{x_k}/s_y) \tag{16-27}$$

where

s_{x_k} = the standard deviation of variable X_i

s_y = the standard deviation of y

Standardized coefficients are bounded by -1 to $+1$; hence the larger (in an absolute sense) the beta coefficient, the more important the variable.

As we will see, caution must be exercised when relating importance of a variable to its regression coefficients whether the coefficients are standardized or not.

Effects of Multicollinearity

Consider the Venn diagram shown in Figure 16-5, part **a.** The shaded area represents the shared variation (that is, overlap) between y and X_1 or the amount of variation in y explained by X_1. In simple regression, the b_1 coefficient reflects the amount of explained variation in y relative to the total variation accounted for by X_1 which is reflected by the shaded portion of the figure.

Figure 16-5, part **b** presents a Venn diagram for a criterion variable (y) and two independent variables $(X_1$ and $X_2)$. Now $a + c$ represents the

[8]Neter, Wasserman, and Kuter, 261.

shared variation between X_1 and y while $b + c$ represents the shared variation between X_2 and y. The area c represents the collinearity between X_1 and X_2. If we regress y on X_1 alone, the regression coefficient would reflect the amount of shared variation given by $a + c$, whereas if we regress y on X_2 alone, the coefficient would reflect the shared variation given by $b + c$. The total shared variation between y and the two independent variables (X_1, X_2) is $a + b + c$. Hence the individual estimates $(a + c)$ and $(b + c)$ overstate the shared variation because the area c is common to both X_1 and X_2. And herein lies the problem of *multicollinearity*. The individual regression coefficients cannot be interpreted because the values are affected by the amount of association between the independent variables themselves. Figure 16-5, part **c** presents a case in which the independent variables are not associated. In such cases, the estimates of the regression coefficients for the multiple regression model will be the same as the estimates obtained from regressing y on each X_1 and X_2 separately; in other words, the multiple regression parameter estimates will be identical to the parameter estimates obtained from fitting two single regression models, one for y and X_1, and one for y and X_2.

E X A M P L E

Table 16-11 presents data for sales volume (y_i), shelf space (X_{1i}) and in-store coupons distributed (X_{2i}) for 10 brands of soap. First let's regress y on X_1. The estimate of b_1 is:

$$b_1 = \sum_i (X_{1i} - \overline{X}_1)(y_i - \overline{y})/\sum(X_{1i} - \overline{X}_1)^2$$

$$= 252/31.5 = 8$$

Hence we would say that for every facing increase in shelf space, sales volume will increase by $800. The intercept term is

$$b_0 = y - b_1\overline{X}_1$$

$$= 77.3 - 8(15.35)$$

$$= -45.5$$

Now let's regress y_i on coupons used (X_2). The estimates of b_0 and b_2 using Table 16-11 can be found to be

$$b_0 = 14.67$$

$$b_2 = 3.75$$

Consider next the multiple regression results. The estimates of b_0, b_1, and b_2, using the data in Table 16-11, are

$$b_0 = -43.97$$

$$b_1 = 7.52$$

$$b_2 = 0.35$$

Hence the multiple regression equation is

$$Y_i = -43.97 + 7.52X_1 + 0.35X_2$$

Table 16-12 presents the estimates of b_1 and b_2 for both the simple regression model and the multiple regression model. Note that there is a relatively large difference between the two models with respect to the estimate of b_2. Interpreting the multiple regression coefficient for $X_2(= .35)$ might lead us to conclude that the number of coupons distributed has little to do with explaining variations in sales volume; however, this would be an incorrect conclusion. In fact, the number of coupons distributed is strongly correlated with sales volume ($r_{y2} = .76$). The prob-

T A B L E 16-11
Illustrative Data for Regression Analysis with Two Independent Variables

	Sales volume (000) y_i	Shelf-space (1,000 inches) X_{1i}	Coupons distributed (000) X_{2i}
1	50	13.0	12
2	57	13.0	14
3	65	14.0	18
4	72	15.0	15
5	77	14.5	13
6	84	15.0	16
7	88	16.0	20
8	90	17.0	18
9	93	17.5	22
10	97	18.5	19

T A B L E 16-12
Estimated Regression Coefficients

	Unstandardized b_1	b_2	Standardized b_1'	b_2'
Simple regression	8.00	3.75	.94	.76
Multiple regression	7.52	.35	.88	.07

lem here is that the number of coupons distributed is also strongly correlated with shelf space; that is, there are more in-store coupons distributed for brands with a large amount of shelf space. In other words, a substantial portion of the variation in sales volume that is explained by the number of coupons is also explained by shelf space. As we discussed earlier, in multiple regression analysis the shared variation between independent variables is partialled out when estimating individual parameters. Notice from Table 16-12 that multicollinearity adversely effects the standardized regression coefficients as well as the unstandardized coefficients.

Coefficient of Multiple Determination: R^2

As with simple regression analysis the coefficient of determination, R^2 represents the proportion of variation in the dependent variable explained by the set of independent variables. R^2 can be calculated from the following relationships:

$$R^2 = RSS/TSS \tag{16-28}$$

or

$$R^2 = 1 - ESS/TSS \tag{16-29}$$

where

$$TSS = \text{the total sum of squares } \sum_i (y_i - \bar{y})^2$$

$$RSS = \text{the regression sum of squares } \sum_i (\hat{y}_i - \bar{y})^2$$

$$ESS = \text{the error sum of squares } \sum_i (e_i - \bar{e})^2 = \sum (y_i - \hat{y}_i)^2$$

and

$$TSS = RSS + ESS$$

E X A M P L E

Table 16-13 presents summary calculations for the *TSS*, *RSS*, and *ESS* for the sales volume data in Table 16-11. The amount of explained variation in sales volume given shelf space and the number of coupons distributed is

$$R^2 = RSS/TSS = 2018.27/2292.1 = .88$$

Hence, 88 percent of the variation in sales volume is explained by a linear relationship with the size of shelf space and the number of in-store coupons distributed. Note, however, that because of the collinearity between shelf space and the number of coupons distributed we cannot make any inferences concerning the explained variation in sales volume accounted for by each of the independent variables separately.

$$\hat{y}_i = b_0 + b_1 X_{1i} + b_2 X_{2i} = -43.97 + 7.52 X_{1i} + .35 X_{2i}$$
$$\hat{y}_1 = -43.97 + 7.52(13) + .35(12) = 57.99$$
$$\hat{y}_2 = -43.97 + 7.52(13) + .35(14) = 58.69$$
$$\hat{y}_3 = -43.97 + 7.52(14) + .35(18) = 67.61$$
$$\hat{y}_4 = -43.97 + 7.52(15) + .35(15) = 74.08$$
$$\hat{y}_5 = -43.97 + 7.52(14.5) + .35(13) = 69.62$$
$$\hat{y}_6 = -43.97 + 7.52(15.0) + .35(16) = 74.43$$
$$\hat{y}_7 = -43.97 + 7.52(16.0) + .35(20) = 83.35$$
$$\hat{y}_8 = -43.97 + 7.52(17.0) + .35(18) = 90.17$$
$$\hat{y}_9 = -43.97 + 7.52(17.5) + .35(22) = 95.33$$
$$\hat{y}_{10} = -43.97 + 7.52(18.5) + .35(19) = 101.80$$

	TSS $\sum_i (y_i - \bar{y})^2$	RSS $\sum_i (\hat{y}_i - \bar{y})^2$	ESS $\sum_i (y_i - \hat{y}_i)^2$
1	745.29	372.88	63.84
2	412.09	346.33	2.86
3	151.29	93.90	6.81
4	28.09	10.37	4.33
5	0.09	58.98	54.46
6	44.89	8.24	91.58
7	114.49	36.60	21.62
8	161.29	165.64	0.03
9	246.49	325.08	5.43
10	388.09	600.25	23.04
	2292.10	2018.27	274.00

Statistical Testing

There are two common statistical tests used in regression analysis: an overall model test and individual coefficient tests. The **overall model test** determines whether the multiple correlation coefficient is statistically significant. That is, is there a statistically significant association between the dependent variable and the set of independent variables? The hypothesis and test statistic are described below.

Overall model test (F-test) Determination of whether the multiple correlation coefficient is statistically significant.

$HO: \beta_1 = \beta_2 = \ldots \beta_p = 0$

HA: at least one β is different from zero

$$TS_c: F_c = \frac{RSS/p}{ESS/(N - p - 1)}$$

$TS_t: F_{t(1-\alpha;\, df\, =\, p,\, n-p-1)}$

DR: Reject HO: if $F_c > F_{t(1-\alpha;\, p,\, n-p-1)}$

E X A M P L E

Let us now consider whether there is a statistically significant relationship between sales volume and shelf space and the number of coupons distributed. From Table 16-13, the F-test statistic for the sales volume data is

$$F_c = \frac{2018.27/2}{274/7}$$

$$= 25.78$$

Letting $\alpha = .05$, the tabled critical value from Table 5 in the Statistical Appendix is $F_{t(1 - .05; 2, 7)} = 4.74$; consequently, we reject the null hypothesis that

$$HO: \beta_1 = \beta_2 = 0$$

and conclude that there is a statistically significant relationship between sales volume and the two independent variables.

Statistical test of each
regression coefficient
Determination of
significance of each
regression coefficient
separately.

The alternative hypothesis states that $HA:$ at least one $\beta_p \neq 0$. For this reason we generally need to perform a **statistical test of each regression coefficient** separately. The appropriate statistical test is described below:

$HO: \beta_p = 0$

$HA: \beta_p \neq 0$

$TS_c: t_c = b_p/SE(b_p)$

$TS_t: t_{t(1 - \alpha; df = n - 1)}$

$DR:$ Reject $HO:$ if $t_c > t_{t(1 - \alpha; n - 1)}$

Most computer software packages providing multiple regression analysis programs will routinely report standard errors of the parameter estimates—i.e., $(SE(b_p))$.

E X A M P L E

Table 16-14 provides summary output from the SPSS multiple regression package for the data we have been analyzing.[9] At the $\alpha = .05$ level, $TS_t = 1.86$; hence from the summary table we can reject the hypothesis that β_1 equals zero, but we cannot reject the hypothesis that β_2 equals zero.

[9]N. H. Nie et al. SPSS: Statistical Package for the Social Sciences (New York: McGraw-Hill, 1975).

T A B L E 16-14
SPSS Output

SPSS--Statistical Package for the Social Sciences
Version 9.0 (nos) March 06, 1984
124400 CM Maximum field length request

Regression example
File Noname (Creation date = 86/08/11.)   86/08/11.   09.10.13.   Page 8

Multiple regression

Dependent variable.. Y
Mean response 77.30000   Std. Dev. 15.95863
Variable(s) entered on step number 1.. X1
                                       X2

Multiple R	.93833	Analysis of variance	DF	Sum of squares	Mean square	F	Significance
R Square	.88046	Regression	2.	2018.09619	1009.04810	25.77824	.00
Adjusted R Square	.84630	Residual	7.	274.00381	39.14340		
Std Deviation	6.25647	Coeff of variability	8.1 PCT				

----- Variables in the equation -----					----- Variables not in the equation -----			
Variable	b	Std error b	F	SIGNIFICANCE	Beta	Variable	Partial	tolerance	F	SIGNIFICANCE
					ELASTICITY					
X1	7.5195502	1.7850286	17.745710	.004	.8818661					
					1.49321					
X2	.35008651	1.0331846	.11481402	.745	.0709338					
					.07563					
(Constant)	-43.971540	17.711960	6.1632544	.042						

All variables are in the equation.

Coefficients and confidence intervals.

Variable	b	Std error	T	95.0 pct confidence interval	
X1	7.5195502	1.7850286	4.2125657	3.2986377	, 11.740463
X2	.35008651	1.0331846	.33884218	-2.0930013	, 2.2931743
CONSTANT	-43.971540	17.711960	-2.4825903	-85.853577	, 2.0895024

Though in the above example we cannot reject the hypothesis that $\beta_2 = 0$, it would be a mistake to conclude that X_2, the number of coupons distributed, has no association with sales volume. Recall that we previously demonstrated that the estimated regression coefficients are affected when the predictor variables are collinear. Moreover, in the presence of multicollinearity, the variance and consequently the standard error of the regression coefficients are also affected. We see, therefore, that in the presence of multicollinearity both the numerator and denominator of the test statistic used to assess the statistical significance of the predictor variables are adversely affected. When the independent variables are correlated, the individual tests of significance for regression coefficients are not, in a strict sense, valid and must be interpreted cautiously. In practice, predictor variables will always exhibit some degree of association; thus the issue is not whether multicollinearity exists, but rather the degree to which the predictors covary.

Model Assumptions

Before concluding our discussion of multiple regression, we must note that there are other assumptions concerning statistical tests in regression analysis. These assumptions concern the distribution of the residuals $e_i = (y_i - \hat{y}_i)$. Specifically, the assumption is that the residuals are normally and independently distributed. Often plots of residuals and other types of residual analysis can provide useful information on whether these assumptions are in place. Residual plots, which are usually available in standard software packages (such as SPSS), are used to determine if there is any pattern to the residuals. If the residuals follow some pattern, then they are generally not normally distributed.[10]

Summary

Assessing the level of association (correlation) between two variables is a common practice in marketing research. In this chapter we have seen that the method used for calculating the correlation depends on which scale(s) of measurement the variables adhere to. Using an incorrect method for calculating the correlation can make a weak association look strong or vice versa.

Regression analysis is a commonly used method for predicting the value of one variable (the dependent variable) when the value of another variable (the independent variable) is determined. Regression analysis is also commonly used to assess the effect of a set of independent variables on a dependent variable. We may also use the multiple regression equation to predict the dependent variable given a specific level for each of

[10]Excellent discussions of residual analysis can be found in N. Draper and H. Smith, *Applied Regression Analysis* (New York: John Wiley & Sons, 1966).

the independent variables. However, interpretation of the individual effect of one of the independent variables on the dependent variable is seriously affected when the independent variables are collinear.

Key Concepts

Association among variables   *Regression analysis*
Measures of correlation   *Coefficient of determination*
Collapsing variable categories *Multicollinearity*

Review Questions

1. Explain the concepts of covariation and correlation.
2. What is the objective in regression analysis?
3. What is the importance of the coefficient of (multiple) determination?
4. How can the importance of a predictor variable be assessed? What are the effects, if any, of multicollinearity?
5. Describe the statistical testing procedures in multiple regression analysis. What assumptions are they predicated on?

Appendixes:
Multivariate Analysis Procedures

$\mathbf{M}$ultivariate analysis can be simply defined as the application of methods that *simultaneously* deal with reasonably large numbers of variables. In other words, multivariate techniques differ from univariate and bivariate analysis in that they direct attention away from the analysis of mean and variance of a single variable, or from the pairwise relationship between two variables, to the analysis of the relationship among three or more variables.

$\mathbf{I}$n this appendix we discuss several of the more popular multivariate techniques used in marketing research; in particular, these techniques are frequently used in various types of *market studies.* In Chapter 17, we discuss and illustrate how these techniques can prove useful in the context of market positioning, market segmentation, and market structure analysis.

Multidimensional Scaling (MDS)

In this appendix we present some technical details on MDS.[1] The discussion is organized in terms of (1) derived distances, (2) nonmetric MDS, and (3) computer software.

DERIVED DISTANCES

The fundamental premise of MDS is that the derived distances in the space should match the original proximities (similarities). MDS programs find the positions in space or the coordinates for each of the objects such that the distances between them will correspond as closely as possible to the proximity values. The success of this process is judged by how well the derived distances in this space match the original proximities.

MDS attempts to determine a set of coordinates called the initial or starting configuration. Distances in the derived space are calculated from these coordinates and evaluated relative to the original proximity values. If the error is large, (that is, if the differences between the derived distances and the proximities are large), then the program moves the coordinates and recomputes the distances in the derived space. This process is repeated until the distances in the derived space adequately fit the data on the basis of some goodness-of-fit criterion (called *stress*).

[1]Much of this material has been adapted from: W. R. Dillon and M. Goldstein, *Multivariate Analysis: Methods and Applications* (New York: John Wiley & Sons, 1984), Chapter 4.

NONMETRIC MDS

Nonmetric MDS assumes that the level of measurement is at the nominal or, at best, ordinal scale. It is quite common for the proximity values to have ordinal properties. In this case, the computation criterion is to relate the rank order of distances to the rank order of the proximity measures. Thus, in contrast to metric MDS, nonmetric MDS procedures yield solutions such that the distances in the derived space are merely in the same rank order as the original data.

An important secondary purpose in this type of analysis is to "metricize" the nonmetric data. Nonmetric MDS programs apply monotone transformations to the original data in order to permit arithmetic operations to be performed on the rank orders of the proximities. A monotone transformation maintains only the rank orders of the proximities. (The logarithm and exponential functions, for example, produce monotone transformations.) Monotone transformations of the data that are as much like the distances as possible are called disparities. As you will shortly see, these disparities, along with the derived distances, are used to judge the adequacy of the reduced space representation.

One popular approach to MDS with ordinal data is Kruskal's *least-squares monotonic transformation.*[2] This approach yields disparities that are a monotonic transformation of the data and that match the distances, in a least-squares sense, as closely as possible. To better understand how the process works consider Table 16A-1. Part **a** of the table shows the lower-half of a hypothetical symmetric matrix of ordinal data on six stimuli.

First notice that immediately below part **a** of Table 16A-1, the data have been arranged into a vector of numbers sorted in ascending order. Part **b** shows the matrix of derived distance, and they too have been arranged in vector form—not in ascending order, but rather in data order. For example, since the second element in the data vector corresponds to matrix position (2,1) with a value of 2, the second element in the distance vector is 1.0; similarly, the last element in the data vector corresponds to matrix position (5,4) with a value of 15, and the last element in the distance vector has the value 8.4. It is now easy to see that if the elements in the distance vector were in the proper order in relation to the data vector, they too would be in ascending order—however, they are not. The procedure is to replace every sequence of two numbers that is out of order with the mean of the two numbers. Part **c** of the table shows how this works. Here NG (no good) indicates two numbers out of ascending order. For example, the distances 2.4 and 2.0 are out of order, and therefore we replace each with their mean value of 2.2. Next, this new value is compared with the number immediately following it and an

---

[2]J. B. Kruskal, "Multidimensional scaling by optimizing goodness of fit to a nonmetric hypothesis," *Psychometrika,* **29,** 1964, 1–27; J. B. Kruskal, "Nonmetric multidimensional scaling: A numerical method," *Psychometrika,* **29,** 1964, 28–42.

T A B L E   16A-1

Kruskal's Least-Squares Monotone Transformation

a. Raw data

```
 0
 2  0
 5  1  0
 3  7  8  0
 9  6  4 15  0
14 12 13 11 10 0
```
Sorted into ascending order:
1 2 3 4 5 6 7 8 9 10 11 12 13 14 15

b. Distances

```
0.0
1.0 0.0
3.2 0.8 0.0
2.4 3.8 4.0 0.0
4.2 2.6 2.0 8.4 0.0
9.2 6.0 7.2 5.4 5.6 0.0
```
Arranged in data order:
0.8 1.0 2.4 2.0 3.2 2.6 3.8 4.0 4.2 5.6 5.4 6.0 7.2 9.2 8.4

c. Least-squares monotonic transformation

```
        OK    OK   NG         NG        OK
      0.8   1.0   2.4   2.0   3.2   2.6   3.8   4.0
            OK    2.2  OK
            OK  2.9 OK
      OK    OK    NG         OK    OK
      4.2   5.6   5.4   6.0   7.2   9.2   8.4
            OK    5.5  OK         OK    8.8
```

d. Disparities

0.8 1.0 2.2 2.2 2.9 2.9 3.8 4.0 4.2 5.5 5.5 6.0 7.2 8.8 8.8

Optimally scaled:

```
0.0
1.0 0.0
2.9 0.8 0.0
2.2 3.8 4.0 0.0
4.2 2.9 2.2 8.8 0.0
8.8 6.0 7.2 5.5 5.5 0.0
```

Source: Dillon, W. R. and M. Goldstein, *Multivariate Analysis: Methods and Applications* (New York: John Wiley & Sons, 1984), 128.

dition check is again undertaken. The next number is 3.2, and no replacement is needed (numbers in the proper order are indicated by OK). The process continues in a similar fashion. It may happen that the mean of two distances is not in the proper order; in such cases the mean of three (or more) distances is then formed. When the correct ordering of all the numbers in the distance vector is achieved, they are taken out of the vector and put back in matrix form. These numbers are now called the disparities. When there are ties in the data the process is altered slightly.

In practice, the process starts with an initial configuration of points

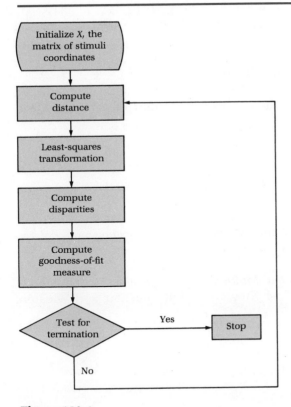

Figure 16A-1

The Nonmetric MDS Procedure. (From Dillon, W. R. and M. Goldstein, *Multivariate Analysis: Methods and Applications.* New York: John Wiley & Sons, 1984, 130.)

(stimulus coordinates), perhaps determined randomly, in a specified dimensionality (number of dimensions). This configuration is moved iteratively to minimize some stress measure, subject to maintaining the monotonicity of the disparities with the original proximities. The process terminates when the value of the stress measure at a given iteration fails to improve by a specified amount from its value at the previous iteration. Figure 16A-1 summarizes the general procedure in flow chart form.

COMPUTER SOFTWARE

There are two requisites for an MDS analysis—a set of numbers, called proximities, which express all (or most) combinations of pairs of similarities within a group of objects, and a computer-based algorithm to implement the analysis. In the last decade or so there has been a rapid increase in the number of computer programs for MDS. Six of the major

MDS computer programs are MINISSA, POLYCON, KYST, INDSCAL/ SINDSCAL, ALSCAL, and MULTISCALE. Note that ALSCAL can be accessed through SAS (Supplemental Library User's Guide, 1980). In addition, there is available MDS(X), which is an integrated series of MDS algorithms with common command language.

The various MDS programs differ in a number of fundamental ways. It is beyond our scope to discuss the mechanics of each computer program.[3]

References

Dillon, W. R. and M. Goldstein, *Multivariate Analysis: Methods and Applications* (New York: John Wiley & Sons, 1984) Chapter 4.

Green, P. E. and F. J. Carmane, *Multidimensional Scaling and Related Techniques in Marketing Analysis* (Boston: Allyn & Bacon, 1970).

Green, P. E. and V. Rao, *Applied Multidimensional Scaling: A Comparison of Approaches and Algorithms* (New York: Holt, Rinehart and Winston, 1972).

---

[3]For a thorough discussion, consult S. S. Schiffman, M. L. Reynolds, and F. W. Young, *Introduction to Multidimensional Scaling* (New York: Academic Press, 1981).

Factor Analysis Techniques

PRINCIPAL COMPONENTS ANALYSIS (PCA)

Assume that n subjects have responded to a questionnaire containing p items. A basic purpose of *principal components* is to account for the total variation among these n subjects in p-dimensional space by forming a new set of orthogonal and uncorrelated *composite* variates. As we shall see, each member of the new set of variates is a linear combination of the original set of measurements. The linear combinations will be generated in such a manner that *each successive composite variate will account for a smaller portion of total variation*. Hence the first composite (that is, *principal component*) will have the largest variance, the second will have a variance smaller than the first but larger than the third, and so on. In general, the number of new composite variables that will be needed to account adequately for the total variation is less than p.

Model Development

Suppose that for a particular subject the observed responses for the p items on the questionnaire are represented by $X' = [X_1, X_2, \ldots, X_p]$. For all subjects let the population variance-covariance matrix of X be given by

$$\Sigma = \begin{bmatrix} \sigma_{11} & \sigma_{12} & \cdots & \sigma_{1p} \\ \sigma_{21} & \sigma_{22} & \cdots & \sigma_{2p} \\ \cdot & \cdot & & \cdot \\ \cdot & \cdot & & \cdot \\ \cdot & \cdot & & \cdot \\ \sigma_{p1} & \sigma_{p2} & \cdots & \sigma_{pp} \end{bmatrix}$$

The elements along the main diagonal of Σ are, respectively, the true population variances of each of the p original variables. The elements off the main diagonal are the true population covariances (that is, the manner in which pairs of original variables relate to each other—positively, negatively, or not at all).

To find the first principal component $Y_{(1)}$, we seek a vector of coefficients $\mathbf{a}' = [a_1, a_2, \ldots, a_p]$ such that the variance of $\mathbf{a}'\mathbf{X}$ is a maximum over the class of all linear combinations of $\mathbf{X}$ subject to the constraint $\mathbf{a}'\mathbf{a} = 1$. The reason for requiring that the coefficients be normalized (that is, $\mathbf{a}'\mathbf{a} = 1$) is that otherwise the variance of $\mathbf{a}'\mathbf{X}$ would increase by making the coordinates of $\mathbf{a}$ arbitrarily large. It can be shown that the set of coefficients $\mathbf{a}$ defining the first principal component is that which corresponds to the largest eigenvalue λ_1 of $\mathbf{\Sigma}$. An eigenvalue is merely the *variance of a particular principal component.* Thus, the largest eigenvalue is the variance of the first principal component $Y_{(1)}$. Moreover, the set of coefficients defining this first principal component is called the eigenvector $\mathbf{a}_{(1)}$. The first principal component is given by $Y_{(1)} = \mathbf{a}'_{(1)}\mathbf{X}$.

The second principal component is obtained by finding a second normalized vector (set of coefficients) $\mathbf{a}_{(2)}$, orthogonal to $\mathbf{a}_{(1)}$, such that $Y_{(2)} = \mathbf{a}'_{(2)}\mathbf{X}$ has the second largest variance (that is, eigenvalue) among all the vectors satisfying the constraints $\mathbf{a}'_{(2)}\mathbf{a}_{(2)} = 1$, $\mathbf{a}'_{(1)}\mathbf{a}_{(2)} = 0$. The process continues until all p sets of coefficients (eigenvectors) are generated in such a manner that each is normalized and orthogonal to the sets of coefficients generated for the other principal components.

The coefficients defining a given principal component have an interesting interpretation. Within the jth component the contribution of variable X_i is given by a_{ij}, where $Y_{(j)} = a_{1j}X_1 + a_{2j}X_2 + \ldots + a_{pj}X_p$. The magnitude and sign of a_{ij} gives the strength and direction of the relationship between X_i and $Y_{(j)}$. It can be shown that the covariance of X_i with the component $Y_{(j)}$ is $\sqrt{\lambda_j}a_{ij}$, where λ_j is the eigenvalue whose associated set of coefficients of *component weights* a_{ij} can be converted into *component loadings* by dividing $\sqrt{\lambda_j}a_{ij}$ by the standard deviation of X_i. Component loadings represent the correlation between each variable X_i and the component $Y_{(j)}$. Note that if all the variables defining X are first standardized, then $\mathbf{\Sigma}$ is a correlation matrix, and since all the variances will then be equal to 1, the scaled weights, $\sqrt{\lambda_j}a_{ij}/s_{xi} = \sqrt{\lambda_j}a_{ij}$, represent the correlation between X_i and $Y_{(j)}$.

How Many Components to Retain

One of our primary objectives in a principal components analysis is dimensionality reduction; hence, if we use all or most of the possible new variates, we are in a sense defeating our purpose. There is a rich class of statistical inference that can be helpful in determining how many components to generate. Most of the available statistical tests are applicable only for large samples and deal with a determination of whether the generated eigenvalues (that is, component variances) appear significantly different from zero. Moreover, many users of these tests do not find them particularly helpful, and hence more ad hoc procedures are commonplace.

When the variance-covariance matrix is the basic input, components are usually generated until some prespecified amount of total variation is accounted for. This, of course, is a very subjective and arbitrary stopping rule. It is, however, the most frequently used rule. In the case of correlation input the "root greater than 1" criterion is frequently employed.[4] This criterion retains only those components whose eigenvalues are greater than 1. The rationale for this rule is that any component should account for more variance than any single variable in the standardized test score space. Both procedures are sensible and are recommended. There are also a number of graphic procedures that can be helpful in determining how many components to retain.

References

Dillon, W. R. and M. Goldstein. *Multivariate Analysis: Methods and Applications* (New York: John Wiley & Sons, 1984).

Gnanadesikan, R. *Methods for Statistical Data Analysis of Multivariate Observations* (New York: John Wiley & Sons, 1977).

Morrison, D. F. *Multivariate Statistical Methods*, 3rd edition (New York: McGraw-Hill, 1976).

FACTOR ANALYSIS[5]

Factor analysis is another linear reduction technique. However, factor analysis has more inherent structure since it assumes a specified model that implies a reduced form of the input matrix; that is, the factor analytic model presumes the existence of a smaller set of factors that can produce exactly the correlation in the larger set of variables.

Model Development

The basic model in factor analysis is usually expressed by

$$\mathbf{X} = \mathbf{\Lambda}\,\mathbf{f} + \mathbf{E} \tag{16A-1}$$

where

$\mathbf{X}$ = p-dimensional vector of observed responses

$\mathbf{\Lambda}$ = $p \times q$ matrix of unknown constants called factor loadings

$\mathbf{f}$ = q-dimensional vector of unobservable variables called common factors

$\mathbf{E}$ = p-dimensional vector of unobservable variables called unique factors

We assume that the variance-covariance matrix of $\mathbf{E}$ is a diagonal matrix, $\mathbf{\Phi}$, with entries ϕ_i^2 and that all covariances between $\mathbf{E}$ and $\mathbf{f}$ are zero.

---

[4]H. F. Kaiser, "The Varimax Criterion for Analytic Rotation in Factor Analysis," *Psychometrika*, Vol. 21, 1958, 187–200.

[5]Much of this material has been adapted from W. R. Dillon and M. Goldstein, *Multivariate Analysis: Methods and Applications* (New York: John Wiley & Sons, 1984), Chapter 3.

The basic model along with the associated assumptions imply that Σ_{XX}, the variance-covariance matrix of $\mathbf{X}$, is expressible as

$$\Sigma_{XX} = \Lambda \Sigma_{ff} \Lambda' + \Phi \tag{16A-2}$$

Standardizing the vector of common factors and assuming that they are pairwise uncorrelated, one is led to

$$\Sigma_{XX} = \Lambda \Lambda' + \Phi \tag{16A-3}$$

To get a better feel for the basic model, let us examine equation (16A-1) in somewhat more detail. Writing (16A-1) in terms of its elements we have

$$\begin{bmatrix} X_1 \\ X_2 \\ \cdot \\ \cdot \\ \cdot \\ X_p \end{bmatrix} = \begin{bmatrix} \Lambda_{11} & \Lambda_{12} & \cdots & \Lambda_{1q} \\ \Lambda_{21} & \Lambda_{22} & \cdots & \Lambda_{2q} \\ \cdot & \cdot & & \cdot \\ \cdot & \cdot & & \cdot \\ \cdot & \cdot & & \cdot \\ \Lambda_{p1} & \Lambda_{p2} & \cdots & \Lambda_{pq} \end{bmatrix} \begin{bmatrix} f_1 \\ f_2 \\ \cdot \\ \cdot \\ \cdot \\ f_q \end{bmatrix} + \begin{bmatrix} E_1 \\ E_2 \\ \cdot \\ \cdot \\ \cdot \\ E_p \end{bmatrix}$$

or

$$X_i = \sum_{j=1}^{q} \lambda_{ij} f_j + E_i \tag{16A-4}$$

This representation shows directly that, for the case of uncorrelated and standardized common factors, the common factor loading λ_{ij} expresses the correlation between the jth factor and the variable X_i. If we do not assume, however, that the common factors are pairwise uncorrelated, then the same interpretation does not prevail.

A further implication of the basic model as shown in equation (16A-1) is that for the case of uncorrelated and standardized common factors, the correlation r_{ij} between any two variables X_i and X_j is expressible in terms of factor loadings by

$$r_{ij} = \sum_{k=1}^{q} \lambda_{ik} \lambda_{jk} \tag{16A-5}$$

Note that from (16A-3)

$$\text{Var}(X_i) = \sigma_{ii} = \sum_{j=1}^{q} \lambda_{ij}^2 + \phi_i^2 \tag{16A-6}$$

and hence we can think of λ_{ij}^2 as the contribution of the common factor f_i to the variance of X_i. The contribution of all the factors to the variance of X_i (that is, $\sum_{j=1}^{q} \lambda_{ij}^2$) is called the *commonality* of X_i; ϕ_i^2 is the uniqueness of X_i and measures the extent to which the common factors fail to account for the variance of X_i. The total contribution of f_j to the variances of all the variables is

$$v_j = \sum_{i=1}^{p} \lambda_{ij}^2 \qquad (16A\text{-}7)$$

and hence the total contribution of all the common factors to the total variance of all the variables is the total commonality

$$v = \sum_{j=1}^{q} v_j \qquad (16\text{-}A8)$$

To summarize,

$$
\begin{aligned}
\text{Total Variance} &= \sum_{i=1}^{p} \sigma_{ii} \\
&= \sum_{i=1}^{p} \sum_{j=1}^{q} \lambda_{ij}^2 + \sum_{j=1}^{p} \phi_i^2 \qquad (16A\text{-}9) \\
&= v + \phi^2 \\
&= \text{total communality} + \text{total uniqueness}
\end{aligned}
$$

Rotation of Factor Solution

When we introduced the notion of factoring the variance-covariance matrix Σ_{xx} (or the correlation matrix), we did not indicate that alternative solutions were possible and may be equally as valid. In fact, if the matrix Λ of factor loadings is postmultiplied by any orthogonal matrix A, then Σ_{xx} will be reproducible through ΛA as well as through Λ. The matrix of factor loadings Λ represents a particular interpretation of the data—that is, the variance-covariance or correlation matrix in terms of a set of factors. The rotated matrix of factor loadings A represents an alternative interpretation of the data that, in a mathematical sense, is equally as valid. The rotational process of factor analysis allows the researcher a degree of flexibility by presenting a multiplicity of views of the same data set in order to aid in interpretation.

Many procedures used to rotate the matrix of factor loadings do so in a manner to achieve simple structure. The major characteristics of simple structure are the following:

1. Any column of the factor loading matrix should have mostly small values, as close to zero as possible.
2. Any given row of the matrix of factor loadings should have nonzero entries in only a few columns.
3. Any two columns of the matrix of factor loadings should exhibit a different pattern of high and low loadings.

The idea of simple structure is not limited to orthogonal rotations but is equally reasonable for oblique rotations—that is, rotations that lead to nonorthogonal solutions.

Most computer software packages for factor analysis contain various rotational procedures. Factor loadings are automatically rotated to achieve certain criteria. Although options are given for oblique rotations, orthogonal rotations are without question the most frequently employed. Kaiser's Varimax method for factor rotation is probably the most popular of the computer-generated procedures.[6] The Varimax method rotates factors so that the variance of the squared factor loadings for a given factor is made large. Most of the popular computer packages use Varimax rotation either with raw factor loadings or with normalized loadings—that is, by first dividing each variable loading by the square root of its commonality. By scaling, all variables are given equal weight in the rotation. However, some authors have argued against such scaling, especially when commonalities are very small.

Because of the computational complexities inherent in generating a matrix of factor loadings, today factor analyses are done almost exclusively by computer. Perhaps the most frequently employed methods are the principal factor solution and the maximum likelihood solution. Discussion of how each procedure operates is beyond our scope. For an in-depth presentation, we recommend the reader to Harman;[7] however, at least for the beginner, a step-by-step discussion of the nuances of each algorithm is not necessary in order to access an available computer package.

HOW DO PRINCIPAL COMPONENTS AND FACTOR ANALYSIS DIFFER?

There continues to be considerable confusion in many quarters about the differences between principal components and factor analysis. Recall that in principal components analysis we find linear combinations of the original variables such that the jth component generated has the jth largest variance. Even though a few components may account for a large portion of the total variance, all p components are needed to recover the correlations exactly. In contrast, the common factor model posits the existence of a number of factors smaller than the number of original variables that will reproduce the correlations exactly but that may not account for as much variance as does the same number of principal components. Finally, it is important to note that while in principal components analysis the factors are linear combinations of the observable variables, in common factor analysis the factors are linear combinations of only the common parts of the variables. Hence, it is understandable

[6]H. F. Kaiser, "The Varimax Criterion for Analytic Rotation in Factor Analysis," *Psychometrika*, Vol. 23, 1958, 187–200; H. F. Kaiser, "Computer Programs for Varimax Rotation in Factor Analysis," *Educational and Psychological Measurement*, vol. 19, 1959, 413–420.
[7]H. H. Harman, *Modern Factor Analysis* (Chicago: The University of Chicago Press, 1967).

that principal components is viewed as variance-oriented, whereas in common factor analysis the specific variance is expressed separately and, as such, it is correlation- or covariance-oriented.

References

Cattell, R. B. *Factor Analysis* (New York: Harper & Brothers, 1952).

Dillon, W. R. and M. Goldstein. *Multivariate Analysis: Methods and Applications* (New York: John Wiley & Sons, 1984).

Rummel, R. J. *Applied Factor Analysis* (Evanston, Ill.: Northwestern University Press, 1970).

Discriminant Analysis[8]

In discriminant analysis we have collected measurements on individuals who belong to one of several groups. The goal is to find linear composites (that is, linear combinations) of the predictor variables that can distinguish the various groups. This is accomplished by finding axes that maximize the ratio of between-groups to within-groups variability of projections onto the axes. In general, with K groups and p predictor variables, there are, in total, $\min(p, K-1)$ possible discriminant axes (that is, linear composites). In most applications, since the number of predictor variables far exceeds the number of groups under study, at most $K - 1$ discriminant axes will be considered.

Determining the number of statistically significant discriminant functions is particularly important. The number of discriminant functions that provide statistically significant among-groups variation essentially defines the dimensionality of the discriminant space. Thus, multiple discriminant analysis can be viewed as a data reduction technique, since it can, by uncovering a small number of discriminant functions (new axes), provide a condensed version of the factors that contribute to the among-group differences.

To better understand how multiple discriminant analysis works, consider Figure 16C-1, which shows the scatterplot for the two predictor variables X_1 and X_2 and three groups. Notice also that two new axes, denoted by Y_1 and Y_2, have been plotted in the space. Imagine now that we want to find the mean projection of each group on each axis by projecting the observations (that is, points) first onto Y_1 and then onto Y_2. Essentially, this is what multiple discriminant analysis does, in that its objective is to find those axes (in this case Y_1 and Y_2) with the property that the ratio of between-groups to within-groups variability is as large as possible. With more than two groups, however, there is an additional constraint. The discriminant functions are generated so that the scores on each new discriminant axis are uncorrelated with the scores on any previously obtained discriminant axis. In other words, Y_1 is the single new

[8]Much of the following discussion is extracted from W. R. Dillon and M. Goldstein, *Multivariate Analysis: Methods and Applications* (New York: John Wiley & Sons, 1984), Chapter 11.

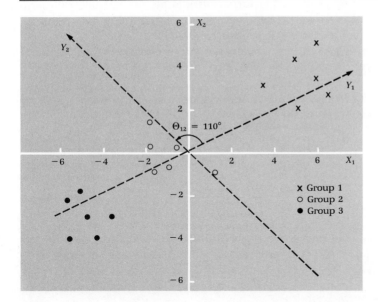

Figure 16C-1

Scatterplot of Hypothetical Data on Two Variables for Three Groups. (From Dillon, W. R. and M. Goldstein, *Multivariate Analysis: Methods and Applications.* New York: John Wiley & Sons, 1984, 396.)

axis that maximizes the ratio of between-groups to within-groups variability; Y_2 is the second new discriminant axis that maximizes the ratio of residual between-groups to within-groups variability (after accounting for the between-groups to within-groups variability that is associated with Y_1), subject to its point projections being uncorrelated with the point projections on Y_1. In addition, as we will see, the discriminant functions are extracted so that the accounted-for variation appears in decreasing order of magnitude.

OBJECTIVES OF MULTIPLE DISCRIMINANT ANALYSIS

The following summarizes five of the objectives that are typically found in multiple discriminant analysis applications.

1. To find linear composites of the predictor variables having the property that the ratio of between-groups to within-groups variability is as large as possible, subject to the constraint that each uncovered linear composite must be uncorrelated with previously extracted composites. The linear composites are computed so that the accounted-for variation appears in decreasing order of magnitude.

2. To determine whether the group centroids are statistically different and the number of statistically significant discriminant axes (that is, the dimensionality of the discriminant space).

3. To successfully assign new observations to one of the several groups, based on the observation's predictor-variable profile and resultant scores on the linear composites.

4. To determine which of the predictor variables contributes most to discriminating among the groups.

5. Identify the dimensions that underlie the discriminant space.

THE APPROACH

Assume that samples of n_i observations are available from the ith group, $i = 1, 2, \ldots, K$, with each observation consisting of p measurements $X' = (X_1, X_2, \ldots, X_p)$. We denote by T the matrix of the total mean corrected sum of squares of cross products for the scores on all $n = \Sigma_i n_i$ observations. That is,

$$\mathbf{T} = \sum_{i=1}^{k} \sum_{j=1}^{n_i} (\mathbf{X}_{ij} - \overline{\mathbf{X}})(\mathbf{X}_{ij} - \overline{\mathbf{X}})' \tag{16C-1}$$

The matrix of sum of squares and cross products for the ith group will be denoted by $\mathbf{W}_i$.

$$\mathbf{W}_i = \sum_{j=1}^{n_i} (\mathbf{X}_{ij} - \overline{\mathbf{X}}_i)(\mathbf{X}_{ij} - \overline{\mathbf{X}}_i)' \tag{16C-2}$$

The within-groups sum of squares are given by

$$\mathbf{W} = \mathbf{W}_1 + \mathbf{W}_2 + \ldots + \mathbf{W}_k \tag{16C-3}$$

The matrix of between-groups sum of squares and cross products can thus be found by the difference

$$\mathbf{B} = \mathbf{T} - \mathbf{W} \tag{16C-4}$$

Define the linear compound $\mathbf{Y} = \mathbf{a}'\mathbf{X}$. With respect to the linear composite $\mathbf{Y}$, the between-groups sum of squares are given by $\mathbf{a}'\mathbf{Ba}$. Similarly, the within-groups sum of squares are $\mathbf{a}'\mathbf{Wa}$. Thus,

$$\lambda = \frac{\mathbf{a}'\mathbf{Ba}}{\mathbf{a}'\mathbf{Wa}} \tag{16C-5}$$

is the ratio of the between-groups to within-groups sum of squares for the K groups on the first linear compound. We wish to maximize λ with respect to $\mathbf{a}$. Therefore, we take the partial derivative with respect to $\mathbf{a}$ and set it equal to zero. After some simplification we have

$$(\mathbf{B} - \lambda\mathbf{W})\mathbf{a} = 0 \tag{16C-6}$$

Though (16C-6) can be solved directly, it is more convenient to premultiply by $\mathbf{W}^{-1}$ and work with

$$(\mathbf{W}^{-1}\mathbf{B} - \lambda\mathbf{I})\mathbf{a} = 0 \tag{16C-7}$$

In this form it can be shown that the maximum value of λ is the largest eigenvalue of the matrix $\mathbf{W}^{-1}\mathbf{B}$, and $\mathbf{a}$ is the corresponding eigenvector, whose elements are the discriminant weights associated with the first linear composite.

In general there will be $r = \min(K - 1, p)$ linear composites. We will denote by λ_j the jth eigenvalue of $\mathbf{W}^{-1}\mathbf{B}$, where $j = 1, 2, \ldots, r$. The relative magnitudes of the respective eigenvalues, λ_j, give the descriptive index of the importance of each of the discriminant axes. For example by expressing each eigenvalue as a percentage of the "total variance" accounted for, that is,

$$\frac{\lambda_j}{\Sigma_j\lambda_j} \tag{16C-8}$$

we can determine which discriminant axes capture the major sources of variation separating the groups.

Associated with each linear composite is a set of discriminant weights (eigenvectors). We will denote by $\mathbf{a}_j$ the set of discriminant weights associated with the jth linear composite (eigenvalue). For interpretation it has become customary to transform the discriminant weights into what are called discriminant loadings. Discriminant weights can be adversely affected by predictor variables that are correlated. Thus, a better way of interpreting the relationship between the predictor variables and a discriminant function is to compute the simple correlation of the variable and the computed discriminant scores for that function. In other words, discriminant loadings are correlations, where the correlation is taken across the observed values of a given variable and the projection of points on a particular discriminant axis.

STATISTICAL TESTS

To assist in determining how many linear composites (that is, axes) to retain, we can use Bartlett's statistic V and its χ^2 approximation to the significance of the eigenvalue of $\mathbf{W}^{-1}\mathbf{B}$. If $\mathbf{X}$ is multivariate normal within each group with equal variance-covariance matrices, the significance of the r discriminant functions can be assessed by computing a logarithmic function of Λ:

$$V = -\{(n - 1) - \tfrac{1}{2}(p + K)\}ln\,\Lambda \tag{16C-9}$$

where Λ is a Wilks' lambda variable. It can be shown that

$$\Lambda = \prod_{j=1}^{r} (1 + \lambda_j)^{-1} \tag{16C-10}$$

Thus, since $-\ln a = \ln(1/a)$, we can write Bartlett's statistic as

$$V = \{(n - 1) - \tfrac{1}{2}(p + K)\} \sum_{j=1}^{r} \ln(1 + \lambda_j) \qquad \text{(16C-11)}$$

The statistic V is approximately distributed as a χ^2 random variable under the null hypothesis that the number of linear composites equals r with $p(K - 1)$ *df*. Thus, if the value of V is greater than a critical point from a χ^2 distribution with $p(K - 1)$ *df*, then we conclude that the discriminant solution is statistically significant. Because the discriminant functions are uncorrelated, the additive components of V are each approximately χ^2 variates. Thus, the significance of, say, the jth eigenvalue λ_j can be assessed by computing

$$V_j = \{(n - 1) - \tfrac{1}{2}(p + K)\}\ln(1 + \hat{\lambda}) \qquad \text{(16C-12)}$$

This statistic under *HO:* is approximately a χ^2 variate with $(p + K - 2j)$ df. Successive tests can be formed by cumulatively subtracting $V_1, V_2, \ldots V_j$, from V.

References

Crask, M. R., and W. D. Perreault. "Validation of Discriminant Analysis in Marketing Research," *Journal of Marketing Research*, February 1977, 60–64.

Dillon, W. R. "The Performance of the Linear Discriminant Function in Nonoptimal Situations and the Estimation of Classification Error Rates: A Review of Recent Findings," *Journal of Marketing Research*, February 1982, 44–46.

Morrison, Donald G. "On the Interpretation of Discriminant Analysis," *Journal of Marketing Research*, May 1969, 156–63.

Cluster Analysis[9]

In many application settings there is reason to believe that the set of objects under study can be clustered into subgroups that differ in meaningful ways. The most commonly used term for the class of procedures that seek to separate the component data into groups is cluster analysis. The cluster analysis procedure typically begins by taking, say, p measurements on each of the n objects. The $n \times p$ matrix of raw data is then transformed into an $n \times n$ matrix of similarity or, alternatively, distance measures where the similarities or distances are computed between pairs of objects across the p variables. Next a clustering algorithm is selected, which defines the rules concerning how to cluster the objects into subgroups on the basis of the inter-object similarities. As we indicated, the goal in many cluster applications is to arrive at clusters of objects that display small within-cluster variation relative to the between-cluster variation. As a final step, the uncovered clusters are contrasted (that is, profiled) in terms of their mean values on the p variables or other characteristics of interest.

CLUSTERING CRITERIA

As we indicated, the researcher wanting to perform a cluster analysis is faced with what appears to be an endless list of clustering algorithms to choose among. For the most part, clustering algorithms depend upon high-speed computer technology for computational efficiency and strive to meet some criterion that essentially maximizes the between-cluster variation relative to the within-cluster variation.

The between cluster variation can be judged by assessing the dis-

[9]Much of this material is taken from W. R. Dillon and M. Goldstein, *Multivariate Analysis: Methods and Applications* (New York: John Wiley & Sons, 1984), Chapter 5.

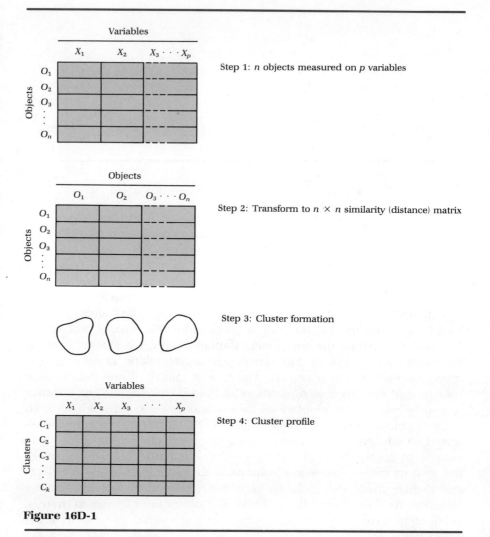

Step 1: *n* objects measured on *p* variables

Step 2: Transform to $n \times n$ similarity (distance) matrix

Step 3: Cluster formation

Step 4: Cluster profile

Figure 16D-1

Overview of Cluster Analysis. (Adapted from W. R. Dillon and M. Goldstein, *Multivariate Analysis: Methods and Applications.* New York: John Wiley & Sons, 1984, 158.)

tance between cluster centers in comparison with the distance of a cluster member to a cluster center. To understand how this criterion can be used to form clusters, imagine starting with a given number of cluster centers chosen arbitrarily, or on judgment, and assigning objects to the nearest cluster center. Next the mean or center of gravity of the resulting clusters are computed, and then objects are juggled back and forth between the clusters, each time recomputing the centers of gravity and the resultant between- and within-cluster variation until the ratio is sufficiently large.

SIMILARITY MEASURES

Fundamental to the use of any clustering technique is the computation of a measure of similarity or distance between the respective objects. These measures can be separated into two broad classes based upon the quality of the data available. With data having metric properties, a distance-type measure can be used, whereas with data having nominal components, a matching-type measure is appropriate.

Distance-Type Measures

Assume data have been collected on n objects or individuals. Let X_{ik}, $i = 1, 2, \ldots, n$, $k = 1, 2, \ldots, p$, be the measurement collected on the ith object or individual for the kth variable. Many measures of distance are special cases of the Minkowski metric defined by

$$d_{ij} = \left\{ \sum_{k=1}^{p} \mid X_{ik} - X_{jk} \mid^{r} \right\}^{1/r} \tag{16D-1}$$

where d_{ij} denotes the distance between the two objects i and j. If we set $r = 2$, then we have the Euclidean distance between objects i and j:

$$d_{ij} = \left\{ \sum_{k=1}^{p} (X_{ik} - X_{jk})^{2} \right\}^{1/2} \tag{16D-2}$$

If $r = 1$, then we have

$$d_{ij} = \left\{ \sum_{k=1}^{p} \mid X_{ik} - X_{jk} \mid \right\} \tag{16D-3}$$

which is referred to as the absolute or city-block metric. The use of the city-block metric results in two objects having the same distance regardless of whether they are two units apart, say, on each of two variables, or one unit apart on one variable and three units apart on the other—assuming, of course, scale units of equal value.

Euclidean distance is not scale invariant. Therefore, the use of raw data should be considered skeptically when computing distances between objects, since distance can be badly distorted by a simple change of scale.

Matching-Type Measures

Matching-type measures, are perhaps better known as association coefficients, appropriate when the data are nominally scaled. These types of similarity measures generally take on values in the range 0 to 1, and are based on the reasoning that two individuals should be viewed as being similar to the extent that they share common attributes.

CLUSTERING TECHNIQUES: HIERARCHICAL AND PARTITIONING METHODS

A rather large number of clustering algorithms have been proposed. There are two popular kinds of clustering techniques. The first group, called *hierarchical* techniques, clusters the clusters themselves at various levels. The second group, called *partitioning* techniques, forms clusters by optimizing some specific clustering criterion.

Hierarchical Techniques

Hierarchical techniques perform successive fusions or divisions of the data. One of the primary features distinguishing hierarchical techniques from other clustering algorithms is that the allocation of an object to a cluster is irrevocable; that is, once an object joins a cluster it is never removed and fused with other objects belonging to some other cluster. *Agglomerative* methods proceed by forming a series of fusions of the *n* objects into groups. *Divisive* methods partition the set of *n* objects into finer and finer subdivisions. Thus agglomerative methods eventually result in all objects falling in one cluster, whereas divisive techniques will finally split the data so that each object forms its own cluster. In either case, the obvious issue is where to stop. The output from both agglomerative and divisive methods is typically summarized by the use of a dendogram, which is a two-dimensional treelike diagram illustrating the fusions or partitions that have been effected at each successive level.

Agglomerative Methods. These methods all proceed in a similar fashion: Each object starts out in its own cluster; at the next level the two closest objects (clusters) are fused; at the third level a new object joins the cluster containing the two objects, or another two-object cluster is formed, with the decision resting on some assignment criterion. The process continues in a similar fashion until eventually a single cluster containing all *n* objects is formed.

Agglomerative methods differ to the extent that alternative definitions of distance or similarity are used in the assignment rule. Two of the more popular agglormerative techniques are described below.

1. *Single linkage, or the nearest-neighbor method.* Single linkage methods use a minimum-distance rule that starts out by first finding those two objects having the shortest distance. They constitute the first cluster. At the next stage one of two things can happen: Either a third object will join the already formed cluster of two, or the two closest unclustered objects are joined to form a second cluster. The decision rests on whether the distance from one of the unclustered objects to the first cluster is shorter than the distance between the two closest unclustered objects. The process continues until all objects belong to a single cluster. For this method, then, the distance

between clusters is defined as the distance between their nearest neighbors.

2. *Complete linkage, or the furthest neighbor method.* This method is exactly opposite to the approach taken in single linkage, in the sense that distance is now defined as the distance between the most distant pair of individuals.

Divisive Methods. Hierarchical divisive methods start by splitting the total pool of objects into two groups. An immediate problem is how to effect the first split. With n objects there is a possibility of $2^{n-1} - 1$ different ways to form subsets of size 2. Hence, even with the recent advances in computer storage capacity, the number of subsets considered will have to be restricted in most realistic applications. Once the initial split is made, objects are moved from one cluster to another, or finer subdivisions of the already formed clusters are made. What distinguishes the various divisive methods is (1) how the initial split is effected and (2) how already formed clusters are subdivided.

Partitioning Techniques

Unlike hierarchical clustering techniques, methods that effect a partition of the data do not require that the allocation of an object to a cluster be irrevocable. That is, objects may be reallocated if their initial assignments were indeed inaccurate. These techniques partition the data based upon optimizing some formal and predefined criterion. The use of partitioning techniques usually assumes that the number of final clusters is known and specified in advance, although some methods do allow the number to vary during the course of the analysis. A popular partitioning method is the *K-Means* clustering procedure.

References

Ball, G. H. *Classification Analysis* (Stanford Research Institute, SRI, Project 5533, 1971).

Cormack, R. M. "A Review of Classification," *Journal of the Royal Statistical Society Series A* (General), 134, pt. 3, 1971, 321–353.

Hartigan, J. A. *Clustering Algorithms* (New York: John Wiley & Sons, 1975).

Johnson, S. C. "Hierarchical Clustering Schemes," *Psychometrika* 32, 241–254.

CASE STUDIES FOR PART V

Case 1: National Wine Tracking Study

The following case exercise is used as an interviewing tool at a New York-based supplier for junior research project directors.

Attached are:

1. A questionnaire
2. A grid page

Your assignment is to prepare a set of data processing cleaning instructions for the grid page.

<u>National Wine Tracking Study</u>
—Main Questionnaire—
Interviewer Do Not Read List for Q's 1-6

1. I'd like to ask you some questions about wine. Please tell me all the brands of wine you can think of. (Probe:) What others? *(Record all mentions on white grid page under Q.1, "Unaided aware.")*
2. What brands of wine do you recall having seen or heard advertised on TV, radio or in magazines recently? (Probe:) What others? *(Record all mentions on white grid page under Q.2, "Unaided advertising.")*
3. What brand of wine did you buy last? *(Record all mentions on white grid page under Q.3, "Bought last.")*

   If no brand is mentioned anywhere in Q's 1, 2, or 3,
   skip to Q.7. Otherwise, continue.
4. And what brand did you buy the time before that? *(Record all mentions on white grid page under Q.4, "Bought time before last.")*
5. What brand are you most likely to buy next? *(Record all mentions on white grid page under Q.5, "Will buy next.")*

7. Have you ever heard of *(brand)*? *(Record "yes" answers on white grid page under Q.7, "Aided aware.")*
(Ask Q.8 for each (*) brand mentioned in Q.1 or Q.7 but not Q.2)

8. Do you recall having recently seen or heard advertising for *(brand)*? *(Record "yes" answers on white grid page under Q.8, "Aided ad aware.")*
(Ask Q.9 for each (*) brand mentioned in Q's 1, 2 or 7 but not Q's 3-4)

9. Have you ever bought *(brand)*? *(Record "yes" answers on white grid page under Q.9, "Ever bought.")*
(Ask Q.10a for each (*) brand mentioned in Q's 3, 4, or 9)

10a. Have you bought *(brand)* in the *past two months*? *(Record "yes" answers on white grid page under Q.10a, "Bought past two months.")*
(Ask Q.10b for each (*) brand mentioned in Q.10a)

10b. How many bottles of *(brand)* did you buy in the past two months? *(Record number legibly on white grid page under Q.10b, "# of bottles.")*

CARD 4 continued   DO NOT READ LIST

	Q.1 Un-aided aware (18)	Q.2 Un-aided advtg (24)	Q.3 Bought last (30)	Q.4 Bought time before last (36)	Q.5 Will buy next (42)	Q.6 Would consider buying (48)	Q.7 Aided aware (54)	Q.8 Aided ad aware (59)	Q.9 Ever bought (64)	Q.10a Bought past two months (69)	Start card 5 Q.10b # of bot.
3—*Almaden 1	1	1	1	1	1	1	1	1	1	1	_____ 6-
Almaden Light 2	2	2	2	2	2						
Almaden Golden 3	3	3	3	3	3						_____ 8-
*B&G.................4	4	4	4	4	4	4	4	4	4		
4—*Black Tower 5	5	5	5	5	5	5	5	5	5		_____ 10-
5—*Blue Nun 6	6	6	6	6	6	6	6	6	6		_____ 12-
*Bolla Or Soave Bolla ..7	7	7	7	7	7	7	7	7	7		_____ 14-
Brolio 8	8	8	8	8	8						
*Carlo Rossi 9	9	9	9	9	9	9	9	9	9		_____ 16-
*Cella 0	0	0	0	0	0	0	0	0	0		_____ 18-
(19)	(25)	(31)	(37)	(43)	(49)	(55)	(60)	(65)	(70)		
The Christian Brothers ...1	1	1	1	1	1	1					
2—*Folonari 2	2	2	2	2	2	2	2	2	2		_____ 20-
Fontana Candida 3	3	3	3	3	3						
Franzia 4	4	4	4	4	4						
6—*Gallo 5	5	5	5	5	5	5	5	5	5		_____ 22-
*Giacobazzi 6	6	6	6	6	6	6	6	6	6		_____ 24-
Gold Seal Catawba 7	7	7	7	7	7						
Great Western 8	8	8	8	8	8						
7—*Inglenook...........9	9	9	9	9	9	9	9	9	9		_____ 26-
Italian Swiss Colony/Colony ...0	0	0	0	0	0	0	0	0	0		
(20)	(26)	(32)	(38)	(44)	(50)	(56)	(61)	(66)	(71)		
Krug 1	1	1	1	1	1	1					
8—*Lancers 2	2	2	2	2	2	2	2	2	2		_____ 28-
Los Hermanos 3	3	3	3	3	3						_____ 30-
9—*Mateus 4	4	4	4	4	4	4	4	4	4		_____ 32-
*Mondavi 5	5	5	5	5	5	5	5	5	5		_____ 34-
*Monterey Vineyards ...6	6	6	6	6	6	6	6	6	6		
*Mouton Cadet (Moo-tawn ka-day) ...7	7	7	7	7	7	7	7	7	7		_____ 36-
Nectarose.............8	8	8	8	8	8						
1—*Partager (Par-ta-jhay) ...9	9	9	9	9	9	9	9	9	9		_____ 38-
10—*Paul Masson (Ma-sahn) 0	0	0	0	0	0	0	0	0	0		_____ 40-
(21)	(27)	(33)	(39)	(45)	(51)	(57)	(62)	(67)	(72)		
*Masson Light.........1	1	1	1	1	1	1	1	1	1		_____ 42-
*Polo Brindisi.........2	2	2	2	2	2	2	2	2	2		_____ 44-
*Prego...............3	3	3	3	3	3	3	3	3	3		_____ 46-

(Continued)

Start card 5

	Q.1 Un-aided aware (21)	Q.2 Un-aided advtg (27)	Q.3 Bought last (33)	Q.4 Bought time before last (39)	Q.5 Will buy next (45)	Q.6 Would consider buying (51)	Q.7 Aided aware (57)	Q.8 Aided ad aware (62)	Q.9 Ever bought (67)	Q.10a Bought past two months (72)	Q.10b # of bot.
11—*Riunite (Ree-u-nee-tee) ..4	4	4	4	4	4	4	4	4	4	4	___ 48-
Ruffino.................5	5	5	5	5	5						
*Sebastiani..............6	6	6	6	6	6	6	6	6	6	6	___ 50-
*Sterling 7	7	7	7	7	7	7	7	7	7	7	___ 52-
12—*Taylor California Cellars (Calif. Cellars) 8	8	8	8	8	8	8	8	8	8	8	___ 54-
*Taylor California Cellars Light 9	9	9	9	9	9	9	9	9	9	9	___ 56-
*Taylor Lake Country 0	0	0	0	0	0	0	0	0	0	0	___ 58-
Taylor (Ask: "could (22)	(28)	(34)	(40)	(46)	(52)	(58)	(63)	(68)	(73)	
you be more specific"). 1	1	1	1	1	1	1					
*Valbon.................2	2	2	2	2	2	2	2	2	2	2	___ 60-
*Vivante................3	3	3	3	3	3	3	3	3	3	3	___ 62-
Yago 4	4	4	4	4	4	4					
Other (specify)											
_____0	0	0	0	0	0	0					
_____0	0	0	0	0	0	0					80-4	80-5
_____0	0	0	0	0	0	0					
None x	x	x	x	x	x						
Don't Know ....y	y	y	y	y	y	y					
23-	29-	35-	41-	47-	53-						

Case 2: Kentucky Fried Chicken

The following provides details on a Kentucky Fried Chicken (KFC) concept study. Based upon the information provided and any statistical tests you feel are appropriate, prepare a statement of findings.

Purpose

The objective of the research is to assess two alternative concept positionings for Kentucky Fried Chicken ("Chicken Superiority" and "Good For You") through a battery of evaluative scaled measurements that address (1) appeal and (2) relevance.

Method and Scope

Two hundred respondents were recruited via central-location shopping mall intercept. Qualified respondents were screened to meet the following requirements:

- Aged 18–49
- Household income *under* $35,000
- At least four visits to a fast-food restaurant in the past month
- Past six month KFC visitor
- Not negative to future KFC visit

556

Sample quotas were set to provide for a respondent sample that con-formed to the following conditions:

- one-half male; one-half female
- one-half with a child aged 6–18 at home; one-half without a child aged 6–18 at home

Detailed Findings

Findings are listed in Tables 1–8.

TABLE 1
Overall Rating of Kentucky Fried Chicken

Base: Total respondents	"Chicken superiority" 200 %	"Good for you" 200 %
Excellent/very good	45	65
Excellent	20	40
Very Good	25	25
Good	15	15
Fair	25	10
Poor	15	10

TABLE 2
Summary of Mean Score Agreement Levels
(7-point scales)

Base: Total respondents	"Chicken superiority" 200 $\overline{X}$	"Good for you" 200 $\overline{X}$
Appeal The way they described Kentucky Fried Chicken was appealing to me personally	3.80 (1.21)*	5.87 (.98)
I really liked the way she talked about Kentucky Fried Chicken	3.77 (1.12)	4.74 (1.01)
Listening to what she said could really make me hungry for Kentucky Fried Chicken	3.45 (1.01)	5.41 (.95)

*Numbers in parentheses give variances.

TABLE 3

Summary of Mean Score Agreement Levels

Base: Total respondents	"Chicken superiority" 200 $\bar{X}$	"Good for you" 200 $\bar{X}$
Relevance		
The Kentucky Fried Chicken experience described here is something I'd like to have more often	3.45 (1.45)*	3.52 (1.21)
She was talking about some things that matter to me when it comes to fast food	3.63 (1.23)	5.87 (1.01)
She described what I really like about eating Kentucky Fried Chicken	3.60 (1.5)	4.89 (1.01)

*Numbers in parentheses give variances.

TABLE 4

Summary of Top-Box Agreement Levels
(Strongly agree)

Base: Total respondents	"Chicken superiority" 200 %	"Good for you" 200 %
■Appeal		
The way they described Kentucky Fried Chicken was appealing to me personally	12	36
I really liked the way she talked about Kentucky Fried Chicken	14	36
Listening to what she said could really make me hungry for Kentucky Fried Chicken	15	40
■Relevance		
The Kentucky Fried Chicken experience described here is something I'd like to have more often	8	15
She was talking about some things that matter to me when it comes to fast food	14	38
She described what I really like about eating Kentucky Fried Chicken	13	18

TABLE 5
Simple Correlation of Attributes to Overall Rating of KFC

Base: Total respondents	"Chicken superiority" 200	"Good for you" 200
■Appeal		
The way they described Kentucky Fried Chicken was appealing to me personally	−.154	.654
I really liked the way she talked about Kentucky Fried Chicken	.200	.589
Listening to what she said could really make me hungry for Kentucky Fried Chicken	.107	.761
■Relevance		
The Kentucky Fried Chicken experience described here is something I'd like to have more often	−.140	.641
She was talking about some things that matter to me when it comes to fast food	−.200	.742
She described what I really like about eating Kentucky Fried Chicken	.109	.451

TABLE 6
Multiple Regression
(Overall rating regressed on specific attribute ratings)

	"Chicken superiority"	
	Regression coefficient	Standard error
Eating Kentucky Fried Chicken is a more enjoyable experience than eating most other fast foods (X_1)	2.89	.50
It made me look forward to the next time I get Kentucky Fried Chicken (X_2)	.56	.42
The way they described Kentucky Fried Chicken was appealing to me personally (X_3)	−1.85	1.01
I really liked the way she talked about Kentucky Fried Chicken (X_4)	−1.01	1.25
This reminds me of a lot of other Kentucky Fried Chicken commercials I've seen in the past (X_5)	−.025	.32

$R^2 = .262; RSS = 16543.21; ESS = 46542.3$

(Continued)

T A B L E 6

Continued   **Multiple Regression**

(Overall rating regressed on specific attribute ratings)

Correlation Matrix

	y	X_1	X_2	X_3	X_4	X_5
y	1.0					
X_1	.67	1.0				
X_2	.23	.45	1.0			
X_3	−.36	−.42	−.67	1.0		
X_4	−.31	−.38	−.42	.50	1.0	
X_5	−.15	−.09	−.16	.25	.10	1.0

T A B L E 7

Multiple Regression

(Overall rating regressed on specific attribute ratings)

	"Good for you"	
	Regression coefficient	Standard error
Eating Kentucky Fried Chicken is a more enjoyable experience than eating most other fast foods (X_1)	2.25	.87
It made me look forward to the next time I get Kentucky Fried Chicken (X_2)	1.32	.35
The way they described Kentucky Fried Chicken was appealing to me personally (X_3)	.87	.25
I really liked the way she talked about Kentucky Fried Chicken (X_4)	1.01	.87
This reminds me of a lot of other Kentucky Fried Chicken commercials I've seen in the past (X_5)	−1.25	.65

$R^2 = .433$; $RSS = 19911.394$; $ESS = 26063.432$

Correlation Matrix

	y	X_1	X_2	X_3	X_4	X_5
y	1.0					
X_1	.59	1.0				
X_2	.58	.65	1.0			
X_3	.46	.23	.32	1.0		
X_4	.40	.21	.29	.89	1.0	
X_5	−.09	.05	.01	−.14	−.25	1.0

Base: Total Respondents	"Chicken superiority" 200 %	"Good for you" 200 %
Age		
18–24	31	26
25–29	24	26
30–34	17	19
35–39	15	14
40–49	13	15
Household size		
One	9	12
Two	19	24
Three	34	22
Four	20	21
Five or more	18	21
Income		
Under $15,000	21	25
$15,000 to under $25,000	38	35
$25,000 to under $35,000	41	40
Race		
White	72	66
Black	25	26
Other non-white	3	8
Markets		
Atlanta	15	15
Chicago	14	14
Detroit	13	13
Houston	23	22
Los Angeles	21	22
Seattle	14	14

Case 3: An Evaluation of One Print Advertisement for Velvet Liqueur

The following case exercise is used as an interviewing tool by Perception Research, Inc., Englewood, New Jersey. The instructions and materials which follow appear as they would if you were interviewing at Perception Research, Inc. Following are

1. A background and objectives statement
2. Discussions of methodology
3. Tables of results

for a short print ad study.

Your assignment is to discuss detailed findings in writing, as if the next step were to give it to the typist. You may include a short summary and conclusions if you wish.

Our purpose is simply to aid in the evaluation of your ability to organize your thoughts, draw insights from the data, and express yourself in writing.

You may type a rough copy or hand write as you normally might do. Please take as much time as you need to produce what you feel is a representative sample of your work.

Background and Objectives

White Palace Partners, Inc. is currently considering a new advertising execution for a proposed new liqueur product called Velvet.

They have requested that PRS evaluate the new execution to determine if it appears to be a viable introductory vehicle for this new product. The *key* objectives of the new execution were:

- An unaided recall score of at least 30 percent
- A purchase intent top box level of at least 15 percent
- A "someone like me" level of at least +25 percent (see user image)

Sample Composition

A total of 75 interviews were conducted among purchasers (past year) and drinkers (past month) of a proprietary liqueur. Participants were half males and half females. In addition, they were half legal drinking age to 34 and half 35–49.

Test Date and Locations

Interviewing was conducted at the PRS test facilities in New Jersey, Florida, California, and Minnesota during March 1984.

Research Procedures

Participants were screened at each shopping mall location. They were not, however, pre-alerted as to the category under consideration.

Qualified respondents were seated in an interviewing booth with a slide projector. Participants were informed that they would be viewing a series of advertisements taken from a magazine. They were allowed to spend as much or as little time as they wished viewing each ad.

Unaided and aided recall was then obtained.

Participants were then re-exposed to the test ad and asked to examine it in detail. A brief verbal interview was then conducted. Questioning focused on

- Future purchase intent and reasons
- Product and user imagery

Detailed Tables

Tabulated information from the questionnaire is listed in Tables 1–6.

T A B L E 1
Unaided Recall

	Base:	Total (75) %
Amaretto di Saronno		69
Kahlua		69
Volkswagen Jetta		65
American Express		63
Hilton Hotel		60
CocoRibe		59
Pentax		52
General Electric		47
Citizens Watches		40
Kool Lights		40
Velvet		*33*
Grand Marnier		31
Test Average*		54

*Excluding Velvet.
Q. Thinking of the ads you just saw, which ones can you remember? Do you recall any other products or companies? Tell me the names of the products and companies you just saw advertised.

T A B L E 2
Total Ad Recall
(Unaided Or Aided)

	Base:	Total (75) %
Kahlua		97
American Express		95
Kool Lights		93
Amaretto di Saronno		91
Citizens Watches		91
Hilton Hotel		91
CocoRibe		87
Volkswagen Jetta		85
Pentax		84
General Electric		75
Grand Marnier		69
Velvet		*61*
Test Average*		87

*Excluding Velvet.
Q. Here is a list of brand names. Some of these brands appeared in the ads you just saw, while others did not. Please tell me those which you definitely remember having seen, even though you may have mentioned them before.

TABLE 3
Purchase Intent

	Base:	Total (75) %
Definitely would buy (5)		7 ⎤ 34
Probably would buy (4)		27 ⎦
Might or might not buy (3)		33
Probably would not buy (2)		24 ⎤ 33
Definitely would not buy (1)		9 ⎦
Mean Rating		3.0

Q. Assuming Velvet were available at your liquor store, how likely would you be to buy a bottle based on what this ad shows and tells you about the brand? Please tell me the statement on the card which comes closest to describing how you feel about buying Velvet?

TABLE 4
Reasons For Purchase Intent

	Base:	Total (75) %
Favorable		51
Product Attributes		37
Taste/Flavor		33
Almond and orange flavor		20
Like almond		7
Would taste good		4
Would taste similar to Amaretto		3
Other Product Attributes		13
Like cordials/liqueurs		7
Italian/imported from Italy		5
Like the color of the liqueur		3
Visual		16
Bottle		13
Like the shape of the bottle		4
Attractive bottle		4
Cut glass bottle		3
Unusual shape bottle		3
Other Visual		8
Almonds in the ad		7
Like the glass		3
Other Favorable		20
Curious/try new products		12
Would buy for company/guests		4
For special occasions		4
Unfavorable		28
Taste/Flavor		23
Dislike almond		11
Wouldn't like orange and almond flavor		8
Would be too sweet		5
Dislike coconut		3
Visual		5
Bottle		3
Other Visual		3
Dark color ad		3
Other Unfavorable		4
Neutral/Conditional		39
Satisfied with current liqueur		11
Not familiar with it		9
Wouldn't buy a bottle until I've tasted it		9
Depends on price		9
Don't drink much liqueur		5

Q. Why do you say that?

Product and User Image Net Differences*

	Total
Base:	(75)
	%

Product Image

High quality (vs. low quality)	+69
Good after dinner (vs. not)	+65
Good for serving to guests (vs. not)	+52
Good straight or on-the-rocks (vs. not)	+47
An Italian liqueur (vs. not)	+44
Has a light orange taste (vs. strong)	+43
Would make a good gift (vs. would not)	+43
Good tasting (vs. is not)	+33
Has a light almond taste (vs. strong)	+23
Different from other liqueurs (vs. similar)	+21
More expensive than other liqueurs (vs. less)	+ 5

User Image

For selective drinkers (vs. drink almost anything)	+68
For people who really know liqueurs (vs. don't)	+35
For women (vs. not for women)	+27
For men (vs. not for men)	+24
For someone like me (vs. not)	+ 1

*Percent selecting the two boxes closest to the description appearing first, minus the percent selecting two boxes closest to the description shown in parentheses, utilizing a 5-point semantic differential scale.

Q. On this card are pairs of phrases which could be used to describe a product such as Velvet or the types of people who might buy a product such as this. For each pair of phrases, please indicate how this ad makes you feel about Velvet by placing an "X" in the space that best reflects your feelings.

TABLE 6
Summary for Key Dimensions

	Velvet (75) %	Previously Tested Velvet Ads					New Product Liqueur Norm %
Base:		A (150) %	B (151) %	C (149) %	D (150) %	E (151) %	
Unaided Recall	33	15	17	26	28	27	32
Total Recall	61	47	50	42	52	38	53
Likes and Dislikes							
Any Likes	NA	71	75	79	80	75	79
Any Dislikes	NA	37	44	48	51	51	49
Net Difference*	NA	+34	+31	+31	+29	+24	+30
Purchase Intent							
Definitely would buy	7 ⌉ 34	1 ⌉ 23	9 ⌉ 31	6 ⌉ 35	5 ⌉ 26	5 ⌉ 29	8 ⌉ 38
Probably would buy	27 ⌋	22 ⌋	22 ⌋	29 ⌋	21 ⌋	24 ⌋	30 ⌋
Product Image—Net Differences*							
High quality	+69	+57	+72	+54	+55	+57	+51
Good after dinner	+65	+75	+76	+70	+70	+74	NA
Good after serving guests	+52	+67	+60	+62	+62	+72	+68
Good straight or on-the-rocks	+47	+71	+72	+71	+66	+69	+65
An Italian liqueur	+44	+49	+89	+68	+81	+68	NA
Has a light orange taste	+43	+39	+23	+32	+39	+39	NA
Would make a good gift	+43	+39	+46	+40	+45	+42	NA
Good tasting	+33	+46	+39	+46	+42	+45	+55
Has a light almond taste	+23	+48	+47	NA	NA	NA	NA
Different from other liqueurs	+21	−3	−8	−7	−5	−13	+18
More expensive than others	+5	+17	+17	+9	+27	+19	+17
User Imagery—Net Differences*							
For selective people	+68	+54	+43	+53	+54	+47	+40
For people who really know liqueur	+35	+48	+47	+50	+51	+54	+41
For women	+27	+46	+58	+57	+65	+64	+65
For men	+24	+27	+19	+29	+34	+35	+15
For someone like me	+1	+25	+34	+29	+28	+27	+29

*Top 2 boxes minus bottom 2 boxes, based on a 5-point scale.

566

Case 4: Consumer Attitudes and Perceptions Toward Seafood When Eating Out—Positioning Phase

In Case Studies for Parts II and IV we introduced details on a study designed to collect information on consumers' attitudes and perceptions toward nontraditional fish consumption when eating out (in particular, see Part II, Case 2). Following is the executive summary for the focus group phase of this study.

Executive Summary

Overall, participants in these focus groups have a favorable attitude toward fish. They are eating more fish today than they ever have in the past and expect that consumption to increase. These consumers are more willing and more likely to try fish when eating out than they are at home. In fact, on many occasions they seem to relate eating out with eating fish.

On the other hand, in spite of the high propensity to eat fish in restaurants, there is significant resistance to trying the nontraditional species that were suggested to the participants in this study. Some participants are familiar with less traditional fish, if only by name, but none speak highly or very favorably about any of them. In some cases perceptions are negative; in many cases they are inaccurate.

In general, it might be said that there is an outright "suspicion" of nontraditional species that project an unpleasurable experience. Those who are not familiar with the species mentioned seem to base their perceptions solely on the name. Other influential negative factors are the image of fish as an animal, its eating habits, appearance, and social behavior. Those who hold these perceptions are not influenced by those who do not, or by those who have had good experiences with nontraditional species.

Participants agree that they eat fish because they like the way it tastes. Health factors are also mentioned as reasons for consuming fish, particularly by the men. Being light and easily digested is mentioned more by the women. Fish is considered a good alternative to red meats but is something generally not served at home. Many participants say they eat fish in restaurants because it is a change from what is prepared at home. This also depends on the amount of trust they put in the reputation of the restaurant and/or chef.

Factors that can either inhibit or promote the selection of fish include the method of preparation, previous experience, and cost. Although fish is not considered to be inexpensive it is generally seen as a good food value. Yet some group participants said price prevents them from trying an unfamiliar fish. The risk of disliking the fish is too great relative to the cost in both dollars and the dining experience. A few participants feel that low-priced fish are of poor quality. Others complain about fish being "smelly" or "bony" or "oily" or "slimy" or "too strong."

The consumption of fish in restaurants does not appear to have a direct correspondence with childhood, geographic, ethnic, or religious exposure or experience.

Several ideas for promoting nontraditional fish were suggested. Both men and women agreed that a description of the fish, its type, taste, and method of preparation enhances the likelihood of their trying it if it is unfamiliar.

Other frequently mentioned suggestions are to serve these fish as appetizers or "specials," or to include them in a combination plate. Free samples give people an opportunity to try unfamiliar fish without the risk. Media suggestions include food preparation programs or morning talk shows with respected authorities like Julia Child.

Also mentioned is the implementation of an industry-wide program, comparable to that of the American Dairy Association, to promote fish in general. This is considered to be a good strategy to make consumers more aware of fish as an alternative to other foods.

Other means suggested to promote unfamiliar fish include:

- Make clear that the fish is fresh and prepared to order (but do not overdo, which causes suspicions)
- Offer in a "specialty" restaurant setting, especially a seafood restaurant
- Price attractively—lower than steaks, for example, but not radically lower than other well-known fish
- Have recommendations come from the restaurant—that is, from the chef, not from waiters or waitresses

In addition, focus group participants were also asked to provide similarity/dissimilarity ratings for eight traditional species of fish:

Fillet of sole	Salmon
Schrod	Cod
Haddock	Halibut
Blue fish	Swordfish

In the next phase of this research study, interest centered on consumers' attitudes and perceptions of nontraditional fish. Specifically, the objectives were to explore:

- current eating-out habits of consumers in non-fast-food restaurants
- attitudes, beliefs, and intentions of consumers concerning the ordering of fish when eating out
- consumers' perceptions of nontraditional fish

- consumers' willingness to try nontraditional fish
- perception of nontraditional fish species' attributes held by consumers
- familiarity of and satisfaction with selected nontraditional fish
- different promotional techniques that might increase consumers' willingness to try nontraditional fish when dining out
- the relationship among "ideal," perceived, and actual attributes of specific nontraditional fish
- characteristics of consumers who would be more willing to try nontraditional fish

Each of the eleven nontraditional fish species

Butterfish	Whiting
Hake	Skate
Mackerel	Eel
Monkfish	Cusk
Squid	Tilefish
Pollock	

were evaluated on eleven attributes and a "willingness to try" measure as shown below:

Criteria	Range of variation	
	(1)	(5)
willingness to try	not very	very
body	soft	firm
flavor	mild	strong
fat content	low	high
oily	not oily	very oily
flaky	not flaky	very flaky
color	white	dark
boniness	not bony	very bony
odor	mild	strong
moisture	dry	moist
fleshiness	lean	meaty
fishiness	not fishy	very fishy

Figure 1 presents the profile for the ideal fish. Table 1 provides mean and percentage rating on "willingness to try" for each nontraditional fish species. Figures 2–12 present perceptual maps for three user groups ("not willing to try," "uncertain," "very willing to try") for each type of nontraditional fish.

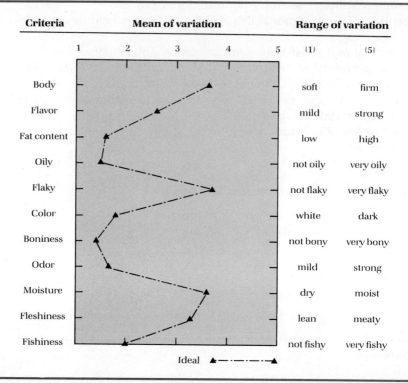

Figure 1

Profile of the ideal fish.

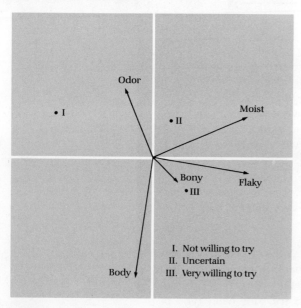

Figure 2

Discriminant analysis of butterfish.

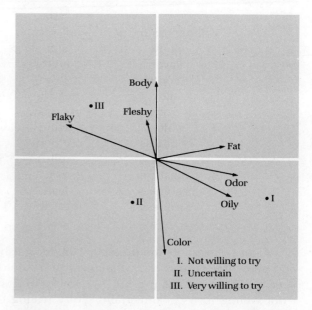

Figure 3

Discriminant analysis of cusk.

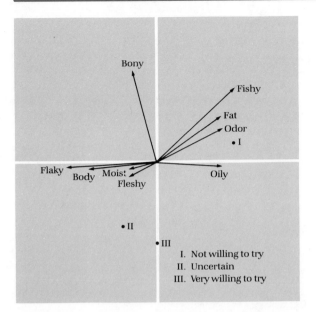

Figure 4

Discriminant analysis of eel.

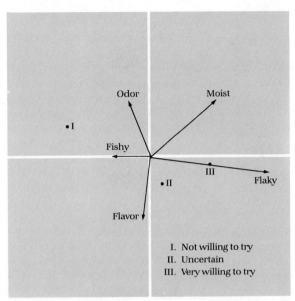

Figure 5

Discriminant analysis of hake.

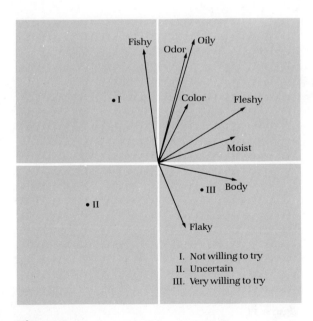

Figure 6

Discriminant analysis of mackerel.

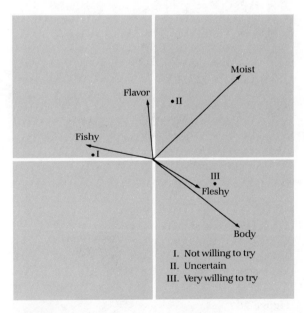

Figure 7

Discriminant analysis of monkfish.

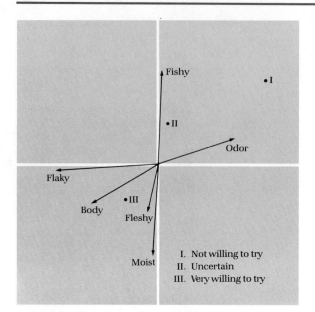

Figure 8

Discriminant analysis of pollock.

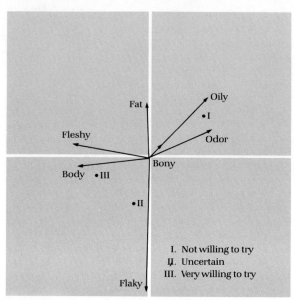

Figure 9

Discriminant analysis of skate.

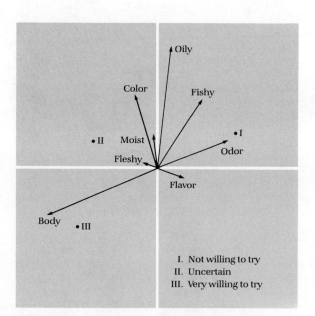

Figure 10

Discriminant analysis of squid.

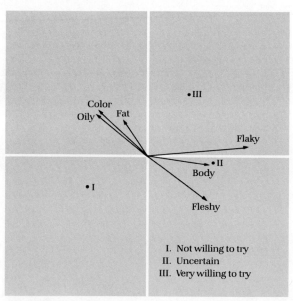

Figure 11

Discriminant analysis of tilefish.

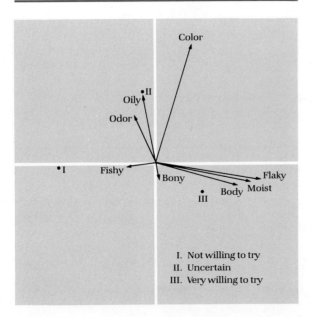

I. Not willing to try
II. Uncertain
III. Very willing to try

Figure 12

Discriminant analysis of whiting.

TABLE 1

**Willingness To Try Nontraditional Fish
[Scale (1) not very willing to (5) very
willing]**

Species	Willingness to try (mean responses)
Butterfish	3.39
Hake	2.96
Mackerel	3.22
Monkfish	2.91
Squid	2.49
Pollock	3.52
Whiting	3.27
Skate	2.52
Eel	2.07
Cusk	2.81
Tilefish	2.41

Species	Not willing (1 & 2)	Uncertain (3)	Very willing (4 & 5)
Butterfish	27%	22%	51%
Hake	39	21	40
Mackerel	35	16	49
Monkfish	42	18	40
Squid	57	12	31
Pollock	24	21	55
Whiting	28	25	47
Skate	51	22	27
Eel	67	12	21
Cusk	43	21	36
Tilefish	51	26	23

Questions

Based upon the results provided, answer the following questions.

1. What are consumers' general attitudes and perceptions of consuming fish when eating out?
2. Recommend a strategy for increasing the consumption of nontraditional fish when eating out.

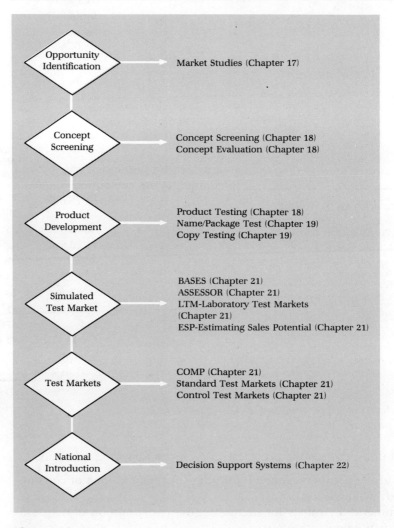

Figure 1

Framework for Part VI.

APPLICATIONS

In Part VI we introduce, discuss, and illustrate basic concepts and implementation of different types of market research studies. Once again we use prototypical marketing research proposals as a framework for discussing the various applications considered in the remaining chapters.

Figure 1 outlines the specific areas considered. Note that our attention focuses primarily on the prelaunch stage of the research cycle. The reasons are simple: (1) the prelaunch stage is a particularly active one in terms of both the variety and volume of marketing research conducted and (2) the prelaunch stage is crucial in determining the ultimate market acceptance of a new product. The reality of the marketplace is that most new products fail. In fact, of the 5,000 new products studied by the advertising agency Dancer Fitzgerald, only about 2 percent, fewer than 100, achieved satisfactory sales volume that would qualify them as even minimal successes. More importantly, it appears that the reason for market failure is marketing related and can be avoided by effective marketing research testing in the prelaunch stage. Specifically, in the 75 consumer product failures studied by *Advertising Age* several years ago, most failures were marketing related, involving "value consumer difference" (36 percent), "poor product positioning" (32 percent), and "no point of difference" (20 percent).

CHAPTER

Market Studies

CHAPTER OBJECTIVES

- Explain what is meant by a product-market.
- Define the philosophy and objectives of market studies.
- Describe the various types of market studies.
- Explain how national market studies are conducted.
- Describe the role of strategic market studies.
- Discuss and illustrate three basic strategic market studies—*positioning studies, market segmentation studies,* and *market structure studies.*
- Acquire an understanding of the various methods used in the three basic types of strategic market studies.

Introduction

An essential ingredient in designing successful marketing strategies is a thorough understanding of the structure of markets and the patterns of competition that exist within the markets. It is difficult to conceive of a situation in which decisions concerning the marketing-mix elements (that is, product design, price, advertising, and distribution) would be made without first acquiring an understanding of the competitive arena. The first step in this process is to define what is meant by a product-market.

A **product-market** consists of (1) a set of products that can be substituted for each other in those use situations where similar benefits are sought and (2) the customers for whom such uses are relevant.[1] In other words, product-markets reflect the fact that individuals seek the benefits that products provide and that their decisions about the available alternatives are based on prior experience or the specific consumption situation that applies.

Product-market The set of products that can be substituted for each other within those use situations where similar benefits are sought and the customers for whom such usages are relevant.

[1]G. S. Day, A. D. Shocker, and R. K. Srivastava, "Customer-Oriented Approaches to Identifying Product-Markets," *Journal of Marketing*, Fall 1979, 10.

576

Acquiring an understanding of a product-market may not be as simple as you might expect. First, the idea that product categories are unique and easily distinguishable is a gross simplification. In many instances, product-market boundaries are amorphous, marked by arbitrary distinctions. For example, consider the snack food product category. In defining this product-market should we include only junk food snacks such as potato chips, pretzels, peanuts, and candy bars, or also fruits, or possibly even yogurt? Unfortunately, in this case, substitutability is a matter of degree and—ultimately—personal preference. Second, because the idea of a unique product-market is an oversimplification, several different distinctions can be made:[2]

1. *Different product types* that serve the same generic need, (pencils and pens) and, therefore, may be perceived as substitutes in the long run, but differ with respect to the specific need satisfied.
2. *Different product variants* that are available within the same overall type (such as low-fat and regular cottage cheese) and serve on certain occasions as substitutes.
3. *Different brands* produced within the same product variant (for example, Coca-Cola and Pepsi-Cola), differentiated on the basis of package design, color, taste, shape, and so forth, and therefore, serve as direct substitutes.

Third, because of the breadth and complexity of consumer need and the availability of a large number of alternatives to satisfy it, there is not a single product-market, but rather several submarkets and strategic segments composed of customers with common uses or applications of the product.

In this chapter we discuss marketing research studies designed to provide information about the composition and structure of a product-market. Although these studies, generically referred to as *market studies*, vary in their scope and orientation, they play a fundamental part in the research process.

PHILOSOPHY AND OBJECTIVES OF MARKET STUDIES

Market studies provide information useful in designing effective marketing strategies. Among other things, they are the principal source of data on category and brand-use patterns, demographic characteristics of users, and customer attitudes and predispositions. Specifically, market studies provide information on

Market studies Marketing research studies designed to provide information about the composition and structure of a product market.

[2]T. Lunn makes these distinctions in "Segmenting and Constructing Markets," in *Consumer Market Research Handbook*, ed. R. M. Worcester (Maidenhead, Berkshire: McGraw-Hill, 1972). A similar discussion can be found in G. S. Day, A. D. Shocker, and R. Srivastava, "Product-Markets," *Journal of Marketing*, Fall 1979, 10–11.

- Incidence of category and brand use
- Brand and advertising awareness
- Use and purchase patterns
- Customer attitudes and perceptions
- Demographic and psychographic user profiles

The information collected in market studies can prove useful in virtually all phases of a product's life cycle. These studies can be used very early in the research process to identify opportunities for new products or line extensions; they provide information that can be used to both segment and structure a product-market; they can be used to analyze differences by market, demographic, attitude, or behavioral segment; they can be used later in a product's life cycle to monitor changes in user profiles, use patterns, and attitudes with a view toward repositioning the product; and they can be used to measure the relative effectiveness of a firm's marketing program.

National market studies
Studies concerned with monitoring changes in the marketplace over time. The information collected includes category and basic-use patterns and customer demographic and psychographic data.

Strategic market studies
Studies focusing on in-depth analysis of a specific product-market; they fall under the umbrella of custom research and are tailored to address specific marketing issues and/or problems.

Positioning studies
Attempts to portray the interrelationships among a set of brands in terms of consumers' perceptions and preferences for these brands.

Segmentation studies
Attempts to identify subgroups of consumers who will respond to a given marketing-mix configuration in a similar manner.

Structure studies
Attempts to define the competitive relationships within a product-market.

TYPES OF MARKET STUDIES

We describe two general types of market studies.

1. **National market studies** monitor changes in the marketplace over time. The information collected includes category and brand-use patterns and customer demographic and psychographic data. The data obtained are used to identify market opportunities, define target audiences, and provide direction for development of marketing strategies. These studies may be conducted annually or more frequently depending upon the activity within the product-market and/or the vulnerability of the manufacturer conducting the study (for example, a leading brand might want to monitor the market continually in order to effectively defend its position against competition). These studies are also sometimes referred to as "tracking studies."

2. **Strategic market studies** focus on an in-depth analysis of a specific product-market. Typically these types of studies fall under the umbrella of custom research and are tailored to address specific marketing issues and/or problems. We discuss and illustrate three types of strategic market studies: **positioning studies, segmentation studies,** and **structure studies.** Positioning studies attempt to portray the interrelationships among a set of brands in terms of consumers' perceptions and preferences for these brands. Segmentation studies attempt to identify subgroups of consumers who will respond to a given marketing-mix configuration in a similar manner. Structure studies attempt to define the competitive relationships within a product-market. In essence all three are used to help marketing managers understand and cope with their competitive environment.

NATIONAL MARKET STUDIES

As we indicated, national market studies are designed to provide basic information on product categories and brands, including use incidence and customer demographics and psychographics, which can be used to monitor changes in the marketplace over time. Exhibit 17-1 presents a prototypical national market study research proposal.

Procedures

Market studies may be conducted through any of the data-collection/interviewing methods we have discussed. Typically, however, interviews are conducted by telephone from a central facility. In cases where brand exhibits are required, door-to-door personal interviews are used. (Recall, however, from Chapter 5, that it is becoming increasingly difficult to conduct door-to-door interviews given the increasing number of working women and the difficulty and cost of getting interviewers to work evenings and weekends.) In both instances a national probability sample of households is employed.

Basic Samples

Sample-size requirements in national market studies are set based upon the various criteria discussed in Chapter 7. Typically, the standard

E X H I B I T   17-1

Market Study Proposal

Brand:	Skweeky Kleen Bar Soap
Project:	Bar Soap National Tracking Study
Background and Purpose:	The Bar Soap Brand Group has requested that a continuous tracking study be conducted in 1986. This study will be a continuation of the 1985 tracking study.

The objectives of this study will be to:

1. Determine track changes in brand awareness and usage since the introduction of new products.

2. Determine changes in volume contribution within the market.

3. Analyze consumer perceptions and measure changes in those perceptions among various market segments.

Research Method:	The 1986 study will be conducted over the course of the year, with monthly waves of interviewing to begin in January. The monthly tracking system was also used in 1985.

As in previous studies, interviewing will be conducted by WATS telephone from a central location. Telephone numbers will be selected via strict probability methods from all working exchanges and numbers in the continental United States. Respondents will be randomly selected within households. A total of 2,400 past-30-day bar soap users will be interviewed (200 per month for the twelve months of January through December 1986).

The basic questionnaire will follow that used in the 1985 study and will include the following question areas:

- Brand awareness (unaided and aided)
- Brand use (ever, past 30 days, most often)
- Number of bars used past 30 days
- Brand ratings for brands used
- Brand ratings for brand ever used but not past 30 days
- Importance of product attributes
- Other diagnostic question areas (to vary)

Timing and Cost: Fieldwork will be conducted monthly, beginning in January. Top-line reports on brand awareness and usage will be provided monthly, while more complete reports will be reported quarterly and when all the interviews are completed. The specific timing will be as follows:

Interview date	Number of interviews	Timing of monthly top-lines	Timing of quarterly top-lines	Final report
January	200	2/13	—	—
February	200	3/13	—	—
March	200	4/10	—	—
1st qtr.	600	—	5/15	—
April	200	5/8	—	—
May	200	6/12	—	—
June	200	7/15	—	—
2nd qtr.	600	—	8/14	—
July	200	8/11	—	—
August	200	9/11	—	—
September	200	10/12	—	—
3rd qtr.	600	—	11/13	—
October	200	11/9	—	—
November	200	12/11	—	—
December	200	1/13	—	—
4th qtr.	600	—	1/23	—
Total	2,400			3/25

The cost of this study will be $100,000 ± 10%.

Selected Supplier: Market Facts, Inc.

minimum sample size in a national market study is 500 category users. This size permits subgroup analysis (such as regional analysis) to be performed. Category users are usually defined as consumers who have used a brand in the product category under study in a recent time period (for example, the past 30 days). For low-incidence or seasonal products a longer time frame is usually used.

If the basic sample does not produce a minimum of 100 respondents in a user group of particular interest, the sample is supplemented to ensure that sufficient respondents are obtained in the desired group. For example, in a national soft-drink market study commissioned by Coca-Cola, a sufficient number of Pepsi users (more than 100) should be present in the sample. The supplemental sample is selected after the basic random sample has been completed. The procedures for selecting the supplemental sample should follow the same guidelines already outlined.

Questions Asked

The standard questions and question order used in prototypical market studies refer to.

- Brand and advertising awareness
- Brand use
- Brand purchase
- Advertising recall
- Open-ended likes/dislikes
- Brand ratings
- Other diagnostic questions
- Classification questions

Usually, the questions asked and question order are standardized to ensure that the data collected are comparable from market study to market study.

Action Standards

This type of market study is descriptive in nature. It is used to formulate or revise marketing strategies. Consequently, action standards are not usually applicable.

Approach to Analysis

Typically, analysis focuses on differences in category incidence, brand awareness and use levels, and changes in these levels over time. Volume contribution based on gender and age is calculated for the category under study and for major brands in the category. Volume contribution is estimated by multiplying the census estimates of the popula-

TABLE 17-1

Volume Contribution Estimates

Age	(1) Census estimate	(2) Incidence (%)	(3) Mean Usage rate (bar/mo.)	(4) Volume contribution (1) × (2) × (3)
			Brand X	
Males				
20–29	9,438	28	1.80	4,756.75
30–34	8,555	25	2.25	4,812.19
35–39	6,869	12	1.95	1,607.35
40–44	5,691	13	1.25	924.79
45–54	5,383	9	.97	469.94
55–59	5,455	7	.63	240.57
60+	14,691	6	.50	440.73
Total males	56,082			
Females				
20–29	9,492	32	2.50	7,593.60
30–34	8,687	28	2.35	5,716.05
35–39	7,164	13	2.10	1,955.77
40–44	5,996	12	1.90	1,367.09
45–54	5,646	5	1.75	494.03
55–59	5,944	4	1.77	420.84
60+	20,083	6	1.55	1,867.72
Total females	63,012			

tion of each group times the incidence of use within the group times the mean rate of use. Table 17-1 demonstrates how volume estimates are calculated. The supplemental sample should be excluded from the data for the purpose of estimating (1) incidence rates of category use, brand awareness, and brand use, and (2) total category demographic volume contribution profiles since—if included—this would bias the representation of the "supplemental" groups in the population. The supplemental sample is combined with the basic sample for the purpose of analyzing specific brand user groups.

STRATEGIC STUDIES

As we indicated, strategic studies are conducted to provide marketing managers with information useful in understanding and coping with their current and future competitive environments. Because of the growing intensity of competition in virtually all areas of business, predicting the reactions of competitors to a firm's own marketing plans is one of the most pressing problems most firms face. Among the crucial managerial questions concerning competition are

- What is driving competition in my industry or in industries I am thinking of entering?
- What actions are competitors likely to take, and what is the best way to respond?
- How will my industry evolve (over time)?
- How can the firm be best positioned to compete in the long run?[3]

In the remaining sections of this chapter we discuss three types of strategic studies designed to provide information on the competitive structure of a product-market. In essence, each of the studies discussed provides insights into the interrrelationships of firms, consumers, and products so that the marketing manager may better understand and predict consumer and competitor reactions to the firm's marketing-mix decisions.

POSITIONING STUDIES

Product positioning studies provide "pictures" or maps of the competitive structure or other relationships among a predetermined set of products or brands. Such maps are based upon judgments by a sample of respondents, familiar with the product category under study, and presumably represent how "the market" perceives the predetermined set of products or brands. **Product maps** provide management with a consumer perspective on competition in the marketplace. When used early in the marketing planning process, product maps can influence the alternative courses of action considered in later stages of the product's life and research cycles. In addition to providing a structure of competitive relationships, product maps have also been used to (1) develop and evaluate strategic plans, (2) track market changes, (3) investigate the relationship between the firm's actions and their market consequences, and (4) position or reposition a brand to appeal to specific consumers.

Product maps Space which represents the perceived relationships among a set of brands; the spatial distance between any two brands represents the degree to which they are perceived as being similar in terms of relevant attributes or preferences.

Philosophy and Objectives

It has been argued that firms compete to the extent that their "products are sufficiently similar so as to be close substitutes in the eyes of the buyer."[4] Product maps graph the notion of close substitutes. Perceptual or preference data are analyzed to produce a representation in spatial form of the perceived relationships among a set of brands. In the product

[3]M. E. Porter, *Competitive Strategy* (New York: Free Press, 1980).
[4]A. Koutsouiannis, *Modern Microeconomics*, 2nd ed. (London: Macmillan, 1979), 8.

map, the closer the distance between any two brands (or products/services) the closer the brands are perceived as being in terms of relevant attributes or preferences.

Product maps consist of two essential elements:

1. A set of axes that reflect the dimensions on which the brands are judged. Typically, these dimensions represent product features or attributes judged to be important to the consumer.
2. A set of coordinates (scores) that can be used to position each brand in the perceptual product space; in essence, the score gives a brand's position on the important features represented by the axes.

A perceptual product map is based on a plot of these coordinate scores in two or three dimensions. The position of a brand on the map shows its similarity to each other brand and the extent to which it possesses the important features that define the dimensions of the space. Thus, the importance (weight) given to a dimension plays a crucial role in determining the derived distance between products in the dimensional space. A sample perceptual product map for the soft-drink product market is shown in Figure 17-1. The map indicates that consumers evaluate soft

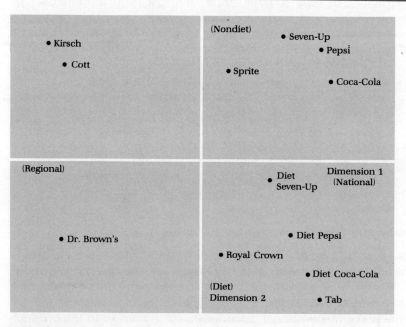

Figure 17-1

Illustrative product map for soft drink market.

drinks on the basis of whether they are diet or regular brands and nationally or regionally distributed. (How the dimensions are uncovered will be discussed later.) According to the product map Diet Coke and Tab are perceived to be very similar in terms of their underlying dimensions and therefore should be judged as highly competitive.

Types of Product Maps

Product maps, regardless of their type, are generated from judgmental data that reflect the way consumers perceive similarities and preferences among competing brands. Though many different types of judgmental data have been used to construct product spaces, the most common forms of product maps use preference or perceptual data. The choice of data affects not only the mode of collection but also the method used to produce the map.

Perceptual product maps are based upon consumers' perceived similarities and dissimilarities among a set of competing brands. The axes defining the resulting perceptual space represent those attributes most relevant to the consumer. For example, a perceptual product space for soft drinks may tell the brand manager that "diet versus regular" and "regional versus national" describe the evaluation process used by consumers. In addition to identifying the relevant dimensions, perceptual product spaces indicate how consumers view the brands of soft drinks along each dimension. Thus, perceptual product spaces represent "psychological" and/or "sociological" positioning.[5] Though direct similarities can be used to generate a perceptual product space, typically construction begins with consumers rating existing brands (and perhaps an ideal brand and/or a fictitious brand) independently on a set of attributes. Respondents are asked to rate their ideal brand so that the resulting perceptual space can be related to preference, if desired; that is, brands closer to the ideal brand are presumed to be preferred. Fictitious brands are often included to help interpret the resulting perceptual space; specifically, fictitious brands can be helpful in interpreting gaps in the perceptual space (if, of course, the fictitious brand occupies the gap) and can be used to infer the relationship of brand alternatives that differ from the set of existing brands used to construct the product map. Typically the scaling of each brand is on either semantic differential scales,[6] bipo-

Perceptual product maps Maps based upon consumers' perceived similarities and differences among a set of competing brands.

[5]For further discussion, see A. D. Shocker and V. Srinivasan, "A Consumer-Based Methodology for the Identification of New Product Ideas," *Management Science*, February 1974, 921–938; A. D. Shocker and V. Srinivasan, "Multiattribute Approaches for Product Concept Evaluation and Generation: A Critical Review," *Journal of Marketing Research*, May 1979, 159–180.

[6]For illustrative examples see M. B. Holbrook and J. Huber, "Separating Perceptual Dimensions from Affective Overtones: An Application to Consumer Aesthetics," *Journal of Consumer Research*, March 1979, 272–283; J. Huber and M. B. Holbrook, "Using Attribute Ratings for Product Positioning: Some Distinctions Among Compositional Approaches," *Journal of Marketing Research*, November 1979, 507–516.

lar adjectives scales,[7] agree-disagree scales,[8] or anchored scales.[9] All of these scale types have been discussed and illustrated in Chapter 10.

Preference product maps attempt to identify how consumers use the perceived dimensions in making evaluations of a brand or in choosing among alternative brands. The axes of the product map in this case reflect those attributes most relevant from the standpoint of consumer preference; in other words, the product map represents the consumer's preference space. Preference data used to generate product maps are typically collected by direct comparisons using a rank-order procedure (see Chapter 10). Essentially each respondent would rank-order each brand in terms of preference, or some variation of a paired comparison approach would be used. With direct rank-order preference data a non-metric multidimensional scaling procedure is typically used to construct the product space (see Appendix 16-A, Chapter 16).

Preference product maps Attempts to position brands in the perceptual space in accordance with those product features or attributes that consumers view as most important in making evaluations of the brand or in choosing among alternative brands.

Methods Used to Generate Product Maps

Three major approaches have been used to generate product maps: multidimensional scaling (MDS), principal components analysis (PCA), and multiple discriminant analysis (MDA).

For discussion purposes, consider Table 17-2 which presents the mean attribute ratings and standardized scores for each of four automobile brands. (We discussed how standardized scores are computed in Chapter 14.) The data were collected in a 1980 study in which 500 individuals rated the VW Rabbit, Plymouth Horizon/Omni, Chevrolet Chevette, and Honda Civic on five product characteristics. The attribute ratings were collected on nine-point rating scales. In the present context the standardized scores (which we will need in computing the location of a brand in the perceptual space) are obtained as follows: First, for each brand and attribute we compute the standard deviation of scores across all 500 respondents; next we subtract the average score for each brand on each attribute (see Table 17-2) from each respondent's original rating and divide by the respective attribute's standard deviation.

Let us now turn our attention to the three common methods of creating product maps. Since all of these methods have been discussed in the Appendix to Chapter 16, the discussion will be brief.

Multidimensional scaling (MDS) can be used on direct comparison (rank-order) judgments regarding the similarities among a set of competing brands (nonmetric MDS) or on derived similarities computed from

Multidimensional scaling Way of mapping that creates a structure in which spatial proximities between brands are consistent with respondent's judgmental data on brand similarities or dissimilarities.

---

[7]For an illustrative example, see P. E. Green and V. Rao, *Applied Multidimensional Scaling* (New York: Holt, Rinehart and Winston, 1972).

[8]For an illustrative example see, J. R. Hauser and G. L. Urban, "A Normative Methodology for Modeling Consumer Response to Innovation," *Operations Research*, July–August 1977, 579–619.

[9]For an illustrative example see Y. Wind, "A New Procedure for Concept Evaluation," *Journal of Marketing*, October 1973, 2–11.

TABLE 17-2
Summary Measures

	Average scores				
	Gas	Style	Reputation	Handling	Safety
Rabbit	7.66	5.02	6.97	6.51	5.15
Chevette	6.61	5.27	6.47	6.12	4.90
Horizon	6.57	5.54	5.35	5.61	4.71
Civic	7.50	5.21	6.02	6.16	4.47
	Standardized Scores				
	Gas	Style	Reputation	Handling	Safety
Rabbit	1.00	−1.12	1.11	1.11	1.18
Chevette	−.83	.05	.39	.05	.31
Horizon	−.90	1.30	−1.24	−1.32	−.35
Civic	.72	−.23	−.27	.16	−1.18

respondent's rating of the brands on a set of product attributes (metric MDS). In either case, MDS creates a structure in which spatial proximities between brands are consistent with respondents' judgmental data on brand similarities or dissimilarities.

In the derived similarity approach, the first step is to compute the Euclidean distance between each pair of brands using the brand attribute ratings (see Chapter 16, Appendix 16-A). Next the Euclidean distances are submitted to a MDS procedure, and the dimensional solutions are examined. Figure 17-2 shows a two-dimensional solution for the automobile data. Notice that the brands are spread out, with each automobile brand occupying its own quadrant. Most notably, Rabbit is positioned to the far right of the origin and Horizon is positioned to the far left. The uncovered dimensions and specifically the position of each brand in the space represents how the brands were perceived on the set of attributes. To interpret the space we can examine the correlation between a brand's rating on each attribute (gas economy, style, and so on) and its position on the two derived dimensions. In practice this is accomplished by simply regressing each of the five attribute (mean) ratings on the brand locations in the perceptual space; in other words, five regressions are run in which each attribute (mean rating) is the dependent variable and the brand coordinates are treated as independent variables. The association between the positions of the brands in the product map and each attribute is given by the standardized regression coefficients (beta weights). The standardized regression coefficients are given in Figure 17-2. Thus reputation, handling, and safety are most associated with dimension 1, where dimension 2 reflects gas economy distinctions. Further technical details on MDS can be found in Chapter 16, Appendix 16-A.

Figure 17-2

MDS two-dimensional solution.

| | Standardized Regression Coefficients | | |
| | Dimension | | |
Attribute	1	2	R^2
(X_1) Gas economy	.31	− .95	.81
(X_2) Style	.74	− .67	.78
(X_3) Reputation	.97	.24	.88
(X_4) Handling	.95	.31	.89
(X_5) Safety	.99	− .14	.91

Principal components analysis A popular approach to factor analysis; uncovers dimensions that are linear combinations of the original attributes such that the uncovered dimensions account for as much variation in the original attribute ratings as possible.

Principal component analysis (PCA) can also be used to uncover the dimensions underlying a product map. PCA uncovers dimensions that are linear combinations of the original attributes such that the uncovered dimensions account for as much variation in the original attribute ratings as possible. The first principal component, Y_1, of the original attributes, $X_1, X_2, \ldots, X_p$, is that linear combination

$$Y_1 = a_{11}X_1 + a_{21}X_2 + \ldots + a_{p1}X_p \tag{17-1}$$

of the attribute ratings whose sample variance

$$s^2_{Y_1} = \sum_i \sum_j a_{i1}a_{j1}s_{ij} \tag{17-2}$$

is greatest; in other words, the first principal component (dimension) contains as much of the total information in all the p original attribute ratings as possible. Similarly, the second principal component, Y_2, is that linear combination of the original attributes which accounts for the maximum amount of the remaining total variation not already accounted for by Y_1. Further technical details regarding principal components were presented in Chapter 16, Appendix 16-B.

In a prototypical product-map application using PCA, the analysis begins with the interattribute correlations computed across respondents and brands. The matrix of interattribute correlations is submitted to a PCA program that determines, among other things, the coefficients (that is, the a's) shown in equation (17-1). These weights, often called **loadings,** give the correlation of the attribute with the respective dimension. For the automobile data the loadings for the first two dimensions extracted from the (5×5) interattribute correlation matrix are shown on the side

Loadings Weights that give the correlation of the attribute with respect to the dimension.

PCA Loadings		
Attribute	Y_1	Y_2
(X_1) Gas economy	.54	.77
(X_2) Style	.67	−.47
(X_3) Reputation	.77	.08
(X_4) Handling	.79	.04
(X_5) Safety	.72	−.27

Location of Brands		
Automobile	Dimension 1	Dimension 2
Rabbit	2.37	1.11
Chevette	0.15	−.71
Horizon	−1.86	−1.36
Civic	−.70	.97

Figure 17-3

PCA perceptual product map.

of Figure 17-3. Consistent with the findings generated from using MDS, the first uncovered dimension reflects reputation, handling, and safety distinctions, whereas the second uncovered dimension is most associated with gas economy.

To position a particular automobile brand in the two-dimensional product space we use equation (17-1) and the results shown in Table 17-2 and the loadings. To illustrate, consider the Rabbit; substituting the respective loadings and standardized scores into equation (17-1) we have for dimension 1

$$Y_1 = .54(1.0) + .67(-1.12) + .77(1.11) + .79(1.11) + .72(1.18)$$
$$= 2.37$$

and for dimension 2

$$Y_2 = .77(1.0) - .47(-1.12) + .08(1.11) + .04(1.11) - .27(1.18)$$
$$= 1.11$$

Thus, the location of the Rabbit automobile in the perceptual product space is (2.37, 1.11). The positions of the other three brands of automobiles are given at the bottom of Figure 17-3. The resulting perceptual product-map is shown in this figure.

In the context of generating product maps, several features of PCA warrant some discussion. First, PCA based upon interattribute correlations uncovers dimensions characterized by descriptive adjectives that mean the same thing to people; that is, PCA focuses on semantic meaning and essentially identifies groups of similar statements. Thus, one can say that PCA produces dimensions characterized by attributes seen as similar by respondents (that is, people agree in their ratings). This means that the attributes that are most important in determining choice behavior could be overlooked if they were relatively independent of other attributes. Second, the importance of a dimension extracted by PCA with correlational input is determined by the number of attributes loading on the dimension and their perceived similarity—the more that are similar the greater the apparent importance of the dimension. Thus, it is conceivable that the dimensions uncovered by PCA can be determined *in advance* simply by determining how many statements about a given aspect of a brand (such as economy) are to be rated by respondents.

Multiple discriminant analysis (MDA) is another approach to uncovering the dimensions underlying a product map. In the context of product mapping applications the brands serve as the groups. Discriminant analysis attempts to distinguish among a set of brands on the basis of a set of product attributes. Specifically, the objective in multiple discriminant analysis is to find axes (dimensions) that maximally separate the groups—that is, the axes maximize between-group to within-group variability. With MDA the axes or dimensions uncovered represent linear combinations of the original attributes that best discriminate between the alternative brands. Letting Z_i denote the ith discriminant function we have

Multiple discriminant analysis Discriminant functions are linear combinations of the original attributes that best discriminate between the alternative brands.

$$Z_i = b_0 + b_{1i}X_1 + b_{2i}X_2 + \ldots + b_{pi}X_p \qquad (17\text{-}3)$$

where b_0 is a constant and the $b_{1i}, b_{2i}, \ldots, b_{pi}$ are discriminant weights that reflect the importance of attribute p in the ith discriminant function. The number of **discriminant functions** retained define the dimensions of the perceptual product map; usually two or three discriminant functions are retained. The location of the brands in the perceptual product space is given by the mean rating on each discriminant function. These mean ratings, called **group centroids,** are obtained by entering average values on each attribute for each brand into each of the first two or three discriminant function equations in turn. Further technical details on discriminant analysis techniques were provided in Chapter 16, Appendix 16-C.

Discriminant functions Axes or dimensions that in some sense account for brand differences.

Group centroids Mean ratings of each brand on each discriminant function.

In MDA product-mapping applications the respondent $\times$ brand $\times$ attribute data are submitted to a discriminant analysis program, with the brands serving as the group factor. The **standardized discriminant function weights (the b coefficients)** indicate the importance of each attribute in distinguishing among the alternative brands. The standardized discriminant function weights for the four-automobile-brand/five attribute data we have been discussing are shown on the side of Figure 17-4. To interpret the dimensions the simple product moment correlation of each attribute with each dimension is also given. Notice that the interpretation of each dimension is consistent with the previous analyses: reputation, handling, and safety have the largest correlation with dimension 1 and gas economy has the largest correlation with dimension

Standardized discriminant function weights (the b coefficients) Measures of the importance of each attribute in distinguishing among the alternative brands.

	Discriminant functions			
	1		2	
Attribute	Weights	Correlations	Weights	Correlations
(X_1) Gas economy	−.43	−.15	.93	.68
(X_2) Style	.66	.21	.25	−.002
(X_3) Reputation	−.75	−.65	−.72	−.42
(X_4) Handling	−.23	−.62	.02	−.04
(X_5) Safety	.10	.42	−.29	−.27

Location of Brands		
Automobile	Z_1	Z_2
Rabbit	−2.15	−.46
Chevette	0.11	−1.13
Horizon	2.45	.44
Honda Civic	−.40	1.15

Figure 17-4

MDA perceptual product map.

2. To locate the brands in the preceptual product space we use equation (17-3), with the standardized weights and the standardized scores shown in Table 17-2. To illustrate, consider the Rabbit automobile; substituting the appropriate standardized weights and standardized scores into equation (17-3) we have for discriminant function 1

$$Z_1 = -.43(1.0) + .66(-1.12) - .75(1.11)$$
$$- .23(1.11) + .10(1.18)$$
$$= -2.15$$

and for discriminant function 2

$$Z_2 = .93(1.0) + .25(-1.12) - .71(1.11)$$
$$+ .02(1.11) - .29(1.18)$$
$$= -.46$$

Thus the location of the Rabbit automobile in the perceptual product space is (−2.15, −.46). The positions of the other three brands of automobiles are given on the side of Figure 17-4. The resulting perceptual product map is shown in this figure.

In general, MDA will produce solutions that differ from those of either PCA or MDS. Differences in solutions are due to the fact that MDA takes into account the within-brand interattribute covariances, and the reduced space will be oriented to variables having relatively large between-brand to within-brand variation. Thus, compared to PCA and MDS, MDA will probably use fewer attributes; however, because the dimensions uncovered by MDA can be directly linked to attributes for which there exist large brand differences, the solution may actually prove more actionable in a managerial sense.

MARKET SEGMENTATION STUDIES

Market segment
Subgroups of consumers who respond to a given marketing-mix strategy in a similar manner.

Put simply, the term **market segment** refers to subgroups of consumers who respond to a given marketing-mix strategy in a similar manner; in other words, segments consist of subgroups of consumers who exhibit differing sensitivities to some marketing-mix element.[10] Though initially the contribution of segmentation analysis to marketing planning was to provide a framework for the analysis of existing data, today its role has expanded to provide a basis for identifying the data needed for strategy development and implementation. **Segmentation research** provides guidelines for a firm's marketing strategy and resource allocation among markets and products and consequently influences all marketing tactical plans and programs. By recognizing consumer heterogeneity, a firm can increase its profitability by segmenting its market.

Segmentation research
Studies that provide guidelines for a firm's marketing strategy and resource allocation among markets and products.

Philosophy and Objectives

Segmentation research has been used to answer a wide variety of questions concerning market response to a firm's marketing strategies—that is, product changes, price changes, new product offerings—and the selection of target markets. Typical management questions that guide market segmentation studies involve such issues as

1. How do the evaluations of a set of new product concepts vary by different respondent groups—males versus females, users versus nonusers of the company's brand, and so on?
2. Are there different promotion-sensitive segments for a new-product concept and how do they differ with respect to product use, concept evaluations, attitudes, and demographic and psychographic profiles?
3. How do the target markets for a new-product concept differ with respect to end benefits sought, product-use characteristics, and other background characteristics?

From these management questions we see that there is an intimate relationship between product positioning and segmentation analysis. To effectively position a product to a specific target of consumers who share certain common characteristics (similar reactions to price, promotion, and the like) presumes that these subgroups of consumers have already been identified—in other words, the market has been segmented. In fact,

---

[10]A comprehensive, critical review of the theory, research, and practice of market segmentation can be found in Yoran Wind, "Issues and Advances in Segmentation Research," *Journal of Marketing Research*, August 1978, 317–37.

it is reasonable to suggest that in order to develop effective marketing strategies, management should employ the concept of segmentation in all studies.

Types of Market Segmentation Studies

Segmentation studies generally follow one of two types of approaches.[11]

1. **A priori segmentation.** In a priori segmentation designs the basis for segmentation—such as usage, brand loyalty, product purchase— is specified in advance of the segmentation analysis. In other words the segments are defined a priori and the analysis centers on profiling the various subgroups of consumers on the basis of product-use characteristics, size, demographic variables, psychographics, and other relevant characteristics.

2. **Post-hoc segmentation.** In post-hoc segmentation designs segments are defined after the fact on the basis of some sort of clustering of respondents on a set of "relevant" characteristics such as benefit sought, need, or attitudes. Once the segments have been formed, they are profiled on the basis of size, product-use characteristics, and respondent background variables.

A priori segmentation Studies where the basis for segmentation, such as use, brand loyalty, and product purchase, is specified in advance of the segmentation analysis.

Post-hoc segmentation Studies where segments are defined after the fact on the basis of some sort of clustering of respondents on a set of "relevant" characteristics such as benefit sought, need, attitudes, and the like.

In a priori segmentation studies the basis for segmentation must be specified in advance. Obviously, management needs and knowledge of the market under study will ultimately determine what base is ultimately used. Yoram Wind, an expert in the theory and practice of segmentation research, has listed several of his "preferred" bases for segmentation.[12]

- Benefits sought (in industrial markets, the criterion used is purchase decision)
- Product preference
- Product purchase and use patterns
- Brand loyalty and switching patterns
- Reaction to new concepts (intention to buy, preference over current brand, and so on)
- Price sensitivity
- Deal-proneness
- Media use
- Psychographic/lifestyle
- Store loyalty and patronage

The choice of descriptor variables to use for the purpose of profiling the segments is a more difficult question. First, there are an enormous number of descriptor variables from which to choose. Second, **actionable descriptor variables** should be used: The information on the discriminating descriptors can be used by management in developing the

Actionable descriptor variables Information on the discriminating descriptors that can be used by management in developing the firm's marketing strategies.

[11]These distinctions, *a priori* and *post-hoc*, were suggested by P. E. Green, "A New Approach to Market Segmentation," *Business Horizons*, February 1977, 61–73.

[12]Y. Wind, "Issues and Advances in Segmentation Research," 320.

firm's marketing strategies. Third, there should be a relationship between the descriptors selected and the basis for segmentation in order for management to identify segments with varying sensitivities to marketing-mix variables on the basis of demographic and other segment descriptors.

Research Design

The research design for a prototypical market segmentation study can be described in terms of the following seven stages.[13]

1. Selection (a priori) or determination (post-hoc) of the basis for segmentation.
2. Selection of a set of segment descriptors (including hypotheses on the possible link between these descriptors and the basis for segmentation).
3. Sample design—mostly stratified and occasionally a quota sample according to the various classes of the dependent variable.
4. Data collection.
5. Formation of the segments based on a sorting of respondents into categories.
6. Establishment of the (conditional) profile of the segments.
7. Translation of the findings about the segments' estimated size and profile into specific marketing strategies, including the selection of target segments and the design or modification of specific marketing strategy.

Note that with the exception of the fifth step, relating to the formation of the segments, and sometimes the third step, relating to the specific sample design used, the research design for both a priori and post-hoc segmentation studies are essentially the same.

Analysis Techniques

Most segmentation studies follow a two-step analysis procedure. In the first stage respondents are classified into segments. In the second stage the various clusters are profiled in terms of key discriminatory variables.

Cluster analysis
Commonly used technique for allocating respondents to segments where respondents are clustered on the basis of benefit sought, need, or other relevant characteristics and where the number and type of segments are determined by the clustering technique being used.

Cluster Membership. In a priori segmentation studies the delineation of clusters is straightforward—typically respondents are simply sorted on the basis of the dependent variable (basis for segmentation). However, some thought should be given to the conceptual implications of the operational definition being used and the sensitivity of the resulting segments to this definition. For example, consider the frequently used segmentation base of brand loyalty, and specifically, the segments of brand-loyal users versus brand-switchers. An immediate question is how should the sample be divided? That is, what operational definition of brand loyalty should be used?

[13]Ibid., 321.

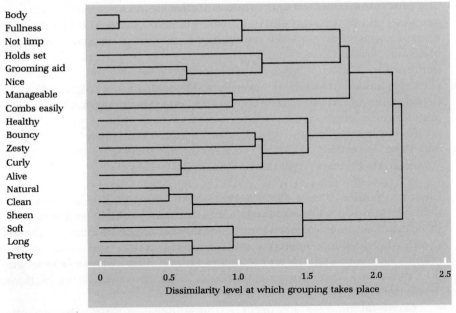

Body
Fullness
Not limp
Holds set
Grooming aid
Nice
Manageable
Combs easily
Healthy
Bouncy
Zesty
Curly
Alive
Natural
Clean
Sheen
Soft
Long
Pretty

0   0.5   1.0   1.5   2.0   2.5
Dissimilarity level at which grouping takes place

Figure 17-5

Structure of nineteen-element word associations for hair shampoos. *Source:*
Paul E. Green, Yoram Wind, and Arun K. Jain. "Analyzing Free-Response Data in
Marketing Research," *Journal of Marketing Research*, February 1973, 45-52.
Reprinted by permission of the American Marketing Association.

In post-hoc segmentation studies, respondents must be allocated to
the various segments in some way.

In **cluster analysis** respondents are clustered on the basis of benefit
sought, need, or other relevant characteristics where the number and
type of segments are determined by the clustering technique being used.
The objective in most cluster applications is to arrive at clusters of objects (that is, people, brands, and the like) that display small within-cluster variation relative to the between-cluster variation. There are a large
number of different clustering algorithms available. Two major types of
clustering techniques are the **bottom-up approach** and the **top-down
approach.** A bottom-up approach builds up clusters—at the beginning
each respondent belongs to his or her own cluster and then clusters are
joined together on the basis of their similarity. A top-down approach
breaks down clusters—at the beginning all respondents belong to one
cluster and then respondents are partitioned into two clusters, then
three clusters, and so on until each respondent occupies his or her own
cluster. In both cases the results are summarized by a tree-like structure
called a **dendogram** that shows which clusters were joined or partitioned at each step. Further details on cluster analysis were given in
Chapter 16, Appendix 16-D.

Figure 17-5 presents an illustration of cluster analysis applied to

Bottom-up approach
Process of building up
clusters—at the beginning
each respondent belongs
to his or her own cluster
and then clusters are
joined together on the
basis of their similarity.
Top-down approach
Process of breaking down
clusters—at the beginning
all respondents belong to
one cluster and then
respondents are
partitioned into two
clusters, then three
clusters, and so on until
each respondent occupies
his or her own cluster.
Dendogram A tree-like
structure that shows
which clusters were
joined or partitioned at
each step.

word associations among a set of hair shampoo adjective descriptors. The clustering is on the individual adjective descriptors rather than on people. The input to the clustering analysis is a matrix of similarities (or dissimilarities) that gives the similarity (dissimilarity) between each pair of adjective descriptors. The dendogram shown in Figure 17-5 presents a bottom-up solution. Adjectives that are most similar (or, equivalently, least dissimilar) in meaning are clustered together first; other adjective descriptors are joined with these primary clusters and then clusters are joined until a single cluster exists. At the first stage "body" and "fullness" are joined; next, "natural" and "clean" merge, then "curly" and "alive," and then "grooming aid" and "nice"; "sheen" then joins the cluster of "natural" and "clean," and the process continues.

Cluster profiles Profiling of each segment in terms of its distinctive features.

Automatic interaction detection algorithm Division of a total sample into mutually exclusive subgroups through a series of splits. Each split is determined by selecting a predictor variable and its categories that maximize the reduction in the unexplained variation in the dependent variable.

Cluster Profiles. Once the segments have been defined and respondents sorted into categories, interest focuses on profiling each segment in terms of its distinctive features. The three most commonly used procedures for profiling segments are (1) simple cross-tabulations, (2) multiple discriminant analysis, and (3) some variant of an **automatic interaction detection algorithm,** such as AID,[14] that searches for interactions in a set of data.

Cross-tabulations are perhaps the simplest approach to profiling segments. With this approach the basis for segmentation (dependent variable) is cross-classified with the segment descriptors (independent variables). Such tables can be used to make distinctive statements about the various segments. Recall, we discussed and illustrated cross-tabulations and methods for analysis in Chapters 14 and 15.

Multiple discriminant analysis has also been frequently used in a segment profiling technique as well as in product positioning. With standard discriminant analysis, the segments serve as the group factor. Segment descriptors are entered in a sequential or stepwise fashion and are assessed with respect to their discriminatory power. The group centroids are used to position each group on the discriminant dimensions and the correlation of each variable with the respective function is used as a means of "interpreting" the space.

AID-like algorithms have been successfully used in a large number of commercial applications. The standard AID procedure is restricted to dichotomous data (binary splits). Put simply, AID sequentially divides a total sample into mutually exclusive subgroups through a series of binary splits. Each split is determined by selecting a predictor variable and its categories that maximize the reduction in the unexplained variation in the dependent variable. The end result of this process is to have one group with a low criterion score and the other with a high criterion score. The process begins by considering, for each predictor variable in turn, the best split defined in terms of the ratio of B_c/T_c, where B_c is the between-groups sums of squares, T_c is the total sums of squares, and the

[14]J. A. Sonquist, *Multivariate Model Building* (Ann Arbor, Survey Research Center, 1970).

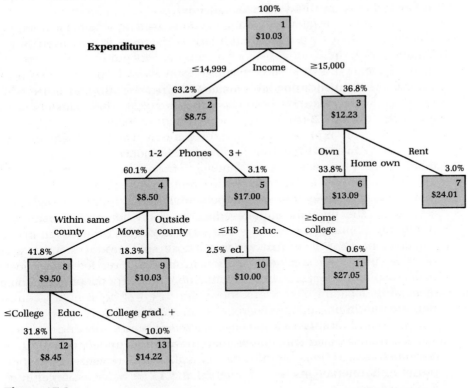

Figure 17-6

AID analysis of average monthly long-distance bill. *Source:* W. R. Dillon and M. Goldstein, *Multivariate Analysis: Methods and Applications* (New York: John Wiley & Sons, 1984), 185.

subscript c is used to denote the criterion variable. Once the binary splits have been formed for each variable, the variable with the highest B_c/T_c is used to partition the total sample, and all other splits are discarded. Next each subgroup is treated as though it were a separate initial sample and the process is repeated on that subgroup with the largest total sums of squares on the criterion variable. The process terminates if the B_c for that unsplit group having the largest T_c is less than some predetermined value, usually expressed as a percentage of the T_c for the entire sample.

    To provide a specific illustration of how AID works consider Figure 17-6, which contains the tree developed from the AID analysis based on average monthly long-distance telephone charges (in dollars) and seven predictor variables. The figure can be read as follows: The entries outside of each box give the variable selected, its best split, and the percentage of the relevant sample—that is, of the previous split—belonging to each partition. The entry in the upper corner in each box numbers the stage in the splitting process. The dollar amount located in the center of each box is the average monthly long-distance telephone expenditure corresponding to the particular profile partition.

The process begins with family income. This variable is most important in the sense of producing the largest decrease in the unexplained variation in monthly long-distance telephone expenditures. The two segments generated at this stage relate to families with incomes less than $15,000, who expend, on the average $8.75 per month, and those with incomes greater than $14,999, who expend $12.23. The segments sizes are, respectively, 63.2 percent and 36.8 percent of the total sample. At the next stage each branch is considered separately. For those families with income less than $15,000, the number of telephones (1 or 2 versus 3 or more) is split on, whereas for families whose income is in excess of $14,999, home ownership (own versus rent) is the splitting factor. Note that the partition segment sample percentages sum to the segment percentage of the immediately preceding partition (for example, for the number of phones, 60.1 + 3.1 = 63.2). The algorithm proceeds in a similar fashion and selects that variable whose split produces the largest decrease in the unexplained variation in expenditures for a previously defined split. It appears that family income, number of telephones, home ownership, location of previous move, and head of household's education are the important predictors. These variables generate twelve distinct segments or clusters based upon the best binary splitting of each.

As a final comment, notice that the asymmetry of the AID tree. Asymmetric trees must be indicative of higher-order effects—that is, the presence of interactions (see Chapters 6 and 15 for a discussion of interaction effects).

Syndicated Services

We discussed syndicated data sources in Chapters 3 and 4. Specifically in Chapter 3 we mentioned the Simmons Research Bureau and SRI International as sources of marketing-related information. Recently, several syndicated services that specifically provide information on target segments have become available.

PRIZM neighborhood life-style clusters Assigns individuals to unique market segments on the basis of where the individual lives; underlying premise is that choice of neighborhood is the most basic consumer decision and one that ultimately reflects lifestyle choices.

PRIZM Neighborhood Life-Style Clusters. PRIZM assigns individuals to unique market segments on the basis of where the individual lives. The premise underlying the PRIZM system is that choice of neighborhood is the most basic consumer decision and one that ultimately reflects lifestyle choices. Census demographics coupled with other lifestyle factors forms the basis of the PRIZM Life-Style Clusters—neighborhoods with statistically similar demographics or lifestyle portraits form the clusters. PRIZM Life-Style Clusters have been used for (1) explaining differences in behavior, responsiveness, and potential profitability, (2) targeting messages and offers and (3) geographically locating prospects.

VALS. We have discussed the VALS system in Chapter 3. The Value and Lifestyles Program of SRI International divides Americans into nine types identified by lifestyle, which are grouped into four categories on the basis of self-image, aspirations, and products used. Survivors and Sustainers are in the Need-Driven category, which accounts for 11 percent of the population; I-Am-Me's, Experientials, and the Societally Conscious are in the Inner-Directed category, 19 percent of the population; Belongers, Emulators, and Achievers are in the Outer-Directed category, 68 percent of the population; and at the very top of the VALS hierarchy are the last type, the Integrateds, a mere 2 percent of the population. Exhibit 17-2 provides a more detailed description of each segment in terms of consumption patterns, media habits, and attitudes.

EXHIBIT 17-2

VAL Segment Profiles

The Need Driven

Survivors

- Consumption patterns: Cigarettes; decaffeinated coffee; over-the-counter painkillers; small heater units
- Media habits: Television game shows and soap operas; afternoon radio
- Attitudes: Despairing; conservative; resigned

Sustainers

- Consumption patterns: Beer; cold cereal; soft drinks; canned and prepackaged foods; cheap cameras
- Media habits: Daytime television; radio news, talk shows, and ethnic programs; classified newspaper ads
- Attitudes: Hopeful; resentful; not concerned with rules

The Outer-Directed

Belongers

- Consumption patterns: American automobiles; garden equipment; canned vegetables
- Media habits: Television soap operas; home magazines; country music
- Attitudes: Conforming; unexperimental; church-, family-, and home-oriented; patriotic

Emulators

- Consumption patterns: Fast foods; cosmetics; weight-lifting equipment; prepared cocktail mixes
- Media habits: Television adventure shows; progressive radio; automotive magazines
- Attitudes: Ambitious; frustrated; envious

Achievers

- Consumption patterns: Luxury cars; high-tech products; golfing; frozen entrees; wine; health and fitness gear
- Media habits: Pay cable TV; business and sports magazines
- Attitudes: Decisive; competitive; in search of fame and material success

Inner-Directeds

I-Am-Me's

- Consumption patterns: Frozen pizza; corn chips; sheet music
- Media habits: Television adventure shows; progressive radio; science and technology magazines
- Attitudes: Spontaneous; receptive to new ideas, situations, and environments; flamboyant

Experientials

- Consumption patterns: Yogurt; mineral water; foreign-made cars; foreign travel
- Media habits: Little television viewing; adult rock and classical music; special-interest magazines
- Attitudes: Idealistic; emotional; liberal; supportive of environmental protection

Societally Conscious

- Consumption patterns: Small cars; tennis and hiking equipment; photography supplies; ethnic foods; natural cheese
- Media habits: Public television; business and science magazines; radio news
- Attitudes: Self-reliant; socially responsible; little faith in government; strong interest in the arts

Integrateds

- Consumption patterns: Outdoor recreation; nonfiction books; imported products
- Media habits: Little television viewing except for sports and documentaries; business, home, and special-interest magazines
- Attitudes: Extremely self-aware; well-adjusted; trusting; supportive of free enterprise

Source: SRI, International.

MARKET STRUCTURE STUDIES

Perceptual product maps provide insights into which products or brands are competitors and so can be used to define the boundaries of a market. Segmentation analysis provides insights into the reasons why a set of products or brands compete and so can be used to explain a market. Neither procedure, however, provides information on the *magnitude* of competition among a set of products or brands. Procedures that attempt to measure the degree of substitutability between a set of competing products or brands fall under the umbrella of **market structure analysis.**

Philosophy and Objectives

The objective in market structure analysis is to determine the degree of substitutability among a set of products or brands. Obviously, before the extent of competitiveness among a set of products or brands can be determined, the relevant product-market must be defined. Hence, most market structure analysis techniques provide product-market boundary definitions as well as some measure of the degree of substitutability among the brands making up the product-market. In general, then, market structure analysis refers to the process of organizing a set of products or brands such that their interrelationships are glaringly apparent.

The importance of accurately characterizing the structure of a market can be illustrated by examining Figure 17-7. The figure shows two alternative hypothetical structures for a limited set of national brand soft drinks. The structures shown in the figure are called **hierarchical** because the brands are partitioned into several nested subsets. In part **A** the soft drink market is structured according to brand name (that is, a *brand-primary* market) whereas in part **B** the structure is attribute-based, partitioned according to regular/sugar-free/caffeine-free/sugar-and-caffeine-free combinations (that is, a *form-primary* market). The implication in the structures depicted in the figure is that consumers in one case first decide on which brand name of soft drink to buy (part **A**), whereas in the other case, consumers first decide on the type of soft drink to buy and then choose the brand (part **B**). Consider now the competitive environment surrounding Sprite. If part **A** of the figure accurately reflects the market structure, then the absence of a diet, caffeine-free product does not hurt Sprite's share of market; in fact, the implication is that introduction of such a product offering would have cannibalistic effects. The situation is different if part **B** of the figure accurately reflects the market structure. If consumers follow an attribute-based strategy, then Sprite can potentially increase its share of market by introducing a regular or diet, caffeine-free product.

Types of Market Structure Studies

Market structure studies can be classified according to (1) type of data used, (2) structure imposed, and (3) approach to analysis.

Data Used. Market structure procedures rely on either purchase or use behavior data or consumer judgmental data.

Purchase or use behavior data provide the most accurate indication of what people do, or have done. **Cross-price elasticity of demand** is a form of purchase/use data that measures the percentage of change

Market structure analysis The process of organizing a set of products or brands in terms of the degree of substitutability or competitiveness.

Hierarchical structure Partitioning of brands into several nested subsets.

Purchase or use behavior data Information providing the most accurate indication of what people do or have done.

Cross-price elasticity of demand The percentage of change in demand for one product divided by the percentage change in price of the second product, assuming that all other factors affecting demand are constant.

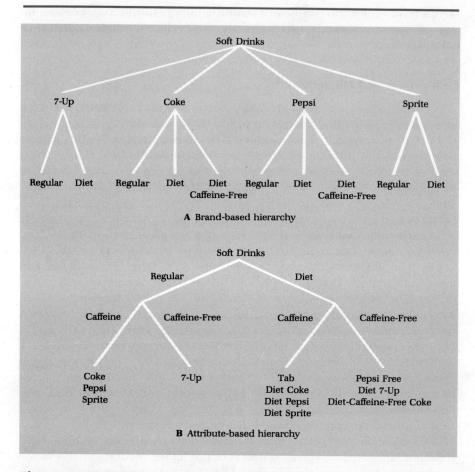

A Brand-based hierarchy

B Attribute-based hierarchy

Figure 17-7

Two hypothetical hierarchies for a limited set of national-brand soft drinks.

Brand switching The
probability of purchasing
Brand X, given that Brand
Y was purchased on the
last purchase occasion.
Judgmental data
Information generally
based on perceptions or
preference—may give
better indications of
future patterns of
consumption.

in demand for one product divided by the percentage change in price of
the second product—assuming that all other factors affecting demand
are constant. A positive cross-price elasticity indicates substitutes and a
negative cross-elasticity indicates complements. **Brand switching** is the
probability of purchasing Brand X, given that Brand Y was purchased on
the last purchase occasion. Brand switching is typically estimated on the
basis of panel data. Purchase history strings are analyzed and the frequency with which purchases of a given brand are preceded by purchases of a different brand are computed. The tacit assumption with this
type of data is that respondents are more likely to switch between close
substitutes than between distant ones and, consequently, brand switching incidences are indicative of brand substitutability.

Judgmental data are based on perceptions or preference and may give better indications of future patterns of consumption. **Decision sequence analysis** uses protocols of consumer decision making that indicate the sequence in which various pieces of information (such as price or brand name) are employed to reach a final decision. Typically, respondents are asked to verbalize what they are thinking as they make purchase decisions in the course of a shopping trip. The verbal account of their decision process is called a protocol. *Perceptual mapping* uses similarity (dissimilarity) data to arrive at a geometric representation of the competitive nature of a market. **Derived substitutability** asks respondents to indicate, in some manner, the degree to which a set of products or brands are substitutes. These data can be collected by simple direct rating scales,[15] free responses,[16] or the dollar metric approach.[17]

Structure Imposed. Market structure studies can be classified according to whether a hierarchical structure is imposed. We introduced an example of hierarchically structured markets in Figure 17-7. In such markets, the products or brands are sequentially partitioned into mutually exclusive and exhaustive subsets. The implicit assumption is that switching is more likely to occur at lower levels in the hierarchy than at higher levels. In other words, brands occupying subsets at lower levels in the hierarchy are presumably very similar to each other (that is, they share certain features), as opposed to brands occupying other subsets higher up in the hierarchy; thus, at lower levels in the hierarchy the flow of switching is higher and the greater is the degree of competition between products or subsets of brands.

Approach to Analysis. There are two general ways to proceed with a market structure analysis. We can assume that no prior knowledge of the structure of the market is known and proceed with the analysis in a purely **exploratory** fashion; in such cases the data alone, in the form of household purchases or consumer judgments, provide the basis for the structure uncovered. In contrast to exploratory analysis, we can use prior knowledge of the presumed relationships among a set of products or brands to infer what the structure should look like and use a method in which we can restrict the system to be consistent with the hypothesized structure. In this sense, we are not relying solely on data, but on a combination of what we actually observe in the marketplace and what we expect to observe based upon our understanding of the product-market under study. This type of an approach to market structure analysis is generally referred to as **confirmatory** since we attempt to confirm or negate a hypothesized structure.

[15] For an illustrative example, see Y. Wind, "The Perception of a Firm's Competitive Position," in *Behavioral Models for Market Analysis*, ed. F. M. Nicosia and Y. Wind (New York: The Dryden Press), 163–81.

[16] For an illustrative example, see P. E. Green, Y. Wind, and A. K. Jain, "Analyzing Free Response Data in Marketing Research," *Journal of Marketing Research*, February 1973, 45–52.

[17] For an illustrative example, see E. A. Pessemier, *Product Management: Strategy and Organization* (Santa Barbara, Calif.: Wiley/Hamilton, 1977), 203–254.

Decision sequence analysis Process that uses protocols of consumer decision making that indicate the sequence in which various pieces of information (such as price or brand name) are employed to reach a final decision.

Derived substitutability Form of judgmental data collection where respondents indicate the degree to which a set of products or brands are substitutes.

Exploratory analysis Type of analysis which assumes that no prior knowledge of the structure of the market is known. In such cases, the data alone provide the basis for the structure uncovered.

Confirmatory analysis Approach that uses prior knowledge of the presumed relationships among a set of products or brands to infer what the structure should look like; also uses a method where we can restrict the parameters of the system to be consistent with the hypothesized structure.

Methods for Investigating Structure

Many methods have been proposed for investigating the competitive structure of a product-market. Though it is not possible to discuss all of them, we describe three behavioral methods in Exhibits 17-3, 17-4, and 17-5. Each of these attempts to partition a market into competitive submarkets under the assumption that relatively high levels of switching among products or brands indicates close substitutes.

"Empirical" Hendry system Method for investigating competitive structure where switching between competitive products is proportional to the product of market shares.

E X H I B I T   17-3

"Empirical" Hendry System

Premise:	Switching between competitive products is proportional to the product of market shares. The theoretical switching matrix is compared with the actual switching matrix. A proposed market partitioning is an adequate representation if switching within and among partitions is proportionate.
Data:	Brand-switching data
Procedure:	1. Propose market partitioning.
	2. Calculate switching constants empirically within and across partitions.
	3. Assess adequacy of proposed structure using goodness-of-fit tests.

Source: M. U. Kalwani and D. G. Morrison, "A Parsimonious Description of the Hendry System," *Management Science*, January 1977, 467–97.

Hierarchical clustering Method of investigating competitive structure where consumers engage in a nonobservable hierarchical choice process.

E X H I B I T   17-4

Hierarchical Clustering

Premise:	Consumers engage in a nonobservable hierarchical choice process. The lower the level in the hierarchy, where the "flow" of switching is higher, the greater the degree of competition between products or partitions.
Data:	Brand-switching data
Procedure:	1. Set up a brand-switching matrix
	2. Choose an approximate *proximity measure* (or similarity index) based on the "flow" of consumers between two products.
	3. Set up the resulting "similarity matrix."
	4. Choose a clustering method.

5. Cluster the proximity matrix.
6. Test and interpret the solution.
7. Compare different hierarchical structures for segment differences.

Source: R. R. Vithala and D. J. Sabavala, "Inference of Hierarchical Choice Processes from Panel Data," *Journal of Consumer Research*, June 1981, 85–96.

EXHIBIT 17-5

Prodegy

Premise:	Consumers, faced with the deletion of a preferred product, will switch to a close competitor. A proposed market structure is adequate if this "forced switching" within partitions is substantially greater than in unstructured markets.
Data:	Forced-choice data or brand-switching data.
Procedure:	1. Propose market partitioning.
	2. Calculate difference in forced switching between structured and unstructured markets.
	3. Assess the adequacy of a proposed structure by using Z-test of differences in proportions.

Prodegy Method of investigating competitive structure where consumers, faced with the deletion of a preferred product, will switch to a close competitor.

Source: G. L. Urban, P. L. Johnson, and J. R. Hauser, "Testing Competitive Market Structures," *Marketing Science*, Spring 1984, 83–112.

Summary

This chapter has described various types of studies that attempt to provide information about the composition and structure of the competitive arena that a firm operates in. National market studies focus primarily on the changes that may have occured in the competitive market over time. Strategic market studies are generally custom research products and focus on an in-depth analysis of a product-market. We considered three kinds of strategic market studies—*positioning studies*, which attempt to define market boundaries on the basis of consumer perceptions or preference; *market segmentation studies*, which attempt to identify segments of consumers who respond to marketing-mix variables in similar ways; and *market structure studies*, which attempt to investigate the extent of competition among a set of alternative brands. All of the studies discussed in this chapter can be used to formulate marketing strategies and to shape the course of subsequent marketing research activities relating to concept and product testing, package testing, advertising research, and test markets.

Key Concepts

National market studies   *Market segmentation studies*
Strategic market studies   *A priori segmentation*
Positioning studies   *Post-hoc segmentation*
Product maps   *Cluster analysis*
Multidimensional scaling   *Cluster profiles*
Principal components   *AID algorithm*
Multiple discriminant analysis   *Market structure studies*

Review Questions

1. Discuss the role and importance of market studies in marketing research and more generally in developing marketing strategies.
2. Discuss the circumstances that would lead you to recommend that a strategic market study be undertaken as opposed to a national market study.
3. As a recent addition to the marketing "team" of a major consumer package firm you are asked to explain how product maps work.
4. Discuss the major research approaches to market segmentation.
5. Can the sellers of industrial and institutional goods and services also benefit from market segmentation and market structure studies? What suggestions can you offer for segmenting and structuring industrial markets?

Concept and Product Testing

- Acquire an understanding of the importance of concept- and product-testing research.
- Describe the different types of concept tests.
- Define the purpose of concept-screening tests.
- Describe the various aspects of concept-screening test procedures.
- Define the purpose of concept-evaluation tests.
- Describe the various aspects of concept-evaluation test procedures.
- Discuss how conjoint analysis is used in concept/product development.
- Describe the role of product testing.
- Define the various types of product tests.
- Provide general guidelines concerning the appropriateness of monadic versus comparative product tests.
- Describe the various aspects of product-test procedures.

Introduction

In this chapter we provide a framework for understanding the practice of *concept* and *product* testing. The single most important determinant of market success is consumer acceptance of a firm's products. A consumer buys a product for its **end benefits**—that is, what the product offers in terms of satisfying the consumer's wants and needs, not simply what the physical product is. Concept- and product-testing procedures are directed at understanding consumer's perceptions of both physical product characteristics and end benefits—and, consequently, the product's ultimate market acceptance. As such, concept and product tests play a necessary and integral role in developing effective marketing strategy.

End benefits What the product offers in terms of satisfying the consumer's wants and needs.

CONCEPT TESTING: PHILOSOPHY AND OBJECTIVES

Concept An idea aimed at satisfying consumer wants and needs.

Put simply, a **concept** is an idea on its way to becoming a marketing strategy. A marketing strategy attempts to convince a target segment of consumers that a particular brand possesses those end benefits that they desire and presents evidence to support this claim. Concepts represent the essence of the product. Thus to be successful, concept testing must capture and effectively communicate the spark of an idea. Typically, concept tests are preceded by an **opportunity analysis** (usually contained within a market study—see Chapter 17), which identifies unfulfilled consumer wants and needs to ensure that the most salient product end benefits are communicated.

Opportunity analysis Research to identify unfulfilled consumer wants and needs.

Concept testing provides a system for reshaping, redefining, and coalescing ideas to arrive at a basic concept for a product with greater vitality and potential for market acceptance. Specifically, concept tests are conducted to:

1. Quantitatively assess the relative appeal of ideas or alternative product positionings that aim the product at different target segments by highlighting those product features most desired by those segments of the population.
2. Provide necessary information for developing the product and product advertising.
3. Indicate those segments of the population where the appeal of the product is likely to be concentrated.

Procedures for concept testing vary greatly, depending on the stage of the research cycle. For example, concept testing can be used to screen new product ideas to identify the most promising concepts. Alternatively, they can be used later in the prelaunch/test-market phase to estimate ultimate consumer demand for the basic product concept before risking national rollout. Finally, concept tests can be used after rollout in established markets to investigate the level of consumer interest in a competitive new product concept in the prelaunch/test market phase, or for line extensions of an existing brand—in this setting, the concept test could also identify the key appeal of the competitive entry and areas where the established brand is particularly vulnerable.

Concept testing has proven effective for most kinds of products, excepting products that are radically innovative and that require significant changes in existing consumption patterns. Because these new products diffuse slowly through the population and require substantial commitment and behavioral change, a consumer's stated intentions with regard to them are likely to be highly unreliable. For example, before their introduction it probably would have been difficult to adequately assess the ultimate impact of personal computers, video games, pregnancy test kits, or other types of radically new technology.

TYPES OF CONCEPT TESTS

There are two broad categories of concept tests.

1. **Concept-screening tests** identify and prioritize those ideas (out of a large number of concepts) with the greatest potential for further testing and development. The screening can be undertaken with respect to (1) many different new product ideas or (2) alternative end-benefit incentives for the same new-product idea. This type of concept testing is generally performed very early in the research cycle.

2. **Concept-evaluation tests** gauge the level of consumer interest in a new product idea and determine the major strengths and weaknesses of the appeal. These tests are performed at various stages of the research cycle—early in the prelaunch stage or just before a test market. Typically, however, they are performed after the process of initial screening and concept refinement.

Concept-screening tests Concept tests for screening new product ideas or alternative end-benefits for a single product idea.

Concept-evaluation tests Concept tests designed to gauge consumer interest and determine strength and weaknesses of the concept.

Concept-screening tests are designed to evaluate a set of ideas *before* significant resources are committed to their development. Most new product ideas are bad ideas, not likely to meet with market acceptance. For example, only two out of 120 new food concepts tested by Custom Research, Inc. received top-box intent scores ("definitely buy") as high as 25 percent.[1] Thus, by employing effective concept-testing procedures, marketing research aids in making optimum use of research and development (R & D) laboratories as well as marketing budgets and management time.

CONCEPT-SCREENING TESTS: IMPLEMENTATION

In concept-screening tests, respondents are exposed to a series of many different new-product concepts or alternative "benefit bundles" for the same product concept to (1) obtain a preliminary indication of market acceptance and (2) identifying which ideas should be singled out for additional development and subsequent testing.

When many new product ideas are involved we refer to the procedure as a **new-product concept-screening test;** when the focus is on alternative end-benefit incentives for a single idea, we refer to the procedure as an **alternative-buying-incentive concept-screening test.** Exhibits 18-1 and 18-2 present prototypical marketing research proposals for these two procedures.

New-product concept-screening test Concept-screening tests that focus on many new product ideas.

Alternative-buying incentive concept-screening test Concept-screening tests that focus on alternative end-benefit incentives for a single idea.

[1]Reported in Jeffrey L. Pope, *Practical Marketing Research* (New York: AMACOM, 1981), 131.

E X H I B I T 18-1

Project Proposal: New-Product Concept-Screening Test

Brand: New products

Project: Concept screening

Background   The New York banking group has developed 12 new product
and   ideas for investment products (services). The objectives of this
Objectives: research are to assess consumer interest in the concepts and
                establish priorities for further development.

Research   Concept testing will be conducted in four geographically
Method: dispersed central-location facilities within the New York
                metropolitan area.

                Each of the 12 concepts plus 1 retest control concept will
                be evaluated by a total of 100 men and 100 women with
                household incomes of $25,000. The following age quotas will
                be used for both male and female groups within the sample:

            18–34   = 50 percent
            35–49   = 25 percent
            50 & over   = 25 percent

                Each respondent will evaluate a maximum of 8 concepts.
                Order of presentation will be rotated throughout to avoid
                position bias.

                Because some of the concepts are in low-incidence product
                categories, user groups will be defined both broadly and
                narrowly in an attempt to assess potential among target
                audiences.

Information to   This study will provide the following information to assist in
Be Obtained: concept evaluation:
                    Investment ownership
                    Purchase interest (likelihood of subscription)
                    Uniqueness of new service
                    Believability
                    Importance of main point
                    Demographics

Action   In order to identify concepts warranting further development,
Standard: top-box purchase-intent scores will be compared to the top-
                box purchase-intent scores achieved by the top 10 percent
                of the concepts tested in earlier concept-screening studies.
                Rank order of purchase-intent scores on the uniqueness,
                believability, and importance ratings will also be considered in
                the evaluation and priorization of concepts for further
                development.

Material
Requirements: Fifty copies of each concept

Cost:	The cost of this research will be $15,000 \pm 10$ percent
Timing:	This research will adhere to the following schedule:

Fieldwork	1 week
Top-line	2 weeks
Final report	3 weeks

Supplier: Market Facts, Inc.

E X H I B I T 18-2

Project Proposal: Alternative Buying Incentive Concept Screening Test

Brand: Suave

Project: Hand lotion buying incentive test

Background and Objectives: The brand group is interested in assessing the potential of a large number of alternative strategies and claims in the hand-lotion market. Accordingly, the objective of this research is to identify key benefits in hand lotion for incorporation in alternative concepts for subsequent testing.

Research Method: Central-location interviews will be conducted in four geographically dispersed markets with 200 adult women who are past-30-day hand-lotion users. Age quotas will be:

age 18–34	45 percent
age 35–54	30 percent
55 +	25 percent

Respondents will be shown a series of benefit statments about hand lotion and asked to rate each in turn on purchase interest, uniqueness, believability, and importance. Order of presentation will be randomized in order to avoid position bias.

Information to Be Obtained:
- Category and brand usage
- Purchase interest
- Purchase frequency (volume)
- Uniqueness
- Believability
- Importance

Action Standard:
- The themes that generate the highest percentage of top-box purchase interest (percent saying "definitely would buy"), will be incorporated into Sauve advertising.
- The statements that best communicate each theme, based on factor-loading scores will be incorporated into Sauve advertising.

Cost and
Timing:

The cost of this research will be $10,000 ± 10 percent. The research will adhere to the following schedule:

Fieldwork	1 week
Top-line	2 weeks
Full tabulations	5 weeks
Final report	2 weeks

Supplier: Final Analysis

Procedures

Presentation of Concepts. In new-product concept-screening tests, a **concept board** is the most frequently used format for presenting product descriptions to respondents. An illustrative concept story board is presented in Figure 18-1. Essentially only two elements are critical in the concept statement:

Concept board
Illustration and copy describing how the product works and its end benefits.

1. Copy describing how the product works and its end benefits.
2. Some type of illustration, most often a simple line drawing.

The copy should be written simply without puffery and exaggeration. Photographs are generally not necessary for most product categories and tend to be expensive (exceptions are categories in which image plays an important part, such as cosmetics). The tendency is to also include price information, although in certain instances it may be omitted. When the name of the manufacturer adds real value to the new-product concept, then it should be explicitly stated.

Interviewing. Concept-screening tests are generally conducted in a central location, although they certainly could be conducted by telephone or mail. Typically, an intercept procedure in either a shopping mall, food store, or other high-traffic location is used. To judge consumer reaction in different markets, the interviewing can be divided among different cities. In new-product concept-screening tests the usual practice is to show each respondent no more than eight new product ideas, whereas in alternative-buying-incentive concept-screening tests each respondent is exposed to a large number (at least ten to fifteen, and possibly many more) of alternatives for the same product idea in order to screen down to a smaller number for subsequent testing. Finally, it is preferable to expose each respondent to a variety of product ideas rather than expose the same respondent to extremely similar concepts.

Focus groups are also frequently used to screen new-product concepts (see Chapter 5); the groups are typically presented with five or six new concepts that provide the focus and orientation for discussion.

Questions Asked. In new-product concept-screening tests the most important questions to ask relate to

Lancia Introduces
Skillet Pizza

Now you can make real homemade pizza without using your oven.

With new SKILLET PIZZA, you can prepare a pizza that's fresher than the frozen variety and as delicious as any from a pizzeria—without turning on your oven.

Each SKILLET PIZZA package contains all the good ingredients you need, formulated to cook up into a perfect pizza in 20 minutes, in your skillet, on top of your stove. There are three flavors—cheese, pepperoni and sausage.

All come with a complete dough mix that only needs to have a half cup of cold water stirred in to form a dough that becomes a light crisp crust. No kneading. No waiting for dough to rise. And you can make the crust as thick or thin as you like.

There's a complete pizza sauce, too, rich and tomato-y, and to top it off in traditional style, a packet of shredded parmesan cheese is included in every package.

Directions are simple. Cook in your skillet, lid ajar, for 13 to 15 minutes. Uncover, cook another 3 to 5, and you have a beautiful golden thick crust pizza, to serve 4. LANCIA SKILLET PIZZA makes pizza the way your family loves it—without even turning on your oven.

Figure 18-1

Illustrative concept story board.

- purchase intent
- purchase frequency (optional)
- uniqueness of the idea
- believability of the idea
- importance of the sales message

In alternative-buying-incentive concept-screening tests respondents are usually asked to rate the concepts, according to some sorting procedure, in terms of how interested they would be in purchasing the product described. Other diagnostic questions typically relate to importance of the sales message, uniqueness, and believability.

Sampling Practices

In concept-screening tests, nonprobability sampling procedures are used. Sample-size determination is based on cost and conventional industry standards (see Table 7-2, Chapter 7).

Action Standard

A new product's top-box intention score is the crucial factor determining whether the concept is singled out for further attention. This score is usually compared to some known normative data for the test category (for example, 25 percent of the respondents must say "definitely would buy" for food products). Diagnostic questions pertaining to importance, believability, and uniqueness are examined with a view toward spotting weaknesses that, if corrected, might justify a concept's being recommended for subsequent testing.

In alternative-buying-incentive concept-screening tests, the focus is on identifying (1) themes that generate the highest percentage of top-box purchase-intent scores and (2) statements that best communicate each theme. Other diagnostic questions pertaining to uniqueness, believability, and importance are used to identify strengths and weaknesses of each alternative-buying-incentive concept.

Analysis Approach

In both types of concept-screening tests, the analysis centers on purchase-intent scores. Standard ways of analyzing the purchase-intent questions are to look at scores for either the top-box ("definitely would buy") or the top two boxes ("definitely would buy" plus "probably would buy") across all of the concepts rated. Obviously, the objective of this analysis is to identify the proportion of potential buyers who have a strong interest in the product.

The diagnostic questions can be analyzed in a number of different ways. For example, the buying-intent score and the unique score for each concept can be plotted. The quadrant of the grid in which each concept is located indicates the likelihood of ultimate market acceptance and the appropriate marketing strategy. To be more specific, each concept falls into one of the following four clusters.[2]

1. **"The me-too or generic products"**—characterized by concepts having high purchase-intent scores but low product-uniqueness scores. In order to be successful, a distinctive advantage needs to be created. Since the risks associated with products that are not really "new" are high these concepts should be viewed with caution.

2. **The winners**—inhabited by concepts having high purchase-intent scores and high product uniqueness scores. As such, these new-product ideas have the greatest chance of meeting with market acceptance.

3. **The long shots**—characterized by concepts having low purchase-intent scores and low product uniqueness scores. Unless the diagnostic data reveals specific correctable weaknesses, these product ideas should be eliminated from further consideration.

4. **The fad or specialty products**—inhabited by concepts having low purchase-intent scores but high product uniqueness scores. These product ideas typically require high profit margins and are characterized by short product-life cycles.

"Me-to" or generic products Concepts with high purchase-intent but low uniqueness scores.

Winners Concepts with high purchase-intent and high uniqueness scores.

Long shots Concepts with low purchase-intent and low uniqueness scores.

Fad or specialty products Concepts with low purchase-intent but high uniqueness scores.

A typical approach in analyzing the results of alternative-buying-incentive concept tests is to cluster the various concept statements on the basis of their respective purchase-intent scores to identify sets of concept statements having similar appeal. We want to identify subgroups of concept statements such that within a given subgroup the concept statements are *homogenous* (small *within-cluster* variation), but across the subgroups the concept statements are *heterogeneous* (large between-cluster variation).

Concept-Evaluation Tests: Implementation

Concept evaluation tests are typically conducted after initial screening and concept refinement. The purpose of a concept-evaluation test is to

1. Assess market potential for each product (or product positioning).
2. Determine a product concept's strengths and weaknesses.
3. Provide an indication as to the market segment in which each proposed product is likely to have the greatest acceptance.

Because concept-evaluation tests involve a forecast of market potential, either in terms of share of market or unit/dollar volume, they are being used increasingly with slight modifications to decide whether to initiate a test market (see Chapter 21). Consequently, if we can determine prior to test marketing that a new product will not likely meet company

[2]Ibid, 138.

objectives with respect to volume or share, the management team may decide to drop the product from further consideration and avoid the costs involved with test markets. In essence, concept-evaluation tests are being used as a "simulated test market" to acquire some perspective on how good the market is with a view toward determining which new-product concepts should go into market testing. For this reason, we will discuss concept-evaluation test services and specific forecasting techniques in Chapter 21, which considers test markets and simulated test-market applications. Exhibit 18-3 presents a prototypical concept-evaluation test-marketing research proposal.

E X H I B I T   18-3

Project Proposal: Concept Evaluation Test

Brand:	Sunshine
Project:	Candy Bar concept test
Background and Objectives:	The brand group has developed three alternative positionings for the Sunshine product. The purpose of this research is to measure the relative appeal of the positionings and to identify market segments in which the product's appeal is likely to be concentrated.
Research Method:	A three-cell monadic concept test will be conducted in geographically dispersed markets. Each concept will be exposed to 200 individuals who are past-30-day candy bar users. The following age quotas, based on category volume, will apply to each cell:

Male	45%	8–11	5%
Female	55%	12–17	20%
		18–34	35%
		35–49	25%
		50 +	15%

Information to Be Obtained:	Purchase interest
	Purchase frequency (volume/week)
	Likes/dislikes
	Believability
	Uniqueness
	Overall/attribute ratings
	Importance of main benefit
	Other diagnostic questions
	Demographics

Action Standard:	The positioning that generates the greatest top-box purchase interest (percent saying "definitely would buy") will be recommended for further development.
Cost:	$22,500 ± 10 percent
Supplier:	Market Facts, Inc.

Procedures

Presentation of Concepts. New-product concepts can be presented to respondents in various ways. For example, concept story boards, commercial advertisements, or actual product prototypes can be used. Because concepts have been previously screened and refined, the number of new-product concepts or positionings being tested is typically small (two to three), and the product description formats tend to be more elaborate and in some cases reflect advertising copy scheduled to be used in actual market tests. In no case is a single concept tested in isolation. When a single concept is under study, either a second concept or a control concept should be included in the design. A control concept should be a product that is available in the marketplace but that has low awareness levels among category users.

Interviewing. As in concept-screening tests, interviews are typically conducted by intercept in a central location; but again, interviewing certainly could be conducted by mail or telephone, depending on budget constraints and study objectives. In order to identify the concept's target market, information on category and brand purchases should be obtained from respondents before they are exposed to the product description. Generally a monadic design (Chapter 10) is used; that is, a separate group of respondents evaluates each alternative concept (or product positioning).

Questions Asked. After exposure to the product description the respondent is asked questions pertaining to

- purchase intent
- purchase frequency (volume)
- key benefit (open-ended question)
- likes/dislikes (open-ended)
- believability (open-ended)
- uniqueness
- overall/attribute ratings
- key benefit importance
- demographics

Sampling Practices

In concept-evaluation tests nonprobability sampling procedures are typically used. Interviews are usually completed on 200 respondents per concept. All respondents should be category users with specific age, sex, and user-group quotas usually determined by total category volume contribution.

Action Standards

In most cases, the concept with the highest top-box purchase-intent score is recommended for further testing. If a sufficient number of concept-evaluation tests have been completed, then category norms can be used. In cases where a control concept has been used, the test concept should be recommended only if its purchase-intent score is at least equal to that obtained by the control concept. The standard practice is to perform a test of the difference in purchase-intent scores (that is, either proportion saying "definitely would buy" or mean rating) for the test and control concepts at some prespecified confidence level (usually at least 80 percent).

Analysis Approach

Once again, the analysis centers on purchase-intent scores, and data on uniqueness, believability, or attribute ratings are used for diagnostic purposes only.

In concept-evaluation tests, the primary objective is to estimate potential trial-purchase levels for the new-product concept. Issues relating to forecasting are discussed in Chapter 22.

CONCEPT/PRODUCT DEVELOPMENT

A useful procedure for concept or product development is conjoint analysis. Recall that we discussed conjoint analysis in the context of attitude-measurement models in Chapter 11. Conjoint analysis is particularly useful in concept and product testing when the potential set of relevant attributes that together define the new concept or product or service can be easily and realistically quantified. Typically, durable concepts, products (including industrial goods),[3] and services lend themselves to this approach to testing.

Overview

Put simply, conjoint analysis provides a way of modeling consumer preferences (or other reactions) for concepts, products, and services that

---

[3]For application of conjoint analysis to industrial goods see F. Acito and T. P. Hustad, "Industrial Product Concept Testing," *Industrial Marketing Management* (1981), 67–73.

are described in terms of bundles of attributes. For example, consider the checking-account services provided by banks. Suppose that this service can be adequately described by the following attributes

- Interest payment
- Automatic teller
- Number of affiliated branches
- Minimum balance required
- Service charge

Suppose further that these attributes are defined as follows:

- Interest payment
    4.5 percent
    5.0 percent
    5.5 percent
- Automatic teller
    Yes
    No
- Number of affiliated branches
    3–5
    6–10
    11 +
- Minimum balance required
    No balance
    $200
    $500
- Service charge
    None
    $.10 per check
    $5.50 per month

Then, conjoint analysis can be used to determine which of the following two checking account configurations each individual has greatest preference for and possibly whether preference for the preferred checking account service is sufficiently great to make it the likely choice:

- Checking account A
    4.5 percent interest paid
    No automatic teller
    3–5 affiliated branches
    No minimum balance required
    No service charge
- Checking account B
    5.5 percent interest paid
    Automatic teller
    6–10 affiliated branches
    $200 minimum balance
    $.10 per check

The first step in the execution of a conjoint study is to determine which attributes are to be included in the study and what their levels will be. It is possible to predict preference only for products that can be described in terms of the attributes included in the study. The selection of attributes should be based on the following criteria:

1. They should capture the essence of any existing or potential products of interest.
2. They should differentiate among products.
3. The range of any quantitative attributes (such as price) should be broad enough to cover all anticipated specifications.

Several additional points are also worth noting. First, attribute definitions should be expressed in terminology from the respondent's point of view. Second, when soft (e.g., intangible or image) attributes are included, perceptual information should also be obtained. Third, it should be logically possible to present each level of each attribute with every level of every other attribute. Fourth, the attributes should represent independent dimensions of the product or service category. Finally, the attributes should be of comparable importance, since the model is based on a compensatory formulation.

Conjoint analysis quantifies each individual's value system associated with the levels of the defining attributes. As we discussed in Chapter 11, this is accomplished analytically by decomposing overall evaluations of a judiciously selected set of multi-attribute products or services. The quantification process results in numbers called utilities which represent that attribute's contribution to the overall evalution.

Validation

One of the primary reasons for conducting a conjoint study is to be able to predict preference for products or services that have not been directly evaluated. Thus, some effort must be made to determine the predictive validity of the conjoint model developed. Ideally, the model's predictions would be compared against actual purchases. If this is not possible, then the model's predictions should be compared to respondent's preferences for products in a "hold-out" set. This requires a hold-out set of products that have been evaluated, in addition to those that have been used to estimate the utilities of the conjoint model. The objective is to compare the model's predictions regarding those products with the actual evaluations. Two measures of predictive validity often used are (1) the percent of correct, first-choice predictions and (2) the median Spearman rank correlation (Chapter 16) between each individual's preference rankings and the model's predictions of those rankings. These measures provide some indication of how the model is doing overall.

Simulation Models

In conjoint analysis, simulating market share consists of determining what proportion of the respondents would choose each product or service in a fully specified set of products. This is accomplished by determining which product or products each respondent would choose and then aggregating the results. The two most commonly used choice models are the first-choice and share-of-preference models.

The first-choice model assumes that each individual always purchases the product for which he or she has the greatest utility. This approach makes the most sense in situations where purchases are infrequent.

The share-of-preference model assumes each respondent purchases products in proportion to his or her utility for the products. This model is generally applied in situations where the products are likely to be purchased frequently.

Market Simulations

Given the ability to predict relative preference and possibly purchase probability with the aid of the choice models just discussed, it is possible to simulate the consequences of (1) the introduction or removal of products and services from the marketplace and (2) modifications in the specifications of existing products or services, both one's own and competitions.

Armed with this kind of information, it is possible to develop products that (1) maximize share, revenue, profits and so on; (2) minimize the cannibalization of existing products or services, and (3) are targeted to specific groups of people. Strategies can also be developed to minimize the impact of changes in competitions' products, and the degree of interest in new products can be assessed.

To achieve these objectives, it is only necessary to observe the effect that variations in the specifications of products have on simulated shares. Because utilities are developed at the individual level, simulations can be performed at any level of aggregation. In addition, by cross-tabulating predicted choice selections with respondent demographics, it can be determined who is buying what; and, by cross-tabulating predicted choice selections between simulations, switching behavior can be studied. Finally, if the need arises, respondents can be weighted to reflect population characteristics or differential purchase frequency or usage (see Chapter 13).

First-choice model Conjoint analysis model that assumes individuals always choose products for which they have greatest utility.

Share-of-preference model Conjoint analysis model that assumes individuals purchase products in proportion to their utility for the products.

PRODUCT TESTING: PHILOSOPHY AND OBJECTIVE

Product tests attempt to answer one of the most basic of questions relating to the ultimate market acceptance of a product: "How does this product perform when evaluated by the consumer?" Performance can be evaluated in isolation, in a competitive frame, against its advertising, or against a formula variation. There is no better way to answer this question than to experience and use the product under real-life conditions. From product testing we learn which product is most acceptable to consumers. Product testing is particularly important in the consumer package-goods industries (food, health and beauty aids, household products, and the like) where physical product improvements can quickly change market shares in a product category and where production/distribution of product prototypes is economically feasible.

Specifically, product tests are conducted for four purposes.

1. *Tests against the competition* seek to identify which of many alternative new formulas is best in terms of being most preferred or measure the performance of the new product relative to other competitive products.
2. *Product improvement* tests attempt to determine whether an improved formula (or construction) should replace the current product.
3. *Cost-savings* tests attempt to determine whether a less-expensive product should replace the current product.
4. *Concept-fit* tests attempt to determine which of several test-product variants most closely resembles what is being communicated by the "product sell."

Monadic products tests Designs where a consumer evaluates only one product, having no other product for comparison.

Comparison product tests Designs where a consumer rates products by directly comparing two or more products.

Sequential monadic designs Comparison tests where a consumer rates one product and then is given a second product to rate independently.

Protomonadic designs Comparison tests where a consumer evaluates one product and then compares it to a second product.

Paired comparison designs Tests where a consumer directly compares two products.

Repeat paired comparison designs Tests where a respondent is given two or more sets of products to compare against each other at two different points in time.

TYPES OF PRODUCT TESTS

There are two broad types of product-test procedures.

1. **Monadic product tests** present the consumer with one product and ask for an evaluation of that product with no other specific product for comparison. Actually, the test product is rated and compared to all other similar products the consumer has ever used and specifically to the product currently being used.
2. **Comparison product tests** present the consumer with two or more products and ask for a comparison and rating of each. There are many different variations of comparison product tests. In **sequential monadic designs,** a respondent tests one product, evaluates it, and then is given a second product to evaluate independently. In **protomonadic designs,** a respondent tests one product, evaluates it, and then is given a second product and compares the two. In **paired comparison designs,** a respondent is given two products to compare against each other. In **repeat paired comparison designs,** a respondent is given two or more sets of products to compare against each other at two different points in time. The objective is to determine whether the respondent chooses between them in the same way on more than one occasion. In **round robin de-**

signs, each of a series of products is tested against each of the others and the results are combined. In **triangle designs,** a respondent is given two blind samples of one product and one blind sample of another product and asked to identify that one that differs from the other two. In **duo-trio designs,** a respondent is given a "standard" product and then asked to determine which of two other products matches it. And, in **discrimination difference designs,** a respondent is asked to determine if one product differs from others.

The advantage of monadic testing is in its realism. In normal situations a respondent uses one product at a time and then determines whether it is acceptable or unaccceptable for repurchase. Monadic tests are designed specifically to test the qualities of the product itself—the frame of reference will be the product the respondent is currently using and all other products in the category. Because of this, the result of a monadic product test may be difficult to interpret, unless norms have been established; for example, what does it mean if 75 percent of the respondents rated the product's taste as "excellent"? In contrast, comparison tests, by their very nature, concentrate on the differences between the products being tested—the paired nature of the test makes comparison product tests more sensitive, all else the same, than monadic product tests; however, it is far more difficult to generalize to the universe of all products.

Round robin designs Test where a series of products is tested against each of the others.

Triangle designs Tests where a respondent is given two samples of one product and one sample of another and asked to identify the one that differs.

Duo-trio designs Test where a respondent is given a standard product and asked to determine which of two other products is most similar.

Discrimination/difference designs Tests where a respondent is asked if one product differs from others.

PRODUCT TESTS: IMPLEMENTATION

Exhibit 18-4 presents a prototypical product-test proposal.

Procedures

Presentation of Products. A crucial issue in presenting the product to respondents is whether to disclose the brand and/or company name. In other words, should products be tested on a "blind" (no identification as to brand) or a "branded," "identified," "open" basis? **Blind testing** is undertaken when (1) new products are being tested where no brand name, packaging, or advertising has been developed as yet, and (2) reactions to the "pure" product, apart from established image values, are desired. Note that the product test described in Exhibit 18-4 calls for a blind test. The reasons for this is that the brand group probably wants to see how consumers rate this product against the leading competitor (Campbell's Soups) without the outside influence of brand image or advertising.

    Branded testing is usually undertaken when (1) measurement of the effects of the brand name, or brand image, on reactions to the products is required and (2) brand identification is so obvious, and its effect on

Blind testing Tests where the brand name of the product is *not* disclosed during test.

Branded testing Test where brand name of product is disclosed during test.

ultimate market acceptance is so inevitable, that there is little point in doing a blind test.

There are four basic principles to follow in preparing the product for testing. First, the product tested should be representative of the product that will ultimately appear in the marketplace. Second, name and packaging materials should be as close as possible to those that will be used when the product goes to the market. Third, sensitivity to what is being tested is necessary; for example, if different formulas are being tested, then make sure all other factors (size, shape, color, and so on) are identical. Fourth, products should be labeled in a fashion that minimizes bias (for example, avoid using letters/numbers that are obviously sequential).

Interviewing. Two research methods predominate in product-testing applications: (1) in-home placement and (2) central location testing.

In-home product testing can be undertaken in a number of different ways. The interviewer may go from door to door to determine whether the respondent qualifies for the test; if the respondent qualifies, then a product is left behind and the interviewer will arrange a time to return when the respondent's reactions to the product will be recorded. On the other hand, if the product test can be conducted quickly (typically the case in taste and smell tests), the interviewer may ask the respondent to test the product right on the spot. An increasingly frequent practice is to have the interviewer initiate contact via the telephone and if the contacted respondent qualifies and is willing to cooperate, then the product is delivered by the interviewer or by mail. The respondent's reaction to the product is recorded, either through a personal interview or by telephone. Another variation of in-home placement is to interview respondents in shopping malls or other high-traffic locations and then give them the products to take home and use. Follow-ups can then be scheduled either by personal interview or via telephone. Still yet another variation of in-home placement is to use a "mail panel," consisting of families who have previously agreed to test products. Products are delivered by mail and, therefore, the product tested must be suitable for mail shipment (see Chapter 5).

E X H I B I T 18-4

Project Proposal: Product Test

Brand:	New Products Hardy Soup
Project:	Campbell versus new Hardy Soup blind product test
Background and Objectives:	R&D has developed a new Hardy Soup in two different flavors (chicken noodle and mushroom). Additionally, each flavor has been developed at two different flavor strengths. The brand

groups has requested that research be conducted to determine (1) whether this product should be considered for introduction, (2) if so, if one or both flavors should be introduced, and (3) which flavor variation(s) would be preferred most by the consumer.

The objective of this research will be to determine consumer preference for each flavor variation of the new product relative to Campbell's Chunky products.

Method: There will be four cells. In each cell, a blind paired product test will be conducted between a different flavor variation of the new product and the currently marketed Campbell's product, as follows:

- Campbell's Chunky Chicken Noodle versus Hardy's Chicken Noodle 1
- Campbell's Chunky Chicken Noodle versus Hardy's Chicken Noodle 2
- Campbell's Chunky Mushroom versus Hardy's Mushroom 1
- Campbell's Chunky Mushroom versus Hardy's Mushroom 2

In each cell, there will be 200 past-30-day ready-to-serve soup/user purchasers.

Respondents will be interviewed in a shopping mall and given both products to take home and try. Additionally, respondents must be positively disposed toward chicken noodle or mushroom flavors in order to be used in the test. Order of product trial will be rotated to minimize position bias. Telephone call-backs will be made after one-week period.

*Action
Standard:*   Each new soup flavor will be considered for introduction if one or more of its flavor variations achieves at least absolute parity with its Campbell's Chunky control.

If for either flavor alternative more than one flavor level variation meets the action standard, the one that is preferred over Campbell's at the highest level of confidence will be recommended to be considered for introduction.

A single sample *t*-test for paired comparison data (two-tail) will be used to test for significance.

*Cost and
Timing:*   The cost of this study will be \$32,000 ± 10 percent.

The following schedule will be established:

Fieldwork	2 weeks
Top-line	2 weeks
Final report	4 weeks

*Research
Firm:*   Market Facts, Inc.

Central-location product testing has become very popular in recent years because in-home placement can be extremely expensive, especially with low-incidence product categories, where the costs of screening and call-backs are expected to be substantial. With central-location testing respondents are screened on location (or recruited by telephone) and invited to the testing location, usually a shopping mall or food store where the research company conducting the product test has rented space. Typically, food products tested are prepared by home economists or trained kitchen personnel and the respondent is invited to taste various samples of two or three of the products being tested and then is asked questions about each item sampled. The major limitation of central-location testing is that the respondent does not get a chance to experience the product in his or her own kitchen, nor does the information obtained reflect the opinions of the respondent's family. Clearly, for products where ease of preparation or application is important—for example, in case of cake mix and furniture polish—some sort of in-home testing is required.

A related issue involves the length of the product test; that is, how long should the test run? Obviously, the respondent should be given ample opportunity to use the product as frequently as is desired and under realistic conditions. Generally, in-home tests last a minimum of a week. In certain situations, an **extended-use product test** is warranted; here the respondent uses the product over a period of weeks or months; for example, it may be important to determine what kind of use or abuse the respondent will give the product over time. In the case of novelty products a **sales wave extended-use product test** is often performed. In sales wave product tests the respondent is given the opportunity to buy the product at intervals coinciding with the normal purchase cycle. This type of product test can (1) identify novelty products that are initially liked, but quickly wear out, (2) isolate target groups, (3) help in forecasting share of market or volume, and (4) identify specific product problems.

Extended-use product test In-home test where respondent is given opportunity to use the product over a period of weeks.

Sales wave extended-use product test Respondent is given opportunity to buy the product at intervals coinciding with the normal purchase cycle.

Questions Asked. The types of questions asked will vary to some extent, depending on the interviewing method. In general, the most important questions to ask relate to

- preference
- overall rating
- attribute ratings
- likes/dislikes
- advantages/disadvantages
- uniqueness
- frequency of use (if applicable)
- who used the product (if applicable)
- when and how was the product used (if applicable)
- use patterns (if applicable)

Sampling Practices

Once again nonprobability sampling designs are frequently used in product-testing applications. The typical approach is to specify age and sex quotas based on total category volume contribution. Standard minimum cell sizes for in-home use tests typically call for 100–200 respondents to be interviewed. In central-location tests the standard minimum cell size is typically 100 respondents, although simple test-versus-competitive-control studies are often conducted with as few as 50 respondents per cell.

Action Standards

The specific criteria for evaluating product tests depend on the stated purpose of the test. The following are action standards for three broad types of product tests.

Tests Versus Competition

1. New products as well as established products should achieve an overall preference difference that is statistically significant at the 90 percent level of confidence in each principal target group.
2. In copy-claim-support tests the test product must achieve significant preferences versus competition at the 95 percent confidence level for superiority claims and at least absolute parity (50 percent) for parity claims.

Product Improvement Tests

1. We should recommend that the improved product replace the current product only if it achieves statistically equivalent preferences over the current product among brand users, and significant preferences (90 percent) among nonusers (or vice versa, depending upon the marketing objectives of the proposed product improvement).
2. In copy-claims-support tests, the improved product must achieve significance preference versus the old product at the 95 percent confidence level for superiority claims and at least absolute parity (50 percent) for parity claims.

Cost Savings Tests

1. We should recommend that the less-expensive product replace the current product only if it achieves parity among current users *and* nonusers of the brand. (Parity equals *not* losing to the current product at greater than some specified level of confidence.)

Analysis Approach

In product-testing applications interest centers on tests of mean differences and/or tests of proportions based on the key evaluative measures (such as overall rating or overall preferences). Guidance for research and development can be derived through an analysis of directional ratings in monadic designs (for example, what percent of respondents felt that the level of sweetness was "too much." "not enough," or "just the right amount"), and preference on specific attributes in paired designs.

Summary

In this chapter we have considered two of the most important practices undertaken in marketing research—concept and product testing. We discussed and illustrated the basic types of concept screening, concept evaluation, and product tests. Through the use of hypothetical marketing research proposals we have attempted to introduce the major issues involved in concept and product testing and to provide specific details on how concept and product tests are implemented.

Key Concepts

Concept screening tests

Concept evaluation tests

Conjoint analysis for concept testing

Product testing

Review Questions

1. Discuss the differences between concept-screening tests and concept-evaluation tests.
2. Explain how conjoint analysis can be used in concept or product development. What are the critical issues in designing conjoint analysis concept or product tests?
3. Why are product tests conducted? Translate each of the reasons for conducting product tests into a number of specific types of product-testing applications.
4. Discuss the various types of product tests. For each of the following products or brands, which type of product test would you recommend and why?
   - New cold tablet
   - Lancia skillet pizza (see Figure 18-1)
   - Spaghetti in a jar

5. Contrast in-home product tests with central-location product tests. For each of the following products or brands, determine whether you would suggest an in-home or central-location product test.

- New cold tablet
- Lancia skillet pizza (see Figure 18-1)
- Spaghetti in a jar

Name and Package Testing

CHAPTER OBJECTIVES

- Describe how names are created and the primary approach to naming a product.
- Define the information typically collected in name-testing studies.
- Describe how name tests are implemented.
- Define the basic functions that a package serves.
- Outline the reasons for conducting a package test.
- Describe how package tests are implemented.

Introduction

The name of a new product and its package design are two integral components that influence ultimate market acceptance. With the advent of self-service retail environments, name and package testing have become more important in the last two decades: Consumer recognition and product visibility are necessarily vital considerations in marketing any product. In this chapter we discuss name- and package-testing research.

NAME TESTS

Names are important because of the information they convey; the name of a product communicates both denotative and connotative meaning. **Denotative meaning** refers to the literal, explicit meaning of a name. **Connotative meaning** refers to the associations that the name provokes beyond its literal, explicit meaning—in other words, the imagery that is associated with a brand name. Specifically, a brand name (1) identifies the product to consumer, retailer, distributor, and manufacturer and (2) differentiates the product from competitive products and conveys physical and emotional benefits.

We don't mean to say that a "good" name will save a bad product. However, in these days of product "me-too-ism," a dull or otherwise inappropriate name can be a severe handicap even to a superior product.

Denotative meaning The literal, explicit meaning of a name.

Connotative meaning The associations that the name implies, beyond its literal, explicit meaning; the imagery associated with a brand name.

630

Recognizing the value of a good name, many companies now make use of commercial-names experts. One such expert is Ira Bachrach, founder of NameLab, a commercial-names factory. For $35,000 or so, Bachrach will assist you in naming your product entry. In Exhibit 19-1 Bachrach comments on the names of several products that you might recognize.

E X H I B I T 19-1

Name Calling*

The Diehard

Value overwhelms metaphor: This is "the best adapted metaphor in the history of brand names," says Bachrach.

Anacin

Strong medicine: The brain doesn't think of pictures so much as of words. Using familiar language elements, or "morphemes," scientific-sounding Excedrin and Bufferin evoke strength. But competing Anacin is perceived negatively, due to its prefix meaning "not."

Nissan Sentra

No name is a good name: "Only recently have car names become rational," says Ira Bachrach, who has devised automobile names for several makers. For Nissan Motor, the message suggested by "Sentra" is safety. The public accepts the coined term to be a quality of the product. But good names aren't always names at all, e.g., "240" works symbolically well for Mercedes-Benz, denoting cool efficiency.

Apple

The genesis of microcomputing: Apple was there first. The marketing challenge back then demanded a symbol of friendliness, trustworthiness, and simplicity—concepts, according to Ira Bachrach, of "nonspecific affect." Thus an innocuous fruit, irrelevant to technology, was appropriate. To Bachrach, it meant something that didn't screw up your utility bill.

Budweiser

A "Bud," not a "Budweiser": A name that becomes short, friendly, and familiar can make its way into the language.

Rainbow (Digital)

No pot of gold: After Apple, micros became packaged goods that demanded specific messages. Thus, Bachrach feels, the amorphous "Rainbow" appeared far too late. Although commendably simple and easy, to the now-informed public it said "noncomputer." And it cast a sense of arbitrarily having been slapped on. "About as amateurish as you can get," observes Bachrach.

*Adapted from Robert A. Manis, "Name-Calling," *Inc. Magazine* (July 1984), pp. 67–74.

Philosophy and Objectives

Obviously, a name should be legible, pronounceable, memorable, and distinctive. However, the denotative and connotative meaning associated with a name should be consistent and support the overall brand strategy plan and corporate direction. Once a name has been decided upon, all of the advertising, packaging, and promotional efforts are directed toward implanting that name in the minds and vocabulary of consumers. Thus, probably the last thing manufacturers want to do is to change the names of their products, although there have been exceptions such as ESSO to EXXON, Datsun to Nissan.

Name-testing research is typically conducted for one or more of the following reasons:

1. To generate new name ideas.
2. To measure legibility and pronounceability.
3. To measure association with product category.
4. To measure distinctiveness.
5. To measure relative ability to project strategy-supporting promises of product use and end-benefits.

Company names
Corporate names attached to the products they market.

Explicit descriptive names Names that are meant to describe the physical product.

Line names Names assigned to a variety of specific products that the company markets.

Implicit imagery names Names that do not literally describe the product, but implicitly and indirectly convey its characteristics.

Created names Names that do not have literal meaning with respect to the characteristics of a product; however, through advertising they may acquire indirect meaning that can reflect favorably on the product.

There are many different strategies in developing names for products. For example, some companies choose to give meaning to a meaningless name like "Kodak," while others choose names like "Rice Krispies," which literally describes the physical product. Approaches to naming a product include[1]

1. **Company names.** Libby, Scott Paper, General Mills, Pillsbury, and Kraft are all examples of companies that attach their corporate names to the products they market. In contrast, other corporations such as General Foods and Proctor & Gamble follow a strategy of using individual brand names for their products.
2. **Explicit descriptive names.** Minute Rice, Rice-A-Roni, Wheat Chex, and Light 'n Lively are all examples of names meant to describe the physical product.
3. **Line names.** These names are assigned to a variety of specific products that the company markets. Betty Crocker, Green Giant, and Aunt Jemima are examples of line names.
4. **Implicit imagery names.** A common strategy is to use a name that does not literally describe the product, but implicitly and indirectly conveys characteristics about the product. Examples include Taster's Choice, Pampers, and Liquid Paper.
5. **Created names.** These names do not have a literal meaning with respect to the characteristics of a product. However, through advertising they may acquire indirect meaning that can reflect favorably on the product. Examples of created names include Aim, Marlboro, Virginia Slims, and Scope.

[1]Parts of the following discussion were adapted from Jeffrey Pope, *Practical Marketing Research* (New York: AMACOM, 1981), 157–58.

6. **Designer names.** These names are associated with individuals who are leading figures of fashion design. They lend their names to mass-marketed fashion and accessories and in some cases even to unrelated products (such as automobiles). Examples include Bill Blass and Yves St. Laurent.

Designer names Names associated with leading figures of fashion design and lent to mass-marketed fashion and accessories.

Procedures

There is no one "right" way to choose a name. Only very general guidelines can be offered. To get some perspective on how names are given to products, consider Exhibit 19-2, which tells the story of COMPAQ, NameLab's biggest success.

A very general procedure for creating a list of new names is to (1) list objectives and benefits of the brand strategy and corporate-direction statement; (2) list appropriate synonyms and antonyms; and (3) combine appropriate objectives and benefits with appropriate synonyms and antonyms to produce a list of "promising" words, prefaces, and suffixes. It is a good practice to never test a new name in isolation. At least two alternatives should be tested for comparison. Note that reactions to a given name may be affected by the other names in the test; therefore, you should exercise extreme caution in comparing the results of one name test with that of another name test.

Name tests are generally conducted in a central location, either at a shopping mall or some other high-traffic location.

Interviewing Practices. The format for presenting names to respondents is quite simple. Each new name is placed on a separate card and the respondent is exposed to either the entire set of names (cards) or a limited set. Actually, the respondent is shown a concept statement containing one of the test names and a brief description of the product. If a brand strategy has been agreed upon, then the product statement should be strategically oriented. The order of the names is rotated from respondent to respondent in order to remove position bias effects. After exposure to each name, the respondent is typically asked to read and pronounce the name and answer other questions.

Questions Asked. Typically name tests collect information on:

1. *Legibility and pronounceability.* Respondents are asked to read and pronounce a single new name at a time.
2. *Association.* Respondents are asked to associate the name with a product category. For example, typical questions are
   - "What type of product do you think this is?"
   - "Which one of the products on this card do you most associate with *(name)?* . . . Which others do you associate with it?"
3. *Distinctiveness.* Respondents may be asked to indicate the distinctiveness of the new name by asking such questions as:
   - "What brand(s) does this *(name)* most remind you of, and why?"
   - "Who do you think manufactured it, and why?"

4. *Imagery and end benefits.* Respondents are asked to use semantic differential scales to describe the new name/product. In such cases, the respondent will be shown a concept statement containing one of the test names and a brief description of the product. Note that product descriptors should (1) adequately cover all of the important end benefits, (2) focus on product-oriented issues like "crunchy" as opposed to name-oriented issues like "sounds good," and (3) be consistent with brand strategy and corporate direction statements. The set of scales can also be used for a competitive product or a respondent's ideal brand.

E X H I B I T 19-2

COMPAQ

NameLab's most notable entry so far came in 1982 on behalf of a tiny start-up that intended to sell portable computers. The founders, two engineers from Texas Instruments Inc., were content to name the company and its product after a local address; hence, Gateway Technology. The little machine presumably could be sold as Gateway, inasmuch as a computer is a "gateway" to some vague, but assuredly noble, end. To scientists, the connection seemed clever enough. But not to the company's prime investors, a partnership headed by Ben Rosen and L. J. Sevin. Justifiably concerned lest Gateway mean little to consumers, and even less to Wall Street, Rosen urged that NameLab be consulted. Enter Ira Bachrach, with his intensively linguistic and peculiarly totemic approach to naming things. Within a few weeks, Gateway was presented with several snappier choices, among them Cortex, Cognipak, and Suntek. Oh, yes—and Compaq.

No one can say for sure that the company might not have done equally well under the banners of Cognipac, Gateway, or even Tip-Top. Nonetheless, as Compaq, the corporation went on to sell $111 million worth of computers in 12 months, a U.S. record for first-year revenues. But this almost didn't come to pass, due to concern that the name might be challenged. In many of its particulars, trademark and service mark law is so vague, confusing, and regionalized that general counsel often prefers the discretion of another choice to the valor of stepping on toes, however unrelated. Gateway's attorneys felt that the proposed new trademark came too close to "Compac," a registered service mark of a trans-atlantic cable switching network owned by ITT Corp., and asked that it be reconsidered. But with a public offering at stake, the board of directors sought a hot name, and Compaq it stayed. "If you ask lawyers, 'Should I go outside?' " Bachrach complains good-humoredly, "they'll say, 'God, you could get run over!' "

An expert in marketing packaged goods from an earlier career in advertising, the 46-year-old Bachrach has discovered that the rules there apply to nonpackaged-goods fields as well. To this discipline he also brings an approach to language developed in his graduate thesis that involves relationships among semantic fragments, by which he tried to win the George Bernard Shaw prize for developing an English phonetic alphabet. (Thuh pryez rhemaynz unwon evun toodae.) As a result, many NameLab creations enjoy multiple effects, sometimes via neologisms with implications that are hidden within ancient but evocative roots. To be sure, Compaq computers could easily have been called "Compacts," but with humdrum impact, weaker suggestiveness, and stage-sharing with cars and cosmetics.

The client had ordered up a word that would be memorable and at the same time "take command of the idea of portableness"; something that would distinguish itself from all the other IBM Personal Computer compatibles. NameLab developed a table of basic word parts called "morphemes," of which 6,200 exist in English. An unabashed morpheme addict, Bachrach fashioned "Compaq" from two "messages," one of which indicated computer and communications and the other a small, integral object. The "com" part came easily. The "pac" followed with more difficulty, since its phonetic notation included endings in "k," "c," "ch," and, possibly, "q." NameLab considered all four of them. When the "q" hit, Bachrach gasped eureka. As a bonus to the assigned burden, "paq" also was affectively scientific, he reasoned, strongly hinting of "somebody trying to do something precisely and interestingly."

As a significant benefit, the "paq" suffix fits neatly into what could become a product family name: Printpaq, Datapaq, Wordpaq, and the like. Combining a corporate name with a product name results, by mere repetition, in consumer acceptance of substance and reliability. "By naming subsequent products '-paq,' " Bachrach reasons, "they get added free exposure. It doesn't cost them a dollar in advertising."

When Compaq's board of directors asked what would happen if the company wanted to produce larger systems under the restrictive 'paq' concept, Bachrach explained that all good solutions are limited. The more general a solution is, he philosophized, the less effective. "Look, if it works," Bachrach told the board, "your name will become the dominant symbol for portable computers, like Xerox is the symbolic identity for copiers. If that happens and several years from now you want to introduce a megasupercomputer, you can always change your company name or use a model that doesn't have a 'paq.' In the meantime, you'll be crying all the way to the bank. A name that's any good," he lectures customers, "is scary. If it isn't, it's not going to accomplish very much."

Source: Robert A. Manis, "Name-Calling," *Inc. Magazine,* July 1984, 67–74.

Frequently the name given to a product is that of a celebrity (for example, "Krystle" perfume). In so-called designer or celebrity name studies, interest centers on:

1. *Familiarity.* How familiar is the celebrity to the target segment?
2. *Appropriateness.* Respondents are asked to indicate the appropriateness of the celebrity and the product category.
3. *Imagery.* Respondents are asked to use semantic differentials to describe the imagery of the celebrity.

Sampling Practices

As we indicated, interviewing for a name test is usually conducted at a high-traffic central location. Standard practice is to use a minimum of 100 category users per name variation and no less than 50 respondents for a subgroup analysis. Specific age and gender quotas may also be imposed, based on total category volume contribution or U.S. census estimates.

Action Standards

Various criteria for name evaluation can be used. Performance criteria include the following:

1. The relative importance of the various measurements.
2. The relative importance of the various descriptors and associations.
3. The resources available to develop a creative name—that is, to render a "meaningless" name "meaningful."

Though the specific criteria for name evaluation will vary, it is important to explain them clearly.

Approach to Analysis

Typically, the approach to analyzing the information collected in name tests is quite straightforward. First, new names are screened as to their legibility and pronounceability. Names that respondents have difficulty reading or pronouncing are generally not candidates for further consideration. With respect to the association, distinctiveness, imagery, and end-benefits data, the typical approach is to use one- or two-tailed tests of proportions and means (see Chapter 15).

PACKAGE TESTS

The package design is one of the most important marketing components for a product. A package serves several basic functions:

1. It contains, protects, and dispenses the product.
2. It provides point-of-purchase advertising.
3. It serves as an attention-getting device.
4. It provides a reminder to current users.
5. It is a source of information about directions, ingredients, and potential cautions.
6. It provides a vehicle for announcing promotions and deals.
7. It promises physical and emotional end benefits.

The package is the piece of information that every consumer sees, and so a better package can make a difference. The importance of package design is exemplified by North American Phillips Lighting Corporation's strategy, described in Exhibit 19-3.

There are many different approaches to package testing. In this chapter we describe only one of them.

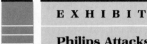

E X H I B I T   19-3

Philips Attacks $2.2 Billion Bulb Market

Consumer awareness begets sales in the $2.2 billion U.S. lighting industry, and North American Philips Lighting Corp. (NAPLC) is counting on a multimillion-dollar ad and marketing program to become America's top-selling lighting line.

The Bloomfield, N.J.-based subsidiary of North American Philips Corp. acquired the Westinghouse lamp division two years ago. Now it's ready to capitalize on the acquisition, and it's counting on redesigned packaging, a major ad program with a heavy network TV emphasis, and mechandising and promotional support for the trade to make it a worldwide leader in lighting.

The media campaign was launched on network TV in the northeast and north central regions during the fourth quarter, with national advertising slated to begin next year. The fall campaign will reach about 50% of U.S. consumers, while the 1986 campaign will reach an estimated 98%. The ads are complemented by an extensive public relations effort which includes TV talk shows and news programming.

The new packaging emerged after a year of study. It incorporates both the Philips and Westinghouse brand names. "When research proves we've established sufficient awareness of the Philips brand, the Westinghouse trademark will be phased out," according to William V. Attardie, Philips' vice president, consumer lighting division.

Studies of consumer buying habits and eye-tracking studies of prototype package designs preceded the selection of the new package design, which brings a unified, color coded, family appearance to the product line.

"The studies also found that consumers view the new packaging graphics as attractive, contemporary, and esthetically pleasing," Attardi said. "Consumers perceived the packaging as respresenting a high-quality product and a brand they could trust."

Philips has converted to a four-bulb pack to appeal to its primary customers: women, most of whom work and prefer larger packages.

Revamped packaging isn't the only tool in NAPLC's arsenal to capture consumers' attention. The company is extending use of its unique "shape of quality" in the line.

The high-quality soft white bulbs are being converted to this distinctive T-shape. The line of 33% Longer Life bulbs will retain the T-shape, as will several high-margin speciality bulbs.

"Consumers will come to recognize these distinctively shaped bulbs as a symbol of our quality," Attardi said.

During a two-stage roll-out, NAPLC personnel will physically change over stores from the old line to the new. To capitalize on impulse buying habits, more money is being channeled into sales promotions.

Computer-generated planograms will help retailers optimize square footage sales, turn rate, and gross return on investment. Trade programs are supported with extensive free-standing newspaper inserts, point-of-purchase material, trade promotions, and ad allowances.

Source: Marketing News, November 22, 1985, 26. Reprinted by permission of the American Marketing Association.

Philosophy and Objectives

Obviously, the package design must work; however, other aspects of the package need to be tested as well. Most consumer-goods package tests are conducted for the following two purposes:

1. To assess the visibility of package alternatives, relative to one another and usually relative to a competitive brand.
2. To assess the ability of package alternatives to convey perceptions of physical and emotional end benefits.

Remember that the purpose of a package test is not to assess the artistic quality of the package design.

Procedures

The procedures involved in package testing research are a bit more involved than those used in name tests. Exposure to the package and measurement of its visibility and image must be carefully controlled. A package design should never be tested in isolation, since a package alternative that may have high visibility scores when tested by itself can lose its impact when placed among competitive products; in addition, when testing packages designed for established products, the product's current package design should be included in the test as a control. Thus, for example, in a test of Life Savers, other products found at the front end of stores—such as Tums rolls, Rolaids rolls, Trident, Certs, and Dentyne—should also be included in the test, even though some of these are in different product categories.

Control over exposure to package alternatives is sometimes accomplished by using slides and a tachistoscope (T-Scope). Slides allow greater control over exposure to the shelf space than if an actual display was used. The use of the T-Scope allows the researcher to control light intensity and exposure duration. Though package alternatives could be tested in actual store environments, either in test markets or in simulated test markets, this is rarely done. The substantial practical and cost considerations involved in producing the product in several different packages generally preclude this approach.

Interviewing Practices. Interviewing is conducted at high-traffic central locations. Because slides are used to project pictures of the various package alternatives, the site must allow for total darkness (with the exception of a safety light) and have a partitioned-off interviewing area where respondents cannot overhear one another. The projector is usually placed ten feet and respondent eight feet from the viewing screen. Before exposure to a test slide, each respondent is run through a "dummy" slide so that the procedure is fully understood.

When the test begins, the respondent is exposed to a single test var-

Figure 19-1

Package slide. (Courtesy Anheuser-Busch Companies.)

iant that shows a picture of a package alternative among those of other products that appear in its normal environment; in other words, the test is monadic, and no respondent is exposed to more than one test variant. The pictures of the test variants are projected from standard 35-mm slides. The slides are constructed so that their longest dimension is on the horizontal, to depict an actual store environment. Pictures are taken against light-gray backgrounds to control for color effects. Typically, there are about 8–12 evenly distributed products per slide, and to minimize bias three random layouts of each test variant are used. Figure 19-1 shows a product-line extension package slide test for Eagle snacks.

Respondents are exposed to each slide at four different intervals: 1/8 second, 1/4 second, 1/2 second, and 1 second. After each exposure, the respondent indicates to the interviewer which brand he or she has seen. When imagery and end benefits data are needed, the respondent is then escorted to a separate area and shown the product. The product can be displayed in a number of different formats; for example, the respondent can be shown a story board, the actual product, or a 35-mm slide.

Questions Asked. Package tests typically focus on "visibility" and "image" areas.

1. *Visibility.* After each exposure (1/8 second, 1/4 second, 1/2 second, and 1 second) the respondent is asked to indicate what he or she has seen.
2. *Image.* Respondents are asked to use semantic differential scales to describe their impressions of the product. The question format is the same as that used in name testing. Note again that the image questions should concentrate on end benefits and product-oriented issues like "sweet" as opposed to package-oriented issues like "looks pretty."

Sampling Practices

Interviewing for a package test is conducted at high-traffic central locations. Standard practice is to use a minimum of 100 category users per test variant and no fewer than 50 respondents for a subgroup analysis. As in name testing, specific age and gender requirements may be established.

Action Standards

Various standards for package-test evaluation can be used. Performance standards include:

1. Whether the package must equal or have greater visibility than the current package designs or competitive packages.
2. Whether the package must equal or better ratings on key issue scales.
3. Whether visibility or image is to receive the greater weight in making the analysis.

Approach to Analysis

The analysis focuses on the visibility and image measures. As in name testing, visibility and image scores are typically tested across alternative package designs with test of proportions and means (see Chapter 15).

Summary

In this chapter we have discussed and illustrated the basic techniques and procedures used in name- and package-testing research. As we have indicated, name and package tests are extremely important marketing research activities simply because much of what is conveyed about a product is communicated through the product's name and package design.

Key Concepts

Name tests
Denotative meaning
Connotative meaning
Company names
Explicit descriptive names

Line names
Implicit imagery names
Created names
Package tests

Review Questions

1. Discuss the primary approaches to naming a product.
2. Describe the key information that should be collected in a name test.
3. Describe the steps in conducting a name test.
4. Why is packaging an important consideration?
5. Describe the steps in conducting a package test. What issues should the researcher be particularly sensitive to?

Advertising Research Practices

CHAPTER OBJECTIVES

■ Understand the many purposes that advertising serves.
■ Define what is meant by advertising effectiveness.
■ Describe and illustrate standard copy-testing practices in the print and television media.

Introduction

In this chapter we consider studies designed to investigate advertising—which many consider to be the major channel of communication between marketers and the public. Advertising effectiveness is a crucial concern to most companies. Advertising serves multiple purposes: It provides information; it can generate favorable attitudes toward a brand; it can lead to favorable intentions to buy; it can cause an individual to buy a brand; and, as is typically the case with durable purchases, it can be used to rationalize a purchase.

Because advertising serves many purposes, measures of its effectiveness may take many different forms. The measures may be qualitative, quantitative, or a combination of both. They may be taken in a laboratory-like setting before a finished advertisement is ready. Alternatively, they may be taken on a finished advertisement either before the advertisement is placed in the media or at various times after it has been placed in the media. Thus, what is being measured, when the measurement is made, and which medium the advertisement is placed in, determine the precise definition of effectiveness.

Most advertising research techniques focus on measuring the effectiveness of an ad in terms of awareness, communicability, and persuasiveness. Typical questions center on

■ Whether the ad creates awareness
■ Whether the ad communicates the benefits of the product
■ Whether the ad creates a predisposition to purchase

Thus, although some may argue that the ultimate goal of advertising is to increase sales, rarely are sales volume or market share directly used to measure the effectiveness of advertising. First, advertising is only one element in the overall marketing mix and it is difficult, if not impossible, to unambiguously separate the effects of advertising from those of in-store promotions, distribution, shelf-position, coupons, and so on. Second, in certain companies, advertising budgets are fixed to sales volume; that is, advertising budgets are allocated as a fixed percentage of sales. In such cases, it may be impossible to isolate the effects of advertising because of the "chicken and egg" syndrome. Third, even when advertising does affect sales directly, there is typically a lag between when the ad is run and the purchases that result from it, which makes measurement difficult. Fourth, the effects of competitive activities (such as new-product introductions, couponing activities, and the like) often cannot be separated from the effect of a given firm's advertising. Fifth, advertising has a cumulative effect so that attempts to isolate the effects of a single ad, especially for an established brand, can be very difficult.

Advertising effectiveness studies are generically referred to as **copy testing.** Copy testing can be undertaken by the advertiser directly, by the advertising agency, or by an independent commercial copy-testing service. Commercial copy-testing firms offer their services to advertisers and advertising agencies and provide an independent means for both the advertiser and the advertising agency to evaluate an ad. Copy-testing services vary greatly, depending on the medium in which the ad is to be placed. We discuss standard copy-testing practices in the *print* and *television* media.

Copy testing Generic term for advertising effectiveness studies.

PRINT AD TESTS

Print ad tests attempt to assess the power of an ad placed in a magazine or newspaper to be remembered, to communicate, to affect attitudes, and ultimately to produce sales. Though in principle all print-testing techniques focus on reactions to the ad itself, the impact of the ad on the perception of the product is also investigated. Exhibit 20-1 presents a prototypical marketing research proposal for a print ad test.

Print ad tests Attempts to assess the power of an ad placed in a magazine or newspaper to be remembered, to communicate, to affect attitudes, and to ultimately produce sales.

Philosophy and Objectives

Put simply, the objective in print ad tests is to make go/no-go decisions regarding the test advertisement. Print ad-testing procedures, which are typically applicable across all brands, provide comparative data that can be used as norms to judge proposed advertisements. For example, in the print ad described in Exhibit 20-1, the new Soft Touch "Soft Drop" print ad will be compared to a past Soft Touch "Lulu" ad tested approximately six months previously.

E X H I B I T 20-1

Print Ad Test: Marketing Research Project Proposal

Brand:	Soft Touch Hand Lotion
Project:	"Soft Drop" print test

Background and Objectives:

A new Soft Touch "Soft Drop" print ad was developed in March 1986 and made available for testing. The Soft Touch "Lulu" ad was tested via the Mapes & Ross print copy test method in September 1985.

The purpose of this research is to determine the effectiveness of the "Soft Drop" ad in generating attention and purchase persuasion relative to the past "Lulu" ad.

Research Design:

The Mapes & Ross print test method will be used. The ad will appear in the May 1986 issue of *Good Housekeeping*. The sample will consist of 200 women, aged 18–65, who are regular readers of women's service magazines *(Family Circle, Good Housekeeping, Ladies' Home Journal, McCalls, Redbook, Woman's Day)*, and have *not* read the *Good Housekeeping* test issue. The test issue will be placed with randomly selected women using door-to-door interviews. Each respondent will be asked to read the magazine as they normally would.

When the test issue is placed, brand preferences for hand and body lotions, and other product categories will be obtained (pre-print exposure). The next day respondents will be recontacted by telephone, and will be asked to describe at least one article as proof of readership. They will then be asked the same brand preference questions as the day before (post-print exposure), and additionally, will be asked to recall and describe six ads appearing in the magazine, including the Soft Touch ad.

Information to be Obtained:

Pre-exposure interview:

- Qualifying demographics
- Brand preference (hand and body lotions plus five additional product categories)

Post-exposure interview:

- Brand preference (hand and body lotions plus five additional product categories)
- Proven recall
- Recall content

Action Standard:

The "Soft Drop" copy approach will be recommended if it performs *significantly higher** than the "Lulu" ad on each of the following measures:

      Brand preference (pre–post) shift
      Proven recall

*Significant difference at the 90 percent or higher level of confidence.

| *Cost &* | The cost for this research will be $6,000 $\pm$ 10 percent. |
| *Timing:* | Time schedule for this research will be: |

	Field work	1 Week
	Top-line	2 Weeks
	Computer tabulations	2 Weeks
	Final report	1 Week
	Total	6 Weeks

| *Research* | Mapes & Ross |
| *Supplier:* | |

Research Design

The research design used in print testing depends on the shape and context in which the ad is presented to the respondent. The four basic types of research designs are described below.[1]

Single Ad. In a **single ad research design** the respondent is exposed to the test ad by itself; that is, the test ad is not shown with other ads, and is not displayed in a magazine. There are two approaches with this type of research design.

- **"Headline" tests.** In headline tests, the focus is on the ad itself. Usually, the respondent is shown two or more headlines and is then asked to indicate the one that is most interesting. After selecting the most interesting headline, the respondent is shown the corresponding ad and asked the usual diagnostics. The advantage of this research design is its approximation to reality; it is reasonable to expect that before a print ad is "seen," the headline must capture the person's attention.
- **Forced exposure tests.** In forced exposure tests, pre- and post-exposure purchase-preference questions are asked. Before the respondent is exposed to the test ad, a purchase-intention question is asked. After exposure to the test ad the respondent is again asked the purchase-intention question and the top-box (or top-two-box) percentages "pre" and "post" are compared. The difference in these percentages is said to reflect the ad's **attitude-shift ability** (that is, the ad's persuasiveness). Thus, this type of research design focuses on the ad's effect on perceptions of the product.

Multiple Ads. In this research design, commonly referred to as **portfolio tests,** an array of ads is prepared. In the portfolio, which resembles a book, each ad is presented on its own page. One of the ads in the portfolio is the test ad; some of the other ads are from the same product

[1]The discussion in this section follows that of Holbert et al., *Marketing Research for the Marketing and Advertising Executive* (American Marketing Association, New York Chapter, Inc., 1981), Chapter 10, pp. 196–199.

Single ad research design Test where respondent is exposed to the test ad by itself; that is, the test ad is not shown with other ads, and it is not displayed in a magazine.

"Headline" test Design where the respondent is shown two or more headlines and is then asked to indicate the one that is most interesting.

Forced exposure tests Design where pre- and post-exposure purchase-preference questions are asked.

Attitude-shift ability The difference between the percentage of the program audience who selected the test brand before viewing the ad or commercial and the percentage who selected it after viewing.

Multiple ads/portfolio tests Test where respondent examines a portfolio of ads, one of which is the test ad.

category and some are frequently from other product categories. The respondent is given the portfolio and asked to leaf through it. After the respondent examines the portfolio, it is taken away and an unaided-recall questioning period begins. Here interest centers on which brands the respondent recalls being advertised and specific information concerning the recalled ads. The test continues by exposing the respondent to the test ad again. The respondent is then asked about specific brand information contained in the ad and its believability. The weakness of portfolio testing lies in its unrealistic settings and the forced (aided) question format feature of this method. On the positive side, it is inexpensive and quick and can be easily interpreted if norms have been developed.

"Dummy-magazine" tests
A test format using a dummy magazine that looks realistic, and which systematically varies the advertisements in such a way that some families receive a dummy magazine containing the test ad and other (matched) families receive a dummy magazine containing no ads at all.

"Dummy-Magazine" Tests. In this research design the effectiveness of the test ad is evaluated before the respondent realizes that he or she is participating in a copy test. Though there are several different ways to implement this design, a typical approach is to print a dummy magazine that looks realistic (that is, contains articles, pictures, editorials, and so on) and systematically vary the advertisements in such a way that some families receive a dummy magazine containing the test ad(s) and other (matched) families receive a dummy magazine containing no ads at all. Several days after placing the dummy magazines in respondent's homes, the respondent is asked a "buffer" question relating to how he or she liked the magazine and product-centered rating questions relating to information presented in the test ads. The product-centered rating questions can be used to make comparisons (such as attitude-shift scores) across the "exposed" and "unexposed" groups. Frequently, recall and comprehension questions are also asked after the product ratings have been collected.

"Real-magazine" tests
Test where interest centers on the "magazine" effect—that is, the context in which the ad appears.
Home placement Test where the current issue of a magazine is given to the respondent one or two days before the issue is scheduled to be available to the general public; at call-back the respondent is asked to indicate all of the ads that were in the issue and specific information on what each ad contains.

"Real-Magazine" Tests. In real-magazine print ad tests, interest centers on the "magazine" effect, that is, the context in which the ad appears. There are two popular varieties of real-magazine testing studies.

- **Home placement.** In this research design readers of a particular magazine are identified. The current issue of the magazine is given to the respondent one or two days before the issue is scheduled to be available to the general public. At the time of placement, each respondent is informed of an intended telephone or personal call-back that will take place the following day in order to ask more questions about the issue.

  In ad-centered home placement tests nothing is specifically said about the test ad. At the time of call-back the respondent is simply asked to indicate all of the ads that were in the issue and specific information on what each ad contains (such as picture, headline, and so forth). Frequently, an "aided" question format is used in which the interviewer asks about the test ad, some other ad, or all ads appearing in the issue. In product-centered home placement tests, the procedure is the same except that at the time of placement, the interviewer asks the respondent for purchase-intention ratings. At call-back, the interviewer asks standard unaided recall, aided recall, and diagnostic questions, and then at the end of the interview asks the purchase-intention questions again. The percentage difference between the "pre" (placement) interview and the "post" (call-back) interview intention scores for the test brand are used as a measure of effectiveness.

- **"Starch" scores.** In this research design, named after Daniel Starch, readers of specific magazines are located and the interviewer determines whether each ad in the issue was remembered; whether the name of the brand or advertiser was read; and whether a substantial portion of the advertisement was read. Based upon this information, the Starch service provides index scores (such as the basic "Recognition Index" report) and other normed data.

"Starch" scores Research design where readers of specific magazines are located and the interviewer determines whether each ad in the issue was remembered, whether the name of the brand or advertiser was read, and whether a substantial portion of the advertisement was read.

Questions Asked

As we indicated, the information collected in print ad tests typically relates to reactions to the ad itself and/or the effects the ad had on perceptions of the product. Typically, interest centers on four key measures:

1. **Recall.** A primary indicator of ad effectiveness is how many people remember having seen the test ad both on an unaided and aided basis. Frequently a **proven total recall** score is computed which gives the percentage of respondents who correctly recalled specific copy or visual elements in the test ad. In addition, specific details on what each respondent saw are also collected. Exhibit 20-2 shows prototypical unaided and aided brand-recall question formats for the print ad test described in Exhibit 20-1.

Recall Measures of how many people remember having seen the test ad both on an unaided and aided basis.
Proven total recall Percentage of respondents in the program audience that correctly recalled copy or visual elements in the test ad or commercial.

E X H I B I T 20-2

Unaided and Aided Question Formats for a Print Ad Test

Unaided Questions

1a. Now, I'd like to change your attention to the ads that appeared in this magazine. Do you remember seeing any ads in this particular magazine for *(fill in product category form below)?* If Yes: What brand of _____ was advertised?

(Note: Record respondent's answer exactly, as close to their pronunciation as possible and/or any remark made on the name. Probe for specific name and type. Repeat for all product categories. Probe for mention of brands advertised in each category until the respondent cannot remember any more brands advertised in that category.)

A. **Pantyhose**

( )YES ( )NO

_____

Brand name (probe for as many
    brands as
    respondent can
    remember.)

_____

Brand name (probe for as many
    brands as
    respondent can
    remember.)

_____

Brand name (probe for as many
    brands as
    respondent can
    remember.)

B. **Toaster ovens**

( )YES ( )NO

_____

Brand name (probe for as many
    brands as
    respondent can
    remember.)

_____

Brand name (probe for as many
    brands as
    respondent can
    remember.)

_____

Brand name (probe for as many
    brands as
    respondent can
    remember.)

C. **Lotions for your body**

( )YES ( )NO

_____

Brand name (probe for as many
    brands as
    respondent can
    remember.)

_____

Brand name (probe for as many
    brands as
    respondent can
    remember.)

_____

Brand name (probe for as many
    brands as
    respondent can
    remember.)

D. **Cosmetic or cosmetic
   studios**   ( )YES ( )NO

_____

Brand name (probe for as many
    brands as
    respondent can
    remember.)

_____

Brand name (probe for as many
    brands as
    respondent can
    remember.)

_____

Brand name (probe for as many
    brands as
    respondent can
    remember.)

E. **Bras**

( )YES ( )NO

_____

Brand name (probe for as many
    brands as
    respondent can
    remember.)

_____

Brand name (probe for as many
    brands as
    respondent can
    remember.)

F. **Men's underwear**

( )YES ( )NO

_____

Brand name (probe for as many
    brands as
    respondent can
    remember.)

_____

Brand name (probe for as many
    brands as
    respondent can
    remember.)

Brand name (probe for as many
brands as
respondent can
remember.)

Brand name (probe for as many
brands as
respondent can
remember.)

Aided Questions

1b. Next, I would like to read off the names of some of the ads in this issue.
Please tell me whether or not you recall seeing them. Please say "yes" for
each ad where you can actually recall some part of the illustration or the
printing well enough to picture it in your mind. *Read the ad list slowly. Give*
the respondent plenty of time to think about each ad. Remind her that we are
only interested in the ads as they appeared in this particular issue.

		YES	NO
	1( ) L'Eggs Sheer Elegance pantyhose	1( )	2( )
Start	2( ) Proctor-Silex toaster oven	1( )	2( )
with	3( ) Johnson's baby lotion	1( )	2( )
item	4( ) Merle Norman cosmetics	1( )	2( )
checked	5(√) Support Can Be Beautiful bras	1( )	2( )
	6( ) Jockey men's underwear	1( )	2( )

2. **Recognition.** Interest typically centers on whether the respondent
can recognize the name of the test brand. For example, a standard
practice is to cut out the name of the brand or the package, or any
other identifying feature, and then ask the respondent to indicate
what the ad is for. Eye-movement copy-testing services are essentially recognition tests in that the purpose is to identify which parts
of the ad the eye moved over.

3. **Diagnostics.** Standard diagnostic questions generally include measures of **believability** and **comprehension**—was the main idea of
the ad believable? Was there any information in the ad that you did
not understand? Diagnostic testing may also include direct evaluation of the ad on bipolar adjective scales. This information is used
to determine the percentage of respondents rating the ad as
"clever," "dull," and so forth and can be compared with normed
data, if available.

4. **Product perceptions.** These questions relate to the ad's effect on
perceptions and/or purchase intentions concerning the test brand.
In product-centered print ad tests, a "pre" (placement) and "post"
(call-back) procedure is used.

Sampling

Interviewing is usually conducted in several geographically dispersed markets with a minimum of 150 respondents per advertisement.
For subgroup analysis, no fewer than 50 respondents are typically used.

Recognition Score
measuring whether the
respondent can recognize
the name of the test
brand.

Diagnostics Measures of
believability and
comprehension.
Diagnostic testing may
also include direct
evaluation of the ad,
perhaps on bipolar
adjective scales.
Comprehension/
believability Percentage of
respondents in the
program audience that
correctly understood/
believed product claims
communicated in the test
commercial.
Product perceptions
Questions relating to the
ad's effect on perceptions
and/or purchase
intentions concerning the
test brand.

Action Standard

The action standards in prototypical print ad tests are specified in terms of the copy-testing service's norms. For example, a typical action standard might say that the advertisement will be recommended if it generates proven total recall levels equal to or better than the norm and/or generates pre-post "Best or Better Brand" levels equal to or better than the norm. Note that in the print ad test marketing research proposal presented in Exhibit 20-1, the action standard is specified with respect to the comparative base "Lulu" ad.

Approach to Analysis

The analysis centers on proven recall and brand preference. Diagnostic measures are secondary.

TELEVISION COMMERCIAL TESTS

Television advertising is much more expensive than print advertising. For example, a 30-second airtime spot on the 1986 Super Bowl Program cost $550,000. Because of this, commercial copy-testing services have become big business. The number of commercial copy-testing services has grown dramatically over the past twenty years. Today, the number of techniques used to evaluate the effectiveness of television commercials is far too large to list. In this section we provide a general overview of television-commercial testing procedures.

Philosophy and Objectives

A television commercial can serve many different purposes. Ultimately it sells the product by conveying a specific appeal to an intended target audience. To accomplish this the television commercial must (1) attract attention, (2) register brand name and packaging, (3) communicate meaningful benefits, and (4) motivate purchase. Put simply, television-commercial testing seeks to determine whether the commercial under study succeeds in doing what it is intended to do. To be more specific, the objectives of television-commercial tests are to

1. Measure the commercial's intrusiveness—attention/recall.
2. Measure what is communicated—comprehension/believability.
3. Measure the impact of the commercial on purchase interest and brand attitudes.

Note that the relative importance of each of these measures will vary depending on the type of commercial being tested. For example, in the case of a new-product introduction, intrusiveness and comprehension may be more important than attitude shift.

Research Design

Methods for evaluating television commercials can be divided into two broad types: *off-air* and *on-air*. **Off-air tests** are "artificial" since the testing takes place in a controlled environment that does not resemble the surroundings in which the individual usually views commercials—that is, in one's home. Off-air tests are used to evaluate the commercial's communication effectiveness before it goes on the air. In contrast, **on-air tests** take place in realistic settings; respondents are asked their reactions to commercials that they have seen in their own home, on their own television sets. At the time of viewing the commercial, the respondent does not know that he or she will be questioned about what they saw.

Off-Air Tests. These tests are designed to evaluate a commercial before it is aired in order to effect changes in the commercials that make it more effective. Off-air testing can take place almost anywhere—in theaters, in shopping malls, in mobile vans, or even in the person's own home using projectors that resemble television sets. Exhibit 20-3 presents a prototypical off-air test marketing research proposal.

Off-air tests Method for evaluating television commercials where the testing takes place in a controlled environment that does not resemble the surroundings in which the individual usually views commercials.

On-air tests Testing that takes place in realistic settings; respondents are asked their reactions to commercials that they have seen in their own homes, on their own television sets.

E X H I B I T 20-3

Off-Air Test Marketing Research Project Proposal

Brand: Colgate

Project: Copy Test "Midnight Delight"

Background and Purpose: A new commercial has been developed—"Midnight Delight." Brand Group is interested in determining its effectiveness.

The objectives of this study will be to determine:
- Brand recall
- Copy recall
- Purchase-intent shifts
- Comparison with previous copy-testing results

Research Method: This research will be conducted using central location mall facilities in Boston, Atlanta, Milwaukee, and San Francisco.

Each commercial will be viewed by 200 past-30-week toothpaste users as follows:

		Age group	Number of respondents
Males	50%	8–11	30
Females	50%	12–17	50
		18–24	25
		25–34	25
		35–49	10
		50 +	10
			150

Action Standard:	This study will be done for information purposes in order to be used in conjunction with previous copy-testing results.
Information to be Obtained:	■ Brand recall ■ Copy recall ■ Pre- and post-purchase interest
Cost and Timing:	The cost for one commercial will be $6,500 ± 10%. The following schedule will be established:

Fieldwork	3 weeks
Top-line	1 week
Final report	3 weeks
Total	7 weeks

Supplier:	Market Facts, Inc.

A popular setting for conducting *off-air* tests is in a theater. Respondents are invited to come to a local theater and view "pilots" of future new television programs. Inserted into the program are several commercials. Before viewing the program each respondent is asked brand-preference information for a number of product categories, including the test-product category, under the pretense of a drawing in which the respondent will receive the product, or cost of the product for which he or she has the strongest preference. After viewing the program (and commercials), respondents are once again asked to express their brand preferences. A "prepost" measure of effectiveness is used to evaluate the test commercial. The attitude shift effect is computed by taking the difference between the percentage of respondents who selected the test brand before viewing the commercial and the percentage who selected it after viewing the commercial. Attitude-shift scores are compared with norms—results of past tests. Typically, comprehension and recall measures are also collected. Two of the best known research firms offering this type of copy-testing service are McCollum/Spielman and Research Systems Corporation.

Tele-Research offers a different type of *off-air* copy testing service. In this approach respondents are intercepted as they enter food stores. In conveniently located trailers, respondents view a series of commercials, one of which is the test commercial; as a reward the respondents are given a book of money-off coupons, one (or more) of which is for the test brand. A control group of respondents is used. They receive the book of coupons but do not view the commercials. The measure of commercial effectiveness used is the difference between the purchase incidence of respondents who viewed the commercials and those who did not.

On-Air Tests. These tests are designed to evaluate a commercial after it has been placed on the air in order to assess whether the commercial does what it is supposed to do in a normal competitive environment.

Two types of *on-air* testing can be distinguished: *on-air single exposure* tests and *on-air multiple* tests.

One of the best known of the single-exposure techniques is **day-after recall.** With this technique, the test commercial is aired in several (three to four) test cities. The next day, a sample of respondents who say they viewed the program on which the test commercial was telecast are interviewed. Viewers of the program are questioned, on an unaided and aided basis, about whether they saw the commercial, and if so, what it said. These measures are compared with norms (such as recall scores for other products in the same or a similar category) in order to judge the relative effectiveness of the test commercial. Two of the best known research firms specializing in day-after recall are Burke Marketing Research and Mapes & Ross. Exhibits 20-4 and 20-5 present illustrative marketing research proposals for these two copy-testing services.

Multiple-exposure techniques attempt to give a better indication of the test commercial's sales effectiveness. In this approach, the test commercial is aired in a test city (or cities) over time. Periodic on-air tests are conducted along with store audits of sales. Controlled cable test services have recently become very popular. With this technique, one campaign is aired in homes in one city, or one side of town, or one side of a city block, and so on, and another campaign is aired in the home of a matched sample. Thus, through repeated (over time) measures of recall and store audits for each group of viewers the relative effectiveness of each campaign can be judged.

Day-after recall (DAR) Single exposure on-air technique where the test commercial is aired in several test cities; the next day, a sample of respondents who say they viewed the program on which the test commercial was telecast are interviewed.

Multiple-exposure techniques Technique where the test commercial is aired in a test city (or cities) over time; periodic on-air tests are conducted along with store audits of sales.

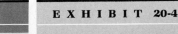

E X H I B I T   20-4

Mapes & Ross 24-Hour Recall Marketing Research Project Proposal

Brand: Schick Moisturizing After Shave

Project: "Cruiser" Mapes & Ross on-air test

Background and Objectives: The Agency has developed a pool-out of the "Macho Feel" campaign, "Cruiser." The commercial will be available in photomatic form.

The objectives of this test will be:

- To measure the commercial's effectiveness in generating attention (related recall).
- To measure the commercial's effectiveness in purchase persuasion (pre/post brand preference).
- To measure the commercial's effectiveness in communicating the key copy points—"Leaves Skin Feeling Good" and "Gives Me Masculine Scent."

Research Design: The traditional Mapes & Ross on-air test method will be used. The sample will consist of 200 male respondents, age 18 and older, in the program audience. The sample specifications will follow recent "Macho Feel" and Mapes & Ross on-air tests. The data will be broken out by 18–34, 35–49, and 50–65 year olds as they fall naturally in the program audience.

The commercial will be shown in Philadelphia, Kansas City, and San Francisco on UHF television channels using movie programs. There will be *one* commercial exposure. In each of the three metropolitan areas, interviewers will telephone a sample of men, age 18 and over, and invite them to view the test program that night. As part of the invitation phase, respondents will be asked for their brand preference (pre-purchase brand preference of Schick Moisturizing After Shave).

The follow-up telephone interviews the *next day* will probe whether the prerecruited respondents watched the program. Next, brand preference (post-purchase brand preference of Schick Moisturizing After Shave) will be repeated to observe the extent to which viewers changed their preference for the brand in the test commercial.

Then respondents will be asked what they recalled about the Schick Moisturizing After Shave commercial followed by rating the brand described in the commercial on product attributes.

Information to be Obtained:

1. Related (proven) recall—percent of respondents in the program audience that correctly recalled one or more copy and/or visual elements in the commercial ("attention" score).
2. Copy/visual recall
3. Pre/post brand preference for Schick Moisturizing After Shave ("purchase persuasion" score).
4. Attribute ratings
   - Makes skin feel good
   - Gives masculine scent
   - Attractive to opposite sex
   - Doesn't burn
   - Doesn't sting
   - Helps nicks or cuts
   - Long lasting scent
   - Contains sun screen

Action Standard:

The "Cruiser" commercial will be compared to the original "Macho Shave" animatic commercial and the Mapes & Ross norms on the following measures:

	Macho Feel	Mapes & Ross All Products Norm
Proven recall	18%	21%
Percent recalling "Leave Skin Feeling Good"	35%	—
Percent recalling "Gives Me Masculine Scent"	28%	—

Pre/post brand preference—Total Respondents	+16.4	+8.1
Pre/post brand preference—Age 18–34	+5.9	—

If the commercial scores below the above scores for the original "Macho Feel" commercial and the Mapes & Ross norms, we will not move forward with the test commercial. Additionally, if "Cruiser" scores lower than "Macho Feel" on pre/post brand preference in the 18–34 age group, we will not move forward with the new commercial.

*Timing and
Cost:*

The time schedule for this research will be:

1½ weeks to set up test/insert commercial into UHF
    movie programs
1   day fieldwork
1   week top-line
2   weeks computer tabulations
2   weeks final report
———————————————————————————
7½ weeks total

The cost for this research will be $11,250 ± 10 percent.

Supplier: Mapes & Ross

E X H I B I T   20-5

**Burke 24-hour-recall Marketing Research
Project Proposal**

Brand: Juicy Fruit

Project: "False Start" Burke on-air test

*Background
and
Objectives:*   The William Wrigley Co. has requested a Burke on-air test for the new copy execution "False Start."

The objective of this research is to measure the communication effectiveness of the "False Start" execution.

*Research
Method:*   A sample of 150 past-30-day chewing gum users in the commerical audience will be interviewed. The air date is scheduled for Tuesday, December 9, on "Moonlighting." Interviewing will be conducted within five metro areas: Boston, Atlanta, Indianapolis, Dallas, and Phoenix.

*Information to
be Obtained:*   ■ Total commerical recall
■ Copy recall
■ Visual recall

*Action
Standard:*   The commercial will be considered acceptable in the areas of memorability and sales message communication if:

(a) it generates 25% or better related recall score,
(b) at least 25% of the commercial audience remembers at least one sales message.

Timing and Cost:	Fieldwork	December 9
	Top-line	December 16
	Final report	January 15

The cost for this research will be $15,000 ± 10%

Research Supplier: Burke Marketing Research

Questions Asked

Though the specific questions asked will depend on which commercial copy-testing service is being used, there are a number of common measures collected in most television commercial tests. Several of these are

1. **Proven total recall**—percentage of respondents in the program audience that correctly recalled copy or visual elements in the test commercial.
2. **Copy recall**—percentage of respondents in the program audience that correctly recalled copy elements in the test commercial.
3. **Visual recall**—percentage of respondents in the program audience that correctly recalled visual elements in the test commercial.
4. **Comprehension/believability**—percentage of respondents in the program audience that correctly understood/believed product claims communicated in the test commercial.
5. **Attitude shift**—the difference between the percentage of the program audience who selected the test brand before viewing the commercial and the percentage who selected it after viewing the commercial.

It is important to note that the specific questions asked are standardized for each copy-testing service so that comparable norms can be developed.

Copy recall Percentage of respondents in the program audience that correctly recalled copy elements in the test commercial.

Visual recall Percentage of respondents in the program audience that correctly recalled visual elements in the test commercial.

Sampling

Sampling practices vary depending on the research design used. In general, interviews are conducted on a minimum of 150 respondents per commercial who are 30-day past users of the product category. Where appropriate, age and gender quotas are based on category volume contribution. The specific test cities used will depend on which copy-testing service is being used and whether the commercial is being tested on-air or off-air. Standard test cities will be discussed in Chapter 21.

Action Standards

The action standards in prototypical television commercial tests are expressed in terms of the copy-testing services' norms or with respect to a specific previous copy test. Each copy-testing service has developed data banks on the effectiveness (that is, recall, attitude-shift, and so forth) of ads across a large number of product categories. For example, in Exhibit 20-4 we see that the Mapes & Ross's all-products norm for proven recall is 21 percent. Thus, a commercial achieving a proven recall score of 30 percent would be viewed as above-average.

Approach to Analysis

Once again the analysis centers on recall and brand preference. As in print testing, diagnostic measures are secondary.

Summary

In this chapter we have described the standard copy-testing procedures used to evaluate the effectiveness of print ads and television commercials. In addition, we have discussed the copy-testing services offered by many of the leading research firms in the industry.

Key Concepts

Copy testing
Print ad tests
Single ad research design
"Headline" test
Forced exposure tests
Multiple ads/portfolio tests
"Dummy magazine" tests

"Real magazine" tests
Home placement
Off-air tests
On-air tests
Day-after recall (DAR)
Multiple-exposure techniques

Review Questions

1. Discuss the issue of ad effectiveness.
2. Describe the basic types of research designs used in the copy-testing print ad tests.
3. What information is usually collected in print ad tests?
4. Discuss the objectives of television commercial tests. Does the importance of each objective vary with the type of commercial being tested?
5. Describe the basic types of research designs used in evaluating television commercials.

CHAPTER

Test Market Studies

CHAPTER OBJECTIVES

■ Describe the information provided by good test market programs.
■ Define the basic steps in test market studies.
■ Explain the procedures used in standard test market audits and controlled test market audits.
■ Discuss and provide a comparative survey of simulated test market services.

Introduction

Because of the highly competitive and risky nature of most product-markets today, management is no longer responsible just for making profits but also for maximizing the company's return on investment (ROI). New-product introductions play a crucial role in determining a company's financial viability and are in fact the lifeblood of most companies. And all indicators are that management expects "new" products to contribute more to profits in five years than they do now.

Unfortunately, however, according to published data about 80 percent of new packaged goods introductions fail and approximately one-third of all nationally distributed new products are withdrawn from the market within one year after introduction. These failure estimates are even more alarming in light of the whole range of marketing research activities (such as concept tests and product tests) that occur prior to national launch. Data indicate that 65 percent of new-product funds are spent on marginal or losing brands.[1] Because not all new-product introductions will eventually succeed, new-product introductions must typically have projected ROI in the 30–40 percent range.

Test market services are designed to help marketing managers make the right decision concerning new products and additions or revisions to existing product lines. The primary purpose of test market studies is

[1]Figures reported by Burke Marketing Services, Inc.

to provide a real-world, in-market exposure for evaluting a product and its marketing program. By using a test market service the marketing manager has the ability to take a proposed national program with all of its separate elements and evaluate them in a smaller, less expensive situation with a view toward determining whether the potential profit opportunity from rolling out the new product or line extension outweighs the potential risks. Good test market programs provide information on such factors as

- Market share of product and/or volume estimates
- Who is buying the product, how often, and for what purpose
- From where purchases are made, and at what price
- What changes in strategy were made by the competition
- What effect the new item has on already-established lines

Test markets are, however, not cheap. Average costs can run over $800,000.

In addition to traditional test markets, this chapter also considers the burgeoning area of simulated test marketing. Simulated test marketing usually involves exposing a few hundred respondents to a commercial or story board for a proposed new product, giving them an opportunity to buy the product, and then following up with telephone interviews with those who used the product to measure their reaction and repeat-purchase intention. Based on these data and other management-supplied information on specific marketing elements, market share and/or volume estimates are projected (that is, forecasted). As we will see, a simulated test market saves time and money and has changed what is looked for in a test market.

Typically, test market results, whether real or simulated, involve a model used to forecast the new product's market share or volume at rollout. Standard forecasting methods will be discussed in Appendix 22-A.

TO TEST OR NOT TO TEST?

Test marketing offers a firm two important benefits:

1. It provides an opportunity to obtain a measure of a product's sales performance under reasonably natural market conditions. As a by-product, management can predict the product's likely national market share, and this forms the basis of the decision about whether to rollout the product nationally.
2. It provides an opportunity, prior to full distribution, for management to identify and correct product or marketing strategy weaknesses, which would be much more difficult and expensive to correct after national rollout.

Despite these benefits, certain issues need to be considered before a decision to test market is made. Test marketing has both direct and indirect costs. Direct costs of test marketing include product costs and marketing investment. Indirect costs involve (1) opportunity costs—revealing a new product idea to a competitor, (2) exposure costs—the name of the company is exposed along with the brand, and (3) internal costs—diversion of employee time and activities (rarely quantified when the cost of the test market is estimated). In essence, whether to test market is a trade-off between reducing uncertainty by collecting additional information at considerable direct and indirect cost and immediately introducing the product nationally by avoiding any delays.

At least four major factors should be considered in determining the efficacy of test marketing:[2]

1. It is necessary to weigh the cost and risk of product failure against the profit and probability of success. If the costs and risks of product failure are low, then a national launch should be considered. On the other hand, high costs coupled with great uncertainty favor the test market approach.

2. The difference in the scale of investment involved in the test versus national launch route has an important bearing on deciding whether to test. If very little difference in manufacturing investment is called for whether a test or national launch is undertaken, then the investment risk favors the national launch approach. On the other hand, where plant investment for a national launch is considerable, but only slight for a test market, the investment risk favors the test launch approach.

3. Another factor to be considered is the likelihood and speed with which the competition will be able to copy your product and preempt part of your national market or overseas market; where they have the technology, they will be developing their own versions of your product—and marketing it if you leave the opportunity open for them to do so.

4. In addition to the investment in plant and machinery that may be involved, every new-product launch is accompanied by a substantial marketing investment that varies with the scale of the launch. Typically, new-product launches call for heavy advertising and promotional expenditure; they require sales-force time, attention, and effort; and they need shelf space in wholesale and retail outlets, sometimes obtained only at the expense of the space already given to the company's existing products. Moreover, if a new product fails, such costs as rebating and reclaiming unwanted stock from customers must be incurred, along with writeoff costs of dealing with unwanted and unusable materials and packaging. Management should also take into account the possible damage that a new product's failure can inflict on the company's reputation, which is a real if not quantifiable cost.

[2]The following discussion was taken from N. D. Cadbury, "When, Where and How to Test Market," *Harvard Business Review*, May-June 1985, 97–98.

BASIC STEPS IN TEST MARKET STUDIES

Once a decision has been made to test a proposed new product or line extension, a number of basic steps should be followed to achieve the desired results with minimum use of time and money.[3] The basic steps outlined below should be followed in sequence and no steps should be omitted.

Step 1: Define Objective

The first step in defining the objectives of a test market is to closely examine the product to be tested. The product being tested could be:

1. A "me too" product—essentially the same as the other brands currently on the market; for example, another women's hair removal cream, basically the same as a dozen others already available.
2. An improved product—an improvement over the other brands currently on the market; for example, a women's hair removal shave cream with a new ingredient that prevents hair growth for up to two weeks.
3. A category extension—a "new" type of brand as compared to other brands currently on the market; for example, a women's hair removal shave cream that disposes of leg and arm hair without the need of a razor and has a "fresh" scent.
4. A "never before" product—the product being tested may be a totally new and unique product, not currently available on the market; for example, a new "pill" taken once every two weeks that retards the growth of arm and leg hair for up to fourteen days.

Obviously, there is a relationship between the type of new product that is to be tested and the risks and rewards associated with ultimate market failure or success. If, for example, the proposed new product entry is a "me too" item, its introduction will require far less cost and time than if the product were a "never before" item requiring a much longer diffusion process.

Typical test market objectives are to project (forecast) such key market indicators as (a) dollar and unit sales volume, and (b) dollar and unit shares. Frequently, these indicators are supplemented by forecasts of inventories and measure of shelf location, facings, price variation, promotion activity, and demographic factors. In effect, test markets measure what is happening in the marketplace at the retail level.

---

[3]This section is based upon material found in *A Telling Look at the 27 Most Frequently Used Test Markets*, Volume III (New York: New York Times Publishing Company, 1982).

Step 2: Plan Strategy

Manufacturing and distribution decisions must be given immediate attention. Once management has decided how the proposed new-product entry will be manufactured, consideration turns to how it will be promoted in the marketplace. With a "me too" product, advertising is crucial, since—in large measure—positioning, strategy, and execution determine its market success or failure. On the other hand, with a "never before" product it is important to get the new entry into the hands of those individuals who will believe the veracity of the advertiser's claims and will have favorable evaluations. Free samples and high-value cents-off coupons can prove to be effective inducements.

Media selection is another important part of developing an overall testing strategy. For example, if the national media plan for a new product uses magazines, then the test market area must have a representative sampling of print so that the necessary projections can be made. Weekend magazines and TV guides published by local newspapers frequently serve as surrogates for national magazines in test markets. Newspapers are particularly effective for ads that require a large amount of explanatory information and for coupons with short expiration dates. Newspapers also have relatively comprehensive reach in their specific geographic area. Finally, no test market area would be selected if it did not have at least three commercial TV stations and some cable TV penetration.

Step 3: Determine Methodology

Having determined the objectives of the test and an appropriate strategy, including a media plan, the next step is to determine the type of test market method that is consistent with the stated objectives; in other words, *how* the test will be conducted and *who* will do the actual testing and auditing. Test markets are a form of field experimentation. In test markets, management attempts to manipulate certain marketing elements while holding others constant in a real-world environment. Consequently, the issues and methods discussed under experimental design in Chapter 6 are extremely important.

There are three general methods from which to choose. Each method described below will be discussed in greater detail later in this chapter.

Simulated test market
Method where various groups of preselected respondents are interviewed, monitored and sampled with the new product; in addition, respondents may be exposed to various media messages in a controlled environment.

1. **The simulated test market.** As we discussed earlier, simulated test markets do not involve an actual "test market," at least not in the traditional sense. Instead, various groups of preselected respondents are interviewed, monitored, and sampled with the new product; in addition, respondents may be exposed to various media messages in a controlled environment. The objective of simulated test markets is to project (forecast) what the new product would do if rolled out nationally.

2. **The standard test market.** With this method, the company's own sales force would be responsible for distributing the new product in the selected test market areas. Sales force personnel would stock the shelves and return at periodic intervals to restock and count movement.

3. **The control test market.** With this method, the entire test market project is handled by an outside research company. The control method includes *mini-market* (or *forced distribution*) tests as well as smaller controlled store panels. The research company handling the test guarantees distribution of the new product in stores that represent a predetermined percentage of the market—hence the term *controlled store panel*. They provide warehouse facilities and use their own field representatives to sell the product and are responsible for shelf-stocking and count movement. Because the guaranteed distribution allows marketing managers to begin advertising and promotion two weeks after a retailer agrees to stock the new product (instead of the usual 60 to 90 days it takes to go through regular distribution channels), faster readings are possible. Controlled store testing can be conducted by electronic or manual auditing. Behaviorscan, AdTel, and Erim are leaders in electronic audit services. Recall that we discussed electronic scanner services in Chapter 4. Market Facts, Market Audits, and Burgoyne provide traditional controlled store audits.

Standard test market
Method where the company's own sales force is responsible for distributing the new product in the selected test market areas. Sales force personnel would stock the shelves and return at periodic intervals to restock and count movement.

Control test market
Method where the entire test market project is handled by an outside research company.

Step 4: Select Markets

Where to test the proposed new product is obviously one of the most important questions facing the marketing manager. Figure 21-1 presents Dancer Fitzgerald's sample list of recommended test markets. The clear trend in test market selecting has been to locate mid-size cities that reflect national demographics. Test market overuse has not been a pressing concern. Most marketing professionals feel that as long as the testing is conducted properly (that is, unobtrusively) the respondent will rarely know that he or she is involved in a test.

There appear to be four overriding factors to consider in selecting a test market:

1. *Number of markets to use.* The more markets that can be used, the better. Results will be more reliable and a greater number of variations can be tested. Geographically dispersed markets should be used whenever possible. When testing an existing product, the general approach is to use a "matched market" strategy in which two markets are chosen for their similarities on several selection criteria such as demography, geography, climate, category image, and competitive brand use.

2. *Size of markets to use.* Reliability and cost are the key here; selected markets should be large enough to give reliable results, but

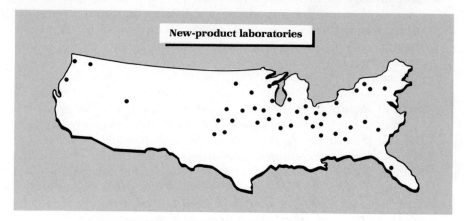

Dancer Fitzgerald Sample's preferred test markets

Area	% U.S. house-holds	TV house-holds	Area	% U.S. house-holds	TV house-holds
1. Cleveland	1.64	1,395.1	22. Albany-Schenectady-Troy, N.Y.	0.56	477.1
2. Pittsburgh	1.44	1.299.0	23. Tulsa, Okla.	0.54	459.2
3. Minneapolis-St. Paul	1.36	1,155.9	24. Wichita-Hutchinson, Kan.	0.50	421.8
4. Seattle-Tacoma	1.33	1,133.7	25. Toledo, O.	0.48	409.3
5. St. Louis	1.22	1,041.0	26. Des Moines, Ia.	0.43	368.8
6. Portland, Ore.	0.92	784.4	27. Syracuse, N.Y.	0.43	364.6
7. Indianapolis	0.92	782.9	28. Green Bay, Wis.	0.42	353.1
8. Cincinnati	0.84	716.4	29. Roanoke-Lynchburg, Va.	0.41	348.3
9. Kansas City, Mo.	0.82	698.6	30. Springfield-Decatur-Champaign, Ill.	0.41	348.1
10. Milwaukee	0.81	686.3			
11. Orlando-Daytona Beach, Fla.	0.79	668.5	31. Rochester, N.Y.	0.41	346.0
12. Nashville, Tenn.	0.76	644.5	32. Omaha, Neb.	0.41	345.5
13. Charlotte, N.C.	0.76	644.1	33. Spokane Wash.	0.38	326.7
14. Columbus, O.	0.74	628.7	34. Cedar Rapids-Waterloo, Ia.	0.37	316.6
15. Buffalo, N.Y.	0.72	615.6	35. Chattanooga, Tenn.	0.34	293.0
16. Oklahoma City	0.71	604.3	36. South Bend-Elkhart, Ind.	0.32	273.7
17. Grand Rapids-Kalamazoo-Battle Creek, Mich.	0.66	560.9	37. Evansville, Ind.	0.31	261.2
18. Salt Lake City	0.65	554.1	38. Fort Wayne, Ind.	0.27	229.2
19. Louisville, Ky.	0.61	515.2	39. Peoria, Ill.	0.25	216.7
20. Dayton, O.	0.56	479.8	40. Greenville-Spartanburg-Asheville, N.C.	0.25	216.1
21. Greensboro-Winston-Salem-High Point, N.C.	0.56	478.6	41. Fargo, N.D.	0.25	211.4
			42. Erie, Pa.	0.18	150.8

TV households in thousands   Source: Dancer Fitzgerald Sample

Figure 21-1

Recommended test market areas.

not so large as to be prohibitively expensive. The standard practice is to use multimarkets comparable in demographics that collectively represent about 2–3 percent of the U.S. population. It is important to note that the larger the market, the greater the likelihood that the competition will gain knowledge of the test and the more expensive is the media buying.

3. *Markets with representative demographics.* Several criteria are important—for example, family size, age levels, income, buying habits, and so forth. If the new product is going to be rolled out nationally, the test market should come as close as possible to matching the demographic average of the nation. In general, the market environment should be consistent with the environment in which the new product will compete when rolled out.

4. *Markets that are isolated.* The test market selected should be relatively isolated in terms of media and physical distribution so as to minimize waste and maximize security. **Spill-in** and **spill-out** are two components of isolation that are frequently examined. Spill-in refers to the amount of outside media coming into a market—the accepted guideline is that if 30–40 percent of a market's population reads another city's newspaper and watches another city's TV station, there is too much spill-in. **Spill-out** refers to the amount of a test market's newspapers and TV being seen and read in distant cities—the 30–40 percent guideline is also used with regard to spill-out. The concern with spill-out is that too much of the advertising effort is going into areas where the new product is not available. Finally, if markets are isolated there is a greater chance to keep the new product hidden from competitors and therefore reduce the chance for competitors to **jam** the test market by reducing price, offering high value coupons, and so on.

If an electronic test market is to be used, the selection of the test markets can be even more problematic. First, selection of test markets is by necessity confined to cities in which the electronic scanner equipment is in operation. Second, a company can be "locked-out" of a possible test city due to a competitor who happens to be testing in the same product category. Exhibit 21-1 summarizes the criteria that should be considered when selecting a test market.

Spill-in The amount of outside media coming into a market.
Spill-out The amount of a test market's newspapers and TV being seen and read in distant cities.

Jamming Practice of reducing price, offering high value coupons and so on in order to disrupt a competitor's test market.

E X H I B I T 21-1

Criteria for Selecting Test Markets

Representative as to population size

Typical per-capita income

Typical purchasing habits

Stability of year-round sales

Relative isolation from other cities

Not easily "jammed" by competitors

Typical of planned distribution outlets

Availability of retailers that will cooperate

Availability of media that will cooperate

Availability of research and audit service companies

Step 5: Execute the Plan

The key consideration in executing the test is to carry out the test marketing as a legitimate *test* and not attempt to guarantee success. In this regard, there are two tendencies to guard against. First, the marketing management team should not confuse paying "attention" with "over-attention." Over-attention can cause the new product to do better in the test market than it will when rolled out nationally—it may be for this reason that only 40 percent of all new products that pass successfully through the testing stage are also successful nationally. Second, the marketing management team should not be over-anxious with respect to repeat-purchase incidence. Repeat purchase of a new product is critical to its eventual success. Frequently, the temptation is to abort a test when the first repeat-purchase-cycle incidences look good. Whether good or bad, repeat-purchase rates should be examined very carefully to determine what may be the culprit (such as media mix, advertising, or the product) or what is leading to success (such as special deals or high-value coupons). In either event, the test should continue at least until the results begin to stabilize. NPD Research, Inc., uses the following guidelines in evaluating repeat purchase rates: 64 percent or more probably means success, 47 percent probably means "maybe," and a rate of 39 percent or less usually means failure.[4]

Step 6: Evaluate the Results

There are four critical areas to keep in mind when evaluating test market results.

1. *The awareness and attitude levels of consumers.* Key awareness information answers the questions: Do consumers know the product exists? Do consumers know what the product does? Do consumers know how much the product costs and where to get it? The awareness level will provide information on the effectiveness of the advertising. The attitude level, on the other hand, provides information on what consumers who have tried (or are aware of) the new product

---

[4]Figures reported by NPD Research, Inc.

think about it. If awareness levels are high, but attitudes are negative, the indication would be that a more extensive advertising (heavier spending) program should be used.

2. *Purchase measures.* Another key factor in evaluating the test is trial and repeat-purchase incidences. Purchase measures, particularly trial, indicate whether or not the advertising and promotion plan has worked.

3. *The effect on competition.* It is very important to monitor the actions of competitors during the testing period. As we indicated, competitors can attempt to jam the test by offering sample products, price reductions, coupons, and the like.

4. *The effect on other products.* What the new product is taking sales from is particularly important. If most of the new product's sales are at the expense of one of the company's other established lines, then there may not be any real market gain. Cannibalization should be closely investigated.

5. *The next step.* After evaluating test market results, the marketing management team can move in one of these directions:

- Go back to Research and Development with an effort to improve the product.
- No go decision—abort the entire project.
- Go decision—give the green light to either launch the new project (or commission a test market if evaluating the results from a simulated test market).

SIMULATED TEST MARKETING METHODS

In the past decade simulated test markets have become increasingly popular. As we indicated earlier, simulated test markets do not involve an actual test market. Instead, preselected individuals are interviewed, monitored, and sampled with the product. The prototypical procedure involves intercepting shoppers at a high-traffic location, sometimes pre-screening them for category usage, exposing the selected individuals to a commercial (or concept) for a proposed new product, giving them an opportunity to buy the new product in a real-life or laboratory setting, and interviewing those who purchased the new product at a later date to ascertain their reaction and repeat-purchase intentions. Based upon trial estimates and repeat-purchase data and management-supplied data on advertising and distribution, the simulated test market result is a projection of share and/or volume and repeat purchases of the product at rollout.

The popularity of simulated test markets can be traced to a number of factors. First, they are relatively fast—a full market evaluation can be finished in 12 to 16 weeks, depending on the service used. Second, they are confidential. The competition does not have the opportunity to jam the test. Third, compared to traditional test markets that can cost in excess of $800,000, they are inexpensive, costing between $60,000 and $85,000, again depending on the service. Finally, the validation evidence indicates that simulated test markets can be quite accurate, with forecast errors generally less than 5 percent.[5] We will return to the issue of accuracy shortly.

History

The first simulated test market was introduced by Yankelovich, Skelly and White, Inc., in 1970. This model, called LTM (Laboratory Test Market), was soon followed by a number of other models. Simulated test markets should not be viewed as substitutes for test markets. From the results of a simulated test market, management can be in a better position to decide not to proceed with a weak product and consequently save the time and money that would have to be committed if a test market were to be conducted; in other words, simulated test markets are generally used to decide whether it is worth the time, cost, and risk of performing a test market. When the decision is to go to test market, simulated test markets also have changed what is expected from the testing. Since the simulated test market gives some indication of what can be expected, the test market can be designed so as to optimize the way in which the new product is priced, promoted, and distributed.

Another significant development in the history of simulated test markets is their use very early on in the new-product development process. Because the costs associated with the product development process increase at each step from raw idea to new-product launch, today simulated test markets are commonly used in the concept- and product-testing stages to get an early reading on sales potential. The objective here is to quickly evaluate a new product's potential so as to lower the risk.

A Comparative Review

Since Yankelovich, Skelly and White's LTM model was introduced in 1968, a large number of other simulated test markets services have appeared. Today, there are five popular simulated test market models in use. These are LTM (Yankelovich, Skelly and White), ASSESSOR (Management Decision Systems),[6] COMP (Elrick and Lavidge), BASES (Burke Marketing Services), and ESP (NPD). Each of these services has its own distinct advantages and disadvantages. In deciding which service to use, the following factors should be considered: (1) cost, (2) time, (3) degree of

---

[5]See, for example, G. L. Urban and G. M. Katz, "Pre-Test-Market Models: Validation and Managerial Implications," *Journal of Marketing Research*, (August 1983), 221–34.

[6]In 1985 Management Decision Systems was acquired by Information Resources, Inc. (IRI).

confidentiality, (4) characteristics of the model, and (5) documentation of overall accuracy of forecasts.

Cost. Cost of conducting a simulated test market will ultimately depend on the product tested and the corresponding category incidence rate, as well as on other specifics concerning how the test is to be conducted. In general, however, ASSESSOR is the most expensive of the simulated test market models, with typical costs in the $60,000 to $80,000 range, whereas BASES and COMP are the least expensive of the simulated test market models, with typical costs in the $40,000 to $60,000 range.

Timing. The time needed to complete a simulated test market will ultimately depend on the use-up rate for the new product being tested. Assuming a two-week use-up rate, the time needed from authorization of design to formal presentation for each of the five simulated test markets services are given below

ASSESSOR	13–14 weeks
COMP	9–10 weeks
LTM	14–16 weeks
BASES	13 weeks
ESP	12–14 weeks

Confidentiality. All market simulation services offer a degree of confidentiality not possible with any type of in-store testing since respondents are screened for security criteria before they are exposed to the advertising or to the product. However, COMP typically offers two options that can increase security. First, with COMP, subjects can be recruited by telephone rather than mall intercept (for an additional cost). Second, COMP offers a product pick-up option, in which they attempt to recover all the product that was distributed during the experiment.

Model Characteristics. The following characteristics are most relevant to our purposes.

1. The BASES model is designed to use the data generated by a general audience. Thus, it is best suited to test (1) new products that address a general audience, (2) innovative new products, and (3) products for which category boundaries are unclear (such as snacks).
2. In simulated test market models that use purchase-intent scales the objective is to link the attitudinal response (purchase intent) to purchase behavior (trial and repeat rate), adjusting for season, region, and advertising and promotion plans. Researchers generally agree, however, that there is some overstatement by consumers concerning purchase intentions; in other words, not all consumers who say they would buy a given product would actually buy it within a given pe-

T A B L E 21-1

Conversion Rate Examples

Purchase intent	Scenario			
	1	2	3	4
Definitely would buy	100%	52%	100%	90%
Probably would buy	0	17	40	30
Might or might not buy	0	8	0	5
Probably would not buy	0	2	0	2.5
Definitely would not buy	0	1	0	2

Source: Y. Lynn et al., "New Product Analysis and Testing," in *Handbook of Business Problem Solving,* ed. K. J. Albert (New York: McGraw-Hill 1980), 4–13 to 4–27.

T A B L E 21-2

Weighting Purchase Intent Scores

Intent scale	Simulated test result	Weights	Estimate of potential trial
Definitely buy	25%	.52	13.00%
Probably buy	30%	.17	5.10%
Might or might not buy	35%	.08	2.80%
Probably not buy	7%	.02	0.14%
Definitely not buy	3%	.01	—
Total	100%		21.04%

riod of time (perhaps a year). The critical element in interpreting the purchase intent is to calibrate the precise "rate of conversion" from this attitudinal response to behavioral measures. Historically, many conversion rates have been used. Four examples of conversion rates used by consumer packaged goods researchers in the U.S. are given in Table 21-1.

Under scenario 1, purchase rates would be taken as 100 percent of the top-box score on the purchase-intent measure. Under scenario 2, purchase rates would be computed by taking 52 percent of the top-box purchase intentions plus 17 percent of the second top-box purchase intentions plus 8 percent of the "might or might not buy" purchase intentions, and so on. In other words, under scenario 2, it is believed that 1 percent of the individuals who indicated that they "definitely would not buy" actually end up purchasing the product. As shown in Table 21-2, based upon scenario 2 weights, the forecasted trial-purchase level for the new product concept is 21.04 percent.

3. All of the simulated test markets models adjust trial rate and repeat-purchase rate by marketing plans—that is, planned advertising spending and distribution levels. The following example illustrates the nature of the adjustment.

E X A M P L E

Estimated trial rate	10.7%
×	×
Total awareness (marketing plan)	50.0%
×	×
% Distribution (marketing plan)	70.0%
=	
Net cumulative trial	3.7%
×	×
Estimated share of choice	28.5%
=	
Ongoing unit share	1.1%

---

4. The LTM model does not use attitude measures to measure the strength of repeat purchase, and thus might not be best suited to a problem that hinges on the relative strength of purchase intention for two highly similar brands.

5. ASSESSOR and COMP both use an attitudinal measure to evaluate strength of repeat purchase and also to generate a brand share forecast independent of the trial-repeat model. However, in the ASSESSOR measure, brand preference, the set of brands is determined by the respondent's "evoked set"; in the COMP measure, attribute ratings, the set of attributes is predetermined by the study design. This preselection of the attributes is an arbitrary element and perhaps a flaw in the COMP model.

Overall Accuracy. Table 21-3 summarizes the reported number of tests conducted and actual validation cases by each of the five simulated test markets models. In evaluating the overall accuracy of any of these services it is necessary to recognize the difficulties inherent in validating the market share/sales volume forecasts. For the most part, the marketing plans (that is, total awareness, percent distribution) used as input into the forecasting models do not match the plan actually used in the new-

TABLE 21-3

Reported Number of Tests and Validations for Five Simulated Test Market Models

	Number of tests conducted		Number of claimed validations
Model	Claimed number	Years reported	
LTM	1,500	1968–1983	500
ASSESSOR	450	1973–1982	44
COMP	200*	1971–1983	90
BASES	1,500	1977–1983	152
ESP	86*	1982 only	30

*Cumulative total not known.

product introduction. And other factors not anticipated in the simulation may affect the new product's performance in the real world. Therefore, in order to validate a result a forecast must be readjusted to match the real-world situation. This assumes, of course, that the client is willing to share this information with the simulation service; however, this is certainly not always the case. Further, there is a certain self-selection process that takes place, since clients who are most pleased with the service are the ones most willing to offer validation information—which affects the ability of the validation data reported to be generalized. A partial exception to these points is BASES, which is linked via Burke Marketing Service to ADTEL and thus has easy access to some parallel in-store test results. Recognizing these points, note the following:

1. ASSESSOR, with 44 validations reported in the *Journal of Marketing Research*, August 1983, offers predictions that fall, on average, 0.8 share points from actual test market data, once the simulation has been adjusted for the real-world data. Approximately 70 percent of the predictions fall within 1.1 share points. These validations represent some 20 percent of the 200 ASSESSOR tests conducted between 1973 and 1982.
2. BASES (BASES II), with 131 validations reported as of 1982 (reflecting both test market and ADTEL validations), offers volume predictions that fall within 5 percent of actual first-year volume 35 percent of the time and within 10 percent of the first-year volume 66 percent of the time once the appropriate adjustments have been made. These validations represent some 15 percent of the approximately 900 total BASES experiences.
3. LTM reports 500 validation cases out of 1,500 total experiences and reports that the predicted share matches the actual share in nine

out of ten cases. However, this information must be considered with caution given that: (1) the reported higher accuracy of LTM versus BASES and ASSESSOR despite the more sophisticated models offered by the latter, (2) the LTM validation findings, unlike the BASES and ASSESSOR reports, have not appeared in a professional journal or been formally presented to a professional conference, and (3) LTM cites a surprisingly high number of validations—approximately one-third of the applications have claimed to have been validated despite the difficulties inherent in obtaining the information necessary for validating the model's prediction. Thus, it may be that the LTM data are, for some reason, not comparable with those for BASES and ASSESSOR.

4. COMP reports 90 validation cases; these cases are reported to demonstrate the system's remarkable accuracy, though no specific data are shown. COMP estimates that approximately 85–90 percent of the validations have fallen within one share point of market data. As with LTM, the reported accuracy seems high relative to ASSESSOR and BASES, the validation data are unpublished, and the number of validations (some 36 percent of total COMP experiences) might lead to question the nature of these validations. However, unlike LTM, COMP offers a model that incorporates both behavioral and attitudinal data and that might appear to have the sensitivity of BASES or ASSESSOR.

5. ESP reports 30 validation cases. Over these cases volume prediction errors average ± 9.9 percent, and were within 10 percent of the first-year volume in 57 percent of the cases. As with the LTM and COMP models, validation data have not been published in a professional journal or been formally presented to a professional conference.

What could account for the inaccuracies in the simulated test market models? First, some of the inaccuracy probably traces to new products that do not fit easily into established product categories—such introductions tend to confound market simulation models. Second, some of the variance surely traces to assumptions that are implicit to the idea of a simulation per se.

Summary

This chapter has been devoted to the topic of test marketing. Pretest and test market studies are designed to provide varying extents of real-world, in-market exposure and evaluation of a product and its marketing program. Because of the risks associated with new-product introduction, pretest and test markets will likely continue to be crucial elements in making more effective marketing decisions.

Key Concepts

New product failure rates

*Benefits of information versus
   costs associated with delay*

Steps in test marketing

Standard test market audits

Controlled test market audits

Simulated test market methods

Review Questions

1. Discuss the reasons for conducting test markets.
2. What factors should be considered in determining the efficacy of test marketing?
3. Describe the steps in test market studies.
4. Why have simulated test market studies become popular?
5. Evaluate the five popular simulated test market models.

Marketing Decision Support Systems (MDSS's)

C H A P T E R   O B J E C T I V E S

- Distinguish MDSS's from other technologically-based advances.
- Discuss those factors that have led to increased reliance on MDSS's.
- Illustrate how management expertise can be married by computer technology to provide a framework for making faster and more accurate marketing decisions.
- Describe what an MDSS is.
- Explain the concept of a decision calculus.
- Discuss the essentials of an MDSS.
- Explain the specific benefits derived from using an MDSS.
- Illustrate those areas in which an MDSS can be particularly useful.
- Outline the issues involved in implementing MDSS's.
- Present several alternative forecasting methods.

Introduction

- "I need to see what each of my product lines has sold in dollars, each month, for the year to date."
- "I need to rank my product lines by dollar sales this year."
- "I need to compare year-to-date advertising expenditures by media against budget targets, with variances expressed as a percentage."
- "I want to designate a target profit level, set some conditions such as price and a first-month sales volume, and then determine what rate of sales growth is needed to reach the profit target; moreover, what are the implications of changing the base conditions?"

The activities described above all illustrate applications that are well-suited for marketing decision support systems (**MDSS's**). What distinguishes the MDSS concept from other technologically-based advances such as management information systems (MIS) and management science (MS) is its humanistic orientation. MIS touted the computer as the solution to management's problems; MS touted mathematical models and experts in "scientific" methods as the solution. MDSS's, on the other hand, position the manager as the solution, equipped, of course, with

MDSS A coordinated collection of data, systems, tools, and techniques, complemented by supporting software and hardware designed for the gathering and interpretation of business and environmental data.

675

the appropriate decision support technology. An MDSS improves the likelihood that a company will achieve its market objectives by amplifying the capabilities of the marketing manager; in particular, MDSS analysis enables marketing managers to identify the financial and volumetric impact of their marketing programs, derived, at least in part, from the bases of information collected through marketing research activities.

This chapter is devoted to a discussion of MDSS technology. Nearly all MDSS's use marketing research information; typically the marketing research department initiates the discussion and negotiation process that leads to the development of an MDSS. The purpose of this chapter is to illustrate how management expertise can be married to computer technology to provide a framework for making faster and more accurate marketing decisions. There are a great many different types of MDSS's; consequently, we will not be able to discuss all of the varieties here. Rather, our goal will be to discuss (1) the reasons for developing MDSS's, (2) the concept of a decision calculus, (3) the essentials of MDSS's, (4) the benefits and payoffs of using an MDSS, (5) areas in which MDSS can enhance decision making, and finally (6) the issues involved in implementation.

WHY AN MDSS?

The answer to this question is simple: competition! For better or worse, competitive environments incubate MDSS's. Because of the competitiveness of most markets, marketing researchers and managers find not only that they are making more decisions, but also that the decisions must be made more quickly and with greater certainty. Coupled with the need to make quicker, more precise decisions is the proliferation of data. A common source of frustration is the knowledge that data relevant to the problem at hand exist somewhere in the organization, but are not easily located, comprehended, formatted, or manipulated. MDSS's promise to provide key marketing managers and researchers with relevant information and the ability to work with it in order to enhance their decision-making capabilities.

A pioneer in the development and dissemination of MDSS's is Professor John D. C. Little of the Sloan School of Management at M.I.T. Little describes an *MDSS* as

> a coordinated collection of data, systems, tools, and techniques with supporting software and hardware by which an organization gathers and interprets relevant information from business and environment and turns it into a basis for marketing action.[1]

MDSS's run the gamut from simply providing information storage capa-

[1] J. D. C. Little, "Decision Support Systems for Marketing Managers," *Journal of Marketing* 43 (Summer 1979), 11.

bilities through statistical analyses to interactive modeling. In all cases, however, the emphasis is on providing support for decision making.

THE CONCEPT OF A DECISION CALCULUS

Decision calculus is a term invented by Little to describe MDSS's that represent an extension of a manager's ability to think about and analyze his or her operation.[2] Specifically, a decision calculus is defined as a model-based set of procedures for processing data and judgments to assist a manager in decision making.[3] According to Little, a decision calculus should be

Decision calculus A model-based set of procedures for processing data and managerial judgments designed to assist a manager in decision making.

1. *Simple.* Understanding can be increased by including only important information in a system. Only when it is demonstrated that detailed information can be understood and used by managers should it be included.
2. *Robust.* A system should not give bad answers; thus a structure should be imposed that inherently constrains answers to a meaningful range of values.
3. *Controllable.* A user should be able to make the system behave in a prescribed way. The user should fully understand how to set inputs to get almost any outputs. Parameters of the system should represent the operation as the manager sees it.
4. *Adaptive.* A system should be able to be updated as new information is available.
5. *Complete.* A system should be able to handle a variety of different phenomena without bogging down.
6. *Easy to use.* A system should allow a manager to change inputs easily and obtain outputs quickly. On-line, conversational input/output and personal computers make this a reality. Good on-line systems facilitate learning by providing user instructions and by allowing the user to get a feel for how the model works through direct experience.

In essence, then, a decision calculus orientation generates a system that brings the model to the manager and makes it a part of him or her.

THE ESSENTIALS OF AN MDSS

An important essential element in an MDSS is a computer. However, contrary to what you might think, computers *cannot* automate complex decision making. Rather, their role is to help retrieve information quickly and manipulate it creatively in order to enhance decision-making capabilities. The key is to get relevant information to the manager as fast as

[2]This section is based on John D. C. Little, "Models and Managers: The Concept of a Decision Calculus," *Management Science*, April 1970, B-466–485.
[3]Ibid., B-470.

he or she can use it. With this in mind, the following describes the important features of an MDSS.[4]

1. It is *computerized.* Computerization brings speed that allows managers to manipulate information in a variety of ways.
2. It is *interactive:* On-line interactive systems provide the manager with menu-driven instructions and allow results to be generated on the spot. A computer programmer is not required and the process is under the direct control of the manager; moreover, the manager need not wait for scheduled reports.
3. It is *flexible:* Flexibility means that the manager can sort, average, total, and manipulate the data in a variety of ways. It allows the manager to access and integrate data from a number of different sources.
4. It is *discovery-oriented:* A discovery orientation means that the manager can search for trends, identify problems, and ask new questions on the basis of the information provided.
5. It *minimizes the frustration quotient:* The system is easy to learn and use. Novice users who are not particularly computer-knowledgeable should be able to use the system easily, initially selecting standard or "default" options so that they can immediately work with the basic system while gradually learning to exercise all of its options.

MDSS's have three essential features: databases, a user interface and a library of analytical and modeling tools. Figure 22-1 depicts these essential characteristics. Notice that the manager interfaces with the system through interactive instruction and display. The central database contains all of the information in the system. Typically, the practice is to "distribute" the MDSS; a network of microcomputers is linked to the control database, which is housed on a mainframe computer or minicomputer. This arrangement puts flexible computing power in the hands of managers, while the MIS group usually remains responsible for the update and integrity of the central database.

Rational database manager *A component of an MDSS that provides the user with the ability to efficiently access and manipulate the data.*

The core of the MDSS is the **rational database manager.** The database manager provides the user with the ability to efficiently access and manipulate the data. The database manager program responds to commands from a user at the CRT screen, extracts the right information from the central database, and arranges it in a specified report format.

The selected data can be analyzed in a variety of ways. The analytical structure is generally organized in terms of subsystems, such as sales analysis, forecasting, advertising evaluation, product line analysis, and market/customer information. The properly formatted data could be loaded into either an electronic spreadsheet, one of many different optimization models, a statistical package subroutine, or a graphics software subroutine. Electronic spreadsheets warrant some special comments since they probably represent the single greatest reason that

---

[4] The following discussion has been adapted from Michael Dressler, Joquin Ives Brant, and Ronald Beall, Decision Support Systems: "What the Hot Marketing Tool of the '80s Offers You," *Industrial Marketing*, March 1983, 51–60.

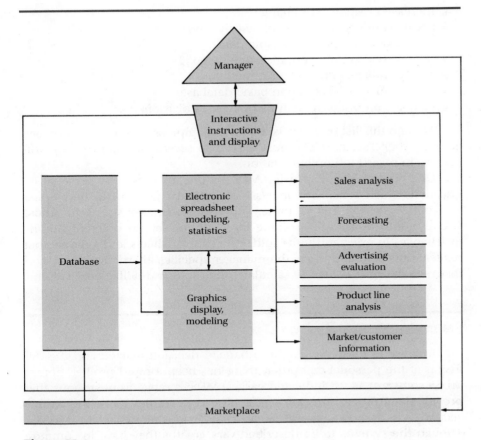

Figure 22-1

Decision support system. (*Source:* Michael Dressler, Joquin Ives Brant, and Ronald Beall, *Industrial Marketing*, March 1983, 54.)

managers have begun to use microcomputers routinely. Electronic spreadsheets appear as a large grid, similar to an accountant's worksheet, on which a manager can revise numbers. They are very useful for adjusting forecasts and for performing operations on a series of numbers; in addition, recently more sophisticated versions of spreadsheets have been available, offering such features as net present value and various forecasting models.

BENEFITS AND PAYOFFS

Proponents of the concept of an MDSS ascribe a number of specific benefits to it. Those frequently cited include:

- Increased staff efficiency—more work in less time
- Increased managerial effectiveness—ability to focus on key issues

- Increased response to change
- Greater understanding of market dynamics
- More extensive use of available data
- More varied set of alternatives evaluated
- Greater reliance on analytical methods
- Development of a common basic database
- Reliance on uniform analysis by various divisions

Though this list of potential benefits is impressive, not all companies embrace MDSS's. An MDSS must overcome several barriers that we will discuss in regard to implementation.

One primary payoff of using MDSS is the ability to answer "what if" questions. Such sensitivity analysis is particularly useful in developing marketing strategy. For example, suppose a manager wants to adjust twelve-month dollar sales-volume forecasts for several different brands for changes in price and units sold. Using spreadsheets and a model that relates units sold and price, the manager specifies alternative prices and instructs the spreadsheet to calculate units sold and dollar sales volume.

ENHANCED DECISION MAKING

Because of the potential for enhanced decision making and the diffusion of the personal computer, there has been a rapid proliferation of MDSS software. As we indicated earlier, MDSS's range from systems that provide data retrieval to statistical analysis to complex modeling. In this section we describe several areas that lend themselves to MDSS's. Though the systems to be described vary greatly, they have in common the ability to enhance a manager's decision-making capabilities.

Sales and Product Analysis

Sales and product analysis is a basic core feature of many MDSS's. Managers tend to be extremely interested in this application because of its critical role in decision making. Typically, an MDSS will allow the manager to see sales or unit volume by product broken down by sales representative and customer segment, by time period, geographical location, and so forth—the level of analysis will simply depend on the specificity of the company's database. Exhibit 22-1 presents several prototypical sales and product analyses obtained with the Acustar™ decision-support system.[5]

[5]ACUSTAR™ is distributed by TYMSHARE, Cupertino, California.

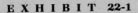
Prototypical Sales and Product Analysis from Acustar™

SOURCE: FACTORY
CATEGORY: COFFEE
GEOGRAPHY: TOTAL U.S.

SALES PERFORMANCE UPDATE
BASIS: 5 MONTH SALES ENDING MAY 1982

PAGE: 1
DATE: 09/19/82
USER: JMH

K= THOUS. M= MILL.	LAST YR Y.T.D. SALES	CURRENT Y.T.D. SALES	INDEX CURRENT Y.T.D. VS YR AGO	Y.T.D. SALES FORECAST	INDEX CURRENT Y.T.D. VS FORECAST	TOTAL 1982 SALES FORECAST	SALES NEEDED TO MEET FORECAST	VOL LAST YR DURING REMAIN MONTHS	INDEX CURRENT TO GO VS YR AGO
TOTAL GENERAL COFFEE CO.	$66,871K	$91,175K	136	$89,267K	102	$227,759K	$136,584K	$160,888K	85
TOTAL IRISH HOST	$12,243K	$14,201K	116	$16,326K	87	$41,308K	$27,107K	$29,065K	93
IRISH HOST 4 OZ	$4,883.9K	$5,564.8K	114	$6,000.0K	93	$16,211K	$10,646K	$11,327K	94
IRISH HOST 8 OZ	$6,256.1K	$7,516.2K	120	$9,125.8K	82	$21,972K	$14,455K	$15,716K	92
IRISH HOST 12 OZ	$1,102.9K	$1,120.0K	102	$1,200.1K	93	$3,125.4K	$2,005.4K	$2,022.6K	99
TOTAL ISLAND SUNSET	$37,271K	$55,525K	149	$51,421K	108	$128,446K	$72,921K	$91,175K	80
ISLAND SUNSET 4 OZ	$8,802.2K	$10,758K	122	$11,014K	98	$26,854K	$16,096K	$18,052K	89
ISLAND SUNSET 8 OZ	$17,288K	$24,949K	144	$23,948K	104	$59,232K	$34,283K	$41,944K	82
ISLAND SUNSET 12 OZ	$11,181K	$19,819K	177	$16,460K	120	$42,360K	$22,542K	$31,180K	72
TOTAL PERFECT CHOICE	$17,357K	$21,449K	124	$21,521K	100	$58,005K	$36,556K	$40,649K	90
PERFECT CHOICE 4 OZ	$5,031.7K	$4,845.4K	96	$5,892.5K	82	$14,236K	$9,390.5K	$9,204.1K	102
PERFECT CHOICE 8 OZ	$9,502.9K	$12,504K	132	$11,938K	105	$33,345K	$20,841K	$23,842K	87
PERFECT CHOICE 12 OZ	$2,822.0K	$4,100.3K	145	$3,690.7K	111	$10,424K	$6,324.2K	$7,602.5K	83

Update Sales Performance

The status reports generated with Acustar offer a method of periodically reviewing market performance versus objectives.

See how your brand is doing year-to-date (YTD). How does it compare to this year's forecast? What is the YTD percent increase or decrease versus last year's sales?

SOURCE: SAMI+MAJERS
CATEGORY: COFFEE

IRISH HOST VS PRIVATE LABEL
REGIONAL PERFORMANCE COMPARISON

PAGE: 1
DATE: 09/19/82
USER: JMH

13 PD END PD#202 3/5/82

K= THOUS. M= MILL.	IRISH HOST				PRIVATE LABEL			
	AREA %CONTRIB TO TOTAL DOLLARS	DOLLAR SHARE OF CATEGORY	AVERAGE PRICE PER POUND	SHARE OF CATEGORY WGTD VAL	AREA %CONTRIB TO TOTAL DOLLARS	DOLLAR SHARE OF CATEGORY	AVERAGE PRICE PER POUND	SHARE OF CATEGORY WGTD VAL
TOTAL U.S.	100.0%	14.2%	$0.92	12.3%	100.0%	9.1%	$0.67	4.7%
NORTHEAST	29.9%	20.2%	$0.89	11.6%	11.8%	5.1%	$0.67	1.1%
MID ATLANTIC	11.8%	20.2%	$0.88	18.6%	7.9%	8.7%	$0.66	8.5%
SOUTHEAST	9.3%	14.8%	$0.91	10.2%	8.6%	8.8%	$0.67	5.0%
MID SOUTH	2.7%	10.4%	$0.93	12.6%	6.3%	15.6%	$0.69	7.0%
CENTRAL	18.9%	17.8%	$0.93	12.2%	16.3%	9.8%	$0.65	4.9%
SOUTHWEST	6.6%	12.4%	$0.96	10.3%	11.6%	14.1%	$0.67	8.9%
NORTHWEST	6.0%	12.4%	$1.01	9.2%	9.2%	12.2%	$0.69	6.9%
SOUTH PACIFIC	11.7%	7.9%	$0.92	13.9%	20.2%	8.8%	$0.65	4.1%
NORTH PACIFIC	3.1%	6.0%	$0.98	8.8%	7.9%	9.7%	$0.68	3.4%

Compare Performance by Region

Compare your brand to a competitor on a region-by-region basis. And answer questions like:
Where and why are private label brands performing better than my brand?
What is my brand's average price per pound by region?

SOURCE: MAJERS+SAMI
CATEGORY: COFFEE
GEOGRAPHY: NEW ENGLAND

MAJOR BRANDS AREA TRENDS

PAGE: 1
DATE: 09/20/82
USER: JMH

K= THOUS. M= MILL.	PD#189 3/6 1981	PD#190 4/3 1981	PD#191 5/1 1981	PD#192 5/29 1981	PD#193 6/26 1981	PD#194 7/24 1981	PD#195 8/21 1981	PD#196 9/18 1981	PD#197 10/16 1981	PD#198 11/13 1981	PD#199 12/11 1981	PD#200 1/8 1982	CURRENT PD#201 2/5 1982	YR AGO PD#188 2/6 1981	52 WEEK PD#201 2/5 1982
ISLAND SUNSET															
1 PD UNIT SHARE......	3.0%	3.0%	2.4%	2.4%	2.2%	2.2%	2.7%	2.8%	2.7%	2.6%	2.3%	1.8%	1.9%	2.8%	2.4%
1 PD PRICE/UNIT	$0.63	$0.64	$0.65	$0.65	$0.65	$0.65	$0.61	$0.60	$0.62	$0.64	$0.66	$0.70	$0.71	$0.63	$0.64
1 PD % WGTD VALUE ...	10.3%	5.7%	0.8%	7.2%	0.8%	0.0%	6.3%	1.0%	1.3%	0.6%	0.0%	0.0%	7.6%	10.0%	3.8%
IRISH HOST															
1 PD UNIT SHARE......	7.5%	7.4%	7.2%	7.2%	7.1%	7.1%	6.8%	6.7%	6.8%	6.9%	7.0%	7.3%	7.2%	8.3%	7.1%
1 PD PRICE/UNIT	$0.65	$0.65	$0.65	$0.65	$0.67	$0.67	$0.67	$0.67	$0.67	$0.68	$0.69	$0.69	$0.69	$0.63	$0.67
1 PD % WGTD VALUE ...	0.0%	0.6%	6.0%	3.2%	0.9%	8.4%	0.9%	0.0%	0.0%	1.4%	0.7%	0.0%	0.8%	1.4%	1.5%
MOUNTAIN HIGHLANDS															
1 PD UNIT SHARE......	6.4%	6.4%	6.4%	6.4%	7.2%	7.2%	7.0%	6.9%	6.5%	6.3%	6.4%	6.5%	6.5%	6.4%	6.6%
1 PD PRICE/UNIT	$0.73	$0.73	$0.74	$0.74	$0.77	$0.78	$0.78	$0.78	$0.79	$0.80	$0.80	$0.80	$0.80	$0.71	$0.77
1 PD % WGTD VALUE ...	0.0%	0.0%	0.0%	0.0%	2.7%	0.4%	0.0%	0.9%	0.4%	0.2%	0.0%	0.0%	0.0%	0.0%	0.4%

Review Trends

Combine information from multiple data sources in one report to obtain a more complete picture of trends in your marketplace.

Sales and Product Forecasting

Making forecasts is intrinsic to the management function. Many managers make forecasts on a routine basis; and, in many cases, the performance of the manager is in large measure determined by the accuracy of the forecasts made.

There are many different forecasting methods. To some, forecasting means making "educated" guesses, while to others, forecasting involves the use of complex mathematical models and procedures.[6] For example, among *judgmental methods*, which are the least sophisticated of the forecasting techniques, are included

- **Salesforce-composite estimates**—forecasts based on the informed knowledge of the firm's salesforce. Sales personnel provide estimates

[6]For more details on various forecasting techniques, see John C. Chambers, Satinder K. Mullick, and Donald D. Smith, *An Executive's Guide to Forecasting* (New York: John Wiley & Sons, 1974); Spyros Makridakis and Steven C. Wheelwright, *Forecasting: Methods and Applications* (New York: Wiley, 1978); Steven C. Wheelwright and Spyros Makridakis, *Forecasting Methods for Management* (2nd ed. New York: John Wiley & Sons, 1977). Douglas Wood and Robert Fildes, *Forecasting for Business: Methods and Application* (New York: Longman Group, 1976).

of future demand. This technique makes use of the relationship between a sales representative and his or her customers in order to develop accurate estimates about future trends. By participating in the forecasting process, the sales representative may have greater confidence in the derived sales quotas and consequently may be more motivated to achieve those quotas. This technique appears well-suited to products that are fairly technical and subject to a changing technology. On the negative side, sales representatives are biased observers. Therefore, few companies use their estimates without some adjustments.

- **Jury of expert opinion**—forecasts based on combining the views of key executives. The views of several key executives are combined in the hope of providing a more accurate forecast of future demand than would be possible with the use of a single estimator. Though this technique is used by all kinds of companies, it is more likely to be adopted by a consumer goods manufacturer or by a service firm than by an industrial marketer. The critical problems with the executive-opinion approach are (1) too much weight is given to opinion, (2) executive's time is infringed upon, and (3) there is no optimal universally-agreed-upon procedure for combining the individual (executives') forecasts.

- **Delphi and related methods**—forecasts based on asking a group of experts for their best estimate of a future event, then processing and feeding back some of the information obtained, and then repeating the process. After a number of cycles the estimate for the group is usually obtained by taking the median on the last set of responses. There are three key features to this approach: (1) *anonymous response*, in which opinions and assignments are obtained anonymously, (2) *interaction and controlled feedback*, in which systematic exercises are used to promote interaction with controlled feedback between rounds, and (3) *statistical group response*, where the estimate of group opinion is obtained by aggregating individual opinions at the final round.

Among the more sophisticated of the forecasting techniques are time series and regression and econometric models.

- **Time series models**—methods that produce forecasts on the basis of statistical analysis of past data. These methods are based on the premise that past data incorporate enduring and identifiable causal relationships that will carry forward into the future. A large number of time series models fall under the umbrella of what can be called smoothing techniques. The notion underlying smoothing techniques is that past data reflect some pattern in the values of the variable to be forecasted along with random fluctuations. By eliminating random fluctuations, smoothing techniques hope to identify the under-

Salesforce-composite estimates A method of forecasting based on the informed knowledge of the firm's salesforce who provide estimates of future demand

Jury of expert opinion A method of forecasting based on combining the views of key executives.

Delphi method A method of forecasting based on asking a group of experts for their best estimate of a future event, then processing and feeding back some of the information obtained, and then repeating the process; on the last set of responses, the median is usually chosen as the best estimate for the group.

Time series models Methods that produce forecasts on the basis of the statistical analysis of past data that presumably incorporate enduring and identifiable causal relationships that will carry forward into the future.

lying pattern in the historical data. Because these models assume that very little is known about the underlying cause of demand and that the future will be similar to the past, they are most useful for short- or medium-term forecasts (usually less than one year). We will discuss and illustrate several time series models in Appendix 22-A.

■ **Regression and econometric models**—methods that produce forecasts based on expressing demand as a function of a certain number of deterministic factors. These models are not necessarily time dependent and therefore can be useful when making long-term forecasts. The development of a model that captures the structure between demand and its underlying causes should lead to a better understanding of the situation and improved accuracy. Appendix 22-A discusses and illustrates how regression analysis is used in a forecasting context.

The features the MDSS's bring to forecasting are speed and the ability to easily play "what if" games. With use of an MDSS the manager need not wait hours or days for the computer runs to be completed by other departments. In addition, forecasts can be quickly updated. Because of direct interaction with the MDSS, the manager can ask questions concerning different scenarios based upon the information provided and his or her intuitive thinking about the future course of events. Exhibit 22-2 presents a prototypical forecasting system that illustrates the speed and flexibility that an MDSS brings to the forecasting task.

E X H I B I T 22-2

MDSS Forecasting System

```
Choose one:> forecast
forecasting methods

      1 Moving Averages (MAv)
      2 Double Moving Averages (DMAv)
      3 Exponential Smoothing (ExS)
      4 Double Exponential Smoothing (DExS)
      5 Regression

Choose one:> MAv
Period to base Moving Average On:> 3
Enter data by year> 1966 28.2, 1967 31.6, 1968 30.5,
1969 31.8, 1970 34.2, 1971 36.3, 1972 39.3, 1973
41.7, 1974 50.0, 1975 46.8, 1976 43.7, 1977 52.1,
1978 63.3, 1979 69.9, 1980 72.3, 1981 76.0, 1982
76.1, 1983 78.0
```

Forecast and Actual

```
What forecast output(s) do you want?
      1 Graph (GRA)        1 Graph actual and
                             predicted
      2 Report (REP)       1 Report actual, forecast,
                             and change
      3 Adjust (ADJ)       1 Adjust the forecast

Choice:> 1
```

Advertising Readership

McGraw-Hill Research has developed an MDSS to assist in understanding the key elements that determine a print ad's effectiveness. McGraw's MDSS makes use of a relatively large database, incorporating over 4,000 advertisements appearing in 26 business publications studied by McGraw-Hill's AD SELL readership program. Each ad is coded for its various physical characteristics, and this information is "married" to the "steps to a sale" readership scores it receives. The readership scores and converted index numbers reported are normed by magazine and issue. The norming procedure employed allows advertisements from different magazines appearing in different issues to be compared. Exhibit 22-3 presents prototypical information from McGraw-Hill's MDSS program.

E X H I B I T 22-3

MDSS: Report (All user responses are circled)

```
Press <CR> key for next screen:;

REPORT identifies the Top and Bottom X% of a
publication ads,
which can be  (1). Single and Multiple Page ads,
             (2). Single-Page ads,
       or    (3). Multiple-Page ads,
by selecting one of the following performance
measures:
    1. Established Contact (EC)
    2. Created Awareness (CA)
    3. Arouse Interest (AI)
    4. Built Preference (BP)
    5. Kept Customer Sold (KCS).

The analysis can be performed for specific
    1. Advertiser
    2. Product Category
    3. Advertiser and Product Category
or  4. Total Data Base.

In addition, you can request information on each ad
scoring in the top and bottom X%. Information is:

    Performance Measures/Issue/Year/Page#/
    Advertiser/Product Category and ONE physical
    attribute.


ID    Ad Page Type

1     Single/Multiple-Page ads
2     Single-Page ads
3     Multiple-Page ads

Enter ID# to select Ad Page Type: ①
```

```
ID      Performance Measure
──      ─────────────────────────────────────
1       EC Establish Contact (attract attention)
2       CA Create Awareness (make prospect aware of
        something not known before)
3       AI Arouse Interest (cause action)
4       BP Build Preference
5       KCS Keep Customer Sold
```

Enter ID# to select Performance Measure: ① Right
(y/n)? ⓨ

```
        ID      Function Type
        ──      ──────────────────────────────
        1       Advertiser
        2       Product Category
        3       Advertiser and Product Category
        4       Total Data Base
```

Enter ID# to select Function Type: ④
Right (y/n)? ⓨ

Enter the Top/Bottom X% that this report will be
based on, e.g. 5 means 5%: ⑩ Right (y/n)? ⓨ

Input ad/sell data normalized by: issue/year
Mean Score Report ==>Ad Page Type: Single/Multiple-
                    Page ads
                    ==>10% of EC with Total Data Base

```
        ID#  #Ads  EC    CA    AI    BP    KCS   Inq/#Ads
        ───  ────  ────  ────  ────  ────  ────  ────────
Top      1    15   96.9  36.4  56.7  60.0  91.1  0.0/0
Bottom   2    15   30.6  70.9  70.0  60.3  72.7  0.0/0
```

Enter ID# to select Item: ① Right (y/n)? ⓨ

```
ID#     Item
───     ──────────────────────────
0       QUIT
1       Perform a T-test
2       Retrieve Ad Information
```

Enter ID # to Select Two Items For T-test:
1. ① Right (y/n)? ⓨ
2. ② Right (y/n)? ⓨ
Enter Significance Level<e.g. 5 means 5%>: ⑤
Right (y/n)? ⓨ

Press <CR> key for next screen:

Ad Page Type: Single/Multiple-Page ads; 10% of EC
Two Tailed T-Test Significance Level: 5% Degree of
Freedom: 28
  A)Top 10%: Total Data Base
      vs
  B)Btm 10%: Total Data Base

		T-value	Prob	Decision
EC	:	45.46	0.00	Reject Ho
CA	:	-4.58	0.00	Reject Ho
AI	:	-1.73	0.09	Accept Ho
BP	:	-0.03	0.97	Accept Ho
KCS	:	1.53	0.14	Accept Ho

*   Null Hypothesis(Ho): There is no difference be-
        tween the mean performance scores for A)
        ads versus B) ads.
**   Accepting/Rejecting Ho confirms/disconfirms that
        there is no difference in the mean perfor-
        mance scores.
*** A positive/negative algebraic sign of T-value
        indicates that, on the average, A) ads
        out/underperform B) ads

Enter ID# to select Item: ② Right (y/n)? ⓨ

ID#	Item
0	QUIT
1	Perform a T-test
2	Retrieve Ad Information

Do you want information on physical characteristics: ⟨yes⟩

ID	Attribute
1	Type of Advertisement
2	Size
3	Color
4	Use of any Color
5	Bleed
6	Insert
7	Location of Ad.
8	L/R hand Page

```
9       Cover Position
10      Inquiry Card
11      800 Number
12      No. of Illustrations
13      Length of Copy
14      Location of Largest Illustration
15      Position of Largest Illustration
16      Insert Card
17      Position of Main Headline
```

Enter ID# to select attribute<0=NO
attribute>: ③ Right (y/n)? ⓨ

```
ID      Report Format
─────────────────────
1       Individual Ad
2       Grouped in a Table
```

Enter ID# to select Report Format: ②
Right (y/n)? ⓨ

Enter q to QUIT display, otherwise hit <CR> key:
Top 10%: Total Data Base

EC	Isu/Yr	Pg#	CA	AI	BP	KCS	Color
98.9	6/83	10	23.2	44.0	52.7	92.0	Four Color
				Product Category:			NOT available
				Advertiser:			NOT available
98.9	5/82	11	37.1	73.2	68.6	95.0	Four Color
				Product Category:			NOT available
				Advertiser:			NOT available
97.8	5/82	32	19.1	37.8	52.9	87.0	Four Color
				Product Category:			NOT available
				Advertiser:			NOT available
95.7	6/83	0	16.8	48.8	93.2	98.0	Four Color
				Product Category:			NOT available
				Advertiser:			NOT available

Do you want to save the output (y/n)? ⓝ

Do you want another analysis (y/n)? ⓝ

Source: McGraw-Hill Research.

ASCID—Advertising Strategy and Copy Information Development

ASCID[7] is an MDSS that aids the manager in evaluating the efficacy of new-brand advertising material. ASCID can be used in pretesting and postevaluation environments. In a pretesting environment, ASCID can screen candidate advertisements and establish a rank-ordering for the ability to "move" a referent brand to a desired position in the existing competitive space. In a postevaluation setting, ASCID can determine the positioning/repositioning effectiveness of a particular copy. ASCID generates a perceptual product space. It accepts as input either direct or derived ratings. The process begins by generating the existing product space and then fits property vectors (if available). The research analyst, using data on the existing competitive environment, is asked to indicate the desired (or ideal) position that best matches brand/company objectives. The desired position reflects the displacement of the referent brand under the assumption that the proposed copy is successful in changing consumer perceptions. On the basis of postexposure rating (either direct or derived), the referent brand is then *repositioned in the existing competitive space.* Various positioning effectiveness measures are computed. The postexposure reposition of the referent brand is accomplished in the *existing* competitive space. Figure 22-2 presents prototypical output from the ASCID MDSS.

Promotion Evaluation

A recent *Marketing News* article described the use of *K-PASA*, Kraft Promotion Analysis Self-Assessment.[8] The system provides brand managers with information on tonnage, share, and so forth as well as promotion information. The system consists of a number of reports. Each report prompts the user for input values and has query capability, reporting, statistical, mathematical, financial and graphical tools. Figure 22-3 shows a baseline application that compares what was sold by week to a base level of sales. By knowing when the promotion occurred, the manager can determine the incremental volume and profit received from each promotion. K-PASA provides quick information on the effects of a promotion on sales and volume. The information can then be divided among such factors as location, discount rate, and promotion period. Other system capabilities include profit-loss reports for each promotion and various options for specialized reports.

---

[7]Further details on ASCID can be found in William R. Dillon, Teresa J. Domzal, and Thomas J. Madden, "Evaluating Alternative Product Positioning Strategies," *Journal of Advertising Research*, Vol. 26, No. 4. August/September 1986, 29–35.

[8]"Modified Computer System Helps Kraft Make Plans," *Marketing News*, 23 May 1986, 31.

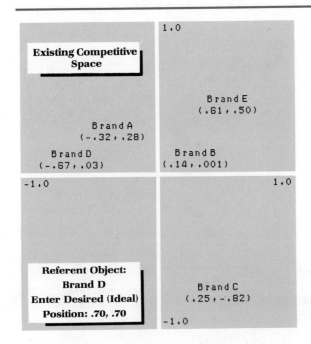

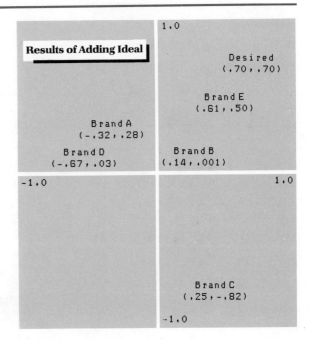

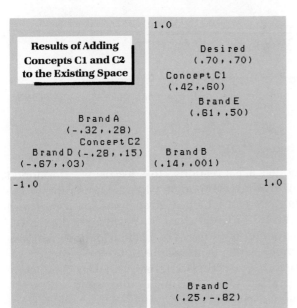

SUMMARY	Coordinates	Effectiveness index (%)
Brand D (Referent)	(-.67, .03)	--
Desired (Ideal)	(.70, .70)	--
Concept C1	(.42, .60)	198.5
Concept C2	(-.28, .15)	102.4

Figure 22-2

ASCID MDSS.

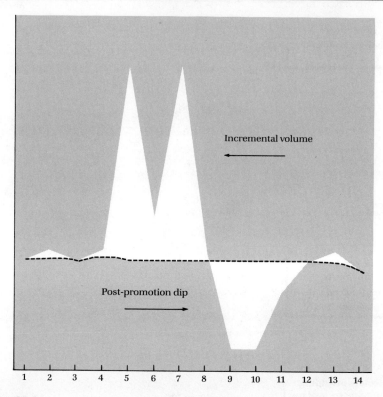

Figure 22-3

K PASA. *Source:* "Modified Computer System Helps Kraft Make Plans," *Marketing News*, 23 May 1986, 31.

Advertising Budget Decisions (ADBUG)

The ADBUG MDSS models sales response to advertising.[9] Developed by John D. C. Little, the ADBUG MDSS models what is happening to the whole industry or product class of which a given brand is a part and what is happening to the brand's market share within the product class.

The ADBUG MDSS is quite easy to use. The basic equations defining the model are few in number while, at the same time, the structure allows the manager to consider the effects on share of advertising, copy and media effectiveness, product-class seasonality and trend, share dynamics, and a variety of nonadvertising effects, such as promotion, competition, and price. Moreover, the system is designed to answer "what if" questions and perform sensitivity analyses.

In order to calibrate a sales response to advertising function, a number of working conditions must be assumed. Specifically, for a given time period, ADBUG MDSS assumes that

[9]The ADBUG MDSS is described in Little, *Management Science*, April 1970, B-466–485.

1. With zero advertising, brand share will fall by a fixed amount; in other words, there is a floor on how much share will fall from its initial value by the end of one time period.
2. With an extremely large advertising expenditure—say, something approaching saturation—brand share will increase by a fixed amount; in other words, there is a ceiling on how much share will increase from its initial value by the end of one time period.
3. There is a level of advertising expenditure that will maintain share at its initial level.
4. Based upon data analysis or managerial expertise, it is possible to determine the effect on share of a 50 percent increase in advertising expenditure over maintenance level.

Time delays are also taken into account. To incorporate time delays, the model defines

long run min = the level that share would eventually decay to in the absence of any advertising expenditures

persistence = the fraction of the difference between share and *long run min* that is retained after decay.

The advertising that goes into the response function in a given time period is determined from the following relation:

adv(t) = [media efficiency *(t)*][copy effectiveness *(t)*][adv dollars *(t)*]

The media efficiency index and the copy effectiveness index are assumed to have reference values of 1.0. If, for example, the brand manager thinks that the efficiency of the media selected in a given time period will likely deliver above-average results, a value greater than 1.0 would be assigned. These indices can be determined subjectively or can be based on data on media costs, segment exposure incidences, copy testing results, and so forth. Other factors, such as price promotion, package changes, product changes, competition, and the like, also affect share and therefore should be either directly or indirectly incorporated into the system. An easy yet effective way to accomplish this is to introduce the concept of a *reference case*, which represents a set of values against which changes can be measured. The reference case includes a referenced time period, not one of the number time periods used in calculations but one set aside to serve as a standard. Thus all time varying effects, including media efficiency and copy effectiveness discussed above, are assigned a value in the reference period.

The final question that must be answered is, "How should advertising be changed to increase profits?" The cumulative contribution after advertising in the last period of the calculation provides the answer to this question. Specifically, a slope parameter for each time period is computed. The slope parameter gives

slope *(t)* = the change in cumulative contribution after advertising in the last period, per unit change in advertising dollars in time *t*.

A positive slope indicates that advertising increases will be profitable, negative, unprofitable, and zero, indifferent.

Operation

The best way to see how the *ADBUG* MDSS operates would be by demonstration at a computer terminal. Short of this, we provide an example. The details are presented in Exhibit 22-4.

E X H I B I T 22-4

ADBUG MDSS (All user responses are circled)

```
Run

Input with data statements?  (n)
Number of periods(max 10) ?  (2)

Reference case conditions
Mkt share at start of period ? .087
Adv rate to maintain share (mm $/period) ?  (4)
Mkt share at end of period
   If adv reduced to zero ?  (.037)
   If adv increased to saturation ?  (.15)
   If adv increased 20% over maintenance rate ?  (.10)
Mkt share in long run if adv reduced to zero ?  (0)
Index of media efficiency ?  (1.2)
Index of copy effectiveness ?  (1.2)
Contribution profit (before adv. exp.)
Expressed in dollars/sales unit ?  (3.68)
Average brand price ($/unit)?  (10.7)
Other data:
Mkt share in previous period ?  (.080)
Product sales rate at start of period (MM
unit/period) ?  (78)
Average price for product($/unit)?  (10.7)

Budget horizon conditions
Consider response to product class advertising ?  (n)
Product has a seasonal or other non adv time effect
?  (n)
Brand share has a non adv time effect ?  (n)
Maintenance advtg varies?  (n)
Media efficiency varies ?  (y)
Index of media efficiency for period
   1          ?  (1.2)
   2          ?  (.9)
```

```
Copy effectiveness varies ? (y)
Index of copy effectiveness for period:
 1          ? (1.2)
 2          ? (.1)
Brand adv rate varies ? (n)
Brand advertising (MM dollars) ? (6.85)

Action code :1=output,2=change,3=stop

Action ? (1)

Period Share  Product      Brand      Contr Brand Contr Cumul Slope
       pct    Sales        sales      bef   adv   aft   contr CC$/$
       units Units Dolrs Units Dolrs  adv   dolrs adv
             (MM)  (MM)  (000) (000) (000) (000) (000) (000)
       ─────────────────────────────────────────────────────────────
    1  11.95   78   835  9320 99726 34298  6850 27448 27448  2.05
    2   5.11   78   835  3988 42671 14676  6850  7826 35274 -0.97

Action ? (3)
```

IMPLEMENTATION ISSUES

Much has been written on implementation of MDSS's.[10] Two issues critical to implementation are factors that affect adoption and implementation success.

Factors Affecting Adoption

Whether or not an organization embraces MDSS's is obviously determined by a number of diverse factors. The following discusses several salient factors that can influence the likelihood of adoption.

Payoffs. The payoffs of adopting an MDSS should be weighed against the cost. We have already described several marketing decision areas that lend themselves nicely to MDSS's. If you recall, the payoff from these systems was quicker, improved decision making. Although, in our opinion, improved decision making that leads to increased profits should be the only payoff criterion considered, there are other possible reasons for building an MDSS—for example, to (1) change the decision-making pro-

[10]See, for example, Steven L. Alter, *Decision Support Systems: Current Practices and Continuing Challenges* (Reading, Mass.: Addison-Wesley, 1980); Randall L. Schultz and Dennis P. Slevin, "Introduction: The Implementation Problem," in *The Implementation of Management Science*, ed. Robert Doktor, Randall L. Schultz, and Dennis P. Slevin (Amsterdam: North Holland, 1979), 1–15; Ralph H. Sprague and Eric D. Carlson, *Building Effective Decision Support Systems* (Englewood Cliffs, N.J.: Prentice-Hall, 1982).

cess, (2) change the organization, (3) establish a power base (a select group of MDSS users), (4) gain attention within the firm and (5) challenge the "old line." In terms of costs, one must consider *time, money,* and *dissonance* (for example, corporate inertia that produces resistance to change coupled with frustration).

Organizational Structure. The structure of an organization with respect to the stability of junior, middle, and top management, management interaction, and the degree of decentralization will affect the adoption of MDSS. In firms that are organized functionally with well-defined roles (jobs) and performance evaluation, it is more likely that the manager will have a personal stake in the adoption of any system that can enhance the quality of decision making.

Corporate Culture. The prevailing norms, beliefs, and myths of each organization also determine how it views MDSS's. How competition is viewed, the toughness and competitiveness of its marketing and sales people, the philosophy concerning market expansion and innovation, the attitude toward risk and decision making will all, to varying degrees, affect the likelihood of adoption.

Players. The quality of an organization's managers ultimately plays an important role in the adoption process. The personal values (such as loyalty, hard work, and discipline) emphasized and attitude toward teamwork also affect whether or not MDSS will be embraced.

Implementation Success

Implementation success means different things to different people. For some, implementation is successful when the manager has directly used the results derived from the MDSS in making a decision. Others believe that the fact that managers do not use the MDSS results directly is simply a sign that the manager is not losing responsibility or control—what is important is the man-model-machine interaction, since it invariably results, albeit indirectly, in a marriage of the MDSS output with the manager's own heuristic knowledge structure. Regardless of how one views implementation success, it is clear that the accent should be on improving the quality of decision making. Improvement implies change, but change alone does not guarantee improvement. An MDSS that improves decision making is "successfully implemented."

A general recommendation concerning implementation problems can be made. All of the available evidence indicates that there are likely to be fewer problems in MDSS's when the managers who must use the system are involved in the development of the system, well before the final decision to implement.

Summary

In this chapter we have attempted to provide a brief introduction to MDSS's. We have concentrated on the practical issues involved in using an MDSS and have illustrated several different types of MDSS's. By now, you should understand the essentials of an MDSS, its payoffs and benefits, and the application areas in which it can be most useful as well as how it fits into the marketing research function.

Key Concepts

MDSS

Decision calculus

MDSS essentials

Rational database manager

MDSS subsystems

MDSS benefits

Judgment-forecasting techniques

Salesforce-composite estimates

Jury of expert opinion

Delphi method

Time series models

Regression and econometric models

MDSS implementation

Review Questions

1. Discuss the concept of a decision calculus and its importance to MDSS.
2. In designing a MDSS what considerations are important?
3. Describe the potential benefits derived from using a MDSS.
4. Discuss three application areas in which a MDSS could potentially prove useful.
5. Comment on the issues that should be considered when implementing a MDSS.

Forecasting Techniques

OVERVIEW

The forecasting techniques described in this appendix are primarily smoothing techniques—that is, moving averages and exponential smoothing. In addition, we present a brief example of how regression analysis can be used as a forecasting technique. Our discussion of smoothing techniques parallels the presentation in Chapter 3 of Wheelwright and Makridakis' book *Forecasting Methods for Management*, which we recommend for the interested reader.[11]

Smoothing techniques use a series of historical data to predict or forecast the value for some future event of the series. For example, if we were interested in forecasting the level of sales for next year we would use the value of sales for some historical period (say the last ten years) to obtain the forecasted value.

The basic notion inherent in smoothing methods is that there is some pattern to the series of data and that this pattern will continue in the future; consequently, past events are drawn upon to predict or forecast future events. The accuracy of the forecast with smoothing techniques depends primarily on (1) the cohesiveness of the series of historical data and (2) how far in the future the forecast is made. Before we present the smoothing methods, let's first take a brief look at these two conditions.

When we use smoothing methods for forecasting, we are assuming that there is some pattern to the data and that each data point in the historical series represents that underlying pattern plus some random fluctuation.[12] Smoothing methods attempt to remove the random fluctuations from the data and base the forecast on the underlying pattern. When the series of data is primarily characterized by random fluctuation there exists little pattern to the data and consequently our forecasts will be based more on randomness than on pattern. Hence, we should not be surprised if our forecast does not predict the future value very well.

[11]Steven C. Wheelwright and Spyros Makridakis, *Forecasting Methods for Management*.
[12]Ibid, 30.

The second element that can affect our forecast is how far into the future we want to predict. We must remember that we are basing the forecast of the future events (forecasted value) on past events. Hence, we are assuming that the environment that produced the past events will exist in the future.

Moving Averages

The method of moving averages uses the average of some specified historical period to forecast the value of a future period. For example, if we use a three-period moving average, then the future period $(t + 1)$ forecast would be the average of the last three data points in the historical series. That is, if we had annual sales data for the historical period 1970 to 1986 and we wanted to forecast sales for the period 1987 the forecast would be the average sales value for the periods 1984, 1985, and 1986. A five-year moving average forecast would use the last five years.

Table 22A-1 contains revenue data for Tootsie Roll, Inc., for the periods 1966 to 1983. We use these data to explicate the method of moving averages. Table 22A-2 presents the forecasted values for a three- and five-period (in this case, years) moving average.

T A B L E 22A-1
Revenue Values for Tootsie Roll, Inc., for the Periods 1966 to 1983

Year	Revenues (millions)
1966	28.2
67	31.6
68	30.5
69	31.8
70	34.2
71	36.3
72	39.3
73	41.7
74	50.0
75	46.8
76	43.7
77	52.1
78	63.3
79	69.6
80	72.3
81	76.0
82	76.1
83	78.0

T A B L E 22A-2
Simple Moving Averages

Year	Actual value	Forecast 3 years	Forecast 5 years
1966	28.2	—	—
67	31.6	—	—
68	30.5	—	—
69	31.8	30.1	—
70	34.2	31.3	—
71	36.3	32.17	31.26
72	39.3	34.1	32.88
73	41.7	36.6	34.42
74	50.0	39.1	36.66
75	46.8	43.67	40.30
76	43.7	46.17	42.82
77	52.1	46.83	44.30
78	63.3	47.53	46.86
79	69.6	53.03	51.18
80	72.3	61.67	55.1
81	76.0	68.4	60.2
82	76.1	72.63	66.66
83	78.0	74.8	71.46
		76.7	74.4

TABLE 22A-3

Double Moving Averages

Year	Actual value	Forecast 3-year single moving average	Forecast 3-year double moving average
1966	28.2	—	—
67	31.6	—	—
68	30.5	—	—
69	31.8	30.1	—
70	34.2	31.31	—
71	36.3	32.17	31.19
72	39.3	34.1	32.52
73	41.7	36.6	34.29
74	50.0	39.1	36.6
75	46.8	43.67	39.79
76	43.7	46.17	42.98
77	52.1	46.83	45.56
78	63.3	47.53	46.84
79	69.6	53.03	49.13
80	72.3	61.67	54.08
81	76.0	68.4	61.03
82	76.1	72.63	67.57
83	78.0	74.8	71.94

Double Moving Averages

This method of forecasting is an extension of the moving average method. The procedure is the same; however, the values used to provide the estimates are the values calculated for the simple moving averages. The estimates resulting from a double moving average for the Tootsie Roll data are presented in Table 22A-3.

When the historical data are characterized by an increasing trend, as with the data shown in Table 22A-1, moving average estimates are always below the actual data. Notice from Table 22A-3 that the single moving average estimates are consistently below the actual data; for example, 31.8 versus 30.1, 34.2 versus 31.31, 36.3 versus 32.17, and so on. In addition, the double moving average estimates are always below the single moving average estimates. To prepare forecasts we use both the single and double moving average estimates. First we must calculate two factors, A and B. Letting S'_{t+1} be the estimate derived from the single moving averages and S''_{t+1} be the estimate derived from double moving averages and n be the number of years used to calculate the moving average, the factors A and B are[13]

[13]Ibid., 43.

T A B L E 22A-4
Double Moving Averages Forecasts

	Actual	(1) Single moving Average	(2) Double moving Average	(3)	A	B	F''_{t+1}
1966	28.2	—	—				
67	31.6	—	—				
68	30.5	—	—				
69	31.8	30.10					
70	34.2	31.30					
71	36.3	32.17	31.19		33.15	.98	34.13
72	39.3	34.10	32.52		35.68	1.58	37.26
73	41.7	36.60	34.29		38.91	2.31	41.22
74	50.0	39.10	36.6		41.6	2.5	44.1
75	46.8	43.67	39.79		47.55	3.88	51.43
76	43.7	46.17	42.98		49.36	3.19	52.55
77	52.1	46.83	45.56		48.1	1.27	49.37
78	63.3	47.53	46.84		48.22	.69	48.91
79	69.6	53.03	49.13		56.93	3.9	60.83
80	72.3	61.67	54.08		69.26	7.59	76.85
81	76.0	68.40	61.03		75.77	7.37	83.14
82	76.1	72.63	67.57		77.69	5.06	82.75
83	78.0	74.80	71.94		77.66	2.86	80.52

$$A = 2S'_{t+1} - S''_{t+1}, \qquad\qquad (22A\text{-}1)$$

and

$$B = \frac{2}{n-1}(S'_{t+1} - S''_{t+1}) \qquad\qquad (22A\text{-}2)$$

The forecasted value is

$$F''_{t+P} = A + BP$$

where P equals the number time periods in the future we wish to forecast. The calculations for the forecasts using both single and double moving averages are provided in Table 22A-4.

Exponential Smoothing

A major limitation to the method of moving averages is that the years used to compute the estimates are given equal weights and any previous years are given zero weights. For example, the estimate for 1987 would be, with a three-year moving average, ⅓ of each of the three preceding years; all years prior to 1984 would receive a zero weight in the estimation of the forecast for 1987.

Intuitively, we would expect future events to be most similar to the most recent historical events; consequently, we would like to develop forecasts whereby the most recent events receive more weight than less recent events. The method of exponential smoothing allows us to apply differential weighting.

Letting F_{t+1} be the forecast for the period $t + 1$ (that is, the next period), the formula for exponential smoothing can be written as

$$F_{t+1} = F_t + \alpha(S_t - F_t) \qquad (22A\text{-}3)$$

where

F_t = forecast for the tth, or last period,

S_t = actual value for the tth, or last period,

α = smoothing constant, which is equal to $\dfrac{1}{n}$

Additional insight into the smoothing constant α can be gleaned by re-writing (22A-3) as

$$F_{t+1} = \frac{1}{n} S_t + \left(1 - \frac{1}{n}\right) F_t \qquad (22A\text{-}4)$$

Now, n represents the number of past years upon which we wish to base our forecast; hence, the fewer the number of past years we base our forecast on, the more the weight given to the most recent observations.

To explicate the method of exponential smoothing, we again use the data shown in Table 22A-1 for values of α equal to .2 and .5. These estimates are shown in Table 22A-5.

When $\alpha = .5$ we are placing more weight on the most recent observation than when $\alpha = .2$. Notice the difference between the forecasts for years 1975 and 1977 for $\alpha = .2$ and $\alpha = .5$. In 1974 there was a considerable jump in revenues from the past period, 1973 (50.0 versus 41.7). When $\alpha = .5$, which does weight the discrepancy more heavily, the forecast for 1975 is considerably closer to the actual value than when $\alpha = .2$.

Additionally, look at the forecast for 1977. In 1976 the level of revenues actually fell from the previous year (43.7 versus 46.8). When $\alpha = .5$ the forecast for 1977 reflected this change and the forecasted value was less than the forecasted value for 1976. However, when $\alpha = .2$ the forecasted value is greater than the previously forecasted value.

Double Exponential Smoothing

From Table 22A-5 we can see that the estimates produced by simple exponential smoothing, like moving averages, are consistently below the actual values. This will always be the case when the actual values are characterized by an increasing trend. To refine our estimate, we use double exponential smoothing. As we will see momentarily, the estimates from double exponential smoothing will also be consistently below the simple exponential smoothing estimates.

Single Exponential Smoothing for $\alpha = .2$ and .5

Year	Actual value	Forecasts F_{t+1} $\alpha = .2$	$\alpha = .5$
1966	28.2	—	—
67	31.6	28.20	28.20
68	30.5	28.90	29.90
69	31.8	29.22	30.20
70	34.2	29.74	31.00
71	36.3	30.63	32.60
72	39.3	31.76	34.45
73	41.7	33.27	36.88
74	50.0	35.00	39.29
75	46.8	38.00	44.65
76	43.7	39.76	45.73
77	52.1	40.55	44.72
78	63.3	42.86	48.41
79	69.6	46.95	55.86
80	72.3	51.48	62.73
81	76.0	55.64	67.52
82	76.1	59.71	71.76
83	78.0	<u>62.98</u>	<u>73.93</u>
		65.98	75.97

The basic method of double exponential smoothing is analogous to the method of double moving averages. That is, we exponentially smooth the already smoothed estimates and use the difference between the two to produce a better estimate of the actual values when there exists a linear trend to the data.

Letting α equal $1/n$, formula (22A-4) can be rewritten as

$$F_{t+1} = \alpha S_t + (1 - \alpha) F_t \qquad (22A-5)$$

where

S_t is the actual value for period t, and
F_t is the forecasted value for period t.

The formula for double exponential smoothing is

$$F''_{t+1} = \alpha F'_{t+1} + (1 - \alpha) F''_t \qquad (22A-6)$$

where

F''_{t+1} is the double exponentially smoothed estimate for period $t + 1$,
F'_{t+1} is the single exponentially smoothed estimate for period $t + 1$,
F''_t is the double exponentially smoothed estimate for period t, and
α is the smoothing constant.

Note that

$$F'_{t+1} = \alpha F_t + (1 - \alpha)F'_t \qquad (22A\text{-}7)$$

The forecasted value F_{t+P} is

$$F_{t+P} = A + BP \qquad (22A\text{-}8)$$

where

$$A = 2F'_{t+1} - F''_{t+1} \qquad (22A\text{-}9)$$

and

$$B = \frac{\alpha}{1 - \alpha} (F'_{t+1} - F''_{t+1}) \qquad (22A\text{-}10)$$

F_{t+P} is the double exponentially smoothed forecast for the pth
   period
$P =$ the number of periods in the future we wish to forecast

Table 22A-6 presents the estimates from the double exponential
smoothing method.

T A B L E 22A-6
Double Exponential Smoothing Forecast

Year	Actual value	S'_t	S''_t	A	B	Forecast ($\alpha = .5$) F_{t+1}
1966	28.2	—	—	—	—	—
67	31.6	28.2	28.2	28.2	0.00	—
68	30.5	29.9	29.05	30.75	0.85	31.6
69	31.8	30.2	29.28	30.77	0.57	31.34
70	34.2	31.0	30.14	31.68	0.68	32.36
71	36.3	32.6	31.37	33.74	1.14	33.88
72	39.3	34.5	32.94	36.06	1.56	37.62
73	41.7	36.9	34.92	38.88	1.98	40.86
74	50.0	39.3	37.11	41.49	2.19	43.68
75	46.8	44.7	40.90	48.50	3.80	52.3
76	43.7	45.7	43.30	48.10	2.40	50.5
77	52.1	44.7	44.00	45.40	0.70	46.1
78	63.3	48.4	46.20	50.60	2.20	52.8
79	69.6	55.9	51.05	60.75	4.85	65.60
80	72.3	62.7	56.88	68.52	5.82	74.34
81	76.0	67.5	62.19	72.81	5.31	78.12
82	76.1	71.8	67.00	76.60	4.80	81.40
83	78.0	73.9	70.45	77.35	3.45	80.80

Evaluating Smoothing Techniques

In our presentation of moving averages and exponential smoothing we arbitrarily chose values for the period of moving averages, or α. In practice these values are typically determined by choosing a number of different values and comparing the accuracy of the forecasts derived. For example, we might choose values of α equal to .2, .25, .3, .35, . . . , .95 and then calculate estimates of sales for each α level. To assess the accuracy we compare the discrepancy between the actual value and the predicted value.

One measure commonly used to compare the accuracy of the forecasted values is the mean absolute error, which is calculated as

$$\sum_{t=1}^{T} \left[\frac{|S_t - F_t|}{S_t} \right] \Big/ T \tag{22A-11}$$

where

S_t is the actual value, and

F_t is the forecast value.

Earlier we described smoothing techniques as methods that use a series of historical data to ascertain any underlying patterns in the data. If the historical series is in fact characterized by an underlying pattern, then the more time periods we use the more likely we are to discover this underlying pattern. That is, we will smooth out the random fluctuations. For this reason, we typically take only the mean absolute error for the last ten or fifteen periods.

In practice the job of the forecaster is simplified by computer software that will rapidly calculate the mean absolute error (or some other accuracy measure) for different values of α and provide the value of α for which mean absolute error is minimized.

Forecasting with Regression

In Chapter 16 we described regression analysis as a statistical method for describing the linear relationship between two (or more) variables. In addition, we showed how regression analysis can be used to forecast values of $y(\hat{y})$, given some value of X. In this case, the values of X would simply be a linear trend representing the different years—that is, 1966 = 1, 1967 = 2, . . . , 1983 = 18. The dependent variable would be the values of revenues for the different years.

Regressing revenues on the time periods yields the following equation:

$$\hat{y}_t = 19.44 + 3.23 \, (X_t) \tag{22A-12}$$

Table 22A-7 presents the forecasted values of revenue for the Tootsie Roll data contained in Table 22A-1 using regression analysis.

TABLE 22A-7

Regression Forecasts

Year	Actual value	Forecast
1966	28.2	22.67
67	31.6	25.90
68	30.5	29.13
69	31.8	32.36
70	34.2	35.59
71	36.3	38.82
72	39.3	42.05
73	41.7	45.28
74	50.0	48.51
75	46.8	51.74
76	43.7	54.97
77	52.1	58.20
78	63.3	61.43
79	69.6	64.66
80	72.3	67.89
81	76.0	71.12
82	76.1	74.35
83	78.0	77.58

CASE STUDIES FOR PART VI

Case 1: To Revive Tab, Coke Stresses "Sassy" Taste Over Sex Appeal

By Ronald Alsop,
Staff Reporter of The Wall Street Journal

For many years, sexy ads sold Tab diet cola. Remember the commercial in which a bikini-clad girl strutted out of the surf while the bouncy jingle, "Tab, Tab cola, for beautiful people," played? That was the most popular Tab advertisement ever, and it ran just three years ago during Tab's heyday.

Now an underdog in the soft-drink wars, Tab is being promoted on TV these days by a wholesome young woman dressed in a man's necktie and a baggy blouse and sweater. Seated at a patio table, she tells how she converted her pal Sheila Dailey from Diet Pepsi, which Sheila once loved, to Tab's new "crisp, sassy, not-too-sweet taste."

While decidedly less saucy than the old ads, this harder-hitting competitive commercial is an important part of Coca-Cola Co.'s stepped-up plans for rejuvenating Tab, which has been overshadowed by Coke's extraordinarily successful diet Coke. Instead of a weight-control pitch for Tab, the new focus is taste.

If Coke succeeds, it will be one for the marketing textbooks. Tab's share of the soft-drink market plunged to 1.8% last year from 4.3% in 1982, according to Beverage Digest, an industry newsletter. Once the fifth-biggest selling soft drink, the 22-year-old brand now is tied for 10th place with Diet 7-Up.

"It's hard to reposition and dress up old brands like Tab and Diet Rite Cola," says Robert Weekes, an executive vice president at Dancer Fitzgerald Sample Inc. His ad agency recently helped 23-year-old Diet Rite stage a comeback.

What made Tab such a success was its loyal female following who guzzled large volumes of the stuff. Women either liked the biting after-

Source: Wall Street Journal, 14 March 1985, 33.

taste or tolerated it as the sacrifice they had to endure to stay slim. Then in 1982 came diet Coke, a sister brand that proved more tasty than Tab and voraciously cannibalized its sales. "We paid so much attention to diet Coke that we forgot to take care of marketing Tab," says Stephen D'Agostino, president of JTL Corp., a large Coca-Cola bottler.

Coke calls the Tab situation "critical" and frets that only 8% of U.S. households bought the brand in the fourth quarter of 1984 (15% bought diet Coke). Tab sales have especially suffered at fountains and in vending machines, but Coke claims that in food stores, sales are starting to inch back up. "We believe Tab can become the No. 2 selling low-calorie cola in food stores, just behind diet Coke," says Sergio Zyman, senior vice president of marketing at Coca-Cola USA. "And we're not smoking any weed when we say that."

But competitors and beverage industry analysts contend that Tab still is on the skids. Says Emanuel Goldman, an analyst at Montgomery Securities: "The erosion is slowing, but we still don't know how big that group of hard-core Tab drinkers is." He projects that Tab sales will drop another 15% this year to about 150 million gallons. That compares with 375 million gallons in 1982.

Coke won't disclose how much money it is spending to push Tab this year but says there will be more TV advertising and cents-off coupons as well as such promotions as a Tab sweatshirt offer and a Tab fitness guide.

Tab's ad budget was estimated at nearly $30 million last summer when Coke switched the account to SSC&B. That ad agency's first campaign, "Tab's got sass," began running in December, and consumer awareness of Tab ads already is growing. "Products that have gone down can rarely be brought back, but the thinking seems good on the new Tab campaign," says Faith Popcorn, president of BrainReserve Inc., a New York marketing firm. "Most soft-drink ads are talking about being part of a group. But with the word 'sass,' Tab may appeal to more rebellious people."

Coke hopes to position Tab as an alternative for consumers who want a tart, dry taste and find NutraSweet artificial sweetener a bit cloying. Tab was reformulated last year to include a blend of saccharin and Nutrasweet, rather than all NutraSweet. Promoting Tab as more palatable than Diet Pepsi's 100% NutraSweet formula may seem cockeyed coming from a company that touts its own diet Coke with 100% NutraSweet as superb tasting. But Coke's goal is to steal business from Diet Pepsi and not hurt diet Coke in the process of rebuilding Tab's sales. The cover of Coke's "Low-Cal Category Leadership Plan" shows a Diet Pepsi can being squeezed into a fizzing, mangled mess.

Pepsico Inc. has chosen not to strike back at Tab or diet Coke. Instead, it is running soft-sell Diet Pepsi commercials featuring celebrities like Geraldine Ferraro and quarterback Joe Montana. "Coke is in a pretty reactive mode," says John Costello, senior vice president, marketing, at Pepsi-Cola USA. "The company seems to have a different advertising approach every eight weeks for Tab and diet Coke."

That's an exaggeration, but the campaign to revive Tab has indeed been rocky. Last summer, Coke introduced the new formula with NutraSweet and saccharin only to be flooded with calls and letters from Tab fans who hated the new taste. Coke stuck with the revised formula, but Mr. Zyman, the marketing executive, says the company may yet develop a more satisfying sweetener blend.

Until recently, Tab also had been plagued by lackluster ads. To rekindle allegiance, Coke tried the slogan, "You're not my diet anything. You're my Tab." But that didn't slow the defections. Then last summer, commercials hailing the new sweetener blend used the tag line, "Let's taste new Tab." Unfortunately, what some consumers thought they heard was "Less taste, new Tab."

Question

1. Coca-Cola is interested in testing the effectiveness of the new Tab advertising theme. Develop a marketing research proposal for assessing the efficacy of the new ad campaign.
2. How can the ASCID MDSS be used to help Coca-Cola in evaluating the new ad campaign?

Case 2: General Foods Gets a Winner With Its Jell-O Pudding Pops

By Janet Guyon,
Staff Reporter of The Wall Street Journal

Of the more than 10,000 new products appearing in grocery stores since 1970, only a score or so have made it to $100 million in annual retail sales. The next on the list is likely to be General Foods Corp.'s Pudding Pops, frozen pudding on a stick.

Aided by a generous $25 million advertising and promotion budget, Jell-O Pudding Pops rang up $65 million in sales during their first eight months in stores' frozen food sections. The product seems certain to reach the $100 million mark by next month, the end of the first year on the market. Pudding Pops are just beginning to appear in West Coast stores, the final step in national distribution, but already they have spurred such companies as Consolidated Foods Corp., Borden Co., Unilever, and Beatrice Foods Co. to come out with competing products.

Pudding Pops have quickly established themselves as General Foods' biggest winner since Maxwell House Master Blend coffee was brought out early in 1981. And the product, with its chocolate, vanilla and banana flavors, has put new life in the company's old Jell-O brand.

Source: Wall Street Journal, 10 March 1983, 33.

Six years or so ago, marketing men at General Foods noticed that consumers weren't eating much Jell-O pudding and gelatin anymore. Growth of both products was declining. People didn't have time to make desserts, and if they did they worried about what the extra calories would do to their waistlines.

By freezing pudding, General Foods figured it could solve the problems. Preparation time was eliminated. Pudding Pops could be taken out of the freezer and eaten anytime as a snack. And they could be pushed as a healthy alternative to ice cream novelties: a two-ounce Pudding Pop has 100 calories, three grams of protein and three grams of fat; a standard three-ounce, chocolate-covered, vanilla ice cream bar has 170 calories, two grams of protein and 13 grams of fat.

The frozen confection market had another attraction for General Foods—ice cream makers who would be Pudding Pops' competition don't spend much on advertising. Ad spending outside of daily newspapers by the entire ice cream industry in 1981 amounted to only about $8.5 million, according to Leading National Advertisers, an advertising measurement service. Network TV advertising doesn't pay because labeling control by state dairy boards keeps ice cream essentially a local business. Ice cream makers spend most of their money on transportation because, unlike frozen foods which are shipped through a grocery's warehouse system, ice cream novelties usually are delivered and put in store cases by independent distributors—a relatively expensive process.

General Foods' ads, featuring long-time Jell-O spokesman Bill Cosby, were first aimed at kids and young mothers. "Mom won't throw you into the old dungeon" for eating Pudding Pops, Mr. Cosby tells a youngster, "because she knows it's made with real pudding." But General Foods has found that half the Pudding Pops sold are consumed by adults, and new ads include adults eating them in the background. The company plans other ads directed solely at adults.

To lick the distribution problem, General Foods made Pudding Pops so they would melt at a higher temperature than ice cream and could be distributed along with the company's frozen Birds Eye vegetables. Ice cream must be transported at 20 degrees below zero Fahrenheit or it will build up ice crystals. Frozen foods are shipped at zero-degree temperature. In California, however, General Foods contracted with Dreyer's Grand Ice Cream Inc., an ice cream maker, to distribute Pudding Pops because Dreyer's has a lock on novelty shelf space in major California groceries.

But distribution has given General Foods some headaches. Grocery store clerks, unaccustomed to the product, sometimes don't replenish Pudding Pops often enough, or they sometimes have put them in the wrong section—with frozen cakes or waffles, for example—where they miss out on shopper impulse buying. As an aid to store clerks, General Foods has made a seven-minute film on the merits of Pudding Pops. More to the point is a sales flier that says, "Many of your customers will go to another store if Jell-O brand Pudding Pops are not available."

Competition so far hasn't been tough, says Richardo De Santis, a manager for Pudding Pops, because no other company is spending nearly what General Foods is devoting to the promotion of its product. Among the competitors, only Consolidated Foods' Popsicle Good n' Puddin bars are available nationally. That is soon to change, however. This May, for example, Beatrice Foods Co. will start a $5 million national ad campaign for its Swiss Miss pudding bars.

Stephen Wholihan, president of Sanna Inc., the Beatrice subsidiary making Swiss Miss, contends that only Beatrice and General Foods, because of their pudding knowledge, have come up with formulas that don't have an icy texture. "A lot of the pudding bars are just fancy Fudgsicles," he says.

"We've taken a major asset—the Jell-O trademark—and used it to get into a whole new business," says Robert Seelert, head of General Foods' $3.3 billion packaged convenience foods business. Now the company wants to widen its horizons. It is [considering introducing] Gelatin Pops, whipped frozen gelatin on a stick.

Question

1. Management at General Foods Corp. was quite satisfied with the success of Pudding Pops. However, with respect to Gelatin Pops, the proposed new product entry, management was concerned about consumer acceptance. Develop a complete research agenda for testing whether Gelatin Pops should be introduced.

Case 3: Global Marketing: Will One Sales Pitch Work Worldwide?

By Christine Dugas

Just about every international marketing or advertising symposium these days has one item at the top of its agenda: going global with the sales pitch. Call it "worldwide branding," "global marketing" or any of the other buzzwords that have been coined to describe it, the idea that marketers should position and pitch their products the same way around the world is the most fiercely debated topic in international marketing. To its advocates, worldwide branding will soon make traditional multinational marketing as archaic as mercantilist theory. To critics, the air castle the globalists have constructed will melt away as soon as it is taken out of the B-school classroom. . . .

Those moves still sound heretical to many marketers who learned their trade in the multinational explosion of the '60s, when U.S. marketing

Source: Adapted from *Marketing and Media Decision,* July 1984, 20-27.

executives shed their homespun style and went native. Multinational companies took great pains to adapt product design, positioning, and marketing to the special conditions of each country they operated in: local managers who grew up in the markets they came to oversee achieved greater and greater levels of autonomy. "I say it's the height of arrogance to assume you can standardize a product and sell it to people around the world," says Eric D. Haueter, VP-corporate development, CPC International. A good many international marketers agree with him. John Lowden, VP-corporate relations and advertising at ITT, calls global marketing "ridiculous."

Even Theodore Levitt, the global guru at Harvard who preaches the doctrine with evangelical fervor, concedes that standardized selling isn't the end of the story. "The wheel of evolution will keep turning," says Levitt. Once global marketers attain the low prices that Levitt believes standardization aims at, competition will swing back to—you guessed it, "product line proliferation, differentiation and upgrading of products to suit more sophisticated tastes."

But that day is a long way off. For the moment, the cycle is going the other way and it is moving on a tide of cultural convergence. Leading social indicators suggest that while all countries have not reached identical levels of development, they are moving in the same direction. Similar patterns can be discerned: increasing divorce rates, school enrollment, number of working women and single person households. "We all know some countries are in better economic shape than others," says Jennifer Stewart, senior VP-research director at Ogilvy & Mather. "But consumer prices went up everywhere in the '70s. Automobile ownership went up everywhere, and the rest of the world is catching up with the U.S.A." Moreover, she notes, psychographic parallels can be seen around the world as well. "There is evidence that the people typologies identified in the U.S. [such as SRI's Values & Lifestyles Program] have their counterparts in other countries."

Psychographic and demographic bonds like these can prove stronger than national spirit. "Take the appeal of coffee," says Mac Cato, managing director of Peterson Blyth Cato, a package design firm. "It is much easier now to appeal to a doctor in Germany and a doctor in Italy than it is to appeal to a doctor in Germany and a steelworker in Germany."

To arrive at a positioning that will cross borders, Cato searches out "a common denominator at the core of a brand. It's a case of simplify, simplify, simplify." After all that whittling away of non-essentials, though, "a brand can be reduced to such a broad common denominator that it loses all its meaning," he cautions.

Once it establishes that positioning, the global marketer can opt for any degree of standardization in how to communicate it. "The real genius in global marketing is knowing when you have to vary the basic plan," says McCann-Erickson president Robert L. James. Goodyear, for instance, is content to provide local managers with a common positioning and advertising strategy. Beyond that, "we're not going to change a country's ability to execute its own marketing objectives as long as the general message of product benefits and product innovation stay the same," says George Lennox, VP-advertising at Goodyear.

Questions

Management for a leading brand of cold tablets in the United States is contemplating the use of a global advertising campaign. Presently the brand manager in each country is responsible for the brand's advertising in that country. A critical factor in the decision is the perception of the brand by consumers with different cultural backgrounds. Specifically, management is focusing on cultural differences with respect to similarity of the brand with its competition and the salient dimensions used to create the similarities.

1. What considerations are important in developing a global marketing strategy?
2. What research projects would you recommend to address management problems?
3. How much would cultural factors affect research methodology?
4. For this specific problem, global positioning strategy for cold tablets, would you recommend one positioning strategy in lieu of another?

Case 4: A Better Potato Chip

By Janet Guyon,
Staff Reporter of The Wall Street Journal

Twenty managers at Frito-Lay Inc. sit at a conference table, nibbling thick, white tortilla chips. The chips taste good, but the managers aren't here for idle munching.

Small tortilla-chip makers in the West have been winning customers who like corn chips to eat with meals, rather than just as a snack. Their paler, blander chips are hurting sales of two Frito stars, Doritos and Tostitos. The chips the Frito managers are sampling, a proposed new offering called Sabritas, are supposed to put a stop to that.

But there are problems. The marketing people want Sabritas to be made only of white corn so they will be pale, but Frito-Lay plants now use yellow corn or a yellow-white mix. Will a new grain bin have to be built for the white corn?

Another thing: The competing chips have a twist tie around the top of the bag. Twist ties are expensive and are a bother to put on. But shoppers might not think of Sabritas the way they do the others if Sabritas' bag doesn't look the same.

Source: Wall Street Journal, 23 March 1983.

Wayne Calloway, the company's president, gives the objectors a meaningful look. "Jerry, Jim, we need to get with this one," he says. "We're already late." A committee is formed to solve the problems so that test marketing can begin. Chief among the problem is getting the right package. This involves many decisions. For example, How should it be sealed? What color should it be? Should it say "potato chips" or "potato crisps"? Should the chips show through a window on the package? Frito figures that for a chip sold nationally, a window costs $1 million to $2 million extra a year.

Question

1. Assume that you are a marketing research analyst at Frito-Lay, Inc., working on the proposed new Sabritas brand. As part of your responsibilities develop a marketing research proposal for a package study.

PART

VII

REPORT PREPARATION

The last major part of this text book consists of a single chapter, Chapter 23, in which we present suggestions for writing and orally presenting the results of a research project. The written report and oral presentation are the culmination of the months of work involved in any marketing research study. They are the "final product" of the study. As such they must be handled in an effective and professional manner.

Presenting the Research

CHAPTER OBJECTIVES

- Explain the issues involved in communicating the research findings to management.
- Discuss the general guidelines for writing the research report.
- Explain the organization of the research project.
- Illustrate how the data should be presented.
- Discuss the general guidelines for the oral presentation.
- Illustrate the use of visual aids.

Introduction

The results of marketing research must be effectively communicated to management. Presenting the results of a marketing research study to management generally involves a formal written research report as well as an oral presentation. The report and presentation are extremely important. First, because the results of marketing research are often intangible (after the study has been completed and a decision is made there is very little physical evidence of the resources such as time, money, and effort, that went into the project), the written research report is usually the only documentation of the study. Second, the written research report and oral presentation are typically the only aspect of a study that many marketing executives are exposed to, and consequently the overall evaluation of the research project rests on how well this information is communicated. Third, since the written research report and oral presentation are typically the responsibility of the marketing research supplier, the communication effectiveness and usefulness of the information provided plays a crucial role in determining whether that particular supplier will be used in the future.

Every research firm and each person writes in a different style. There really isn't one right style for a report; furthermore, clear writing and effective speaking are individual skills that require constant honing. Nevertheless, there are some basic principles for writing a research report

clearly and making an oral presentation. These principles provide a p
spective on style that can help in communicating the critical essence o
a marketing research study.

WRITTEN REPORT

As we indicated, the written report is of critical importance since (1) it is the basis upon which decisions are ultimately made and (2) it serves as a historical record. Preparing a research report involves other activities besides writing; in fact, writing is actually the last step in the preparation process. Before writing can take place, the results of the research project must be fully understood and thought must be given to what the report will say. Thus, preparing a research report involves three steps: *understanding, organizing,* and *writing*.

Usually, before any writing is started, the marketing research supplier will sit down with a marketing person from the sponsoring firm to review data and discuss specific requirements. This "meeting" can take place over the telephone, but more often it takes place in person. The first step at the meeting is to outline the major findings and to arrange them in order of priority. As we will shortly see, a report generally follows the marketing issues defined in the "Background and Objectives" section of the marketing research proposal (Chapter 1). All report requirements are clearly explicated at this time. The meeting confirms specific dates for the delivery of the report and for other data, if requested, to be available. These dates should be consistent with the time schedule on the marketing research proposal.

The marketing research supplier is responsible for report writing. What the client (sponsoring firm) wants is a well-analyzed, tersely written report. Typically, the marketing research analyst or some other marketing executive at the sponsoring firm will be responsible for the final editing and for writing the "Marketing Implications and Recommendations" section. Whether you eventually end up writing research reports at a supplier house, become a marketing research analyst who must edit and write specific sections of the research report, or become a brand manager or other marketing executive who must react to and use the information communicated in written research reports, there are several aspects of report writing that you should be aware of.

General Guidelines

The guidelines you would follow in writing any report or research paper should be followed when you write a marketing research report.

- *Think of your audience.* Marketing researchers are primarily involved in planning and conducting marketing research studies; however, the information gleaned from the study is ultimately of importance

717

keting managers, who will use the results to make decisions.
he written report must be understood by them. Don't be
echnical and use too much jargon; in other words, direct the
d content of the research report to the audience who will
ly use it.

se yet complete. On the one hand, a written report should
lete in the sense that it stands by itself and no additional
on is needed. Remember, that for the majority of people
the report, it will likely be their only exposure to the proj-
e other hand, the report must be concise: It must focus on
l elements of the project and must exclude unimportant
sues and findings. The "Background and Objectives" sec-
proposal can help in discerning what is important.

_ *the results and draw conclusions.* The marketing managers who read the report are expecting to see interpretive conclusions about the information presented in the research report. Thus,
before you write you must understand in an overall sense what the
results mean and be able to describe them in a few sentences. Simply reiterating facts presented in tables and exhibits won't do.

Report Format

The organization of the written research report essentially follows
the format used in developing the research proposal. The following outline is the suggested format for writing the research report.

    I. Title Page
   II. Table of Contents
  III. Introduction
     A. Background and Objectives
     B. Methodology
       ■ Sample
       ■ Procedure
       ■ Questionnaire
     C. Action Standard
  IV. Management Summary
     A. Key Findings
     B. Conclusions
     C. Marketing Implications and Recommendations
   V. Detailed Findings
     A. Evaluation Measures
     B. Diagnostic Measures
     C. Profile Composites
  IV. Appendices
     A. Questionnaire
     B. Field Materials
     C. Statistical Output (supporting tables not included in body)

The following discussion considers each major component of the research report.

Title Page. The title page should contain:

1. a title that accurately conveys the essence of the study
2. the date
3. the agency (typically a marketing research supplier) submitting the report
4. the organization that has sponsored the study, and
5. the names of those persons who should receive the written report

Table of Contents. The table of contents lists:

1. the sequence of topics covered in the report, along with page references, and
2. the various tables and exhibits contained in the report along with page references

Introduction. The introduction section of the report gives details on the research project with respect to (1) background and objectives, (2) methodology, and (3) action standards. This section closely follows the research proposal except that any technical jargon that might have been used in the research proposal should be translated into everyday terms for the report. This section tells the reader why the study was conducted, how it was conducted, and how the results are evaluated.

Management Summary. The management summary is perhaps the most important component of the written report, since many of the management team who are designated to receive the report will read only this section. For this reason, the management summary must be clearly and concisely written. Only key findings are presented, accompanied by interpretive conclusions. Exhibit 23-1 provides a prototypical management summary.

Detailed Findings. The detailed findings section provides information on key measures collected in the study. Typically, findings are reported for: (1) **evaluative measures** such as purchase interest, which help answer the question, "What happened?"; (2) **diagnostic measures,** such as likes/dislikes and attribute ratings, which help answer the question, "Why did it happen?"; and finally (3) **profile composites**—of heavy users, for instance—which help answer the question, "Whom did it happen to?" In all cases, detailed findings are reported in order of importance with *unaided*-question format results reported first, followed by *aided*-question format results. This section, which is usually written by the sponsoring firm, specifically focuses on the marketing problem at hand, and, more importantly—based upon the research findings and conclusion—attempts to provide action alternatives that can potentially solve the problem.

Evaluative measures
Research findings that help answer the question, "What happened?"

Diagnostic measures
Like/dislike and attribute ratings that help answer the question, "Why did it happen?"

Profile composites
Research findings that answer the question, "Whom did it happen to?"

E X H I B I T 23-1

Management Summary

The revised edition of the Westbank Access Account commercial, "Money Crazed II" performs somewhat better than its predecessor, "Money Crazed." "Money Crazed II" generates greater brand name registration on an unaided basis (while performing at parity on total recall) and communicates a broader spectrum of benefits (combined accounts, banking ease, higher interest rates, fee savings) than the earlier version (convenient access and check-bouncing protection). Both versions are seen as relevant, creating positive attitudes toward Westbank, entertaining, and realistic, while being deficient in news value and generating "purchase" motivation.

- "Money Crazed II" is at least as intrusive as "Money Crazed." While no differences emerge between the two ads for total recall (with nearly 9 in 10 viewers recalling the Westbank Access Account brand name), the revised execution ("Money Crazed II") achieves levels of unaided brand name recall (64 percent) that are significantly higher than levels realized for the original "Money Crazed" execution (50 percent).
- Although "Money Crazed II" is an improvement over "Money Crazed," the executional device is still prominent in communication playback (40 percent mention at least one executional element in "Money Crazed II" 52 percent for "Money Crazed"). Importantly, nearly 7 in 10 "Money Crazed II" viewers and better than half of all "Money Crazed" viewers recall some services. Key areas of playback for each execution are outlined below:

"Money Crazed"	*"Money Crazed II"*
24 hour banking	checking/savings in one account
easy access to money	interest rates (high/er)
checks won't bounce	transferring money
get cash fast	fee savings

Responses to the bank service recall and main point questions were quite similar to those cited above.

- Consumers evaluated the Westbank Access Account ad on a series of Viewer Response Profile characteristics in order to yield information on entertainment value, empathy, confusion, familiarity, relevance, and brand reinforcement. "Money Crazed II" is rated at parity on most items vis-à-vis "Money Crazed," although "Money Crazed" was thought to be more entertaining, realistic, and provided a message individuals could identify with.

On the positive side, both executions were found to be relevant, reinforce favorable brand attitudes, provide entertainment value, and present their respective messages in a realistic manner. Both commercials were also judged as being weak in providing news value and a message that bank customers would identify with.

- Interest in opening a Westbank Access Account (after exposure to the ad) is relatively low, with both versions performing at parity on this measure: 14 percent of "Money Crazed" viewers said that they "definitely/probably would open an Access Account" while 11 percent of "Money Crazed II" respondents made the same assertion.

Appendix. The appendix contains information that will not be of primary interest to all readers of the research report. The sampling plan, copies of the questionnaire, details on the interviewing procedures and general field instructions, and in-depth statistical tables are generally relegated to the appendix.

Presenting the Data

Easy-to-understand tables and graphics will greatly enhance the readability of the written research report. All tables and figures appearing in the report should contain (1) an identification number to permit easy location, (2) a title that conveys the contents of the table, and (3) table **banner heads** (containing column labels), table **stub heads** (containing row labels), and figure **legends,** which define specific elements in the figure (or exhibit).

Figure 23-1 displays prototypical illustrations of how data can be presented in tabular and graphic form. Three commonly used graphic presentations are shown: the pie chart, the bar chart, and the line chart.[1] (Recall that we have already discussed graphic representations of data in Chapter 14.)

Pie Chart A pie chart is a circle divided into sections where the size of each section corresponds to a portion of the total. Part B of Figure 23-1 displays the market share, given in Part A of the figure, in the form of four pie charts. Notice that each section of each pie reflects a brand's market share in the respective region.

Bar Chart A bar chart displays data in the form of vertical (or horizontal) bars where the length of each bar reflects the magnitude of the variable of interest. Parts C and D of Figure 23-1 display two types of bar charts for the market share data given in Part A.

Line Chart A line chart represents another way of presenting data. Part E presents a line chart for the market share data given in Part A of the figure. Compared to bar charts, line charts are superior when (1) the data involve a long time period, (2) several series are involved, (3) the emphasis is on the movement rather than the actual amount, (4) trends of frequency distributions are presented, (5) a multiple-amount scale is used, or (6) estimates, forecasts, interpolation, or extrapolation are to be shown.[2]

ORAL PRESENTATION

In many instances, the oral presentation is as important in determining how the overall project is received as is the written research report. Typically, major projects require a series of "informal" oral reports

Banner heads Table column labels.
Stub heads Table row labels.
Legends Explanations of specific elements in a figure.

Pie chart Graphic device; a circle divided into sections where the size of each section corresponds to a portion of the total.

Bar chart Graph that displays data in the form of vertical (or horizontal) bars where the length of each bar reflects the magnitude of the variable of interest.
Line chart Graph where data points are connected by lines.

---

[1]As we indicated in Chapter 14, care must be exercised when making a comparison across regions and/or brands since different vertical scalings are used.

[2]M. E. Spear, *Practical Charting Techniques* (New York: McGraw-Hill, 1969), 74.

Part A: Market Shares by Region

Brand	Region			
	North	South	East	West
A	.10	.35	.12	.30
B	.15	.25	.18	.05
C	.30	.08	.35	.11
D	.20	12	.10	.14
E	.25	.20	.25	.40

Part B: Market Share by Region (Pie Chart)

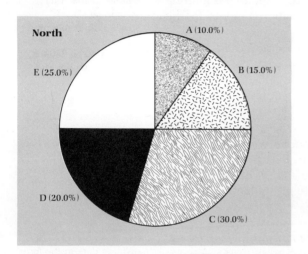

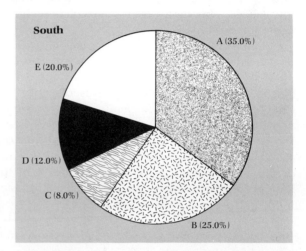

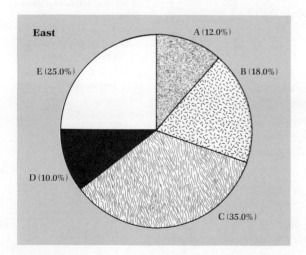

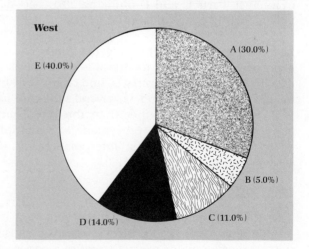

Figure 23-1

Three commonly used graphic presentations: the pie chart, the bar chart, and the line chart.

Part C: Market Shares by Region (Bar Chart)

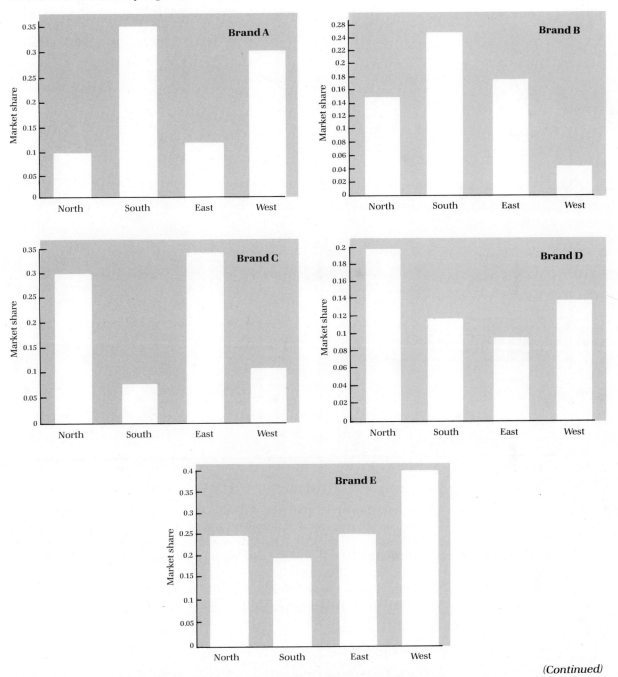

(Continued)

Part D: Market Shares by Region (Bar Chart)

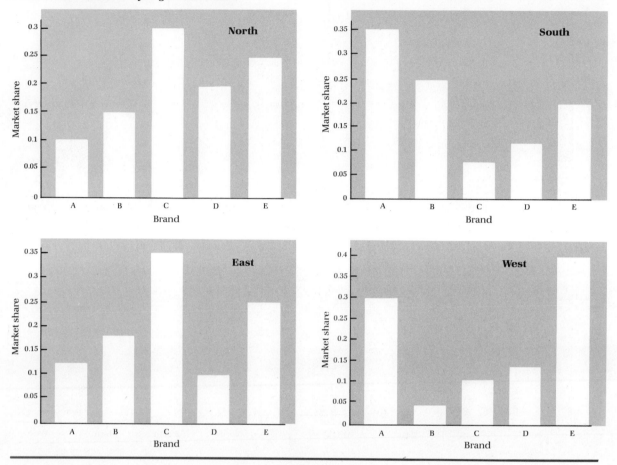

as well as a "formal" oral presentation at the conclusion of the study. The formal oral presentation given to the management team of the sponsoring firm can take place before or after the written research report has been distributed. The oral presentation provides the management team with the opportunity to ask questions and have points clarified, and, most importantly, allows members of the team to think aloud about the interpretation of the research findings.

General Guidelines

To a large extent the general guidelines for written reports apply equally well to oral presentations. In addition, the following suggestions may prove useful.

Part E: Market Shares by Region (Line Chart)

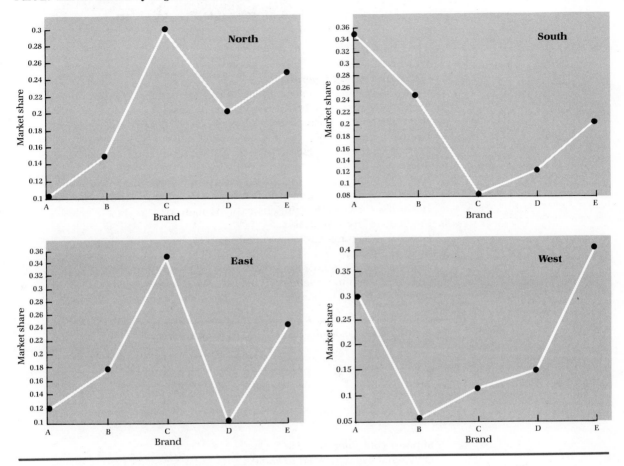

1. Prepare a written script or detailed outline for the presentation.
2. Begin the presentation with a discussion of the background of the study, the research objectives, and the method used.
3. Make extensive use of visual aids.
4. Practice the presentation several times in front of a "live" audience.
5. Check audio-visual equipment thoroughly before the presentation.

Exhibit 23-2 presents guidelines by Decker Communications, Inc., a consulting firm specializing in seminars on effective communication techniques, on the secrets to a memorable presentation.

Visual Aids

Visual aids are of critical importance to the oral presentation. Exhibit 23-3 presents several principles to consider when using visual aids.

EXHIBIT 23-2

Seven Secrets to a Memorable Presentation

1. **The "So-What Test"**
   What are three benefits to my listeners?
2. **Attention-Getting Opening**
   What will grab my listeners' attention and focus their interest on my topic?
3. **Two Experiences, Brief Stories or Examples**
   What personal or business related experiences support my key points?
4. **Quote(s)**
   What did somebody else say that is relevant to my topic or situation?
5. **Analogies**
   How can I compare my ideas with examples familiar to my audience? Statistical comparisons? Humorous stories? Metaphors? Future projections—"what if's—"? Vivid descriptions easily visualized?
6. **Pictures in my Visual Aids**
   How can I help my audience picture and remember the situation?
7. **Strong Closing**
   A day, a week, a month from now, what do I want my listeners to *do*? What do I want them to *remember*? To *know*? What lasting *feeling* do I want them to *feel*? If all they remember is my last statement, *what counts most?*

Source: Decker Communications, Inc. (San Francisco, 1982).

EXHIBIT 23-3

Principles in Using Visual Aids

Support your *point of view*
Only what listeners *need to know*
Information in *bite-size pieces*
Visual means *visual* (not just letters and numbers)
Big, bold and brilliant
Always *appropriate*
Rule of threes (maximum of six)
Don't read (look at visual, then talk to listeners!)

Source: Decker Communications, Inc. (San Francisco, 1982).

Overhead projector acetates, graphic poster boards, and 35-mm slides can prove effective in communicating the research findings. Figure 23-2 presents several different types of prototypical 35-mm slide formats.[3] Today, visual aids like the ones shown in Figure 23-2 can be constructed on a personal computer with the use of computer graphics software

[3]Available from Great Graphics, a Division of Interactive Market Systems, 19 West 44th Street, New York, NY 10036.

GREAT GRAPHICS™

Only Great Graphics offers such a complete range of
standard formats for instant, inexpensive visualization of
your data, text, or ideas.

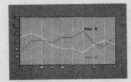

LINE
CHART

3-D BAR
CHART

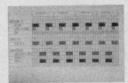

FLOW
CHART

TEXT
CHART

HORIZONTAL
BAR CHART

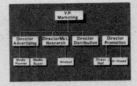

ORGANIZATIONAL
CHART

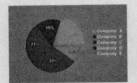

PIE
CHART

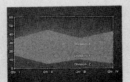

AREA
CHART

LOGOS

BUILD-UPS

MAPS

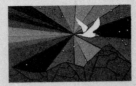

3-D designs, symbols, visuals, images, artwork
from our extensive library to illustrate and
enhance your material.

Figure 23-2

Different types of 35-mm slide formats. (Reprinted by permission of Great
Graphics.)

packages.[4] (Recall again that we have already discussed graphic representations of data in Chapter 14.)

By way of summary, Exhibit 23-4 provides the pros and cons, along with the *do's and don'ts* of using flip charts, overhead projectors, and slides.

E X H I B I T 23-4

Visual Aids

Flip Charts—Best for smaller, more informal groups

Pro
Quick and easy to prepare
Inexpensive
Easy to use
Flexible
Interactive with group

Con
Limited audience size
Limited control
Quality is limited/or costly
Bulky to carry

Techniques
Do:
Consider visibility/readability
Prepare in advance, fill in data
Speak to listeners, *not chart!*
Pencil notes lightly on side
Remove after use
Use color
Use to record sensitive questions
Turn page to reach conclusion
Don't:
Put too much information/detail on
Talk to the chart
Play with marking pen or pointer
Write too small or too light

Overhead Projector—most versatile

Pro
Quick and easy
Fully-lit room
You can turn it on and off
Face your listeners
Portable
Almost any size group
Use overlays
Inexpensive
Easy last-minute changes

---

[4]*PC-Slide*—available from Great Graphics, a Division of Interactive Market Systems, 19 West 44th Street, New York, NY 10036.

Con	Limited full-color effect
	Poor photo projection
	Screen placement
	Sometimes it is "less professional"
Techniques	*Do:*
	Use revelation
	Turn light on and off
	Have a friend change transparencies
	Locate transparency in advance
	Use pencil as a pointer
	Place screen in corner
	Make notes on frame
	Use overlay technique
	Don't:
	Put too much information/detail on
	Talk to machine
	Leave light on
	Be married to machine

Slides—Best for formal, structured speeches

Pro	Excellent visual effect
	Directed light
	Very professional
	Colorful and creative
	Portable
	Any size group
	Easily reproducible
Con	Lack of control (canned)
	Limited eye contact (lose eye contact)
	Lead time required (last minute changes difficult)
	Cost factors
Techniques	*Do*:
	Keep a light on *you*
	Reveal a "line at a time"
	Show in 6-slide segments
	Show 5 seconds per slide
	Dry run for sequence
	Don't:
	Think that slides are your presentation—*You are!*
	Read slides
	Fidget with remote control
	Beware . . . early morning or after lunch

Source: Decker Communications, Inc. (San Francisco, 1982).

Summary

The written report and oral presentation are the culmination of the months of work involved in any marketing research study. They are the "final product" of the study and cannot be handled in a slipshod manner. Both written report and oral presentation should follow the general guidelines that apply to any report or presentation—in marketing or in sociology, history, philosophy. In addition, elements specific to a marketing research report require special attention; the management summary is an example. Good reports and presentations will get the attention they deserve—and will most likely get more business for the supplier. To conclude:

- Think of your audience.
- Be concise yet complete.
- Understand the results and draw conclusions.
- Begin an oral presentation with a discussion of the study, the research objectives and the methodology used.
- Use visual aids.

Key Concepts

Research report   *Report format*
Oral presentation   *Management summary*

Review Questions

1. What general guidelines would you follow when writing a research report?
2. Briefly discuss the recommended format for a research report.
3. What general guidelines would you follow when preparing an oral presentation?
4. How important are visual aids in an oral presentation?
5. Comment on the following statement: "Although visual aids are of critical importance to the oral presentation, it really doesn't matter whether one uses flip charts, an overhead projector, or slides."

CASE STUDIES FOR PART VII

Case 1: Consumers' Attitudes and Perceptions Toward Seafood When Eating Out—Report Phase

Case Studies for Parts II, IV, and V examined various data on consumers' attitudes and perceptions toward nontraditional fish consumption when eating out. This case study presents additional information in Tables 1–4 and Figures 1–11. (This material was graciously provided by Dr. Robert C. Lewis, Department of Hotel Administration, University of Massachusetts.)

Question

1. Prepare an oral report scheduled for 20 minutes making use of the relevant information presented here, as well as in Parts II, IV, and V.

TABLE 1
Sample and Population Profiles

	n	Sample (%)	Population (%)
Sex			
Male	553	29	48
Female	1,376	71	52
Age			
Less than 29	301	15.6	48
30–39	510	26.4	14
40–49	387	20.1	10
50–59	346	17.9	11
Greater than 60	386	20.0	18
1983 household income			
Less than 15,000	160	11.3	42
15,000 to 24,999	240	16.9	27
25,000 to 34,999	341	24.0	16
35,000 to 49,999	338	23.8	9
Greater than 50,000	341	24.0	5

(continued)

Race

Caucasian	1,827	94.7	96
Hispanic	5	0.3	4
Black	13	0.7	(non-white)

Religion

Catholic	937	54.2	45
Non-Catholic	792	45.8	55

Hometown Residence

Coastal areas	1,160	60.5	53
Noncoastal areas	757	39.5	47

T A B L E 2

Behaviors and Attitudes Toward Eating Out

Behaviors

Eating Out Frequency per Month

			95% CI
Luncheon	mean	6.06	5.77 to 6.36
	SD	5.87	
Dinner	mean	5.30	5.10 to 5.51
	SD	4.40	

Frequency of Ordering Fish per Month

Luncheon	mean	3.06	2.88 to 3.24
	SD	2.93	
Dinner	mean	3.22	3.08 to 3.36
	SD	2.78	

Attitudes Scale (1) strongly disagree to (5) strongly agree

	Mean	SD	Strongly Disagree (1 & 2)	Strongly Agree (4 & 5)
Enjoy going to restaurants	4.39	.87	3%	84%
Think about nutrition	3.15	1.33	32	43
Think about calories	2.78	1.37	42	32
For special occasions only	2.29	1.32	61	20
Concerned about price	3.37	1.25	22	48
Enjoy different restaurants	4.25	.96	6	81
Try entrees never had before	3.12	1.28	32	39
Order what I don't eat at home	4.30	1.04	6	82

T A B L E 3
Familiarity with Nontraditional Fish*

A. Awareness and Trial

	Never heard of	Heard of, never tried	Eaten, did not like	Eaten, liked
Butterfish	56.5%	26.3%	2.1%	11.1%
Dogfish	41.8	49.8	2.0	2.3
Hake	33.8	43.5	4.8	13.4
Eel	4.8	64.6	11.3	15.5
Skate	25.5	58.4	3.6	8.3
Tilefish	63.3	26.6	1.4	4.4
Herring	2.0	30.8	22.5	41.4
Mackerel	1.1	18.1	26.7	51.4
Monkfish	39.8	36.1	4.0	15.3
Pollock	7.4	24.7	13.2	50.9
Squid	5.0	44.0	17.0	29.9
Whiting	26.5	35.4	2.9	28.0
Cusk	46.3	33.0	3.6	12.9

B. Experience of Tryers

	Liked	Not liked
Butterfish	84%	16%
Hake	74	26
Skate	70	30
Tilefish	76	24
Monkfish	79	21
Whiting	82	18
Cusk	78	22
Dogfish	54	46
Eel	58	42
Herring	65	35
Mackerel	66	34
Pollock	79	21
Squid	64	36

*Percentages do not add to 100% due to missing responses.

T A B L E 4

Influences in Not Trying Nontraditional Fish
Scale (1) not at all influential to (5) extremely influential

A. Mean and standard deviation

Variable	Mean	Standard deviation
Name of fish	2.69	1.55
Risk of not liking	3.36	1.42
Unfamiliarity	3.36	1.40
Expected taste	3.60	1.30
Past experience	3.55	1.45
Trust in restaurant	3.58	1.40
Image of the fish	3.33	1.46
Social behavior of the fish	2.30	1.48

B. Percent of respondents

Variable	Not influential 1 & 2	Very influential 4 & 5
Name of fish	49%	34%
Risk of not liking	28	50
Unfamiliarity	28	51
Expected taste	19	58
Past experience	24	57
Trust in restaurant	22	60
Image of the fish	28	51
Social behavior of fish	60	23

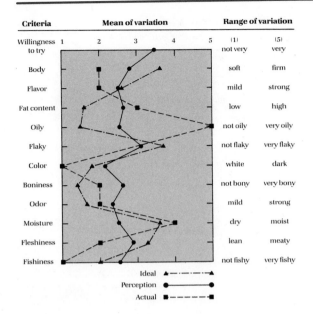

Figure 1

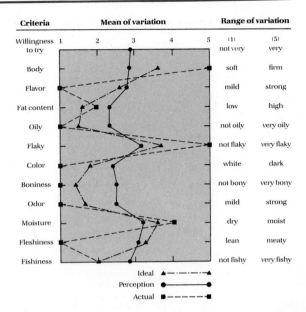

Figure 2

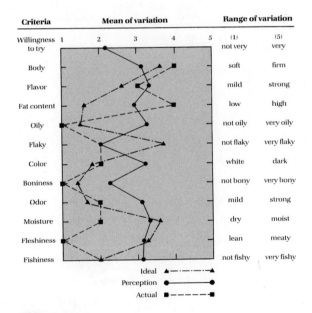

Figure 3

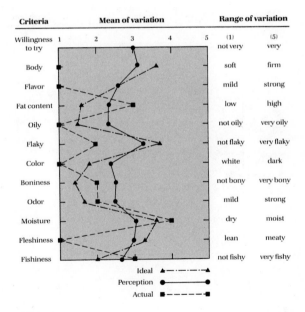

Figure 4

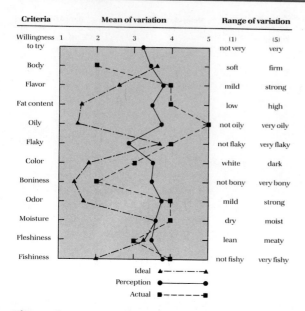

Figure 5

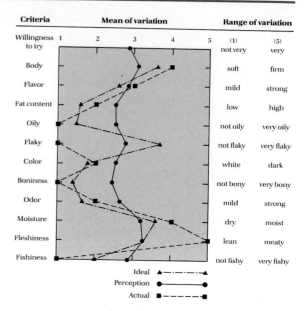

Figure 6

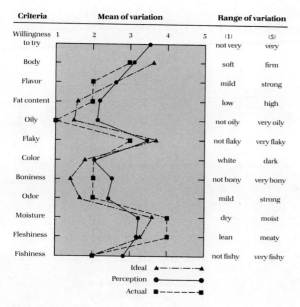

Figure 7

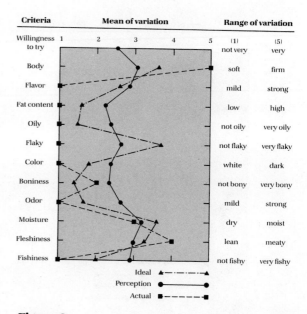

Figure 8

736

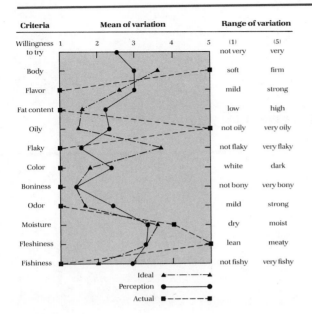

Figure 9

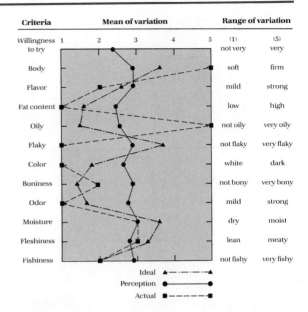

Figure 10

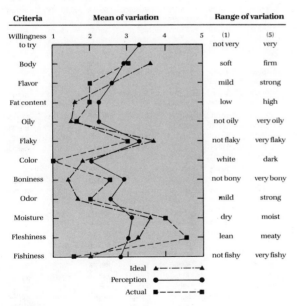

Figure 11

Statistical Appendix

T A B L E 1
Random Number Table

Line/Col.	(1)	(2)	(3)	(4)	(5)	(6)	(7)	(8)	(9)	(10)	(11)	(12)	(13)	(14)
1	10480	15011	01536	02011	81647	91646	69179	14194	62590	36207	20969	99570	91291	90700
2	22368	46573	25595	85393	30995	89198	27982	53402	93965	34095	52666	19174	39615	99505
3	24130	48390	22527	97265	76393	64809	15179	24830	49340	32081	30680	19655	63348	58629
4	42167	93093	06243	61680	07856	16376	39440	53537	71341	57004	00849	74917	97758	16379
5	37570	39975	81837	16656	06121	91782	60468	81305	49684	60072	14110	06927	01263	54613
6	77921	06907	11008	42751	27756	53498	18602	70659	90655	15053	21916	81825	44394	42880
7	99562	72905	56420	69994	98872	31016	71194	18738	44013	48840	63213	21069	10634	12952
8	96301	91977	05463	07972	18876	20922	94595	56869	69014	60045	18425	84903	42508	32307
9	89579	14342	63661	10281	17453	18103	57740	84378	25331	12568	58678	44947	05585	56941
10	85475	36857	53342	53988	53060	59533	38867	62300	08158	17983	16439	11458	18593	64952
11	28918	69578	88231	33276	70997	79936	56865	05859	90106	31595	01547	85590	91610	78188
12	63553	40961	48235	03427	49626	69445	18663	72695	52180	20847	12234	90511	33703	90322
13	09429	93969	52636	92737	88974	33488	36320	17617	30015	08272	84115	27156	30613	74952
14	10365	61129	87529	85689	48237	52267	67689	93394	01511	26358	85104	20285	29975	89868
15	07119	97336	71048	08178	77233	13916	47564	81056	97735	85977	29372	74461	28551	90707
16	51085	12765	51821	51259	77452	16308	60756	92144	49442	53900	70960	63990	75601	40719
17	02368	21382	52404	60268	89368	19885	55322	44819	01188	65255	64835	44919	05944	55157
18	01011	54092	33362	94904	31273	04146	18594	29852	71685	85030	51132	01915	92747	64951
19	52162	53916	46369	58586	23216	14513	83149	98736	23495	64350	94738	17752	35156	35749
20	07056	97628	33787	09998	42698	06691	76988	13602	51851	46104	88916	19509	25625	58104
21	48663	91245	85828	14346	09172	30163	90229	04734	59193	22178	30421	61666	99904	32812
22	54164	58492	22421	74103	47070	25306	76468	26384	58151	06646	21524	15227	96909	44592
23	32639	32363	05597	24200	13363	38005	94342	28728	35806	06912	17012	64161	18296	22851
24	29334	27001	87637	87308	58731	00256	45834	15398	46557	41135	10307	07684	36188	18510
25	02488	33062	28834	07351	19731	92420	60952	61280	50001	67658	32586	86679	50720	94953
26	81525	72295	04839	96423	24878	82651	66566	14778	76797	14780	13300	87074	79666	95725
27	29676	20591	68086	26432	46901	20849	89768	81536	86645	12659	92259	57102	80428	25280
28	00742	57392	39064	66432	84673	40027	32832	61362	98947	96067	64760	64584	96096	98253
29	05366	04213	25669	26422	44407	44048	37937	63904	45766	66134	75470	66520	34693	90449
30	91921	26418	64117	94305	26766	25940	39972	22209	71500	64568	91402	42416	07844	69618
31	00582	04711	87917	77341	42206	35126	74087	99547	81817	42607	43808	76655	62028	76630
32	00725	69884	62797	56170	86324	88072	76222	36086	84637	93161	76038	65855	77919	88006
33	69011	65795	95876	55293	18988	27354	26575	08625	40801	59920	29841	80150	12777	48501
34	25976	57948	29888	88604	67917	48708	18912	82271	65424	69774	33611	54262	85963	03547

35	09763	83473	73577	12908	30883	18317	28290	35797	05998	41688	34952	37888	38917	88050
36	91567	42595	27958	30134	04024	86385	29880	99730	55536	84855	29088	09250	79656	73211
37	17955	56349	90999	49127	20044	59931	06115	20542	18059	02008	73708	83517	36103	42791
38	46503	18584	18845	49618	02304	51038	20655	58727	28168	15475	56942	53389	20562	87338
39	92157	89634	94824	78171	84610	82834	09922	25417	44137	48413	25555	21246	35509	20468
40	14577	62765	35605	81263	39667	47358	56873	56307	61607	49518	89656	20103	77490	18062
41	98427	07523	33362	64270	01638	92477	66969	98420	04880	45585	46565	04102	46880	45709
42	34914	63976	88720	82765	34476	17032	87589	40836	32427	70002	70663	88863	77775	69348
43	70060	28277	39475	46473	23219	53416	94970	25832	69975	94884	19661	72828	00102	66794
44	53976	54914	06990	67245	68350	82948	11398	42878	80287	88267	47363	46634	06541	97809
45	76072	29515	40980	07391	58745	25774	22987	80059	39911	96189	41151	14222	60697	59583
46	90725	52210	83974	29992	65831	38857	50490	83765	55657	14361	31720	57375	56228	41546
47	64364	67412	33339	31926	14883	24413	59744	92351	97473	89286	35931	04110	23726	51900
48	08962	00358	31662	25388	61642	34072	81249	35648	56891	69352	48373	45578	78547	81788
49	95012	68379	93526	70765	10592	04542	76463	54328	02349	17247	28865	14777	62730	92277
50	15664	10493	20492	38301	91132	21999	59516	81652	27195	48223	46751	22923	32261	85653
51	16408	81899	04153	53381	79401	21438	83035	92350	36693	31238	59649	91754	72772	02338
52	18629	81953	05520	91962	04739	13092	97662	24822	94730	06496	35090	04822	86774	98289
53	73115	35101	47498	87637	99016	71060	88824	71013	18735	20286	23153	72924	35165	43040
54	57491	16703	23167	49323	45021	33132	12544	41035	80780	45393	44812	12515	98931	91202
55	30405	83946	23792	14422	15059	45799	22716	19792	09983	74353	68668	30429	70735	25499
56	16631	35006	85900	98275	32388	52390	16815	69293	82732	38480	73817	32523	41961	44437
57	96773	20206	42559	78985	05300	22164	24369	54224	35083	19687	11052	91491	60383	19746
58	38935	64202	14349	82674	66523	44133	00697	35552	35970	19124	63318	29686	03387	59846
59	31624	76384	17403	53363	44167	64486	64758	75366	76554	31601	12614	33072	60332	92325
60	78919	19474	23632	27889	47914	02584	37680	20801	72152	39339	34806	08930	85001	87820
61	03931	33309	57047	74211	63445	17361	62825	39908	05607	91284	68833	25570	38818	46920
62	74426	33278	43972	10119	89917	15665	52872	73823	73144	88662	88970	74492	51805	99378
63	09066	00903	20795	95452	92648	45454	69552	88815	16553	51125	79375	97596	16296	66092
64	42238	12426	87025	14267	20979	04508	64535	31355	86064	29472	47689	05974	52468	16834
65	16153	08002	26504	41744	81959	65642	74240	56302	00033	67107	77510	70625	28725	34191
66	21457	40742	29820	96783	29400	21840	15035	34537	33310	06116	95240	15957	16572	06004
67	21581	57802	02050	89728	17937	37621	47075	42080	97403	48626	68995	43805	33386	21597
68	55612	78095	83197	33732	05810	24813	86902	60397	16489	03264	88525	42786	05269	92532
69	44657	66999	99324	51281	84463	60563	79312	93454	68876	25471	93911	25650	12682	73572
70	91340	84979	46949	81973	37949	61023	43997	15263	80644	43942	89203	71795	99533	50501
71	91227	21199	31935	27022	84067	05462	35216	14486	29891	68607	41867	14951	91696	85065
72	50001	38140	66321	19924	72163	09538	12151	06878	91903	18749	34405	56087	82790	70925
73	65390	05224	72958	28609	81406	39147	25549	48542	42627	45233	57202	94617	23772	07896
74	27504	96131	83944	41575	10573	03619	64482	73923	36152	05184	94142	25299	84387	34925
75	37169	94851	39117	89632	00959	16487	65536	49071	39782	17095	02330	74301	00275	48280
76	11508	70225	51111	38351	19444	66499	71945	05422	13442	78675	84031	66938	93654	59894
77	37449	30362	06694	54690	04052	53115	62757	95348	78662	11163	81651	50245	34971	52924
78	46515	70331	85922	38329	57015	15765	97161	17869	45349	61796	66345	81073	49106	79860
79	30986	81223	42416	58353	21532	30502	32305	86482	05174	07901	54339	58861	74818	46942
80	63798	64995	46583	09785	44160	78128	83991	42865	92520	83531	80377	35909	81250	54238
81	82486	84846	99254	67632	43218	50076	21361	64816	51202	88124	41870	52689	51275	83556
82	21885	32906	92431	09060	64297	51674	64126	62570	26123	05155	59194	52799	28225	85762
83	60336	98782	07408	53458	13564	59089	26445	29789	85205	41001	12535	12133	14645	23541
84	43937	46891	24010	25560	86355	33941	25786	54990	71899	15475	95434	98227	21824	19535
85	97656	63175	89303	16275	07100	92063	21942	18611	47348	20203	18534	03862	78095	50136
86	03299	01221	05418	38982	55758	92237	26759	86367	21216	98442	08303	56613	91511	75928
87	79626	06486	03574	17668	07785	76020	79924	25651	83325	88428	85076	72811	22717	50585
88	85636	68335	47539	03129	65651	11977	02510	26113	99447	68645	34327	15152	55230	93448
89	18039	14367	61337	06177	12143	46609	32989	74014	64708	00533	35398	58408	13261	47908
90	08362	15656	60627	36478	65648	16764	53412	09013	07832	41574	17639	82163	60859	75567
91	79556	29068	04142	16268	15387	12856	66227	38358	22478	73373	88732	09443	82558	05250
92	92608	82674	27072	32534	17075	27698	98204	63863	11951	34648	88022	56148	34925	57031
93	23982	25835	40055	67006	12293	02753	14827	23235	35071	99704	37543	11601	35503	85171
94	09915	96306	05908	97901	28395	14186	00821	80703	70426	75647	76310	88717	37890	40129
95	59037	33300	26695	62247	69927	76123	50842	43834	86654	70959	79725	93872	28117	19233
96	42488	78077	69882	61657	34136	79180	97526	43092	04098	73571	80799	76536	71255	64239
97	46764	86273	63003	93017	31204	36692	40202	35275	57306	55543	53203	18098	47625	88684
98	03237	45430	55417	63282	90816	17349	88298	90183	36600	78406	06216	95787	42579	90730
99	86591	81482	52667	61582	14972	90053	89534	76036	49199	43716	97548	04379	46370	28672
100	38534	01715	94964	87288	65680	43772	39560	12918	80537	62738	19636	51132	25739	56947

Abridged from *Handbook of Tables for Probability and Statistics*, second edition, edited by William H. Beyer (Cleveland: The Chemical Rubber Company, 1968.) Reproduced by permission of the publishers, The Chemical Rubber Company.

T A B L E 2

Cumulative Standard Unit Normal Distribution

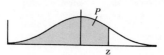

Values of P corresponding to Z for the normal curve. Z is the standard variable. The value of P for $-Z$ equals one minus the value of P for $+Z$, e.g., the P for -1.62 equals $1 - .9474 = .0526$.

Z	.00	.01	.02	.03	.04	.05	.06	.07	.08	.09
0	.5000	.5040	.5080	.5120	.5160	.5199	.5239	.5279	.5319	.5359
.1	.5398	.5438	.5478	.5517	.5557	.5596	.5636	.5675	.5714	.5753
.2	.5793	.5832	.5871	.5910	.5948	.5987	.6026	.6064	.6103	.6141
.3	.6179	.6217	.6255	.6293	.6331	.6368	.6406	.6443	.6480	.6517
.4	.6554	.6591	.6628	.6664	.6700	.6736	.6772	.6808	.6844	.6879
.5	.6915	.6950	.6985	.7019	.7054	.7088	.7123	.7157	.7190	.7224
.6	.7257	.7291	.7324	.7357	.7389	.7422	.7454	.7486	.7517	.7549
.7	.7580	.7611	.7642	.7673	.7704	.7734	.7764	.7794	.7823	.7852
.8	.7881	.7910	.7939	.7967	.7995	.8023	.8051	.8078	.8106	.8133
.9	.8159	.8186	.8212	.8238	.8264	.8289	.8315	.8340	.8365	.8389
1.0	.8413	.8438	.8461	.8485	.8508	.8531	.8554	.8577	.8599	.8621
1.1	.8643	.8665	.8686	.8708	.8729	.8749	.8770	.8790	.8810	.8830
1.2	.8849	.8869	.8888	.8907	.8925	.8944	.8962	.8980	.8997	.9015
1.3	.9032	.9049	.9066	.9082	.9099	.9115	.9131	.9147	.9162	.9177
1.4	.9192	.9207	.9222	.9236	.9251	.9265	.9279	.9292	.9306	.9319
1.5	.9332	.9345	.9357	.9370	.9382	.9394	.9406	.9418	.9429	.9441
1.6	.9452	.9463	.9474	.9484	.9495	.9505	.9515	.9525	.9535	.9545
1.7	.9554	.9564	.9573	.9582	.9591	.9599	.9608	.9616	.9625	.9633
1.8	.9641	.9649	.9656	.9664	.9671	.9678	.9686	.9693	.9699	.9706
1.9	.9713	.9719	.9726	.9732	.9738	.9744	.9750	.9756	.9761	.9767
2.0	.9772	.9778	.9783	.9788	.9793	.9798	.9803	.9808	.9812	.9817
2.1	.9821	.9826	.9830	.9834	.9838	.9842	.9846	.9850	.9854	.9857
2.2	.9861	.9864	.9868	.9871	.9875	.9878	.9881	.9884	.9887	.9890
2.3	.9893	.9896	.9898	.9901	.9904	.9906	.9909	.9911	.9913	.9916
2.4	.9918	.9920	.9922	.9925	.9927	.9929	.9931	.9932	.9934	.9936
2.5	.9938	.9940	.9941	.9943	.9945	.9946	.9948	.9949	.9951	.9952
2.6	.9953	.9955	.9956	.9957	.9959	.9960	.9961	.9962	.9963	.9964
2.7	.9965	.9966	.9967	.9968	.9969	.9970	.9971	.9972	.9973	.9974
2.8	.9974	.9975	.9976	.9977	.9977	.9978	.9979	.9979	.9980	.9981
2.9	.9981	.9982	.9982	.9983	.9984	.9984	.9985	.9985	.9986	.9986
3.0	.9987	.9987	.9987	.9988	.9988	.9989	.9989	.9989	.9990	.9990
3.1	.9990	.9991	.9991	.9991	.9992	.9992	.9992	.9992	.9993	.9993
3.2	.9993	.9993	.9994	.9994	.9994	.9994	.9994	.9995	.9995	.9995
3.3	.9995	.9995	.9995	.9996	.9996	.9996	.9996	.9996	.9996	.9997
3.4	.9997	.9997	.9997	.9997	.9997	.9997	.9997	.9997	.9997	.9998

Taken with permission from Paul E. Green: *Analyzing Multivariate Data* (Hinsdale, Illinois: The Dryden Press, 1978).

T A B L E 3
Upper Percentiles of the *t* Distribution

v^*	.75	.90	.95	$1 - \alpha$ .975	.99	.995	.9995
1	1.000	3.078	6.314	12.706	31.821	63.657	636.619
2	.816	1.886	2.920	4.303	6.965	9.925	31.598
3	.765	1.638	2.353	3.182	4.541	5.841	12.941
4	.741	1.533	2.132	2.776	3.747	4.604	8.610
5	.727	1.476	2.015	2.571	3.365	4.032	6.859
6	.718	1.440	1.943	2.447	3.143	3.707	5.959
7	.711	1.415	1.895	2.365	2.998	3.499	5.405
8	.706	1.397	1.860	2.306	2.896	3.355	5.041
9	.703	1.383	1.833	2.262	2.821	3.250	4.781
10	.700	1.372	1.812	2.228	2.764	3.169	4.587
11	.697	1.363	1.796	2.201	2.718	3.106	4.437
12	.695	1.356	1.782	2.179	2.681	3.055	4.318
13	.694	1.350	1.771	2.160	2.650	3.012	4.221
14	.692	1.345	1.761	2.145	2.624	2.977	4.140
15	.691	1.341	1.753	2.131	2.602	2.947	4.073
16	.690	1.337	1.746	2.120	2.583	2.921	4.015
17	.689	1.333	1.740	2.110	2.567	2.898	3.965
18	.688	1.330	1.734	2.101	2.552	2.878	3.922
19	.688	1.328	1.729	2.093	2.339	2.861	3.883
20	.687	1.325	1.725	2.086	2.528	2.845	3.850
21	.686	1.323	1.721	2.080	2.518	2.831	3.819
22	.686	1.321	1.717	2.074	2.508	2.819	3.792
23	.685	1.319	1.714	2.069	2.500	2.807	3.767
24	.685	1.318	1.711	2.064	2.492	2.797	3.745
25	.684	1.316	1.708	2.060	2.485	2.787	3.725
26	.684	1.315	1.706	2.056	2.479	2.779	3.707
27	.684	1.314	1.703	2.052	2.473	2.771	3.690
28	.683	1.313	1.701	2.048	2.467	2.763	3.674
29	.683	1.311	1.699	2.045	2.462	2.756	3.659
30	.683	1.310	1.697	2.042	2.457	2.750	3.646
40	.681	1.303	1.684	2.021	2.423	2.704	3.551
60	.679	1.296	1.671	2.000	2.390	2.660	3.460
120	.677	1.289	1.658	1.980	2.358	2.617	3.373
∞	.674	1.282	1.645	1.960	2.326	2.576	3.291

Taken with permission from Table III of R. A. Fisher and F. Yates: *Statistical Tables for Biological, Agricultural, and Medical Research,* published by Oliver & Boyd Ltd., Edinburgh, 1963.

$^*v$ = degrees of freedom

T A B L E 4
Selected Percentiles of the χ^2 Distribution

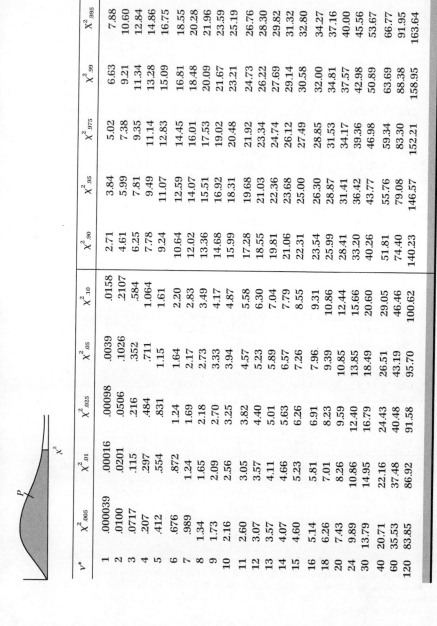

v*	$\chi^2_{.005}$	$\chi^2_{.01}$	$\chi^2_{.025}$	$\chi^2_{.05}$	$\chi^2_{.10}$	$\chi^2_{.90}$	$\chi^2_{.95}$	$\chi^2_{.975}$	$\chi^2_{.99}$	$\chi^2_{.995}$
1	.000039	.00016	.00098	.0039	.0158	2.71	3.84	5.02	6.63	7.88
2	.0100	.0201	.0506	.1026	.2107	4.61	5.99	7.38	9.21	10.60
3	.0717	.115	.216	.352	.584	6.25	7.81	9.35	11.34	12.84
4	.207	.297	.484	.711	1.064	7.78	9.49	11.14	13.28	14.86
5	.412	.554	.831	1.15	1.61	9.24	11.07	12.83	15.09	16.75
6	.676	.872	1.24	1.64	2.20	10.64	12.59	14.45	16.81	18.55
7	.989	1.24	1.69	2.17	2.83	12.02	14.07	16.01	18.48	20.28
8	1.34	1.65	2.18	2.73	3.49	13.36	15.51	17.53	20.09	21.96
9	1.73	2.09	2.70	3.33	4.17	14.68	16.92	19.02	21.67	23.59
10	2.16	2.56	3.25	3.94	4.87	15.99	18.31	20.48	23.21	25.19
11	2.60	3.05	3.82	4.57	5.58	17.28	19.68	21.92	24.73	26.76
12	3.07	3.57	4.40	5.23	6.30	18.55	21.03	23.34	26.22	28.30
13	3.57	4.11	5.01	5.89	7.04	19.81	22.36	24.74	27.69	29.82
14	4.07	4.66	5.63	6.57	7.79	21.06	23.68	26.12	29.14	31.32
15	4.60	5.23	6.26	7.26	8.55	22.31	25.00	27.49	30.58	32.80
16	5.14	5.81	6.91	7.96	9.31	23.54	26.30	28.85	32.00	34.27
18	6.26	7.01	8.23	9.39	10.86	25.99	28.87	31.53	34.81	37.16
20	7.43	8.26	9.59	10.85	12.44	28.41	31.41	34.17	37.57	40.00
24	9.89	10.86	12.40	13.85	15.66	33.20	36.42	39.36	42.98	45.56
30	13.79	14.95	16.79	18.49	20.60	40.26	43.77	46.98	50.89	53.67
40	20.71	22.16	24.43	26.51	29.05	51.81	55.76	59.34	63.69	66.77
60	35.53	37.48	40.48	43.19	46.46	74.40	79.08	83.30	88.38	91.95
120	83.85	86.92	91.58	95.70	100.62	140.23	146.57	152.21	158.95	163.64

Adapted with permission from *Introduction to Statistical Analysis* (2d ed.) by W. J. Dixon and F. J. Massey, Jr., McGraw-Hill Book Company, Inc., 1957.

*v = degrees of freedom

T A B L E 5
Selected Percentiles of the F Distribution

$F_{.90(v_1, v_2)}$ $\alpha = 0.1$

$F_{.90(v_1, v_2)}$ $\alpha = 0.1$

v_2 \ v_1	1	2	3	4	5	6	7	8	9	10	12	15	20	24	30	40	60	120	∞
1	39.86	49.50	53.59	55.83	57.24	58.20	58.91	59.44	59.86	60.19	60.71	61.22	61.74	62.00	62.26	62.53	62.79	63.06	63.33
2	8.53	9.00	9.16	9.24	9.29	9.33	9.35	9.37	9.38	9.39	9.41	9.42	9.44	9.45	9.46	9.47	9.47	9.48	9.49
3	5.54	5.46	5.39	5.34	5.31	5.28	5.27	5.25	5.24	5.23	5.22	5.20	5.18	5.18	5.17	5.16	5.15	5.14	5.13
4	4.54	4.32	4.19	4.11	4.05	4.01	3.98	3.95	3.94	3.92	3.90	3.87	3.84	3.83	3.82	3.80	3.79	3.78	3.76
5	4.06	3.78	3.62	3.52	3.45	3.40	3.37	3.34	3.32	3.30	3.27	3.24	3.21	3.19	3.17	3.16	3.14	3.12	3.10
6	3.78	3.46	3.29	3.18	3.11	3.05	3.01	2.98	2.96	2.94	2.90	2.87	2.84	2.82	2.80	2.78	2.76	2.74	2.72
7	3.59	3.26	3.07	2.96	2.88	2.83	2.78	2.75	2.72	2.70	2.67	2.63	2.59	2.58	2.56	2.54	2.51	2.49	2.47
8	3.46	3.11	2.92	2.81	2.73	2.67	2.62	2.59	2.56	2.54	2.50	2.46	2.42	2.40	2.38	2.36	2.34	2.32	2.29
9	3.36	3.01	2.81	2.69	2.61	2.55	2.51	2.47	2.44	2.42	2.38	2.34	2.30	2.28	2.25	2.23	2.21	2.18	2.16
10	3.29	2.92	2.73	2.61	2.52	2.46	2.41	2.38	2.35	2.32	2.28	2.24	2.20	2.18	2.16	2.13	2.11	2.08	2.06
11	3.23	2.86	2.66	2.54	2.45	2.39	2.34	2.30	2.27	2.25	2.21	2.17	2.12	2.10	2.08	2.05	2.03	2.00	1.97
12	3.18	2.81	2.61	2.48	2.39	2.33	2.28	2.24	2.21	2.19	2.15	2.10	2.06	2.04	2.01	1.99	1.96	1.93	1.90
13	3.14	2.76	2.56	2.43	2.35	2.28	2.23	2.20	2.16	2.14	2.10	2.05	2.01	1.98	1.96	1.93	1.90	1.88	1.85
14	3.10	2.73	2.52	2.39	2.31	2.24	2.19	2.15	2.12	2.10	2.05	2.01	1.96	1.94	1.91	1.89	1.86	1.83	1.80
15	3.07	2.70	2.49	2.36	2.27	2.21	2.16	2.12	2.09	2.06	2.02	1.97	1.92	1.90	1.87	1.85	1.82	1.79	1.76
16	3.05	2.67	2.46	2.33	2.24	2.18	2.13	2.09	2.06	2.03	1.99	1.94	1.89	1.87	1.84	1.81	1.78	1.75	1.72
17	3.03	2.64	2.44	2.31	2.22	2.15	2.10	2.06	2.03	2.00	1.96	1.91	1.86	1.84	1.81	1.78	1.75	1.72	1.69
18	3.01	2.62	2.42	2.29	2.20	2.13	2.08	2.04	2.00	1.98	1.93	1.89	1.84	1.81	1.78	1.75	1.72	1.69	1.66
19	2.99	2.61	2.40	2.27	2.18	2.11	2.06	2.02	1.98	1.96	1.91	1.86	1.81	1.79	1.76	1.73	1.70	1.67	1.63
20	2.97	2.59	2.38	2.25	2.16	2.09	2.04	2.00	1.96	1.94	1.89	1.84	1.79	1.77	1.74	1.71	1.68	1.64	1.61
21	2.96	2.57	2.36	2.23	2.14	2.08	2.02	1.98	1.95	1.92	1.87	1.83	1.78	1.75	1.72	1.69	1.66	1.62	1.59
22	2.95	2.56	2.35	2.22	2.13	2.06	2.01	1.97	1.93	1.90	1.86	1.81	1.76	1.73	1.70	1.67	1.64	1.60	1.57
23	2.94	2.55	2.34	2.21	2.11	2.05	1.99	1.95	1.92	1.89	1.84	1.80	1.74	1.72	1.69	1.66	1.62	1.59	1.55
24	2.93	2.54	2.33	2.19	2.10	2.04	1.98	1.94	1.91	1.88	1.83	1.78	1.73	1.70	1.67	1.64	1.61	1.57	1.53
25	2.92	2.53	2.32	2.18	2.09	2.02	1.97	1.93	1.89	1.87	1.82	1.77	1.72	1.69	1.66	1.63	1.59	1.56	1.52
26	2.91	2.52	2.31	2.17	2.08	2.01	1.96	1.92	1.88	1.86	1.81	1.76	1.71	1.68	1.65	1.61	1.58	1.54	1.50
27	2.90	2.51	2.30	2.17	2.07	2.00	1.95	1.91	1.87	1.85	1.80	1.75	1.70	1.67	1.64	1.60	1.57	1.53	1.49
28	2.89	2.50	2.29	2.16	2.06	2.00	1.94	1.90	1.87	1.84	1.79	1.74	1.69	1.66	1.63	1.59	1.56	1.52	1.48
29	2.89	2.50	2.28	2.15	2.06	1.99	1.93	1.89	1.86	1.83	1.78	1.73	1.68	1.65	1.62	1.58	1.55	1.51	1.47
30	2.88	2.49	2.28	2.14	2.05	1.98	1.93	1.88	1.85	1.82	1.77	1.72	1.67	1.64	1.61	1.57	1.54	1.50	1.46
40	2.84	2.44	2.23	2.09	2.00	1.93	1.87	1.83	1.79	1.76	1.71	1.66	1.61	1.57	1.54	1.51	1.47	1.42	1.38
60	2.79	2.39	2.18	2.04	1.95	1.87	1.82	1.77	1.74	1.71	1.66	1.60	1.54	1.51	1.48	1.44	1.40	1.35	1.29
120	2.75	2.35	2.13	1.99	1.90	1.82	1.77	1.72	1.68	1.65	1.60	1.55	1.48	1.45	1.41	1.37	1.32	1.26	1.19
∞	2.71	2.30	2.08	1.94	1.85	1.77	1.72	1.67	1.63	1.60	1.55	1.49	1.42	1.38	1.34	1.30	1.24	1.17	1.00

Adapted with permission from *Biometrika Tables for Statisticians*, Vol. I (2nd ed.), edited by E. S. Pearson and H. O. Hartley, Cambridge University Press, 1958. *v_1 = degrees of freedom for numerator. **v_2 = degrees of freedom for denominator

T A B L E 5—Continued
Selected Percentiles of the F Distribution

$F_{.95(\nu_1, \nu_2)}$ $\alpha = 0.05$

ν_2** \ ν_1*	1	2	3	4	5	6	7	8	9	10	12	15	20	24	30	40	60	120	∞
1	161.40	199.50	215.70	224.60	230.20	234.00	236.80	238.90	240.50	241.90	243.90	245.90	248.00	249.1	250.10	251.10	252.20	253.30	254.30
2	18.51	19.00	19.16	19.25	19.30	19.33	19.35	19.37	19.38	19.40	19.41	19.43	19.45	19.45	19.46	19.47	19.48	19.49	19.50
3	10.13	9.55	9.28	9.12	9.01	8.94	8.89	8.85	8.81	8.79	8.74	8.70	8.66	8.64	8.62	8.59	8.57	8.55	8.53
4	7.71	6.94	6.59	6.39	6.26	6.16	6.09	6.04	6.00	5.96	5.91	5.86	5.80	5.77	5.75	5.72	5.69	5.66	5.63
5	6.61	5.79	5.41	5.19	5.05	4.95	4.88	4.82	4.77	4.74	4.68	4.62	4.56	4.53	4.50	4.46	4.43	4.40	4.36
6	5.99	5.14	4.76	4.53	4.39	4.28	4.21	4.15	4.10	4.06	4.00	3.94	3.87	3.84	3.81	3.77	3.74	3.70	3.67
7	5.59	4.74	4.35	4.12	3.97	3.87	3.79	3.73	3.68	3.64	3.57	3.51	3.44	3.41	3.38	3.34	3.30	3.27	3.23
8	5.32	4.46	4.07	3.84	3.69	3.58	3.50	3.44	3.39	3.35	3.28	3.22	3.15	3.12	3.08	3.04	3.01	2.97	2.93
9	5.12	4.26	3.86	3.63	3.48	3.37	3.29	3.23	3.18	3.14	3.07	3.01	2.94	2.90	2.86	2.83	2.79	2.75	2.71
10	4.96	4.10	3.71	3.48	3.33	3.22	3.14	3.07	3.02	2.98	2.91	2.85	2.77	2.74	2.70	2.66	2.62	2.58	2.54
11	4.84	3.98	3.59	3.36	3.20	3.09	3.01	2.95	2.90	2.85	2.79	2.72	2.65	2.61	2.57	2.53	2.49	2.45	2.40
12	4.75	3.89	3.49	3.26	3.11	3.00	2.91	2.85	2.80	2.75	2.69	2.62	2.54	2.51	2.47	2.43	2.38	2.34	2.30
13	4.67	3.81	3.41	3.18	3.03	2.92	2.83	2.77	2.71	2.67	2.60	2.53	2.46	2.42	2.38	2.34	2.30	2.25	2.21
14	4.60	3.74	3.34	3.11	2.96	2.85	2.76	2.70	2.65	2.60	2.53	2.46	2.39	2.35	2.31	2.27	2.22	2.18	2.13
15	4.54	3.68	3.29	3.06	2.90	2.79	2.71	2.64	2.59	2.54	2.48	2.40	2.33	2.29	2.25	2.20	2.16	2.11	2.07
16	4.49	3.63	3.24	3.01	2.85	2.74	2.66	2.59	2.54	2.49	2.42	2.35	2.28	2.24	2.19	2.15	2.11	2.06	2.01
17	4.45	3.59	3.20	2.96	2.81	2.70	2.61	2.55	2.49	2.45	2.38	2.31	2.23	2.19	2.15	2.10	2.06	2.01	1.96
18	4.41	3.55	3.16	2.93	2.77	2.66	2.58	2.51	2.46	2.41	2.34	2.27	2.19	2.15	2.11	2.06	2.02	1.97	1.92
19	4.38	3.52	3.13	2.90	2.74	2.63	2.54	2.48	2.42	2.38	2.31	2.23	2.16	2.11	2.07	2.03	1.98	1.93	1.88
20	4.35	3.49	3.10	2.87	2.71	2.60	2.51	2.45	2.39	2.35	2.28	2.20	2.12	2.08	2.04	1.99	1.95	1.90	1.84
21	4.32	3.47	3.07	2.84	2.68	2.57	2.49	2.42	2.37	2.32	2.25	2.18	2.10	2.05	2.01	1.96	1.92	1.87	1.81
22	4.30	3.44	3.05	2.82	2.66	2.55	2.46	2.40	2.34	2.30	2.23	2.15	2.07	2.03	1.98	1.94	1.89	1.84	1.78
23	4.28	3.42	3.03	2.80	2.64	2.53	2.44	2.37	2.32	2.27	2.20	2.13	2.05	2.01	1.96	1.91	1.86	1.81	1.76
24	4.26	3.40	3.01	2.78	2.62	2.51	2.42	2.36	2.30	2.25	2.18	2.11	2.03	1.98	1.94	1.89	1.84	1.79	1.73
25	4.24	3.39	2.99	2.76	2.60	2.49	2.40	2.34	2.28	2.24	2.16	2.09	2.01	1.96	1.92	1.87	1.82	1.77	1.71
26	4.23	3.37	2.98	2.74	2.59	2.47	2.39	2.32	2.27	2.22	2.15	2.07	1.99	1.95	1.90	1.85	1.80	1.75	1.69
27	4.21	3.35	2.96	2.73	2.57	2.46	2.37	2.31	2.25	2.20	2.13	2.06	1.97	1.93	1.88	1.84	1.79	1.73	1.67
28	4.20	3.34	2.95	2.71	2.56	2.45	2.36	2.29	2.24	2.19	2.12	2.04	1.96	1.91	1.87	1.82	1.77	1.71	1.65
29	4.18	3.33	2.93	2.70	2.55	2.43	2.35	2.28	2.22	2.18	2.10	2.03	1.94	1.90	1.85	1.81	1.75	1.70	1.64
30	4.17	3.32	2.92	2.69	2.53	2.42	2.33	2.27	2.21	2.16	2.09	2.01	1.93	1.89	1.84	1.79	1.74	1.68	1.62
40	4.08	3.23	2.84	2.61	2.45	2.34	2.25	2.18	2.12	2.08	2.00	1.92	1.84	1.79	1.74	1.69	1.64	1.58	1.51
60	4.00	3.15	2.76	2.53	2.37	2.25	2.17	2.10	2.04	1.99	1.92	1.84	1.75	1.70	1.65	1.59	1.53	1.47	1.39
120	3.92	3.07	2.68	2.45	2.29	2.17	2.09	2.02	1.96	1.91	1.83	1.75	1.66	1.61	1.55	1.50	1.43	1.35	1.25
∞	3.84	3.00	2.60	2.37	2.21	2.10	2.01	1.94	1.88	1.83	1.75	1.67	1.57	1.52	1.46	1.39	1.32	1.22	1.00

$F_{.975(v_1, v_2)}$ $\alpha = 0.025$

v_2 \ v_1	1	2	3	4	5	6	7	8	9	10	12	15	20	24	30	40	60	120	∞
1	647.8	799.5	864.2	899.6	921.8	937.1	948.2	956.7	963.3	968.6	976.7	984.9	993.1	997.2	1001	1006	1010	1014	1018
2	38.51	39.00	39.17	39.25	39.30	39.33	39.36	39.37	39.39	39.40	39.41	39.43	39.45	39.46	39.46	39.47	39.48	39.49	39.50
3	17.44	16.04	15.44	15.10	14.88	14.73	14.62	14.54	14.47	14.42	14.34	14.25	14.17	14.12	14.08	14.04	13.99	13.95	13.90
4	12.22	10.65	9.98	9.60	9.36	9.20	9.07	8.98	8.90	8.84	8.75	8.66	8.56	8.51	8.46	8.41	8.36	8.31	8.26
5	10.01	8.43	7.76	7.39	7.15	6.98	6.85	6.76	6.68	6.62	6.52	6.43	6.33	6.28	6.23	6.18	6.12	6.07	6.02
6	8.81	7.26	6.60	6.23	5.99	5.82	5.70	5.60	5.52	5.46	5.37	5.27	5.17	5.12	5.07	5.01	4.96	4.90	4.85
7	8.07	6.54	5.89	5.52	5.29	5.12	4.99	4.90	4.82	4.76	4.67	4.57	4.47	4.42	4.36	4.31	4.25	4.20	4.14
8	7.57	6.06	5.42	5.05	4.82	4.65	4.53	4.43	4.36	4.30	4.20	4.10	4.00	3.95	3.89	3.84	3.78	3.73	3.67
9	7.21	5.71	5.08	4.72	4.48	4.32	4.20	4.10	4.03	3.96	3.87	3.77	3.67	3.61	3.56	3.51	3.45	3.39	3.33
10	6.94	5.46	4.83	4.47	4.24	4.07	3.95	3.85	3.78	3.72	3.62	3.52	3.42	3.37	3.31	3.26	3.20	3.14	3.08
11	6.72	5.26	4.63	4.28	4.04	3.88	3.76	3.66	3.59	3.53	3.43	3.33	3.23	3.17	3.12	3.06	3.00	2.94	2.88
12	6.55	5.10	4.47	4.12	3.89	3.73	3.61	3.51	3.44	3.37	3.28	3.18	3.07	3.02	2.96	2.91	2.85	2.79	2.72
13	6.41	4.97	4.35	4.00	3.77	3.60	3.48	3.39	3.31	3.25	3.15	3.05	2.95	2.89	2.84	2.78	2.72	2.66	2.60
14	6.30	4.86	4.24	3.89	3.66	3.50	3.38	3.29	3.21	3.15	3.05	2.95	2.84	2.79	2.73	2.67	2.61	2.55	2.49
15	6.20	4.77	4.15	3.80	3.58	3.41	3.29	3.20	3.12	3.06	2.96	2.86	2.76	2.70	2.64	2.59	2.52	2.46	2.40
16	6.12	4.69	4.08	3.73	3.50	3.34	3.22	3.12	3.05	2.99	2.89	2.79	2.68	2.63	2.57	2.51	2.45	2.38	2.32
17	6.04	4.62	4.01	3.66	3.44	3.28	3.16	3.06	2.98	2.92	2.82	2.72	2.62	2.56	2.50	2.44	2.38	2.32	2.25
18	5.98	4.56	3.95	3.61	3.38	3.22	3.10	3.01	2.93	2.87	2.77	2.67	2.56	2.50	2.44	2.38	2.32	2.26	2.19
19	5.92	4.51	3.90	3.56	3.33	3.17	3.05	2.96	2.88	2.82	2.72	2.62	2.51	2.45	2.39	2.33	2.27	2.20	2.13
20	5.87	4.46	3.86	3.51	3.29	3.13	3.01	2.91	2.84	2.77	2.68	2.57	2.46	2.41	2.35	2.29	2.22	2.16	2.09
21	5.83	4.42	3.82	3.48	3.25	3.09	2.97	2.87	2.80	2.73	2.64	2.53	2.42	2.37	2.31	2.25	2.18	2.11	2.04
22	5.79	4.38	3.78	3.44	3.22	3.05	2.93	2.84	2.76	2.70	2.60	2.50	2.39	2.33	2.27	2.21	2.14	2.08	2.00
23	5.75	4.35	3.75	3.41	3.18	3.02	2.90	2.81	2.73	2.67	2.57	2.47	2.36	2.30	2.24	2.18	2.11	2.04	1.97
24	5.72	4.32	3.72	3.38	3.15	2.99	2.87	2.78	2.70	2.64	2.54	2.44	2.33	2.27	2.21	2.15	2.08	2.01	1.94
25	5.69	4.29	3.69	3.35	3.13	2.97	2.85	2.75	2.68	2.61	2.51	2.41	2.30	2.24	2.18	2.12	2.05	1.98	1.91
26	5.66	4.27	3.67	3.33	3.10	2.94	2.82	2.73	2.65	2.59	2.49	2.39	2.28	2.22	2.16	2.09	2.03	1.95	1.88
27	5.63	4.24	3.65	3.31	3.08	2.92	2.80	2.71	2.63	2.57	2.47	2.36	2.25	2.19	2.13	2.07	2.00	1.93	1.85
28	5.61	4.22	3.63	3.29	3.06	2.90	2.78	2.69	2.61	2.55	2.45	2.34	2.23	2.17	2.11	2.05	1.98	1.91	1.83
29	5.59	4.20	3.61	3.27	3.04	2.88	2.76	2.67	2.59	2.53	2.43	2.32	2.21	2.15	2.09	2.03	1.96	1.89	1.81
30	5.57	4.18	3.59	3.25	3.03	2.87	2.75	2.65	2.57	2.51	2.41	2.31	2.20	2.14	2.07	2.01	1.94	1.87	1.79
40	5.42	4.05	3.46	3.13	2.90	2.74	2.62	2.53	2.45	2.39	2.29	2.18	2.07	2.01	1.94	1.88	1.80	1.72	1.64
60	5.29	3.93	3.34	3.01	2.79	2.63	2.51	2.41	2.33	2.27	2.17	2.06	1.94	1.88	1.82	1.74	1.67	1.58	1.48
120	5.15	3.80	3.23	2.89	2.67	2.52	2.39	2.30	2.22	2.16	2.05	1.94	1.82	1.76	1.69	1.61	1.53	1.43	1.31
∞	5.02	3.69	3.12	2.79	2.57	2.41	2.29	2.19	2.11	2.05	1.94	1.83	1.71	1.64	1.57	1.48	1.39	1.27	1.00

T A B L E 5—Continued

$F_{.99(v_1, v_2)}$ $\alpha = 0.01$

v_2 \ v_1	1	2	3	4	5	6	7	8	9	10	12	15	20	24	30	40	60	120	∞
1	4052	4999.5	5403	5625	5764	5859	5928	5982	6022	6056	6106	6157	6209	6235	6261	6287	6313	6339	6366
2	98.50	99.00	99.17	99.25	99.30	99.33	99.36	99.37	99.39	99.40	99.42	99.43	99.45	99.46	99.47	99.47	99.48	99.49	99.50
3	34.12	30.82	29.46	28.71	28.24	27.91	27.67	27.49	27.35	27.23	27.05	26.87	26.69	26.60	26.50	26.41	26.32	26.22	26.13
4	21.20	18.00	16.69	15.98	15.52	15.21	14.98	14.80	14.66	14.55	14.37	14.20	14.02	13.93	13.84	13.75	13.65	13.56	13.46
5	16.26	13.27	12.06	11.39	10.97	10.67	10.46	10.29	10.16	10.05	9.89	9.72	9.55	9.47	9.38	9.29	9.20	9.11	9.02
6	13.75	10.92	9.78	9.15	8.75	8.47	8.26	8.10	7.98	7.87	7.72	7.56	7.40	7.31	7.23	7.14	7.06	6.97	6.88
7	12.25	9.55	8.45	7.85	7.46	7.19	6.99	6.84	6.72	6.62	6.47	6.31	6.16	6.07	5.99	5.91	5.82	5.74	5.65
8	11.26	8.65	7.59	7.01	6.63	6.37	6.18	6.03	5.91	5.81	5.67	5.52	5.36	5.28	5.20	5.12	5.03	4.95	4.86
9	10.56	8.02	6.99	6.42	6.06	5.80	5.61	5.47	5.35	5.26	5.11	4.96	4.81	4.73	4.65	4.57	4.48	4.40	4.31
10	10.04	7.56	6.55	5.99	5.64	5.39	5.20	5.06	4.94	4.85	4.71	4.56	4.41	4.33	4.25	4.17	4.08	4.00	3.91
11	9.65	7.21	6.22	5.67	5.32	5.07	4.89	4.74	4.63	4.54	4.40	4.25	4.10	4.02	3.94	3.86	3.78	3.69	3.60
12	9.33	6.93	5.95	5.41	5.06	4.82	4.64	4.50	4.39	4.30	4.16	4.01	3.86	3.78	3.70	3.62	3.54	3.45	3.36
13	9.07	6.70	5.74	5.21	4.86	4.62	4.44	4.30	4.19	4.10	3.96	3.82	3.66	3.59	3.51	3.43	3.34	3.25	3.17
14	8.86	6.51	5.56	5.04	4.69	4.46	4.28	4.14	4.03	3.94	3.80	3.66	3.51	3.43	3.35	3.27	3.18	3.09	3.00
15	8.68	6.36	5.42	4.89	4.56	4.32	4.14	4.00	3.89	3.80	3.67	3.52	3.37	3.29	3.21	3.13	3.05	2.96	2.87
16	8.53	6.23	5.29	4.77	4.44	4.20	4.03	3.89	3.78	3.69	3.55	3.41	3.26	3.18	3.10	3.02	2.93	2.84	2.75
17	8.40	6.11	5.18	4.67	4.34	4.10	3.93	3.79	3.68	3.59	3.46	3.31	3.16	3.08	3.00	2.92	2.83	2.75	2.65
18	8.29	6.01	5.09	4.58	4.25	4.01	3.84	3.71	3.60	3.51	3.37	3.23	3.08	3.00	2.92	2.84	2.75	2.66	2.57
19	8.18	5.93	5.01	4.50	4.17	3.94	3.77	3.63	3.52	3.43	3.30	3.15	3.00	2.92	2.84	2.76	2.67	2.58	2.49
20	8.10	5.85	4.94	4.43	4.10	3.87	3.70	3.56	3.46	3.37	3.23	3.09	2.94	2.86	2.78	2.69	2.61	2.52	2.42
21	8.02	5.78	4.87	4.37	4.04	3.81	3.64	3.51	3.40	3.31	3.17	3.03	2.88	2.80	2.72	2.64	2.55	2.46	2.36
22	7.95	5.72	4.82	4.31	3.99	3.76	3.59	3.45	3.35	3.26	3.12	2.98	2.83	2.75	2.67	2.58	2.50	2.40	2.31
23	7.88	5.66	4.76	4.26	3.94	3.71	3.54	3.41	3.30	3.21	3.07	2.93	2.78	2.70	2.62	2.54	2.45	2.35	2.26
24	7.82	5.61	4.72	4.22	3.90	3.67	3.50	3.36	3.26	3.17	3.03	2.89	2.74	2.66	2.58	2.49	2.40	2.31	2.21
25	7.77	5.57	4.68	4.18	3.85	3.63	3.46	3.32	3.22	3.13	2.99	2.85	2.70	2.62	2.54	2.45	2.36	2.27	2.17
26	7.72	5.53	4.64	4.14	3.82	3.59	3.42	3.29	3.18	3.09	2.96	2.81	2.66	2.58	2.50	2.42	2.33	2.23	2.13
27	7.68	5.49	4.60	4.11	3.78	3.56	3.39	3.26	3.15	3.06	2.93	2.78	2.63	2.55	2.47	2.38	2.29	2.20	2.10
28	7.64	5.45	4.57	4.07	3.75	3.53	3.36	3.23	3.12	3.03	2.90	2.75	2.60	2.52	2.44	2.35	2.26	2.17	2.06
29	7.60	5.42	4.54	4.04	3.73	3.50	3.33	3.20	3.09	3.00	2.87	2.73	2.57	2.49	2.41	2.33	2.23	2.14	2.03
30	7.56	5.39	4.51	4.02	3.70	3.47	3.30	3.17	3.07	2.98	2.84	2.70	2.55	2.47	2.39	2.30	2.21	2.11	2.01
40	7.31	5.18	4.31	3.83	3.51	3.29	3.12	2.99	2.89	2.80	2.66	2.52	2.37	2.29	2.20	2.11	2.02	1.92	1.80
60	7.08	4.98	4.13	3.65	3.34	3.12	2.95	2.82	2.72	2.63	2.50	2.35	2.20	2.12	2.03	1.94	1.84	1.73	1.60
120	6.85	4.79	3.95	3.48	3.17	2.96	2.79	2.66	2.56	2.47	2.34	2.19	2.03	1.95	1.86	1.76	1.66	1.53	1.38
∞	6.63	4.61	3.78	3.32	3.02	2.80	2.64	2.51	2.41	2.32	2.18	2.04	1.88	1.79	1.70	1.59	1.47	1.32	1.00

Glossary

A posteriori comparisons
Techniques used to determine which of the means are statistically different once the null hypothesis is rejected.

A priori segmentation
Studies where the basis for segmentation, such as use, brand loyalty, and product purchase, is specified in advance of the segmentation analysis.

Acquiescence bias Tendency to agree or disagree with all statements.

Action standards A basis for defining the performance criterion that will be used in evaluating the results of a marketing research study.

Actionable descriptor variables Information on the discriminating descriptors that can be used by management in developing the firm's marketing strategies.

Affect A person's feelings toward an object. Feelings denote the person's overall evaluation (like/dislike, goodness/badness) of an object.

Affect referral Model based on consumers forming wholistic images of the various alternatives and the consumer chooses the best alternative from the set of products/brands available. The consumer choice is driven by one's overall impression and little or no cognitive processing of attribute-based beliefs is required.

After-only design Experiment that exposes respondents to a single treatment condition followed by a post-exposure measurement.

After-only with control design Experiment where a control group is added to the standard after-only design to control for extraneous sources of bias.

Aided questions Questions that provide clues to potentially help the respondent recall more accurately.

Aided recall Respondents are asked if they remember a commercial for the brand being tested.

Alpha (α) level The likelihood of committing Type I error.

Alternative-buying incentive concept-screening test Concept-screening tests that focus on alternative end-benefit incentives for a single idea.

Alternative form reliability Method of calculating reliability; the same subjects are measured at two different times, usually two weeks apart, with two scales designed to be similar in content but not so similar that the scores on the scale administered first affect the scores on the scale administered after two weeks have elapsed.

Alternative hypothesis A competing hypothesis to the null.

Analysis of covariance (ANCOVA) A means of statistical control where the effects of the confounding variable on the dependent variable are removed by a statistical adjustment of the dependent variable's mean value within each treatment condition.

Analysis of variance (ANOVA) A way to test hypotheses of no differences among means for more than two independent samples. ANOVA is applicable whenever we have interval measurement on k independent groups.

The Arbitron County Coverage Report Report that measures audiences in every county in the continental United States.

Arbitron information on demand (AID) An interactive computer-based system that provides the basis for Arbitron custom reports for clients.

Arbitron Marketing Research A customized research service offered by Arbitron.

Attitude A learned predisposition to respond in a consistently favorable or unfavorable manner with respect to a given object. The three components of attitude are cognition, affect, and conation.

Attitude-shift ability The difference between the percentage of the program audience who selected the test brand before viewing the ad or commercial and the percentage who selected it after viewing.

Audit A formal examination and verification of either how much of a product has sold at the store level (retail audit) or how much of a product has been withdrawn from warehouses and delivered to retailers (warehouse withdrawal audits).

Automatic interaction detection algorithm Division of a total sample into mutually exclusive subgroups through a series of splits. Each split is determined by selecting a predictor variable and its categories that maximize the reduction in the unexplained variation in the dependent variable.

Balanced scale Scale using an equal number of favorable and unfavorable categories.

Banner The variables that span the columns of the cross-tab; generally represents the subgroups being used in the analysis.

Bar chart Graph that displays data in the form of vertical (or horizontal) bars where the length of each bar reflects the magnitude of the variable of interest.

Bayesian decision analysis Process that bases the decision on how large a sample to draw on both the expected value of the information obtained by the sample and the cost of taking the sample.

Before-after design Experiment where a measurement is taken from respondents before they receive the experimental treatment condition; the experimental treatment is then introduced, and post-treatment measurement is taken.

Before-after with control design Experiment that adds a control group to the basic before-after design; the control group is never exposed to the experimental treatment.

Behavioral intentions A person's intentions to perform a specific behavior with regard to an object.

Between group variation Between-group differences in scores for groups that were exposed to different treatments—represents "explained" variation.

Bibliographic databases Computerized files that contain citations to journal articles, government documents, technical reports, market research studies, newspaper articles, dissertations, patents, and so on.

Blind guessing   Using informed intuition to determine how many units to sample.

Blind testing   Tests where the brand name of the product is not disclosed during test.

Bottom-up approach   Process of building up clusters—at the beginning, each respondent belongs to his or her own cluster and then clusters are joined together on the basis of their similarity.

Box and whisker plots   A graphic technique that provides information about central tendency, variability, and shape of distribution.

Brand switching   The probability of purchasing Brand X, given that Brand Y was purchased on the last purchase occasion.

Branded testing   Test where brand name of product is disclosed during test.

Buying power index (BPI)   A weighted index that converts three basic elements—population, effective buying income, and retail sales—into a measurement of a market's ability to buy, expressed as a percentage of U.S. potential.

Cartoon completion test   Projective technique that presents respondents with a cartoon of a particular situation and asks them to suggest the dialogue that one cartoon character might make in response to the comment(s) of another cartoon character.

Case   The unit of analysis for the study.

Casewise deletion   Strategy for missing responses where any case, respondent, is removed if any of his or her reponses are identified as missing.

Causality   Relationship where a change in one variable produces a change in another variable. One variable affects, influences, or determines some other variable.

Cell matching   Sample balancing procedure that involves adjusting each cell individually to match the corresponding population frequency.

Check-in   Procedure by which questionnaires are checked for quota completion and to see that screening questions, skip patterns, open-ended question probing, and so forth have been properly conducted.

Chi-square test statistic   Measure of the goodness of fit between the numbers observed in the sample and the numbers we should have seen in the sample given the null hypothesis is true.

Classification variable   Variable used to place each population element into a particular subpopulation.

Cleaning   A check of all internal consistencies, all possible codes, and all impossible punches.

Closed-ended questions   Questions for which the respondent has a limited number of answer choices.

Clusters   Groups or collections of sampling units.

Cluster analysis   Commonly used technique for allocating respondents to segments where respondents are clustered on the basis of benefit sought, need, or other relevant characteristics and where the number and type of segments are determined by the clustering technique being used.

Cluster profiles   Profiling of each segment in terms of its distinctive features.

Cluster sampling   Design where a sample of clusters is first selected and then a decision on which sampling units to include in the sample is made.

Code sheets   Forms that give instructions to the coders about how each question is to be handled.

Coding   Assignment of a numerical value (code) or alphanumerical symbol to represent a specific response to a specific question along with the column position that the designated code or symbol will occupy on a data record.

Coefficient of determination (r^2)   The ratio of explained to total variation.

Coefficient of variation (C_y)   A measure of relative dispersion given by dividing the population mean by its (true) standard deviation.

Cognitions A person's knowledge, opinions, beliefs, and thoughts about the object.

"Cold" mail surveys Surveys in which questionnaires are sent to a "cold" group of individuals who have not previously agreed to participate in the study.

Company names Corporate names attached to the products they market.

Comparative scaling (nonmetric scaling) Scaling process in which the subject is asked to compare a set of stimulus objects directly against one another.

Comparison product tests Designs where a consumer rates products by directly comparing two or more products.

Compensatory models Models based on weighting, either through an adding or averaging combinatorial rule, attribute-based information concerning the alternative product/brands under consideration such that the presence of one or more attributes can compensate for the absence of other attributes.

Completely randomized factorial designs Generic name for class of designs where each level of a particular treatment is crossed with each level of another treatment.

Compositional models Models that focus on the relationship between evaluative judgments and subjective attribute perceptions.

Comprehension/believability Percentage of respondents in the program audience that correctly understood/believed product claims communicated in the test commercial.

Computer-assisted telephone interviewing (CATI) Survey systems involving a computerized survey instrument. The survey questionnaire is either entered into the memory of a large mainframe computer, into a small microprocessor, or even into a personal computer. The interviewer reads the questions from the CRT screen and records the respondent's answers directly into the computer memory banks by using the terminal keyboard or special touch- or light-sensitive screens.

Concept An idea aimed at satisfying consumer wants and needs.

Concept board Illustration and copy describing how the product works and its end benefits.

Concept/construct Names given to characteristics that we wish to measure.

Concept-evaluation tests Concept tests designed to gauge consumer interest and determine strength and weaknesses of the concept.

Concept-screening tests Concept tests for screening new product ideas or alternative end-benefits for a single product idea.

Concept tests Collection of information on purchase intentions, likes/dislikes, and attribute ratings in order to measure the relative appeal of ideas or alternative positioning and to provide direction for the development of the product and the product advertising.

Concomitant variation The degree to which a variable (X) thought to be a cause covaries with a variable (y) thought to be an effect.

Conditional rank orders Procedure that takes each object in turn as a standard for comparison. Each respondent is asked to rank the remaining objects in order of their similarity to this standard.

Confidence interval Range into which the true population value of the characteristic being measured will fall, assuming a given level of certainty.

Confirmatory analysis Approach that uses prior knowledge of the presumed relationships among a set of products or brands to infer what the structure should look like; also a method where we can restrict the parameters of the system to be consistent with the hypothesized structure.

Confounds or confounding variables Extraneous causal factors (variables) that can possibly affect the dependent variable and, therefore, must be controlled.

Conjoint analysis Decompositional approach in which respondents react to various products, brands, concepts, in terms of overall preference, where the various objects being evaluated reflect a predetermined combination of attributes in some systematic way.

Connotative meaning The associations that the name implies, beyond its literal, explicit meaning; the imagery associated with a brand name.

Constant sum scale Procedure where respondents are instructed to allocate a number of points or chips among alternatives according to some criterion—for example, preference, importance, and so on.

Constitutive definition Specifications for the domain of the construct of interest so as to distinguish it from other similar but different constructs.

Construct validity Determination of whether the independent and dependent variables in a study adequately represent the intended theoretical constructs.

Content validity Indication of the representativeness of the content of a measurement scale; focuses on whether the scale items adequately cover the entire domain of the construct under study.

Continuous rating scale (graphic rating scale) Procedure that instructs the respondent to assign a rating by placing a marker at the appropriate position on a line that best describes the object under study.

Control population Sample known to be representative of the population distribution with respect to the variables of interest.

Control test market Method where the entire test market project is handled by an outside research company.

Controlled store testing Audit where the supplier takes over warehousing and distribution of test product as well as total control of test variables within the market under examination—in addition to the basic task of measuring product sales.

Convenience samples Studies in which respondent participation is voluntary or which leaves the selection of sampling units primarily up to the interviewer.

Convergent validity Indication of the extent to which measurement scales designed to measure the same construct are related.

Copy recall Percentage of respondents in the program audience that correctly recalled copy elements in the test commercial.

Copy testing Generic term for advertising effectiveness studies.

Covariation A systematic relationship between the level of one variable and the level of some other variable.

CPM (cost-per-thousand) Cost-efficiency calculation that represents a television program's ability to deliver the largest target audience at the smallest cost.

Cramer's contingency coefficient (V) Measure of the degree of association between nominal variables which is appropriate for any size contingency table.

Created names Names that do not have literal meaning with respect to the characteristics of a product;

however, through advertising they may acquire indirect meaning that can reflect favorably on the product.

Creation Situation where a respondent recalls an event that did not actually occur.

Criterion of internal consistency An individual item satisfies the criterion of internal consistency if the item score significantly correlates with the attitude score.

Criterion or dependent variable The variable to be predicted.

Criterion validity *(predictive validity)* Indication of whether the measurement scale behaves as expected in relation to other constructs.

Cronbach's alpha Mean reliability coefficient calculated from all possible split-half partitions of a measurement scale.

Cross-price elasticity of demand The percentage of change in demand for one product divided by the percentage change in price of the second product, assuming that all other factors affecting demand are constant.

Cross-sectional surveys Collection of informative data from a number of different respondents at a single point in time.

Cross-tabulation Common method for describing frequency distributions of two variables simultaneously.

Custom research services Tailor-made, one-of-a-kind studies.

Day-after recall (DAR) Single exposure on-air technique where the test commercial is aired in several test cities; the next day, a sample of respondents who say they viewed the program on which the test commercial was telecast are interviewed.

Debriefing Procedure of asking respondents to explain their answers, to state the meaning of each question, and to describe any problems they had with answering or completing the questionnaire.

Decision calculus A model-based set of procedures for processing data and managerial judgments designed to assist a manager in decision making.

Decision sequence analysis Process that uses protocols of consumer decision making that indicate the sequence in which various pieces of information (such as price or brand name) are employed to reach a final decision.

Decompositional models Models that use overall evaluative judgments instead of set criteria to make inferences about product/brand attributes that presumably were themselves used to form those overall evaluative judgments.

Delphi method A method of forecasting based on asking a group of experts for their best estimate of a future event, then processing and feeding back some of the information obtained, and then repeating the process; on the last set of responses, the median is usually chosen as the best estimate for the group.

Demand artifacts Those aspects of the experiment that cause respondents to perceive, interpret, and act upon what is believed to be the expected or desired behavior.

Dendogram A tree-like structure that shows which clusters were joined or partitioned at each step.

Denotative meaning The literal, explicit meaning of a name.

Dependent variable The response measure under study in an experiment whose value is determined by the independent variable.

Depth interview ("one-on-one") Sessions in which free association and hidden sources of feelings are discussed, generally through a very loose, unstructured question-guide administered by a highly skilled interviewer. Attempts to uncover underlying motivations, prejudice, attitudes toward sensitive issues, etc.

Derived similarities Similarity data constructed or derived from the respondent's ratings of each stimulus on a set of verbal descriptors. The respondent is presented with each object and asked to evaluate it on a number of adjectives.

Derived substitutability Form of judgmental data collection where respondents indicate the degree to which a set of products or brands are substitutes.

Description Collecting basic descriptive data on the company, competitors, customers, served markets, and other aspects of the external environment.

Designer names Names associated with leading figures of fashion design and lent to mass-marketed fashion and accessories.

Diagnostic measures Like/dislike and attribute ratings that help answer the question, "Why did it happen?"

Diary panels Samples of households that have agreed to provide specific information regularly over an extended period of time. Respondents in a diary panel are asked to record specific behaviors as they occur, as opposed to merely responding to a series of questions.

Directory-based sampling designs Sample where telephone numbers are selected from the directory in some prescribed way.

Directory databases Computerized files composed of information about individuals, organizations, and services.

Direct or positive association Relationship where, as the value of one variable increases (decreases), there is a tendency for the value of the other variable to increase (decrease).

Direct similarities The case where respondents are presented with object pairs and asked to judge their similarity.

Discriminant functions Axes or dimensions that in some sense account for brand differences.

Discriminant validity Indication of extent to which the measurement scale is novel and not simply a reflection of some other variable.

Discrimination/difference designs Tests where a respondent is asked if one product differs from others.

Discussion guide Agenda that establishes the plan of the focus group interview, including the topics to be covered and sometimes the time allocated to each topic.

Disproportional or optimal allocation Double weighting scheme where the number of sample elements taken from a given stratum is proportional to the relative size of the stratum and the standard deviation of the distribution of the characteristic under consideration among all elements in the stratum.

Dollar metric scale (graded paired comparison) Scale that extends the paired comparison method by asking respondents to indicate which brand is preferred and how much they are willing to pay to acquire their preferred brand.

Double-barreled questions Questions in which two opinions are joined together.

"Dummy-magazine" tests A test format using a dummy magazine that looks realistic, and which systematically varies the advertisements in such a way that some families receive a dummy magazine containing the test ad and other (matched) families receive a dummy magazine containing no ads at all.

Duo-trio designs Test where a respondent is given a standard product and asked to determine which of two other products is most similar.

Editing process Review of the questionnaires for maximum accuracy and precision.

Electronic scanner services Services that record information on *actual* purchase behavior, as opposed to human reported behavior, through electronic optical checkout devices.

"Empirical" Hendry system Method for investigating competitive structure where switching between competitive products is proportional to the product of market shares.

End benefits What the product offers in terms of satisfying the consumer's wants and needs.

Error component Those factors that cause the person's observed scale score to differ from the person's true score.

Estimation of effects Method of handling nonresponse error by linking nonresponse rates to nonresponse effects; to estimate the effects of nonresponse, nonresponse size is linked to estimates of differences between respondents and nonrespondents.

Evaluation Judging the success of what has been done or the likelihood of future success.

Evaluative measures Research findings that help answer the question, "What happened?"

Experimental design Research concept where the researcher has direct control over at least one independent variable and manipulates at least one independent variable.

Experimental effect Impact of the treatment conditions on the dependent variable. Each treatment condition's effect indicates the influence of that condition on the dependent variable.

Explanation An attempt to describe the conditions under which events vary or to identify its antecedents, causes, or effects so as to understand the event under study.

Explicit descriptive names Names that are meant to describe the physical product.

Exploratory analysis Type of analysis which assumes that no prior knowledge of the structure of the market is known. In such cases, the data alone provide the basis for the structure uncovered.

Extended-use product test In-home test where respondent is given opportunity to use the product over a period of weeks.

External secondary data Data available outside the organization from libraries and syndicated services.

External validity Determination of whether the research findings of a study (cause-and-effect relationships) can be generalized to and across populations of persons, settings, and times.

Fad or specialty products Concepts with low purchase-intent but high uniqueness scores.

Field experimental environments Natural settings; experiments undertaken in the environment in which the behavior under study would likely occur.

Finite population correction factor (fpc) Correction for overestimation of the estimated variance (standard deviation) of a population parameter (such as a mean, or proportion) when the target sample represents 10–20 percent or more of the target population.

First-choice model Conjoint analysis model that assumes individuals always choose products for which they have greatest utility.

Focus group interview Interview where the interviewer listens to a group of individuals, belonging to the appropriate target market, talk about an important marketing issue.

Follow-ups Ways of contacting the respondent periodically after the initial contact.

Foot-in-the-door technique Method of reducing nonresponse involves first getting respondents to complete a relatively short, simple questionnaire and then, at some later time, asking them to complete a larger questionnaire on the same general topic.

Forced exposure tests Design where pre- and post-exposure purchase-preference questions are asked.

Forced itemized rating scale Procedure in which a respondent indicates a response on a scale, even though he or she may have "no opinion" or "no knowledge" about the question.

Frequency distribution The number of respondents who chose each alternative answer as well as the percentage and cumulative percentage of respondents answering.

Full profile procedure Technique that simultaneously presents the respondent with a complete set of attribute descriptors. A stimulus card presents respondents with an attribute descriptor for each attribute included in the study; and respondents are asked for an evaluation of the product alternative defined by the selected attribute descriptors appearing on the card.

Full-service suppliers External parties that perform all aspects of a research project.

Full-text databases Computerized files containing the complete text of the source documents that make up the database.

Funnel sequence The procedure of asking the most general (or unrestricted) question about the topic under study first, followed by successively more restricted questions.

Gap Difference between the operational population and the target population.

Graduated buying power indexes Indexes that correlate product potential and buying power of households with low income, moderate income, or high income.

Gross incidence Product/category use incidence for the entire population.

Group centroids Mean ratings of each brand on each discriminant function.

"Headline" test Design where the respondent is shown two or more headlines and is then asked to indicate the one that is most interesting.

Hierarchical clustering Method of investigating competitive structure where consumers engage in a nonobservable hierarchical choice process.

Hierarchical structure Partitioning of brands into several nested subsets.

History Threat to internal validity; refers to those specific events that occur simultaneously with the experiment, but that have not been controlled for.

Home placement Test where the current issue of a magazine is given to the respondent one or two days before the issue is scheduled to be available to the general public; at call-back the respondent is asked to indicate all of the ads that were in the issue and specific information on what each ad contains.

Homoscedasticity In the population the variance of the variable being tested is the same in all samples.

Hypothesis An assumption or guess the researcher or manager has about some characteristic of the population being sampled.

Implicit imagery names Names that do not literally

describe the product, but implicitly and indirectly convey its characteristics.

Imputed response Approach to missing responses where the respondent's answers to other questions asked are used to impute or deduce an appropriate response to the missing question.

Independent consultants Individuals with unique and specialized marketing skills hired for research projects by the client or the research supplier.

Independent samples The measurement of the variable of interest in one sample in no way affects the measurement of the variable in the other sample.

Independent variable A factor in an experiment over which the experimenter has some control; if the experimenter manipulates its value, this is expected to have some effect upon the dependent variable.

Industry standards Those rules of thumb, developed from experience, that have become standard industry guidelines for determining how large a sample to draw.

Instrumentation Threat to internal validity; refers to changes in the calibration of the measurement instrument or in the observers or scorers themselves.

Interactive effects of selection bias Threat to external validity; situation where the improper selection of

respondents interacts with experimental treatment conditions to produce misleading and unrepresentative results.

Internal consistency reliability Method of calculating reliability, the item scores obtained from administering the scale are in some way split in half and the resulting half scores are correlated. Large correlations between split-halves indicate high internal consistency.

Internal secondary data Data available within the organization—for example, accounting records, management decision support systems, and sales records.

Internal validity Determination of whether the experimental manipulation actually produced the differences observed in the dependent variable.

Interquartile range Difference between the 75th and 25th percentile.

Interval scale Measurement device that allows us to tell how far apart two or more objects are with respect to the attribute and consequently to compare the difference between the numbers assigned. Because the interval scale lacks a natural or absolute origin, the absolute magnitude of the numbers cannot be compared.

Inverse or negative association Relationship where, as the value of one

variable increases (decreases), the value of the other variable decreases (increases).

Inverted funnel sequence Sequence inverted in the sense that the questioning begins with specific questions and concludes with the respondent answering the general question.

Item analysis Procedure for checking scale items to ensure that Likert's criterion of internal consistency is satisfied.

Itemized rating scale The respondent is provided with a scale having numbers and/or brief descriptions associated with each category and asked to select one of the limited number of categories, ordered in terms of scale position, that best describes the object under study.

Jamming Practice of reducing price, offering high value coupon and so on in order to disrupt a competitor's test market.

Judgmental data Information generally based on perceptions or preference—may give better indications of future patterns of consumption.

Judgmental sampling Studies where respondents are selected because it is expected that they are representative of the population of interest and/or meet the specific needs of the research study.

Jury of expert opinion A method of forecasting based on combining the views of key executives.

Laboratory experimental environment Research environment constructed solely for the experiment. The experimenter has *direct control* over most, if not all, of the crucial factors that might possibly affect the experimental outcome.

Latent theoretical construct Construct that is not directly observable.

Leaving them blank Procedure whereby missing data are recorded as blanks.

Likert scales Scaling technique where a large number of items that are statements of beliefs or intentions are generated. Each item is judged according to whether it reflects a favorable or unfavorable attitude toward the object in question. Respondents are then asked to rate the attitude object on each scale item in terms of a five-point category-labeled scale.

Limited-service suppliers External parties that specialize in only one or just a few aspects of a research project.

Line chart Graph where data points are connected by lines.

Line marking Similarity judgments recorded by making a mark on a 5-inch line anchored by the phrases "Exact same" and "Completely different."

Line names Names assigned to a variety of specific products that the company markets.

Loaded questions Questions that suggest what the answer should be or indicate the researcher's position on the issue under study.

Loadings Weights that give the correlation of the attribute with respect to the dimension.

Local field services Outside party used by market research suppliers to collect interviews.

Longitudinal surveys Questioning of the same respondents at different points in time.

Long shots Concepts with low purchase-intent and low uniqueness scores.

Magnitude estimation Scale in which respondents assign numbers to objects, brands, attitude statements, and the like so that ratios between the assigned numbers reflect ratios among the objects on the criterion being scaled.

Mail diary services General term for services involving a sample of respondents who have agreed to provide information such as media exposure and purchase behavior on a regular basis over an extended period of time.

Mail surveys Data collection method that involves sending out a fairly structured questionnaire to a sample of respondents.

Mall-intercept personal survey Survey method using a central location test facility at a

shopping mall; respondents are intercepted on a convenience basis while they are out shopping.

Manipulation Setting the levels of an independent variable to test a specific cause-and-effect relationship.

Marginal matching Sample balancing procedure that involves matching the sample to control population or census on each of the variables separately.

Mark-sensed questionnaire Format that requires answers to be recorded with a special pencil in an area coded specifically for that answer and which can be read by a machine.

Market penetration studies Collection of information on such measures as awareness, trial, and past-thirty-day usage, where the objective is usually to track brand awareness, purchase, and usage levels.

Market segment Subgroups of consumers who respond to a given marketing-mix strategy in a similar manner.

Market structure analysis The process of organizing a set of products or brands in terms of the degree of substitutability or competitiveness.

Market studies Marketing research studies designed to provide information about the composition and structure of a product market.

Marketing decision support system (MDSS) Computer-based procedures and methods that regularly generate, store, analyze, and disseminate relevant marketing information.

Marketing research The systematic gathering, recording, processing, and analyzing of marketing data, which—when interpreted—will help the marketing executive to uncover opportunities and to reduce risks in decision making.

Marketing research suppliers The primary data gathers and analysts who execute studies and/or take ultimate responsibility for all technical aspects of a research project.

Matching Involves matching respondents on one or several background characteristics or other factors before assigning them to treatment conditions.

Maturation Threat to internal validity; refers to changes in biology or psychology of the respondent that occur over time and can affect the dependent variable irrespective of the treatment conditions.

Mean The average value.

Measurement Process of assigning numbers to objects to represent quantities of attributes.

Measurement definitions Specifications as to how unobservable constructs are related to their observable counterparts; that is, the procedure that provides a correspondence between the concept and the real world.

Measurement scales Measurement devices that can be distinguished according to the underlying assumptions regarding the correspondence of numbers assigned to the properties of objects and the meaningfulness of performing mathematical operations on the numbers.

Median Value halfway between the highest and lowest values.

"Me-to" or generic products Concepts with high purchase-intent but low uniqueness scores.

Mode Most frequently occurring response.

Monadic products tests Designs where a consumer evaluates only one product, having no other product for comparison.

Mortality Threat to internal validity; refers to the differential loss (refusal to continue in the experiment) of respondents from the treatment condition groups.

Multicollinearity Correlation among independent variables. Multicollinearity causes problems in interpreting the individual regression coefficients because the values are affected by the amount of association between the independent variables themselves.

Multidimensional scaling (MDS) Scaling technique that attempts to uncover how consumers perceive the relationships among products or brands by identifying the relevant dimensions along which products or brands are compared. MDS is a mathematical tool that enables us to represent the proximities between objects spatially as in a map.

Multiple ads/portfolio tests Test where respondent examines a portfolio of ads, one of which is the test ad.

Multiple discriminant analysis Discriminant functions are linear combinations of the original attributes that best discriminate between the alternative brands.

Multiple-exposure techniques Technique where the test commercial is aired in a test city (or cities) over time; periodic on-air tests are conducted along with store audits of sales.

Multiple regression model Model that considers the general case of more than one independent variable.

Mutual exclusivity Condition where the response choices to a question do not overlap with one another.

National market studies Studies concerned with monitoring changes in the marketplace over time. The information collected includes category and basic-use patterns and customer demographic and psychographic data.

Negative association Relationship where high (low) values of one variable are associated with low (high) values of another variable.

Nets   Basic category headings.

Net incidence   The factored-down gross incidence which includes all target population qualifications.

New-product concept-screening test   Concept-screening tests that focus on many new product ideas.

No or zero association   A situation in which there is no systematic relationship between the level of one variable and the level of another variable.

Nominal scales   Measurement device where the numbers assigned allow us to place an object in one and only one of a set of mutually exclusive and collectively exhaustive classes with no implied ordering.

Noncomparative scaling (monadic scaling)   Scaling method whereby the respondent is asked to evaluate each object on the scale provided independently of the other objects being investigated.

Nondirectory sampling designs   Telephone survey samples that do not make direct use of telephone directories. Instead, numbers are prescriptively added to working exchanges (also called prefixes).

Nonequivalent before-after with control quasi design   Experimental design similar to the before-after with control design except not utilizing a random assignment rule. Respondents are first matched on one or a set of relevant background factors to produce two groups of matched pairs and then one group receives experimental treatment.

Nonexperimental designs/ex post facto   Research that entails no manipulation. The effect outcome is observed and then an attempt is made to find the "causal factor" that indicates why the effect occurred.

Nonprobability samples   Form of sampling where there is no way of determining exactly what the chance is of selecting any particular element or sampling unit into the sample.

Nonresponse error   Error that occurs because not all of the respondents included in the sample respond; in other words, with nonresponse, the mean true value (on the variable of interest) of these sample respondents who do respond may be different from the entire sample's true mean value (on the variable of interest).

Nonsampling error   Degree to which the mean observed value (on the variable of interest) for the respondents of a particular sample agree with the mean true value for the particular sample of respondents (on the variable of interest).

Normal equations/ordinary least-squares   Formulas that produce a regression line such that Σe_i^2 is minimized.

NTI-NAD (Nielsen Television Index, National Audience Demographics)   A report combining viewing and audience characteristics used to identify a program (or programs) that will potentially reach the most appropriate and largest target audience.

Null hypothesis   The hypothesis that is tested.

Numeric databases   Computerized files that contain original survey data such as time series data.

Observational methods   Observation of behavior directly or indirectly by human or mechanical methods.

Off-air tests   Method for evaluating television commercials where the testing takes place in a controlled environment that does not resemble the surroundings in which the individual usually views commercials.

Omission   Interviewing condition that occurs when a respondent cannot recall that an event has occurred.

On-air tests   Testing that takes place in realistic settings; respondents are asked their reactions to commercials that they have seen in their own homes, on their own television sets.

On-line vendors   Intermediaries used to access databases rather than going directly to the database producer.

One-sample proportion test   Test of the hypothesis that a proportion is equal to some prespecified value.

One-tail hypothesis test   Test used when the alternative hypothesis is directional—the entire region of rejection is in one tail of the distribution.

Open-ended question format Questions where no fixed-response alternatives are presented; instead, the respondent is permitted to respond freely to the question presented by the interviewer.

Operational population The sampling frame that is used.

Opportunity analysis Research to identify unfulfilled consumer wants and needs.

Optical scanning Direct machine reading of numerical values or alphanumeric codes and transcription onto cards, magnetic tape, or disk.

Order bias Condition where brands receive different ratings depending on whether they were shown first, second, third, etc.

Ordinal scales Measurement device where the response alternatives define an ordered sequence so that the choice listed first is less (greater) than the second, the second less (greater) than the third, and so forth. The numbers assigned do not reflect the magnitude of an attribute possessed by an object.

Overall model test (*F*-test) Determination of whether the multiple correlation coefficient is statistically significant.

Overregistration Condition that occurs when a sampling frame consists of sampling units in the target population *plus* additional units as well.

Package testing A system for assessing the visibility of package alternatives, relative to

one another and usually to a competitive brand, and the ability to package alternatives to convey product end-use benefits.

Paired comparison Scale that presents the respondent with two objects at a time and asks the respondent to select one of the two according to some criterion.

Paired comparison designs Tests where a consumer directly compares two products.

Pairwise deletion Strategy for missing responses that involves using all of the available nonmissing data for each calculation.

Pearson product moment correlation Measure of the linear association between interval or ratio scaled variables.

Perceptual product maps Maps based upon consumers' perceived similarities and differences among a set of competing brands.

Personal in-home survey Survey that involves asking questions of a sample of respondents face-to-face in their homes.

Physical control An attempt to hold constant the value or level of the extraneous variable.

Pie chart Graphic device; a circle divided into sections where the size of each section corresponds to a portion of the total.

Point-biserial correlation coefficient Coefficient that measures the association

between a dichotomous variable and an interval scaled variable.

Positioning A system for determining how to set the mix elements of product, price, promotion, and distribution so as to maximize appeal of a product to a particular target population.

Positioning studies Attempts to portray the interrelationships among a set of brands in terms of consumers' perceptions and preferences for these brands.

Positive association Relationship where high (low) values of one variable are associated with high (low) values of another variable.

Post-hoc segmentation Studies where segments are defined after the fact on the basis of some sort of clustering of respondents on a set of "relevant" characteristics such as benefit sought, need, attitudes, and the like.

Postcoding Coding specifications designated after the questionnaires have been returned from the field.

Power of the test (1 − β) The probability of making a correct decision of rejecting the null hypothesis (*HO:*) when in fact it is false.

Precision Level of uncertainty about the characteristics of the construct being measured.

Precoding Procedure of assigning a code number to every possible response to an open-ended question.

Precommercialization stage Developmental stage of a product, characterized by much marketing research activity designed to ensure that the launched product will be successful in matching or exceeding management's performance objectives.

Prediction The attempt to make statements about future events on the basis of the effects of past, current, or proposed events.

Predictor or independent variable The variable upon which the prediction is based.

Preference product maps Attempts to position brands in the perceptual space in accordance with those product features or attributes that consumers view as most important in making evaluations of the brand or in choosing among alternative brands.

Prescription Selecting a course of action based upon the objectives of the study and identifying relevant alternatives and their likely consequences.

Pretest markets A system for providing management with information on the likely share or volume a new product will capture prior to conducting a test market.

Primary data Data collected for a specific research need; they are customized and require specialized collection procedures.

Primary sampling units (PSUs) Clusters used at the first stage of sampling.

Principal components analysis A popular approach to factor analysis; uncovers dimensions that are linear combinations of the original attributes such that the uncovered dimensions account for as much variation in the original attribute ratings as possible.

Print ad tests Attempts to assess the power of an ad placed in a magazine or newspaper to be remembered, to communicate, to affect attitudes, and to ultimately produce sales.

Prior notification Method of reducing nonresponse that involves sending potential respondents an advance letter to notify them of the impending telephone or personal contact.

PRIZM neighborhood life style clusters Assigns individuals to unique market segments on the basis of where the individual lives; underlying premise is that choice of neighborhood is the most basic consumer decision and one that ultimately reflects lifestyle choices.

Probability proportional to size (PPS) sampling Design where clusters are sampled at the first stage with probability proportional to the number of sampling units in the cluster.

Probability sampling designs Samples drawn in such a way that each member of the population has a known, nonzero chance of being selected.

Prodegy Method of investigating competitive structure where consumers, faced with the deletion of a preferred product, will switch to a close competitor.

Product maps Space which represents the perceived relationships among a set of brands; the spatial distance between any two brands represents the degree to which they are perceived as being similar in terms of relevant attributes or preferences.

Product-market The set of products that can be substituted for each other within those use situations where similar benefits are sought and the customers for whom such usages are relevant.

Product perceptions Questions relating to the ad's effect on perceptions and/or purchase intentions concerning the test brand.

Product target AID A microcomputer that categorizes television viewers by their purchasing patterns.

Profile composites Research findings that answer the question, "Whom did it happen to?"

Project proposal A research written description of the key research design factors that define the proposed study.

Projective techniques A class of techniques which presume that respondents cannot or will not communicate their feelings and beliefs directly; provides a structured question format in which respondents can respond indirectly by projecting their own feelings and beliefs into the situation while they interpret the behavior of others.

Proportional allocation Sampling design guaranteeing that stratified random sampling will be at least as efficient as SRS. The number of elements selected from a stratum is directly proportional to the size of the stratum.

Protocol analysis Procedure where the respondent "thinks aloud" while completing the questionnaire.

Protomonadic designs Comparison tests where a consumer evaluates one product and then compares it to a second product.

Proven total recall Percentage of respondents in the program audience that correctly recalled copy or visual elements in the test ad or commercial.

Proximities Any set of numbers that express the amount of similarity or difference between pairs of objects.

Purchase-intent scales Procedure attempting to measure a respondent's interest in a brand or product.

Purchase or use behavior data Information providing the most accurate indication of what people do or have done.

Q-sort scales Rank-order procedure in which objects are sorted into piles based on similarity with respect to some criterion.

Qualitative research methods Techniques involving small numbers of respondents who provide descriptive information on their thoughts and feelings not easily projected to the whole population.

Quantitative research methods Technique involving relatively large numbers of respondents and designed to generate information that can

be projected to the whole population.

Quasi-experimental designs Experimental designs in which the researcher is unable to achieve complete control over the scheduling of the treatments or cannot randomly assign respondents to experimental treatment conditions.

Quota sampling Design that involves selecting specific numbers of respondents who possess certain characteristics known, or presumed to affect, the subject of the research study.

Radio and television AID Analysis of a station's audience by selected demographics, specific geography, or nonstandard time periods.

Random digit directory sample designs Samples of numbers drawn from the directory, usually by a systematic procedure. Selected numbers are modified to allow all unlisted numbers a chance for inclusion.

Random sampling error Error caused because the particular sample selected is an imperfect representation of the overall population and therefore the true mean value for the particular sample of respondents (on the variable of interest) differs from the true mean value for the overall population (on the variable of interest).

Random sources of error Denoted by X_R, component made up of

transient personal factors that affect the observed scale score in different ways each time the test is administered.

Randomization Process by which respondents are randomly assigned (e.g., pulling a respondent's name out of a hat) to treatment conditions for the purpose of controlling extraneous factors in an experimental setting.

Range Difference between largest and smallest values of distribution.

Rank-order scale Scale in which respondents are presented with several objects simultaneously and requested to "order" or "rank" them.

Rating The percent of all households that have at least one television set viewing a program for at least six minutes out of every fifteen minutes that the program is telecast.

Ratio scales Measurement device with the same properties as interval scales. In addition, ratio scales have a natural or absolute origin.

Rational database manager A component of an MDSS that provides the user with the ability to efficiently access and manipulate the data.

Raw data Respondent's answers to questions as they are contained on the questionnaire.

Reactive or interactive effects of testing Threat to external validity that occurs when a preexposure measurement increases or decreases the respondent's sensitivity or responsiveness to the experimental treatment conditions and thus leads to unrepresentative results.

"Real-magazine" tests Test where interest centers on the "magazine" effect—that is, the context in which the ad appears.

Realistic research environment Situation similar to the normal situation in which the behavior under study would naturally occur.

Recall Measures of how many people remember having seen the test ad both on an unaided and aided basis.

Recognition Score measuring whether the respondent can recognize the name of the test brand.

Record A string of coded data in a machine-readable format.

Refusal conversion (persuasion) Method of reducing nonresponse; skilled interviewers reduce the proportion of refusals by not accepting a refusal to a request for cooperation without making an additional plea.

Region of rejection A cut point often referred to as a critical value; if the value of the test statistic falls to the right or the left of this critical value, we reject the null hypothesis.

Regression analysis Procedure that determines how much of the variation in the dependent variable can be explained by the independent variable.

Regression and econometric model Methods that produce forecasts based on expressing demand as a function of a certain number of deterministic factors.

Regression line A line fitted to the data that in some sense best captures the functional relationship.

Related samples The measurement of the variable of interest in one sample can affect the measurement of the variable in some other sample.

Relative tolerance level (r) The difference between the estimate and its unknown true population value expressed as a percentage.

Reliability The extent to which measures are free from random error and yield consistent result.

Reliability coefficient Measure that indicates the amount of systematic variation, relative to the total observed scale variation.

Repeat paired comparison designs Tests where a respondent is given two or more sets of products to compare against each other at two different points in time.

Replacement Approach to reducing nonresponse; included in the survey are the addresses (or telephone numbers) of nonrespondents from an earlier survey that used similar sampling procedures. When a response is obtained in the current survey, the interviewer replaces the nonresponse address with an address for a nonresponse in a previous study.

Repositioning A strategy that defines a new role (new users or uses) for an aging product in the marketplace.

Research life cycle Research activities in distinct stages matched to the unique needs of the product during each stage of its life cycle (prelaunch, rollout, and established markets).

Residual An error term representing the difference between the actual and predicted values of the dependent variable.

Response error Error that occurs because respondents (who do respond) may give inaccurate answers or a respondent's answers may be misrecorded.

Response rates The total number of respondents sent questionnaires who complete and return them expressed as a percentage.

Round robin designs Test where a series of products is tested against each of the others.

Salesforce-composite estimates A method of forecasting based on the informed knowledge of the firm's salesforce who provide estimates of future demand.

Sales wave extended-use product test Respondent is given opportunity to buy the product at intervals coinciding with the normal purchase cycle.

Sample Subset of respondents from the overall target population.

Sample balancing Procedure where the sample is weighted to match the general population on specific characteristics before tabulating other variables to estimate their population distribution.

Sampling frame An explicit list of individuals or households eligible for inclusion in the sample.

Sampling interval Computed by taking n/N together with r, the chosen.

Sampling units The elements that make up the population.

Sampling variable Variable that represents the characteristic of the population that we wish to estimate.

Scale transformations Procedures for transforming data by one of a number of simple arithmetic operations to make comparisons across respondents and/or scale items.

Scatter diagram A bivariate plot of two variables.

Secondary data Data that have been collected for another project and have already been published. Sources can be in-house or external.

Secondary sampling units (SSUs) Sampling units selected at the second stage of sampling.

Segmentation studies Attempts to identify subgroups of consumers who will respond to a given marketing-mix configuration in a similar manner.

Selection bias Threat to internal validity; refers to the improper assignments of respondents to treatment conditions.

Self-administered CRT interview An interviewing method where the respondent sits at a computer terminal and answers the questionnaire by using keyboard and screen.

Self-perception theory Theory proposing that individuals come to know their attitudes through interpreting the causes of their behavior. To the extent that one's behavior is attributed to internal causes and not to circumstantial pressures, a positive attitude toward the behavior develops, and these attitudes, or self-perceptions, exert a direct influence on subsequent behavior.

Semantic differential scale Semantic scales utilizing bi-polar adjectives as end points.

Semantic scale Procedure where respondents describe their feelings on a rating scale with end points or categories associated with labels having semantic meaning.

Sentence completion Projective technique where respondents are asked to complete a number of incomplete sentences with the first word or phrase that comes to mind.

Sequential monadic designs Comparison tests where a consumer rates one product and then is given a second product to rate independently.

Share The percent of households with television set on who are tuned to a specific program at a specific time.

Share-of-preference model Conjoint analysis model that assumes individuals purchase products in proportion to their utility for the products.

Simple one-stage cluster sampling One-step design where first stage clusters are selected by SRS and within each selected cluster all sampling units are chosen.

Simple random sampling Design guaranteeing that every sample of a given size as well as every individual in the target population has an equal chance of being selected.

Simple two-stage cluster sampling Design where the clusters at the first stage are selected by SRS, and at the second stage the sampling units are selected probabilistically by SRS from each sample cluster— so that the same fraction of sampling units is drawn from each sample cluster.

Simple Weighting Procedures that attempt to remove nonresponse bias by assigning weights to the data that in some sense account for nonresponse.

Simulated test market Method where various groups of preselected respondents are interviewed, monitored and sampled with the new product; in addition, respondents may be exposed to various media messages in a controlled environment.

Single ad research design Test where respondent is exposed to the test ad by itself; that is, the test ad is not shown with other ads, and it is not displayed in a magazine.

Single-response formats Scaling technique that involves asking the respondent to make a judgment about the object in question.

Single-stage cluster sample One-step design where, once the sample of clusters is selected, every sampling unit within each of the selected clusters is included in the sample.

Skewed distribution Distribution where one tail is fat, while the other is thin.

Snowball design Sample formed by having each respondent, after being interviewed, identify others who belong to the target population of interest.

Sorting Procedure that involves presenting the respondent with the total stimulus set and asking him or her to sort the set into groups of like objects.

Spearman's rank-order correlation coefficient Measure of linear association between variables that have ordinal scale properties.

Split-halves Scale items split in terms of odd- and even-numbered items or randomly.

Spill-in The amount of outside media coming into a market.

Spill-out The amount of a test market's newspapers and TV being seen and read in distant cities.

Spurious association Inappropriate causal interpretation of an observed association.

Standard deviation Index of variability in the same measurement units used to calculate the mean.

Standard error ($s_{\bar{y}}$) Indication of the reliability of an estimate of a population parameter; it is computed by dividing the standard deviation of the sample estimate by the square root of the sample size.

Standard test market Method where the company's own sales force is responsible for distributing the new product in the selected test market areas. Sales force personnel would stock the shelves and return at periodic intervals to restock and count movement.

Standardized discriminant function weights (the b coefficients) Measures of the importance of each attribute in distinguishing among the alternative brands.

Standardized research services Studies conducted for different clients, but always in the same way.

Stapel scale Procedure using a single criterion or key word and instructing the respondent to rate the object on a scale.

"Starch" scores Research design where readers of specific magazines are located and the interviewer determines whether each ad in the issue was remembered, whether the name of the brand or advertiser was read, and whether a substantial portion of the advertisement was read.

Statistical conclusion validity Involves drawing inferences about whether two variables covary.

Statistical hypothesis test Test that determines the probability of observing a sample mean of $\bar{x}$ if indeed the population mean (or hypothesized mean) is μ.

Statistical test of each regression coefficient Determination of significance of each regression coefficient separately.

Statistically significant finding Indication that our notions (hypotheses) about a population are likely given the sample evidence.

Storage instantaneous audimeter Instrument that continuously monitors and records television viewing in terms of when the set was turned on, what channels were viewed, and for how long.

Store audits Studies that monitor performance in the marketplace among dollar and unit sales/share, distribution/out of stock, inventory, price, promotional activity, and feature ads.

Strategic market studies Studies focusing on in-depth analysis of a specific product-market; they fall under the umbrella of custom research and are tailored to address specific marketing issues and/or problems.

Stratified sampling Design that involves partitioning the entire population of elements into subpopulations, called strata, and then selecting elements separately from each subpopulation.

Structure studies   Attempts to define the competitive relationships within a product-market.

Structured interview   Method of interviewing where the questions are completely predetermined.

Stub   Delineates the response formats to be used in the cross-tab. Stubs make up the rows of the cross-tab.

Substitutions   Method of handling nonresponse; nonresponses are replaced with other substitute respondents expected to respond.

Surrogate situations   Use of experimental settings, test units and/or treatment conditions that differ from those to be encountered in the actual setting that the researcher is interested in; threat to external validity.

Survey   A method of gathering information from a number of individuals (the respondents, who collectively form a sample) in order to learn something about a larger target population from which the sample was drawn.

Symmetric distribution Distribution where values on either side of the center of the distribution are the same.

Syndicated research services   Market research suppliers who collect data on a regular basis with standardized procedures. The data are sold to different client customers.

Systematic sampling   Design where the target sample is generated by picking an arbitrary starting point (in a list) and then picking every nth element in succession from a list.

Systematic sources of error Denoted by X_s, component made up of stable characteristics that affect the observed scale score in the same way each time the test is administered.

Tab houses   Outside suppliers that perform tabulating work and other analyses when neither the client nor the marketing research supplier has the necessary computing resources.

Target AID   Categorization of audiences by lifestyle, purchasing habits, and economic standing.

Target population   The population of interest; contains the sampling units (and elements) that possess the information sought by the survey.

Telephone surveys   Survey that involves phoning a sample of respondents drawn from an eligible population and asking them a series of questions.

Telescoping   Condition that occurs when a respondent compresses time, or remembers an event as occurring more recently than it actually occurred.

Test markets   A system that allows the marketing manager to evaluate the proposed

national marketing program in a smaller, less expensive situation with a view toward determining whether the potential profit opportunity from rolling out the new product or line extension outweighs the potential risks.

Testing   Threat to internal validity; refers to the consequences of taking before-and-after exposure measurements on respondents.

Test-retest reliability   Method for calculating reliability; respondents are administered identical sets of scale items at two different times under similar conditions. The reliability coefficient is computed by correlating the scores obtained from the two administrations.

Thematic apperception test (TAT)   Projective technique presenting respondents with a series of pictures or cartoons in which consumers and products are the primary topic of attention.

Third person/role playing Projective technique that presents respondents with a verbal or visual situation and asks them to relate the feelings and beliefs of a third person to the situation, rather than to directly express their own feelings and beliefs about the situation.

Time series models   Methods that produce forecasts on the basis of the statistical analysis of past data that presumably incorporate enduring and identifiable causal relationships that will carry forward into the future.

Time series quasi design Experiment that involves periodic measurements on some group or individual, introduction of an experimental manipulation, and subsequent periodic measurement.

Tolerance level The allowable difference permitted between the estimate and its known true population value.

Top-box intention scores The percentage of individuals who indicate that they "definitely" would buy.

Top-down approach Process of breaking down clusters—at the beginning all respondents belong to one cluster and then respondents are partitioned into two clusters, then three clusters, and so on until each respondent occupies his or her own cluster.

Top-line reports Highlights of the study's results given to the marketing executive before all of the data have been tabulated.

Total survey error The difference between the overall population's true mean value (on the variable of interest) and the mean observed value (of the variable of interest) obtained from the particular sample of respondents.

Total variation Sum of between variation plus within variation.

Tracking System for measuring the key sales components of customer awareness and trial and repeat purchases.

Tradeoff procedure Technique where the respondent is asked to consider two attributes at a time—to rank the various combinations of each pair of attribute descriptors from a most preferred to least preferred.

Treatment Term for that independent variable that has been manipulated.

Triangle designs Tests where a respondent is given two samples of one product and one sample of another and asked to identify the one that differs.

True-score model A person's (true) specific attitude toward buying and using the brand, denoted by X_T.

Two-factor after-only with control design Experiment differing from the after-only with control group designs by having more than one independent variable.

Two-independent-sample test Test whether the observed proportion (mean) in one sample is equal to the observed proportion (mean) in another sample.

Two-tail hypothesis test Test used when the alternative hypothesis is nondirectional—the region of rejection is in both tails of the distribution.

Type I error Situation occurring when the null hypothesis is in fact true, but is nevertheless rejected on the basis of the sample data.

Type II or beta (β) error Situation occurring when we fail to reject the null hypothesis

(HO:) when in fact the alternative *(HA:)* is true.

Unaided recall Respondents are asked if they remember seeing a commercial for a product in the product category of interest.

Unaided questions Questions that do not provide any clues to the answer.

Unbalanced scale Scale using an unequal number of favorable and unfavorable scale categories.

Underregistration Condition that occurs when a sampling frame contains fewer sampling units than the target population.

Unstructured interview Method of interviewing where questions are not completely predetermined and the interviewer is free to probe for all details and underlying feelings.

Utility scale values Ratings that indicate how influential each attribute level is in the consumer's overall evaluations.

Validation Procedure where between 10 and 20 percent of all respondents "reportedly" interviewed are recontacted by telephone and asked a few questions to verify that the interview did in fact take place.

Variable (re)specification Transformation of data that creates new variables and/or collapses the categories of existing variables in order to respecify a variable into a form consistent with the aims of the study.

Verification   Procedures aimed at ensuring that data from the original questionnaires have been accurately transcribed onto computer cards, magnetic tape or disk.

Visual recall   Percentage of respondents in the program audience that correctly recalled visual elements in the test commercial.

Winners   Concepts with high purchase-intent and high uniqueness scores.

Within-group variation Within group sum of squares; reflects differences in scores for respondents in the same group—represents "unexplained" variation.

Word association   Projective technique where respondents are presented with a list of words, one at a time, and asked to indicate what word comes immediately to mind.

Name Index

BrainReserve Inc., 708
Brant, Joquin Ives, 678n, 679
Bristol-Meyer Co., 202-204
Bromo Seltzer, 22
Brooks, R. M., 237n
Brown, H. J., 95
Brown & Williamson, 66
Burdick, R. B., 240n
Burger King, 441, 442, 446, 464, 466-467, 471-472
Burgoyne, 123, 664
Burke Marketing Research, Inc., 30, 76, 123, 127, 173, 174, 187, 214, 653, 656, 668
Bush, A. J., 153n
Business Communications Company, 83
Business Index, 82
Business Information Guidebook, 80
Business Information Sources, 81
Business Periodical Index, 82
Buspar, 202-204
Butler, E. W., 151n

Cadbury, N. D., 660n
Cagner, Shelly, 119n
Calahan, D., 139n
Calloway, Wayne, 714
Campbell, D. R., 295n
Campbell, P. T., 166n, 167n, 181n
Carby, Tom, 272
Carlson, Eric D., 695n
Carmone, F. J., 341n
Carpenter, E. H., 237n
Carroll, J. D., 341n
Carter-Wallace Inc., 203
Case, P. B., 151n, 310n
Cateora, P. C., 382n
Caterpillar Tractor Co., 194
Cato, Mac, 712
Cattell, R. B., 543
Cattin, P., 341n
Chambers, John C., 682n
Chapman, D. W., 242n
Chartmaster, 444
Chemical Rubber Company, 739
Chen, C. C., 102
Child, Julia, 568
Chooz, 22
Christenson, J. A., 237n
Christian Herald, 19
Christian Science Monitor, 82
Chrysler Corporation, 386-388
Chudnoff, M., 26n, 131n
CIRR/Corporate and Industry Research Reports Index, 83
Ci2 System, 377
Clark, V. A., 148n
Clarke, Roberta, 71
Coca-Cola Company, 41-42, 51, 161-162, 577, 581, 707-709
Cochran, W., 255n, 267n

Cohen, J., 508n
Coke, 41-43, 51-52, 707-709
Cole, E., 76n
Colgate, Craig, 81
Collins, M., 151n
Colombotos, J., 150n
COMP, 668-673
Compaq, 633, 634-635
Compuserve, Inc., 97, 98
Connolly, Jay, 395, 396
Consolidated Foods Corp., 709, 711
Control Data, 116
Cook, T. D., 166n, 167n, 181n
Coombs, C. H., 286n
Cooper, Stanford L., 147n
Coors (Adolph) Company, 39-40
Cormack, R. M., 553
Cosby, Bill, 710
Cosmopolitan, 19
Costello, John, 708
Council of American Survey Research Organizations (CASRO), 37
County and City Data Book, 84
Cox, E. P., II, 310n
Cox, Michael, 146n
Coyle, B. W., 295n
CPC International, 712
Craig, S., 382n
Crask, M. R., 548
CRC Information Systems, Inc., 377
CREST Report, 113
Cronbach, L. J., 167n, 292n
Crossley, Archibald, 20
Cuadra Associates, Inc., 97
Cullwick, D., 137n

D'Agostino, Stephen, 708
Dailey, Sheila, 707
Dallas Pen Co., 68
Dancer Fitzgerald Sample Inc., 194, 195, 663, 707
Daniell, Lorna M., 81
D'Arcy MacManus Masius, 201
Davidson, J. H., 48n
Day, G. S., 576n, 577n
Dayton, Michell, 479n
Decker Communications, Inc., 726, 729
Deeter, William, 21
Deming, W. E., 419n
De Santis, Richardo, 711
Dey, K. V., 67
Dialog Information Service Inc., 97, 98, 103
Diet Rite Cola, 707
Di-Gel, 22
Dillman, D. A., 237n, 239n, 241n, 346n, 358n, 363n, 364n
Dillon, William R., 330n, 532n, 543, 544n, 548, 549n, 597, 690n
Directory of Directories, 81

Directory of On-Line Databases, 95, 97
Dixon, W. J., 742
Doktor, Robert, 695n
Domzal, Teresa, 690n
Donnelley Demographics, 103, 104
Donnelley Marketing Information Services, 103
Douglas, S. P., 382n
Dow Jones News/Retrieval, 97, 98
Draper, N., 528n
Drayton, L., 109n
Dressler, Michael, 678n, 679
Dreyer's Grand Ice Cream Inc., 710
Dunning, B., 139n
DuPont (E. I.), 34

Eastman, R. O., 19
Eastman Research Bureau, 19
Edsel, 40-41
Effective Online Searching, 102
Ehrhart-Bobic Associates, 123
Electronic Questionnaire Design and Analysis with CAPPA, 376-377
Elrick and Lavidge, 30, 668
Encyclopedia of Associations, 81
Encyclopedia of Business Information Sources, 81
Encyclopedia of Information Systems and Services, 97
Erdos & Morgan, 378
ERIM, 123, 126
Esmark Inc., 393
ESP, 668-673
Ethridge, James M., 81

F & S Index: Europe, 82
F & S Index: International, 82
F & S Index: United States, 82
Federal Home Loan Bank Board, 394
Federal Home Mortgage Corp., 393
Ferber, R., 109n
Ferraro, Geraldine, 708
Festinger, L., 286n
Figueroa, Oscar, 80
Fildes, Robert, 682n
Final Analysis, Inc., 180, 612, 652
Findex: The Directory of Market Research Reports, Studies and Surveys, 83
Fineberg, Stephen E., 503n
Firtle, N., 305n
Fishbein, M., 312n, 319n, 320n
Fisher, R. A., 741
Fiske, D. W., 295n
Ford Motor Company, 17, 40-41
Forecasting Methods for Management, 698
1411 Co., 271-272
Freddie Mac, 395, 396
Freddie Mae, 394
Freeman, J., 151n

Frerichs, R. R., 148n
Freund, John E., 460n
Frey, J. H., 239n
Friedman, H. H., 310n
Frito-Lay Inc., 713-714
Frost & Sullivan, 80, 83
Fuchs, Hanno, 21n

Gale Research Company, 97
Gallanis, D., 21n
Gallegos, J. G., 239n
Gallup, George, 19
Gardner, Burleigh, 288, 288n
Gateway Technology, 634
Gaviscon, 22
Gelusil, 22
General Electric Company, 19
General Foods, 152, 632, 709-711
General Mills, 632
General Motors Corporation, 388
Geo, 17
Gershon, Samuel, 202
Giges, Nancy, 42n, 168n
Gillette, 68-69
Ginsburger, G., 109n
Givon, A. M., 310n
Glasser, Gerald J., 145n, 147n
Goldberg, Harold, 203
Golden, P., 26n
Golden, R., 131n
Goldman, Emanuel, 708
Goldstein, M., 330n, 532n, 543, 544n,
    549n, 597
Goodyear, 712-713
Graves, R. M., 239n
Gray, Edwin, 394, 395
Green, Paul E., 335n, 340n, 341n, 376,
    586n, 593n, 595, 603n, 740
Greenblatt, David, 204
Guilford, J. P., 290n
Guinan, Edward J., 271, 272
Gulliksen, H., 294n

Haire, J. F., Jr., 153n
Haire, Maison, 137n
Haley, R. I., 310n
Hall, J. L., 95
Hansen, R. A., 240n
Harman, H. H., 542, 542n
Harper, R. N., Jr., 386-388
Harper, Roy W., 201, 202
Hartigan, J. A., 553
Hartley, H. O., 743
Hartley, Robert F., 40n
Hatch, T. E., 44n
Hauck, Mathew, 146n
Haueter, Eric D., 712
Hauser, J. R., 34n, 586n, 605
Hays, William L., 433n, 454n, 499n
Hess, John M., 135n
Hicks, Charles R., 451n, 474n, 476n
Higgins, Keven T., 70

Hiiz, N. H., 429n
Hochstim, J. R., 148n
Hoel, Paul G., 436n, 514n
Hoffmann-La Roche Inc., 202
Holbrook, M. B., 585n
Hollart, N., 26n, 131n
Holmes, Lee, 396
Home, 17
Home Testing Institute (HTI), 141
Honomichl, Jack J., 19n, 20n, 31n,
    42n, 145n
Hotheimer, Fritz S., 138n
Hovland, C. I., 319n
Huber, J., 585n
Hull, C. H., 429n
Hunt, Shelly D., 375n
Hursch, G. D., 376n
Hustad, T. P., 618n
Hutton (E. F.) & Company, 83

IMS International, 28, 30, 32, 122
INDSCAL/SINDSCAL, 536
Information Industry Marketplace,
    97
Information Resources, Inc. (IRI),
    126
*Information Sourcebook for
    Marketers and Strategic
    Planners*, 81
International Research Associates,
    20
*International Statistics Index: A
    Guide to the Statistical
    Publications of International
    Intergovernmental
    Organizations*, 83
International Telephone and
    Telegraph (ITT), 634

Jacobs, B., 305n
Jaeger, R. J., 223n
Jain, Arun K., 341n, 595, 603n
James, Robert L., 712
Jell-O Pudding Pops, 709-711
Jenkings, J. G., 429n
Johnson, P. L., 605
Johnson, R. J., 341n
Johnson, Richard M., 336n, 338n,
    377
Johnson, S. C., 553
Johnston, J., 341n
Journal of Advertising Research, 20
Journal of Consumer Research, 20
Journal of Marketing, 82
Journal of Marketing Research, 20
JTL Corporation, 708

Kaiser, H. F., 539n, 541, 542n
Kalwani, M. U., 604
Kanuk, L., 138n, 139n
Katz, D., 286n
Katz, G. M., 44n, 668n

Kaufman, I. M., 137n
Kedia, K., 376
Kentucky Fried Chicken, 556-561
Keon, J., 234n
Kerlinger, F. N., 290n, 308n
Kidder, Peabody & Company, Inc.,
    83
King, R. L., 135n
Kish, Leslie, 234n, 238n, 241n, 255n
Klecka, William R., 147n
Klompmaker, J. E., 138n
Knapp Communications
    Corporation, 17-18
Knox, M. Z., 135n
Koutsouiannis, A., 583n
Kraft, 632
Kruskal, J. B., 341n, 533, 533n
Kutener, Michael J., 498n, 521n
KYST, 536

Landon, E. L., Jr., 146n
Lansing, J., 109n
Lazarsfeld, Paul, 20
Leading National Advertisers, 710
Lee, G., 216n
Leefer, J. R., 310n
Lehman Brothers Kuhn Loeb, 66
Lemeshow, S., 267n
Lennox, George, 713
Lerner, David, 353n
Leslie, L., 236n
Levitt, Theodore, 712
Levy, P. S., 267n
Lewis, Robert C., 396n
Libby, 632
Liebetrau, Albert M., 504n
Liebowitz, David, 68
Liggett & Myers, 66-67
Likert, Rensis, 20
Lindley, J. D., 138n
LINMAP, 341
Little, John D. C., 676, 677, 677n, 692
Lockley, L. L., 20
London, E. Laird, Jr., 147n
Lord, F. M., 290n
Lorillard, 65-66
Los Angeles Times, 82
Lotus 1-2-3, 444
Louis Harris Poll, 394
Lovelock, C. H., 137n
Lunn, T., 577n

Maalox, 22
Madden, Thomas J., 690n
Magilavy, L. J., 239n
Makridakis, Spyros, 682n, 698, 698n
Management Decision Systems, 668
Manis, Robert A., 631n, 635, 639
Mann, Maurice, 395, 396
Mapes & Ross, 645, 653, 655, 657
M/A/R/C, 378
Market Audits, 663

Market Fact's Consumer Mail Panel (CMP), 141

Market Facts, Inc., 30, 50, 123, 137, 183, 190, 378, 580, 611, 617, 625, 663

Marketing and Research Counselor's National Neighborhood Panel (NNP), 141

Marketing News, 288, 690

Marketing Research Association (MRA), 37

Marketing Science, 20

Market Research Corporation of America (MRCA), 111

Mars, Inc., 21

Martin, Warren S., 506n

Massey, F. J., Jr., 742

Maxwell, John C., Jr., 66

Mayer, Charles S., 384n

Mayros, Van, 81

Mazis, M. B., 310n

McCann-Erickson, 712

McCollum/Spielman, 30, 176

McConnell, J. D., 172n

McDonald's, 441, 442, 468, 471-472

McGraw-Hill Research, 685-686

Mead Data Central, 97, 98

Mead-Johnson Pharmaceutical, 202, 204

Meehl, P. E., 167n

Melugin, Ed, 68

Mercury Savings Association, 394

Meringolo, Salvatore M., 75n

Metro-Mail, 116

Metz, J., 109n

Metzger, Dale D., 145n, 147n

Milk of Magnesia, 22

MINISSA, 536

MONANOVA, 341

Mondale, Walter, 13

Monroe, K. B., 236n

Montana, Joe, 708

Montgomery Securities, 708

Morrison, Donald G., 548, 604

Moskowitz, H. R., 305n

Mullick, Satinder K., 682n

MULTISCALE, 348

Mylanta, 22

NameLab, 631, 633-635

National Association of Home Builders, 394

National Audience Demographics, 115

National Family Opinion (NFO), 111-113, 141, 378

National Newspaper Index, 82

National Purchase Diary Panel (NPD), 109, 111, 113

National Sporting Goods Manufacturers Association, 80

National Trade and Professional Association of the United States, 81

Neiman, Judith S., 71

Neter, John, 498n, 521n

New Jersey State Tourist Commission, 276

New Product News, 34

News Net, 97, 98

New York Times, 82, 95, 97

New York Times Index, 82

New York Times Info. Bank, 95, 97

NFO Digest, 109

Nicosia, F. M., 603n

Nie, N. H., 526n

Nielsen, Arthur C., 20

Nielsen (A. C.) Company, 20, 27, 30, 32, 111, 114, 120, 126

Nielsen Retail Index, 121

Nielsen Television Index, 114-115

Nikhil, Rishiyur S., 376

Nordberg, Olivia Schieffelin, 89

North American Phillips Lighting Corporation, 636-637

Novick, M. R., 290n

NPD Research, Inc., 30, 378, 666, 668

Nunnally, J. C., 278n, 290n, 292n

NutraSweet Company, 7

Ogilvy & Mather, 7, 712

Online Bibliographic Databases, 95

Online Bibliographic Searching: A Learning Manual, 102

Osgood, C., 312n

O'Shaughnessy, John, 44n

Ossip, Al, 153n

Page, R. L., 138n

Parfitt, J. H., 109n

PEAC, 11-13

Pearson, E. S., 743

Pen Shop, 68-69

People, 7, 66

Peoria Journal Star, 195

Pepsico Inc., 42, 51-52, 161-162, 577, 581, 707, 708

Pepsi-Cola USA, 708

Pepto Bismol, 22

Perception Research, Inc., 561-562

Performance Test, 205-207

Perreault, W. D., 548

Pessemier, E. A., 301n, 603n

Peter, J. P., 290n

Peters, Thomas J., 14, 14n

Peterson Blyth Cato, 712

Philadelphia Inquirer, 82

Philip Morris, 65-67

Pillsbury, 632

Pilot Pen Corp., 68

POLYCON, 536

Popcorn, Faith, 708

Pope, Jeffrey L., 135n, 609

Porter, M. E., 583n

Power (J. D.) & Associates, 17

Predicasts, 83

Predicasts *Basebook*, 83

Predicasts *Forecasts*, 84

PREFMAP, 341

Pring, David C., 383n

Proctor & Gamble, 34, 632

Rafael, J. E., 155n

Rakel, Robert, 203

Rao, V., 586n

Reader's Digest, 7, 384

Reagan, Ronald, 13

Recordimeter, 114-115

Rentschler, Frederick B., 392-393

Restaurant Association of America, 273

Reynolds (R. J.), 65-67

Reynolds, M. L., 536n

Rich, C. L., 145n

Rich, M. Farnsworth, 104

Richard, L. E., 151n

Rickels, Karl, 204

Robinson, L. M., 240n

Rogers, T. F., 148n

Rolaids, 22

Roper, Elmo, 20

Rosen, Ben, 634

Rosenberg, M. J., 319n

Rosenthal, R., 171n

Rosnow, R. L., 171n

Rummel, R. J., 543

Saari, B. B., 295n

Sabavala, D. J., 605

Sales and Marketing Management, 84

Salomon Brothers, 395

SAMI, 30, 32, 76, 122-123

Sanna Inc., 711

Sawtooth Software, Inc., 377

Sawyer, A. G., 171n, 193n

Schaffer, William D., 479n

Schewe, C. D., 240n

Schiffman, S. S., 536n

Schlaiffer, P., 221n

Schmitt, N., 295n

Schultz, Randall L., 695n

Schweizer, S., 102

Scientific Press (The), 376

Scott Paper, 632

Scripto, 68

Searle (G. D.), 5

Sendak, P. E., 193n

Sevin, L. J., 634

Shane, Leonard, 394, 396

Shapira, Z., 310n

Sharing Marketing Decisions with Diary Panels, 109n, 113

Shaw, George Bernard, 634

Shaw, Ronald, 68

Shepard, R. N., 341n

Sheth, J., 151n

Shocker, A. D., 576n, 577n, 585n
Silk, A. J., 44n
Simmons Market Research Bureau, Inc., 88
Slevin, Dennis P., 695n
Smith, Donald D., 682n
Smith, H., 528n
Smith, Scott M., 376n
Smith-Barney, 80
Snickers, 21
Social Research, Inc., 288
Soft Goods Information Service (SGIS), 113
Sonquist, J. A., 596n
Southwestern Bell, 271
Sparkman, Richard D., Jr., 375n
Spear, M. E., 721n
Sprague, Ralph H., 695n
SRI International, 89
Srinivasan, V., 585n
SRI Values and Lifestyles, 89
Srivastava, R. K., 576n, 577n
Standard & Poor's *Statistical Service*, 84
Stanley, S. T., 166n, 167n
Starch, Daniel, 19, 353n
State and Metropolitan Area Data Book, 84
Statistical Abstract of the United States, 84
Statistical Package for the Social Sciences, 429
Statistical Reference Index: A Selective Guide to American Statistical Publications from Private Organizations and State Government Sources, 83
Steinbrenner, K., 429n
Stevens, J., 151n
Stevens, S. S., 282n
Stewart, David W., 77n
Stewart, Jennifer, 712
Stiff, R., 137n
Stocking, Carol, 349n
Stroh Brewery, 201-202
Study of Media and Markets, 88
Suci, G., 312n
Sudler & Hennessey, Inc., 22, 23
Sudman, Seymour, 109n, 145n, 146n, 234n, 347n, 349n, 353n, 357n, 361n
Sumichrast, Michael, 394
Summers, G. F., 292n
Sunrise Movers, 272
Survey of Buying Power, 84, 85, 87

Survey Research Center, 20
Swift/Hunt-Wesson Inc., 393
SYSDAT, 444
System Development Corporation, 97, 98

Tab, 707-709
Talarzyk, W. W., 161n
Tannebaum, P., 312n
Telenet, 101
Telmar Media Systems, 97, 98, 99, 104
Telser, E., 148n, 150n
Texas Instruments Inc., 634
Thematic Apperception Test (TAT), 136
Thurstone, L. L., 300n
Time, 7
Time, Inc., 122
Tootsie Roll, Inc., 699-700, 705
Topicator: Classified Article Guide to the Advertising/ Communications/Marketing Periodical Press, 82
Toys for All, 69-70
TRACE, 11-12
Tuchfarber, Alfred J., Jr., 147n
Tulle, D. S., 151n
Tums, 22
TV Guide, 7
Twidt, Dick Warren, 27n
Tyebjee, T. T., 148n

Unilever, 709
Uninet, 101
United States Bureau of the Census, 80, 84, 104-105, 141
United States Census of Population, 211
United States Food and Drug Administration (FDA), 202
United States League of Savings Institutions, 394
Upjohn Co., 203, 204
Urban, G. L., 34n, 44n, 586n, 605, 668n
Users' Guide: 1980 Census of Population and Housing, 104

Valium, 202-204
Value and Lifestyles Program, 599-600
Vao, V., 335n
Villarreal, Julio, Jr., 272

Vithala, R. R., 605
Vu/Text Information Services, Inc., 82, 97, 99

Wainer, Howard, 442n, 443, 444
Walker, B. J., 240n
Wall Street Journal, 82
Wall Street Journal Index, 82
Warburg, Paribas, Becker Inc., 395
Warner-Lambert Company, 22
Washington Post, 82
Wasserman, Paul, 81
Wasserman, William, 498n, 521n
Waterman, Robert H., 14, 14n
Weeks, Robert, 707
Welkowitz, J., 508n
Werner, Michael, 81
Westinghouse, 637
Whalen, B., 155n, 156n
Wharton School of Business, 201
Wheelwright, Steven C., 682n, 698, 698n
White, Percival, 20
White Palace Partners, Inc., 562
Wholihan, Stephen, 711
Wijk, G., 240n
Wilcox, James, 375n
Wildt, A. R., 310n
Williams-Jones, J., 236n
Wilson, Elmo, 20
Wind, Yoram, 201, 335n, 353n, 586n, 592n, 593, 593n, 595, 603n
Winkle, Charles, 80
Winkler, Robert L., 499n
Wittink, D. R., 341n
Woman's Day, 7
Wonnacott, Ronald J., 462n
Wonnacott, Thomas H., 462n
Wood, Douglas, 682n
Worcester, R. M., 577n
Worthing, P. M., 193n
Wrigley (William) Co., 655
Wyeth Laboratories, 203

Yankelovich Monitor, 89
Yankelovich, Skelly and White, Inc., 89, 668
Yates, F., 741
Yellow Pages, 271-272
Yokopenic, P. A., 148n
Young, F. W., 536n
Young & Rubican, 22

Zyman, Sergio, 708

Subject Index

field operations and, 55-56
layout of, 361-375
logical flow in, 357-361
mail panels and, 141-142
mail surveys and, 137-140
mark-sensed, 412
pretesting, 375-376
response formats in, 353-357
Questions
aided, 353
closed-ended, 56, 355-357, 407
diagnostic, 614
double-barreled, 352
filter, 359-360
loaded, 350
open-ended, 56, 131, 354-355, 407, 408-410
unaided, 353
Quota samples, 232-234

Radio
evaluative methods for, 116-118
information on demand, 119
diary panels and, 109
Random digit directory designs, 146
Randomization, 165
Random numbers, 165, 738-739
Random sampling errors, 235
Random sources of error, 291
Range, 436
interquartile, 436-437
Rank-order correlation coefficient, 499-501
Rank-order scales, 302-303
Rating, 114, 117
Rational database manager, 678
Ratio-scaled variables, 496-499
Ratio scales, 286
Raw data, 404
Reactive effects of testing, 170-171
Realistic marketing research environment, 24-25, 158
"Real-magazine" tests, 646-647
Recall, 647
copy, 656
day-after, 653
proven total, 647, 656
visual, 656
Recognition, 649
marketing planning and, 45-47
Record, 367
Reference case, 693
Refusal conversion, 240
Region of rejection, 455
Regression
forecasting and, 705-706
ordinary least-squares, 341, 515
Regression analysis, 494, 511-528
multiple, 519-528
simple, 511-519
Regression coefficient, 488
standardized, 520-521

Regression coefficient—cont'd
statistical test of, 526
Regression line, 512-513
Regression models, 684
Related samples, 463
Relative tolerance level, 250
Reliability, 288, 290-294
alternative form, 293-294
construct validity and, 288-289
internal consistency, 292-293
measurement of, 291-294
test-retest, 292
theory of, 291
Reliability coefficient, 220-221, 292
Repairable failure, 35
Repeat paired comparison designs, 622
Replacement, nonresponse and, 242-243
Repositioning, 21, 36
Research environments, 24-25, 158
Research life cycle, 33
Research methods
qualitative, 131
quantitative, 131
Research reports
marketing decision support, 686-689
oral, 721-729
visual aids and, 725-729
written, 717-729
Residual, 513
Response bias, mail panels and, 142
Response errors, 235-236, 346
Response latency, 131
Response rates
improvement of, 237-241
mail panels and, 142
mail surveys and, 139-140
mall-intercept surveys and, 153
personal in-home surveys and, 151
telephone surveys and, 148-149
Restaurant industry, case study, 273-274, 555-561
Revised probability, 62
Round robin designs, 622-623

Sales analysis, 680-682
Salesforce-composite estimates, 683
Sales forecasting, 682-685
Sales wave extended-use product tests, 626
Sample balancing, 416-418
Sample control
mall-intercept surveys and, 152-153
personal in-home surveys and, 150
self-administered CRT interview and, 155
telephone surveys and, 145-148

Samples, 55, 128
convenience, 232
independent, 463
judgmental, 232
national market studies and, 579-581
nonprobability, 223, 231-234
probability, 223-231
purposive, 209
quota, 232-234
related, 463
Sample size, 218-223
blind guessing and, 218
simple random sampling and, 249-250
statistical precision and, 219-221
stratified sampling and, 259-260
systematic sampling and, 253-254
Sampling, 55, 211-212
cluster, 229-231
procedures for, 263-267
concept-evaluation tests and, 618
concept-screening tests and, 614
data collection in, 217-218
design considerations in, 212
incidence rates in, 216-217
international considerations in, 383
name tests and, 635-636
package tests and, 640
print ad tests and, 649
probabilistic, 4
probability proportional to size, 230, 264-267
product tests and, 627
sampling frames in, 215-216
simple random, 224
population proportions and, 269
procedures for, 245-254
stratified, 225-227
population proportions and, 270
procedures for, 254-263
systematic, 224-225
procedures for, 251-254
target populations in, 213-215
television commercial tests and, 656
Sampling designs
directory-based, 146, 147
nondirectory, 146-148
probability, 209, 221
Sampling frames, 215-216
mail surveys and, 138
telephone surveys and, 145-146
Sampling gap, 216
Sampling interval, 252
Sampling units, 213
primary, 229
secondary, 229
Sampling variables, 225